1

UNDERSTANDING AND INTERPRETING
HEMATOLOGICAL INVESTIGATIONS

BY

DR. AGOURRAM TAIEB

B.Sc. M.Sc. D.Sc (MEDICAL)

aberdeen university
press services

Printed in the United States of America
ISBN: 978-0-578-01786-0

This book is printed on 8" x 11", perfect binding, 60# cream interior paper, black and white interior ink, 100# white exterior paper, full-color exterior ink. Prices are subject to change.

Cover Title Designed by Aberdeen University Press Services.

Understanding and Interpreting Hematological Investigations
First Edition
Dr. Agourram Taieb

"To my parents, who taught me I could do anything;
my beloved wife, Hoda, who believed that I could do anything;
and my kids; Tarik, Adel ,Reda, Yassine & Amina,
For whom I would do anything."

I turn finally to Dr LAZRAK NICOLE, always sensitive to the problems
of education and continuing medical education, my most sincere and heartfelt gratitude
for the attention she has brought to my training since 1974, and I wish to express my gratitude
to all my colleagues and professors of hematology at laboratoire du Maghreb au Maroc.

-Agourram Taieb-

ACKNOWLEDGMENTS

No matter how this thesis is attributed, its contents are actually the fortunate product of a concerted effort by a large, number of professors in hematology of different countries, over a five years period. Since I started my PhD adventure, five years ago, I have received help, advice and support from many people, to all of whom I am really thankful.

Pr Whitney Williams played a major role in this study; I cannot thank you enough for your advice and guidance and for your willingness to support me through the discovery process- thanks for all of your insightful feedback and words of encouragement for permitting me to use your data in my thesis research.

I would like to thank, Pr Peter Robert Galbraith; I had learnt several new hematology lessons, which would keep me ahead in my personal and academic careers. I would like to thank you once again Dr Galbraith, for giving me such a great opportunity to study with you.

I would like to acknowledge the following professors for their help in completing this thesis: Pr John Ross, Pr David G. king. Pr John Lewis Young Jr

I would like to express my gratitude to all those who gave me the written permission to copy some information related to the field of hematology and to all those who gave me the possibility to complete this thesis: Pr Nivaldo Medeiros, Pr Duane W. Sears, Pr Amos M Cohen, Pr Zandecki Marc and Pr John Meletis. Thanks for allowing me to use your images on my thesis.

This thesis really catalogs the hard work of a number of individuals who contributed many of the ideas discussed. Each was extremely helpful in providing guidance on organization, presentation, conceptualization, and technical details. Of course, the mistakes remain mine.

I am very grateful to Pr Han Myint from the University of Colorado who gave me the possibility to refresh my knowledge in hematological malignancies from fundamentals to recent advances including novel therapies.

I thank all of the teachers at Harvard Medical School who helped me with proofreading the hematology tutorial and Intensive Review of internal Medicine (IRIM 2005). I have learned more about internal medicine, the cancer biology and more courses in hematology/oncology and pathology than I ever thought I would. Their enthusiasm for the use of cases study in hematology is both admirable and inspirational. Thanks to you Dr Sanjiv Chopra, M.D. The IRIM 2005 is excellent and worthy of review over and over again. This undoubtedly enriched my skill and knowledge.

I would like to thank all people who have helped and inspired me during my doctoral study. I especially want to thank Prof Gary E. Kaiser, Prof Nghia Duc (Andy) Nguyen, Dr Arthur O. Anderson and Pr Charles E.Hess at University of Virginia for their perpetual help.

This graduate thesis marks a great achievement of my professional life, which would not have been possible without the immense support and great affection of several people. I would like to extend my sincere gratitude to all of them here.

Last, but not least, the biggest personal thanks goes to my sons Tarik, Adel, Reda, Yassine and Amina. Thanks-I love you all. Believe it or not, the "five more years" is finally over!

This thesis is dedicated to my wife, HODA, who has always encouraged me to pursue my dreams. Whose patience, support, and impeccable understanding allowed me to write this thesis?

I thank my family and friends who have helped me get through this very long and intensive project.

Thanks to God for my life through all tests in the past five years. You have made my life more bountiful. May your name be exalted, honored, and glorified.

ABSTRACT

Hematology is the subspecialty of internal medicine concerned with disorders of the blood, bone marrow and lymphatic systems.

Hematologists are called in for cases of suspected blood disorders when the diagnosis is unclear or specialized medical care is needed. They coordinate total patient care, working, where needed, with surgeons, radiation therapists, gynecologists or other specialists.

Not everyone with a blood problem needs a hematologist. Many blood problems are diagnosed and managed by general internists. When special knowledge in diagnosis and treatment is required, the skills of a hematologist are called upon. Treatments may include therapeutic phlebotomy, bone marrow aspiration, core bone marrow biopsy, and chemotherapy or other special therapy.

Fundamental to the training of health care providers and physicians interested in hematology and medical oncology is the acquisition of knowledge concerning the basic scientific principles that underlie our understanding of cancer biology.

To gain an understanding of the role of the various clinical labs in the diagnosis of benign hematologic diseases

To acquire expertise in the preparation and interpretation of pathologic material, in particular bone marrow aspirates and biopsies, lymph node biopsies, in the diagnosis of hematologic disorders.

To use hospital resources to appropriately gather information needed for the interpretation of the laboratory testing.

To gain familiarity with the laboratory methods used to diagnose hematologic disorders, including the use of the automated blood counters, coagulation testing, and protein and hemoglobin electrophoresis

To become familiar with the procedures involved in blood banking

To gain expertise in the preparation and interpretation of bone marrow aspirates and biopsies

To gain familiarity with the use of immunostaining

The Clinical laboratory hematology specialists are often called upon to lend their expertise to help solve myriad problems that emerge from both routine and specialized laboratory testing:
- Blood smears: RBC size, shape, and hemoglobinization, WBC number and kind and distribution, recognizing abnormal WBC, estimating platelet number, granule content, clumping, recognizing unusual cells, recognizing blood parasites, malaria, Babesia, Erlichia, filarial
- Bone marrow aspirates – differential counts, myeloid, erythroid, lymphoid differentiation, megakaryocyte number and morphology, histiocyte inclusions
Bone marrow biopsies – cellularity, tumor infiltration, megakaryocyte number,
Correlation of aspirates and biopsies
Cytochemistry
Histopathologic techniques in diagnosis
- Correlation of morphology of the bone marrow aspirate and biopsy, histochemistry, immunochemistry, flow cytometry and clinical presentation to arrive at a diagnosis in patients with leukemia and lymphoma
Cytogenetics, including fluorescence in-situ hybridization (FISH)
Hemoglobinopathies – sickle S, Hb C, and other, managing exchange transfusions
Thalassemias – beta, alpha
- Serum protein electrophoresis
Monoclonal gammopathies in serum, urine and CSF

The Hematologist must recognize abnormalities and know how to correct them. They monitor, screen, and troubleshoot analytical devices including calibration, quality control, "on the fly" or run-by-run assessment, statistical control of observed data, and recording normal operations. To maintain the integrity of the laboratory process, the hematologist recognizes factors that could introduce error and rejects contaminated or sub-standard specimens.

A hematologist role is to provide accurate laboratory results in a timely manner. These results are used to confirm a diagnosis or to monitor treatment. Safeguards ensure accuracy. Safeguards include experimental controls, calibration of laboratory instruments, delta checks (changes within a normal series of results), and periodic surveys.

Hematologists are usually hidden from view.

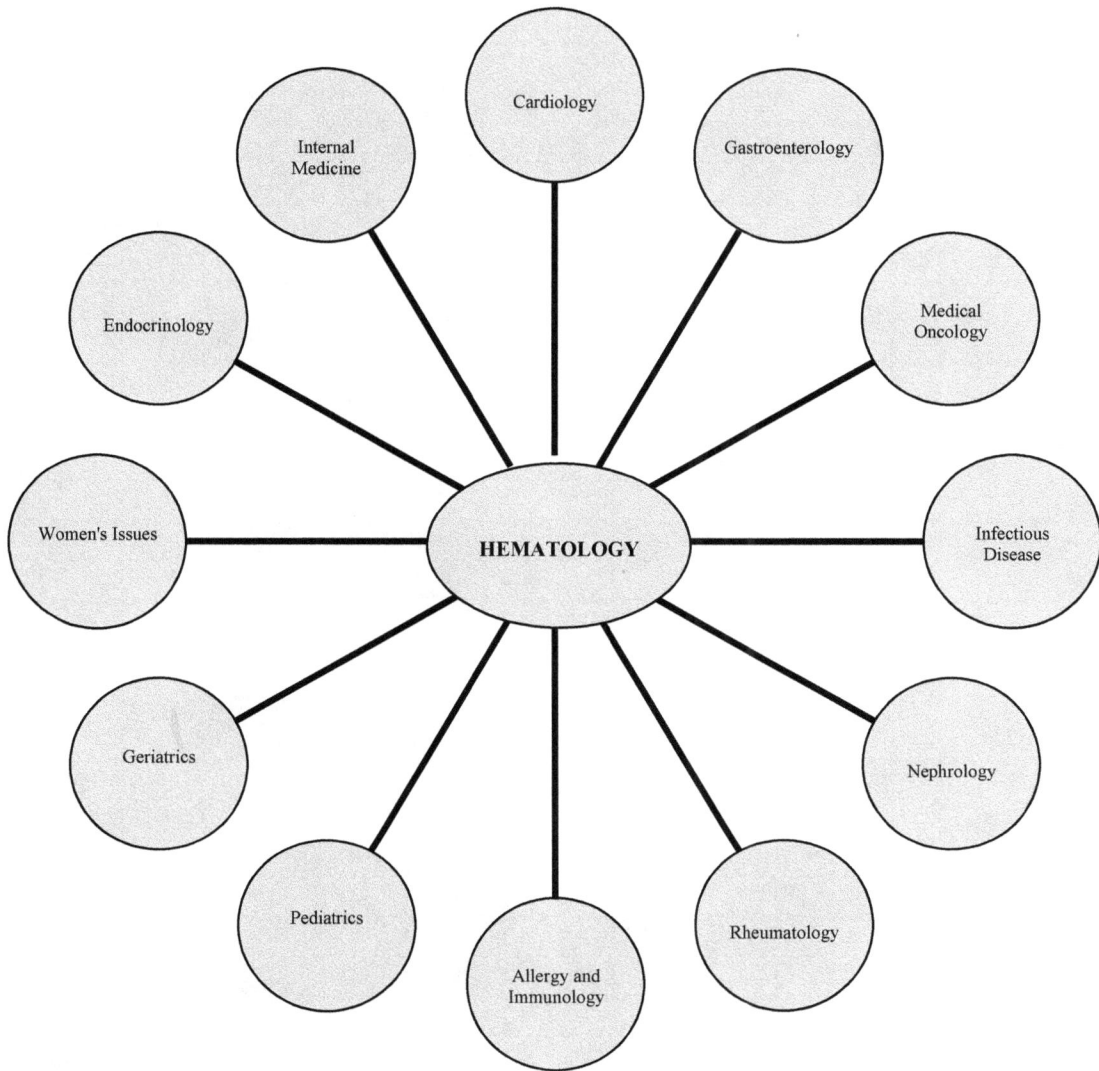

TABLE OF CONTENTS

11

PART ONE: BASIC LABORATORY CONCEPTS

In order to understand what goes wrong in cancer, it is important to understand how normal cells work. The first step is to discus the structure and basic functions of cells.

CHAPTER ONE: CELL BIOLOGY

History and Theory

In 1665, The English scientist Robert Hook made an observation that would change basic biological theory and research for ever .While examining a dried section of cork tree with a crude light microscope; he observed small chambers and named them cells. Within a decade, researchers had determined that cells were not empty but instead were filled with a watery substance called cytoplasm.

Over the next 175 years, research led to the formation of the cell theory, first proposed by the German botanist Matthias Jacob Schleiden and the German physiologist Theodore Schwann [i]in 1838 and formalized by the German research Rudolf Virchow in 1858. In its modern form, this theory has four basic parts:

The cell is the basic structural and functional unit of life; all organisms are composed of cells.
 All cells produced by the division of preexisting cells. Each cell contains genetic material that is passed down during process of reproduction.
All basic chemical and physiological function – for example – repair, growth, movement, immunity, communication, and digestion, are carried out inside of cells ,
The activities of cells depend on the activities of sub cellular structures within the cell. These sub cellular structures include organelles, the plasma membrane and if present, the nucleus.

The cell theory leads to two very important generalities about cells and life in general:

Cells are a live , this means cells can take energy (which , depending on the cell type , can be in the form of light , sugar, or other compounds) and building materials (proteins ,carbohydrates, and fats) , and use these to repair themselves and make new generations of cells (reproduction) .
The characteristics and needs of an organism are in reality the characteristics and need s of the cells that make up the organism

Cell Structure and Function

The proper function of human bodies is dependent on smaller structures, or organs, such as the heart or lung. The tiny cells that make up these organs actually contain within them smaller structures called organelles. Those organelles help the cells to perform their job. In cancer, changes to these organelles can cause the individual cells and ultimately the entire organism to have serious problems.
 An organelle is a sub cellular structure that has a specific function .Every cell in the body is enclosed by a cell membrane. The cell membrane separates the material outside the cell (extra cellular) from the material inside the cell (intra cellular). It maintains the integrity of a cell and controls passage of materials into and out of the cell. All material within a cells must have access to the cell membrane for the need exchange.

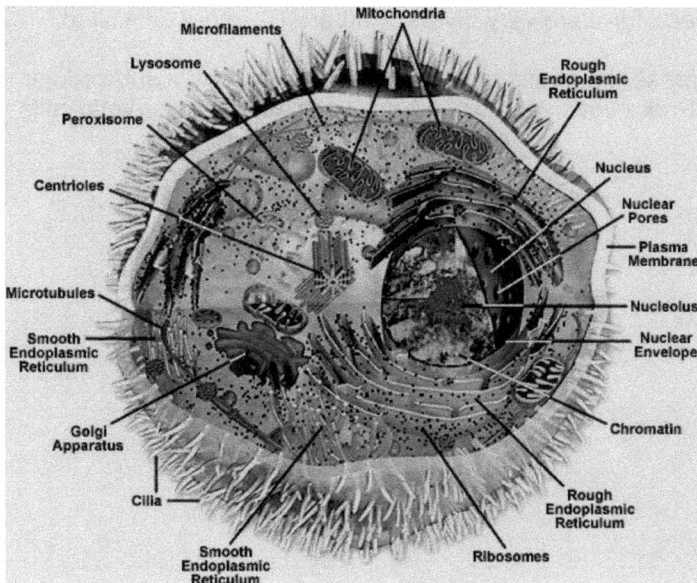

http://training.seer.cancer.gov; funded by the U.S. National Cancer Institute's Surveillance, Epidemiology and End Results (SEER) Program, via contract number N01-CN-67006, with Emory University, Atlanta SEER Cancer Registry, Atlanta, Georgia, U.S.A. Used with permission.

* The cell membrane is a double layer of phospholipids molecules. Proteins in the cell membrane provide structural support, form channels for passage of material, act as receptor sites, function as carrier molecules, and provide identification markers.

Cells are surrounded by a membrane. This membrane has many functions, some of which are listed here:

- To maintain all the cell contents within it
- To protect the cell
- To allow for selective permeability
- To enable signal transduction

* The nucleus, formed by a nuclear membrane around a fluid nucleoplasm, is the control center of the cell; threads of chromatin in the nucleus contain deoxyribonucleic acid (DNA), the genetic material of the cell. The nucleus is a dense region of ribonucleic acid (RNA) in the nucleus and is the site of ribosome formation.

* The cytoplasm is the gel like fluid inside the cell. It is the medium for chemical reaction. It provides a platform upon which other organelles can operate within the cell

All of the function for cell expression; growth and replication are carried out in the cytoplasm of the cell. Within the cytoplasm, materials move by diffusion, a physical process that can work only fort short distances.

* Cytoplasmic organelles are little organs that are suspended in the cytoplasm of the cell. Each type of organelles has a definite structure and a specific role in the function of the cell. Examples of cytoplasmic organelles are mitochondrion, ribosome, endoplasmic reticulum, Golgi apparatus, and lysosomes.

The structural and functional characteristics of different types of cells are determined by the nature of the proteins present. Cells of various types have different functions because cell structure and function are closely related .It is apparent that a cell that is very thin is not well suited for protective function. Bone cells do not have an appropriate structure for nerve impulse conduction. Just as there are many cell types, there are varied cell functions.

The generalized cell functions include movement of substances across the cell membrane, cell division to make new cells, and protein synthesis.

The survival of the cell depends on maintaining the difference between extra-cellular and intra-cellular material .Mechanisms of movements across the cell membrane includes simple diffusions, osmosis, filtration, active transport, endocytosis, and exocytosis.

A part from these similarities cell structure and form are very diverse and are therefore difficult to generalize.

One major difference among cells is the presence or absence of a nucleus, which is a sub-cellular structure that contains the genetic material. Prokaryotic cells lack a nucleus, whereas eukaryotic cells contain a nucleus.

The Nucleus

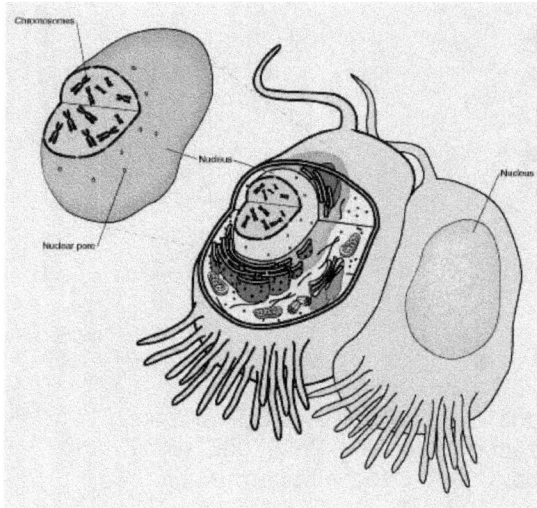

Courtesy of National Human Genome Research Institute

The nucleus is the brain of eukaryotic cells. Usually the nucleus is round and the largest organelle in the cell. It is surrounded by a membrane , called the nuclear envelope .The envelope is riddled with holes , called nuclear pores , that allow specific materials to pass in and out of the nucleus , just like proteins in the cell membrane regulate the movement of molecules in and out the cell itself . Attached to the nuclear envelope is the endoplasmic reticulum. The nucleus is surrounded by the cytoplasm inside a cell. The nucleus houses the DNA which stores genetic information for a cell. The DNA contains instructions for the production of the cell's proteins and for reproduction to construct proteins, the DNA is copied to messenger RNA in the process called transcription .The mRNA goes to the ribosome , either in the nucleus , or in the endoplasmic reticulum , where the actual construction of the proteins takes place .   Structurally, the nucleus is composed of three main parts, the nucleolus, the nuclear envelope, and the chromatin. The nucleolus contains ribosomes, RNA, DNA, and proteins.

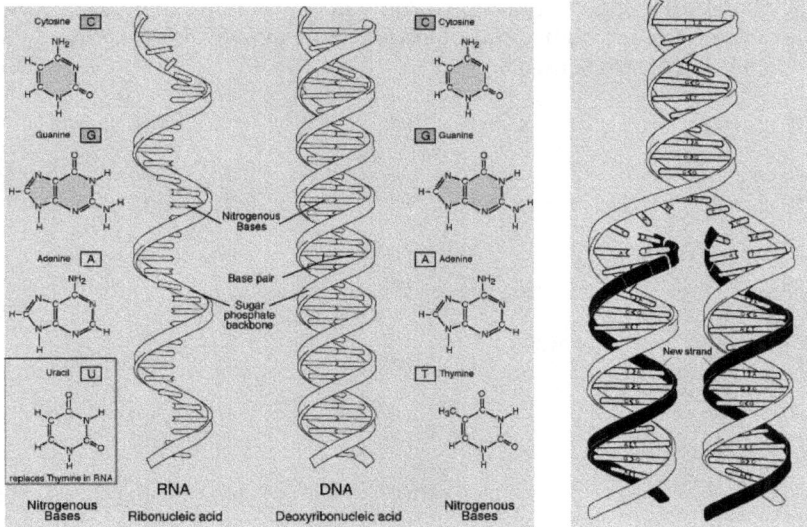

Courtesy of National Human Genome Research Institute

The nucleus regulates all cell activity. It does this by controlling the enzymes present. DNA contains the information for the production of the proteins. This information is encoded in the four DNA bases: Adenine (A).Guanine (G). Cytosine (C). Thymine (T). The specific sequence of the bases tells the cell what order to put the amino-acids. DNA bases pair up with each other A with T, C with G, to form units called bases pairs. Each base is also attached to a sugar molecule and a phosphate molecule. Together, a base, sugar, and phosphate are called a nucleotide. Nucleotides are arranged in two long strands that form a spiral called a double helix.

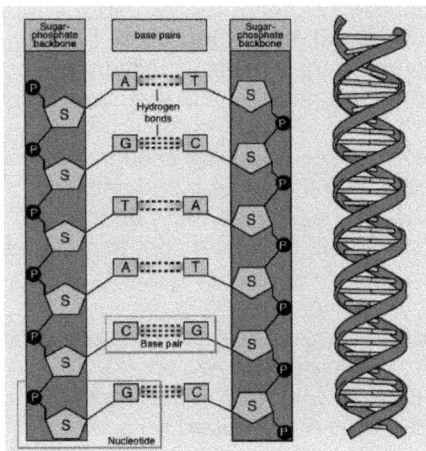

Courtesy of National Human Genome Research Institute

An important property of DNA is that it can replicate, or make copies of itself. Each strand of DNA in the double helix can serve as a pattern for duplicating the sequence of bases. This is critical when cell divide because each new cell needs to have an exact copy of the DNA present in the old cell.

There are three processes that enable the cell to manufacture proteins: Replication, transcription, and translation. First, the DNA is replicated, so that there are two identical copies of the DNA. Then, the DNA is transcribed into RNA [Just like DNA, RNA is composed of a four letter alphabet .However, the Thymine (T) in DNA is replaced by a Uracil (U) in RNA], which then translated, or read by tRNA to make the proteins.

There are two major types of material within the nucleus.
1) The "nucleoplasm": the jelly-like matrix within which all other materials within the nucleus "float".

2) 'Chromatin": this material is easily stained (Hence the name.) Chromatin is the name that describes nuclear material that contains the genetic code. It is composed of DNA and its associated protein histone which forms the long strands called "chromosomes".

The Chromosomes

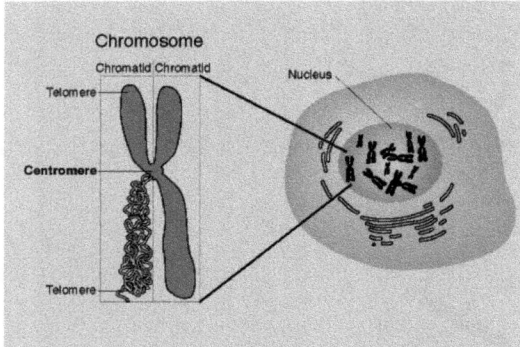

Courtesy of National Human Genome Research Institute

It is well known that DNA (deoxyribonucleic acid) is the blueprint of life. DNA provides the codes for the structural and enzymatic proteins that make up every cell. DNA is packaged into units called chromosomes. The chromosome number varies in different species. In humans there are 46 chromosomes, or 23 pairs of chromosomes (diploid), in every cell except the mature egg and sperm which have a set of 23 chromosomes (haploid). If the chromosomes in a single cell were stretched out and laid end to end, the DNA would be two meters long

Chromosomes are visible only during cell division, when the DNA is supercoiled and condensed to facilitate distribution into daughter cells. Cell division in somatic cells (mitosis) results in the creation of daughter cells with the same number of chromosomes as the original cell, a total of 46 chromosomes. Cell division in the germ cells, eggs and sperm (meiosis), results in the creation of daughter cells with half the number of chromosomes as the original cell, a total of 23 chromosomes. This reduction in the number of chromosomes is important so that the original number of 46 chromosomes is restored following fertilization of the egg by the sperm.

The chromosome constitution of an individual (karyotype) can be analyzed following tissue culture of an appropriate sample. The most commonly used sample is blood (using the white blood cells or lymphocytes) since it is the most accessible. However, other samples are used depending upon the indication: amniotic fluid cells, to analyze the karyotype of the fetus; products of conception, to analyze the cause of a miscarriage or stillbirth; bone marrow cells, to diagnose the presence or type of leukemia; and skin, to determine the presence of another cell line (mosaicism).

Since cells have to be grown in culture, it is important that samples are received in the laboratory within 24 to 48 hours after collection. The cells are grown in media for three days to two weeks depending on the sample source. Cell division is arrested during metaphase, when the chromosome material is condensed. Following hypotonic treatment and fixation, the cells are dropped on a slide and then stained. At least 20 metaphase spreads are analyzed and 2 or 3 metaphase spreads are photographed. The chromosomes are arranged to create a karyotype.

Chromosomes vary in size and in shape. The pairs of autosomal chromosomes are arranged in a karyotype from the biggest, #1, to the smallest, #22. The sex chromosomes are placed to the right of the smallest autosomal chromosomes. Based upon size and shape, chromosomes are divided into eight groups: A (1 to 3), B (4 and 5), C (6 to 12), D (13 to 15), E (16 to 18), F (19 and 20), G (21 and 22) and the sex chromosomes, XX in females and XY in males.

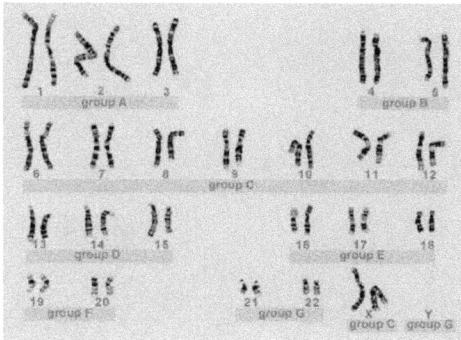

http://learn.genetics.utah.edu/units/disorders/karyotype/chrompictures.cfm

Each chromosome has a centromere, region which contains the kinetochore, a microtubule organizing centre responsible for attachment of the chromosome to the spindle apparatus at mitosis. The two sister chromatids are principally held together at the Para centric heterochromatin at opposite ends of the centromic region. Centromere divides the chromosome into two arms, the short arm (p arm) and the long arm (q arm). When the short arm is nearly as long as the long arm, the chromosome is said metacentric, if it is shorter, the chromosome is said sub-metacentric, when it is very short, but still visible, the chromosome is said to be sub-telocentric, when extremely short, virtually, the chromosome is said acrocentric.

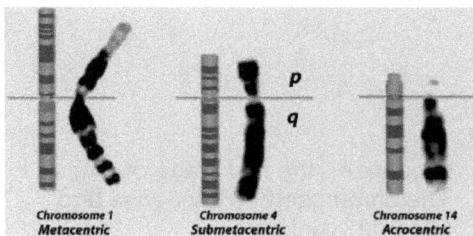

http://learn.genetics.utah.edu/units/disorders/karyotype/chrompictures.cfm

Each numbered chromosome is unique and can distinguish from another by size, the location of the centromere and the pattern of dark and light bands.

To "read" a set of human chromosomes, scientists first use three key features to identify their similarities and differences:

Size. This is the easiest way to tell two different chromosomes apart.

Banding pattern. The size and location of Giemsa bands on chromosomes make each chromosome pair unique.

Centromere position. Centromeres are regions in chromosomes that appear as a constriction. They have a special role in the separation of chromosomes into daughter cells during mitosis cell division (mitosis and meiosis).

Using these key features, scientists match up the 23 pairs -- one set from the mother and one set from the father.

Life Cycle of Cell

Most eukaryotic cell lives according to an internal clock, that is, they proceed through a sequence of phases called the cycle.

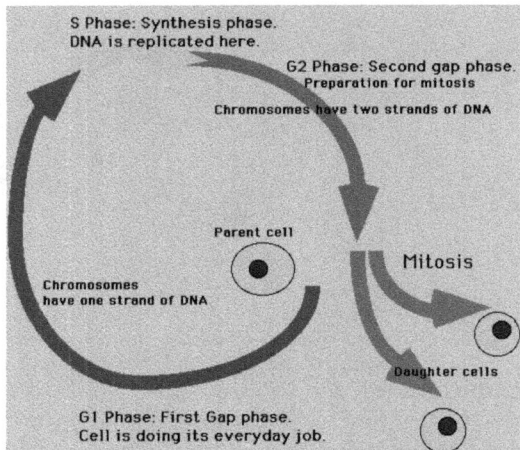

Mitosis

The stages of the cell cycle can be broken down into five stages:
Interphase, Prophase, Metaphase, Anaphase, Telophase

Interphase
Is the "resting" or non-mitotic portion of the cell cycle?
It is comprised of G1, S, and G2 stages of the cell cycle.
DNA is replicated during the S phase of Interphase

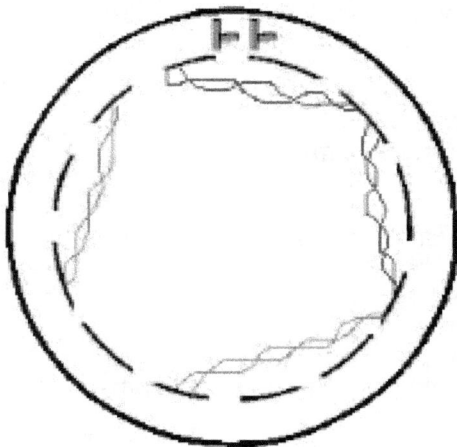

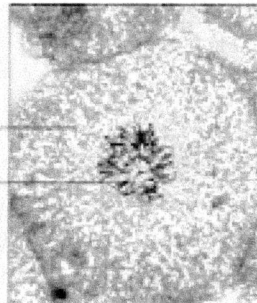

Prophase - the first stage of mitosis.
The chromosomes condense and become visible
The centrioles form and move toward opposite ends of the cell ("the poles")
The nuclear membrane dissolves
The mitotic spindle forms (from the centrioles in animal cells)
Spindle fibers from each centriole attach to each sister chromatid at the kinetochore
Compare Prophase to the Prophase I and to the Prophase II stages of mitosis.

7

Metaphase
The Centrioles complete their migration to the poles
The chromosomes line up in the middle of the cell ("the equator")
Compare Metaphase to the Metaphase I and to the Metaphase II stages of mitosis.

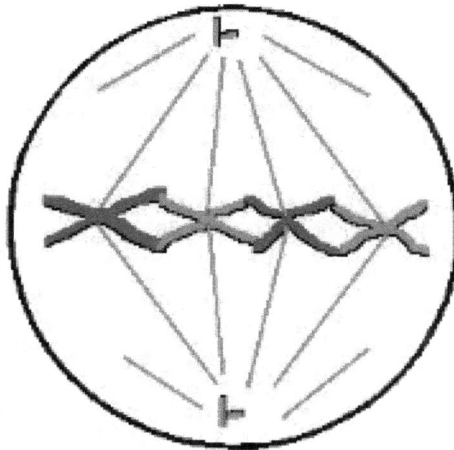

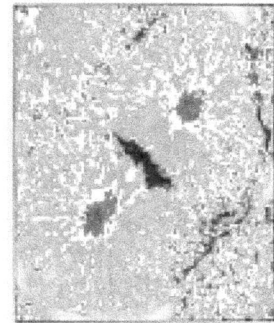

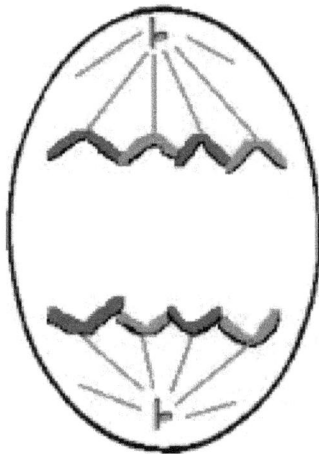

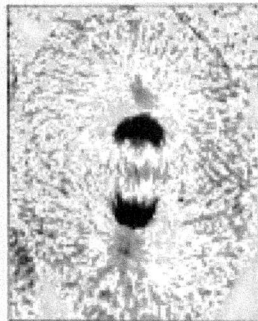

Anaphase
Spindles attached to kinetochores begin to shorten.
This exerts a force on the sister chromatids that pulls them apart.
Spindle fibers continue to shorten, pulling chromatids to opposite poles.
This ensures that each daughter cell gets identical sets of chromosomes
Compare Anaphase to the Anaphase I and to the Anaphase II stages of mitosis.

Telophase
The chromosomes decondense
The nuclear envelope forms
Cytokinesis reaches completion, creating two daughter cells
Compare Telophase to the Telophase I and to the Telophase II stages of mitosis.

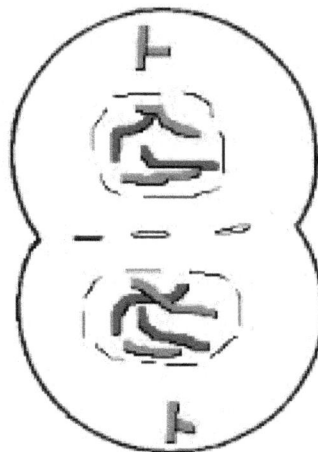

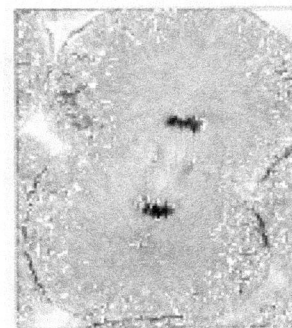

Courtesy of the University of Illinois at Chicago, department of Biological Sciences

Cytokinesis Divides the Cytoplasm

In animal cells, cytokinesis occurs by a process known as cleavage

First, a cleavage furrow appears cleavage furrow = shallow groove near the location of the old metaphase plate.

A contractile ring of actin microfilaments in association with myosin, a protein
Actin and myosin are also involved in muscle contraction and other movement functions
The contraction of a the dividing cell's ring of microfilaments is like the pulling of drawstrings
The cell is pinched in two cytokinesis in plant cells is different because plant cells have cell walls. There is no cleavage furrow. During telophase, vesicles from the Golgi apparatus move along microtubules to the middle of the cell (where the cell plate was) and coalesce, producing the cell plate. Cell-wall construction materials are carried in the vesicles and are continually deposited until a complete cell wall forms between the two daughter cells.

Chromosome Separation Is the Key Event of Mitosis

Mitotic spindle fibers are the railroad tracks for chromosome movement.
Spindle fibers are made of microtubules.
Microtubules are lengthened and shortened by the addition and loss of tubulin subunits.
Mitotic spindle shortening during anaphase is a result of the loss of tubulin subunits.
A kinetochore motor is the engine that drives chromosome movement.
Multiple studies have shown that the kinetochore contains motor proteins that can "walk" along the spindle fiber during anaphase.
These proteins presumably remove tubulin subunits, shortening spindle fibers and facilitating the chromosome movement.

Meiosis Is a Special Type of Cell Division That Occurs in Sexually Reproducing Organisms
Meiosis reduces the chromosome number by half, enabling sexual recombination to occur.
Meiosis of diploid cells produces haploid daughter cells, which may function as gametes.
Gametes undergo fertilization, restoring the diploid number of chromosomes in the zygote
Meiosis and fertilization introduce genetic variation in three ways:
 1- Crossing over between homologous chromosomes at prophase I
 2- Independent assortment of homologous pairs at metaphase I:
Each homologous pair can orient in either of two ways at the plane of cell division.
 3- The total number of possible outcomes = 2n (n = number of haploid chromosomes).
Random chance fertilization between any one female gamete with any other male gamete
The Role of Sexual Reproduction in Evolution
Sexual reproduction in a population should decline in frequency relative to asexual reproduction.
Asexual reproduction-No males are needed, all individuals can produce offspring.
Sexual reproduction-only females can produce offspring, therefore fewer are produced.
Sexual reproduction may exist because it provides genetic variability that reduces susceptibility of a population to pathogen attack.
    The stages of meiosis can be broken down into two main stages, Meiosis I and Meiosis II
a- Meiosis I can be broken down into four substages: Prophase I, Metaphase I, Anaphase I and Telophase I
b- Meiosis II can be broken down into four substages: Prophase II, Metaphase II, Anaphase II and Telophase II

Meiosis I

Prophase I - most of the significant processes of Meiosis occur during Prophase I
The chromosomes condense and become visible
The centrioles form and move toward the poles
The nuclear membrane begins to dissolve
The homologs pair up, forming a tetrad
Each tetrad is comprised of four chromatids - the two homologs, each with their sister chromatid
Homologous chromosomes will swap genetic material in a process known as crossing over (abbreviated as XO)
Crossing over serves to increase genetic diversity by creating four unique chromatids

Metaphase I
Microtubules grow from the centrioles and attach to the centromeres
The tetrads line up along the cell equator

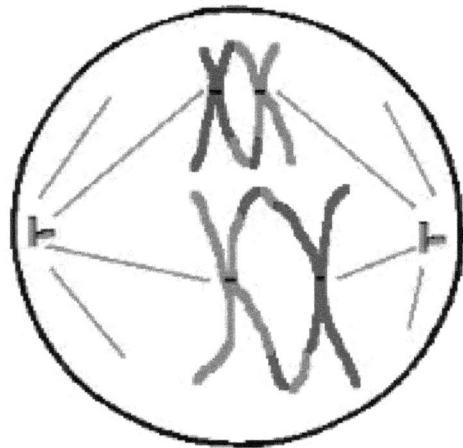

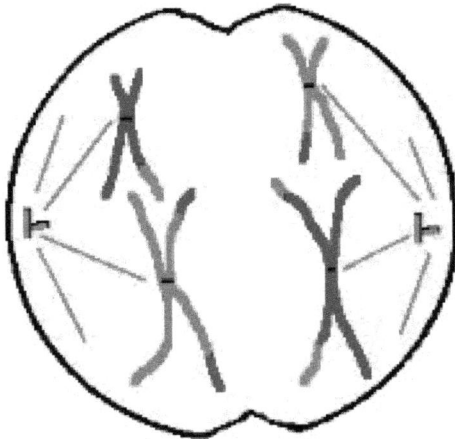

Anaphase I
The centromeres break and homologous chromosomes separate (note that the sister chromatids are still attached)
Cytokinesis begins
.

Telophase I
The chromosomes may decondense (depends on species)
Cytokinesis reaches completion, creating two haploid
daughter cells

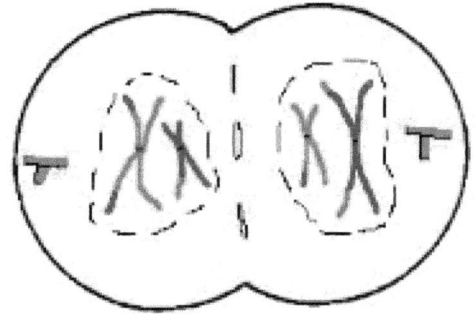

Courtesy of the University of Illinois at Chicago, department of Biological Sciences

Meiosis II

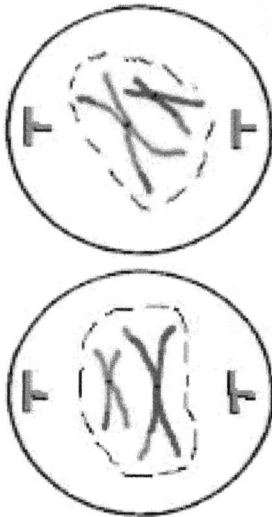

Prophase II
Centrioles form and move toward the poles
The nuclear membrane dissolves

Metaphase II
Microtubules grow from the centrioles and attach to the centromeres
The sister chromatids line up along the cell equator

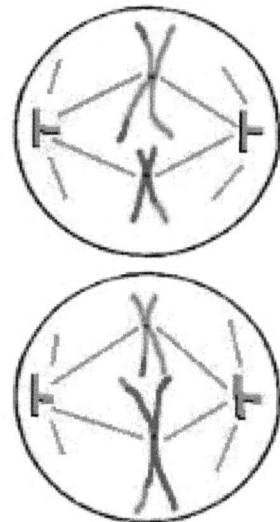

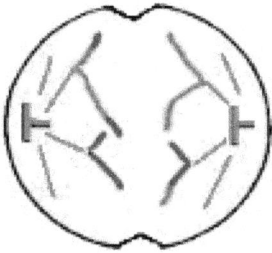

Anaphase II
The centromeres break and sister chromatids separate
Cytokinesis begins

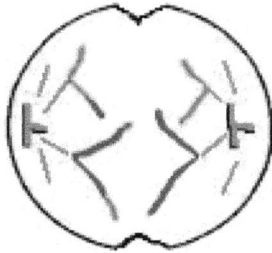

Telophase II
The chromosomes may decondense (depends on species)
Cytokinesis reaches completion, creating four haploid
daughter cells

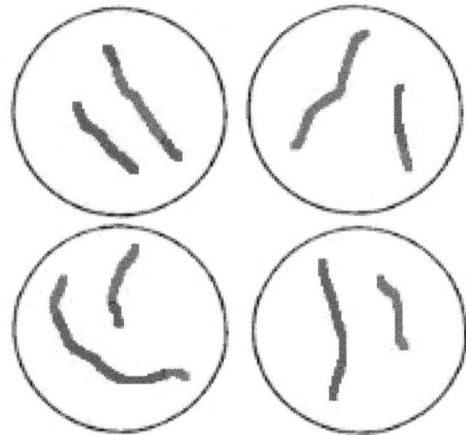

Courtesy of the University of Illinois at Chicago, department of Biological Sciences

The Consequences of Meiotic Mistakes

Nondisjunctions occur when homologous chromosomes fail to separate at meiosis I or when chromatids fail to separate at meiosis II.
Fertilization can result in embryos that are 2n + 1 (a "trisomy") or 2n − 1.
Abnormal copy numbers of one or more chromosomes is usually, but not always, fatal (Example: Down syndrome)
Polyploidy can occur when whole sets of chromosomes fail to separate at meiosis I or II.
The resulting 2n gametes, if fertilized by normal sperm, create 3n zygotes (triploid).
Organisms with an odd number of chromosome sets cannot produce viable gametes.

CHAPTER TWO: CANCER BIOLGY

The cell cycle stops at several check-points and can only proceed if certain conditions are met. There are several safeguards built into the cell division process to assure that cells do not divide unless they have completed the replication process correctly and that the environmental conditions in which the cells exist are favorable for cell division.

Many of the future of cancer cells are due to the defects in the genes that control cell division. Cancer cells do not obey these rules and will continue to grow and divide.

When a cell receives the message to divide, it goes through the cell cycle, which includes several phases for the division to be completed. Check-points a long each step of the process makes sure that everything goes the way it should. Many processes are involved in cell reproduction and all these processes have to take place correctly for a cell to divide properly. If anything goes wrong during this complicated process, a cell may become cancerous.

Cell cycle checkpoints are used by the cell to monitor and regulate the progress of the cell cycle. Checkpoints prevent cell cycle progression at specific points, allowing verification of necessary phase processes and repair of DNA damage. The cell cannot proceed to the next phase until checkpoint requirements have been met.

Several checkpoints are designed to ensure that damaged or incomplete DNA is not passed on to daughter cells. Two main checkpoints exist: the G1/S checkpoint and the G2/M checkpoints. G1/S transition is a rate-limiting step in the cell cycle and is also known as restriction point. An alternative model of the cell cycle response to DNA damage has also been proposed, known as the post replication checkpoint

P53 plays an important role in triggering the control mechanisms at both G1/S and G2/M checkpoints.

DNA replication and chromosome distribution are indispensable events in the cell cycle control. Cells must accurately copy their chromosomes, and through the process of mitosis, segregate them to daughter cells. The checkpoints are surveillance mechanism and quality control of the genome to maintain genomic integrity. Checkpoint failure often causes mutations and genomic arrangements resulting in genetic instability. Genetic instability is a major factor of birth defects and in the development of many diseases, most notably cancer. Therefore, checkpoint studies are very important for understanding mechanisms of genome maintenance as they have direct impact on the ontogeny of birth defects and the cancer biology.

Genetic Change

A cancer cell is a cell that grows out of control. Unlike normal cells, cancer cells ignore signals to stop dividing, to specialize, or to die and shed. Growing in an uncontrollable manner and unable to recognize its own natural boundary, the cancer cells may spread to areas of the body where they do not belong.

In a cancer cell, several genes change (mutate) and the cell becomes defective.

Genes are the basic units of heredity. Serve two roles in cancer, some contribute to the development of cancer and others protect individuals from cancer.

Within each chromosome, there are many hundreds to thousands of genes. Genes Are segmented of DNA that tells the cell to do a specific task, usually to make a particular protein. Each protein has a specific job for function in the body, for example, some proteins help muscle cells contact, certain proteins help one cell divide into two, while others prevent the cell from dividing too often. Each human cell has a bout 30,000 genes, each one makes a protein with a unique function.

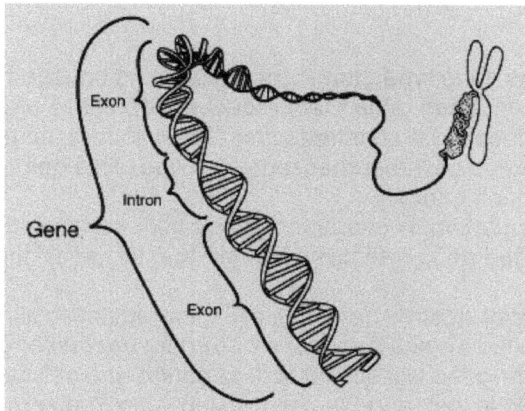
Courtesy of National Human Genome Research Institute

A cell uses its genes selectively-that is it will activate, or "turn on" the genes it needs at the right moment. This process allows for the different kinds of cells needed to make up different organs like the brain and the liver. Some genes stay active all the time to produce proteins needed for basic cell function. Others shut down when their job is finished and start again later if needed. A mutated (altered or changed) gene may tell the cell to make an abnormal protein, which no longer function properly. This may not have any effect at all, or it may lead to a disease. Some disease like sickle cell anemia is caused by gene mutations that are passed from parent to child. These types of diseases are considered to be hereditary.

  - Hereditary mutations are genes changes that come from a parent and therefore exist in all cells of the body, including reproductive cells (sperm or egg cells). The mutation can be passed from generation to generation. These are also called germline mutations. This type of mutation is a major factor for 5 to 10% cancer.

  - Acquired mutation (most cancers are caused by acquired mutation). An acquired mutation occurs when DNA in a cell changes during the person's life. This can be caused by environmental influences such as exposure to radiation or toxins. These types of mutations are not hereditary. They are not in every cell of the body like the hereditary mutations but only in the tumor or cancer cells. These are also called sporadic or somatic mutations.

  Mutations may also occur in a single cell within an early embryo. As all the cells divide during growth and development, the individual will have some cells with the mutation and some cells without the genetic change. This situation is called mosaicism.

  Some genetic changes are very rare; others are common in the population. Genetic changes that occur in more than 1 percent of the population are called polymorphisms. They are common enough to be considered a normal variation in the DNA. Polymorphisms are responsible for many of the normal differences between people such as eye color, hair color, and blood type. Although many polymorphisms have no negative effects on a person's health, some of these variations may influence the risk of developing certain disorders.

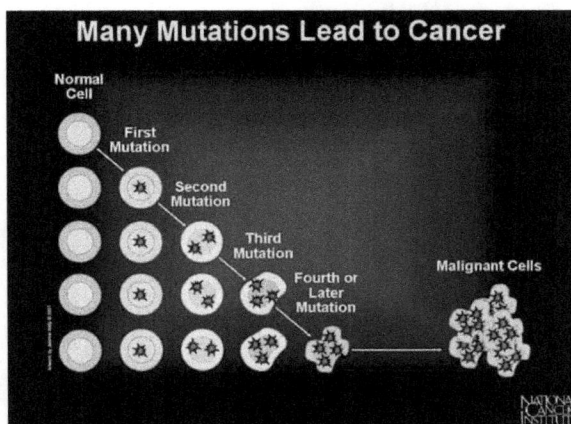
Courtesy of National Cancer Institute

Genes of Cancer

There are two general types of genes mutations. One type, dominant mutation, is caused by an abnormality in one gene in pair. An example is a mutated gene that produces a defective protein that causes the growth-factor receptor on a cell's surface to be constantly "on" when, in fact, no growth factor is present. The result is that the cell receives a constant message to divide. This dominant "gain of function gene" is often called an oncogene (onco= cancer).

The second gene type of mutation, recessive mutation, is characterized by both genes in the pair being damaged. For example, a normal gene called p53 produces a protein that turns "of" the cell cycle and thus helps to control cell growth.

The primary function of the p53 genes is to repair or destroy defective cells, thereby controlling potential cancerous cells. This type of gene is called an anti-oncogene or tumor suppressor gene. If only one p53 gene in the pair is mutated, the other gene will still be able to control the cell cycle. However, if both genes are mutated, the "off"swith is lost, and the cell division is no longer under control.

Abnormal cell division can occur either when active oncogenes are expressed or when tumor suppressor genes are lost. In fact, for a cell to become malignant, numerous mutations are necessary. In some cases, both types of mutations- dominant and recessive- may occur.

More than 100 oncogenes are now recognized, and undoubtedly more will be discovered in the future. Scientists have divided oncogenes into the 5 different classes:
- Growth factors
- Growth factors receptors
- Signal transducers
- Transcription factors
- Programmed cell death regulators

As scientists learn more about oncogenes, they may be able to develop drugs that inhibit or stop them. Many agents that target oncogenes are currently in development as
Potential anticancer drugs and some have already been approved by the US Food and Drug Administration (FDA) for clinical use.

Tumor suppressor genes are normal genes that slow down cell division, repair DNA mistakes, and tell cells when to die (a process known as apoptosis or programmed cell death). When tumor suppressor genes don't work properly, cell can grow out of control, which can lead to cancer.

About 30 tumor suppressor genes have been identified:
- Genes that control cell division
- Genes that repair DNA
- Cell suicide genes

An important difference between, oncogenes and tumor suppressor genes is that oncogenes result from activation (turning on) of proto-oncogenes, but tumor suppressor genes causes cancer when they are inactivated (turned off).

The lost complicated examples of cellular dynamics occur when a cell changes, or differentiates to carry out a specialized function. This process often is marked by a change in the microscopic appearance, or morphology of the cell.

Angiogenesis and Tumor Biology

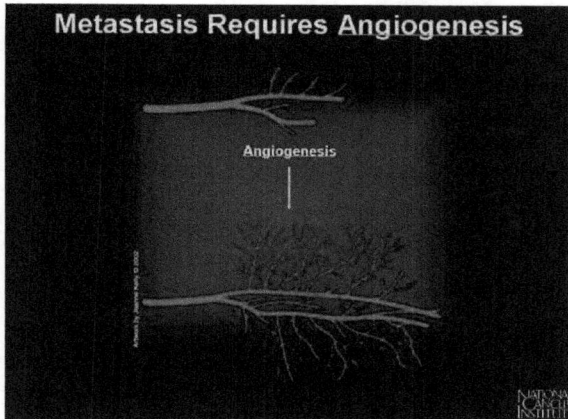

Courtesy of National Cancer Institute

Angiogenesis is important in embryogenesis, when it is tightly regulated by specific activators for a short time and then down regulated. Normal adult's blood vessels (BV) are quiescent, except in some disease states.

Tumor angiogenesis refers to: the development of new BV from existing BV. There are discreet steps:

*Post capillary venules show degradation of basement membranes.
*Endothelial cells migrate toward the tumor and form tubular structures.
*Incompetent basement membrane leaks macromolecules.

The body is made up of many types of cells. Normally, cells grow and divide to produce new cells in a controlled an orderly manner. Sometimes, however, new cells continue to be produced when they are not needed. As a result, a mass of extra tissue (tumor) may develop. A tumor can be benign (not cancerous) or malignant (cancerous).

Cells in malignant tumors are abnormal and divide without control or order. These cancerous cells can invade and damage nearby tissue, and spread to other parts of the body (metastasize).

If a tumor is suspected to be a malignant, a medical doctor removes a simple of tissues or the entire tumor in a procedure called a biopsy. A pathologist examines the tissue to determine whether the tumor is benign or malignant. The pathologist can also determine the tumor grade and identify other characteristics of the tumor cells.

The American joint commission on cancer recommends the following guidelines for grading tumors.

GX= Grade cannot be assessed (undetermined grade).
G1= Well-differentiated (low grade).
G2= moderately differentiated (Intermediate grade).
G3= poorly differentiated (High grade).
G4=Undifferentiated (High grade).

"American joint committee on cancer. AJCC Cancer Staging Manual. 6th Ed. New York, NY: Spring, 2oo2

Cancer Classification

Cancers may be categorized based on the function/location and stages of tumor progression of the cells from which they originate.

The following terms are commonly used to distinguish tumors of different origin. From a histological standpoint there are hundreds of different cancers, which are grouped into five major categories:

- Carcinoma
- Sarcoma
- Leukemia
- Lymphoma
- Myeloma

In addition, there are also some cancers of mixed types.

-Carcinoma refers to a malignant neoplasm of epithelial origin or cancer of the internal or external lining of the body. Carcinomas malignancies of epithelial tissue account for 80 to 90% of all cancer cases. Carcinomas are divided into two major subtypes: Adenocarcinoma, which develops in an organ or gland, and squamous cell carcinoma, which originates in the squamous epithelium.

-Sarcoma refers to cancer that originates in supportive and connective tissues such as bones, tendons, cartilages, muscles and fat. Examples of sarcomas are: Osteosarcoma (bone). Rhabdomyosarcoma (skeletal muscle).

-Leukemia is cancer of the bone marrow. The disease is often associated with the over production of immature white blood cells. These immature cells do not perform as well as they should, therefore the patient is often prone to infection. Example of leukemias includes lymphocytic leukemia and granulocytic leukemia.

-Lymphoma develops in the glands or nodes of the system, a network of vessels, nodes, and organs (specially the spleen, tonsils, and thymus). The lymphomas are sub classified into two categories: Hodgkin's lymphoma and non-Hodgkin's lymphoma.

-Myeloma is a cancer involving the plasmacytes responsible for the production of antibodies.

Stages of Tumor Progression

1-Hyperplasia: The altered cell divides in an uncontrolled manner leading to an excess of cells in that region of the tissue mixed types: The components may be within one category or from different categories. Some examples are: Adenosquamous carcinoma and carcinosarcoma.
The cells have a normal appearance but there are too many of them.

2- Dysplasia: additional genetic changes in the hyperplasic cells lead to even more abnormal growth. The cells and the tissue no longer look normal. The cells and tissue may become disorganized.

3 - Carcinoma in-situ: Cells of this type are said to be differentiated or anaplasic. A key facet of in situ growth is that the cells are contained within the initial location and have not yet crossed the basal lamina to invade other tissue. The abnormal cells are all in on location.

4- Malignant tumors: These tumors have the ability to invade surrounding tissues and/or spread (metastasize).

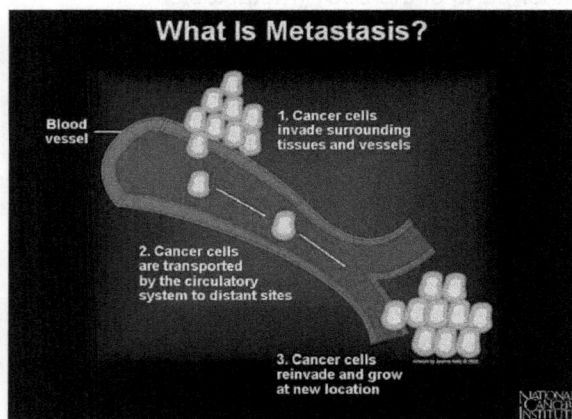

Courtesy of National cancer Institute

Some tumors do not progress to the point where they invade distant tissues. Such tumors are said to be benign. Because they do not spread beyond their initial location, they are not considered to be cancerous.

CHAPTER THREE: GENERAL CYTOGENETICS

Cytogenetics is the science that combines the methods and findings of cytology and genetics in the study of abnormal chromosomal structure and numbers in evaluating particular disease states.

Chromosome analysis

Normally chromosomes can't be seen with a light microscope but during cell division they become condensed enough to be easily analyzed at 1000X. To collect cells with their chromosomes in this condensed state they are exposed to a mitotic inhibitor which blocks formation of the spindle and arrests cell division at the metaphase stage.

A variety of tissue types can be used to obtain chromosome preparations. Some examples include peripheral blood, bone marrow, amniotic fluid, and products of conception. Although specific techniques differ according to the type of tissue used, the basic method for obtaining chromosome preparation is as follow:
1 - Sample log-in and initial setup.
2 -Tissue culture (feeding and maintaining cell cultures).
3 -Addition of a mitotic inhibitor to arrest at metaphase.
4 -Harvest cells. The step is very important in obtaining high quality preparation. It involves exposing the cells to a hypotonic solution followed by a series of fixative solutions. This causes the cells to expand so the chromosomes will spread out and can be individually examined.
5 -Stain chromosome preparations to detect possible numerical and structural changes.

Virtually all routine clinical Cytogenetic analyses are done on chromosome preparations that have been treated and stained to produce a banding pattern specific to each chromosome. This allows for the detection of subtle changes in chromosome structure. The most common staining treatment is called G-banding. A variety of other staining techniques are available to help identify specific abnormalities. Once stained metaphase chromosome preparations have been obtained they can examined under the microscope. Typically 15-20 cells are scanned and counted with a least 5 cells being fully analyzed. During a full analysis each chromosome is critically compared band-for-band with its homolog. It is necessary to examine this many cells in order to detect clinically significant mosaicim or clonality.

Following microscope analysis, either photographic or computerized digital images of the best quality metaphase cells are made. Each chromosome can then be arranged in pairs according to size and banding pattern into a karytotype. The karytotype allows the Cytogeneticist to even more closely examine each chromosome for structural changes. A written description of the karytotype which defines the chromosome analysis is then made.

Chromosome abnormalities

Although chromosome abnormalities can be very complex there are two basic types: numerical and structural. Both types can occur simultaneously.
Numerical abnormalities involve the loss and/or gain of a whole chromosome and can include both autosomes and sex chromosomes. Generally chromosome loss has a greater effect on an individual than does chromosome gain although these can also have severe consequences. Cells which have lost a chromosome are monosomy for that chromosome while those with an extra chromosome show trisomy for the chromosome involved. Nearly all autosomal monosomies die shortly after conception and only a few trisomy conditions survive to full tem. The most common autosomal numerical abnormality is Down syndrome. Curiously, a condition called triploidy in which there is an extra copy of every chromosome (69 totals), can occasionally survive to birth but usually die in the newborn period. Another general rule is that or gain of an autosome has more severe consequences than loss or gain of a sex chromosome. The most common sex chromosome abnormality is monosomy of the X chromosome (45, X) or Turner syndrome. Another fairly common example is Klinefelter syndrome (47, XXX). Although there is substantial variation within each syndrome, affected individuals often lead fairly normal lives. Occasionally an individual carries an extra chromosome which can't be identified by its banding pattern, these are called marker chromosomes. The introduction of FISH techniques has been a valuable tool in the identification of marker chromosomes.

Structural abnormalities involve changes in the structure of one or more chromosomes.

There are three of the more common types:

1 - Deletions involve loss of material from a single chromosome. The effects are typically severe since there is a loss of genetic material.

2 - Inversions occur when there are two breaks within a single chromosome and the broken segment flips 180(invert) and reattaches to form a chromosome that is structurally out-of-sequence. There is usually no risk for problems to an individual if the inversion is of familial origin (has been inherited from a parent). There is a slightly increased risk if it is a de novo (new) mutation due possibly to an interruption of a key gene sequence.   Although an inversion carrier may be completely normal, they are at a slightly increased risk for producing a chromosomally unbalanced embryo. This is because an inverted chromosome has difficulty pairing with its normal homolog during meiosis, which can result in gametes containing unbalanced derivative chromosomes if an unequal cross-over event occurs

3 - Translocations involve exchange of material between two or more chromosomes. If a translocation is reciprocal (balanced) the risk for problems to an individual is similar to that with inversions: usually none if familial and slightly increases if de novo. Problems arise with translocations when gametes from a balanced parent are formed which do not contain both translocation products. When such a gamete combines with a normal gamete from the other parent the result is an unbalanced embryo which is partially monosomic for one chromosome and partially trisomic for the other.

Numerical and structural abnormalities can be further divided into two main categories: constitutional, and acquired. Sometimes individuals are found who have both normal cell lines. These people are called mosaics and in the vast majority of these cases the abnormal cell line has a numerical chromosome abnormality. Structural mosaics are extremely rare. The degree to which an individual is clinically affected usually depends on the percentage of abnormal cells. A routine Cytogenetic analysis typically includes the examination of at least 15-20 cells in order to rule out any clinically significant mosaicism.

Limitations of conventional cytogenetic studies

- Low sensitivity compared to FISH and PCR
- At least 2 of 20 metaphases must have same chromosomal anomaly to call clonal.
- Results may be misleading if cells of interest did not proliferate.
- Malignant cells sometimes grow less well in culture than normal cells.
- The cell type for each metaphase is unknown.
- Cryptic chromosomal defects are not detected: t(15;17), t(9;22), in 5% of CML, and t(12;21) in B cell ALL.

Fluorescence In-Situ Hybridization

Fluorescence In-Situ Hybridization is a method used to identify specific parts of chromosome. For example, if we know the sequence of a certain gene, but we don't know on which chromosome the gene is located, we can use FISH to identify the chromosome in question and the exact location of the gene. Or, if we suspect that has been a translocation in a chromosome, we can use a probe that spans the site of breakage/translocation. If there has been no translocation at that point, we will see one signal, since the probe hybridizes to one place on the chromosome. If however, there has been a translocation, we will see two signals, since the probe can hybridize to both ends of the translocation point.

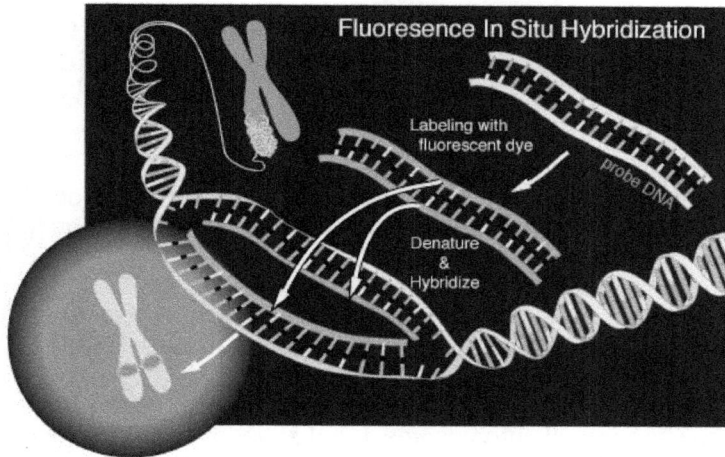

Fluoresence In Situ Hybridization

Labeling with fluorescent dye

probe DNA

Denature & Hybridize

Courtesy of National Human Genome Research Institute

Each probe is specific to one region of a chromosome (pair), and is labeled with fluorescent molecules throughout its length.
 - Each microscope slide contains many metaphases.
 - Each metaphase consists of the complete set of chromosomes, one small segment of which each probe will seek out and bind itself to.

The first step is to break apart (denature) the double strands of DNA in both the probe DNA and the chromosome DNA so they can bind to each other. This is done by heating the DNA in a solution of formamide at a high temperature (70C).
Next, the probe is placed on the slide and a glass coverslip is placed on top. To prevent evaporation; the edges of the coverslip are sealed with rubber cement. The slide is then placed in a 37C incubator overnight for the probe to hybridize with the target chromosome.
Overnight, the probe DNA seeks out its target sequence on the specific chromosome and binds to it.
 The next day, the coverslip is removed, and the slide is washed in a salt/detergent solution to remove any of the probes that did not bind to chromosomes. A differently colored fluorescent dye is added to the slide to stain all of the chromosomes so that they may be viewed using a fluorescent light microscope.
 Although metaphase spreads are useful to visualize specific chromosomes and the exact region to which the probe binds, sometimes a general count of chromosome number or presence/absence of a probe signal is enough to give information (XX vs. XY chromosomes, trisomy 21 etc).In this case, cell nuclei in which the chromosomes are not condensed enough to view as separate objects can be use. These are called interphase nuclei, and they greatly outnumber metaphases on any given slide.
 Two (or more) different probes labeled with different fluorescent tags can be mixed and used at the same time. The chromosomes are then stained with a third color for contrast. This gives a metaphase or interphase cell with three colors which can be used to detect two different chromosomes at the same time, or to provide a "control probe" in case one of the other target sequences are deleted and a probe cannot bind to the chromosome.
 The nomenclature of human chromosomes is based on several international consensus conferences. The convention is to first state the total chromosome number, followed by the sex chromosome constitution:
46, XX normal female
46, XY normal male
The description of abnormal karyotypes can be complicated. Examples of the more common designations are as follows:
[del] deletion
[t] translocation
[dup] duplication
[Ter] terminal
[ins] insertion
[mat] maternal origin
[i] Isochromosome

[pat] paternal origin
[inv] inversion
[+] additional chromosome
[r]ring chromosome

    By convention, the total chromosome count and sex chromosomes are followed by a notation indicating the type of chromosome abnormality that is present. The abnormality is defined using one of the above designations followed by the number of the chromosome(s) that is involved, and the band(s) at the site of the breakpoint. See the examples below.

46, XY, del (22) (q21) a male with 46 chromosomes and a deletion on chromosome 22, with a breakpoint at band q21

46, XX, inv (7) (p11; q22) a female with 46 chromosomes and an inversion on chromosome 7, with breakpoints at bands p11 and q22

46, XX, t (1; 6) (p23; q21) a female with 46 chromosomes and a translocation between chromosomes 1 and 6 with breakpoints at band p23 on the short arm of chromosome 1 and at band q21 on the long arm of chromosome 6

47, XX, +21 a female with an extra copy of chromosome 21, trisomy 21 or Down syndrome

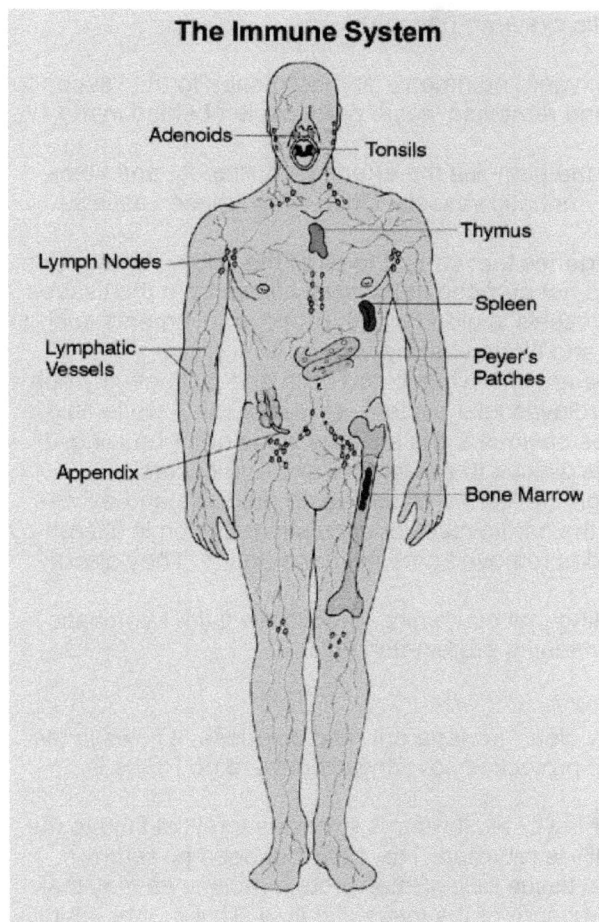

The Immune System

Adenoids — Tonsils

Thymus

Lymph Nodes

Spleen

Lymphatic Vessels — Peyer's Patches

Appendix — Bone Marrow

http://www.healthcare.utah.edu/healthinfo/adult/infectious/immune.htm

CHAPTER ONE: THE LYMPHATIC SYETEM=LYMPH

The human body has two circulatory systems! These are the cardiovascular system and the lymphatic system. The differences between these two systems are:

The cardiovascular system= (Blood) and the lymphatic system= (Lymph).

Blood is responsible for collecting and distributing oxygen, nutriments and hormones to the tissues to the entire body. Lymph is responsible for collecting and removing waste products left behind in the tissues.

Blood flows in a closed continuous loop throughout the body via the arteries, capillaries, and veins. Lymph flows in an open circuit from the tissues into lymphatic vessels. Once within these vessels, lymph flows in only one direction.

Blood is pumped. The heart pumps blood into the arteries that carry it to all of the body. Veins return blood from all parts of the body to the heart. Lymph is not pumped. It passively flows from the tissues into the lymph capillaries. Flow within the lymphatic vessels is aided by other body movements such as deep breathing and the action of nearby muscles and blood vessels.

Blood consist of the liquid plasma that transports the red and white blood cells and platelets. Lymph that has been filtered and is ready to return to the cardiovascular system is clear or milky white fluid.

Blood is visible and damage to blood vessels causes obvious signs such as bleeding or bruising. Lymph is invisible and damage to lymphatic system is difficult to detect until swelling occurs.

Blood is filtered by the kidney. All blood flows through the kidney where waste products and excess fluids are removed. Necessary fluids are returned to the cardiovascular circulation. Lymph is filtered by lymph nodes located throughout the body. These nodes remove some fluid and debris. They also kill pathogens and some cancer cells.

Blood vessel damage or insufficiency produces swelling that containing low-protein fluid. Lymphatic vessel damage or insufficiency produces swelling containing protein-rich fluid.

The lymph is an alkaline (pH>7.0) fluid that is usually clear, transparent, and colorless, it flows in the lymphatic vessel and bathes tissues and organs in its protective covering. There are no RBCs in lymph and it has lower protein content than blood.

The lymphatic system has three primary functions. First of all, it returns excess interstitial fluid to the blood. Of the fluid that leaves the capillary, a bout 90% is returned. The 10% that does no return becomes part of the interstitial fluid that surrounds the tissue cells. Small protein molecules may leak through the capillary wall and increase the osmotic pressure of the interstitial fluid. This further inhibits the return of the fluid into the capillaries, and fluid tends to accumulate in the tissue spaces. If this continues, blood volume and blood pressure decrease significantly and the volume of tissue fluid increases, which results in edema (swelling).

Lymph capillaries pick up the excess interstitial fluid and proteins and return them to the venous blood. After the fluid enters the lymph capillaries, it's called lymph.

The second function of the lymphatic system is the absorption of fats and fat-soluble vitamins from the digestive system and the subsequent transport of these substances to the venous circulation.

The third and probably most well known function of the lymphatic system is defense against invading microorganisms and disease.

Lymph nodes and other lymphatic organs filter the lymph to remove microorganisms and other foreign particles.

The body uses the lymphoid system to enable lymphocytes to encounter antigens and it is here that adaptive immune responses are initiated. The lymphoid system consists of primary lymphoid organs, secondary lymphoid organs, and lymphatic vessels.

a. Primary lymphoid organs

The bone marrow and the thymus constitute the primary lymphoid organs. Both B-lymphocytes and T-lymphocytes are produced from stem cells in the bone marrow. B-lymphocytes mature in the bone marrow while T-lymphocytes migrate to the thymus and mature there. After maturation, both B-lymphocytes and T-lymphocytes circulate through and accumulate in secondary lymphoid organs.

b. Lymphatic vessels

Lymphatic vessels are responsible for flow of lymph within the lymphoid system and are a part of the body's fluid recirculation system. The liquid portion of the blood, called plasma, constantly leaks out of capillaries to deliver oxygen and nutrients to cells of the surrounding tissue. Once in the tissue, the plasma is now called tissue fluid. While most of this tissue fluid re-enters capillaries and is returned directly to the bloodstream, some fluid enters lymph vessels as lymph. The lymph flows through regional lymph nodes and eventually enters the circulatory system at the heart to maintain the fluid volume of the circulation.

c. Secondary lymphoid organs

Adaptive immune responses require antigen-presenting cells, such as macrophages and dendritic cells, and ever changing populations of B-lymphocytes and T- lymphocytes. These cells gather to detect antigens in secondary lymphoid organs.

The secondary lymphoid organs include highly organized lymphoid organs such as lymph nodes and the spleen, as well as less organized accumulations of lymphoid organs scattered strategically throughout the body. These latter include the tonsils and the appendix.

The mucosa-associated lymphoid tissue or MALT refers to the diffuse system of small concentrations of lymphoid tissue found in various sites of the body such as the gastrointestinal tract, thyroid, breast, lung, salivary glands, eye, and skin. MALT is populated by loose clusters of T-lymphocytes, B-lymphocytes, plasma cells, activated T_h cells, and macrophages. MALT can be subdivided into:
GALT (gut-associated lymphoid tissue, such as the Peyer's patches in the lining of the small intestines)
BALT (bronchial-associated lymphoid tissue in the bronchi)
SALT (skin-associated lymphoid tissue beneath the epidermis)
NALT (nose-associated lymphoid tissue)
LALT (larynx-associated lymphoid tissue)
CALT (conjunctiva-associated lymphoid tissue in the eye)

Lymph nodes contain many reticular fibers that support fixed macrophages and dendritic cells as well as everchanging populations of circulating B-lymphocytes and T-lymphocytes. When microorganisms and other antigens enter tissues, they are transported by tissue fluid into the lymph vessels. Lymph vessels, in turn, carry these antigens, now in the lymph, to regional lymph nodes. Here the microbes and other antigens in the lymph encounter changing populations of B-lymphocytes, are filtered out and phagocytosed by the fixed macrophages and dendritic cells, and are presented to changing populations of T-lymphocytes. Approximately 25 billion different lymphocytes migrate through each lymph node every day.

Like the lymph nodes, the spleen contains many reticular fibers that support fixed macrophages and dendritic cells as well as everchanging populations of circulating B-lymphocytes and T-lymphocytes. When microorganisms and other antigens enter the blood, they are transported by the blood vessels to the spleen. Here they encounter changing populations of B-lymphocytes, are filtered out and phagocytosed by the fixed macrophages and dendritic cells, and are presented to changing populations of T-lymphocytes.

Microorganisms and other antigens entering the respiratory tract, gastrointestinal tract, eye, and skin encounter macrophages, dendritic cells, and the changing populations of B-lymphocytes and T-lymphocytes in MALT.

Lymphatic Vessels

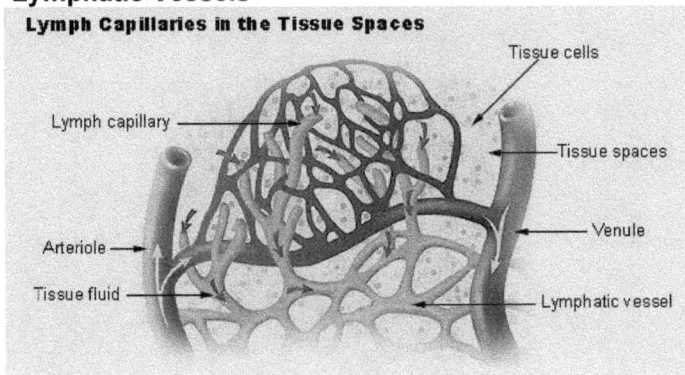

Lymph Capillaries in the Tissue Spaces

http://training.seer.cancer.gov

24

Unlike blood vessels, only carry fluid away from the tissues. The smallest lymphatic vessels are the lymph capillaries, which begin in the tissue spaces as blind-ended sacs. Lymph capillaries are found in all regions of the body except the bone marrow, central nervous system, and tissues, such as the epidermis, that lack blood vessels. The wall of the lymph capillaries is composed of the endothelium in which the simple squamous cells overlap to form a simple one-way valve. This arrangement permits fluid to enter the capillary but presents lymph from leaving the vessel.

The microscopic lymph capillaries merge to form lymphatic vessels. Small lymphatic vessels join to form larger tributaries, called lymphatic trunks, which drain large regions. Lymphatic trunks merge until the lymph enters the two lymphatic ducts. The right lymphatic duct drains lymph from the upper right quadrant of the body. The thoracic duct drains all the rest.

Like veins, the lymphatic tributaries have thin walls and have valves to prevent backflow of blood. There is no pump in the lymphatic system like the heart in the cardiovascular system. The pressure gradients to move lymph through the vessels come from the skeletal muscle action, respiratory movement, and contraction of smooth muscle in vessel walls.

Lymph Nodes

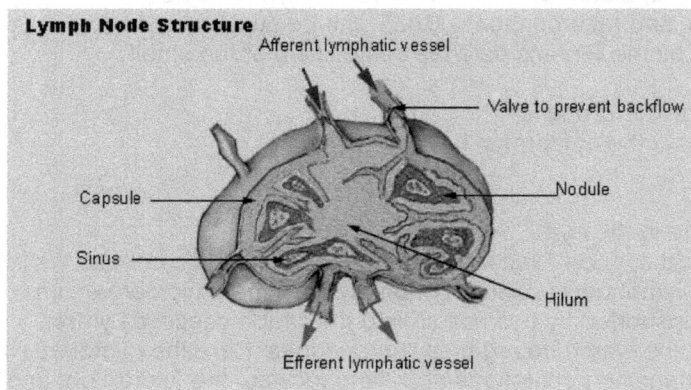

http://training.seer.cancer.gov;

Lymph nodes are small bean-shaped structures that are usually less than 2.5 cm length. They are widely distributed throughout the body along the lymphatic pathways where they filter the lymph before it is returned to the blood. Lymph nodes are not present in the central nervous system. There are three superficial regions on each side of the body where lymph nodes tend to cluster. These areas are the inguinal nodes in the groin, the axillaries' nodes in the armpit, and the cervical nodes in the neck.

The typical lymph node is surrounded by a connective tissue capsule and divided into compartments called lymph nodules. The lymph nodules are dense masses of lymphocytes and macrophages and are separated by spaces called lymph sinuses. Several afferent lymphatic vessels, which carry lymph into the node, enter the node on the convex side. The lymph moves through the lymph sinuses and enters an efferent lymphatic the efferent vessel leaves the node at an intended region called the hilum.

Tonsils

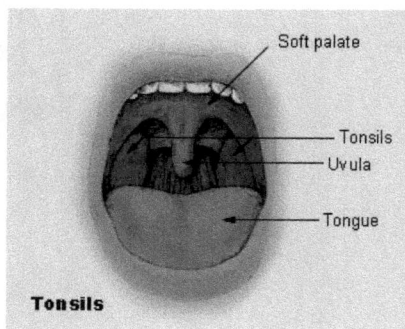

http://training.seer.cancer.gov

Tonsils are clusters of lymphatic tissue just under the mucous membranes that line the nose, mouth, and throat (pharynx). There are three groups of tonsils. The pharyngeal tonsils are located near the opening of the nasal cavity into the pharynx. When these tonsils become enlarged they may interfere with breathing and are called adenoids. The palatine tonsils are the ones that are located near the opening of the oral cavity into the pharynx. Lingual tonsils are located on the posterior surface of the tongue, which also places them near the opening of the oral cavity into the pharynx. Lymphocytes and macrophages in the tonsils provide protection against harmful substances and pathogens that may enter the body through the nose or mouth.

Thymus

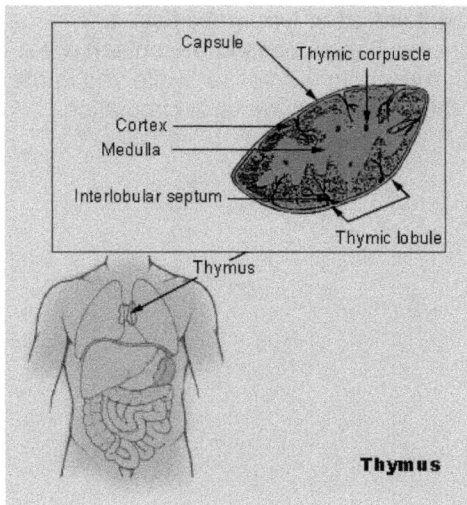

http://training.seer.cancer.gov

The thymus is a soft organ with lobes that is located anterior to the ascending aorta and posterior to the sternum. It is relatively large in infants and children but after puberty it begins to decrease in size so that in older adults it is quite small. The primary function of the thymus is the processing and maturation of special lymphocytes called T-cells. While in the thymus, the lymphocytes do not respond to pathogens and foreign agents. After the lymphocytes have matured, they enter the blood and go to other lymphatic organs where they provide defense against disease. The thymus also produces a hormone, thymosin, which stimulates the maturation of lymphocytes in other lymphatic organs.

Spleen

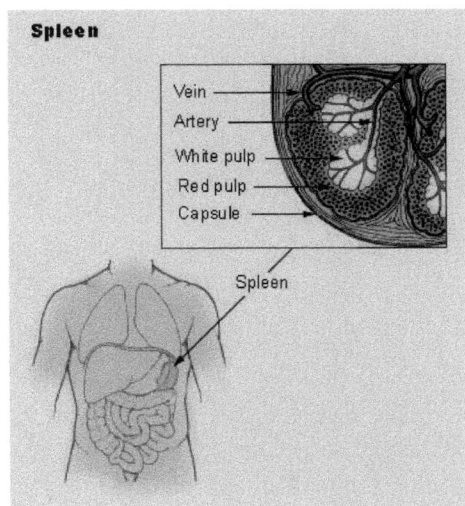

http://training.seer.cancer.gov

The spleen is located in the upper left abdominal cavity, just beneath the diaphragm, and posterior to the stomach. It is similar to a lymph node in shape and structure but it is much larger. The spleen is the largest lymphatic organ in the body. Surrounded by a connective tissue capsule, which extends inward to divide the organ into lobules, the spleen consists of two types of tissue called white pulp and red pulp. The white pulp is lymphatic tissue consisting mainly of lymphocytes around arteries. The red pulp consists of venous sinuses filled with blood and cords of lymphatic cells, such as lymphocytes and macrophages. Blood enters the spleen through the splenic artery, moves through the sinuses where it is filtered, the leaves through the splenic vein.

The spleen filters blood in much the way that the lymph nodes filter lymph. Lymphocytes in the spleen react to pathogens in the blood and attempt to destroy them. Macrophages then engulf the resulting debris, the damaged cells, and the other large particles. The spleen, along with the liver, removes old and damaged erythrocytes from the circulating blood. Like other lymphatic tissue, it produces lymphocytes, especially in response to invading pathogens. The sinuses in the spleen are a reservoir for blood. In emergencies such as hemorrhage, smooth muscle in the vessel walls and in the capsule of the spleen contracts. This squeezes the blood out of the spleen into general circulation.

CHAPTER TWO: THE CARDIOVASCULAR SYSTEM= BLOOD

The cardiovascular system is sometimes called the blood-vascular or simply the circulatory system. It consists of:
-blood
-heart
-blood vessels (arteries, arterioles, capillaries, venules and veins)
Blood is a connective tissue composed of a liquid portion called plasma (the matrix) and a cellular portion consisting of various cells and cell fragments. Blood contained in the circulatory system is pumped by the heart around a closed circle or circuit of vessels as it passes again and again through the various circulations of the body.
Blood carries the following to the body tissues:
-Nourishment.
-Electrolytes.
-Vitamins.
-Antibodies.
-Heat.
-Oxygen.
Blood carries the following away from the body tissues:
-Waste matter.
-Carbon dioxide.
Blood has the following major characteristics:
-denser and more viscous than water
-temperature of 38 degrees Celsius
-pH that normally ranges between 7.35 and 7.45
-constitutes about 8% of total body weight
-average volume of 5 to 6 liters in adult males and 4 to 5 liters in adults females

Component of Blood

Blood consists of a liquid component, the plasma, and formed elements, as we call the solid component. Inorganic components of plasma include the major electrolytes sodium, chloride, and potassium ions, among which the salt, sodium chloride, is predominant.
Plasma also contains soluble proteins, the most abundant of which is serum albumin. The primary purpose of albumin is to transport fatty acids, which are not terribly soluble in an aqueous environment by themselves. Albumin also serves to transport lipid-soluble hormones such as steroids. Another major component is carbonic anhydrase, which catalyzes the conversion of dissolved carbon dioxide to bicarbonate anion and back. Carbonic anhydrase is essential toward maintaining the pH of blood and extra cellular fluids within physiological limits. Other plasma proteins of interest include Immunoglobulins, fibrinogen, and clotting factors.

The term serum refers to the liquid component of clotted blood. Serum differs from plasma in that it lacks the formed elements and clotting factors, but retains the electrolytes and soluble proteins, including antibodies.
Blood to which an anticoagulant has been added will not clot. Blood cells will settle to the bottom of the tube leaving plasma at the top of the tube. Blood to which no anticoagulant has been added will clot. Blood cells get caught in the clot leaving serum behind.
Proteins make up 6-8% of the blood. They are about equally divided serum albumin and a great variety of serum globulins.
After blood is withdrawn from a vein and allowed to clot slowly shrinks. As it does so, a clear fluid called serum is squeezed out. Thus:
Serum is blood plasma without fibrinogen and other clothing factors.
The serum proteins can be separated by electrophoresis. The separated proteins appear as distinct bands. The most prominent of these and the one that moves closest to the positive electrode is serum albumin.
Serum albumin is made in the liver, binds many small molecules for transport through the blood, and helps maintain the osmotic pressure of the blood. The other proteins are the various serum globulins. They migrate in the order (alpha globulins, beta globulins, gamma globulins).Most antibodies are

gamma globulins. Therefore gamma globulins become more abundant following infections or immunization. The gamma globulins are produced by cells of the immune system.

Albumin is the smallest of the plasma proteins and is just small enough to pass through capillary walls. In normal circumstances this leads to the small amount of leakage into the interstitial fluid. In severe kidney disease large amounts of albumin are able to leak out through the damage kidney tubules and can be detected in the urine. Because the liver can quickly and easily replace lost albumin the body may lose large amounts of the protein without showing signs of disease.

The blood plasma contains inorganic ions which are important in regulating cell function and maintaining homeostasis. For example depletion of potassium may occur following severe diarrhea and vomiting. Potassium affects cells excitability and severe loss will cause muscle weakness and abnormalities of the cardiac impulse. The same problems may result in severe sodium depletion. Lack of sodium in the plasma will result in a reduction in the overall volume of extra cellular fluid which in turn leads to a drop in blood pressure causing weakness, dizziness, mental confusion and fainting.
In addition to proteins and inorganic ions the blood plasma carries a wide range of substances in transit to various tissues throughout the body. Nutrients are carried in the blood plasma. The most abundant, is glucose which is the primary source of energy for cell metabolism. Other nutrients in transit in the plasma include amino acids, fatty acids, triglycerides, cholesterol and vitamins. Waste products of metabolism are also transported by the plasma including urea, uric acid and creatinine from the kidneys and bilirubin from the gall bladder.

Hormones, such as cortisol and thyroxin are also transported around the body in plasma attached to plasma proteins. Other substances can be transported in the plasma the most obvious examples being drugs and alcohol.

The formed elements are all cells or parts of cells, including the following:

- Erythrocytes or red blood cells (RBCs).
- Leukocytes or white blood cells (WBCs).
        - Granular leukocytes (granulocytes):
                    - Neutrophiles.
                    - Eosinophiles.
                    - Basophiles.
        - Agranular leukocytes (agranulocytes):
                    - Lymphocytes.
                        .B-cells
                        .T–cells
                        . Natural killer cells
        - Monocytes.

    - Platelets (which are cell fragment).

Red Blood Cells (Erythrocytes) =RBCs

Greater than 99% of the formed elements in blood are erythrocytes.
A healthy adult male has about 5.4 million erythrocytes per microliter; a healthy adult female has a bout 4.8 million erythrocytes per microliter.
Each RBC is a flexible, biconcave disc that lacks a nucleus and other organelles.
The cytosol of each RBC contains about 280 million dissolved hemoglobin molecules.
Each hemoglobin molecule consists of four globin chains and four heme groups.
 Hemoglobin can bind reversibly to oxygen (to form oxyhemoglobin); this permits erythrocytes to transport oxygen from the lungs to other tissues of the body.
Hemoglobin can also bind reversibly to carbon dioxide (to form carbaminohemoglobin); this permits erythrocytes to transport carbon dioxide from the tissues to the lungs to be expelled.
Hemoglobin also plays a role in regulation of blood flow and blood pressure.
 Erythrocytes live only approximately 120 days due to absence of organelles; the latter results in an inability to replace plasma membrane components that are damaged as RBCs squeeze through narrow capillaries.

Erythropoiesis starts in the red bone marrow and progresses through the following successive stages of differentiation:
-proerythroblast
-reticulocyte that enters the bloodstream
-erythrocyte
Hypoxia stimulates the kidneys to release erythropoietin which in turn stimulates Erythropoiesis.

ABO blood types

There are two major blood group systems; each is based on the presence or absence of genetically determined cell-surface antigens called isoantigenes or agglutinogens:

-ABO Blood grouping system
-Rh blood grouping system
The ABO Blood Group was the first to be discovered (in 1900) and is the most important in assuring safe blood transfusion. The table shows the four ABO phenotypes present in the human population.

	Group A	Group B	Group AB	Group O
Red blood cell type				
Antibodies present	Anti-B	Anti-A	None	Anti-A and Anti-B
Antigens present	A antigen	B antigen	A and B antigens	None

http://en.wikipedia.org/wiki/ABO_blood_group_system

For example, people with type A blood will have the A antigen on the surface of their red cells. As a result, anti-A antibodies will not be produced by them because they would cause the destruction of their own blood. However, if B type blood is injected into their systems, anti-B antibodies in their plasma will recognize it as alien and burst or agglutinate the introduced red cells in order to cleanse the blood of alien protein

Individuals with type O blood do not produce ABO antigens. Therefore, their blood normally will not be rejected when it is given to others with different ABO types. As a result, type O people are universal donors for transfusions, but they can receive only type O blood themselves. Those who have type AB blood do not make any ABO antibodies. Their blood does not discriminate against any other ABO type. Consequently, they are universal receivers for transfusions, but their blood will be agglutinated when given to people with every other type because they produce both kinds of antigens.

A, B, and H antigens have a basic structure that is formed on oligosaccharide chains. These chains are attached to proteins or lipid molecules on the red cell surface. Each chain is made of 4 sugar molecules that are linked in one straight line or branched. Immunodominant sugars present at the terminal ends of the chains confer ABO antigen specificity.

~ A antigen has N-acetylgalactosamine
~ B antigen has D-galactose
~ H antigen has L-fucose

~ O has no additional sugar (H structure).

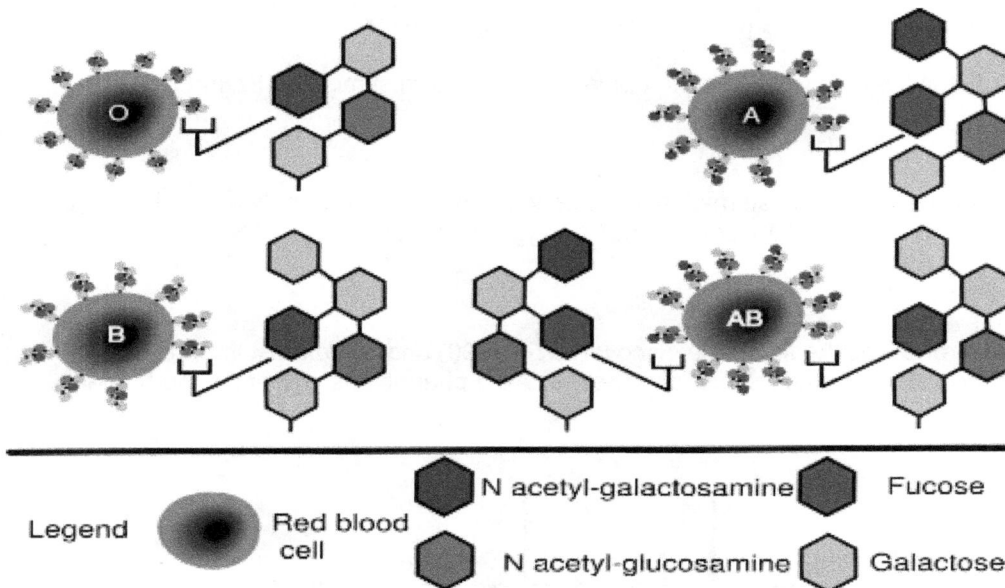

The inheritance of at least one of the H genes is required for normal ABO expression. Group O individuals (genotype OO) will only have the H antigen on their surface.

The two major alleles at the H locus are H and h. The H gene product (L-fucosyltransferase) adds L-fucose to the precursor substance. The h gene is an amorph and results in little or no production of L-fucosyltransferase. If both h genes are inherited (hh), the Bombay phenotype (Oh) occurs. Bombay is a rare blood type originally found in India, but has been found elsewhere in the world. To date, about 130 cases have been reported, with most in India. These individuals did not inherit the H allele and are genetically hh. Because they do not have the H antigen, they will not react with anti-H. Bombay individuals are very rare and can only receive blood from another Bombay. Since they do not have the H substance, they have antibodies towards H, A, and B antigens (all blood types!).

These are two principle subgroups of A. Both subgroups of A are not dinstinguished very well with routine anti-A, however, they can be serologically dinstinguished based on the reactivity with human anti-A_1. When anti-A_1 is added,
- A_1 cells will agglutinate
- A_2 cells will not agglutinate

The majority (80%) of the A and AB population are A_1 or A_1B; the remaining 20% are A_2 or A_2B. Unlike the A_1 gene, the A_2 gene produces a transferase that doesn't convert the H substance into the A antigen very well. As a result, an A_2 individual has significantly fewer antigen sites (75% less) than an A_1 individual. Individuals who are are A_2 or A_2B may produce anti-A_1. Of course, this occurence is small. Anti-A_1 is found in 1-8% of A_2 individuals and 22-30% of A_2B individuals.

It is easy and inexpensive to determine an individual's ABO type from a few drops of blood. A serum containing anti-A antibodies is mixed with some of the blood. Another serum with anti-B antibodies is mixed with the remaining sample. Whether or not agglutination occurs in either sample indicates the ABO type. It is a simple process of elimination of the possibilities. For instance, if an individual's blood sample is agglutinated by the anti-A antibody, but not the anti-B antibody, it means that the A antigen is present but not the B antigen. Therefore, the blood type is A.

Genetic Inheritance Patterns

ABO blood types are inherited through genes on chromosome 9, and they do not change as a result of environmental influences during life. An individual's ABO type is determined by the inheritance of 1 of 3 alleles (A, B, or O) from each parent. The possible outcomes are shown below:

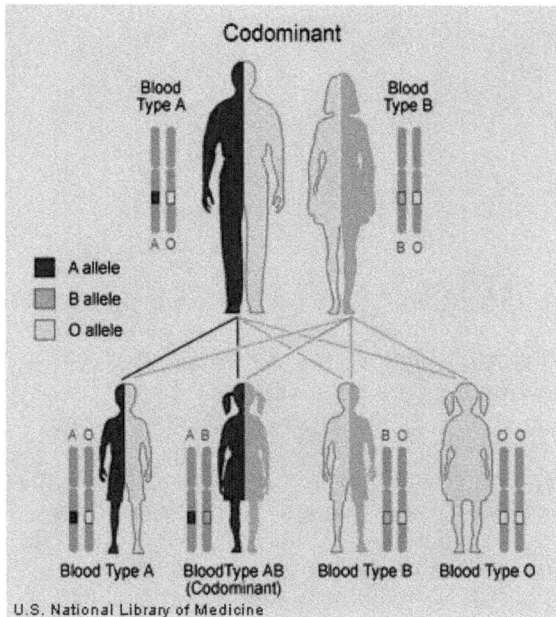

Courtesy of U.S. National Library of Medicine

Both A and B alleles are dominant over O. As a result, individuals who have an AO genotype will have an A phenotype. People who are type O have OO genotypes. In other words, they inherited a recessive O allele from both parents. The A and B alleles are codominant. Therefore, if an A is inherited from one parent and a B from the other, the phenotype will be AB. Agglutination tests will show that these individuals have the characteristics of both type A and type B blood.

In 2007, Danish and French investigators reported the properties of two bacterial glycosidase that specifically remove the sugars responsible for the A and B antigens. This discovery raises the possibility of being able to treat A, B, Or AB blood with these enzymes and thus convert the blood to group O, the "universal donor".

Rh Blood types

The Rh system is named for the rhesus monkey in which they were first discovered.
There are a number of Rh antigens. Red cells that are "Rh positive" express the one designated D. About 15% of the population have no RhD antigens and thus are "Rh negative".

The major importance of the Rh system for human health is to avoid the danger of RhD incompatibility between mother and fetus.

Mother-fetus incompatibility occurs when the mother is Rh- (dd) and the father is Rh+ (DD or Dd). Maternal antibodies can cross the placenta and destroy fetal red blood cells. The risk increases with each pregnancy. The first time an Rh- woman becomes pregnant; there usually are not incompatibility difficulties for her Rh+ fetus. However, the second and subsequent births are likely to have life-threatening problems. The risk increases with each birth. In order to understand why first born are normally safe and later children are not, it is necessary to understand some of the placenta's functions. Nutrients and the mother's antibodies regularly transfer across the placental boundary into the fetus, but her red blood cells usually do not (except in the case of an accidental rupture). Normally, anti-Rh+ antibodies do not exist in the first-time mother unless she has previously come in contact with Rh+ blood. Therefore, her antibodies are not likely to agglutinate the red blood cells of her Rh+ fetus.

Rh type mother-fetus incompatibility occurs only when an Rh+ man fathers a child with an Rh- mother. Since an Rh+ father can have either a DD or Dd genotype, there are 2 mating combinations possible:

father

	D	D
d (mother)	Dd	Dd
d	Dd	Dd

100% Rh+ children

father

	D	d
d (mother)	Dd	dd
d	Dd	dd

50% Rh+ children

Only the Rh+ children (Dd) are likely to have medical complications. When both the mother and her fetus are Rh- (dd), the birth will be normal.

Mother-fetus incompatibility problems can result with the ABO system also. However, they are very rare--less than .1% of births are affected and usually the symptoms are not as severe. It most commonly occurs when the mother is type O and her fetus is A, B, or AB. These problems in a baby are usually treated successfully without blood transfusions.

During birth, there is often a leakage of the body's red cells into the mother's circulation. If the baby is Rh positive (having inherited the trait from its father) and the mother Rh negative, these red cells will cause her to develop antibodies against the RhD antigen. The antibodies, usually of the IgG class, do not cause any problems for that child, but can cross the placenta and attack the red cells of subsequent Rh positive fetus. This destroys the red cells producing anemia, jaundice and elevated bilirubin levels. The disease, called erythroblastosis fetalis or hemolytic disease of the newborn may be so severe as to kill the fetus or even the newborn infant. It is an example of an antibody-mediated cytotoxicity disorder.

Bombay Phenotypes

It is important to be cautious in predicting the ABO blood type of children based on the phenotypes of their parents. This is due to the fact that a third antigen (H) on the surface of red cells can prevent the expected ABO blood type from occurring.
Normally, if an A blood type mother has an O type child; the father is expected to be type O or at least to carry the O allele (OO, AO, or BO genotype).

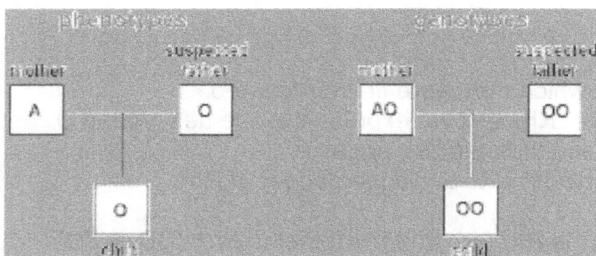

The child has inherited an O allele from both parents. However, an O blood type child can also be born to parents who do not have the O allele if a recessive form of the allele for the H antigen also is inherited from both parents.

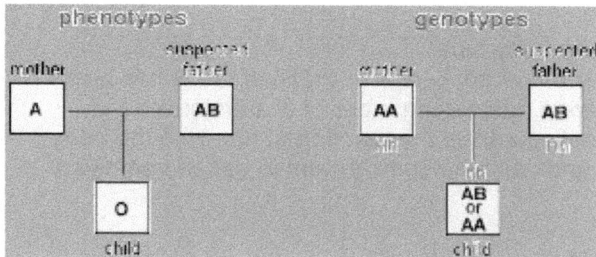

The H antigen is a precursor to the A and B antigens. For instance, the B allele must be present to produce the B enzyme that modifies the H antigen to become the B antigen. It is the same for the A allele. However, if only recessive alleles for the H antigen are inherited (hh), as in the case above, the H antigen will not be produced. Subsequently, the A and B antigens also will not be produced. The result is an O phenotype by default since a lack of A and B antigens is the O type. This seemingly impossible phenotype result has been referred to as a Bombay phenotype because it was first described in that Indian city.

The ABO blood system is further complicated by the fact that there are two subtypes of type A and two of AB. These are referred to as A_1, A2, A1B, and A_2B.

Several other blood group antigens have been identified in humans. Some example: MN, Duffy, Lewis, Kell. They, too, may sometimes cause
-transfusion reactions and even
-hemolytic disease of the newborn

In cases where there is no ABO or Rh incompatibility It is probable that as the RBCs age they become less deformable due to diminishing efficiency of ion pumping mechanisms and as a result they are no longer able to pass through the filtering system of the spleen and are thus removed by being literally eaten up white blood cells in a process known as phagocytosis.

Aged RBCs are removed by the spleen, liver and the bone marrow. Although it appears that the spleen is most active their relative importance to each other under normal circumstances is uncertain. Certainly we know that individuals who have lost their spleen are able to function normally with few limitations.

RBCs have a specialized cytoskeleton in order to maintain their shape. This composes of an actin/spectrin network held together by another protein called ankyrin. A condition known as Hereditary Spherocytosis is caused by an abnormal arrangement of the internal cytoskeleton of RBCs. In this condition the ankyrin binding of spectrin is absent. As a result the cell membrane is not adequately braced and is too easy deformed. Individuals who suffer the condition have spherical RBCs which are abnormally fragile and do not resist osmotic pressure. The most common disorder is anemia in which an inadequate hemoglobin supply causes weakness, pallor and sometimes, breathlessness. It may be the result of impaired RBC functioning or increased RBC destruction.

The most common cause is iron deficiency. Iron is essential for the formation of hemoglobin and a deficiency in the diet means that cells formed in the bone marrow are pale-staining (hypochromic) and smaller than normal (microcytic).

Excessive RBC destruction usually occurs if the RBCs produced are structurally abnormal in some way and are therefore liable to damage in their passage around the body. Any such cells are removed prematurely and in excess by the spleen resulting in hemolytic anemia this often due to a genetic abnormality such as Hereditary Spherocytosis or Sickle cell anemia.

ABO Antibodies

Sugar linkages of A, B, and H antigens also occur in other biologic material such as bacteria, dust, food, and other widely distributed agents constituting powerful and continuous antigenic stimuli. Healthy individuals react to those stimuli by producing antibodies against those antigens foreign to their own system. ABO antibodies are actually not "naturally occurring", they should instead be termed "non-red blood cell stimulated".

• Group A serum contains anti-B
• Group B serum contains anti-A
• Group AB serum contains no antibodies
• Group O serum contains anti-A, anti-B, and anti-A, B

34

Anti-H

There are two types of anti-H: cold reacting and the Bombay type.

Cold reacting agglutinin – found occasionally in the serum of an A_1 or A_1B (most of the H has been converted to A and/or B antigens. The following shows a decreasing order of H substance: $O > A_2 > B > A_2B > A_1 > A_1B$. Commercial anti-H lectin closely parallels the reaction of anti-H in the body.

Bombay anti-H – has a wide thermal range (4-37°C) and can bind complement to cause hemolysis

Anti-A, B

This antibody is found in the serum of group O individuals. It reacts with A, B, and AB cells. It is predominately IgG, with small portions being IgM. Anti-A, B is one antibody; it is not a mixture of anti-A and anti-B antibodies.

Anti-A1

Group O and B individuals contain anti-A in their serum. However, the anti-A can be separated into different components: anti-A and anti-A_1. Anti-A_1 only agglutinates the A_1 antigen, not the A_2 antigen. There is no anti-A_2.

Non-red cell stimulated

Anti-A and anti-B occur so regularly after environmental exposure, they are considered "naturally occurring". There is no recognizable immunizing agent (pregnancy or transfusion) that leads to their appearance. The majorities are IgM, but small amounts are IgG.

Red cell stimulated

These types of antibodies have a known stimulus and are associated with pregnancy or transfusion. In pregnancy, there may be an ABO incompatibility with the fetus; with transfusion, there may be an ABO incompatibility with blood or plasma. Characteristics of these antibodies are:
• Usually IgG
• Active at 37°C
• Titer and avidity increase
• Difficult to inhibit
• More common in group O, but may occur in group A or B

White Blood Cells (Leukocytes) = WBCs

WBCs use the blood as a means of transport from their origination in the bone marrow to their major sites of activity. The majority of the functions of the WBCs occur when they leave the blood circulation to enter other body tissues.

There are five main types of WBCS:

- Neutrophils   =   35 – 75 %.
- Eosinophils   =   1 – 5 %.
- Basophils   =   0 - 1%.
- Lymphocytes =   15 - 45%.
- Monocytes   =   1 - 10%.

White blood cells
-Are much less numerous than red (the ration between the two is around 1:700).
-Have a nucleus and do not contain hemoglobin.
-Participate in protecting the body from infections.

A wide variety of leukocytes participate in an immune response. However, only the lymphocytes posses the attributes of diversity: specificity, memory, and self/non self recognition. All of the other cells have an accessory function: activation of lymphocytes, phagocytosis/antigen clearance, and secretion of cytokines.

Neutrophils

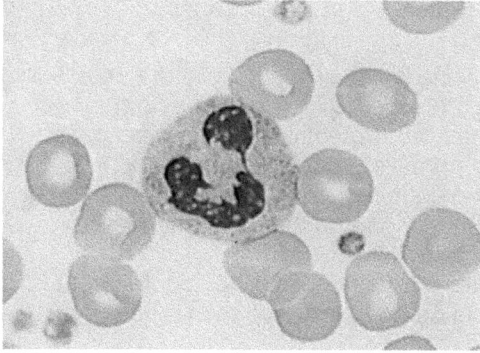

The Neutrophil is a small cell, about 9-10 um in diameter, and is the most abundant leukocyte in blood, accounting for 35-75% of all leukocytes. 5% of these are band cells; the remainders possess segment nuclei (2-5 lobes). The Neutrophil has been referred to as a first line of defense, meaning that it is the first defensive cell type to recruited to a site of inflammation; however, there are other inflammatory cells already present (such as the mast cell). The Neutrophil begins its 2-week lifespan in the bone marrow, with the commitment of a hematopoietic stem cell to myeloblastic differentiation. Even before this cell ceases proliferation, during the promyelocytic stage of the mitotic phase, it begins to produce storage granules called primary or azurophil granules, which are abundant in young newly formed neutrophils, contain certain cationic proteins and defensins that can kill bacteria, proteolytic enzymes like elastase, and cathepsin G to breakdown proteins, lysozyme to break down bacterial cell wall, and characteristically, myeloperoxidase (MPO), which is involved in the generation of bacterial compounds. Specific granules are made in the myelocyte stage, and continue to be produced for some time during the post mitotic phase. Because these granules appear second, they are also known as secondary granules.

Most of the Neutrophils formed in the bone marrow never enter the blood; instead they are phagocytosed by bone marrow macrophages. The bone marrow contains about 30 times more Neutrophils than blood. This excess of bone marrow neutrophils provides a buffer against neutrophils depletion and enables the body to respond to various challenges with massive out-pouring neutrophils. The most well-known causes of neutrophils release into the blood are infections. The method they use to kill invaders is called phagocytosis which involves engulfing and digesting the pathogen so that it winds up enclosed in phagosome (phagocyte vesicle). But this is only the first step, because the more challenging task of destroying the microorganisms remains. Indeed, some pathogens have special, effective mechanisms for frustrating this destruction step.

The next step is the fusion of lysosomes with the phagosome. The result is called a phagolysosome. Lysosomes are derived from the Golgi apparatus, much like secretion vesicles, but their contents are focused on destroying microorganisms.

The neutrophils are short-lived, having a life span of a few hours to a few days, and do not multiply. They circulate in the blood for around 6 hours and if they are not recruited, they undergo apoptosis. In tissue, they function for several hours and die. However, the bone marrow makes about 80,000,000 new neutrophils per minute to replace these.

Eosinophils

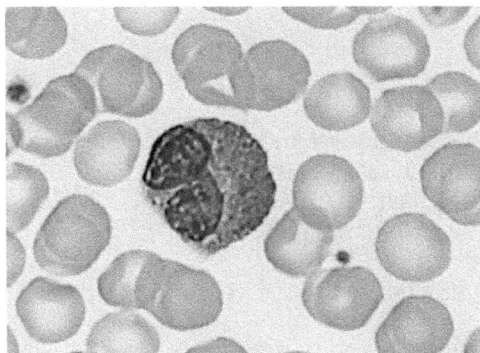

In normal blood, Eosinophils amount to about 1 to 5% of the white blood cells, their natural role is to defend us against parasites. They accumulate wherever allergic reactions like those in asthma take place. In fact allergies such asthma are probably a malfunction of our protective mechanism against parasites. The toxins from the granules are important for killing parasites, but in asthma they are released inappropriately and damage the lining of the air passages. It is one of the objectives of asthma treatment to stop Eosinophils from accumulating in young lungs and to stop those already there from causing damage. Steroid inhalers have a key role in doing this.

These large specific granules are the principal identifying feature of Eosinophils. They contain four distinct cationic proteins which exert a range of biological effects on host cells and microbial targets:

-Major basic protein.

-Eosinophil cationic protein.

-Eosinophil derived neurotoxin. And

-Eosinophil peroxidase.

These proteins have major effects not only on the potential role of Eosinophils in host against helminthes parasites, but also in contributing to tissues dysfunction and damage in Eosinophils related inflammatory and allergic diseases. In addition, histaminases and a variety of hydrolytic lysosomes enzymes are also present in the large specific granules.

Eosinophils also participate in hypersensitivity reactions, especially through two lipid inflammatory mediators, leukotriene (LTC4) and platelet activating factor (PAF).

They are capable of phagocytosis but primarily they release their contents into the surrounding environment to kill microbes extracellularly. They secrete leukotrienes, prostaglandins, chemicals that promote inflammation by causing vasodilatation (and increasing capillary permeability. They also secrete various cytokines) such as IL-1, IL-2, IL-4, IL-5, IL-6, IL-8, IL-13, and TNF alpha.

The Eosinophils functional activity, like the immune response in general, may be beneficial or harmful for the organism. Compared to neutrophils, Eosinophils have limited phagocytic activity which is mainly aimed at killing multicellular parasites.

In addition to the acute release of protein, cytokine and lipid mediators of inflammation, Eosinophils likely contribute to chronic inflammation, including the development of fibrosis. Eosinophils are the major source of the fibrosis-promoting TGF-B in nodular sclerosing Hodgkin's disease. Their life span is 8-12 days.

Basophils

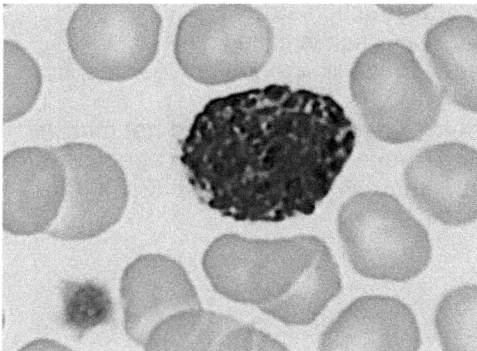

=Hematocell (Prof Zandecki Marc). Used with permission=

Basophils are the smallest circulating granulocytes with relatively the least known function. They arise in the bone marrow, and following maturation and differentiation, are released into the blood circulation. If they are adequately stimulated they may settle in the tissues.

They contain special cytoplasmic granules which store mediators of inflammation. The extra cellular release of the mediators is known as degranulation and may be induced by:

Physical destruction, such as high temperature, mechanical trauma, ionizing irradiation, etc,

Chemical substances, such as toxins, venous, proteases,

Endogenous mediators, including tissue protease, cationic proteins derived from Eosinophils and neutrophils,

Immune mechanisms which may be IgE-dependent

Basophils in the bloodstream represent only < 1% of circulating white blood cells, and are not phagocytic. Their life span is probably a few hours to a few days.

Monocytes

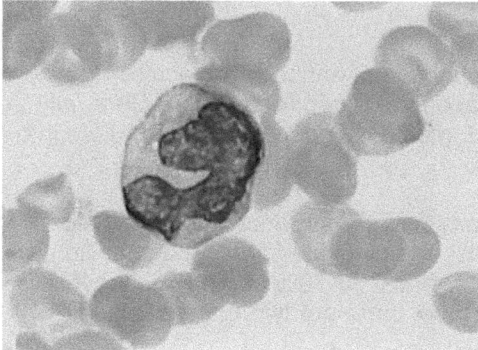

=Hematocell (Prof Zandecki Marc). Used with permission=

Monocytes circulate in the blood and lymph (represent 1 to 10% of the WBCs). Monocytes which migrate from the bloodstream to other tissues are called macrophages. Monocytes are usually identified in stained smears by their large bilobate nucleus.
Their development takes in the bone marrow and passes through the following steps: stem cell-committed stem cell – monoblast – promonocyte –monocyte (bone marrow)-monocyte (peripheral blood) - macrophage (tissue). Monocyte differentiation in the bone marrow proceeds rapidly (1.5 to 3 days). During differentiation, granules are formed in monocyte cytoplasm and these can be divided as in neutrophils into at least two types. However, they are fewer and smaller then their neutrophil counterparts (azurophil and specific granules). Their enzymes content is similar.
The blood Monocytes are young cells that already posses migratory, chemotactic, pinocytic, and phagocytic activities.
Cells which derive from monocyte include the:
   -Kupffer cells of the liver.
   -Sinus lining cells of thee spleen and lymph nodes.
   -Pulmonary alveolar macrophages.
   -Free macrophages in the synovial, pleural and peritoneal fluid.
   -Dendritic antigen presenting cells.

Lymphocytes

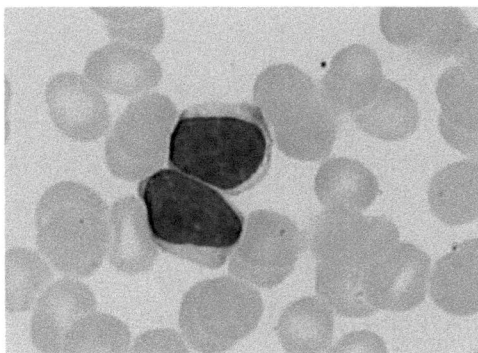

=Hematocell (Prof Zandecki Marc). Used with permission=

Lymphocytes normally represent 25-40% of the WBCs (1,500-4,500/mm^3 of blood).

   a. Lymphocytes mediate the adaptive immune responses.

b. Only a small proportion of the body's lymphocytes are found in the blood. The majority are found in lymphoid tissue. In fact the collective mass of all the lymphocytes in the human body is about the same as the mass of the brain!

c. Lymphocytes circulate back and forth between the blood and the lymphoid system of the body.

d. They have a life span of days to years.

e. There are 3 major populations of lymphocytes:

1. B-lymphocytes (B-cells) mediate humoral immunity, the production of antibody molecules against a specific antigen, and have B-cell receptors (BCR) on their surface for antigen recognition. Generally 10-15% of the lymphocytes are B-lymphocytes. Once activated, most B-lymphocytes differentiate into antibody-secreting plasma cells.

2. T-lymphocytes (T-cells) are responsible for cell-mediated immunity, the production of cytotoxic T-lymphocytes (CTLs), activated macrophages, activated NK cells, and cytokines against a specific antigen. They also regulate the adaptive immune responses. Generally 60-70% of the lymphocytes are T-lymphocytes. Based on biochemical markers on their surface, there are two major classes of T-lymphocytes:

a. T4-lymphocytes (CD4$^+$ T-lymphocytes) have CD4 molecules and T-cell receptors (TCRs) on their surface for protein antigen recognition. They function to regulate the adaptive immune responses through cytokine production.

b. T8-lymphocytes (CD8$^+$ T-lymphocytes) have CD8 molecules and T-cell receptors (TCRs) on their surface for protein antigen recognition. They differentiate into cytotoxic T-lymphocytes (CTLs).

c. NKT cells (natural killer T-cells) are a subset of lymphocytes that bridge the gap between innate and adaptive immunity. They have T-cell receptors (TCRs) on their surface for glycolipid antigen recognition. Through the cytokines they produce once activated, NKT cells are essential in both innate and adaptive immune protection against pathogens and tumors. They also play a regulatory role in the development of autoimmune diseases and transplantation tolerance.

3. NK cells (natural killer cells are lymphocytes that lack B-cell receptors and T-cell receptors. They kill cells to which antibody molecules have attached through a process called antibody-dependent cellular cytotoxicity (ADCC). They also kill human cells lacking MHC-I molecules on their surface.

Blood Platelets (Thrombocytes) = PLTs

Platelet Structure

Thrombocytes are not true cells, but rather cytoplasmic fragments of a large cell in the bone marrow, the megacaryocytes. As megacaryocytes develop into giant cells, they undergo a process of fragmentation that results in the release of over 500 to 1,000 platelets per megakaryocyte. The dominant hormone controlling megacaryocytes development is thrombopoietin (TPO).

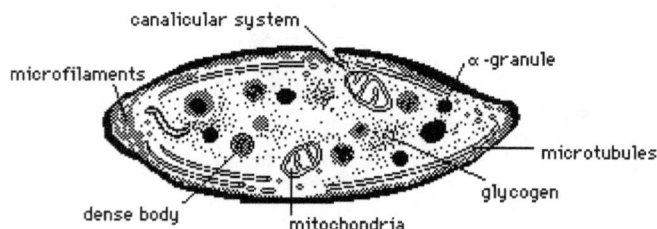

©2007. Rector and visitors of the University of Virginia
Charles E. Hess, M.D. and Lindsey Krstic, B.A. Used with permission

Platelet granules are of two types: alpha granules and dense bodies.
Alpha granules contain Platelet Derived Growth Factor, platelet factor 4, Factors V & XIII and fibrinogen.

Dense bodies contain serotonin, nucleotides (ADP) and calcium. Lysosomes containing hydrolytic enzyme are also present.

The central portion of a platelet stains purple with Wright's stain and is referred to as the granulomere. The peripheral portion stains clear and is called the hyalomere. Platelet contents include glycogen granules. The open canalicular system, which is composed of canaliculi formed from invaginations of the platelet plasma membrane, mitochondria, occasional Golgi elements and ribosome's. Platelets have several types of membrane-bound granules which contain a number of constituents including fibrinogen and several growth factors.

Platelet activation occurs when injury to the vessel wall exposes sub-endothelial components, especially collagen. Platelets adhere to the damaged area and become cohesive to other platelets. This aggregation leads to the formation of a platelet plug, which prevents further blood loss and allows the repair process to begin.

Severe reduction in the number of circulating platelets results in thrombocytopenia. It is a condition which causes spontaneous bleeding as a reaction to minor trauma. This is due to failure of the platelets to seal over microscopic breaches in blood vessel walls. In the skin this is manifest by a reddish-purple blotchy rash. This can be either small blotches (purpura) or large bruise (ecchymoses).

The platelet count in the circulating blood is normally between 150 and 450 million per milliliter of blood. Newborn babies have a slightly lower level, but are normally within the adult range by three months of age. Many factors can influence an individual's platelet count including exercise and racial origin. The average life span of platelet in the blood is 10 days.

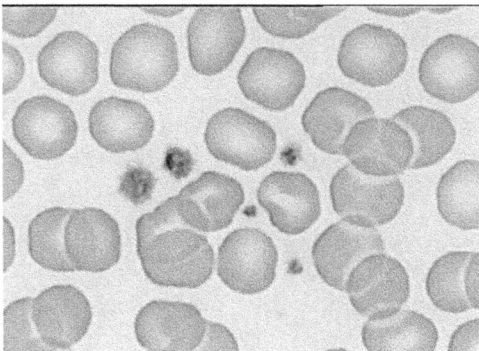

=Hematocell (Prof Zandecki Marc). Used with permission=

Platelet: Function

Platelets play a key role in maintaining vascular integrity by sealing vessels with damaged endothelium and initiating the repair process.

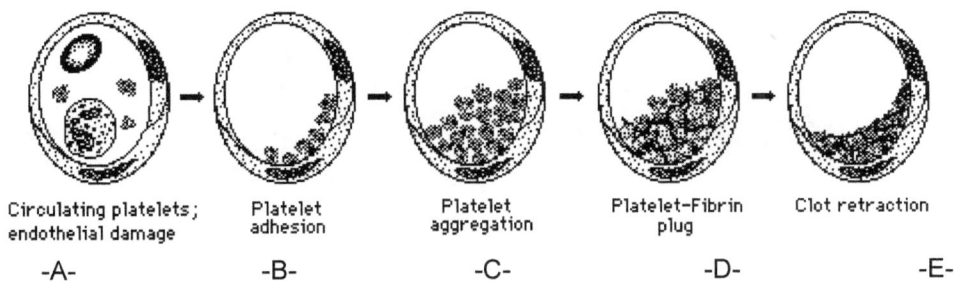

Circulating platelets; endothelial damage	Platelet adhesion	Platelet aggregation	Platelet-Fibrin plug	Clot retraction
-A-	-B-	-C-	-D-	-E-

A - Normal platelets in the blood stream have a discoid shape and have little or no interaction with other platelets or endothelium.

Endothelial damage, specifically exposure of underlying collagen, triggers platelet adhesion. First, von Willebrand's factor (vWF) binds to subendothelial collagen. This results in conformational changes in vWF allowing vWF to bind to the GP Ib receptor on platelets.

Exposure of the basement membrane and release of tissue factor from damaged endothelialcells serves to activate coagulation pathways.

B- Following adhesion, proteins and soluble products interact with platelet membrane receptors to cause activation. At time of activation, platelets become spherical and develop cytoplasmic hair-like filipodia. The GP IIb/IIIa receptor complex Ds conformation allowing binding of fibrinogen. The contents of the alpha and dense granules are secreted. All of the above lead to platelet aggregation.

α granules		dense granules
plt factor 4	vWF	ADP/ATP
PDGF	Factor V	calcium
fibronectin	Factor XIII	serotonin
B-thromboglobulin	fibrinogen	

C- The contents of platelet granules are discharged, exponentially magnifying the accumulation of platelets and fibrin at the site of injury. This process is known as platelet aggregation, the end result of which is formation of a platelet-fibrin plug or thrombus.

D- The fibrin gives the platelet mass strength allowing it to function as a secure patch and a protected base for repair and healing.
Note that many of the platelets appear as empty sacks having discharged their granules.

E- Clot retraction is a function in which the central portion of the platelet attaches to fibrin strands at nodes (cross-over points) and platelet filipods attach to single fibrin strands. Actin in the filipods and myosin in the platelet body contract, shortening the fibrin strands and shinking the platelet-fibrin plug.This process requires large amounts of energy (platelet ATP) and calcium.

CHAPTER THREE: THE IMMUNE SYSTEM

Introduction to the Pathogens

The immune system has evolved to protect us from infectious disease. Disease-causing microorganisms (pathogens) can be classified as viruses, bacteria, fungi, or protozoan parasites. Macroscopic helminths (worm) parasites can also cause infection.

{1} Viruses are obligate intracellular parasites, meaning they can only be replicated inside living cells using the host cell's metabolic machinery. They range in size from 20 nm to 1,000 nm (1 mm) in diameter and come in many different shapes. Viruses are composed of a nucleic acid (DNA or RNA) genome, a protein coat (capsid), and sometimes a lipid envelope which has been modified from the host cell's plasma membrane. The outermost layer of the virus (capsid or envelope) has protein receptors that must bind to specific host cell membrane glycoproteins before the virus can enter the cell and begin its replication cycle. The virus enters via endocytosis or by fusing the viral envelope with the host cell membrane. Once inside the host cell, uncoating removes the capsid and exposes the nucleic acid. Host cell enzymes under viral control, along with viral enzymes in some cases, replicate the viral nucleic acids and synthesize mRNA and viral proteins. In general, DNA viruses are replicated and assembled in the host cell nucleus (proteins are made on the ribosomes and migrate into the nucleus), while RNA viruses are replicated and assembled in the host cell cytoplasm. Virus subunits are combined assembly-style to make new virions. One infecting virion provides the information for the cell to make thousands to millions of progeny virions. Enveloped virions leave the cell by budding, taking with them a covering of host cell membrane modified with virus receptor proteins. Infected cells may produce enveloped viruses for many hours or days before they die. Non-enveloped virions usually accumulate in the cell to a large "burst size", at which point the cell lyses and the virions are free to bind and infect other cells. Important antigens recognized by the immune system include external envelope or capsid proteins, structural proteins inside the virion, and viral enzymes required for replication.

{2} Pathogenic bacteria (singular: bacterium) are single celled microorganisms. Bacteria may be free-living in the environment or in plant, insect, or animal hosts. Some are obligate pathogens that depend on hosts for some key nutrients but living outside host cells, while others are obligate intracellular parasites that require some nutrients or enzymes found only inside host cells. Bacteria are prokaryotic organisms that have a circular DNA genome and enzyme systems inside a lipid bilayer plasma membrane, covered with a cell wall of peptidoglycan that gives the cells their characteristic shape. Mycoplasmas are unusual in lacking a cell wall. Bacteria range from 100 nm to 5 mm in size. They are classified by their shape (rod/bacillus, sphere/coccus, or spiral/spirillum) and by the structure of their cell wall. Gram positive bacteria have a thick peptidoglycan layer outside their plasma membrane. Gram negative bacteria have a thin peptidoglycan layer and an outer (lipid bilayer) membrane (OM) containing Lipopolysaccharide (LPS). Some bacteria also have a carbohydrate capsule, slime layer, or waxy coating to protect them from drying and from the immune system. Some bacteria have short hairy processes called fimbriae (singular fimbria) or pili (singular: pilus) that allow them to adhere to host tissues. Some have long flagella (singular: flagellum) for locomotion. Bacteria reproduce by binary fission, each parent cell giving rise to two identical daughters. The immune system recognizes many antigens on bacteria, including LPS, sugars, and proteins of pili and flagella.

{3}Fungi (singular: fungus) are eukaryotic organisms. They have a lipid bilayer plasma membrane and membranes surrounding organelles in the cytosol. Their genetic material is DNA, which they transcribe into messenger RNA and translate into proteins. They may be unicellular (yeasts), multicellular (filamentous fungi), or exist in both forms (dimorphic fungi). Most pathogenic fungi are opportunistic pathogens: they cause disease only when the host's immune system is weakened. Of the true fungal pathogens, most can live freely in the environment and do not need humans to survive. Of those that are found only on humans, all are extracellular pathogens; many live on the outer surfaces of the body. Fungi can reproduce by sexual or asexual processes.

{4}A wide range of sizes and life styles is found in the protozoan parasites. Protozoan parasites are unicellular eukaryotic organisms. They often have several life cycle stages that have different appearances, antigens, and habitats. During some stages sexual reproduction takes place, while during other stages reproduction is asexual. Some protozoan parasites can live freely in the environment as well as inside a host. Some depend on insect or arthropod vectors to transmit them from host to host and to complete their life cycle. Some are obligate human or animal parasites.

{5}Helminths (worm) parasites are macroscopic, ranging in size from 0.3 mm to 25 meters long. They are multicellular with specialized organs and undergo sexual reproduction. Many helminthes can infect humans and domestic animals, causing serious disease. In addition, they can provoke allergic reactions by their persistent presence in host tissues. Helminthes often live freely or attached in the intestine, but some can also penetrate into the body where they can seriously damage internal organs and the brain.

{6} Normal flora. Think of the body as an elongated donut, with the digestive tract forming the hole and therefore "outside" the body. Other external regions that do not completely penetrate the body are the respiratory tract, the urogenital tract, and the conjunctiva of the eye. The respiratory, urogenital, and much of the digestive tract are composed of specialized epithelial cells forming mucous membranes. Mucin, cilia, and tight junctions between the cells block entry of microorganisms. All internal regions of the body, including the circulation, brain and spinal column, organs, bone, fat, and connective tissue, should be free of microorganisms (sterile). The presence of microbes in blood, urine, or cerebrospinal fluid is indicative of infection.
Beginning at birth, the skin and mucous membranes of humans and animals are colonized with microbes, mostly bacteria. In general, normal flora are not invasive and do not usually cause disease. They occupy niches which supply their requirements for nutrients, oxygen and space to reproduce. They may provide some benefits to the host in the form of secreted vitamins, or some discomfort as they produce gas from undigested food. Cellulose-digesting microbes are essential for ruminant animal nutrition. Normal flora physically blocks the attachment of pathogens or secretes bacteriocins, molecules that inhibit pathogen growth. Prolonged antibiotic treatment that kills normal flora can result in serious disease from pathogens that now find living space. Normal flora can be opportunistic pathogens, causing disease if they enter the body through a wound, surgical incision, following dental work, or on a catheter.

An Overview of Phagocytic Defense

Phagocytic cells include neutrophils, Eosinophils, monocytes, macrophages, dendritic cells, and B-lymphocytes.
Phagocytosis is the primary method used by the body to remove free microorganisms in the blood and tissue fluids. The body's phagocytic cells are able to encounter these microorganisms in a variety of ways:

a. Infection or tissue injury stimulates mast cells, basophiles, and other cells to release vasodilators, to initiate the inflammatory response. Vasodilatation results in increased capillary permeability, enabling phagocytic white blood cells such as neutrophils, monocytes, and eosinophils - as well as other leukocytes - to enter the tissue around the injured site. The leukocytes are then chemotactically attracted to the area of infection. In other words, inflammation allows phagocytes to enter the tissue and go to the site of infection. Neutrophils are the first to appear and are later replaced by macrophage.

b. Lymph nodules are unencapsulated masses of lymphoid tissue containing fixed macrophages and ever changing populations of B-lymphocytes and T-lymphocytes. They are located in the respiratory tract, the liver, and the gastrointestinal tract and are collectively referred to as mucosa-associated lymphoid tissue or MALT. Examples include the adenoids and tonsils in the respiratory tract and the Peyer's patches on the small intestines. Organisms entering these systems can be phagocytosed by fixed macrophages and dendritic cells and presented to B-lymphocytes and T-lymphocytes to initiate adaptive immune responses.

c. Tissue fluid picks up microbes and then enters the lymph vessels as lymph. Lymph vessels carry the lymph to regional lymph nodes. Lymph nodes contain many reticular fibers that support fixed macrophages and dendritic cells as well as everchanging populations of circulating B-lymphocytes and T-lymphocytes. Microbes picked up by the lymph vessels are filtered out and phagocytosed in the lymph nodes by these fixed macrophage and dendritic cells and presented to the circulating B-lymphocytes and T-lymphocytes to initiate adaptive immune responses. The lymph eventually enters the circulatory system at the heart to maintain the fluid volume of the circulation.

d. In addition, Langerhans' cells - immature dendritic cells - are located throughout the epithelium of the skin, the respiratory tract, and the gastrointestinal tract where in their immature form they are attached by long cytoplasmic processes. Upon capturing antigens through pinocytosis and phagocytosis and becoming activated by proinflammatory cytokines, the dendritic cells detach from the epithelium, enter lymph vessels, and are carried to regional lymph nodes. By the time they enter the lymph nodes, they have matured and are now able to present antigen to the everchanging populations of naive T-lymphocytes located in the cortex of the lymph nodes.

e. The spleen contains many reticular fibers that support fixed macrophages and dendritic cells, as well as everchanging populations of circulating B-lymphocytes and T-lymphocytes. Blood carries microorganisms to the spleen where they are filtered out and phagocytosed by the fixed macrophages and dendritic cells and presented to the circulating B-lymphocytes and T-lymphocytes to initiate adaptive immune responses.

f. As mentioned above under fixed macrophages, there are also specialized macrophages and dendritic cells located in the brain (microglia), lungs (alveolar macrophages), liver (Kupffer cells), kidneys (mesangial cells), bones (osteoclasts), and the gastrointestinal tract (peritoneal macrophages).

The adaptative immune system

The body has two immune systems: innate immunity and adaptive immunity.

1. Innate immunity is antigen-nonspecific defense mechanisms that a host uses immediately or within several hours after exposure to almost any microbe. This is the immunity one is born with and is the initial response by the body to eliminate microbes and prevent infection.

Unlike adaptive immunity, innate immunity does not recognize every possible antigen. Instead, it is designed to recognize molecules shared by groups of related microbes that are essential for the survival of those organisms and are not found associated with mammalian cells. These unique microbial molecules are called pathogen-associated molecular patterns or PAMPS and include LPS from the gram-negative cell wall, peptidoglycan and lipotechoic acids from the gram-positive cell wall, the sugar mannose (a terminal sugar common in microbial glycolipids and glycoproteins but rare in those of humans), bacterial and viral unmethylated CpG DNA, bacterial flagellin, the amino acid N-formylmethionine found in bacterial proteins, double-stranded and single-stranded RNA from viruses, and glucans from fungal cell walls. In addition, unique molecules displayed on stressed, injured, infected, or transformed human cells also act as PAMPS. (Because all microbes, not just pathogenic microbes, possess PAMPs, pathogen-associated molecular patterns are sometimes referred to as microbe-associated molecular patterns or MAMPs.)

Most body defense cells have pattern-recognition receptors for these common PAMPS and so there is an immediate response against the invading microorganism. Pathogen-associated molecular patterns can also be recognized by a series of soluble pattern-recognition receptors in the blood that function as opsonins and initiate the complement pathways. In all, the innate immune system is thought to recognize approximately 10^3 of these microbial molecular patterns.

The innate immune responses do not improve with repeated exposure to a given infection and involve the following:

Phagocytic cells: leukocytes such as neutrophils, eosinophils, and monocytes; tissue phagocytic cells in the tissue such as macrophages;

Cells that release inflammatory mediators: inflammatory cells in the tissue such as macrophages and mast cells; leukocytes such as basophils and eosinophils; Natural killer cells (NK cells; and Molecules such as complement proteins, acute phase proteins, and cytokines.

2. Adaptive (acquired) immunity refers to antigen-specific defense mechanisms that take several days to become protective and are designed to react with and remove a specific antigen. This is the immunity one develops throughout life.

An antigen is defined as a substance that reacts with antibody molecules and antigen receptors on lymphocytes. An immunogen is an antigen that is recognized by the body as nonself and stimulates an adaptive immune response. For simplicity we will use the term antigen when referring to both antigens and immunogens. The actual portions or fragments of an antigen that react with antibodies and lymphocyte receptors are called epitopes.

As we will see below, the body recognizes an antigen as foreign when epitopes of that antigen bind to B-lymphocytes and T-lymphocytes by means of epitope-specific receptor molecules having a shape complementary to that of the epitope. The epitope receptor on the surface of a B-lymphocyte is called a B-cell receptor and is actually an antibody molecule called surface immunoglobulin (sIg). The receptor on a T-lymphocyte is called a T-cell receptor (TCR).

It is estimated that the human body has the ability to recognize 10^7 or more different epitopes and make up to 10^9 different antibodies, each with a unique specificity. In order to recognize this immense number of different epitopes, the body produces 10^7 or more distinct clones of both B-lymphocytes and T-lymphocytes, each with a unique B-cell receptor or T-cell receptor. Among this large variety of B-cell receptors and T-cell receptors there is bound to be at least one that has an epitope-binding site able to fit, at least to some degree, any antigen the immune system eventually encounters. With the adaptive immune responses, the body is able to recognize any conceivable antigen it may eventually encounter.

The downside to the specificity of adaptive immunity is that only a few B-cells and T-cells in the body recognize any one epitope. These few cells then must rapidly proliferate in order to produce enough cells to mount an effective immune response against that particular epitope, and that typically takes several days. During this time the pathogen could be causing considerable harm, and that is why innate immunity is also essential.

Adaptive immunity usually improves upon repeated exposure to a given infection and involves:
Antigen-presenting cells (APCs) such as macrophages and dendritic cells;
The activation and proliferation of antigen-specific B-lymphocytes;
The activation and proliferation of antigen-specific T-lymphocytes; and
The production of antibody molecules, cytotoxic T-lymphocytes (CTLs), activated macrophages, and cytokines.

There are two major branches of the adaptive immune responses: humoral immunity and cell-mediated immunity.

1. Humoral immunity: humoral immunity involves the production of antibody molecules in response to an antigen and is mediated by B-lymphocytes.

2. Cell-mediated immunity: Cell-mediated immunity involves the production of cytotoxic T-lymphocytes, activated macrophages, activated NK cells, and cytokines in response to an antigen and is mediated by T-lymphocytes.

The Immune System: Cells and Organs.

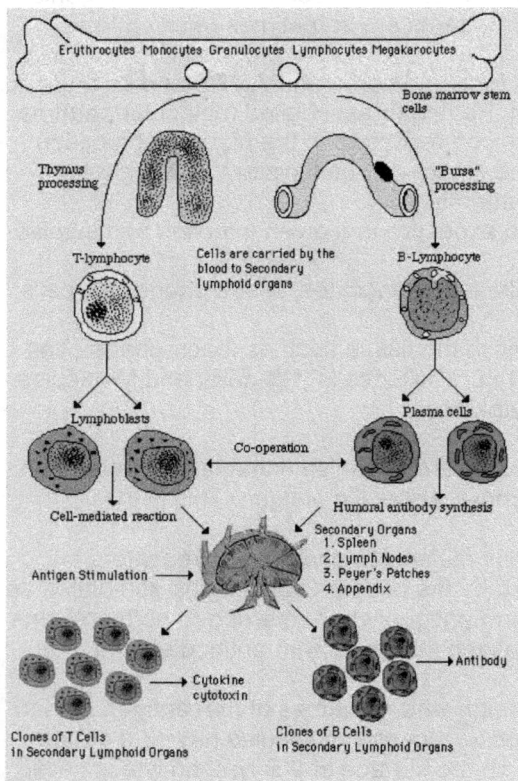

http://uhaweb.hartford.edu/bugl/immune.htm

A system is a regularly interacting or interdependent group of items forming a unified whole. The immune system is the collection of cells and organs that work together to provide immunity. Immune system cells, the white blood cells or leukocytes, wander the body to detect localized infections. Immune system organs provide locations where leukocytes mature and where they interact efficiently with antigen to become fully active effector cells and memory cells. Effector cells eliminate antigen, while memory cells make a more efficient response to a repeat antigen exposure.

The primary (central) immune organs are where white blood cells mature. Hematopoiesis, the development of white blood cells, occurs in the bone marrow. Pluripotent, self-renewing stem cells divide and differentiate into all types of functional blood cells. At each stage of differentiation (stem cell --> progenitor cell --> mature cell), cells become more restricted in their potential than their precursors. During Hematopoiesis, lymphocytes acquire their specific antigen receptors (one specificity per cell), co-receptors required for response to antigen, cytokine receptors, and adhesion molecules that target the cells to particular immune organs. Hematopoiesis is regulated by growth factors, growth factor receptors, and programmed cell death (apoptosis). T cells complete their development in the thymus, an organ in the chest above the heart. The thymus is relatively large in infants and children when T cell development is highest. It begins to shrink at puberty, although some T cell maturation occurs throughout life. Antigen is NOT required for the development of mature antigen-specific T and B lymphocytes.

Phagocytes include two types of leukocytes: blood monocytes, called macrophages when they leave the circulation and enter the tissues, and Polymorphonuclears leukocytes (PMNs or granulocytes), primarily neutrophils. Macrophages are large cells with round nuclei that can put out long pseudopodia to surround antigen. PMNs have lobed nuclei and many granules in their cytoplasm. Macrophages and PMNs engulf and kill pathogens, especially bacteria. Eosinophils kill parasites, especially helminths (worm parasites). Macrophages and PMNs bind common surface molecules on pathogens or antibody-coated pathogens; phagocytes are not antigen-specific and are part of innate immunity. Macrophages also produce cytokines that attract other leukocytes and make blood vessels leaky, leading to inflammation. Dendritic cells (DC) can be phagocytic under certain circumstances and, along with macrophages and B cells, are Antigen-Presenting Cells (APC) which helps stimulate T cell activation.

Lymphocytes are antigen-specific leukocytes responsible for adaptive immunity. They are small, round cells with little cytoplasm and round nuclei. Lymphocytes have membrane receptors that bind antigen; each lymphocyte recognizes one specific antigen. Antigen receptor on B lymphocytes is called membrane immunoglobulin (mIg or antibody) or BCR (B Cell Receptor). Antigen receptor on T lymphocytes is called T Cell Receptor (TCR). Each lymphocyte has about 100,000 copies of its membrane antigen receptor. Lymphocytes specific for many diverse antigens are produced continually in the absence of antigen exposure. When a lymphocyte encounters its specific antigen and receives the proper co stimulatory signals, it proliferates and differentiates into a clone of effector cells with the same antigen specificity. Natural Killer (NK) cells are large granular lymphocytes that lack specific antigen receptors. However, they recognize and respond to altered tissue typing (MHC) proteins present on virus-infected and cancer cells. NK cells are part of the innate immune system.

Secondary (peripheral) lymphoid organs are designed to bring together leukocytes and antigen. Peripheral lymphoid tissues are present throughout the body. Clusters of lymphocytes and specialized antigen-collecting epithelial cells called M cells line the mucous membranes of the respiratory, digestive, and urogenital systems where contact with pathogens is highest. With the tonsils, appendix, and Peyer's patches, they are called the Mucosal Associated Lymphoid Tissues (MALT). Other peripheral lymphoid organs are the spleen, where blood-borne antigens (especially bacteria) encounter the immune system, and lymph nodes, where antigens from the tissues are collected. Fluid leaves the blood circulation at the capillaries and bathes the tissues, supplying nutrients and washing away waste products. The fluid, called lymph, then collects in the lymphatic vessels and passes through the lymph nodes on its way back to the blood circulation. If the tissues are infected, antigen is carried to the nearby (draining) lymph nodes where it comes in contact with phagocytes and lymphocytes to initiates an adaptive immune response. Lymphatic vessels transport lymph and cells from the lymph nodes back into the blood circulation. At any given time many leukocytes recirculate throughout the body and are present in high numbers in the peripheral blood circulation. Expression of adhesion molecules on endothelial cells lining the blood vessels is increased by inflammatory cytokines to signal leukocytes to enter the tissues or the secondary lymphoid organs in response to antigen.

Cell mediated immunity

Adaptive T cell-mediated immunity is driven by activation of T cells: cytotoxic T cells activated by endogenous antigen to kill infected cells, and helper T cells activated by exogenous antigen to stimulate macrophage killing of endosomal pathogens. Note that the pathogens targeted by cellular immunity are protected from antibody and complement binding by their intracellular locations. Adaptive humoral immunity also usually involves T cell activation to produce cytokines that stimulate B cell antibody synthesis. Naïve resting T cells are stimulated by antigen peptide presented on Class I MHC to cytotoxic CD8 T cells or Class II MHC to helper CD4 T cells, along with co-stimulatory signals from APC, to proliferate and differentiate into clones of fully activated effector T cells. Only professional APC (Dendritic cells, macrophages, and B cells) have both Classes I and Class II MHC and can deliver co-stimulatory signals. Activated T cells perform their effector functions when they encounter MHC-presented peptide on their target cells.

Effector Cells in Adaptive Immunity				
	Effector T Cell	Pathogen Location	Antigen Presentation	Target Cell Action
Cellular Immunity	Tc CD8 cytotoxic	Cytoplasm	Infected cell MHC I	Infected cell apoptosis
	Th1 CD4 inflammatory	Macrophage vesicles	Macrophage MHC II	Macrophage activation to kill pathogen
Humoral Immunity	Th2 CD4 helper	Extracellular	APC MHC II	B cell antibody production

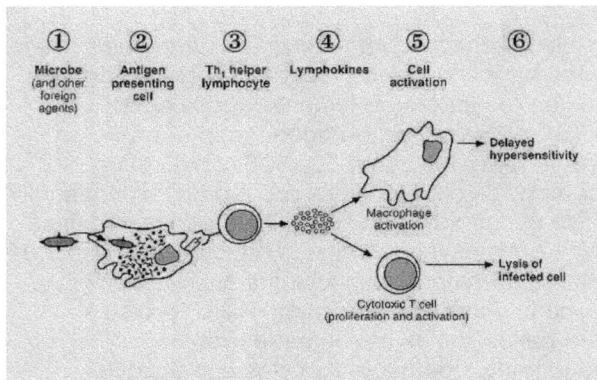

http://uhaweb.hartford.edu/bugl/immune.htm

Lymphocytes of the cell-mediated system defend against bacteria and virus inside the host's cells, and against fungi, protozoan, and worms. T-cells
Some stem cells originating in the red bone marrow migrate to and mature in the thymus gland to become virgin T-cells each with its own unique T-cell Receptor protein. When a virgin T-cell encounters an antigen that it recognizes plus the appropriate secondary signal it divides to give rise to a population of effectors cells.
Each T-cell is equipped with antigen-specific receptor molecules that enable it to recognize just one type of antigen fragment attached to an MHC molecule. If a t-cell finds a matching antigen on a presenting cell and if that presenting cell offers the appropriate signals, the T-lymphocyte responds in two major ways. One is to enlarge and repeatedly divide, thereby increasing the number of cells that react to the antigen. The others is to secrete lymphokines (cytokines such as interleukin), proteins that directly inhibit the pathogen or that recruit other cells to join in the immune response.

Helper T-cells which activate B-cells (and therefore antibody production). Helper T-cells recognize Class II MHC molecules, which are only found on macrophages and B-cells.

Cytotoxic T-cells that kill virus-infected cells. Cytotoxic T-cell only recognizes Class I MHC molecules cradling a specific antigen. These cells are stimulated to reproduce by specific helper T-cells. Cytotoxic T-cells by recognizing specific antigens in association with Class I MHC molecules, can bind to any cell of the body infected by that particular antigenic invader. If docking is successful the cytotoxic T-cells releases a protein called perforin which creates lesions in the infected cells 's membrane leading to the cells lysis-spilling out the invader and other chemicals which quickly attract other lymphocytes and macrophages.
Suppressor T-cells which somehow suppresses the positive feedback characteristic of the immune response
Memory T-cells act as a "reserve army".

Humoral immunity

Humoral immunity refers to antibody production, and all the accessory processes that accompany it: Th2 activation and cytokine production, germinal center formation and isotype switching, affinity maturation and memory cell generation. It also refers to the effector functions of antibody, which include pathogen and toxin neutralization, classical complement activation, and opsonin promotion of phagocytosis and pathogen elimination.

B cells need two signals to initiate activation. Most antigens are T-dependent, meaning T cell help is required for maximal antibody production. With a T-dependent antigen, the first signal comes from antigen cross linking BCR and the second from the Th2 cell. T dependent antigens contain protein so that peptides can be presented on B cell Class II MHC to Th2 cells, which then provide co-stimulation to trigger B cell proliferation and differentiation into plasma cells. Isotype switching to IgG, IgA, and IgE and memory cell generation occur in response to T-dependent antigens.

Some antigens are T-independent, meaning they can deliver both the antigen and the second signal to the B cell. Mice without a thymus (nude or athymic mice) can respond to T-independent antigens. Many bacteria have repeating carbohydrate epitopes that stimulate B cells to respond with IgM synthesis in the absence of T cell help.

T-dependent responses require that B cells and their Th2 cells respond to epitopes on the same antigen. T and B cell epitopes are not necessarily identical; for example, T cells respond well to internal viral proteins while B cells produce neutralizing antibodies to viral coat proteins. (Once virus-infected cells have been killed and unassembled virus proteins released, B cells specific for internal proteins can also be activated to make opsonizing antibodies to those proteins.) Attaching a carbohydrate to a protein can convert the carbohydrate into a T-dependent antigen; the carbohydrate-specific B cell internalizes the complex and presents peptides to Th2 cells, which in turn activate the B cell to make antibodies specific for the carbohydrate.

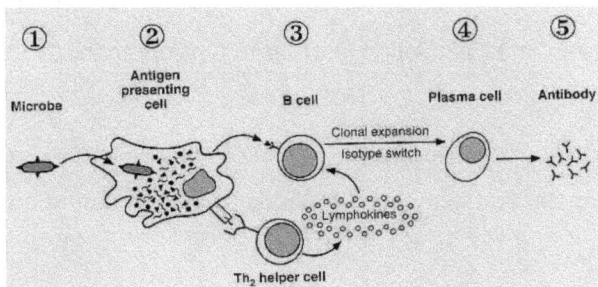

http://uhaweb.hartford.edu/bugl/immune.htm

When a virgin B-cell encounters an appropriately displayed and a secondary signal (usually found on a Helper t-cells) it is prompted to divide, giving rise to a population of effectors called plasma cells. Specific antibodies secreted by plasma (B-cells) aid phagocytes. The circulating antibodies defend mainly against toxins, free bacteria, and virus present in body fluids (humors). B-cells originate in the red bone marrow and the fetal liver. Virgin B-cells mature to become plasma cells or memory B-cells by presenting a processed antigen to a corresponding helper T-cells which releases interleukin1. When activated B-cells form an unmistakably extensive rough endoplasmic reticulum used to manufacture up to 2000 identical antibody proteins per second for 4 – 5 day life span of these cells. The others B-cells become long-lived memory cells.

Antibodies, also called immunoglobulins, constitute the gamma globulin part of the blood proteins. They are soluble proteins secreted by the plasma offspring (clones) of primed B cells. There are large proteins composed of four polypeptides joined in the shape of a Y. two chains are small and two large. All four polypeptides have constant regions that are the same for every antibody (of a class) and variable region tailored to a specific foreign particle (antigen).

3- Antibodies inactivate antigens by, neutralization, agglutination, precipitation, activation of complement:

a. Neutralization occurs when antibodies block viral binding sites or coat a toxin.

b. Agglutination (gluing together) in which antibodies with multiple binding sites sick large groups of particulate antigens (such as bacteria) together making the whole mess easier to dispose of, by macrophages, and other phagocytes. Agglutination is possible because each antibody molecule has 2 antigen binding sites and can cross link adjacent antigens.

c. Precipitation of soluble antigens by a similar process makes these numerous molecules easier for phagocytes to find and engulf.

d. Certain interactions between antibody and antigen activate the complement system.

Antibodies (Immunoglobulins)

Molecular structure

Humoral Immunity refers to the production of antibody molecules in response to an antigen. These antibody molecules circulate in the blood and enter the tissue via inflammation. Humoral immunity is most effective against bacteria, bacterial toxins, and viruses prior to these agents entering cells. Antibodies or Immunoglobulins are specific glycoprotein configurations produced by B-lymphocytes and plasma cells in response to a specific antigen and capable of reacting with that antigen.

There are 5 classes or isotypes of human antibodies:

IgG (Immunoglobulin G; 4 subclasses, IgG1-4)

IgG makes up approximately 80% of the serum antibodies.
IgG has a half-life of 7-23 days depending on the subclass.
IgG is a monomer and has 2 epitope-binding sites.
The Fc portion of IgG can activate the classical complement pathway.
The Fc portion of IgG can bind to macrophage and neutrophils for enhanced phagocytosis.
The Fc portion of IgG can bind to NK cells for antibody-dependent cytotoxicity or ADCC.
The Fc portion of IgG enables it to cross the placenta. (IgG is the only class of antibody that can cross the placenta and enter the fetal circulation.)
High levels of IgG feedback to B-lymphocytes to prevent their activation in order to turn off antibody production

IgM (Immunoglobulin M)

IgM makes up approximately 13% of the serum antibodies and is the first antibody produced during an immune response.
IgM has a half-life of about 5 days.
IgM is a pentamer and has 10 epitope-binding sites.
The Fc portions of IgM are able to activate the classical complement pathway. IgM is the most efficient class of antibody for activating the classical complement pathway.
Monomeric forms of IgM are found on the surface of B-lymphocytes as B-cell receptors.

IgA (Immunoglobulin A; 2 subclasses, IgA1-2)

IgA makes up approximately 6% of the serum antibodies where it has a half-life of approximately 6 days.
IgA is found mainly in body secretions (saliva, mucous, tears, colostrum and milk) as secretory IgA (sIgA) where it protects internal body surfaces exposed to the environment by blocking the attachment

of bacteria and viruses to mucous membranes. While only 6% of the antibodies in the serum are IgA, secretory IgA is the most immunoglobulin produced.

IgA is made primarily in the mucosal-associated lymphoid tissues (MALT).

IgA appears as a dimer of 2 "Y"-shaped molecules and has 4 epitope-binding sites and a secretory component to protect it from digestive enzymes in the secretions.

The Fc portion of secretory IgA binds to components of mucous and contributes to the ability of mucous to trap microbes.

IgA can activate the lectin complement pathway and the alternative complement pathway.

IgD: (Immunoglobulin D)

IgD makes up approximately 0.2% of the serum antibodies.

IgD is a monomer and has 2 epitope-binding sites.

IgD is found on the surface of B-lymphocytes (along with monomeric IgM) as a B-cell receptor or sIg where it may control of B-lymphocyte activation and suppression.

IgD may play a role in eliminating B-lymphocytes generating self-reactive autoantibodies.

IgE (Immunoglobulin E)

IgE makes up about 0.002% of the serum antibodies with a half-life of 2 days.

Most IgE is tightly bound to basophils and mast cells via its Fc region.

IgE is a monomer and has 2 epitope-binding sites.

IgE is made in response to parasitic worms (helminths) and arthropods. It is also often made in response to allergens. (Allergens are antigens causing allergic reactions.)

IgE may protect external mucosal surfaces by promoting inflammation, enabling IgG, complement proteins, and leucocytes to enter the tissues.

The Fc portion of IgE can bind to mast cells and basophils where it mediates many allergic reactions. Cross linking of cell-bound IgE by antigen triggers the release of vasodilators for an inflammatory response.

The Fc portion of IgE made against parasitic worms and arthropods can bind to eosinophils enabling opsonization. This is a major defense against parasitic worms and arthropods.

Each day an average adult produces approximately three grams of antibodies, about two-thirds of this IgA.

The simplest antibodies, such as IgG, IgD, and IgE, are "Y"-shaped macromolecules called monomers. A monomer is composed of four glycoprotein chains: two identical heavy chains and two identical light chains. The two heavy chains have a high molecular weight that varies with the class of antibody. The light chains come in two varieties: kappa or lambda and have a lower molecular weight. The four glycoprotein chains are connected to one another by disulfide (S-S) bond and non-covalent bonds. Additional S-S bonds fold the individual glycoprotein chains into a number of distinct globular domains. The area where the top of the "Y" joins the bottom is called the hinge. This area is flexible to enable the antibody to bind to pairs of epitopes various distances apart on an antigen.

The two tips of the "Y" monomer are referred to as the Fab portions of the antibody. The first 110 amino acids or first domain of both the heavy and light chain of the Fab region of the antibody provide specificity for binding an epitope on an antigen.

The amino acid sequence of the first domain of both the light chain and the heavy chain shows tremendous variation from antibody to antibody and constitutes the variable domains of the antibody. This is because each B-lymphocyte, early in its development, becomes genetically programmed through a series of gene-splicing reactions to produce a Fab with a unique 3-dimensional shape capable of fitting some epitope with a corresponding shape.

The various genes the cell splices together determine the order of amino acids of the Fab portion of both the light and heavy chain; the amino acid sequence determines the final 3-dimensional shape. Therefore, different antibody molecules produced by different B-lymphocytes will have different orders of amino acids at the tips of the Fab to give them unique shapes for binding epitope. The antigen-binding site is large enough to hold an epitope of about 5-7 amino acids or 3-4 sugar residues. Epitopes bind to the Fab portion of the antibody by reversible, non-covalent bonds.

The bottom part of the "Y", the C terminal region of each glycoprotein chain, is called the Fc portion. The Fc portion, as well as one domain of both the heavy and light chain of the Fab region has a constant amino acid sequence that defines the class and subclass of each antibody. The Fc portion is responsible for the biological activity of the antibody, however, the Fc portion only becomes

biologically after the Fab component has bound to its corresponding antigen. Depending on the class and subclass of antibody, biological activities of the Fc portion of antibodies include the ability to:
Activate the complement pathway (IgG & IgM).
Bind to phagocytes (IgG).
Bind to mast cells, basophiles, and eosinophils (IgE).
Bind to NK cells (IgG).
Determine the tissue distribution of the antibodies, that is, to what tissues types the antibody molecules are able to go.
Individual "Y"-shaped antibody molecules are called monomers and can bind to two identical epitopes. Antibodies of the classes IgG, IgD, and IgE are monomers.
Two classes of antibodies are more complex. IgM is a pentamer, consisting of 5 "Y"-like molecules connected at their Fc portions by a "J" or joining chain. Secretory IgA is a dimer consisting of 2 "Y"-like molecules connected at their Fc portions by a "J" chain and stabilized to resist enzymatic digestion in body secretions by means of a secretory component.

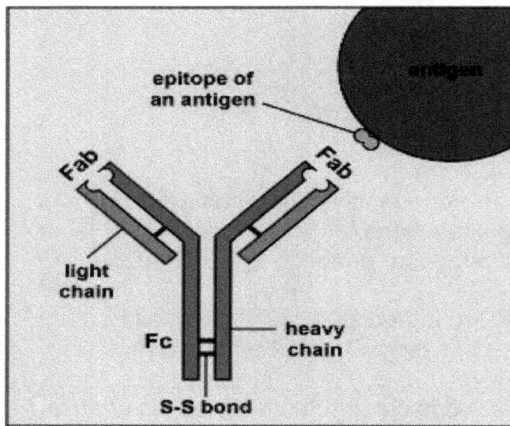

The Fab portion of the antibody has specificity for binding an epitope of an antigen. The Fc portion directs the biological activity of the antibody.

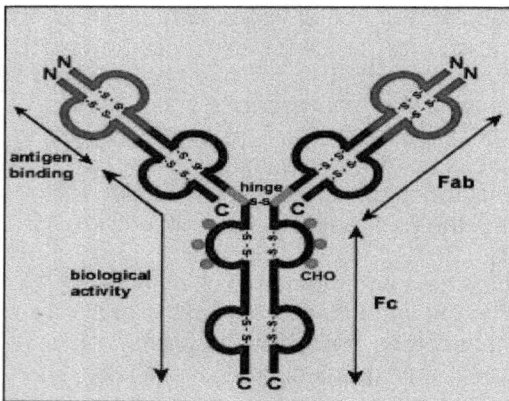

The Fab portion of the antibody has the complementarity-determining regions (red) providing specificity for binding an epitope of an antigen. The Fc portion (purple) directs the biological activity of the antibody. (S-S = disulfide bond; N = amino terminal of glycoprotein; C = carboxy terminal of glycoprotein; CHO = carbohydrate.)

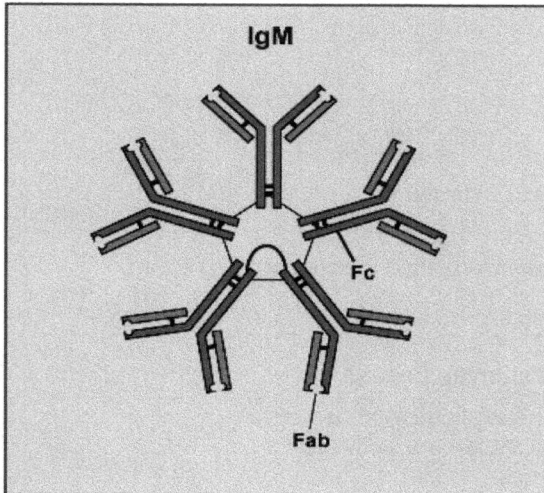

IgM is a pentamer and, therefore, has 10 Fab sites

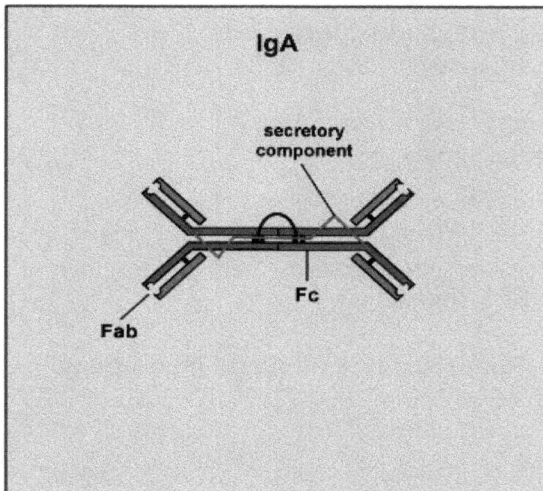

Secretory IgA is a dimer and has 4 Fab sites. A secretory component helps protect it from digestion in body secretions.

=Microbiology (Prof Gary E. Kaiser). Used with permission=

Biological Functions

Properties of Antibody Isotypes			
Isotype	% of total Ig (adult serum)	Biological half-life (days)	Biological Functions
IgA$_1$	11-14	5.9	Pathogen neutralization in mucosal secretions
IgA$_2$	1-4	4.5	
IgD	0.2	2-8	Membrane BCR
IgE	0.004	1-5	Mast cell histamine release
IgG$_1$	45-53	21-24	Pathogen neutralization in tissues Classical complement activation Opsonization NK cell ADCC Transplacental transfer
IgG$_2$	11-15	21-24	Pathogen neutralization in tissues
IgG$_3$	0.03-0.06	7-8	Pathogen neutralization in tissues Classical complement activation Opsonization NK cell ADCC Transplacental transfer
IgG$_4$	0.015-0.045	21-24	Pathogen neutralization in tissues Transplacental transfer
IgM	10	5-10	Classical complement activation Membrane BCR (monomer)

Adapted from Leffell, M. S., A. D. Donnenberg, and N. R. Rose Handbook of Human Immunology. CRC Press, Boca Raton, 1997.

(Pathogen) Antigen

Antigens were originally defined as non-self molecules which bound specifically to antibodies. In practice, the term antigen is used to mean any molecule recognized by the immune system.

Antigens which induce adaptive immunity are called immunogens. All immunogens are antigens, and are usually called antigens unless their ability to induce an immune response is being discussed. Some antigens, called haptens, are not immunogenic unless they are covalently linked to immunogenic carriers (usually proteins). Haptens can bind antibodies once the antibodies are produced, but haptens will not induce antibody synthesis on their own. Small non-protein organic molecules, for example the antibiotic penicillin, are haptens.

Immunogenicity

Immunogenicity is influenced by

- The chemical nature of the antigen.
- The antigen's size.
- The antigen's usual presence in the body.
- Antigen dose and route and timing of administration.
- Whether the antigen is easily phagocytosed.
- Whether antigen is efficiently presented to T cells on MHC.
- The maturity of the immune system, and specific lymphocytes.
   That immunogenicity depends on the immune system as well as on the antigen.
Immunogenicity is generally higher for proteins than for other organic molecules. Protein antigens, which are the predominant sort that activate helper T cells, consequently induce more B cell antibody

production, synthesis of IgG or IgA, and generation of memory B and T cells. T-independent antigens, which activate only B cells, induce IgM synthesis but not other adaptive immune responses.

Immunogenicity increases with molecular size and complexity. Haptens are generally non-proteins or they are too small to be immunogenic unless they are covalently attached to a carrier protein molecule. Some carbohydrate antigens can stimulate B cells to secrete IgM in the absence of T cell help but do not elicit IgG or memory cells. Human infants make poor responses to carbohydrate antigens, so early vaccinations with bacterial polysaccharide antigens employ protein carriers. Aggregated proteins are easily phagocytosed and more immunogenic than soluble proteins. Adjuvants, including bacterial products, alum, or oil emulsification of antigen, attract and activate antigen-presenting cells (Dendritic cells and macrophages) and slow antigen release to prolong exposure and improve immunogenicity.

Each part of the antigen bound by a unique antibody is called an epitope. Most proteins have several epitopes that are recognized by different B cells and induce a polyclonal antibody response. In a polyclonal response, several clones of B cells each make different antibodies, all able to bind to the same antigen but at different epitopes.

Epitopes may be shared by closely related antigens (cross-reactivity), so that antibody made to tetanus toxoid binds tetanus toxin. A protein epitope may be a linear sequence of amino acids or it may be assembled by protein folding. Epitopes with definite three-dimensional shapes and charged amino acids are particularly well recognized by antibodies. External membrane and cell wall molecules, often present in many copies on the pathogen, are common B cell antigens. A small peptide of 4-6 amino acids could fit into an antibody binding site, but larger proteins have more extended epitopes across their surfaces.

Active immunity

Active immunity is induced by exposure to antigen. Antigen dose and the route and timing of antigen contact, as well as immunogenicity, influence the magnitude and nature of the immune response. Very high or very low doses of antigen induce tolerance, the inability to respond to that antigen, while intermediate doses induce immunity. We are generally tolerant to cell-bound and soluble antigens present in our own bodies. Oral tolerance to foods is common, although some foods induce allergic reactions.

Antigens encountered in body tissues through subcutaneous or intramuscular injection are carried by lymph and macrophages into the lymph nodes, where they usually elicit formation of serum IgG antibody. Antigens encountered by mucosal routes (orally or in the respiratory or urogenital tracts) are taken up by M cells and induce secretory IgA production. IgE is often made to worm parasites and to protein allergens such as pollen that are encountered at low doses across mucus membranes. Introducing antigens into the blood stream requires larger doses for inducing immunity, as the majority of antigen is quickly removed and destroyed in the spleen and liver reticuloendothelial systems (RES).

Exogenous (extracellular) pathogens and their toxins, and endogenous (intracellular) pathogens encountered when they are extracellular, induce formation of antibodies by B cells with the help of Th2 cells. Intracellular pathogens elicit formation of cytotoxic T cells (Tc) to kill virus-infected cells or of inflammatory cytokine-producing Th1 cells to promote macrophage destruction of engulfed pathogens. A virus must be capable of infecting and replicating in a host cell to induce formation of cytotoxic T cells, but both live and killed viruses induce antibody formation. Mycobacteriums that survive inside macrophage phagosome induce Th1 activation.

Upon initial (primary) contact with an antigen, a lag of several days occurs before increased antibody production or cellular immunity can be detected. During this time the innate immune response is occurring. Macrophages and neutrophils engulf and destroy the pathogens; complement is activated to stimulate inflammation and pathogen lysis; NK cells kill virus-infected host cells; and cytokine production results in inflammation, increased body temperature (fever), and increased Hematopoiesis.

If antigen is not removed by innate immune mechanisms, adaptive immune effectors are activated. Antigen in the tissues is carried by macrophages, PMNs, and Dendritic cells to nearby secondary lymphoid organs where it stimulates lymphocytes to become immune effector cells. Measures of adaptive immune effector functions such as plasma antibody, increase for about 10-14 days after antigen contact, plateau for several days, and, when antigen has been successfully eliminated, and drop but remain higher than in unimmunized individuals. The predominant antibody made during the primary immune response is IgM. Upon secondary antigen contact, the lag period is shorter, the peak response higher, and increased antibody levels may persist for weeks or months. IgG (or IgA for mucosal antigens) is the predominant antibody made during secondary immune responses.

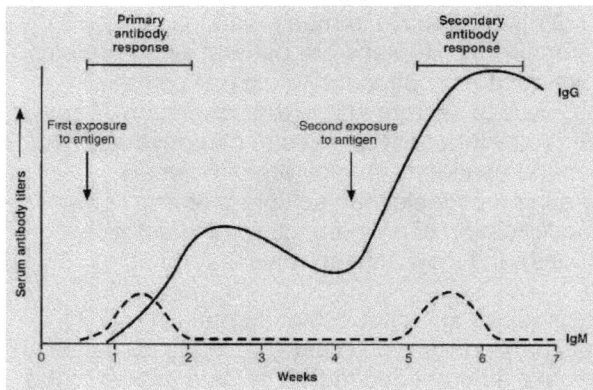

Cluster of Differentiation

The identification of membrane "markers" on immune system cells has been instrumental in the identification and characterization of functional cell types. B cells, helper T cells, and cytotoxic T cells, as well as some of their immature precursors, look identical under the light microscope but have very different functions. Plasma membrane molecules unique to distinct functional cell types were identified by making antibodies to intact cells and studying the ability of those antibodies to bind to or inhibit the activities of different cells. An international CD (Cluster of Differentiation) classification system insures that every antibody identified as anti-CD4, for example, binds the same molecule (not necessarily the same epitope).

Although we call the membrane CD antigens "markers" because they help us identify cells, they are on the membrane to serve as receptors for antigens or cytokines or binding molecules on other cells. CD antigens have been identified on many different immune cells and on cells outside the immune system

Selected Leukocyte Membrane Markers		
Cell Type	Marker	Function
B cells	mIgM and mIgD	Binds antigen
	Igα Igβ (CD79 α β)	Transducers binding signal
	CD 19, CD 21, CD 81	Co-receptors to enhance signaling
activated B cells, Dendritic cells, macrophages	B7.1 (CD 80), B 7.2 (CD86)	Co-stimulator for T cell activation, binds T cell CD28 (binds CTLA-4 for inactivation of T cells)
activated B cells, Dendritic cells, macrophages	CD40	Co-stimulator for APC activation, binds T cell CD40L (CD154)
Dendritic cells	CD209 (DC-SIGN)	Binds ICAM-3 on naïve T cells
T cells	TCR	Binds antigen peptide on MHC
	CD3	Transducers binding signal
activated T cells	CD40L (CD154)	Binds CD40 to communicate with APC
	CD28	Binds B cell B 7.1 and B7.2 to activate T cell
	CTLA-4	Binds APC B 7.1, 7.2 to inactivate T cells
T & NK cells	CD2	Adhesion molecule, binds CD58 (LFA-3)
Th	CD4	Binds class II MHC, co-receptor to

		enhance signaling
Tc	CD8	Binds class I MHC, co-receptor to enhance signaling
NK cells	CD56	Adhesion molecule
Monocyte/macrophages, neutrophils	CD64 (FcγRI)	Binds antigen-bound IgG
Monocyte/macrophages, neutrophils, NK cells	CD16 (FcγRIII)	Binds antigen-bound IgG; low-affinity Fcγ Receptor
Granulocytes and Monocytes	CD 114	Binds G-CSF growth factor
All hematopoietic cells	CD45 (CLA, B220, T200)	Augments signaling
Antigen presenting cells: B cells, Macrophages, and Dendritic cells	Class II MHC	Antigen presentation to Th cells
All nucleated cells	Class I MHC	Antigen presentation to Tc cells

Antibodies to unique CD antigens can be used to purify particular cell populations. Some of the commonly used techniques involve linking the antibodies to plastic dishes, beads, or paramagnetic particles. The desired cells bind to the specific antibodies, and other cell types can be washed away. The use of fluorescent antibodies to CD antigens in flow cytometry allows for the quantification of different cell types (and the amount of marker on each cell) as well as their purification.

Immunodeficiency: An Overview

Immunodeficiency results in an inability to combat certain diseases and may be of two types: primary or secondary. Primary immunodeficiency is usually an immunodeficiency that one is born with. In the case of secondary immunodeficiency, one is born with normal immune responses but some secondary factor or occurrence causes a decrease in immune responses.

Primary Immunodeficiency

A primary immunodeficiency is usually an immunodeficiency that one is born with. Until recently, primary immunodeficiencies were defined as a rare recessive genetic defect in the immune responses that involved the development of B-lymphocytes, T-lymphocytes, or both and resulted in multiple, recurrent infections during infancy. Depending on the disorder, the lymphocytes in question were either completely absent, present in very low levels, or present but not functioning normally. These disorders represent the conventional immunodeficiencies.
However, based on our increased understanding of the human genome and immune responses it now appears that there are a multitude of common, less severe primary immunodeficiencies involving just one or more of the huge number of genes involved in the immune responses. These so called novel primary immunodeficiencies involve the decreased ability to combat just a single type of infection or a narrow range of infections.

Conventional Immunodeficiencies

The conventional primary immunodeficiencies were grouped as follows:

B-lymphocyte Disorders

There may be greatly decreased humoral immunity but cell-mediated immunity, mediated by T-lymphocytes, remains normal.
    1. Agammaglobulinemia

Few if any antibodies are produced and there are reduced B-lymphocyte numbers. The person is very susceptible to recurrent infections by common pyogenic bacteria such as Staphylococcus aureus, Streptococcus pyogenes, Streptococcus pneumoniae, Neisseria meningitidis, and Hemophilus influenzae.These bacteria have antiphagocytic capsules that are normally eliminated by antibodies through opsonization.

Examples include:
- X-linked agammaglobulinemia
- Autosomal recessive agammaglobulinemia
    2. Hypogammaglobulinemia/Isotype Defects
 Decreased general antibody production or decrease production of a single isotype of antibody
 Examples include:
IgG2 subclass deficiency. A person is unable to produce the subclass of IgG called IgG2 but can produce other classes of antibodies. There is increased susceptibility to bacterial infections.
Selective IgA deficiency. A person is unable to make IgA but can produce other classes of antibodies. There is increased susceptibility to bacterial infections and certain prozozoan infections.
Combined Variable Immunodeficiency (CVID). Hypogammaglobulinemia with normal or decreased numbers of B-lymphocytes.
More severe forms such as agammaglubulinemia are treated with artificially-acquired passive immunization - periodic injections of large amounts of immune globulin (IG or IVIG).

T-lymphocyte Disorders

  There is little or no cell-mediated immunity if the disorder involves T8-lymphocytes and/or T4-helper lymphocytes. There may also be decreased humoral immunity if there is a disorder involves T4-helper lymphocytes.
    1. MHC Expression Defects
MHC-I deficiency. Decreased levels of MHC-I production and reduced T8-lymphocyte numbers.
Bare lymphocyte syndrome. Decreased levels of MHC-II, decreased numbers of T4-lymphocytes, and decreased T4-dependent antibody production by B-lymphocytes.
    2. T-Lymphocyte Signaling Defects
Wiskott-Aldrich syndrome. Defective T-lymphocyte activation and defective leukocyte mobility
Proximal TCR signaling defects. Defective cell-mediated immunity and defective T4-dependent antibody production by B-lymphocytes.
    3. Familial Hemophagocytic Lymphohistiocytosis
Perforin deficiencies. Defective CTL and NK cell function; uncontrolled activation of macrophages and CTLs.
Granule fusion defects. Defective CTL and NK cell function; uncontrolled activation of macrophages and CTLs.
X-linked lymphoproliferative syndrome. Defective CTL and NK cell function; uncontrolled activation of macrophages and CTLs. Uncontrolled Epstein-Barr virus - induced B-lymphocyte proliferation.

Combined B- and T-lymphocyte Disorders (Severe Combined Immunodeficiency Disease or SCID)

  These deficiencies affect both humoral immunity and cell-mediated immunity. There is a defect in both B-lymphocytes and T-lymphocytes, or just T-lymphocytes in which case the humoral deficiency is due to the lack of T4-helper lymphocytes.
    1. Cytokine-Signaling Defects
    2. Defects in Nucleotide Salvage Pathways
    3. Defects in V (D) J Recombination (Combinatorial Diversity)
    4. Defective Thymus Development

The thymus is needed for the development of T-lymphocytes from stem cells.
DiGeorge syndrome. Shows decreased levels of T-lymphocytes, normal levels of B-lymphocytes, and reduced antibody levels.
Defective pre-TCR checkpoint. Shows decreased levels of T-lymphocytes, normal or reduced levels of B-lymphocytes, and reduced antibody levels.

Innate Immunity Disorders

- Chronic granulomatous disease.
- No oxygen-dependant killing pathway in phagocytes.

- Recurrent intracellular bacterial and fungal infections.
- Leukocyte adhesion deficiencies.
- Defective leukocyte adhesion, diapedesis, and migration.
- Recurrent bacterial and fungal infections.
- Chediak-Higashi syndrome.
- Defective vesicle fusion and lysosomal function in neutrophils, dendritic cells, macrophages and other cells,
- Recurrent infections by pyogenic bacteria.

Novel Immunodeficiencies

While the rare conventional primary immunodeficiencies mentioned above are still very important, based on our increased understanding of the human genome and immune responses it now appears that there are a multitude of common, less severe primary immunodeficiencies.
These so called novel primary immunodeficiencies relate to an individual's own unique genetics and can involve one or more of many immunity genes, ranging from any of the huge number of genes conferring protective immunity in general, to individual genes conferring specific immunity to a single pathogen.
It is now thought that almost every person suffers from one form of primary immunodeficiency or another. Unlike the classical primary immunodeficiencies, however, these primary immunodeficiencies involve the decreased ability to combat just a single type of infection or a narrow range of infections.

Examples include:
- Disorders of the interleukin-12/interferon-gamma pathway appear to make individuals more susceptible to Mycobacterium and Salmonella infections.
- Disorders of the TLR-3 pathway make individuals more susceptible to herpes simplex virus encephalitis.
- Disorders of the toll-interleukin 1 receptor/nuclear factor kappa B pathway make individuals more susceptible to staphylococcal and pneumococcal infections.
-Disorders of properdin and terminal components of the complement pathways make individuals more susceptible to Neisseria infections.
People with chronic sinusitis that does not respond well to treatment have decreased activity of TLR-9 and produce reduced levels of human beta-defensin 2, as well as mannan-binding lectin needed to initiate the lectin complement pathway.

Secondary Immunodeficiency

In the case of secondary immunodeficiency, one is born with normal immune responses but some secondary factor or occurrence causes a decrease in immune responses. Secondary immunodeficiency is induced by factors such as:
1- Malnutrition. Inhibits lymphocyte maturation and function.
2-Some viruses, e.g., HIV. Depletes T4-lymphocytes.
3-Irradiation - exposure to X-rays and gamma rays- Causes a decreased production of lymphocyte precursors in the bone marrow.
4-Cytotoxic drugs such as many used in cancer chemotherapy- Causes a decreased production of lymphocyte precursors in the bone marrow.
5-Corticosteroids – anti-inflammatory steroids- Damages lymphocytes.
6-Leukemias, cancers of the lymphoid system, metastases- Reduces areas for lymphocyte development.
7-Aging- Adaptive immunity, especially cell-mediated immunity, tends to deminish with aging.
8-Removal of the spleen- Decreased ability to remove microbes that enter the blood

A secondary immunodeficiency of current notoriety is of course Acquired Immuno Deficiency Syndrome or AIDS, a secondary immunodeficiency caused by Human Immunodeficiency Virus (HIV). HIV, via its gp120, primarily infects cells with CD4 molecules and chemokine receptors on their surface, namely, T4-helper lymphocytes, macrophages, and dendritic cells. The median incubation period for AIDS is around 10 years.
During early or acute HIV infection the virus primarily infects and destroys memory T4-lymphocytes which express the chemokine receptor CCR5 and are very abundant in mucosal lymphoid tissues. Here HIV also encounters the dendritic cells located throughout the epithelium of the skin and the

mucous membranes where in their immature form called Langerhans cells they are attached by long cytoplasmic processes. The envelope glycoproteins gp41 and gp120 of HIV contain mannose-rich glycans that bind to mannan-binding proteins (pattern recognition receptors; also called lectin receptors) on the dendritic cells.

Upon capturing antigens through pinocytosis and phagocytosis and becoming activated by pro-inflammatory cytokines, the dendritic cells detach from the epithelium, enter lymph vessels, and are carried to regional lymph nodes. By the time they enter the lymph nodes, the dendritic cells have matured and are now able to present antigens of HIV to naive T-lymphocytes located in the lymph nodes in order to induce adaptive immune responses.

At this point the infection has transitioned from the acute phase to the chronic phase. The chronic phase of HIV infection is characterized by viral dissemination, viremia, and induction of adaptive immune responses. The viremia allows the viruses to spread and infect T4-helper lymphocytes, macrophages, and dendritic cells found in peripheral lymphoid tissues.

During the chronic phase of HIV infection, the lymph nodes and the spleen become sites for continuous viral replication and host cell destruction. During most of this phase, the immune system remains active and competent and there are few clinical symptoms. A steady state-infection generally persists where T4-lymphocyte death and T4-lymphocyte replacement by the body are in equilibrium. In a person infected with HIV, somewhere between one and two billion of these T4-cells die each day as a result of HIV infection and must be replaced by the body's lymphopoietic system in the bone marrow. It is estimated that 10 billion virions are produced and cleared in an infected individual each day. However, the enormous turnover of T4-lymphocytes eventually exhausts the lymphopoietic system and it becomes unable to replace the T4-cells being destroyed. A variety of mechanisms then eventually lead to immunodeficiency.

Mechanisms of HIV-induced immunodeficiency include:

1- Direct HIV-induced cytopathic effect on infected T4-lymphocytes. This can occur through:
2-Increased cell permeability as a result of gp41 expression in the host cell membrane and viral release by budding;
3-Inhibition of host cell protein synthesis as a result of viral replication within the infected cell; and
4-Fusion of infected T4-cells with numerous uninfected T4-cells resulting in syncytia formation
5-Killing of HIV-infected T4-cells by cytotoxic T-lymphocytes or CTLs
6-Killing of HIV-infected T4-cells by antibody-dependent cytotoxicity or ADCC
7-Apoptosis of T4-cells as a result of chronic activation by HIV and by cytokines
8-Shedding of gp120 molecules by HIV. This subsequently triggers a series of events that cause the adaptive immune system to become less and less effective, primarily by altering the normal balance of immunoregulatory T_h1 and T_h2 cells in the body.
9-Impaired function of HIV infected macrophages and dendritic cells.

To further complicate problems; during the replication of HIV the reverse transcriptase of HIV exhibits a high error rate as it transcribes the RNA genome into DNA. As a result, HIV readily mutates to become more immunoresistant, more drug resistant, and able to change the preferred cell type it is able to infect.

Progression to AIDS is marked by a viral load that progressively increases in number while the immune system weakens as a result of the destruction of increasing numbers of T4-lymphocytes and the inability of the body to continually replace these destroyed cells. As will be seen in Unit 5, the loss of T4-helper lymphocytes leads to a marked decline in cells called cytotoxic T-lymphocytes (CTLs), the primary cells the body's immune responses use to destroy virus-infected cells. Once a person progresses to full-blown AIDS he or she becomes susceptible to a variety of opportunistic infections by:

Bacteria such as Mycobacterium avium complex (MAC), Salmonella, and Nocardia;
Protozoa such as Cryptosporidium and Toxoplasma;
Viruses such as cytomegalovirus (CMV), herpes simplex viruses types 1 and 2 (HSV-1, HSV-2), and varicella zoster virus (VZV);
Candida, Cryptococcus, Coccidioides, Histoplasma, and Pneumocystis
There is also an increased incidence of tumors, such Epstein-Barr virus-associated B-cell lymphomas, other lymphomas, cervical cancer, and Kaposi's sarcoma. Wasting syndrome and encephalopathy are also common.

Complement Deficiencies

The complement system refers to a series of proteins circulating in the blood and bathing the fluids surrounding tissues. The proteins circulate in an inactive form, but in response to the recognition of molecular components of microorganism, they become sequentially actived, working in a cascade where in the binding of one protein promotes the binding of the next protein in the cascade.

There are 3 complement pathways that make up the complement system: the classical complement pathway, the lectin pathway, and the alternative complement pathway. The pathways differ in the manner in which they are activated and ultimately produce a key enzyme called C3 convertase:

1. The classical complement pathway is activated by antigen-antibody complexes.

2. The lectin pathway is activated by the interaction of microbial carbohydrates with mannose-binding lectin (MBL) in the plasma and tissue fluids.

3. The alternative complement pathway is activated by C3b binding to microbial surfaces and to antibody molecules.

The end results and defense benefits of each pathway, however, are the same. All complement pathways carry out 6 beneficial innate defense functions. Proteins produced by the complement pathways:

1. Trigger inflammation;

2. Chemotactically attract phagocytes to the infection site;

3. Promote the attachment of antigens to phagocytes (enhanced attachment or opsonization;

4. Cause lysis of gram-negative bacteria and human cells displaying foreign epitopes;

5. Plays a role in the activation of naive B-lymphocytes; and

6. Remove harmful immune complexes from the body.

Complement has several roles in host defense and immune regulation. If a complement component is lacking in an individual the problems encountered depend on which pathway is affected.

Deficiency of C1, C4, C2 (classical pathway) are associated with recurrent infections by encapsulated bacteria which require the triad of antibody, complement and neutrophils to respectively bind to, opsonise and phagocytose and kill these bacteria. These patients can instead or in addition suffer from conditions which result from inefficient clearance of immune complexes (glomerulo-nephritis, lupus erythematosus (these are commonly manifested as renal damage, joint problems and rashes)). A small number of patients do not appear to experience any disease.

Deficiency of C3 results in severe problems with recurrent infection and with immune complex mediated disease because of the central position of C3 in the complement pathways.

Deficiencies of alternative pathway components (Properdin, Factor D) are relatively rare. Properdin deficiency is usually associated with a single episode of bacterial meningitis whilst factor D deficiency is commonly associated with recurrent respiratory tract infections.

Despite the potency of the terminal pathway in causing bacterial lysis, deficiency of C5, C6, C7, C8 and C9 are associated with recurrent infection with only one group of bacteria, Neisseria. Deficient patients commonly present with recurrent meningococcal meningitis. There is no specific treatment of complement deficiency so immunizations and antibiotics are used to respectively reduce the risk and treat infections.

Auto-Immunity

Auto-immunity is the situation in which the host's immune system can be demonstrated to exhibit reactivity to self antigens. It is not always accompanied by any disease. Auto-immune disease is the situation in which a disease is associated with demonstrable immunity. Auto-immunity is simply acting as tissue damaging responses may occur as a consequence of involvement of the immune system, especially when these responses are exaggerated. This is known as hypersensitivity. In some, but not all instances, the immune response is targeted against self.

Auto-immune diseases can be divided into organ-specific and non-organ specific. Organ specific means the auto-immunity is directed against a component of one particular type of organ (the cells of the adrenal glands, causing Addison's disease). In non –organ specific auto-immune disease, the auto-immunity is directed against an antigen that is present at many different sites and can include involvement of several organs (antibody against DNA, resulting in the disease systemic lupus erythematosus (SLE)). In Sjogren's syndrome, patients experience dry eyes and mouth, caused by the production of auto-antibodies against salivary ducts, and rheumatoid arthritis. Auto-immunity may be the result of attack by antibodies, cells or both.

T- Cells may attack antigens found within the thyroid gland in auto-immune thyroiditis (Hashimoto's disease), which is an example of an organ-specific auto-immune disease, and was the first anti-immune disease to be described. In this disease, there are also antibodies to thyroid antigens, which may interfere with uptake of iodine. Thus, both antibodies and immune cells contribute to this disorder. Some of the antibodies are probably harmless, since not all patients with thyroid antibodies have any evidence of functional impairment. In this situation, antibodies serve as markers of auto-immunity. Likewise, T-Cells may attack the beta cells within the islets of Langerhans in the pancreas, resulting in insulin-dependent diabetes mellitus. In SLE, there are circulating immune complexes of DNA-anti DNA. This may settle at various sites (glomerular basement membrane, or dermo-epidermal junction of skin). By contrast, in Graves disease (hyperthyroidism), there is an auto-antibody which binds to the thyrotropin stimulating hormone receptor (TSH receptor), but instead of blocking, it mimics the TSH signal and stimulates instead.

More often, many different microorganisms have been associated with a single autoimmune disease, which indicates that more than one infectious agent can induce the same disease through similar mechanisms. Since infections generally occur well before the onset of symptoms of autoimmune disease, clinically linking a specific causative agent to a particular autoimmune disease is difficult. This difficulty raises the question of whether autoimmune diseases really can be attributed to infections.

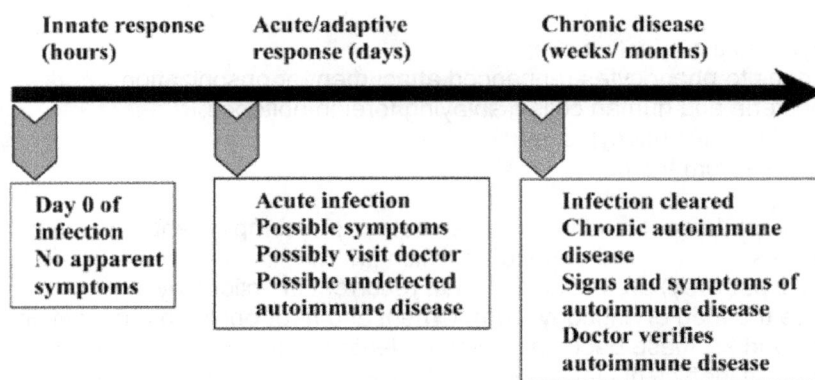

Innate response (hours)	Acute/adaptive response (days)	Chronic disease (weeks/ months)
Day 0 of infection No apparent symptoms	Acute infection Possible symptoms Possibly visit doctor Possible undetected autoimmune disease	Infection cleared Chronic autoimmune disease Signs and symptoms of autoimmune disease Doctor verifies autoimmune disease

Sources: Fairweather D, Rose NR. Women and autoimmune diseases. Emerg Infect Dis. 2004 November. Available from http://www.cdc.gov/ncidod/EID/vol10no11/04-0367.htm

Infections occur before the onset of symptoms of autoimmune disease, making links to specific causative agents difficult. When a person is first infected (day 0), usually no symptoms are apparent. Signs and symptoms of autoimmune disease are clearly present and easily confirmed by physicians during the chronic stage of autoimmunity. However, the infection has been cleared by this time, making it difficult to establish that an infection caused the autoimmune disease.

Human Autoimmune Diseases

Human Autoimmune Diseases			
Disease	Auto antigen	Symptoms	Extent*
Type II: antibodies to cell surface molecules			
Autoimmune hemolytic anemia	Rh blood group antigens, I antigen	Lysis of RBC by complement and FcR⁺ cells, anemia	O
Autoimmune thrombocytopenic purpura	Platelet integrin GpIIb:IIIa	Abnormal bleeding	O
Goodpasture's syndrome	Basement membrane Type IV collagen	Glomerulonephritis, pulmonary hemorrhage	O
Graves' disease	Thyroid-stimulating hormone receptor	Thyroid over-activity	O
Hashimoto's thyroiditis	Thyroglobulin, thyroid peroxidase	Thyroid under-activity	O
Hypoglycemia	Insulin receptor (agonist)	Low blood glucose	O
Insulin-resistant diabetes	Insulin receptor (antagonist)	High blood glucose, ketoacidosis	O
Myasthenia gravis	□ chain of nicotinic acetylcholine receptor	Progressive weakness	O
Pemphigus vulgaris	Epidermal cadherin	Skin blisters	O
Pernicious anemia	Intrinsic factor, gastric parietal cells	Anemia	O
Rheumatic fever	Streptococcal cell wall antigens; antibodies cross-react with heart muscle	Arthritis, myocarditis, heart valve scars	O
Spontaneous infertility	Sperm antigens	Infertility	O
Type III: Immune complex disease			
Ankylosing spondylitis	Immune complexes	Damage to vertebrae	S
Mixed essential cryoglobulinemia	Rheumatoid factor IgG complexes	Systemic vasculitis	S
Rheumatoid arthritis	Rheumatoid factor IgG complexes	Arthritis	S
Systemic lupus erythematosus (SLE)	DNA, histones, ribosomes, snRNP, scRNP	Glomerulonephritis, vasculitis, rash	S
Type IV: T cell-mediated disease			
Experimental autoimmune encephalomyelitis (EAE), multiple sclerosis (MS)	Myelin basic protein, proteolipid protein, myelin oligodendrocyte glycoprotein	Brain invasion by CD4 T cells, weakness	S
Hashimoto's thyroiditis	Thyroid antigen(s)	Thyroid under-activity	O
Insulin-dependent (Type I) diabetes mellitus (IDDM)	Pancreatic □ cell antigen(s)	□ cell destruction	O
Rheumatoid arthritis	Unknown synovial joint antigen	Joint inflammation and destruction	S

*O = organ-specific, S = systemic

When autoimmune disease is caused by auto antibodies, the antigen can often be identified and the disease mechanism classified as Type II or Type III hypersensitivity. In autoimmune hemolytic anemia, antibodies to red blood cell antigens initiate complement lysis and phagocytosis of RBC in the spleen reticuloendothelial system (RES). Antibodies to platelets and neutrophils can also cause depletion of these cells in the RES, although leukocytes are more resistant to complement lysis than are erythrocytes. Treatment for autoimmune hemolytic anemia can involve removal of the spleen. Complement activation in levels too low to lyse cells results in damaging inflammation due to chemotaxis of neutrophils and macrophages and their activation and production of cytokines. ADCC can also result in tissue damage and cell death. An example of antibody-mediated autoimmunity is seen in Hashimoto's thyroiditis, where antibodies to thyroid enzymes or hormones result in damage to the thyroid.

Antibodies to cell surface receptors may stimulate or inhibit receptor function. Antibodies to TSH receptor in the thyroid stimulate thyroid hormone production and induce hyperthyroidism (overactive thyroid) in Grave's Disease. Antibodies to the receptor for acetylcholine, a neurotransmitter, and block nervous system signals to muscle cells and leads to myasthenia gravis, a progressive muscle weakness. Antibodies to insulin receptor have been shown in some cases to mimic insulin function and cause low blood sugar and in other cases to block insulin function and cause high blood sugar. Antibodies to basement membrane Type IV collagen, present in the kidney, lungs, and inner ear, cause Type II hypersensitivity in Goodpasture's syndrome. Antigens must be accessible for antibody-mediated autoimmune disease to occur. Type IV collagen is exposed in the kidney, so Goodpasture's syndrome always results in kidney disease. In general, only smokers also get lung damage with Goodpasture's syndrome, because damage from smoking exposes collagen in the lung. Hearing is rarely lost even though Type IV collagen is also present in the inner ear because it is hidden from the immune system.

In Systemic Lupus Erythematosus (SLE), IgG production too many self antigens results in tissue damage throughout the body (systemic or system-wide disease). Since these self-antigens are present in all cells, antibody can bind and form immune complexes that activate complement whenever cells are damaged. Phagocytes are attracted and damage more cells, resulting in Type III hypersensitivity. Genes associated with SLE include those for proteins involved in antigen clearance, tolerance induction, and organ-specific disease susceptibility. Persisting infection can also lead to Type III hypersensitivity, where continuing antibody production to a pathogen cause tissue damage at the site of infection. An example is Lyme arthritis seen in some people infected with Borrelia burgdorferi, the spirochete that causes Lyme disease.

IgG auto antibodies may be transferred across the placenta and cause transient symptoms in the newborn infant. Damage is usually not permanent; removal of maternal antibodies can be accomplished with plasmapheresis.

T cell-mediated damage results in several autoimmune diseases, including multiple sclerosis, rheumatoid arthritis, and insulin-dependent diabetes. It is more difficult to identify autoimmune T cells and the antigen to which they are responding than it is to identify antibodies and their antigens.

Specificity of autoimmune T cells may be identifiable in animal models of disease, such as experimental autoimmune encephalitis (EAE), a model for multiple sclerosis where disease is induced by injection of myelin basic protein. Both CD8 and CD4 T cells have been implicated in IDDM pathology. Th1 cells are associated with both EAE and rheumatoid arthritis.

Since autoimmune disease is mediated by normal immune mechanisms, controlling the disease without making the patient susceptible to infection is the greatest challenge.

Another problem is that diseases of autoimmune origin are allocated to different medical specialties based on the organ system immediately affected. Autoimmune diseases of the blood, for example are treated by hematologists, those of the nervous system by neurologists, those of the endocrine system by endocrinologists and those of the joints and muscles by rheumatologists. This compartmentalization has hampered communication among physicians and scientists interested in autoimmune diseases.

Gender influence

Women tend to be affected more often by autoimmune disorders; nearly 79% of autoimmune disease patients in the USA are women. Also they tend appear during or shortly after puberty. It is not known why this is the case, although hormone levels have been shown to affect the severity of some autoimmune diseases such as multiple sclerosis. Other causes may include the presence of fetal cells in the maternal bloodstream. The reasons for the sex bias in the autoimmune diseases are unclear but may include such factors as sex-related differences in immune responsiveness, response to infection, sex steroid effects, and sex-linked genetic factors.

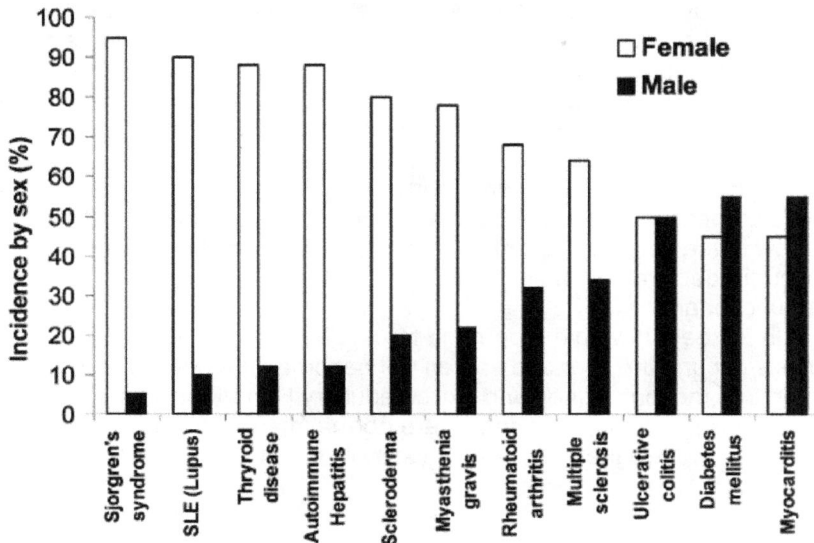

PART THREE: THE NORMAL HEMATOPOIETIC SYSTEM

CHAPTER ONE: OVERVIEW OF HEMATOPOIESIS

Hematopoiesis is the formation and development of blood cells. A steady blood cell population is maintained by production of new cells and destruction of old cells.

The first blood cells formed are RBCs. At 2 to 8 weeks primitive nucleated erythroid cells are found in the yolk sac, they contain hemoglobin but don't mature to fully develop RBCs.

During the 2nd month extramedullary Hematopoiesis develops yolk sac cells migrate to the liver. Granulocytes also appear in the liver during the 2nd month and all adult organs are recognizable. The spleen also contributes to Hematopoiesis at this point.

During the 4th month medullary Hematopoiesis develops when the bone marrow begins to contribute to Hematopoiesis.

During the 5th month bone marrow takes over as chief production site and continues throughout life. At birth the liver and spleen have ceased production of blood cells and Hematopoiesis is occurring in the red bone marrow of almost every bone (axial and appendicular skeletons). As a child develops and matures (beginning at 4 years) the hematopoietic activity begins to move to the axial skeleton (flat bone, skull, ribs, sternum, clavicle, vertebrae, and pelvic bones) and proximal ends of long bones (humerus and femur). This move is completed by age 18.

Remaining marrow cavities are replaced with fat (yellow bone marrow). By age 40 the marrow in sternum, ribs pelvis and vertebrae is composed of equal amounts of hematopoietic tissues and fat.

In times of great demand the marrow in the long bone shafts may become hematopoietic again.

Extramedullary Hematopoiesis occur under two conditions:

1- If the bone marrow is no longer functional.

2- When the bone marrow is not able to keep up with the demand for blood cells.

When extramedullary Hematopoiesis occurs, the liver and spleen will become enlarged. In some diseases the marrow may re-expand into the long bones and extramedullary Hematopoiesis can occur in the liver, spleen and lymph nodes. This occurs in condition where normal marrow sites are replaced by abnormal tissue as in myelofibrosis, or where there is intensive stimulation of Erythropoiesis as in thalassemia.

The Bone Marrow and Hematopoiesis

There are two important interacting components:

    1- A hierarchy of stem cells

    2- The hematopoietic inductive microenvironment

Stem cells at various levels interact with:

-Growth factors

-Integrins (adhesion molecules)

-Cytokines generated by the immune system.

-Chemokines which regulate traffic.

Pluripotent stem cells populate the blood with all its lineages. Each stem cell division yields an identical stem cell (termed self renewal) and a daughter who may differentiate into a lineage committed stem cell. Lineage committed stem cells have a decreased proliferation capacity. This "hierarchy of stem cells" maintains normal polyclonal Hematopoiesis during life. Progression down the hierarchy is associated with loss/gain of:

-Specific cell markers.

-Receptor.

-Adhesion molecules.

-Chromatin openness.

- Access to epigenetic transcription factors, and loss of proliferation potential.

The stromal matrix plays an important role in presenting growth factors and nutrients to developing blood cells. There are lineage specific regions "niches" which provide the molecular basis for homing of transplanted stem cells. Sinusoids are lined with specialized endothelial cells which play an important role by producing factors which regulate growth and differentiation.

    The unique supportive microenvironment stem cell niche

* regulates proliferation and differentiation

* supports survival and inhibits apoptosis

* presents growth factors and nutrients to developing blood cells

Immature cells have receptors which bind them to: proteoglycan molecules on the matrix and to receptors on stromal cells (macrophages, fibroblasts, fat cells and endothelial cells)
Maturing blood cells:
Lose adherence receptors, become deformable.
Migrate through cytoplasm of lining endothelial cell to enter sinusoids.
Platelets are the exception. Megacaryocytes form part of the sinusoidal wall. They form long processes of proplatelets which fragment into nascent platelets.

Growth factors regulate growth and differentiation (erythropoietin, GM-CSF and G-CSF, thrombopoietine) also prevent apoptosis important for homeostasis.

Hematopoietic cells are programmed to self destruct but can be rescued from apoptosis by:
- Specific growth factors
- Certain gene products
- Specific antigen
- Some virus (EBV).

Defects in apoptosis pathway are very important in causing diseases such as chronic lymphocytic leukemia (CLL), and in enhancing resistance to chemotherapy in malignancy.

Induction of apoptosis is a therapeutic strategy in resistant CLL. Inappropriate apoptosis is a disease mechanism in myelodysplastic syndromes. Apoptosis is induced by chemotherapy and resistance to chemotherapy is associated with blocked apoptosis.

The Different Hematopoietic Lineages

All blood cells develop from Pluripotent stem cells that are found in the red bone marrow. Stem cells make up 10% of cord blood cells and <1% of all adults blood cells. Stem cells are able to proliferate as well as differentiate into the different types of blood cells. They are also able to renew themselves. It is now generally accepted that all blood cells are made from a relatively few "uncommitted" cells which are capable of mitosis and of differentiation into "committed" precursors of each of the main types of blood cell.

The polyphyletic theory maintains that the blood cells originate from two or more specific primitive cells.

The Unitarian theory states that the cells of the circulating blood have a common origin from one type of cell.

The Pluripotent stem cell is the progenitor of two multipotential stem cell lines: the myeloid and the lymphoid lines. Myeloid stem cells are precursors of granulocytes, Monocytes, RBCs and platelets; lymphoid stem cells are precursor of lymphocytes.

The myeloid stem cell becomes the CFU-GEMM (colony forming unit, granulocyte-erythrocyte-monocyte-megacaryocytes).

GFU terminology comes from tissue culture of cells where marrow cells were injected and colonies of cells would appear.

GFU-GEMM leads to formation of:
- BFU (burst forming unit erythroid)
- CFU-Meg (megacaryocytes)
- CFU-GM (granulocyte, monocyte/macrophage)
  - CFU-G
  - CFU-M
  - CFU-Eo
  - CFU-Bas

Using routine hematology laboratory analysis, we cannot identify the cells up to this point by morphology alone. They are identified by surface receptor analysis.

The lymphoid cell line becomes the pre-B lymphocyte and pre-T lymphocyte.

http://www.embryology.ch/anglais/qblood/popupblood/q01blut/stammzellen.html

Pools of Hematopoietic Activity

Bone marrow

Stem cell pool- comprised of multipotential stem cells and unipotential committed colony-forming unit, all of which are morphologically unidentifiable.

Proliferating pool- cells are capable of DNA synthesis and are undergoing mitosis. Storage pool-mature cells that are stored for later release into the peripheral blood and cells that are maturing. They are no longer capable of mitosis.

Peripheral blood

Circulating pool- functioning cells in bloodstream, in transit to tissues, the blood we draw for evaluation comes from this pool.

Marginating pool- Primarily a term used fro white blood cells. The cells are adhered to walls of blood vessels and are ready to move through into the tissues (diapedesis). There is constant movement between the circulating and marginating pools.

At a given time the ration of cells in the circulating pool to the marginating pool is 50:50. Neutrophils move freely between the two pools of circulation in peripheral blood.

Maturation of Blood Cells

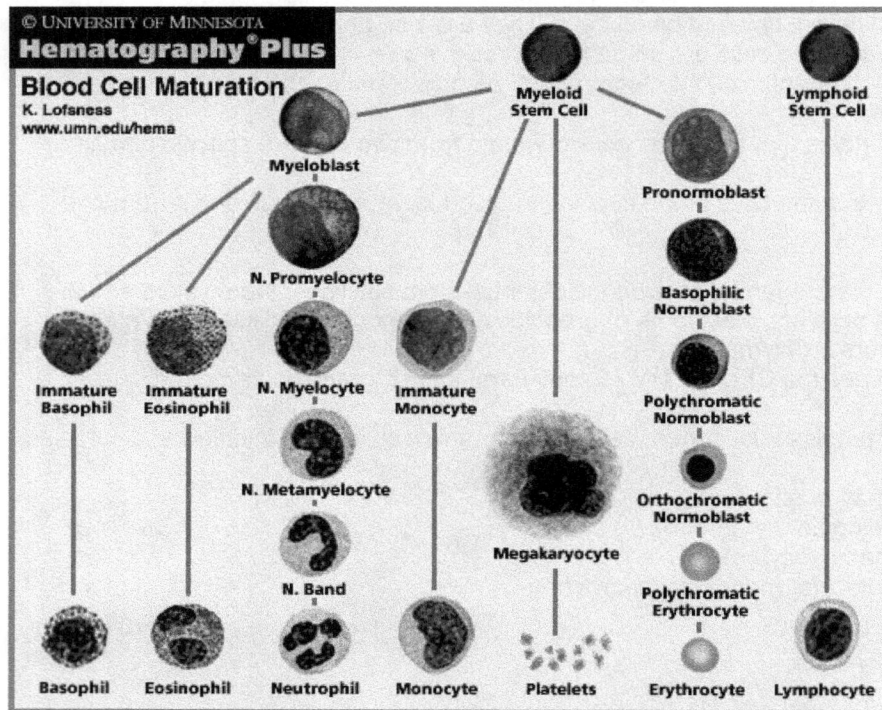

http://www1.umn.edu/hema/pages/matchart.html

Blood cells go through several stages of development; these cells do not jump from one stage to the other but undergo this maturation gradually. It is important to keep this fact in mind, because many times the cell being studied may be in between the two stages described (when this occurs, the cells is generally given the name of the more mature stage).

As a cell is transformed from the primitive blast stage to the mature form found in the blood, there are changes in the cytoplasm, nucleus, and cell size. All three of these changes will occur gradually and at the same time.

Cytoplasm Maturation

The immature cytoplasm will generally stain a deep blue (basophilic) due to the high content of RNA present. As the cell matures, there is a gradual loss of cytoplasmic RNA and therefore a lessening of the blue color. In certain of the cells (for example, the myeloid cells) granules will appear in the cytoplasm as the cell matures. At first the granules are few and relatively non specific. As the cell matures further, these granules will increase in number and take on specific characteristics and functions. The amount of cytoplasm, in relationship to the rest of the cell, will usually in crease as the cell matures.

Nuclear Maturation

The nucleus of the immature cell is round or oval and will be very large in proportion to the rest of the cell. As the cell matures, the nucleus will decrease in relative size and take on various shapes. The nucleus chromatin will transform from a fine delicate pattern to become more and clumped in the mature form, and the staining properties will change from a reddish-purple to a blue-purple. Nucleoli, present in the early stages of the cell, will gradually disappear as the cell ages.

Cell Size

Overall cell size generally decreases as the cell matures. It will usually become smaller in size.

CHAPTER TWO: ERYTHROPOIESIS

Erythron refers to all the erythrocytes and their precursors in the blood, bone marrow or at extramedullary sites. Erythropoiesis is the development of erythrocytes.

Early committed erythroid precursors (BFU-E) generate colonies of 500 or more RBCs in 7-10 days in methylcellulose culture. CFU-E, a late stage erythroid progenitor, generates colonies of only 8 to 64 RBCs in 2 days.

Proerythroblast ultimately generate 16 RBCs. 10% die in marrow due to "ineffective erythropoiesis".

Erythropoietic tissue originates in the yolk sac then moves to the liver and spleen during fetal life. Eventually erythropoiesis settles in the medullary cavity of the skeleton. By about 18 years of age the axial skeleton and proximal ends of the long bones is the site of erythrocyte production.

Nutriments needed for Effective Erythropoiesis

. Amino acids (proteins) - for globin production
. Iron – for heme production
. Vitamins B12, B6, and folic acid
. Erythropoietin (EPO) is a hormone that controls erythropoiesis. Its production and release is governed by:
- The need to keep the normal oxygen carrying capacity of the blood at a steady state based on the normal turnover of erythrocytes.
-The oxygen content of tissues (hypoxia leads to increased production).

Erythropoietin acts primarily at CFU-E stage of committed erythroid cells, it also acts at the BFU-E stage to a lesser degree.

Stages of erythropoiesis

Proerythroblast= Rubriblast

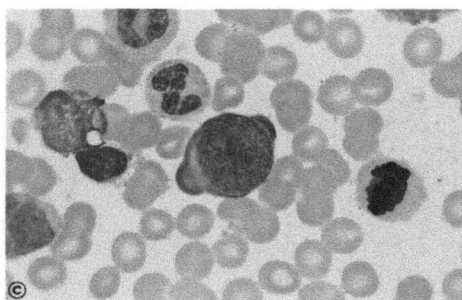

=Atlas of Hematology (Nivaldo Medeiros, MD). Used with permission=

SIZE OF THE CELL	18-25um.
SHAPE OF THE CELL	Round/slightly oval, moderate to large.
N:C RATION	4:1
CYTOPLASM	greatly basophilic, perinuclear halo
NUCLEUS	large, round occupying 80% of the cell
CHROMATIN	The nuclear chromatin is fine (immature) and one to three nucleoli are present.
MARROW	1- 5%
BLOOD	NOT PRESENT

Basophilic Erythroblast = Prorubricyte

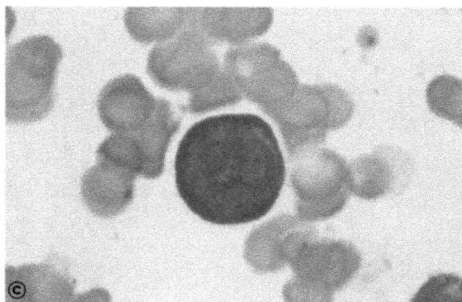

=Atlas of Hematology (Nivaldo Medeiros, MD). Used with permission=

SIZE OF THE CELL	14-18um.
N:C RATIO	3:1
SHAPE OF THE CELL	round, sometimes deformed by surrounding cells
CYTOPLASM	still plainly basophilic
NUCLEUS	round/centrally located
CHROMATIN	somewhat coarser, disappearance of nucleoli
MARROW	1- 7%
BLOOD	NOT PRESENT

Polychromatophilic Erythroblast= Rubricyte

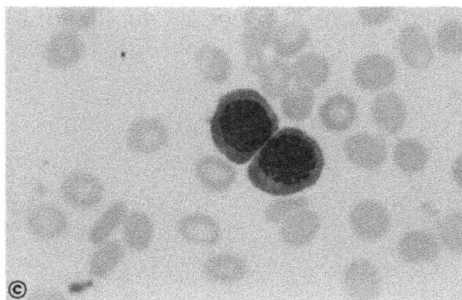

=Atlas of Hematology (Nivaldo Medeiros, MD). Used with permission=

SIZE OF THE CELL	10 -12um
SHAPE OF THE CELL	Round, sometimes deformed by surrounding cells.
CYTOPLASM	Gray-blue (intermediate) corresponds to the superimposition of basophilia (remnant of RNA from the earliest stages) and acidophilia (progressive increase in hemoglobin content
NUCELUS	Round
CHROMATIN	more clumped
MARROW	2- 20%
BLOOD	NOT PRESENT

Acidophilic Erythroblast= Metarubricyte

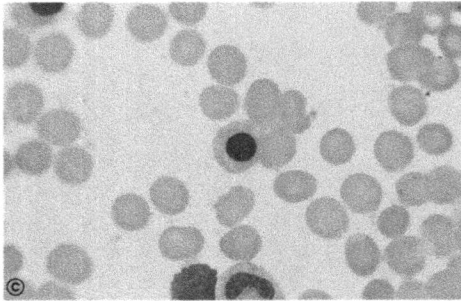

=Atlas of Hematology (Nivaldo Medeiros, MD). Used with permission=

SIZE OF THE CELL	8-12um
SHAPE OF THE CELL	round often deformed by surrounding cells
CYTOPLASM	pink or more or less that of surrounding RBCs.
NUCLEUS	small round
CHROMATIN	dark with intense condensation
MARROW	5- 15%
BLOOD	NOT PRESENT.

Reticulocytes

After the nucleus has left the orthochromatic erythroid, the cytoplasm corresponds to a reticulocyte: some RNA and mitochondria are still present and confer a grayish or bluish color to these cells. Supravital stains (such as brilliant Cresyl bleu) are used in routine conditions to ascertain number of peripheral blood reticulocyte (0.5- 2.0%).

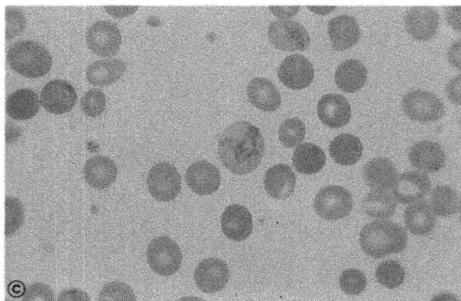

=Atlas of Hematology (Nivaldo Medeiros, MD). Used with permission=

General overviews of cellular changes

Cell volume decreases as the cell matures. On the average the size goes from proerythroblast measuring 25 microns to a mature erythrocyte measuring 7 microns in diameter.
Chromatin condenses. The proerythroblast has very fine chromatin; the acidophil erythroblast has solid chromatin and the mature erythrocyte has none.
Nucleoli disappear by the basophilic erythroblast.
Nuclear shape remains round.
N:C ratio decreases.

RNA activity decreases in cytoplasm resulting in lighter blue cytoplasm as the cell matures. The proerythroblast cytoplasm is deep blue, and the polychromatophilic erythroblast cytoplasm is pinkish blue, the pink coming from the beginning of hemoglobin production.

Hemoglobin production begins at the polychromatophilic normoblast and increases as the cell matures. There is a gradual shifting of predominantly blue to predominantly pink cytoplasmic color as the cell matures to an erythrocyte. A mature erythrocyte has no blue color in the cytoplasm. Mitochondria activity decreases.

The nucleus is eventually extruded. The orthochromatic erythroblast is last stage with a nucleus. Blue color of cytoplasm due to presence of RNA indicating protein synthesis.

Pink color of cytoplasm due to presence of hemoglobin production, Perinuclear halo indicates mitochondria and Golgi apparatus surround the nucleus. These structures do not pick up stain.

The proerythroblast undergoes 4 cell divisions over a period of 72 hours to produce 16 acidophilic normoblasts. This occurs in the bone marrow. The nucleus is extruded to form the reticulocyte. This also takes place in the bone marrow. The reticulocyte matures for another 48 hours in the bone marrow before being released into the peripheral blood as the mature red blood cell. The red blood cell has a life-span of approximately 120 days in the circulating blood.

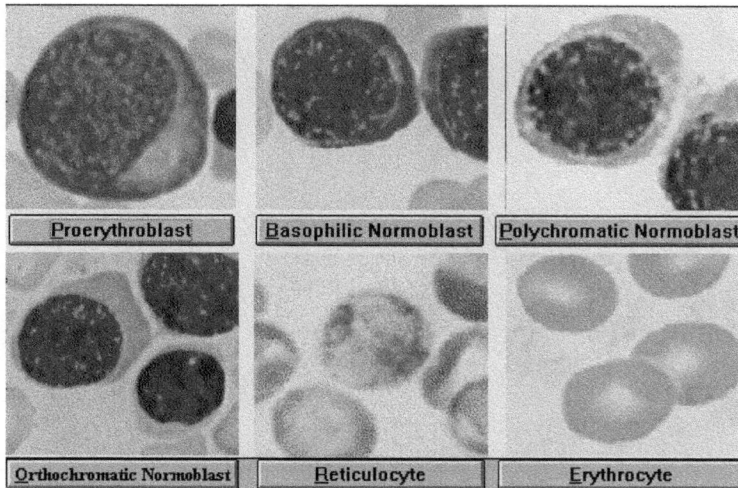

| Proerythroblast | Basophilic Normoblast | Polychromatic Normoblast |
| Orthochromatic Normoblast | Reticulocyte | Erythrocyte |

=The Hematology Unit (Prof .Amos M. Cohen). Used with permission=

CHAPTER THREE: GRANULOPOIESIS

Committed granulocytic progenitors (CFU-C) generate colonies of differentiating/maturing myeloid cell in methylcellulose or agar culture.

The size of their colonies is relatively small because myeloid cells die upon reaching the metamyelocyte stage in agar culture.

In bone marrow metamyelocyte undergo further maturation in the marrow granulocyte reservoir before entering the bloodstream as polymorph nuclear neutrophils (PMN).

PMN are about equally distributed between the axial circulating and marginated granulocyte pools, and in health are maintained within a relatively narrow range

Clonal abnormalities may result in development of leukemia.

Granulocyte colony stimulating factor (G-CCF) acts as a "granulopoietin" somewhat analogous to erythropoietin and thrombopoietin.

G-CCF stimulates proliferation, maturation, differentiation and function of end stage PMN.

G-CCF also rescues granulocytic precursors from apoptosis in vitro.

The CCF has different specificities, and GM-CCF and G-CCF are commercially available.

In vivo sources of CSF include marrow macrophages, stromal and endothelial cells and activated T-cells.

Stages of Granulopoiesis

Myeloblast

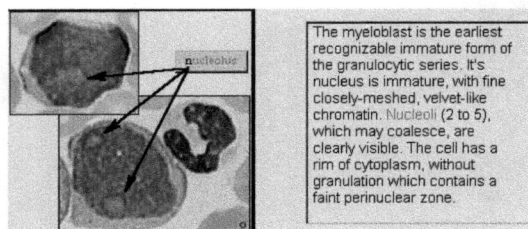

The myeloblast is the earliest recognizable immature form of the granulocytic series. It's nucleus is immature, with fine closely-meshed, velvet-like chromatin. Nucleoli (2 to 5), which may coalesce, are clearly visible. The cell has a rim of cytoplasm, without granulation which contains a faint perinuclear zone.

=The Hematology Unit (Prof .Amos M. Cohen). Used with permission=

SIZE OF THE CELL	18-22 microns
SHAPE OF THE CELL	Large cell, oval, sometimes round
N:C RATIO	High 70 to 80%.
NUCLEUS	Grossly oval or quadrangular, irregular rarely round
CYTOPLASM	Basophilic, and either no or only a few red azurophilic granules are present.
CHROMATIN	Fine with reticular appearance. Has a diffuse pattern, and 1 to 5 nucleoli are visible.
BONE MARROW	1- 5%.
BLOOD	NOT PRESENT

Promyelocyte

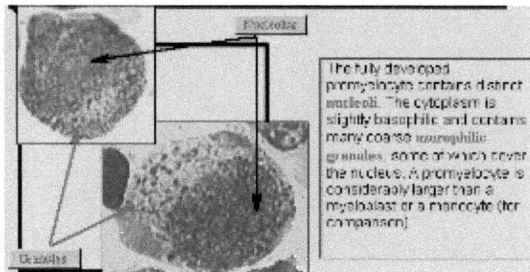

The fully developed promyelocyte contains distinct nucleoli. The cytoplasm is slightly basophilic and contains many coarse neutrophilic granules, some of which cover the nucleus. A promyelocyte is considerably larger than a myeloblast or a monocyte (for comparison).

=The Hematology Unit (Prof .Amos M. Cohen). Used with permission=

SIZE OF THE CELL	20- 25 microns
SHAPE OF THE CELL	Oval or round
NUCLEUS	Oval is often eccentric
N:C RATION	50%.
CYTOPLASM	Pale blue contains a few to many non specific granules
CHROMATIN	May become a little coarser, although it will still be relatively immature. Two or three nucleoli are present
BONE MARROW	1- 6%
BLOOD	NOT PRESENT.

Neutrophil Myelocytes

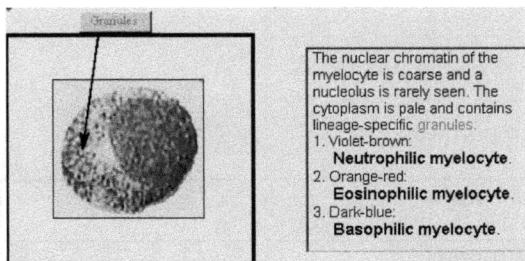

The nuclear chromatin of the myelocyte is coarse and a nucleolus is rarely seen. The cytoplasm is pale and contains lineage-specific granules.
1. Violet-brown:
   Neutrophilic myelocyte.
2. Orange-red:
   Eosinophilic myelocyte.
3. Dark-blue:
   Basophilic myelocyte.

=The Hematology Unit (Prof .Amos M. Cohen). Used with permission=

SIZE OF THE CELL	15-18 microns
SHAPE OF THE CELL	Oval or round
NUCLEUS	Eccentric and oval
N:C RATION	50%
CYTOPLASM	Abundant, without any basophilia, and numerous small red- brown or lilac granules are present
CHROMATIN	begins to clump nucleoli are no longer visible
BONE MARROW	5 – 20%.
BLOOD	NOT PRESENT

Neutrophil Metamyelocyte

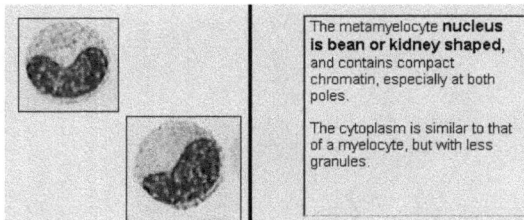

The metamyelocyte **nucleus is bean or kidney shaped,** and contains compact chromatin, especially at both poles.

The cytoplasm is similar to that of a myelocyte, but with less granules.

=The Hematology Unit (Prof .Amos M. Cohen). Used with permission=

SIZE OF THE CELL	14-20 microns
SHAPE OF THE CELL	Oval or round
NUCLEUS	Indented, with a horseshoe-shaped appearance
CHROMATIN	Condensed, elongation and constrictions of the nucleus give rise to band cells and eventually to polymorphs
CYTOPLASM	Few azurophilic and neutrophilic granules
BONE MARROW	10 – 25%.
BLOOD	NOT PRESENT

Band Neutrophil

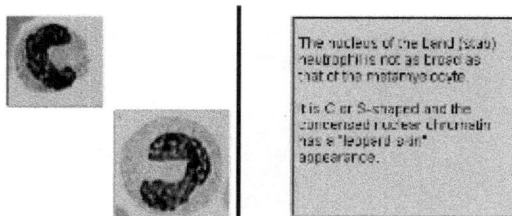

The nucleus of the band (stab) neutrophil is not as broad as that of the metamyelocyte.

It is C or S-shaped and the condensed nuclear chromatin has a "leopard skin" appearance.

=The Hematology Unit (Prof .Amos M. Cohen). Used with permission=

SIZE OF THE CELL	14- 20 microns
SHAPE OF THE CELL	Oval or round
NUCLEUS	Semicircular
CHROMATIN	Condensed. Nucleoli: not visible.
CYTOPLASM	Neutrophilic granules
BONE MARROW	5-20%.
BLOOD	1-5%.

Eosinophil Precursors

In rare instances in normal human bone marrow precursors younger than myelocyte are found, easily identified due to their orange granules. As their number is quite low they are counted together with myelocyte in bone marrow differential.

In Eosinophil series there is one sole type of granules, which progressively mature and acquire their peculiar eosinophilic color.

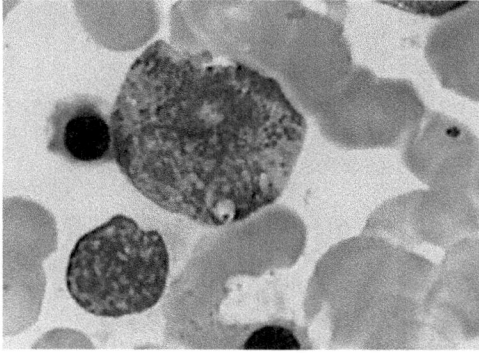

Eosinophil Myelocytes

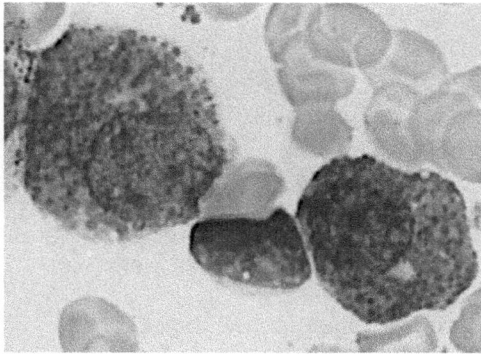

Eosinophil Metamyelocyte

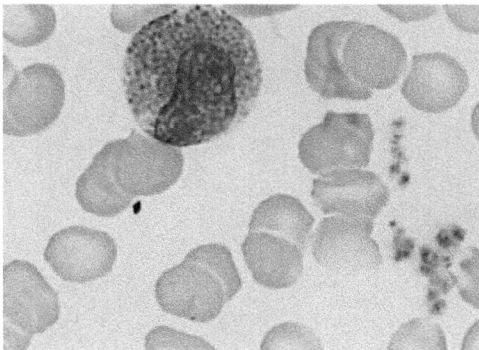

= Hematocell (Prof Marc Zandecki). Used with permission=

Basophils

Cells of this series are easy to identify, due to their large and coarse dark purple or dark red granules. Frequently distributed throughout the cell, they cover the nucleus and in normal conditions it is often difficult to ascertain characteristics of the nucleus. As overall number of Basophils is usually very low, all cells are counted together within the differential.

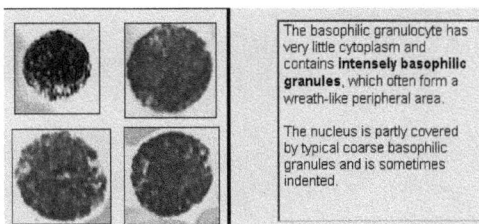

The basophilic granulocyte has very little cytoplasm and contains **intensely basophilic granules**, which often form a wreath-like peripheral area.

The nucleus is partly covered by typical coarse basophilic granules and is sometimes indented.

=The Hematology Unit (Prof .Amos M. Cohen). Used with permission=

General Maturation Changes

1- Overall cell size generally decreases as the cell matures.

2- The nucleus decreases in size and starts to indent at the metamyelocyte stage and is segmented into up to 5 lobes at the segmented neutrophil stage.

3- The nuclear chromatin pattern changes fine (immature) to coarse as the cell matures. The coarseness indicates mitotic inactivity (no more mitosis).

4- Nucleoli disappear by the myelocyte stage. Nucleoli are composed of RNA and are associated with cell division.

5- The amount of cytoplasm increases as a cell matures. N:C ratio decrease from 4:1 to 1:1.

6- Primary non specific granules start to appear at the promyelocyte stage.

7- Secondary specific granules start to appear at the myelocyte stage.

8- Overall cytoplasmic color goes from blue to neutral. The intensity of blue of the cytoplasm indicates the amount of RNA present.

General Appearance changes

The nucleus in immature cells is large because it is physiologically active. The nucleus contains euchromatin (light, loose, and active with nucleoli) if the cell is engaged in mitosis. The nucleus contains heterochromatin (dark, clumped, inactive) if the cell cannot divide.

Cytoplasm will be rich with RNA (blue) if a lot of protein synthesis is occurring (the RNA produces protein such as antibodies, cytokines or proteins associated with cell division). If there is an abundance of protein production, the Golgi apparatus (part of the endoplasmic reticulum that prepares the protein for secretion) will be very prominent as a clear area near the nucleus (perinuclear clear area).

The specific cytoplasmic granules will have various shapes and colors dependent on their content. Secondary granules are different color, Eosinophils have red granules, and Basophils have deep purple to black that may obscure the nucleus and/or cytoplasm. Basophils granules are water soluble and may wash out in poorly fixed smears and appear as empty areas in the cytoplasm. This gives the cytoplasm a white appearance.

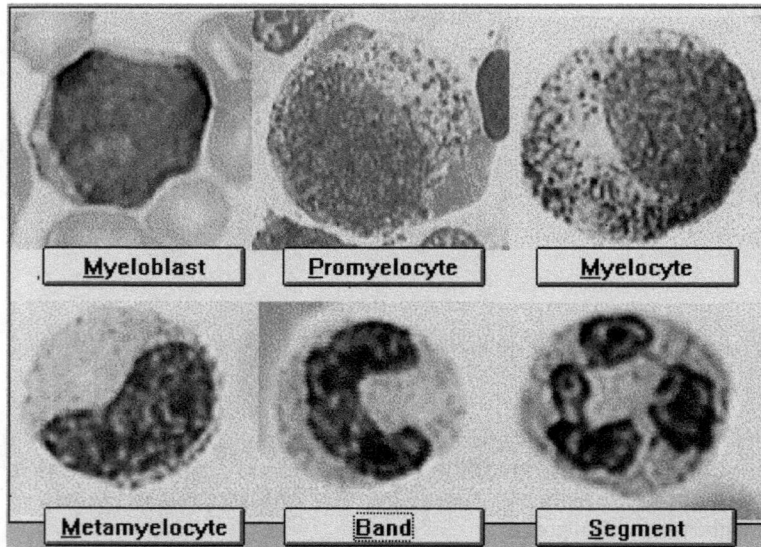

| Myeloblast | Promyelocyte | Myelocyte |
| Metamyelocyte | Band | Segment |

=The Hematology Unit (Prof .Amos M. Cohen). Used with permission=

CHAPTER FOUR: MONOCYTOPOIESIS

These two cells are the same cell type; they are Monocytes in the blood, and become macrophages when they migrate into the tissue.

Like all blood cells, monocytes develop from pluripotential stem cell. The first committed cell along the monocyte development tract is the monoblast, a cell type virtually identical in morphology to the myeloblast of the granulocytic series. Monoblast develop into promonocyte, a large cell with a slightly indented nucleus. Promonocyte develop into mature monocyte.

Monoblast

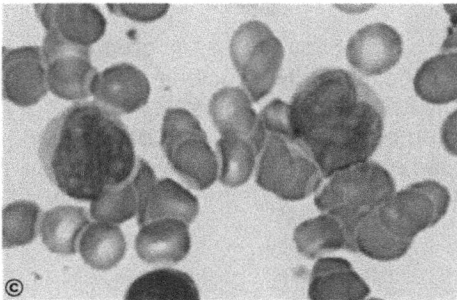

=Atlas of Hematology (Nivaldo Medeiros, MD). Used with permission=

SIZE OF THE CELL	12-20 microns
SHAPE OF THE CELL	Oval, sometimes round
NUCLEUS	Ovoid, round, or irregular
CHROMATIN	Fine, coarse or clumped
CYTOPLASM	Non granular and has moderate basophilic to blue-grey coloration.
BONE MARROW	< 1%
BLOOD	NOT PRESENT

Macrophage

The macrophage is a large cell with a diameter ranging up 20 microns. It is characterized by abundant cytoplasm that appears sky blue to grey in color and many contain azurophilic granules that vary in size and number. Vacuoles are common. Phagosome may be observed with ingested matter. The nucleus is usually eccentric and may be indented, oval, or elongated. The chromatin material appears spongy and will take on lilac to reddish purple color with Wright's stain. One or more nucleoli may be seen. Macrophages (structural elements of bone marrow), tend to be found on the edge of the blood film due to their large size.

CHAPTER FIVE: MEGACARYOPOIESIS

Thrombopoiesis has two phases, proliferation and differentiation of megakaryocytic progenitor cells and the complex process of maturation.

This involves a variable number of endoreduplications, cytoplasmic growth maturation, fragmentation (formation of proplatelets) and direct release of platelets with their specific structural components, into sinusoidal blood. The platelets last for about 10 days before being removed by liver and spleen. The number of platelets can increase 10- fold in times of need.

Thrombopoietin (TPO), IL-11, IL-6 and GM-CSF stimulate megacaryocytes proliferation in vitro. Thrombopoietin, made predominantly in the liver, has circulating levels that inversely correlate with platelet mass because platelets have receptors that remove this growth factor from the circulation. Platelet transfusion, then, may impair the recovery of megacaryocytes. Also, abnormal platelets as in essential thrombocythemia may not clear this growth factor, resulting in continuous platelet production. Platelets are not cells but rather pieces of megacaryocytes.

Several endomitoses (nuclear divisions without further cell division) that occur into early precursors lead to large cells (30 to 100 microns in diameter) named megacaryocytes (MK). Nucleus becomes progressively distorted whereas cytoplasm matures, and ultimately fragments into platelets (up to 2000/MK). Total number of Mk is low (0.02 to 0.05% of all nucleated bone marrow cells) but, as they are very large, they are easily observed at low magnification out the edges of the smears and their amount is usually only and estimate (low, normal, or high density).

Megakaryoblast

The first recognizable cell from the series, large cell (25 to 35 microns) cytoplasm is basophilic and granules are not yet visible. Nucleus is irregular in shape or bilobed and chromatin is dark and homogenous. Nuclear/cytoplasmic ration is high, nucleoli are not visible.

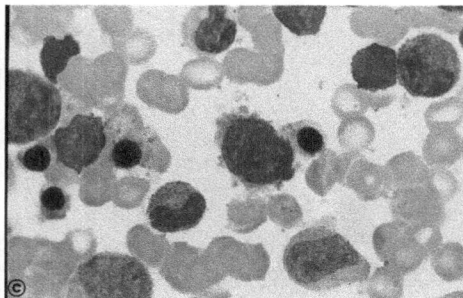

= Atlas of Hematology (Nivaldo Medeiros, MD). Used with permission=

Promegacaryocytes

Large size up to 50 microns, large nucleus, and irregular in shape may even show slight lobulation, cytoplasm usually abundant, blue, with pink spots, sometimes contains big vacuoles. Granules begin to form. Chromatin becomes coarser. In stage II, part of cytoplasmic basophilia disappears, there is an increase in the irregularity of nuclear contour.

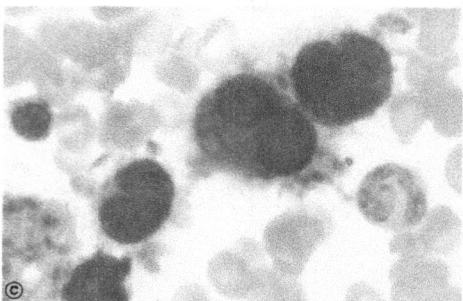

= Atlas of Hematology (Nivaldo Medeiros, MD). Used with permission

Megacaryocytes

The largest cell found in the normal bone marrow (30 to 100 microns).Part of the cytoplasm is pink and finely granular, usually has an irregular peripheral border. The granules will begin to aggregate into little bundles which dud off from the cell to become platelet. The nucleus is multilobulated and irregular. Chromatin is heavily packed; cytoplasm is large, pale blue and pink, with fine granules. External membrane is not always clearly visible, generating platelet processes that fragment into platelets.

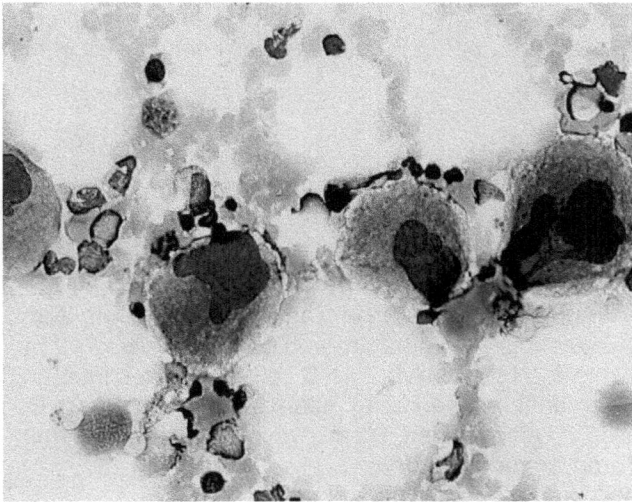

= Hematocell (Prof Marc Zandecki). Used with permission=

As shown here, platelet process cytoplasm of mature megacaryocytes elongates into the lumen of medullary sinusoids; these long and thin ribbons of cytoplasm ultimately fragment and generate platelets. Some platelet processes may be occasionally observed on bone marrow smears.

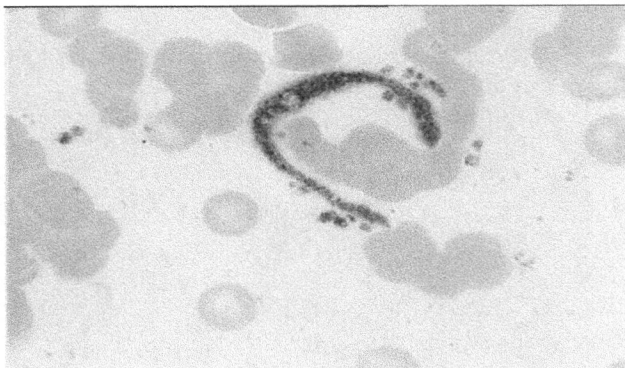

= Hematocell (Prof Marc Zandecki). Used with permission=

CHAPTER SIX: LYMPHOPOIESIS.

This shows the normal pattern of lymphoid cell development from an immature bone marrow lymphoblast precursor, through the lymph node stages, to the final endpoint of a plasma cell. The exact stages and progression of this maturing process are unknown, and thus aspects of this depiction may be controversial.

The lymphocytes are ubiquitous; they are produced in the lymph nodes, spleen, thymus, and bone marrow. If the maturation begins in the marrow, the lymphocyte is designated to be B-type, if the cell matures in the thymus; it is a T-type.

The immune system is remarkable for its ability to respond to a great many antigens, including newly synthesized compounds which did not exist until recently. Unusual properties of antibody diversity include the presence of variable and constant regions on the same polypeptide chain and identical V regions used with different C regions. Somatic recombination for generating antibody and TCR diversity is unique among mammalian genes. Successful synthesis of both H and L chains and their expression on the membrane are necessary for the development of B cells and mark the stages in that development.

Major stages of development in lymphocytes are:
1- Expression of antigen receptor.
2- Testing for appropriate antigen recognition properties (self tolerance).
3- Activation by antigen.
4- Differentiation.

B cells development

B cell development begins in the fetal liver and continues in the bone marrow throughout our lives. The table below illustrates the stages of B cell development. Once a B cell can express both mu and L chains on its membrane, it is officially a B cell. However, it is still immature and can be easily killed by contact with self antigen until it also expressed membrane IgD. The mature B cell that moves into the periphery can be activated by antigen and become an antibody-secreting plasma cell or a memory B cell which will respond more quickly to a second exposure to antigen. B cells which fail to successfully complete B cell development undergo apoptosis (programmed cell death).

Stages in B Cell Development							
	stem cell	early pro-B cell	late pro-B cell	large pre-B cell	small pre-B cell	immature B cell	mature B cell
H chain genes	germline	D-J joining	V-DJ joining	VDJ rearranged	VDJ rearranged	VDJ rearranged	VDJ rearranged
L chain genes	germline	germline	germline	germline	V-J joining	VJ rearranged	VJ rearranged
Surface Ig	none	none	none	□ chain in pre-B receptor	□ chain in cytoplasm and on surface	membrane IgM	membrane IgM and IgD
RAG, TdT expression	no	yes	yes	no	yes	yes	no
Surrogate L chain expression	no	yes	yes	yes	no	no	no
Ig expression	no	yes	yes	yes	yes	yes	yes
btk*	no	little	yes	yes	yes	yes	yes
Membrane markers	CD34	CD34 CD45 (B220) Class II	CD45R Class II CD19 CD40	CD45R Class II pre-B-R CD19 CD40	CD45R Class II pre-B-R CD19 CD40	CD45R Class II IgM CD19 CD40	CD45R Class II IgM IgD CD19 CD21 CD40

Following proliferation, small pre-B cells (no longer dividing) undergo V-J joining on one L chain chromosome. Once L chain has been successfully synthesized, it is expressed with muchain on the cell membrane and the cell is called an immature B cell. Immature B cells are very sensitive to antigen binding, so if they bind self antigen in the bone marrow they die. B cells that do not bind self antigen express membrane IgD with their IgM about the time they leave the marrow and become mature naive (resting) B cells.

T cells development

T cell development occurs in the thymus; the thymus microenvironment directs differentiation as well as positive and negative selection. Lymphoid progenitors which have developed from hematopoietic stem cells in the bone marrow migrate to the thymus to complete their antigen-independent maturation into functional T cells. In the thymus, T cells develop their specific T cell markers, including TCR, CD3, CD4, or CD8, and CD2. T cells also undergo thymic education through positive and negative selection.

Cell differentiation markers, are valuable in describing the development of mature, functional T-cells. In mice, some marrow stem cells stain faintly for the Thy-I (theta) antigen but do not express CD-4 or CD8 antigens. "Double negative cells that express Thy-I and JIld markers are apparently ready for differentiation because they can be induced to express markers of mature T- cells in vitro and in vivo. No all double negative thymocytes can be considered T-cell precursors, however. Class I MHC antigens and common lymphocyte antigen (CD-5) are expressed on precursor T-cells throughout intrathymic and extrathymic maturation. Expression of CD-2 (TII, SRBC receptor) molecules by immature T-cells is believed to facilitate formation of T-cell aggregates and adhesive interactions with thymic epithelial cells through binding with lymphocyte-function associated antigen (LFA-3) expressed on cell membranes. As pre-T cells infiltrate the thymic epithelium they lose surface TL (thymic lymphoma) antigen, express more Thy-I copies and begin to express CD-4 and CD-8 antigens. Double positive (CD-4+, CD-8+) T-cells that express antigen receptor are regarded as immature "cortical" cells that will differentiate into specific accessory T-cells after exposure to antigens and/or help from other T-cells. A proportion of peripheral blood T-cells express both CD-4 and CD-8 indicating that simultaneous expression does not prevent these cells from exiting the thymus. Expression of a single functional phenotype such as CD-4 (helper) or CD-8 (suppressor, cytotoxic) is associated with entry into the thymic medulla, exit to the periphery and inclusion in the recirculating pool. The L3T4 marker (mouse equivalent of CD-4) identifies the helper T-cell and does not react with the Lyt-I antigen on it or any other lymphocyte. Some CD-4 T-cells have been identified that have cellular cytotoxicity as a principal function. The CD-8 (Lyt-2 in mouse) expressing T-cell functions as suppressor cells or are responsible for class I MHC restricted, antigen specific cellular cytotoxicity against virally infected target cells and tumor cells. CD-8 cells are also present in the recirculating pool but cannot be negatively selected from efferent lymph by antigen as are CD-4 helper cells. The CD-8 T-cell is also able to return to the thymic cortex after emigrating while the CD-4+ T-cell is barred from returning unless the thymic perivascular microenvironment is altered as in Myasthenia Gravis. Some CD-8+ and all double positive cells appear to be short-lived because they rapidly disappear from the circulation after adult thymectomy or low level total body irradiation which effects thymic cortical lymphocytes. Acquisition of MHC haplotype restriction is one of the most intriguing aspects of T-cell development in the thymus. During maturation in the Thymus a dramatic selection takes place. Only those T-cell clones that express receptors capable of recognizing antigen in conjunction with the allelic forms of the MHC proteins expressed by thymic epithelial cells (or marrow-derived mononuclear cells) can mature fully. Mature helper T-cells are "restricted" to responding to antigen associated with the class II MHC antigen they saw in the thymic environment regardless of their own genotype. The same is true for mature cytotoxic T-cells who must recognize the class I MHC antigens, they saw during development, simultaneously with the viral or tumor antigen in order to deliver the lethal hit. Specificity for the foreign antigen is not sufficient to activate the respective T-cell if the antigen is expressed on an antigen-presenting-cell or target cell that has MHC antigens different from those that were seen during intrathymic development.

The T-cell antigen receptor is analogous to membrane immunoglobulin in B-cells. The T-cell receptor is composed of two polypeptides (alpha, beta or gamma, delta) associated in the membrane with CD3 and a number of accessory molecules such as CD4/CD8 and CD2. The T-cell receptor complex binds to immunogenic peptides only if they are presented within MHC antigens of antigen presenting cells or target cells. "Processed and presented" antigens are bound in a cleft lined by the polymorphic regions of the MHC antigens (Bjorkman et al 1987) which forms them into "recognizable" 10 angstrom alpha helices. At the gene level, the alpha and beta chain genes are like immunoglobulin heavy chain genes where variable, diversity, joining and constant gene segments are rearranged prior to expression of the protein on the T-cell membrane. This genetic rearrangement and expression is believed to occur after the pre-T cell arrives in the thymus and before it leaves for the periphery. Unlike immunglobulin, the T-cell receptor for antigen cannot effectively bind antigen except in the context of MHC gene products expressed on accessory target cells.

Lymphoblast

  Lymphoblats are 12-20 micron in diameter with a round to oval nucleus, sometimes eccentric in location, the nucleus to cytoplasm ratio is about 4:1 and the periphery of both the nucleus and the cell may be irregular in outline. The fine highly dispersed nuclear chromatin stains a light reddish-purple, and one or two pale blue colorless large nucleoli are visible. The cytoplasm is usually agranular and deeply to moderately basophilic, with marginal (peripheral) intensity a common characteristic.

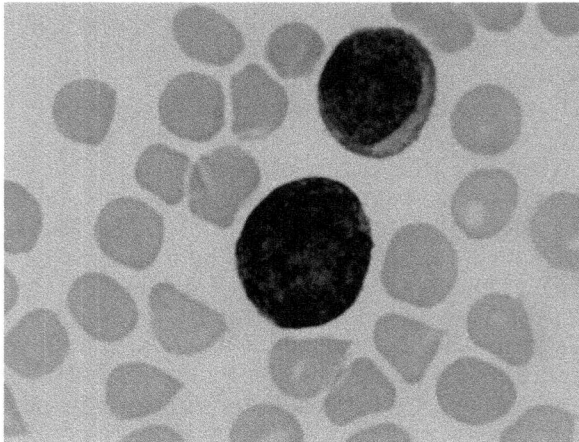

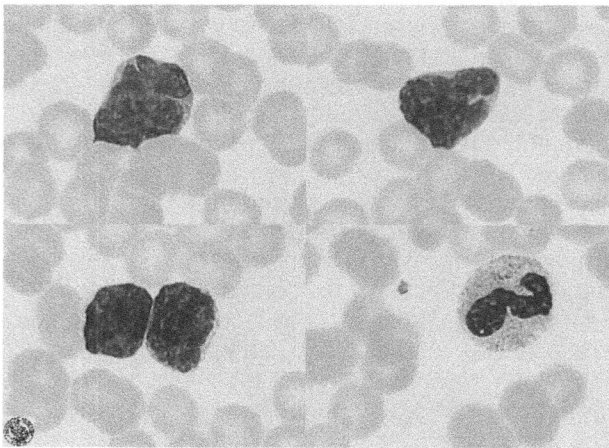

= Hematocell (Prof Marc Zandecki). Used with permission=

Plasmablast

The diameter ranges from 18 to 25 Microns. The cytoplasm is abundant, basophilic, and non-granular. The perinuclear halo may be present representing the active region of the Golgi body. The nucleus will be characterized by clumps of chromatin somewhat similar to the lymphocytes, but the clumping is moderately greater. The generally round nucleus is eccentric with a round to oval shape. Nuclear to cytoplasm ratio is 4:1 several nucleoli are present but may be difficult to see. This stage may not be seen in the bone marrow.

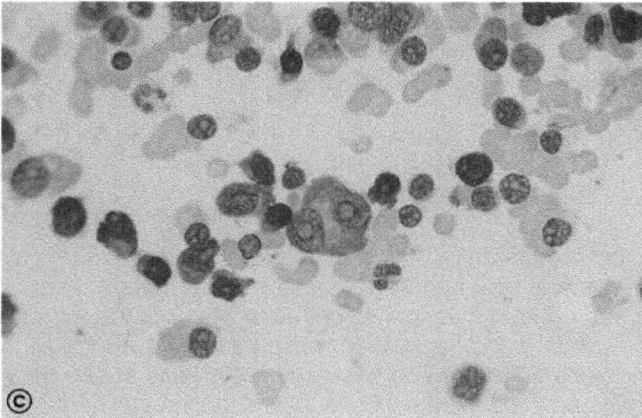

= Atlas of Hematology (Nivaldo Medeiros, MD). Used with permission=

Proplasmacyte

this cell has a diameter ranging from 15 to 25 Microns. The cytoplasm continues to be strongly basophilic (usually more blue than the 'blast' form). The volume of cytoplasm is greater than the plasma blast and is non-granular. Edges of the cytoplasm may appear ragged. The perinuclear halo is obvious. The reddish-purple nucleus continues it eccentric position and is round to oval in shape. The nuclear to cytoplasm ration is 3:1 or higher. Nucleoli may be observed. This cell is usually not observed in bone marrow. If seen, then it may be an indicator of multiple myeloma.

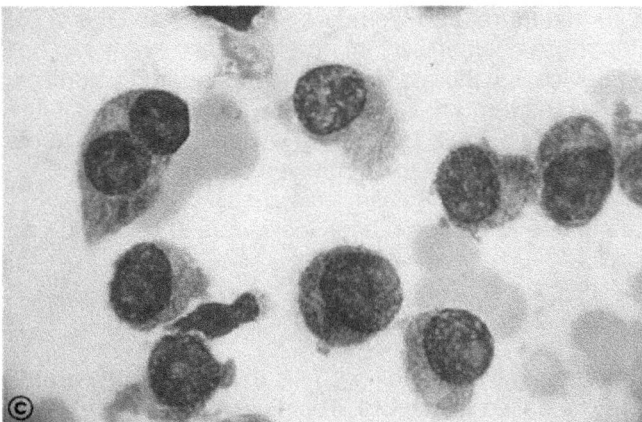

=Atlas of Hematology (Nivaldo Medeiros, MD). Used with permission=

PART FOUR: BASIC CONCEPTS OF HEMATOLOGY

Hematology may be simply defined as the study of blood but actually involves the following:

1-Analysis of the concentration, structure, and function of blood, its elements, and products

2-Quantification and differentiation of cells based upon their morphology. Stain specific elements of the cell and detect cellular antigens.

Hematology, in the decade of the 1940's, was characterized by having only a few routine determinations (examples: bleeding time, platelet count, hemoglobin, hematocrit, WBC count, RBC count, and differential), new has become sophisticated to include cytochemical markers, cell surface markers, measurement of cell volumes, identifying reactive alterations, and identification of neoplastic changes in cell populations. Coagulation enzymes studies, once mysterious, are now automated system.

CHAPTER ONE: QUANTIFICATION CONCEPT

Quantification infers the precise measurement of a substance that results in a numerical value. Hematology was at one time characterized by the manual counting and measurement of blood cells, hemoglobin, packed cell volumes (hematocrit), and blood coagulation procedures. Many of the manual derived values are now obtained by automated cell counters. Certain manual counts, once relying on Thoma and similar pipettes, now employs the Unopette systems. The hemocytometer was at one time the basis of all counting procedures is now used for spinal fluids, semen counts, and synovial fluid counts. Some testing methods remain essentially unchanged, only being adapted to an automated system. An example is the prothrombin time, once performed by adding patients plasma to a test tube followed by addition of thromboplastin was tilted back and forth until the fibrin clot was observed visually. This procedure is now performed by an automated instrument that uses an optical density detector.

Automated Cell Counting and Evaluation

Electronic Impedance

This concept is employed by coulter cell counters (coulter), some cell-Dyn instruments (Abbott). Sysmex counting instruments (Baxter), and Cobas cell counters (Roche).
Instrumentation requires that the sample be diluted to a point that there is minimal number of cells passing through an aperture at the same time.
The aperture or counting orifice is manufactured so that there are electrodes on either side. The solution in which the cells are suspended is an electrolyte solution so that an electrical current can be created between the two electrodes. The counting device is calibrated to draw a designated volume through the counting orifice or aperture. A cell that passes through the aperture will cause a momentary interruption of electrical current between the two electrodes which will cause a pulse to be generated. This weak pulse can be amplified, measured, counted, and displayed on a screen.
The size of the cell will determine the amount of interruption (also called resistance), and can be correlated to cell size. This information can be transmitted to a microprocessor and used to provide an accurate cell count and help identify the types of cells.

Light Scatter and Flow Cytometry

The blood cell is subjected fluid dynamics and made to flow in single line. This called hydrodynamic focusing. Each cell will pass through a detection device called a flow cell. This flow cell will have a laser device focused on it and as the cell passes through the laser light path, it will scatter light in several directions. The unit has one detector that captures the forward scatter light (FSL), and a second detector that is scattered (side scattered or SS) at a 90* or orthogonal angle. This principle allows for differentiating between granulocytes, lymphocytes, and monocytes.
Laser light is a monochromatic light focused on a detection device through the use of mirrors and prisms. Laser light is preferred because of it properties of intensity, stability, and monochromatism. In

those flow cytometer systems that utilize fluorescent dye labeling, the Argon laser is preferred. The Krypton laser is often selected as a second laser system when dual lasers are employed.

The leukocytes are forced to move past this laser light beam in a single file arrangement. The light that strikes each WBC can be measured as reflected or scattered light. This phenomenon is called "optical scatter". The detector used to collect the light scattered by each cell is called a photomultiplier tube. The cell with its internal and external features determines the quantity and character of the light scatter. Light that strikes the cell is scattered at angles proportional to its structural features. Each cell as it passes into the laser beam is measured according to its cells size, number of nuclear lobules, and distribution of dye in the cell if present.

Light that is scattered 180 to the light source is called forward-angle light scatter (designated as FALS or FS). FALS is used to determine cell density or volume which relates to cell size. Light that is scattered 90 to the light source is designated as side scatter or SS. This right angle light scatter is a function of the cell contents revealing information about the nuclear complexity and cellular granularity. The information from these detectors is processed by a microprocessor and will appear in designated areas on a histogram screen. This cell information posted to a screen is called bitmap. The computer is the heart of this instrumentation coordinating all decisions regarding data collection, cell sorting, and analysis.

The characteristics of each type of blood cell determines the nature of the scatter which can designated as high, moderate, or low light scatter. If the FALS and SS from a leukocyte is low, then this would be interpreted as lymphocyte. High FALS and high SS would indicate a neutrophil.

Fluorescent dyes can be used to stain certain components of the cell or may be bound to an immunological molecule that binds to a specific receptor on a cell membrane. Fluorochrome will become excited by different wavelengths of light. This permits the counting of specific tags independently. A flow cytometer with the capability detect different types of dye tags can be used to perform a differential leukocyte count. This type of cytometry can analyze single cells at rates of 50,000 cells per minute. If one it's counting reticulocytes, then they must be stained with a special stain.

Application of Flow Cytometry

Flow cytometry represents a technology that has been developed and expanded aver the past 30 years. It has greatly affected the ability of the laboratory to provide data to diagnose hematological malignancies. This technology may be applied in the following ways:
1- Count and size cells (erythrocytes and leukocytes).
2- Perform differential WBC counts.
3- Analyze up to 10,000 cells per second.
4-Count reticulocytes and platelets
5- Immunophenotyping with monoclonal antibodies.
6- Perform basic lymphocyte screening panels.
7- Perform immunocytochemistry and immunofluorescence staining.
8- Cell sorting into subpopulations.
9- Detect fetal cells and hemoglobin.
10- Detection of malarial parasites.
11- DNA content analysis.
12- Enzyme studies.
13- RNA content.

Flow cytometry employs low voltage DC electrical impedance, laser light technology, non-laser light technology, radio-frequency (high-voltage electromagnetic) current, fluorescence techniques. This technology can examine such things as blood, bone marrow, body fluids, lymph nodes, needle aspirations, solid tumors, and splenic tissues.

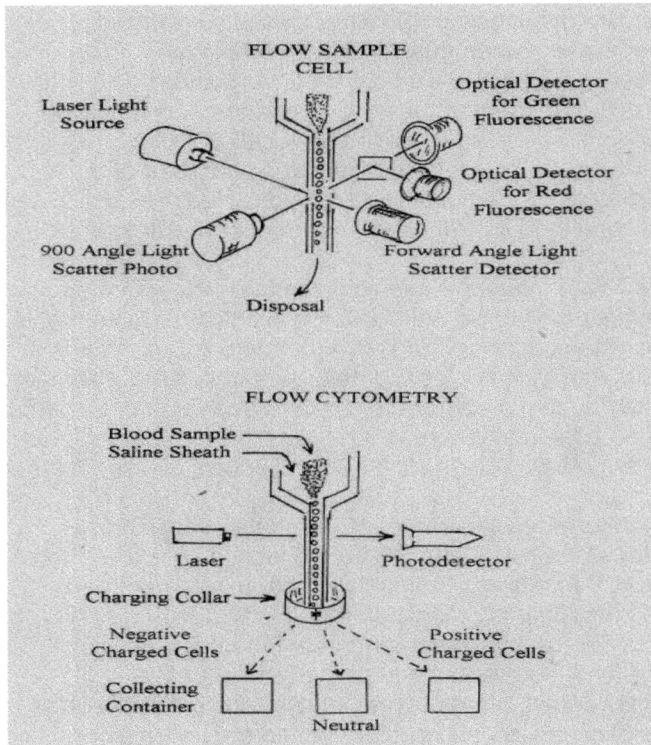

Histogram for WBCs

Volume histograms can be performed for erythrocytes, leukocytes, and/or platelets. These types of histograms will provide an approximate number of cells on the y-axis and the cell size on the x-axis. The leukocyte histogram requires an EDTA blood specimen, isotonic saline, and a lysing reagent. Coulter technology provides a histogram analysis that requires the ability to dilute and shrink the WBCS.

There are three analysis groups:

1-Lymphocytes, including reactive lymphocytes

2-Granulocytes which include metamyelocytes, bands, neutrophils, basophils, and eosinophils

3-Mononuclear cells comprised of monocytes, plasma cells, myelocytes, promyelocytes, and blasts.

If the volume of the cells ranges from 35 to 90 fl, then they are designated as lymphocytes. Volumes of 90 to 160 fl comprises the mononuclear cells whereas those cells that have a volume ranging between 160 to 450 fl would be designated as neutrophils. The instrument will provide a relative number estimate on the vertical (y-axis) and the volume on the horizontal (x-axis). If peaks appear in the histogram that does not fit the normal expected graph, the analysis system will flag those areas. This is an indicator that a visual review of the patient's blood smear is in order. Performing a manual differential would be determined by laboratory criteria.

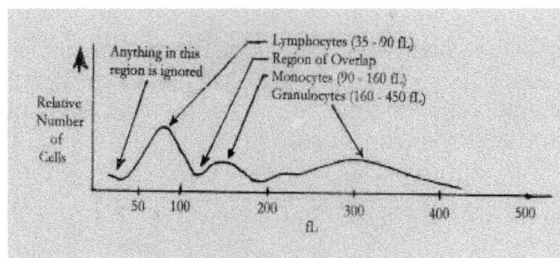

Flags (alert signals) occur when the instrument detects abnormal patterns. The following are examples of cues that the instrument detects:

* Cells that are sized and fall between the lymphocytes and mononuclear cells.
* Cells that activate this alert signal are: increased basophils, increased eosinophils, larger than normal lymphocytes, plasma cells, and certain blast cells.

* If the alert indicates a peak between the mononuclear and granulocyte region, then the cause could be increased immature granulocytes, certain blast cells, and eosinophils.
Cells with sizes falling below 35 fl (the coulter counter can detect cells from the WBC histogram as small as 30fl; it is programmed to ignore those cells between 30 and 35fl). The region on the histogram below 35fl should be clear.

* If there is a leukocytosis due to increased neutrophils, then the peak may occur in the far right region of the histogram.
* An increase in the mononuclear cell population.

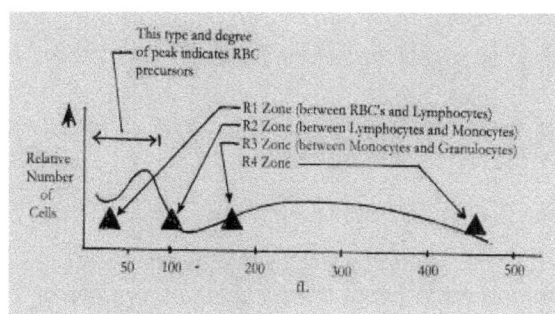

[1] If the peak occurs in R1, then one or more of the following may be indicated:
A- RBC precursors
B- Non-lysed RBC
C- Cryoglobulins
D- Giant or clumped platelets
[2] If the peak occurs in R2, then one or more of the following may be indicated:
A- Blast cells
B- Basophilia
C- Eosinophilia
D- Plasma cells
E- Abnormal and/or variant lymphocytes
[3] If the peak occurs in R3, then one or more of the following may be indicated:
A- Abnormal cells populations
B- Eosinophilia
C- Immature granulocytes
[4] If the peak occurs in R4, then there most likely an absolute granulocytosis (shift-to-right).
[5] Any abnormal peak display will require a manual differential.

Histogram for RBCs

This technology uses EDTA- anticoagulated blood and a diluting fluid. The instrument counts those cells with volume sizes between 36 fl and 360 fl as erythrocytes. A deviation in the shape and position of the RBC histogram becomes an indicator of changes that are occurring in the sight and/or shape of the erythrocytes. The Mean Corpuscular Volume (MCV) is calculated from a designated area under the peak. The Red blood cell Distribution Width (RDW) is calculated from same data used to calculate the MCV.
Information derived from the RBC histogram can be used with test values obtained for Hgb, Hct, RBC count, MCH, and MCHC can provide information to assess erythrocyte problems in the patient. If the RBCS are larger than normal, the curve will shift toward the right. If the RBCS are smaller than normal the curve will shift to the left. If the histogram curve is bimodal, then there is two populations of red blood cells as might be seen when a patient received a blood transfusion. Other conditions that will

cause a bimodal distribution curve are cold agglutinin disease, hemolytic anemia with schistocytes present, or anemia with different size cell populations.

The RBC histogram can measure cells as small as 24 fl. Those cells that are counted in the 24 to 36 fl range are rejected as RBCS and not included in the RBC count. Leukocytes are present in the diluted fluid containing RBCS, but their numbers are statistically insignificant in the count. The instrument computer can be calibrated to compensate for the presence of leukocytes. If the leukocytes count is significantly elevated, the erythrocyte histogram will be affected.

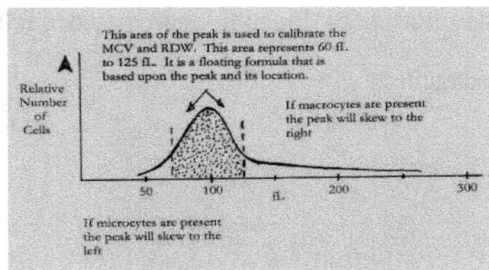

Histogram of Platelets

Platelet derived histograms (via the electrical impedance method) are obtained from volume sizes of 2 to 20 fl. The instrument is designated to count the particles in a range of 0 to 70 fl. The actual count is derived from the "best-fit" log-normal curve which generally falls in the 2 to 20 fl range. The actual counting takes place in the RBC aperture.

With the application of computer technology, two other parameters can be obtained from the platelet histogram:

[1] Mean Platelet Volume (MPV). This is a mathematical calculation to determine the average size of the platelets. The average MPV range= 7 to 10 fl. If the MPV is > 10 fl, then this indicates that immature platelets are being released, which may be due to a normal clotting activity in the body or some pathology may be developing or ongoing. The MPV is also knows as the platelet index (PI) and is analogous to the MCV. The MPV is decreased in aplastic anemia, megaloblastic anemia, chemotherapy, heterozygous thalassemia, and Wiskott-Aldrich syndrome. The MPV is increased in sickle cell anemia, following splenomegaly, and idiopathic thrombopenic purpura.

[2] Platelet Distribution Width (PDW). This is analogous to the Red cell Distribution Width. It compares the uniformity of platelet size. Normal values are less than 20%. Increased values are observed in aplastic anemia, megaloblastic anemia, chronic myelogenous leukemia and chemotherapy. Actual causes for increased PDW values are known but may be due to dysfunctional megacaryocytes development. If erythrocyte fragments are being counted as platelets, the PDW will falsely elevated because it broadens the platelet volume distribution curve.

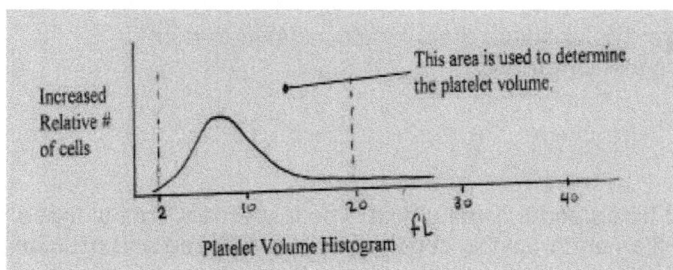

Platelet Volume Histogram

Automated Hematology Analyzer XT-2000i (Megaflex Maroc)

The XT-2000i illuminates the specimen by a semiconductor laser beam and separates the cells using three signals from each cell, i.e., forward scatter, side scatter and side fluorescence. The forward scattered light intensity indicates the cell volume, while side scattered light indicates the cell contents such as nucleus and granules. The side fluorescence indicates the amount of DNA and RNA.

Differentiation Principle

The application of optical methods for leukocyte differential counts began over 100 years ago when Paul Ehrlich demonstrated that it was possible to stain nuclear and cytoplasm cell structures.

Fluorescence flow cytometry as used in the XT-2000i (the combination of a semiconductor laser with suitable polymethine dyes) enables a WBC differential, a Reticulocytes and Thrombocytes measurement, as well as Erythroblasts analysis.

The analytical core is rounded off by the RBC/PLT channel for erythrocyte and thrombocyte determination, based on DC impedance measurement with hydrodynamic focusing, as well as the WBC/BASO channel for total leukocyte count and basophil measurement. The latter relies on an optical measuring principle: The detection and analysis of side and forward scattered light.

WBC and the Diff channel

In this channel, 4-part differential is prepared (neutrophils, lymphocytes, monocytes, eosinophils) by detecting – after specific staining of white blood cells- their side scatter light and their side fluorescence light. The polymethine dye contained in STROMATOLOLYZER-4DS penetrates the leukocytes and stains cell nuclei as well as cytoplasmic organelles. The higher the intracellular RNA content (abnormal cells in comparison with normal cells). The higher the side fluorescence signal. This will result not only in immature granulocytes, but also atypical lymphocytes being shown in areas of significantly higher fluorescence intensity, as compared with neutrophils or, respectively, lymphocytes and monocytes. Thus, beyond the 4-part diff analysis, fluorescence flow cytometry is able to specifically detect and quantify immature granulocytes, as well as activated cells (atypical lymphocytes).

WBC and Baso channel

In this channel the XT-2000i uses forward and side scatter signals. An acidic reagent causes lyse and shrink red blood cells (ghosts), platelets (ghosts) and white blood cells (bare nuclei) with the exception of basophils. Thus, the white blood cell and the basophil counts are derived from this channel.

The surfactant in STROMATOLYZER-FB produces red blood cell and platelet ghosts and bare nuclei of WBC except for basophils, the resulting volumetric differences between basophils and other cells are analyzed using the forward scatter and side scatter information.

Forward light scatter intensity indicates cell volume, and side scatter reflect the complexity of cellular residues, Shrunk cells and basophils are clearly separated by FSC and SSC. Residual nuclei are also separated from ghosts. The sum of basophiles and bare nuclei is the total WBC count.

Ret channel

Reticulocyte analytics is used in the diagnostics and monitoring of anemias. The essential advantage of flow cytometry reticulocyte analysis (versus microscopic counting) is the method's much higher sensitivity and its exemplary precision.

The channel supplies, aside from the count, the differentiation of reticulocytes in different maturity stages and a counting value for thrombocytes (PLT-fl) which is based on fluorescence measurement and being superior under certain conditions to the counting value from the RBC channel which is based on impedance measurement. The polymethine dye contained in RET-SEARCH stains the RNA and DNA in the cells such that reticulocytes are separated from erythrocytes via their difference in RNA content, and the separation from leukocytes will be via the difference in RNA and DNA content. Leukocytes contain more DNA than reticulocytes contain RNA. WBCS are mush more fluorescent.

The reticulocyte differentiation in three different fractions of differently high fluorescence activity and the index of the immature reticulocyte fraction (IRF) will enable statements on the Erythropoietic activity of the bone marrow.

The XT-2000i counts PLT by way of PLT-O method and PLT-I method. Former method is based on the electrical resistance and the latter one utilizes forward scattegram and side scattegram. When the histogram of PLT does not show the abnormality, PLT count is derived by PLT-I. On the country, PLT count is based on the PLT-O when the histogram shows some unusual. If the result of PLT is introduced by PLT-O method, the mark"&" is attached to right side of PLT count.

PLT-I method is superior to PLT-O in the view of reproducibility because of the counting number.

Collection of Blood Specimens

Hematological laboratory procedures are based upon the examination of blood specimens. To obtain valid results, specimens must be properly collected, processed, and recorded. Blood specimens are usually obtained by either venous or capillary puncture. The source of the specimen is determined chiefly by the quantity of blood required to perform the laboratory procedures and the age and condition of the patient.

There is generally little difference in blood counts performed on venous or capillary blood if a free-flowing capillary blood specimen is obtained. Valid blood counts cannot be made when capillary specimens are not taken from a free-flowing sample or when they are obtained from cyanotic or calloused areas or areas of local stasis. White blood cells counts made on blood obtained from such sources can vary as much as 1000-1500 cells per cu mm from their real value. For general purposes, however, venous samples are preferable since they allow for multiple and repeated hematological examinations and provide a sufficient quantity of blood for performing any other required laboratory procedure. Further, with venous blood the chances of error are reduced because operations are made under ideal conditions and repeat operations are possible. In situations where there are limitations on the quantity of blood that can be obtained, that is, in small infants or extensive burn cases, micro quantitative methods are satisfactory for performing an analysis on a specimen obtained by capillary.

Phlebotomy Collections

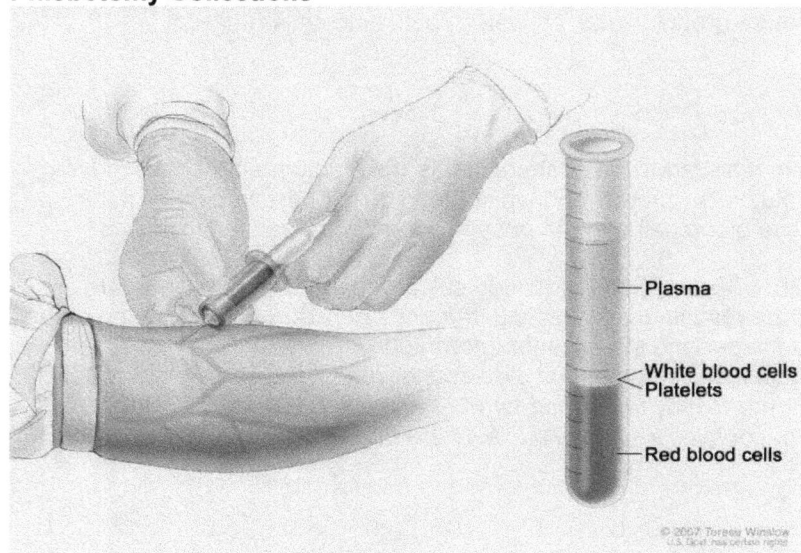

- Plasma
- White blood cells
- Platelets
- Red blood cells

Courtesy of the National Cancer Institute

Identify the patient.
Verify any patient diet restrictions.
Assemble supplies for the venipuncture and put on gloves.
Reassure the patient.
Position the patient if necessary.
Verify the paperwork and blood collecting tubes.
Select the venipuncture site.
Clean the venipuncture site.
Place the tourniquet 3- 4 inches above the venipuncture site.

Perform the venipuncture.

Mix those tubes with additives by gentle inversion as each tube is collected.

Release the tourniquet and remove it.

Place gauze or cotton ball over the puncture site, and then remove the needle as you firmly position the gauze over the wound. Allow the patient to hold if firmly in place with the other hand.

Remove last tube from vacutainer needle.

Replace needle sheath and discard in biohazard container.

Label the requisition with the time collected.

Event of an Adverse Reaction

The two most common adverse reactions are syncope and hematoma. In the event of beginning syncope (the patient indicates that they feel faint), stop the phlebotomy procedure immediately, and quickly removing the needle and releasing the tourniquet. If the patient in sitting lowers the patient's head, have the patient take deep breaths. And apply cool wet cloths/compresses to the back of the neck. A drink of cold water is often helpful. If the patient faints and collapses, lower the patient to the floor to a supine position. Apply cold compresses. The patient will recover, feeling foolish and somewhat embarrassed. Reassure the patient that this is not an uncommon happening and that all is well.

The second adverse reaction is the sudden development of hematoma. This is the result of a substantial amount of blood leaking into the surrounding tissues from around the needle (which may be due to the bevel of the needle protruding partially from the vein).If swelling is observed around the area of the needle, stop the phlebotomy procedure and remove the needle and tourniquet. Apply a cotton ball or gauze pads as the needle is withdrawn and apply a firm pressure to the site fro a minimum of two minutes.

Caution: If a firm pressure is not applied to the venipuncture site or held for an appropriate amount of time after the collection of blood, a hematoma may develop.

Discussion

Cleanliness is essential when performing a venipuncture.

It is most important that correct technique be practiced in order to ovoid unnecessary pain to the patient, prevent tissues damage, secure a good representative blood specimen, and prevent contamination of the specimen or infection of the patient.

Syringes and needles must be thoroughly inspected for damage or malfunction.

If difficulty is experienced in entering the vein or a hematoma begins to from, release the tourniquet and promptly withdraw the needle and apply pressure to the wound.

Vigorous pulling on the plunger of the syringe can collapse the vein, produce hemolysis of the blood specimen, or cause air to enter the syringe.

When repeated venipuncture have to be performed on one patient, it is advisable to select different sites for blood withdrawal.

Remove the tourniquet as early as possible once a good flow of blood has been established.

Prolonged application of the tourniquet results in partial stasis of blood and changes many quantitative values of blood components.

Blood draw by venipuncture often stored for a period of time before it is analyzed. For this reason, certain general precautions must be followed in order to ensure a valid analysis. Before withdrawing blood from its container, make sure the blood sample is thoroughly but gently mixed. Blood containers should be tightly stoppered at all times to prevent drying or contamination. Store the blood specimen in the refrigerator. Blood counts should be done within 3 hours after collection. Under no circumstances should blood taken for hematological examination be stored overnight.

Anticoagulants

Anticoagulants are used to prevent the clotting of the blood specimens and the reagent employs should not bring about alteration of blood components.

Unfortunately, many anticoagulants can alter cell structures as well as coagulation.

The choice of anticoagulant will depend on the analysis to be made.

* Ethylene-diamine-tetra-acetate (EDTA) is the anticoagulant of choice for the most hematological analysis. This anticoagulant causes a minimum of distortion to the cells and platelets. Calcium is chelated, blocking the coagulation cascade phenomenon.

  * Heparin does not alter the size of cellular component. It is, in fact, the standard for comparison of anticoagulant distortion. Inhibits coagulation by interfering with thrombin

  * Sodium citrate is the anticoagulant of choice for coagulation studies. It prevents coagulation by binding the calcium of the blood in a soluble complex. If there is platelet satellite phenomenon, collect a blood specimen in this anticoagulant for retesting.

  * No anticoagulant. This tube has a red and gray marbled stopper. This tube contains an internal silicone coating to facilitate uniform clotting.

CHAPTER TWO: DIFFERENTIATION CONCEPTS

Differentiation in hematology generally employs manual discrimination and evaluation of blood cells under a microscope. There are three classes of cells that are distinguished: leukocytes, thrombocytes, and erythrocytes. This required preparation of blood smear that is stained with Wright's stain or some other special stain.

When observing leukocytes
(1) - Note the size, shape, and color,
(2) - Rank the cells according to their predominance,
(3) -What malignant or non-malignant changes are present.
   When observing erythrocytes
(1)- Note the size, shape, and color,
(2)- How much deviation occurs for typical, biconcave shape, and
(3)-If immature forms are present
   Thrombocytes are to be observed with the same care. The smear is to be examined for the presence of parasites (example: malaria, trypanosomiasis, or babesiosis).

Preparation and Staining of Blood Smears

The type of blood cells found in the peripheral blood smears may be of diagnostic and prognostic importance. For this reason proper preparation and staining of blood films is essential for the identification and study of different kinds of leukocytes. The appearance of erythrocytes and thrombocytes will often give important clues that help distinguish between different types of diseases or other physical changes.

There are two basic methods for the preparation of blood smears: the cover slip and the slide methods. The cover slip method has certain advantages over the slide method; distribution of cells is like that of the in vivo circulation. The principal disadvantage of the latter method is that coves lips are very fragile and easily broken during processing.

The slides and cover glasses must be chemically clean and dry. New slides must first be washed with soapy water and rinses thoroughly with distilled water. The slides are then placed in beaker of 95 percent ethyl alcohol. As the slides are needed, dry them with a soft, lint free cloth. The slides may be reused by properly cleaning them and making sure they are not chipped or scratched.

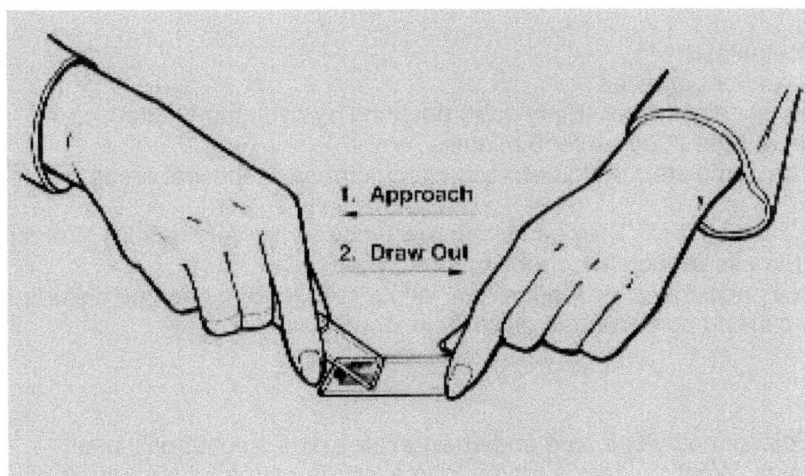

1. Approach
2. Draw Out

[1] A drop of blood is paced on one end of 3" by 1" glass slide and using a spreader slide at an angle of approximately 25 to 45 degree, a wedge type smear is made and allowed to dry.

[2] Smears may be made using two covers glasses. A drop of blood is placed in the center of one of the cover glasses. The other cover glass is placed over the drop of blood so that the corners of each

cover glass form an eight-pointed star. The two cover glasses are pulled apart and allowed to dry face up.

The slides, if not to be immediately stained, must be fixed within two hours to prevent distortion and deterioration. Methanol is the preferred fixative, once stained, if a slide is to be retained, should be "cover-slipped" to prevent stain deterioration. Color will begin to fade in about 2 years on an "uncovered" slide.

Appearance of a Good Quality Wedge-Shaped Smear

Look for a thick band at the application point. The cells will be stacked, overlapping, and closely spaced. The WBCs tend to be of small size in this area. In the thin and feathery portion, an increase in artifacts will be observed due to the wide separation of cells. Wide spaces are characteristic between the cells. The cells tend to be thinner, with a larger sized appearance. Do not evaluate RBC morphology in the thick and thin areas. The intermediate region of the slide is characterized by cells that do not touch or almost do so. The monocytes and granulocytes tend to be settled out in the "sliding" process near the lateral edges of the slide. They can also b noted in large numbers in the feathery area of the slide. Lymphocytes tend to randomly distribute on the slide. Other factors to look for are [1] absence of waves, holes, and ridges and [2] a smooth and event appearance.

The wedge-type blood smear is the most widely procedure for blood films. Concerns are:
[1] A tendency for poor distributed of nucleated cells, monocytes and neutrophils tend to accrue in the feathered end of the wedge smear, leaving the central examination area deficient.
[2] Lymphocytes differential counts may be artificially increased because of the tendency of monocytes and neutrophils to appear in the feathered edge.
[3] Trauma to cells is greater in the wedge preparation increasing the number of basket or smudge cells.
[4] Too large of a drop of blood will produce a thicker smear. This causes nucleated cells to shrink and stain very intensely. Red blood cells tend to from Rouleaux's so that they cannot be evaluated.
[5] A large angle on the spreader slide causes a thick smear.
[6] Spreading the film too fats promotes a thick a smear.
[7] Too small of a drop of blood usually results in a blood film that is too small and/or thin. This results in more spheroid shaped RBCs, distorted RBC shapes, increases numbers of smudges cells, and more nucleated cells accumulate on the periphery of the smear.
[8] Spreading the film too slow promotes a thin smear.

Buffy Coat Smear

The Buffy coat preparation may be required in the following are suspected:
[1] A blood specimen that is pancytopenic and abnormal, immature or reactive cell densities are low.
[2] Examining a patient diagnosed with megaloblastic anemia for nucleated red blood cells and/ or hypersegmented neutrophils.
[3] Looking for plasma cells.
[4] Tumor cells in blood indicating metastasis.
[5] Facilitate the search for bacteria and/or parasites

Smears can be prepared from the white cell layer (Buffy coat) obtained by centrifuging the blood slowly in a Wintrobe hematocrit tube at 500- 800 rpm for 5 minutes.

It is important that the blood film be completely dried before staining; otherwise the wet areas will wash off the slide.

Protect blood slides from insects such as flies. They can clean raw blood slides very rapidly. Protect slides from areas of high humidity. Excessive moisture rends to hemolyze RBCs.

Slides should be stained as soon as possible after preparation. White cells tend to become distorted and disintegrated very rapidly, thus causing considerable difficulty in identification.

Staining of Blood Smears

Wright's stain is composed of oxidized methylene blue and eosin azures. It is a commonly used modification of the Romanowsky stains. Wright's stain is made up in absolute methanol (serves as a fixative) to be a solution of acid dye (eosin) and a basic dye (methylene blue). The quantity of dye used in making up Wright's stain is designed to produce a neutral compound. The basic dyes in this stain have an affinity for the acidic components in the cells (nucleus and some cytoplasmic structures) imparting a violet-blue color. The "azures" will impart red-purple coloration, augmenting the polychrome nature of the stain. The acidic dyes have an affinity for the basic components, hemoglobin and eosinophilic granules, imparting a orange-red color. Neutrophil granules contain a slightly predominate amount of acidic substances which will stain weakly with the azure component of the dye. The polychrome nature of Wright's stain procedures a complex staining pattern that will facilitate visual identification of most cells in circulation.

The HEMA-TEK 2000 Slide Stainer is a fully automated, bench-top instrument designated specifically for use in hematology. If is a self-contained, precision instrument that accepts, conveys, fixes, stains, and delivers dry blood smear preparations that are spread on standard 1"x 3" glass slides. The slides are stained at a rate of one slide per minute.

The macroscopic appearance of stained blood film will have a pinkish to pinkish-blue tone. The microscopic view will show the following:

RBCs have a pink to orange color.

Lymphocytes have a dark purple or blue nucleus and cytoplasm is sky blue to medium blue.

The nucleus of neutrophils stains dark purple or blue and the granules in the cytoplasm are lilac or pink to violet.

The nucleus of the monocytes is light purple to grey-blue and the cytoplasm is grey-blue with fine red granules.

The nucleus of the eosinophils stains like that of the neutrophils, but the large cytoplasmic granules stain orange-red.

The nucleus of basophils stains like that of the neutrophils, but the large cytoplasmic granules stain dark blue-black.

Platelets take on a light blue to purple stain with violet to purple granules.

The Microscope

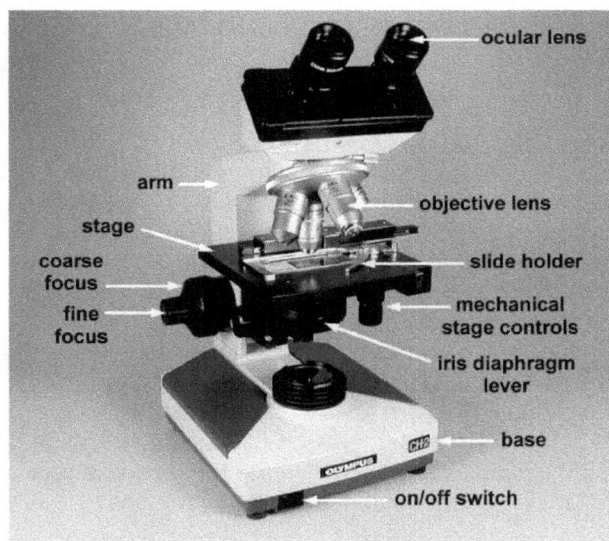

Olympus CH-2 Microscope

Summary observation procedures

1. Before you plug in the microscope, turn the voltage control dial on the right-hand side of the base of the microscope to 1. Now plug in the microscope and turn it on.

2. Place the slide in the slide holder, center the slide using the two mechanical stage control knobs under the stage on the right-hand side of the microscope, and place a rounded drop of immersion oil on the area to be observed.

3. Rotate the white-striped 100X oil immersion objective until it is locked into place. This will give a total magnification of 1000X.

4. Turn the voltage control dial on the right-hand side of the base of the microscope to 9 or 10. Make sure the iris diaphragm lever in front under the stage is almost wide open, (toward the left side of the stage, and the knob under the stage on the left-hand side of the stage controlling the height of the condenser is turned so the condenser is all the way up.

5. Watching the slide and objective lens carefully from the front of the microscope, lower the oil immersion objective into the oil by raising the stage until the lens just touches the slide. Do this by turning the coarse focus away from you until the spring-loaded objective lens just begins to spring upward.

6. While looking through the eyepieces, turn the fine focus towards you at a slow steady speed until the specimen comes into focus. (If the specimen does not come into focus within a few complete turns of the fine focus control and the lens is starting to come out of the oil, you missed the specimen when it went through focus. Simply reverse direction and start turning the fine focus away from you.)

7. using the iris diaphragm lever, adjust the light to obtain optimum contrast.

8. When finished, wipe the oil off of the oil immersion objective with lens paper, turn the voltage control dial back to 1, turn off the microscope, unplug the power cord, and wrap the cord around the base of the microscope.

9. Alternate focusing technique is to first focus on the slide with the yellow-striped 10X objective by using only the coarse focus control and then without moving the stage, adds immersion oil, rotates the white-striped 100X oil immersion objective into place, and adjusts the fine focus and the light as needed.

When observing very large specimens remove the slide holder and place the specimen directly on the stage. It is recommended to use the optional specimen clip for oil immersion objectives.

Examination of Blood Smear

Blood smear examination is an integral part of a hemogram. Blood smear analysis allows quantitation of the different types of leukocytes (called the differential count).Estimation of the platelet count, and detection of morphologic abnormalities that may be indicators of pathophysiologic process. In some instances, a diagnosis may be evident. Deriving full value from blood smear examination requires a well-prepared, well-stained blood smear and some basic skills in the methods of assessment. Though some automated hematology analyzers provide a differential count as part of their output, this does not fully take the place of microscope exam by an experienced observer.

The examination starts with a microscope view to evaluate the quality of the smear based on overall appearance. The microscope analysis begins on lower power (10x), primarily to assess cellular distribution, staining quality, and to select an area where the RBCs are barely touching each other. This area is used to conduct a complete assessment of the cellular elements on higher magnification. On hi-dry (40x), the slide is principally scanned to obtain a WBC estimate. All of the detailed analysis of the cellular elements is performed using oil immersion. This final microscope examination is performed at 50x or 100x oil immersion and includes:

1-Assessment of RBC morphology
2-AWBC differential
3-The identification of abnormal or peculiar leukocytes
4-The number and morphology of the platelets
5-The identification of intra-and extra-cellular elements
6-Assessment of any organisms present

Estimation of the number of Platelets and Leukocytes

Platelet evaluations are a routine part of the WBC differential. The normal procedure is to count 15-20 RBCs and note the number of platelets present. Normal is one platelet per 15-20 RBCs. If there is < 1 platelet/ 15-20 RBCs, the platelets are decreased and the count is expected to be decreased. If there are > 1 platelet/ 15-20 RBCs, the platelets are increased and the count is expected to be increased. One recommended procedure is to count the number of platelets in ten "oil-immersion field" and calculate an average number of platelets per "oif". The count is to be conducted in the monolayer of the blood smear where the RBCs are not over-lapping. Next multiply the average number of platelets times 20,000 and this will give estimated platelets/ mm3. When you are estimated the number of platelet on a stained blood film, report as average number of platelets per oil immersion field (oif).

If approximately 3 to 4 WBCs are observed per "oif", then the WBC count is expected to be in the normal range. If less than this. The count is low. If greater than five WBCs, the count is expected to be elevated.

Correction of WBC Count

This correction is initiated when nucleated red blood cells (NRBC) are encountered on a differential. The number of NRBCs must be enumerated per 100 leukocytes. A corrected count may be reported by using the following formula:

$$\text{Corrected WBC count} = \frac{\text{\# of uncorrected WBCs (X) 100}}{100 + \text{Number of NRBCs/ 100WBCs}}$$

Sample problem: [1] 25 NRBCs counted on differential/ 100WBCs, [2] uncorrected WBCs count = 13,500/mm3, [3] corrected WBC count = 10,800/mm3.

4-3-Blood Smear Preparation for Parasites

Malaria is the most commonly studied parasite in blood. There are four species of malarial parasites. Other blood parasites that may be encountered are Babesia organisms, Trypanosoma species, and Leishmania species.
To prepare the blood, use finger tip or fresh EDTA. Prepare 2- 3 thin smears using the wedge technique. Allow to air dry. To prepare the thick smears, place 2- 3 drops of blood in the center of the slide. Use the corner of a second slide, spread the drop of blood to the size of a dime and allow to air dry. Proceed as follows:
Fix the thin smears in methanol, but DO NOT fix the thick smears.
Place the thin and thick blood smears in 1/10 dilution of Giemsa stain, using buffered distilled water at pH = 6.8. Allow to stain for 30 minutes.
Remove the slides from the Giemsa stain and gently rinse under running tap water and allow to air dry. View microscopically. On the thick smear, WBC nuclei and platelet debris will be seen.

The Blood Smear Strategies

The following should be adhered to minimize the appearance of artifacts:
[1] Do not stain a peripheral blood smear until it is properly fixed Use methanol fixative adjusted to a pH = 8.4.
[2] Watch the staining time. Do not allow Wright's stain to remain on slide or methanol will evaporate and cause precipitation of dye molecules.
[3] If water is present in methanol, ring-shaped, refractive artifacts will appear on erythrocytes. Do not confuse with RBC inclusions.
[4] Do not evaluate RBC hemoglobin content at end of slide.
[5] Do not evaluate smear along edges, the cells tend to be distorted or elongated. This is an artifact of spreading.
[6] When examining the thin edges of the film and crenated RBCs (or echinocytes) are noted, if the spicules are uniform, do not report, this is an artifact.
[7] If you wipe the oil from a stained smear, it is possible from the tissue to damage RBCs, causing them to appear as schistocytes.
[8] If you see a RBC with a distinct colored outer circle with a well defined clear center, without gradation, it is an artifact, not hypochomia. Hypochromia is characterized by gradation from the outer edge to the central area of pallor.

Others things that can cause RBC artifacts are:

1-Delays in making smears

2- Too hot or too cold temperatures in lab.

3- The smear dries too slowly.

4- Polycythemia (increased blood viscosity).

5- The presence of abnormal proteins.

6- Ph to acidic or alkaline, causing changes in the erythrocyte's internal environment.

7- Pressing too hard on the spreader slide as the smear forms.

The Blood Smear Evaluation

[1] Perform the differential count in the monolayer in the middle portion of the slide.

[2] avoid the thick regions because the cells tend to "bunch up" and obscure abnormalities. If the entire slide appears to have cells stacked on top of each other, the slide is too thick.

    A. When the smear was made, the angle of the spreader slide was too large.

    B. To correct, make a new slide with a smaller angle of the spreader slide.

[3] If the end of the smear does not have a feather edge, the angle of the spreader slide was too large or its edge had cracks and/or chips. Use a spreader slide with a smooth, sharp edge.

[4] If cells are to faint to be seen, the staining time was too short. Make a new smear and repeat by staining a longer time.

[5] If the problem in #4 is not attributed to inadequate staining, look at the rinse duffer. Its pH may be to acidic, Remove the problem by using an appropriate with a pH of 6.8.

[6] If there are holes in the smear, the slide contained some form of contamination on its surface. Use only high quality slides to eliminate this problem.

[7] If unidentifiable things are seen on the slide, it may be the result of using a dirty slide.

[8] If the cells are so dark the nuclei cannot be distinguished, the slide was over stained. Slides like these may have visible precipitate stain. Make a new smear and stain a shorter time.

[9] If the problem in #7 is not over staining, then the pH on the buffer rinse may be too alkaline. Resolve the problem by using an appropriate buffer with a pH of 6.8.

[10] Rate the staining qualities.

    A. The thicker areas stain darker and have more artifacts.

    B. Is the stain quality good or poor? The slide may need to be restained.

[11] The normal size of the RBC is 6.0 to 9.0uM, with the 0 = 7.8 uM.

[12] When evaluating the erythrocytes for abnormalities (such as cell size and shape, it is recommended that the degree (if any) of anisocytosis, poikilocytosis, and Hypochromia be noted.

    A. If the RBCs are distorted and proper classification is compromised, then the anticoagulant being used may be a problem or the slide was not allowed to dry properly.

    B. Change to a different anticoagulant and/or allow the slide to thoroughly air dry.

    C. Making blood smears from a finger stick may be the best solution to cell distortion.

[13] If one or more of the three abnormalities are present, look for RBC inclusions examples: Howell-jolly bodies, Pappenheimer bodies, and Heinz bodies.

[14] When observing leukocytes, note the size of the cell.

    A. Small is no smaller than an erythrocyte. Lymphocytes are the only WBCs that are expected to fall in this size category. This size ranges from 8.0 to 10.0 uM. (Hint: The nucleus of a small lymphocyte is about the same size as that of a RBC).

    B. Medium size describes most neutrophils. This size ranges from 9.0 to 15.0 uM.

    C. Large is characteristic of monocytes. This size ranges from 14.0 to 20.0 uM.

[15] Notice the shape of the nucleus.

    A. Neutrophils have a segmented nucleus.

    B. Bands tend to have a "U" or "C" shaped nucleus, but can be "S" shaped.

    C. The nucleus of the lymphocyte tends to be round.

    D. The monocyte is characterized by a convoluted, sprawling nucleus.

    E. A notched nucleus may be observed in the lymphocyte and metamyelocyte.

[16] Evaluate the texture of the nucleus.

    A. If the nucleus is dense and dark, it is pycnotic (neutrophil).

    B. A close knit nucleus is seen in the lymphocyte.

    C. A ropy, spongy-like nucleus is typical for the monocyte.

    D. Fine featured, with little or not texture, may indicate and immature leukocyte.

[17] Consider the chromatin pattern.

    A. Is it smooth or coarse?

B. Is the parachromatin (light staining areas) visible?

[18] Are nucleoli present or absent?

[19] Look at the cytoplasm of leukocyte.

A. large, distinctively colored granules feature the eosinophil and basophil.

B. the neutrophil has fine granules evenly distributed in the cytoplasm.

C. The lymphocyte has a homogenous, light blue colored cytoplasm.

D. A grayish coloration characterizes the monocyte.

E. Compare the staining characteristics around the inside periphery of the cytoplasmic membrane with that on the outside of nuclear membrane. Very immature cells tend to exhibit basophilia at the periphery. Lymphocytes are characterized by light staining about the nucleus (perinuclear halo).

F. Compare the ratio of the cytoplasm to the nucleus.

[20] Abnormalities to watch for in the leukocytes are:

A. Unusual granulation (example: toxic granulation in neutrophils due to a severe infection).

B. Cytoplasmic vacuolation which may be observed in all WBCs.

a. Vacuolated neutrophils observed in severe infections.

b. Infectious mononucleosis causes vacuolation in lymphocytes.

c. Normal monocytes may exhibit some vacuolation.

d. Toxic chemicals/drugs can cause vacuolation in any WBC.

C. Disintegrating cells occur when the cytoplasmic membrane ruptures and the cytoplasm and nuclear contents are somewhat intact (the cell can still be identified). This occurs among all cells and is usually negligible. If there are large numbers present on the slide, which may indicate pathology. Remember that such cells may be the result of making a slide from old blood or improperly making a blood smear. Follow lab protocol in reporting disintegrating cells.

D. Inclusion bodies in the cytoplasm of leukocytes may be an indicator of a pathological condition.

[21] If the differential count is too high for certain leukocytes, one may count the same fields more than once. Repeat count and watch the scanning technique to avoid repeating fields.

PART FIVE: HEMOGRAM

The Complete Blood Count (CBC) test is an automated count of the cells in the blood. A standard CBC includes the following:

1-Number of white blood cells (WBC).
2-Number of red blood cells (RBC).
3-Hemoglobin content (Hgb)
4- Hematocrit (Hct).
5- Mean corpuscular volume (MCV).
6-Mean corpuscular hemoglobin (MCH)
7-Mean corpuscular hemoglobin concentration (MCHC)
8-Platelet count and volume

The results of a CBC can provide information about not only the number of cell types but also can give an indication of the size, shape, and some of the physical characteristics of the cells. In addition, a WBC differential may be ordered and can be done on the same instrument or performed manually. Significant abnormalities in one or more of the cell populations may require visual confirmation by observing a blood smear under a microscope.

CHAPTER ONE: THE RED BLOOD CELL

The erythrocyte is a biconcave disc (to maximize surface area for exchange), with flexibility (to fit through capillaries), and negative surface charges (to repel other cells). With no nucleus, it cannot synthesize proteins, and no mitochondria. Three areas of RBC metabolism are crucial for RBC survival and function. Normal RBC survival time in peripheral blood is 120 days.
RBC membrane
Hemoglobin structure and function
RBC metabolic pathways

Structure and Function

RBC Membrane

The round, biconcave nature of the erythrocyte membrane gives it maximum surface area that is advantageous for gaseous exchange and increased deformability. It composition is approximately 50% protein, 40% lipids, and 10% carbohydrates. Morphologically it is composed of two layers of phospholipids, arranged so that the polar surface the inside and outside of the cell. The non-polar groups are directed to the center of the membrane layer.

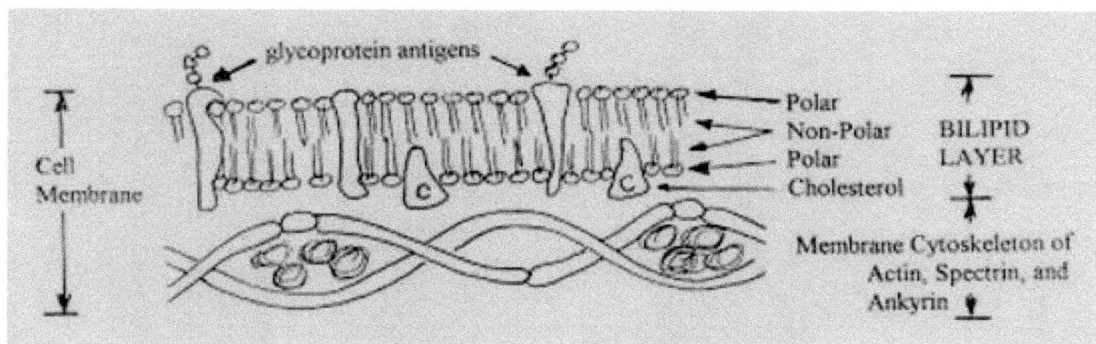

http://www.clt.astate.edu/wwilliam/hem_i_erythrocytes_morphology_and__physiology.htm

The proteins in the RBC membrane account for its shape, structure, and ability to change shape. These proteins are also the channels and pumps to move ions and other molecules in, out, and across the membrane. Some of the proteins function as receptors, many of the proteins function as the RBC antigens (ABO, and Rh), other proteins have enzymatic capability, and all in some degree or another help to stabilize the membrane, If the molecular composition of the RBC membrane changes, the membrane is affected including changes in its shape or ability to transport ions and molecules. If the cholesterol content of the membrane increases, the membrane takes on the appearance of a Target cell (has a centrally stained area and resembles a target). Acanthocytes (has irregular, spiny projections). Decreased spectrin causes decreased membrane; the cell may become Spherocytes (small spherical-appearing cells with no central pallor). If proteins are lost, for whatever reason, the integrity of the membrane is compromised and hemolysis will result. It has been found that some of the RBC membrane antigens are essential for membrane integrity.

RBC Metabolic Pathways

Erythrocytes must be able to metabolize in order to remain viable. The cell has the ability to metabolize glucose through the glycolysis cycle (Embden-Meyerhof anaerobic pathway) for ATP production. ATP is needed to run the membrane pumps (example: Na+ and K+ exchange) which helps to control membrane integrity and cell osmolarity. Energy is required to maintain cell function, membrane shape, and to protect the lipid composition of the cell.

The glycolysis of glucose to ATP provides energy through the Leubering-Rapoport shunt, allows the RBC to regulate oxygen transport during conditions of hypoxia or acid-base imbalance, and permits the accumulation of 2,3-DPG which is essential for maintaining normal oxygen tension.

Hexose monophosphate shunt, metabolizes 5- 10% of glucose, protects the RBC from oxidative injury, most common defect is deficiency of the enzyme glucose-6-phosphate dehydrogenase (G-6PD). If the pathway is deficient, intracellular oxidants can't be neutralized and globin denatures the precipitates. The precipitates are referred to as Heinz bodies.

Methemoglobin reductase pathway maintains iron in the ferrous (Fe^{++}) state, in the absence of the enzyme, Methemoglobin accumulates and it cannot carry oxygen.

Normal Adult Hemoglobin

Hemoglobin (Hgb) is a red colored, conjugated, large molecular weight protein that makes up about 28% of the RBC mass. Most of the RBC mass is water. Each adult hemoglobin molecule (designated as Hgb A) consists of a quaternary protein molecule that consists of four globin (polypeptide) sub-units. The four globin chains constitute a tetramer. Two of the sub-units are designated as alpha chains and other two sub-units are the beta chains. Each sub-unit contains one heme structure which binds the oxygen molecule to form oxyhemoglobin.

The hemoglobin chain is manufactured in the cytoplasm of the cell by the ribosomes. Hemoglobin synthesis begins in the basophilic normoblast. By the time the developing erythrocyte has matured to Metarubricyte stage, about 66% of the hemoglobin formation has been completed. The completion of hemoglobin synthesis occurs in the reticulocyte. The heme structure is manufactured in the mitochondria and cytoplasm in five basic steps.

The Krebs cycle provide a porphyrin precursor in the mitochondrion,

The formation of the porphyrin ring occurs in the cytoplasm,

The porphyrin rings are assembled into the coproporphyrin III (CPG),

The CPG molecule is transferred into the mitochondrion for transforming to protoporphyrin IX (PPG). The final step is inserting a single ferrous molecule to form heme.

Heme is expelled from the mitochondrion to the cytoplasm where it combines with alpha or beta globin to form a hemoglobin monomer. Two alphas and two betas combine to form the hemoglobin tetramer. The function of hemoglobin is to transport oxygen to the tissues and return carbon dioxide to the lungs. Each erythrocyte contains about 300 million hemoglobin molecules and there are about 30 trillion RBC in the average adult body. One gram of hemoglobin can combine with 1.34 ml of oxygen. In one liter of blood, about 195 ml of oxygen is bound to hemoglobin and 3ml of oxygen is carried in free form.

The globin chain determines the classification of the type of hemoglobin:
1- Hemoglobin A1 is the normal adult hemoglobin. This hemoglobin is the major oxygen carried in the human from about three months to death. It appears in the fifth month of gestation. This Hgb type makes up to 97% of normal Hgb.

2- Hemoglobin F. This is hemoglobin normal to the fetus. Appearing about the fifth week of gestation, it will increase and peak about the seventh month, and can make up to 95% of the total hemoglobin. About the time of birth the amount of Hgb F will be reduced to about 80% of the total hemoglobin, as the developing body increased the rate of Hgb A1 production. About six months after birth, Hgb A1 has almost totally replaced Hgb F. By the child's third birthday, <2.0% of the total Hgb is the F type. Hemoglobin F has a higher affinity for oxygen and can "pick-up" the low levels of placental or uterine oxygen. It consists of two alphas and two gamma globin. Hgb F is easier to oxidize to Methemoglobin and it did also more resistant to alkaline denaturation than other hemoglobin.

3- Hemoglobin Gower 1. This is an embryonic Hgb, found in trace amounts. It consists of two zeta and two epsilon globins. It can be detected on the first three months of embryonic life.

4- Hemoglobin Gower 2. This is the most important of the embryonic hemoglobin's and will make up as much 60% of the total embryonic Hgb. it persists only during the first three months of life. It consists of two epsilon and two alpha globins.

5- Hemoglobin Portland. This is an embryonic Hgb, found in trace amounts. It consists of two gamma and two zeta globins.

6- Hemoglobin A2. This hemoglobin type makes up to 3.5% of normal adults Hgb and consists of two alpha and two teta globins. It appears late in the fetal life and is not produced in any significant quantities. It is designated as a minor Hgb.

Normal values
Male: 14-18 g/dl
Female: 12-16 g/dl.

Abnormal Hemoglobin

Carboxyhemoglobin
a. Oxygen molecules bound to heme are replaced by carbon dioxide.
b. slightly increased levels of Carboxyhemoglobin are present in heavy smokers and as a result of environmental pollution.
c. Can revert to oxyhemoglobin.
Methemoglobin
a. Iron in the hemoglobin molecule is the ferric (Fe^{+++}) state instead of the ferrous (Fe^{++}) state. Incapable of combining with oxygen
b. Can occur as a result of strong oxidative drugs or to an enzyme deficiency.
c. Can revert to oxyhemoglobin
Sulfhemoglobin
a. hemoglobin molecule contains sulfur
b. Caused by certain sulfur-containing drugs or chronic constipation
c. Cannot revert to oxyhemoglobin and may cause death.

Breakdown of the RBC

Toward the end of 120 day life span of the RBC, it begins to break down. This is about 1% of RBCs per day.
The membrane becomes less flexible.
The concentration of cellular hemoglobin increases.
Enzyme activity, especially glycolysis, diminishes.
Aging RBCs are removed from the circulation by the reticuloendothelial system (RES) which is a system of fixed macrophages. These cells are located all over the body, but those in the spleen are the most efficient at removing old RBCs.
As the RBC circulates in vessels with a large diameter, the cell is a typical biconcave cell. When it circulates through capillaries, the diameter reduces to 2 to 3 uM and the cell must "squeeze" through. In this process, the cell experiences physical and osmotic stresses that causes the loss of much of it internal plasma. This ability to migrate through a channel smaller than the cell is called deformability. A repeated passage through the capillaries is traumatic and results in the significant changes in the cell membrane which leads to its removal from circulation. The rupture of the membrane allows the escape of hemoglobin. Hemoglobin is degraded to heme and globin. The globin polypeptide chain is degraded to smaller peptide units and joints the amino acid pool. The heme is degraded to iron and the porphyrin ring macrophage. The ring is opened by the enzyme heme oxidase to produce carbon monoxide and biliverdin, the biliverdin is converted to unconjugated bilirubin and carried to the liver by

albumin, a plasma protein. Bilirubin is conjugated in the liver and excreted into the intestine, where intestinal flora converts it to urobilinogen. Most urobilinogen is excreted in the stool, but some is picked up by the blood and excreted in the urine. Conjugated (indirect) and conjugated (direct) bilirubin ca used to monitor hemolysis. Remember that 90% of RBCs are destroyed extravascularly, and 5- 10% are destroyed intravasularly

The Hematocrit

Synonyms: packed cell volume, "crit". The hematocrit (Hct) is the percentage of the total volume of blood that is occupied by packed red blood cells. It is the simplest and most accurate of the laboratory procedures. The Hct results are preferred (as a rule) over that of the RBC count and allows for calculation of the indices. Regarding the manual Hct, the following is applicable:
The buffy coat can provide a "rough" estimate of the WBC count. A rule-of-thumb estimate is a buffy coat of 1.0% is generally represents a normal WBC count.
The buffy coat is not to be included as part of Hct reading.
A distinctly colored plasma layer can indicate the presence an icteric condition.

Normal values are as follows:
Male: 42-53%.
Female: 36-48%.

Significance of the RBC Indices

The indices are set of mathematical calculations that define the size and hemoglobin content of erythrocytes. They require measurement of Hgb (g/dl), Hct (%), and the RBC count (mm3). The relationship among size, Hgb, and Hct was mathematically determined by Wintrobe in the 1922s. Three formulas were developed to describe RBC morphology and to aid in the classification of anemia. With the general availability of electronic cell counters, RBC cell indices are now automatically measured in all blood count determinations.
3-1 MCV (Mean Corpuscular Volume) defines the size of the red blood cells and is expressed as femtoliters (fl) or as cubic microns. The normal range for MCV is 80 to 100 fl. MCV below 80 suggest RBCs are smaller in size, whereas MCV values above 100 suggest RBCs that are larger then normal.

MCV =Hct x 10/ RBC count
Example: RBC count = 5.0 (millions per microliter).
Hct = 45%.
MCV = 90 fl.

3-2 MCH (Mean Corpuscular Hemoglobin) quantify the amount of hemoglobin per red blood cell. The normal values for MCH are 27 to 31 (picograms).

MCH = Hgb x 10/ RBC count
Example, Hgb = 15 g/dl, RBC count = 5.6 millions/ mm3
MCH = 27 pg.

3-3 MCHC (Mean Corpuscular Hemoglobin Concentration) is considered to be an absolute value and expresses the concentration of hemoglobin in terms of average weight in the volume of the RBC. The normal values for MCHC are 34 to 36%.

MCHC =Hgbx100/ Hct
Example, Hgb = 10 g/dl, Hct = 30%.
MCHC= 33%.

3-4 RDW (Red Cell Distribution Width) is a mathematical calculation (built into the automated instrumentation) that uses the MCV and RBC count to measure the variation in the RBC volume distribution. The following formula is used:
SD [RBC volume distribution] x 100/MCV= RDW %.
The normal range is 11.5 to 14.5 %. RDW values should be interpreted with caution and only after evaluating the blood smear and histogram. If there is a true increase in the variation of the cell sizes, the base of the RBC histogram should be broader. Remember, when you are examining a blood smear, to see up to 6% variation in RBC sizes is not abnormal.

The Reticulocyte

The reticulocyte is an index to RBC turnover. Once the nucleus is extruded from the Metarubricyte, it takes 4- 5 days for the reticulocyte to loose it reticulum and become a mature RBC, The "retic" cell spends about three days in the bone marrow. It is slightly larger than the mature RBC and when stained with Wright's stain, it appears polychromatic. The blue tones are referred to as polychromasia or diffuse basophilia. About the third day, the retic cell moves into general blood circulation. It will take approximately another 24 hours for the RNA reticulum to disappear from the cell. If there is a demand by the body for more RBCs in general circulation, then more retic cell be shifted into blood stream earlier then normal. These larger and more immature forms will b seen on the blood smear as polychromatic retics. Because they are the more immature forms, they will circulate in the general circulation longer. The more severe the anemia or blood loss, the greater the number of shifted retics. The normal count for the adults is 0.5% to 2.0%. For the newborn, retic counts of 2.5% to 6.5% are considered normal. The newborn's retic count will fall to the adult level in about two weeks.

Reticulocyte Production Index

The hematocrit is an index to the degree of anemia. Hct values have been interpolated into time factors for calculating the reticulocyte production index (RPI). An Hct range of 40% to 49% has the designation of 1.0. For an Hct of 30% to 39%, the designation is 1.5. An Hct of 20% to 29% become 2.0 and an Hct of 10% to 19% become 2.5. Consider the following table to show the correction of the Hct with bone marrow and peripheral blood.

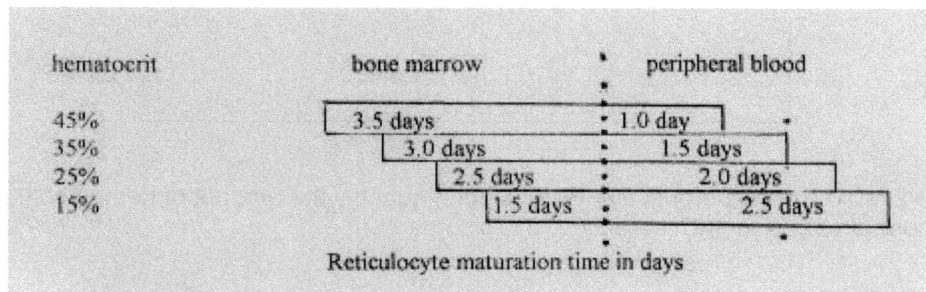

hematocrit	bone marrow	peripheral blood
45%	3.5 days	1.0 day
35%	3.0 days	1.5 days
25%	2.5 days	2.0 days
15%	1.5 days	2.5 days

Reticulocyte maturation time in days

The RPI become an indicator of the degree of bone marrow response to anemia. This calculation is a shift correction for the corrected reticulocyte count. The formula is as follows:

$$RPI = \frac{\% \text{ retic count (x) Hct (L/L)}/ 0.45 (L/L)}{\text{Maturation time in peripheral blood}}$$

Example: retic = 6.5%. Hct =0.26 Mtpb= 2.0
RPI = 1.88. This means that the RBC production rate has increased by 1.88 times. This would be deemed to be an inadequate response. By convention, it is agreed that a RPI value less than 2.0 is an inadequate response. A RPI value of 3.0 is considered to be an appropriate bone marrow response to anemia.
The corrected reticulocyte count (CRC) is also called the Hct correction and retic index. A lab report of a relative retic count may give the appearance of an elevated retic count when it isn't. The CRC

adjusts the actual number of reticulocytes to Hct, giving a more reliable estimate. The formula is as follows:

$$CRC = \frac{Hct\ (L/L)}{0.45} \times \%\ retic,$$

If patient's retic count is 6.5% and the Hct is 0.28, then CRC = 4.04%.
A normal CRC is 1% if the Hct is between 40 to 49%. If the Hct is from 25 to 35% and the CRC falls between 2 and 3%, then the retic cell production is normal. For an Hct that is less than 25%, the CRC should be between 3 and 5%. The retic production index is the preferred method for determining if there is normal production of reticulocytes.

Morphological Changes

Examination of the peripheral blood smear should be considered, along with review of the results of peripheral blood count and red blood cells indices, an essential component of the initial evaluation of all patients with hematological disorders. The examination of the blood film stained with Wright's stain frequently provides important clues in the diagnosis of anemias and various disorders.
Reporting anisocytosis (size), poikilocytosis (shape), stain variations (Hypochromic, normochromic, and hyperchromic). A grading scale that is applicable for grading anisocytosis and poikilocytosis is the following description. RBC anomalies may be graded on a scale of normal, slight, and 1+ to 4+ as follows:
Normal = less than 5% of RBCs differ in shape, size, or hemoglobin intensity from the surrounding pattern of normal round, discoid RBCs.
Slight = approximately 5% to 10% of the RBCs differ from the normal cells.
1+ = 10% to 25% differ from the normal cells.
2+ = 25% to 50% difference from the normal cells.
3+ = 50% to 75% differ from the normal cells.
4+ = > 75% differences from the normal cells.

Erythrocytes size varies from microcytic to normocytic to macrocytic. Microcytic is characterized by [1] a MCV = < 80 fl and [2] size = < 6 micron. Microcytes are observed in iron-deficiency anemia thalassemia. Normocytic is characterized by [1] MCV = 80 to 100 fl and [2] size = 6 to 9 micron. Macrocytosis, observed in hepatic diseases and vitamin B12 and folic acid deficiency anemia's are distinguished by a MCV = > 100 fl and size = >9 micron.
Poikilocytosis indicates a variation in the shape of erythrocytes. A deviation for the normal discoid shape of the erythrocytes is the result of a chemical or physical alteration in the red blood cell membrane or the actual contents of the cell. Because of the variety of shapes seen in erythrocytes, specific names have been assigned to the red blood cell to describe it shape.
Erythrocytes hemoglobinization is describes as normochromic, hypochromic, or hyperchromic. A normochromic RBC describes the presence of a normal of hemoglobin in the cell and that it stains uniformly, evenly. It's MCH = 27 to 32 pg and the MCHC = 31 to 37%. Hypochromasia (Hypochromia) indicates that the RBC contains a decreased amount of hemoglobin. This is one of the most common forms of abnormal erythrocytes, seen in iron-deficiency anemia and thalassemia. It may also be seen in any Hemoglobinopathies. The MCH =< 27 pg and the MCHC = < 31%. The following illustration will assist you in grading the degree of hypochomia.
Hypochromasia (hyerchromia) implies a heavy staining of the red blood cell. Usually it is difficult to correlate over saturation of the hemoglobin in the erythrocyte. This type of appearance is seen in extra thick RBCs or spherocytosis.
For appropriate interpretation of the morphology of erythrocytes, one concentrates on areas of the slide where the red cells appear singly and have central pallor. Examination of erythrocytes far out on the feathered edge discloses erythrocytes lacking central pallor, whereas in thick areas of the slide the morphology of the erythrocytes is distorted by contact between cells.
Artifactual changes of erythrocytes occur commonly on peripheral blood films. Cytoplasmic vacuolization of red cells is an artifact. Echinocytes (crenated red cells) are frequently caused by hyper tonicity or alkalinity of the staining solution. Stomatocytes may form when the staining solution is too acidic. When target cells appear in one area of the slide and not in another, they are artifacts because naturally occurring target cells will be distributed evenly throughout the slide.

Poikilocytes

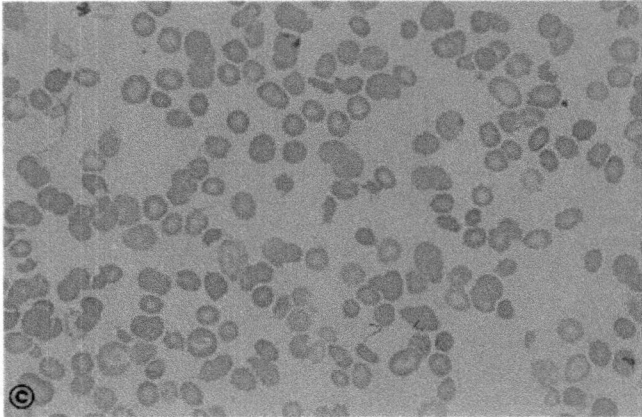

Poikilocytosis describes the variety of non specific shapes that may be observed in RBCs. Poikilocytosis is an irreversible alteration of the cell membrane and is an indicator of abnormal erythropoiesis due to bone marrow effects and/or abnormal RBC destruction. This is one of the most common forms of abnormal RBC morphology. There is a poikilocytosis expression that occurs as the RBCs ages (senescence). The RBC will become pinched, pitted, or notched as the membrane breaks down and sloughs off.

Spherocytes

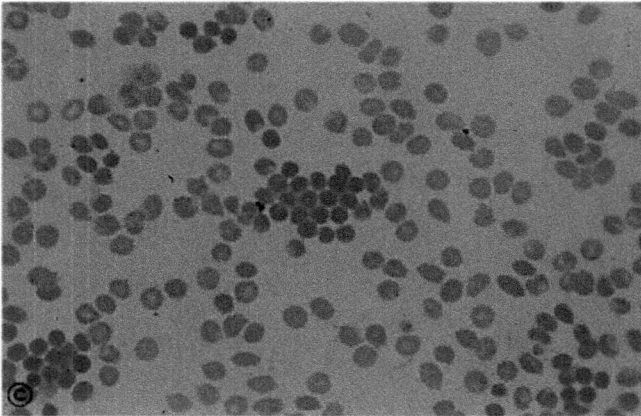

The Spherocyte is an erythrocyte in which the biconcave disc profile is lost. It appears as a smaller and denser RBC. It is also called a hyperchromic microspherocyte. The Spherocyte is formed when there is a defect in the membrane function. The sodium pump causes Na+ retention which increases water retention, increasing the intravascular volume. This cell is observed in immune induced hemolysis, post blood transfusions, and congenital anemia.

Acanthocytes

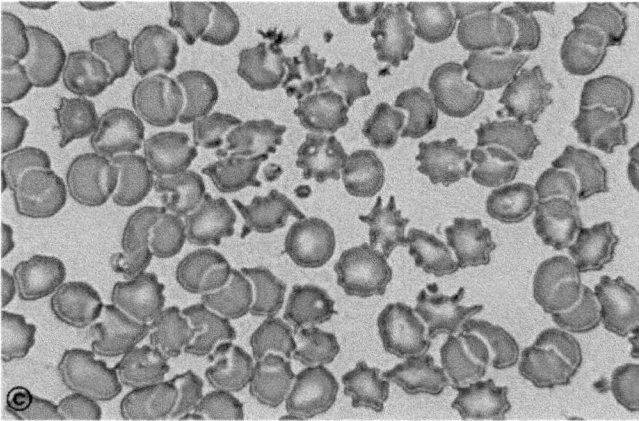

The acanthocyte is an abnormally crenated RBC. It is the consequences of a defect in the cell membrane. These cell types are observed in abetalipoproteinemia, liver disorders, and lipid metabolism disorders. Remember that acanthocytes should not be observed in a normal stained blood film. When they are seen, be sure to indicate their presence.

Burr cells

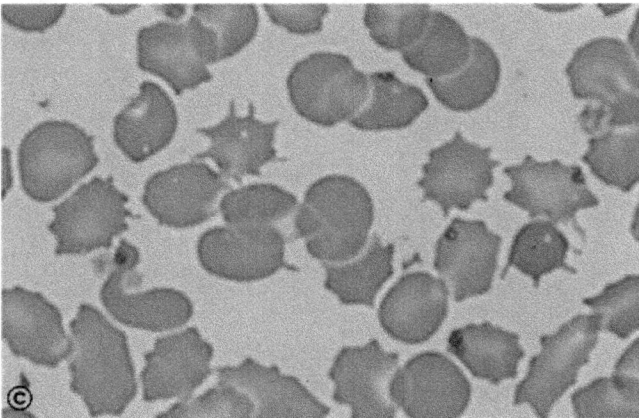

The burr cells are characterized by abnormal cytoplasmic projections, but not to the same extent as that of the acanthocyte. It is characterized by regular pointed projections with regular shape curves. There is an overall uniform spacing. These cells are observed in uremia, acute blood loss, stomach cancer, and pyruvate kinase deficiency.

Schistocytes

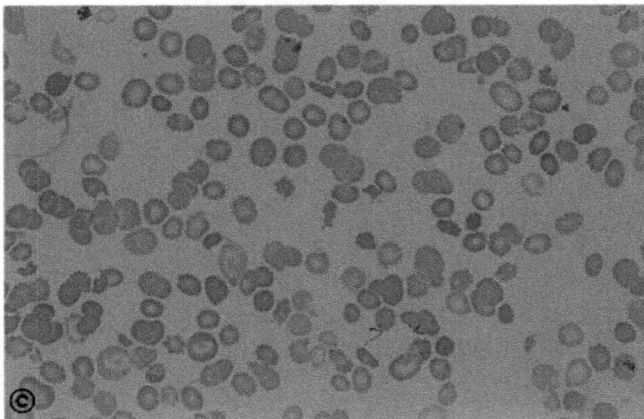

= Atlas of Hematology (Nivaldo Medeiros, MD). Used with permission=

Fragmented cells are fragments of erythrocytes with wide variation in sizes and shapes, usually microcytic in size. Schistocytes are seen in vascular lesions, uremia, microangiopathic hemolytic anemias; hemolytic anemia's caused by physical agents, and disseminated intravascular coagulation (DIC), whenever there is blood vessel pathology present. Schistocytosis is the result of mechanical trauma in the spleen and interaction with intravascular fibrin strands.

Elliptocytes/Ovalocytes

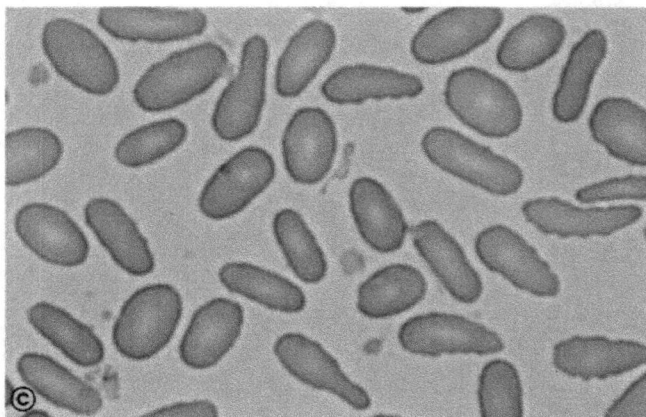

= Atlas of Hematology (Nivaldo Medeiros, MD). Used with permission=

Normally about 5% to 10% of the circulating RBCs are oval. These cells are formed after the erythrocytes mature and leave the bone marrow. Patients diagnosed with elliptocytosis tend to have normal shaped reticulocytes. The mechanism that causes elliptocytes is not known. There is known to be a hereditary defect present in the RBC cytoskeletal proteins (the spectrin chain). These cells observed in varying percentages in iron deficiency anemia, leukemia associated anemia, thalassemia, and dyserythropoiesis. Patients with congenital elliptocytosis may demonstrate up to 90% distinctly oval shaped cells.

Target cells (codocytes)

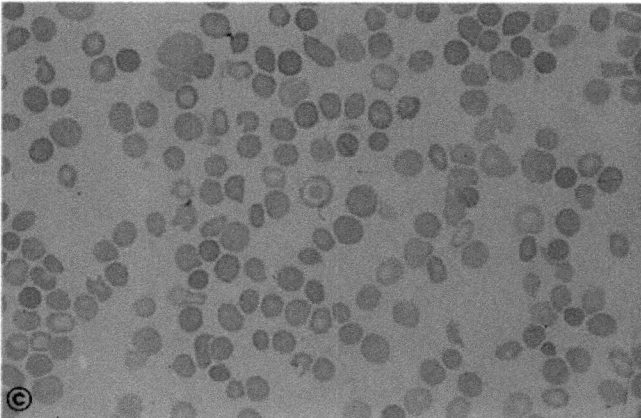

This cell is characterized by an abnormally thin membrane with increase incorporation of cholesterol into the cell membrane. It appears because of misdistributions of abnormal hemoglobin or certain materials being deposited into the cell membrane. These cells are more resistant to hypotonic lysis. It is observed in hemoglobinipathies, hepatic diseases, iron deficiency anemia, hemolytic anemia, and splenectomy

Stomatocytes

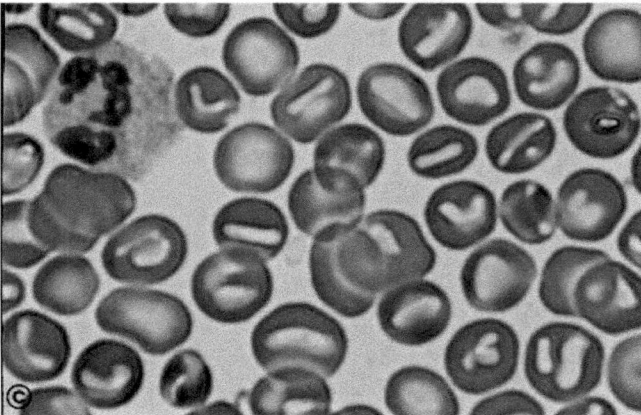

These cells are characterized by an alteration in the permeability of the cell membrane to sodium. It is observed in liver disease, alcoholism, electrolyte imbalance, hereditary stomatocytosis, infectious mononucleosis, lead poisoning, malignancies, and thalassemia minor.

Dacryocytes

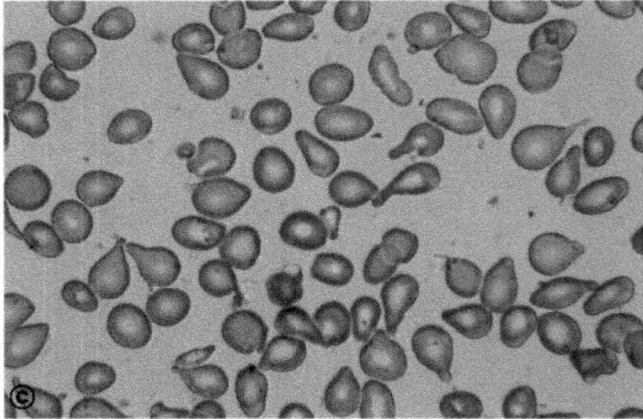

The cell has a definite tear drop shape and length of the "tail" may vary from cell to cell. Small areas of pallor may be present on the cell. The tear-drop cell is observed in pernicious anemia, thalassemia, myeloid Dysplasia, severe anemia, and hemolytic anemia.

Basophilic stippling

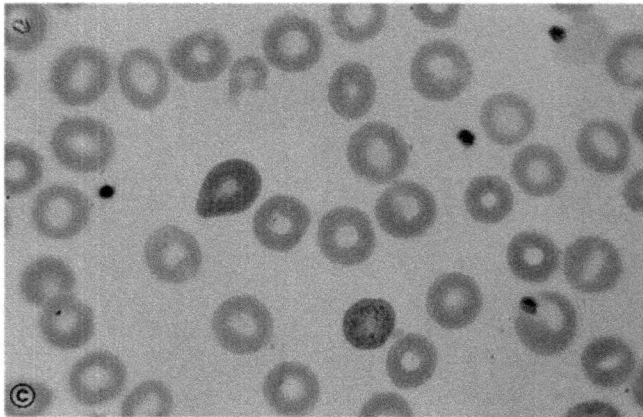

Basophilic stippling (also called punctuate basophilia), is characterized by the presence of numerous granules in the erythrocyte. These blue granules may be fine or coarse and may be intense in color. The granules are aggregates of ribosomes and are evenly distributed in the cell. They are observed in lead poisoning, hemoglobinipathies, alcoholism, and megaloblastic anemia.

Howell-Jolly bodies

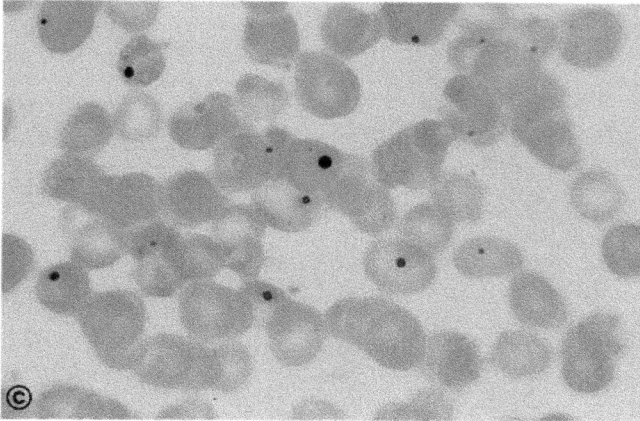

=Atlas of Hematology (Nivaldo Medeiros, MD). Used with permission=

The Howell-Jolly body are round, purple staining nuclear DNA fragments. They are usually observed in the mature erythrocyte, but may also be seen in the nucleated and immature red blood cell. As a rule, only one Howell-Jolly body is seen per cell and some times two.

Cabot ring

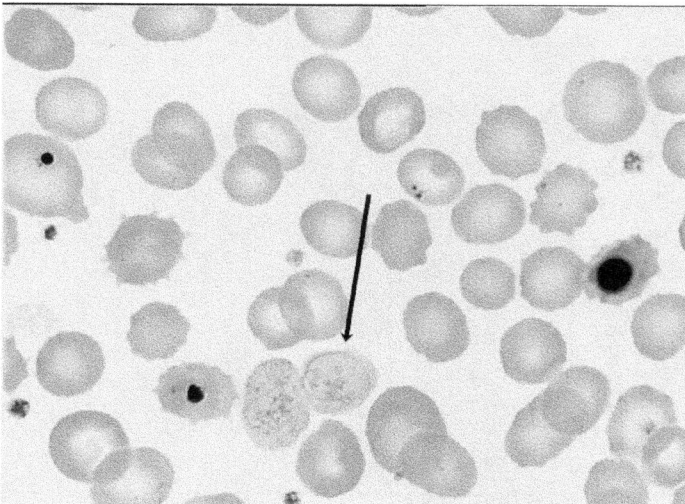

= Hematocell (Prof Marc Zandecki). Used with permission =

The Cabot ring is a purple staining ring-like filament. This inclusion may be present as a double or triple ring. If observed, it is most likely to be seen in severe anemia and lead poisoning. It is generally thought to be due to abnormal erythropoiesis.

Drepanocytes

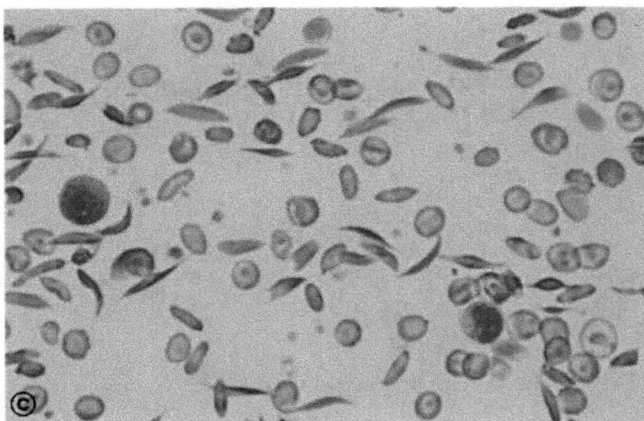

=Atlas of Hematology (Nivaldo Medeiros, MD). Used with permission=

They are associated with the disorder, sickle cell anemia. Like the target cell, sickle cells are resistant to hypotonic lysis. There are two basic types of sickle cells; [1] the oat cell, slightly sickled variation, and/or holly leaf. These RBC collapses into these shapes when there is a reduced oxygen atmosphere. In the presence of a normal oxygen atmosphere, the cells revert to the normal discoid shape. [2] The second type form very discoid filamentous forms. In the presence of a reduced oxygen atmosphere these cell form, but when the oxygen pressure is normalized, they do not revert back to the normal discoid shape. Sickle cells are also observed in hemoglobin SBeta- thalassemia anemia and hemoglobin SC anemia.

Hemoglobin crystals

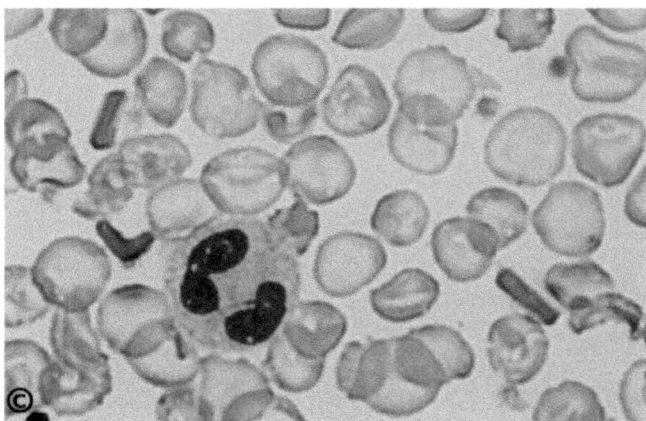

=Atlas of Hematology (Nivaldo Medeiros, MD). Used with permission=

 Hemoglobin crystals are seen as tetragonal crystals, found in hemoglobin C and hemoglobin Sc disease. If the condition is severe, then up to 10% of the RBCs may contain these crystals. In the case of hemoglobin SC disease, the crystals may show greater variation. Hemoglobin C crystals may be demonstrated by washing the red blood cells and suspending them in sodium citrate. Hemoglobin C crystals are precipitated polymers of the beta chains of hemoglobin A.

Rouleaux's formation

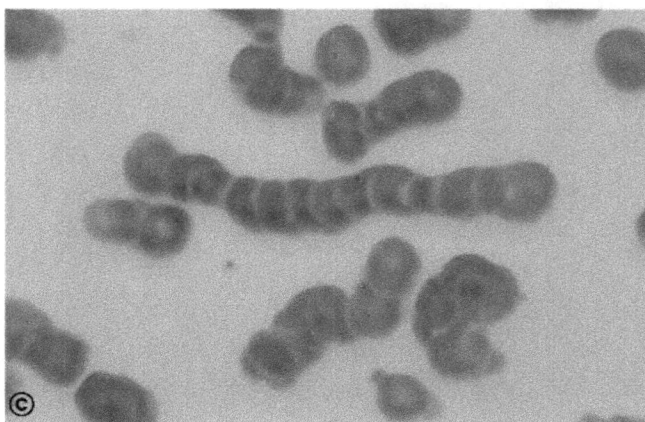

= Atlas of Hematology (Nivaldo Medeiros, MD). Used with permission=

Rouleaux's formations are RBCs arranged in rows or stacks. They are sometimes present as a slide artifact due to a delay in the spreading of blood or the settling out phenomenon in the thick portion of the blood smear. Rouleaux's appear in chronic inflammatory disorders, multiple myeloma, hyerproteinemia, and Waldenstrom's Macroglobulinemia. Increased amount of fibrinogen in the blood can cause Rouleaux's formation. If Rouleaux's is noted in the thick portion of the stained blood film but not in the thin portion, it is probably an artifact, but represents some pathologic problem, report as follows: if the cells are arranged in aggregates of 3 to 4 RBCs report as 1+; if aggregates of 5 to 10 RBCs, then report as 2+, and if the aggregates are so numerous that only a few free RBCs, report as 3+.

Agglutination

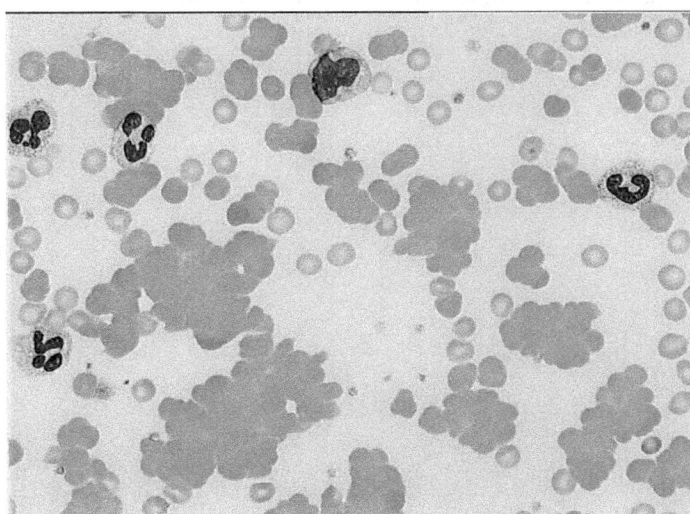

=Hematocell (Prof Marc Zandecki). Used with permission=

Agglutination occurs when cold agglutinations or autoimmune hemolytic anemia are present. The RBCs do not stack as in Rouleaux's, they will clump randomly. If agglutination is present then the automated RBC counts and cell sizing will not be reliable.

Microspherocytes

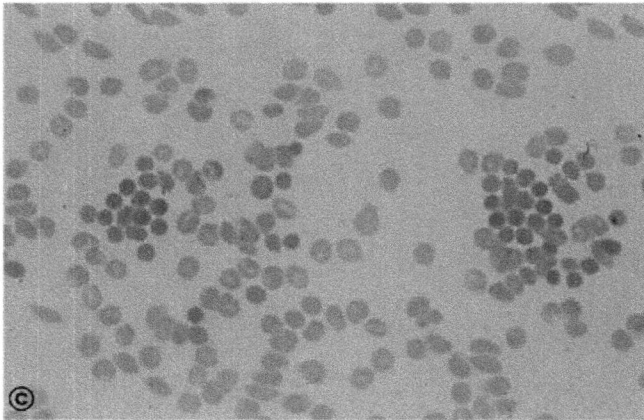

Microspherocytes appears in the blood as small round cells and are the result of intravascular hemolysis. This cell type is seen in patient who receives burns over a minimum of 15% of their bodies. It is though that the heat, which the burned part of the body experiences, exerts a direct effect upon the RBCs to produce fragmentation, budding, and microspherocyte formation. Experiments conducted by heating RBCs to 49degree Celsius demonstrated this fragmentation phenomenon of erythrocytes. These cells are mechanically and osmotically fragile and are rapidly removed from circulation. This phenomenon is characterized by tiny cell diameters of 2 to 4 micron and a MCV that is < 60 fl. There is hemolytic anemia disorder in which the cell membrane protein (spectrin) is abnormal. The RBC will fragment, producing similar fragments as seen in burn patients. These RBC fragments are called "pyropoikiloctyes".

Red blood cell count generally contributes little clinical information. Hemoglobin and hematocrit determination are usually preferred. The RBC count is important for the calculation of the indices. Erythrocytes numbers fluctuate in both health and disease. A decrease in the RBC count is known as erythropenia or oligocythemia. An increase in the RBC count is known as erythrocyosis.

CHAPTER TWO: WHITE BLOOD CELL

Leukocytes numbers fluctuate in health and disease. If the WBC count drops below the normal range (4000 cell/uL), then the condition is leucopenia. If the count is elevated over (10,000 cell/uL), then the condition is leukocytosis. These conditions are due to depression or stimulation of bone marrow and others elements. The WBC count in children tends to fluctuate more widely than adults in disease. WBC counts tend to be higher in the afternoon than in the morning. Strenuous exercise and emotional ups-and-downs will promote an increase in the WBC count. WBC counts can be employed to follow the effectiveness of treatment therapies.

Absolute and Relative Count

The absolute count means to be free from mixture, to have no restrictions. In the laboratory, it is an expression of the numbers of each cell type/up of blood. It is a means of imparting additional information. It is a mathematical calculation that determines the actual number of a cell type so that it is increase or decrease may be known. To calculate the absolute count, the relative count must be known. Use the following formula:

Absolute count = total WBC count (x) relative count.

	Relative count (%)	Absolute count (cell/uL)
Total WBCs		4,000-10,000
Myelocytes	0	0
Metamyelocytes	0-1	0-100
Bands	2-5	80-500
Neutrophils	35-70	1,400-7,000
Eosinophils	0-5	<500
Basophils	0-1	<100
Lymphocytes	15-45	600-4,500
Monocytes	1-10	40-1,000

Cell Biology and Disorders of Neutrophils

The granulocyte pool is a generic term that describes four storage sites (called compartments), containing elevated concentrations of neutrophils. The first compartment is the bone marrow pool. Three levels can be identified in this compartment: proliferation, maturation, and storage. The proliferation role is characterized by the presence of myeloblasts, promyelocytes, and myelocytes. The maturation level is evidence by metamyelocytes and bands. The actual storage pool consists of bands and neutrophils, which are ready to be moved immediately into circulation.
The second compartment is the peripheral blood pool. The predominate leukocyte is the segmented neutrophil, making up to 70% of the total number of WBCs. Bands may found, but will not exceed 2%-5% of the total count in normal condition.
The third compartment is the marginal pool and will contain about 50% of the total number of neutrophils in the body. These are those WBCs that adhere to the blood vessel walls and those that migrate (diapedesis) into the tissues.
The fourth pool is the tissue pool and consists only of those neutrophils found in the body tissues.

2-1- Neutrophil function

Primary function is phagocytosis which occurs in three stages.
A-Migration and diapedesis
1- Chemotaxis is the presence of directional migration which occurs under the guidance of chemo attractants which are produced by the site of injury.
2- The neutrophil transforms from smooth and round to rough and flat.
3- Diapedesis is the movement of the neutrophil through the vessel wall.

B-Opsonization and recognition
> 1- Opsonization is the mechanism which facilitates recognition and attachment to the organism to be ingested.
> 2- After the bacteria are coated by immunoglobulin and complement, it is referred to as an opsonin.

C-Phagocytosis: ingestion, killing and digestion.

1- The cytoplasm of the neutrophil forms a pseudopod which surrounds and envelops the microorganism forming a vacuole called a phagosome.

2- Cytoplasmic granules migrate to the vacuole and release their lytic contents which kill and digest the organism.

Response to infection: Neutrophilia

More Pluripotent stem cells are committed to become granulocytes.

1-The generation time of myelocytes is shortened.

2-Myelocytes undergo an extra division.

3-The transit time through the bone marrow is shortened.

4-Leukemoid reaction is an advanced degree of leukocytes in the blood that is not a result of leukemia. The absolute neutrophil count (ANC) is increased. These changes occur with bacterial and viral infection, pregnancy, massive trauma, drug reactions and other toxic states.

5-The cytochemical stain, Leukocyte Alkaline Phosphatase, is used to differentiate Leukemoid reaction from Chronic Myelogenous Leukemia (CML).

6-Morphologic changes are the presence of toxic granulation, Dohle bodies and cytoplasmic vacuolization.

The Schilling hemogram/Classification

Schilling (German pathologist) noticed that the granulocyte series increased in the number of immature cells during pathological disorders. He modified the Arneth count to a simpler form to include the granulocytic evaluation.

The Schilling Hemogram is a WBC differentiation scheme that evaluates the percentage of neutrophils per 100 WBCs. Schilling introduced the phrases "shift-to-the left" to indicate more immature granulocytes cells and " shift-to-the-right" to indicate an increase in mature granulocytes. His scheme was to set up the reading scale so that the more immature granulocytes would be listed on the left and the mature forms on the right. The scale reads thus:[a] myeloblasts and promyelocytes, [b] myelocytes, [c] metamyelocytes-slightly indented forms, [d] metamyelocytes-band form, and [e] segmented neutrophils. He determined the normal value to be: [a] = 0%, [b] = 0%, [c] = o%, [d] =1 to 5%, [e] = 35 to 70%.

Schilling also identified two types of shifts-to-the-left:

[1] Regenerative shift=to-the-left, characterized by a rapid rate of the production of WBCs with a significantly elevated WBC count. He noted this shift in appendicitis and acute sepsis.

[2] Degenerative shift –to-the-left, characterized by lower WBC count and the number of immature granulocytes expected in circulation are depressed by toxins that interfere with the maturation of the granulocyte. He observed this shift in typhoid fever, brucellosis, pernicious anemia, and TB.

Schilling pointed out that in the normal recovery of a patient, a shift-to-the-right would occur characterized by an increase in lymphocytes and eosinophils before other clinical symptoms became obvious. If the shift-to-the-left persisted, it was a poor prognostic sign.

The Arneth count

Arneth (German pathologist) classified neutrophils according to their age, based upon the number of lobes in the nucleus of neutrophil. He described five age neutrophil age groups:

[1] A single round or indented nucleus as the youngest cell = 5%,

[2] Two distinct nuclear divisions as the next youngest cell = 35%,

[3] Three distinct nuclear division as middle age = 41%,

[4] Four distinct nuclear divisions = 17%,

[5] Five or more distinct nuclear divisions as the oldest cell = 2%.

This classification has some merit but is time consuming for routine laboratory use; therefore it is seldom referred to. It has used in determining hypersegmentation of neutrophils in vitamin B12 deficiency anemia

Filament and non-filament cells

This was a classification scheme that stated that a filament cell included those cells that contained a lobe or segment connected by a filament. There were the neutrophils, eosinophils and basophils. The non-filament cells included myelocytes, metamyelocytes, bands, lymphocytes, and monocytes. It could also contain the more immature forms not listed. If this scheme were employed, a normal differential would appear as follows:

		Schilling-type diff	filament/non-filament diff
Non filament	Normal range%		35%
Myelocytes	0		
Metamyelocytes	0		
Bands	2-5	2	
Lymphocytes	15-40	28	
Monocytes	1-10	5	
Filament			65%
Neutrophils	35-70	60	
Eosinophils	0-5	4	
Basophils	0-1	1	

Hypersegmentation in the granulocytes

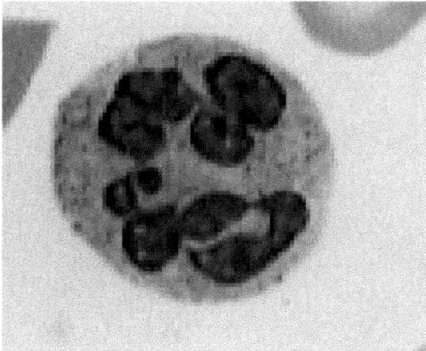

©2007. Rector and visitors of the University of Virginia
Charles E. Hess, M.D. and Lindsey Krstic, B.A. Use with permission

Hypersegmentation indicates changes of abnormal leucopoiesis in granulocytes. This is the presence of increased nuclear lobes in neutrophils, eosinophils, or basophils. For the neutrophil, the appearance of cells with five or more lobes indicates abnormal DNA synthesis which may indicate megaloblastic anemia due to a vitamin B12 and /or folic deficiency. It has been associated with a benign hereditary hypersegmentation disorder.
Patients under rhG-CSF (recombinant human granulocyte colony stimulating factor) therapy have demonstrated hypersegmentation. Hypersegmentation does appear in patients with long term chronic infections. In aged neutrophils, as nuclear deterioration takes place, there may be a temporary pseudo-hypersegmentation phenomenon. Generally hypersegmentation is considered to be an indicator of megaloblastic anemia.

Hyposegmentation in the granulocytes

118

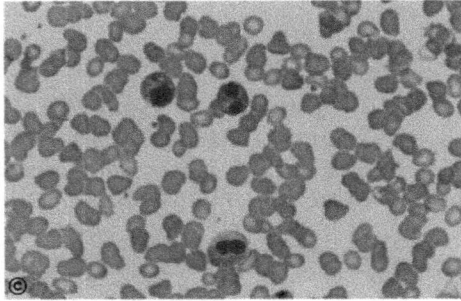

=Atlas of Hematology (Nivaldo Medeiros, MD). Used with permission=

Hyposegmentation is a condition in which the nucleus contains only two lobes or no lobes at all. This condition is characteristic of Pelger-Huet anomaly, a benign autosomal dominant (Homozygous) or a recessive (Heterozygous) disorder. The heterozygous condition is characterized by neutrophils whose nuclear shape appears as a dumbbell or pair of eyeglasses (hence the term" pince-nez". The chromatin clumping and cytoplasmic characteristics are similar to that in the mature normal lobed neutrophil. Neutrophil, with the Hyposegmentation nucleus in an infectious state, the chromatin material appears coarser and more heavily clumped. In the homozygous state, the nucleus does not form lobes but appears as an oval or round nucleus. There is a pseudo-Pelger-Huet condition in which the hyposegmented neutrophil appears bilobed. This is an acquired condition in which trilobed neutrophil are present. This acquired condition occurs due to drug ingestion or a malignancy. Remember do not confuse Pelger-Huet neutrophils with bands or metamyelocytes (the chromatin in the Pelger-Huet is more condensed and coarser than the band or metamyelocyte.

Toxic granulations

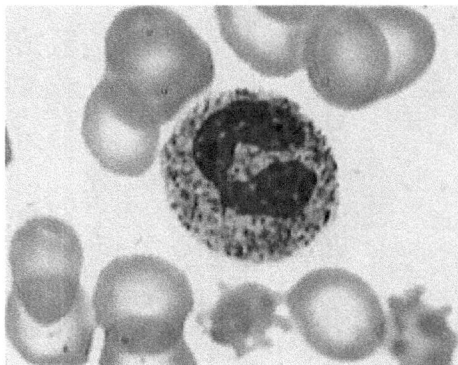

©2007. Rector and visitors of the University of Virginia
Charles E. Hess, M.D. and Lindsey Krstic, B.A. Used with permission

Toxic granules are found in the cytoplasm of neutrophils and must be included in the differential report. It represents a transient change in the cytoplasmic morphology of the neutrophils due to infectious or toxic agents. These are medium to large size dark blue-black granules formed from primary granules which suggest a non specific reactive change. Primary granules, in the neutrophils of normal healthy individuals, are not visible with Wright's stain. Toxic granules tend to cluster in the cytoplasm and not all neutrophils will be affected. If there are a greater number of neutrophils presenting with toxic granulation, this may indicate a more serious prognosis. Toxic granules are graded on a scale of 1+ to 4+. The true toxic granule is composed of peroxidases and acid hydrolases. Toxic granulations are seen in bacterial infections, toxemia of pregnancy, vasculitis, burns, malignancy, or chemotherapy.
Vacuolation in the neutrophil may be better indicator of a bacterial infection than toxic granulation. Also called toxic vacuolation, these are clear, unstained, round areas in the cytoplasm. They are usually most obvious in severe infections.

Dohle body

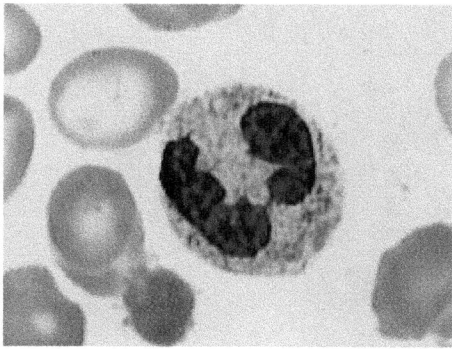

The Dohle body is a cytoplasmic inclusion composed of ribosomal RNA (aggregates of rough endoplasmic reticulum) arranged in parallel rows found in neutrophils and bands. These inclusions stain readily with Wright's stain. In a stained blood film prepared from a non-anticoagulant blood sample, the inclusion tends to stain a bluer coloration.

The Dohle body tends to be found in close proximity to the cell membrane. These inclusions are seen in pregnancy, bacterial infections, burns, cancer, aplastic anemia, and toxic conditions. If toxic granulations are present then look for Dohle bodies.

May-Hegglin anomaly is large blue cytoplasmic inclusions resembling Dohle bodies are found in neutrophils and sometimes lymphocytes and monocytes. Thrombocytopenia and giant platelets are also seen in this anomaly.

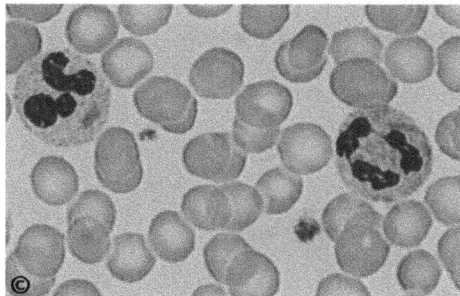

Neutropenia

Neutropenia is the reduction in the number of neutrophils, occurs when the absolute count drops below 1000/uL. If the count drops below 500/uL, then there is a serious risk of severe infections. Suppression of the neutrophil count may be due to some medications (penicillin, ibuprofen, phenytoin, and chlorpropamides), severe infections that cause the outflow of neutrophils into the tissue spaces to exceed the body's ability to replace them, or increased loss of WBCs (as seen in a splenectomy). Neutropenia may be observed in young children as a transient disorder due to viral causes (influenza A and B, rubella, hepatitis A and B, and respiratory syncytial virus). It can be an acquired secondary disorder associated with aplastic anemia, bone marrow malignancy, or vitamin B12 and/or folic acid deficiency.

Alder's anomaly

Prominent dark-staining coarse cytoplasmic granules are found in neutrophils, eosinophils, basophils, monocytes and sometimes lymphocytes. Granules are precipitated mucopolysaccharides.

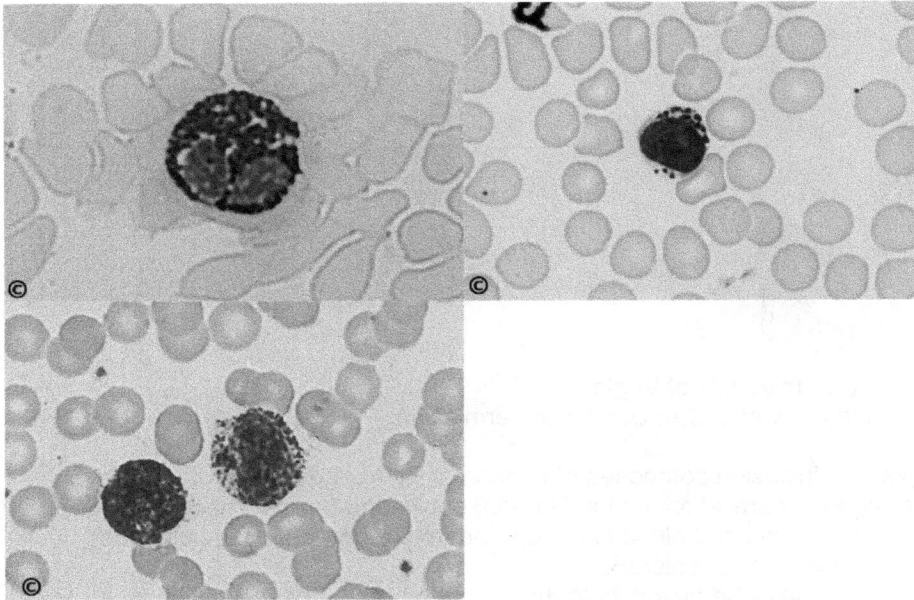

=Atlas of Hematology (Nivaldo Medeiros, MD). Used with permission=

The Chediak-Higashi syndromes

The CHS is a rare autosomal recessive condition associated with abnormally large leukocyte granules resulting from fusion of lysozymes. This disorder may affect granulocytes, leukocytes, and monocytes. Chemotaxis and phagocytosis is defective. Platelets lack dense granules and platelet function is abnormal. Giant melanosomes in occular and skin tissues result in hypopigmentation.

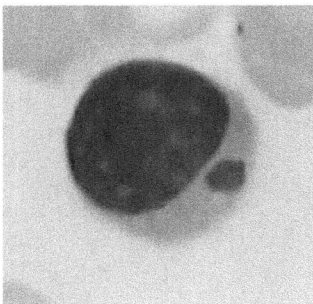

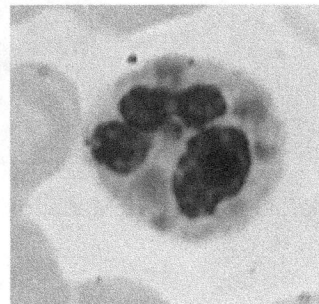

©2007. Rector and visitors of the University of Virginia
Charles E. Hess, M.D. and Lindsey Krstic, B.A. Used with permission

CELL BIOLOGY AND DISORDERS OF LYMPHOCYTES

The lymphocyte exists as subpopulations consisting of small, medium and large lymphocytes. Some professionals classify the lymph cell into only two subpopulations (small and large).

Small lymphocyte

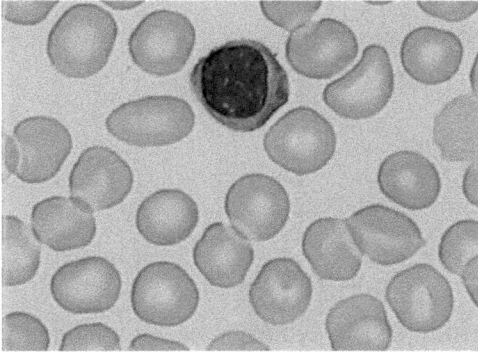

= Hematocell (Prof Marc Zandecki). Used with permission=

The small lymphocyte measures from 8.0 to 10.0 uM, somewhat larger than a RBC. The cytoplasm is characterized as a thin rim about the nucleus. The color of the cytoplasm is dependent upon the properties of the stain being used and will range from a sky blue color to a dark blue coloration. Occasional azurophil granules may be observed. The nucleus to cytoplasm ration ranges from 5:1 to 3:1. The nucleus is about the size of a normal RBC and may be used to estimate the size of the RBC. The nucleus is characterized by a clumped, dense chromatin pattern (designated as the block type). There are no visible nucleoli. The cytoplasm of the mature lymphocyte, regardless of its size stains from a very light blue or almost colorless to a sky blue or even darker blue. This is due to the variety of stain that is being used. If the lab uses modified forms of Wright's stain, then cytoplasm variations will also be seen.

Medium lymphocyte

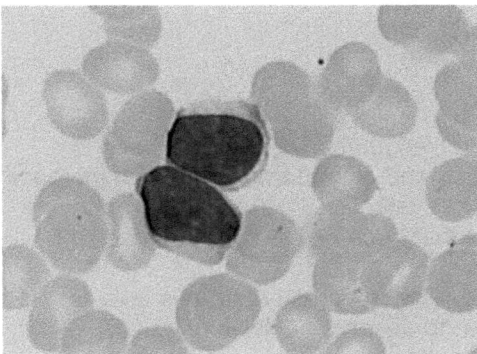

= Hematocell (Prof Marc Zandecki). Used with permission =

The medium or moderate lymphocyte measures from 10 to 12 uM. There is more abundant cytoplasm than in the small lymphocyte. The cytoplasm often stains lighter than of the small lymphocyte, from a sky blue to a medium blue. A few azurophil granules may be seen in the cytoplasm. The nucleus will be rounding, oval, or intender; with the chromatin appearing less dense than in the small lymphocyte. The chromatin will have a clumped appearance. There are no visible nucleoli.

Large lymphocyte

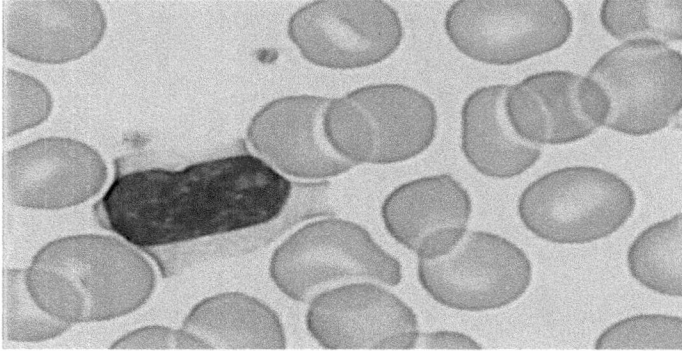

=Hematocell (Prof Marc Zandecki). Used with permission =

The large lymphocyte is characterized by a diameter of 12 to 16 uM. The cytoplasm is very abundant, tending to be clear or pale blue in color. Basophilic colors have been reported. Non-specific azurophilic granules may be seen. The cytoplasmic outline may be irregular. The nucleus is usually round, oval, or indented. The chromatin pattern is coarse. Nucleoli are not visible, the nucleus is eccentric.

Reactive lymphocytes

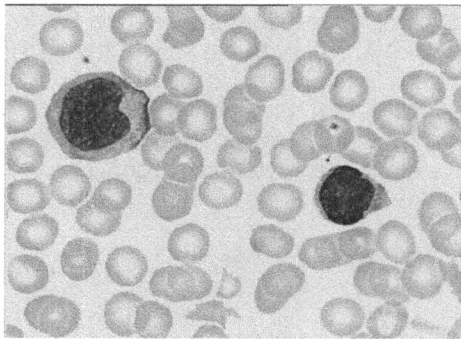

= Hematocell (Prof Marc Zandecki). Used with permission=

The reactive lymphocyte represents a morphological variation in the lymphocyte that has been exposed to antigenic stimulus. It is characterized by size variation and often demonstrates an increase in cytoplasmic mass. This is due to an increase in DNA and RNA synthesis. The reactive lymphocyte is often larger than large lymphocytes. They are T-lymphocytes that become cytotoxic to infected B-lymphocytes.

The nucleus may be oval, round, indented, or irregular in shape. The chromatin pattern is less pachychromatic, being designated as intermediate. It is possible to observe nuclei in reactive lymphocytes that have a "Blast" appearance. Nucleoli may be faintly visible.

The cytoplasm is usually abundant and demonstrates varying shades of basophilia. The basophilia may distribute in variable patterns within the cytoplasm. Azurophilic granules may be present. The Golgi apparatus may be observed. The presence of vacuoles is not unusual and may even give a "bubbly" or "foamy" appearance to the cell.

The reactive lymphocyte is seen in infectious mononucleosis, cytomegalovirus, HIV, infectious hepatitis, organ transplants, and serum sickness. The term "atypical" is often used to describe reactive lymphocytes. Other terms that have been used to describe the reactive lymphocyte are: Turk cell and Downey cell.

Downey cell classification

This classification method was implemented to describe the lymphocytes observed in infectious mononucleosis. This group structured the reactive lymphocyte into three categories. When classifying lymphocytes under the Downey classification, be sure to note the appearance of the cytoplasm and the quantity and distribution of the chromatin structure.
[1] Downey cell type I.

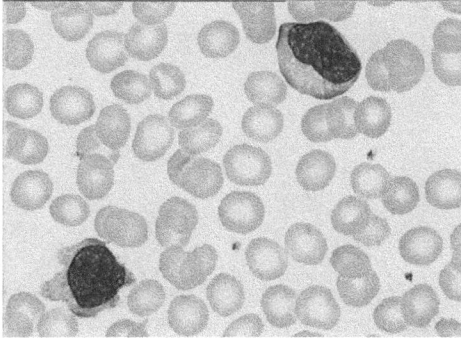

= Hematocell (Prof Marc Zandecki). Used with permission =

The nucleus is irregularly shaped. If the nucleus is round or oval, it may be intended. The nuclear chromatin resembles that of a mature lymphocyte. The cytoplasm is basophilic and may be foamy appearing at times. Vacuoles are present.

Downey cell type II.

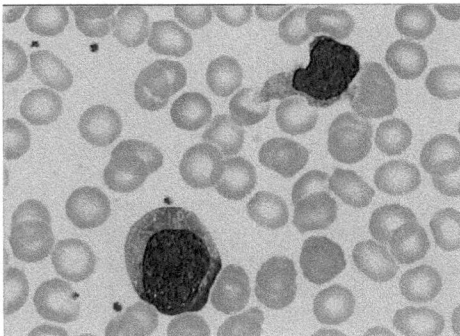

= Hematocell (Prof Marc Zandecki). Used with permission =

The nucleus is characterized by coarser appearing chromatin, but is less so than in the type I cell. The cytoplasm is characterized by an irregular border and is increased in quantity. The cytoplasm is usually characterized by light blue staining cytoplasm around the nucleus but a more intense blue color at the periphery, giving the appearance of basophilia. Radial basophilia may be present. Vacuolation will less in type I and azurophilic granules may be seen on occasions.

Downey cell type III.

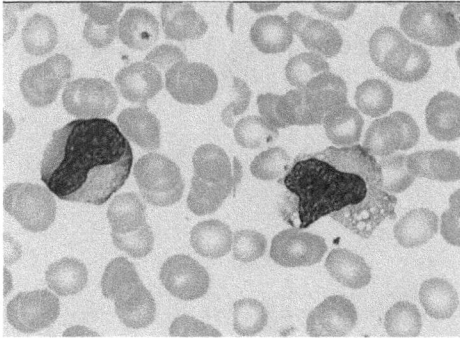

= Hematocell (Prof Marc Zandecki). Used with permission=

The nucleus may resemble the immature lymphocyte and nucleoli (one to four) may be visible. There is an increased in cytoplasmic basophilia. The cytoplasm is abundant and tends to flows around the red blood cells. The cell is larger than types I and II.

Large Granular lymphocytes

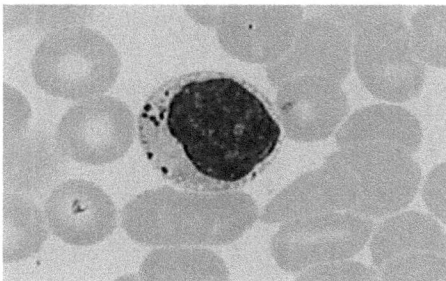

= Hematocell (Prof Marc Zandecki). Used with permission =

This is a sub-population of lymphocytes that make up 5% to 10% of the circulating lymphocytes. These cells are also called (NK or Natural Killer) morphologically they contain azurophilic granules in their cytoplasm. These cells produce interferon and interleukin-2. Their functional role is designated as destroying tumor cells,

The Monocyte and Reactive lymphocyte

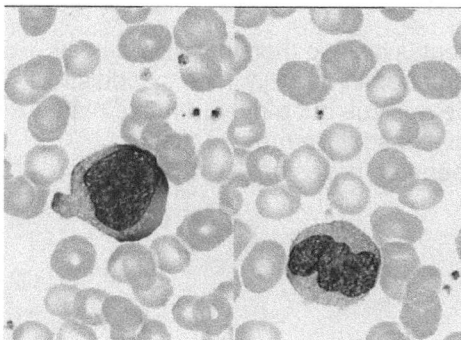

= Hematocell (Prof Marc Zandecki). Used with permission =

	MONOCYTE	REACTIVE LYMPHOCYTE
Chromatin	Lacy, loosely Woven, or ropy	Variable, fine and dispersed to clumped (especially at Membrane periphery)
Cytoplasm	Blue-grey	Pale blue to deeply Basophilic, it tends to Stain unevenly.
Granules	numerous very Fine red granules That gives a ground glass appearance	A few obvious azurophilic may be present.
Nucleolus	absent	May be present
Nucleus	Convoluted, Horseshoe, kidney- Shaped, oval, or Round	Variable shapes from round, elongated, irregular to stretched out
Shape	Pleomorphic, pseudopodia May be present, resists indentation by surrounding cells	Pleomorphic and is easily indented by the surrounding cells
Size	12 to 20 uM	10 to 30 uM
Vacuoles	absent to numerous, Small to large	occasionally present

Plasma cells

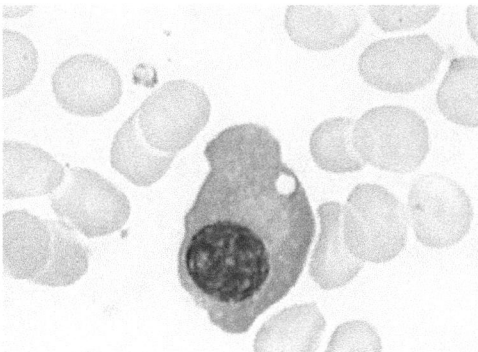

=Hematocell (Prof Marc Zandecki). Used with permission=

 The conversion of lymphocyte to the plasma cell begins when the B-lymphocyte is antigenically stimulated. One of the first steps in the transformation is the enlargement of the B-lymphocyte. The nucleus will manifest visible nucleoli. The cytoplasm becomes basophilic. A clear halo-like area will appear close to the nucleus indicating enlargement of the Golgi body. This clear area is designated as the perinuclear halo. At this stage, the B-lymphocyte is a reactive lymphocyte. The transformation continues and the Plasmablast is formed, to produce a cell that is more efficient at the production of antibodies. The plasma cell will be characterized by the synthesis and release of specific immunoglobulins.

CHAPTER THREE: PLATELETS DISORDERS

Platelet disorders are the most common cause of abnormal bleeding. They can be quantitative or qualitative disorders. Bleeding manifestations are characterized by mucocutaneous bleeding like bruising, nose bleeding, and menorrhagia, and bleeding after hemostatic stress, such as after tonsillectomy and adenoidectomy, dental extraction , and, rarely post-partum.

Platelets circulate in a concentration of 150,000-450,000 cells/ml. of the total body platelets, about 70% stay in the circulation while the remaining 30% are continually but transiently sequestered in the spleen. Platelets remain in circulation for an average of 10 days. Most platelets are removed from the circulation by the spleen and by Kupffer cell in the liver after senescence, but a constant small fraction is continually removed through involvement in maintenance of vascular integrity.

Risk of bleeding

The risk of bleeding is inversely proportional to the platelet count.
1- 50,000-150,000= No symptoms (no treatment generally required).
2- 20,000-50,000= First symptoms (generally need to begin therapy)
3- 10,000-20,000= life-threatening (generally requires hospitalization)
4- <10,000= Risk for spontaneous intracranial hemorrhage.

Evaluation of patient with low platelets count

A)-History
Has the patient ever had a normal platelet count?
B) - Carefully review medication
C)-Ask about other conditions which may be associated with low platelets
. Liver Disease/hepatitis
. Thyroid Disease- both hypo and hyper-
. Infections: Viral, rickettsial
. Pregnancy
D)- Ask about other conditions which may be associated with ITP
. Lupus, CLL, Lymphoma
E)-Physical
. Evaluate for Lymphadenopathy and splenomegaly
. Look for stigmata of bleeding
. Blood blisters' and oral petechiae
F) Laboratory Data
. CBC, Platelet count, blood smear
. Check B12 and folate levels.
. Consider doing a bone marrow aspiration and biopsy.
. Exclude DIC, coagulation screens (PT/PTT/Fib/Dim)
. Shistocytes: Microangiopathy
. Blasts: Leukemia
. Microthrombocytopenia with immunodeficiency: Wiskott-Aldrich syndrome
. Inclusion granules in WBCs and albinism: Chediak-higachi

Pseudo thrombocytopenia

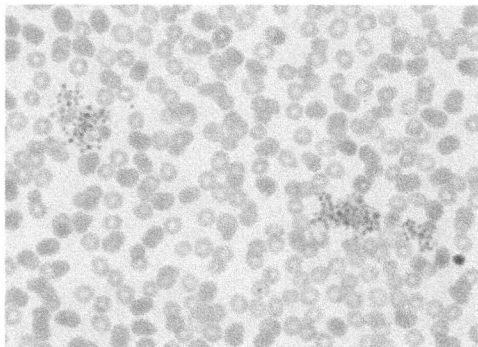

Pseudo thrombocytopenia is an erroneous diagnosis of thrombocytopenia that is the result of platelet clumping. Clumping results from collection of blood in EDTA (seen in 0.3% of patients). The clumping cause the automatic counters to undercount platelets and leads to the low platelet count.

This clumping is not known to be associated with any pathology. Reading the blood smear is the most common way to confirm the clumping and correct the platelet count.

Remember platelet numbers should be evaluated both by a hematology analyzer and by examination of a stained peripheral smear. Microscopic examination of the smear is essential to confirm thrombocytopenia (< 10 platelet per 1000x field without significant clumping of platelets, particularly in the feathered edge of the smear. If thrombocytopenia is an isolated finding without clinical signs, a separate sample should be evaluated to rule out spurious thrombocytopenia due to clumping or clot formation.

When enlarged platelets are easily found in the case of thrombocytopenia, peripheral blood destruction or utilization/consumption is likely since the bone marrow has the ability to produce platelets. The thrombocytopenia simply indicates that the bone marrow is not capable of keeping up with the peripheral destruction or utilization/consumption process. It no enlarged platelets are seen, decreased bone marrow production is much more likely, and detailed evaluation of the bone marrow with fine needle aspiration and possible core biopsy is essential to further characterize the thrombocytopenia.

Platelet satellitism refers to the formation of a platelet rosette that is characterized by four or more platelets on the cytoplasm margin of a neutrophil or band. If is an in –vitro phenomenon and is seen almost exclusively in smears prepared form EDTA-anticoagulant blood. Platelet satellitism has been reported in a variety of clinical conditions including Behcet's disease, lymphomas. However, its occurrence is not known to be associated with specific disorders. When pronounced, platelet satellitism may cause spuriously reduced platelet counts (pseudo-thrombocytopenia).

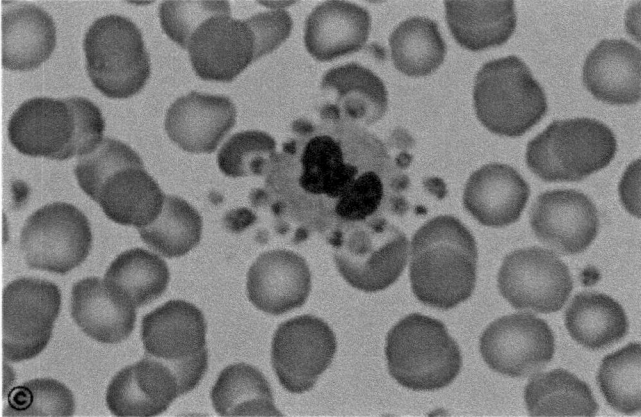

=Atlas of Hematology (Nivaldo Medeiros, MD). Used with permission=

Quantitative disorders

1- Thrombocytopenia usually is an acquired disorder due to:

Decreased production
Bone marrow impairment
Malignancies
Drugs, congenital conditions,
Increased destruction
Autoimmune hemolytic anemia
LE, ITP
Drugs sensitivity
Excessive consumption
DIC, TTP
Excessive dilution
Abnormal distribution
Sequestration by the spleen or the liver

2- Idiopathic Thrombocytopenic Purpura

Resulting from an unknown cause though it often follows a viral infection
Believed to be antibody mediated- may produce a specific platelet autoantibody.
Spontaneous remission occurs in approximately 80% of the cases.

3- Thrombocytosis

Temporary rise in the number of circulating platelets; secondary to stimulus. Platelets do have normal function.
Surgery, particularly splenectomy (since spleen normally contains 20 – 30% of the platelets)
Childbirth
Acute blood loss
Inflammation
Cancer
Exercises
Drugs
Normal function, return turnover level

4- Thrombocythemia
Due to uncontrolled overproduction. Platelets function is abnormal (Myeloproliferative disorders)

Qualitative disorders

1- Glanzmann's thrombasthenia is an inherited deficiency of thrombasthenin causing abnormal platelets aggregation, clot retraction and bleeding time.
2- Bernard-Soulier Syndrome is also inherited and is a deficiency of a membrane glycoprotein. Giant platelets with coarse granulation and vacuoles may be seen, platelet adhesion, aggregation, and bleeding time are abnormal.
3- Von Willebrand's disease is an inherited deficiency of the Willebrand factor (part of the factor VIII molecules), resulting in abnormal platelet adhesion and bleeding time as well as abnormal PTT (due to factor VIII defect).
4- Acquired qualitative defects may results from uremia (due to toxic effect on platelets) drugs (aspirin, certain antibiotics, alcohol), viral infections.
5- Gray platelets syndromes (deficient alpha granules).
6- Delta storage pool deficiency (deficient dense granules).

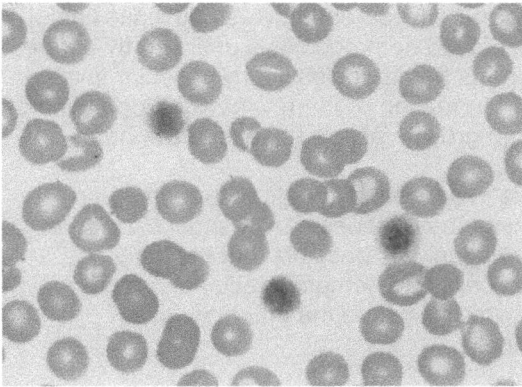

PART SIX: BONE MARROW ASPIRATION

Bone Marrow Development

The hematopoietic stem cell that gives rise to all formed elements of the blood has a peripatetic life cycle. It travels to multiple sites as embryogenesis provides appropriate microenvironments. Early in development, stem cells located in the dorsal mesentery near the primitive aorta migrate through loose connective tissues to the yolk sac. The progeny rapidly divide and develop into precursors of erythroid, myeloid, monocytoid, lymphoid, megakaryocytic and endothelial cell types. Hematopoietic, lymphoreticular and endothelial cells are interdependent and intimately associated as they divide and differentiate within the organizing yolk sac. Blood cells undergo multiple obligatory interactions with endothelial cells and stromal components as they travel from the yolk sac to new sites of hematopoiesis or as they enter and leave the interstices of non-lymphoid tissues.

The location of hematopoiesis shifts from the yolk sac to the developing live where clonal hematopoietic colonies expand in close proximity to endoderm-derived hepatocytes and sinus lining cells (Rossant et al, 1986). The liver remains the major site of fetal hematopoiesis until shortly before birth when stem cells travel by blood to the spleen that supports hematopoiesis until vascular invasion of cartilaginous bones begins the process of ossification and formation of marrow cavity. Population of the developing marrow may be facilitated by chemotactic and growth factors released from bone matrix and connective tissue cells.

The bone marrow remains the primary site of hematopoiesis in adults until death, although some hematopoietic stem cells in connective tissue of the abdominal mesenteries can be induced to form hematopoietic colonies by cytokines released during inflammation. It is possible that the initial development of the blood-forming tissues, migration of stem cells and hematopoietic precursors may be controlled by receptor-ligand interactions and cytokines which regulate the entry, survival, proliferation and differentiation of hematopoietic progenitor cells.

Adult Bone Marrow

The bone marrow is the site of origin of all T- and B- cells, mononuclear phagocytes, platelets, erythrocytes, and other leukocytes in the adult. The aggregate volume and weight surpasses that of the liver. The bone marrow is divided into wedge-shaped hematopoietic compartments filled with proliferating and differentiating blood cells in connective tissue matrices bordered by venous sinuses. Monoclonal antibody-detected phenotypes and reactions for enzymes expressed at stages of differentiation show progressive hematopoietic cell maturation from immaturity in areas near bone to full differentiation at the vascular interface. Radial venous sinuses that merge with a central longitudinal vein are major components of mouse bone marrow structure. Blood cells complete maturation immediately adjacent to the dilated vascular channels into which they will emigrate.

The microenvironment of the bone marrow is produced by a unique endothelium and connective tissue stroma combined with locally deposited cytokines that regulate compartmentalization, proliferation and differentiation of hematopoietic stem cells. Adventitial cells lining the interstitial side of venous sinuses extend cytoplasmic processes into the hematopoietic compartment, making contact with numerous cells. Stromal cells are essential for regulation of hematopoietic cell development. In situ hybridization with probes for allotypic markers proved that stromal cells are capable of transferring the hematopoietic microenviroment of the donor after allogeneic bone marrow transplantation. One way marrow stroma assists hematopoiesis is through the glycosaminoglycan-rich extracellular matrix that binds and distributes growth factors such as granulocyte-myelocyte colony stimulating factor (GM-CSF).

The vascular system of the marrow is anatomically closed with little leakage. Mature cells are transported from interstitium to venous sinus through cytoplasmic apertures in the endothelium. Location of immature cells at sites far removed from the venous sinuses requires that maturing cells acquire sufficient motility to approach the blood vascular interface. Accidental release of cycling hematopoietic cells is prevented because motility is suppressed during cell division. Tidal blood flow through dilated venous sinuses gently supports peripheralization of hematopoietic cells that leave marrow compartments to lodge in other environments as soon as they are able. The marrow monitors and controls release of hematopoietic cells to the periphery by mechanisms that are still unknown. Noradrenergic nerve fibers penetrate into the bone marrow with arteries and follow them deep into regions within the cellular marrow adjacent to the central venous sinus. A few fine varicosities branch

131

from the perivascular plexus to supply aggregates of hematopoietic cells that lay within areas of marrow close to venous sinuses. Little is known of the function of bone marrow innervation outside of its assumed role in controlling blood flow.

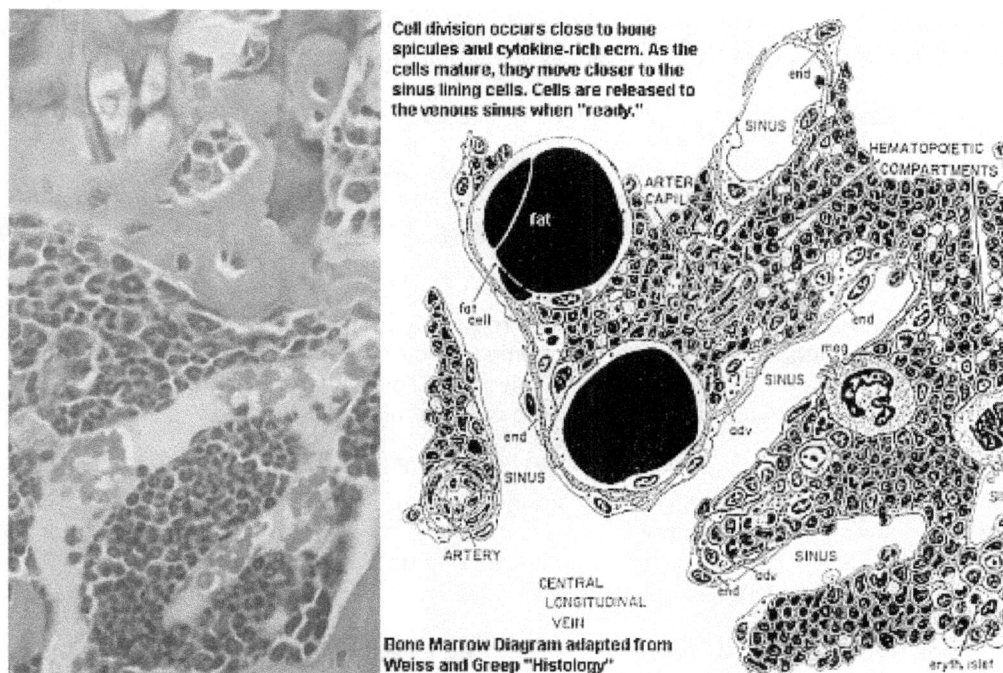

Cell division occurs close to bone spicules and cytokine-rich ecm. As the cells mature, they move closer to the sinus lining cells. Cells are released to the venous sinus when "ready."

Bone Marrow Diagram adapted from Weiss and Greep "Histology"

=Immunology Lecture (Dr. Art Anderson's). Use with permission=

Two different types of technic are available for the study of bone marrow. These two methods give information which is supplementary rather than complementary:
1- A small amount of bone marrow may be obtained by needle aspiration, and from this material a thin smear can be prepared and stained with Wright's stain.
2- Fixed thick sections of bone marrow stained with hematoxylin and eosin may be prepared from material obtained needle aspiration or from material obtained by surgical biopsy of the bone marrow.

In thin smears stained with Wright's stain, individual cells can be identified and
Fine morphologic details can be observed.
In thick sections identification of individual cell types is not possible. On the other hand, the histologic pattern and cellularity of the marrow can be observed in thick sections but not in thin smears. Judging the cellularity of the marrow from thin smears may be misleading.

The disadvantages of surgical biopsy of the bone marrow are that it is a more complicated procedure than needle aspiration from the standpoint of convenience to the patient, danger involved, expense and time, and it involves the coordination efforts of the internist, surgeon and pathologist. Preparations of thick sections from aspirated material are usually quite satisfactory.

Cytologic study of cells aspirated from bone marrow may be of great value in the diagnosis of hematologic disease and in the understanding of the pathologic physiology of the hematopoietic tissues. Because of this, it is fortunate that the marrow cavity of many bones is easily accessible with a minimal amount of discomfort or danger to the patient, and that marrow can be obtained with only moderate experience and skill on the part of the operator. Unfortunately, the procedure is of limited value and will not solve all types of hematologic problems. Therefore, it is important to have clearly in mind the situations where marrow examination can be expected to yield crucial information which cannot be extracted from the history, physical examination, or examination of the blood.

Indications and Limitations

Examination of thin smears of bone marrow is most helpful in those conditions in which diagnosis cells are observed in the bone marrow but are not usually present in the blood. These conditions are:
1- Multiple myeloma.
2- Tumor cells metastazing from prostate, breast, lung, kidney and others tissues.
3- Gaucher's disease.
4- Niemann-pick disease.
5- Kala-azar.
6- Histoplasmosis.
7- Megaloblastic anemia.

A second situation in which examination of thin smears is frequently helpful is in the group of conditions characterized by pancytopenia. If the pancytopenia is the result of leukemia in the "aleukemic" form, marrow examination will permit an unequivocal diagnosis to be made. Marrow examination is particularly helpful in ruling out the diagnosis of leukemia in those patients with pancytopenia from some other cause.

Examination of bone marrow smears is of little or no diagnostic value in microcytic hypochromic anemia, post hemorrhagic anemia, hemolytic anemia, hemorrhagic disorders, lymphoma, anemia of nephritis, anemia of infection, polycythemia, myelosclerosis, infectious mononucleosis, chronic myelogenous leukemia, or in chronic lymphocytic leukemia.

Paraffin sections made from particles of bone marrow removed by aspiration are particularly of value in patients with undiagnosed hematologic disease in disclosing the presence of granulomatous lesions. Such lesions have been found in the bone marrow of patients with tuberculosis, sarcoidosis, brucellosis, Histoplasmosis, infectious mononucleosis and malignant lymphoma. Sections are also of value:
1- In detecting the invasion of marrow by myeloma cells, carcinoma cells and Gaucher cells.
2- In studying the cellularity and histologic architecture of the marrow.

The cellularity of the bone marrow is of particular interest in the diagnosis of aplastic anemia and the histologic pattern is of interest in the diagnosis of myelofibrosis.

The value of bone marrow examination is limited in diseases which involves the marrow in a patchy fashion since the lesion may be missed completely. This statement applies to both thin smears and thick sections, but, of course, more to the former than to the latter. In some patients, no marrow at all will be obtained after repeated attempts at various sites. Furthermore, "dry taps" are more common in patients with granulomatous lesions, myelofibrosis, and metastatic carcinoma than in normal subjects or patients with myeloid or erythroid hyperplasia. This is because these lesions are frequently associated with some fibrosis of the marrow and the cells remain fixed in the marrow cavity. Surgical biopsy of the marrow is indicated in those patients in whom such lesions are suspected and in whom one or more "dry taps" have been obtained.

The only contraindication to marrow aspiration is in hemophilia and related disorders.
Although marrow examination potentially may permit infection or serious hemorrhage, these two complications rarely occur when proper technic is used. Excessive bleeding sometimes occurs in patients with thrombocytopenia but it can usually be satisfactorily controlled by pressure over the site of the puncture. The only serious complication of marrow aspiration is cardiac tamponade when the lower plate of the sternum is perforated as a result of inexperience or carelessness.

Technic

The physician or pathologist will perform the actual procedure and the laboratorian assists. A special aspiration needle is used, usually a Jamshidi or Westerman-Jensen needle. These needles allow the collection of bone tissue and marrow. The site of the biopsy is selected and the subcutaneous are anesthetized.

The needle is then inserted to periostum and additional anesthesia is injected. The next step is an incision to facilitate the insertion of the biopsy needle. The biopsy needle is advanced through the bone marrow into the medullary (marrow) cavity. Approximately 2.0 ml of marrow is aspirated using a 10 ml syringe. The marrow is ejected onto a watch glass or Petri dish and slides are immediately made. True marrow is characterized by the presence of spicules, tiny pale grey-white fragments in the blood. A minimum of then slides should be made.

Site of Puncture

Various sites may be used for the puncture.

1- The sternum is very satisfactory and is the most commonly used site in adults. Marrow will be found at this site even in infants of one to two years of age. The chief disadvantage in using the sternum is that the patient can observe the procedure and may have considerable apprehension due to the proximity of the sternum to the heart. In children the sternal site is less satisfactory than other sites because of the difficulty in completely immobilizing the chest during the procedure, and because the sternal-marrow cavity is quite shallow and the possibility of perforation into mediastinum, although remote, is always present. When the sternum is used, the upper portion of the bone, between the second and third ribs in the midline, is most suitable, and the needle is inserted perpendicular to the bone with the guard set at depth of 1 cm. for adults or at 0.2 to 0.6 cm. for a child.

2- Iliac crest puncture is extremely satisfactory in infants and children and in apprehensive adults and has the advantage that no vital centers are near the site of puncture. The patient is placed on his back or side and the bone marrow needle is inserted into the ilium from the lateral approach about 2 cm. below the anterior superior spine.

3- Spinous process puncture may be performed with the patient in the sitting position or lying face downward. The lumbar and lower thoracic vertebrae are the most satisfactory. With the guard set at 1.5 to 2.0 cm. the needle is inserted directly into the end of the spinous process, midway between the upper and the lower border. Occasionally the needle must be advanced a few mm. at a time to secure marrow.

4- Tibia is the safest bone to puncture in children from birth to 4 to 5 years. This site also has advantage of being easily immobilized. The needle with the guard set at a bout 2 cm. is inserted just below the tubercle on the medial or anterior aspect. The bone may be quite hard in the older infant and considerable pressure may be necessary to penetrate into the marrow cavity.

Aspiration

The procedure should be discussed with either the patient or the parent or both in order to prevent undue apprehension. If after this the patient is still apprehensive, it is well to administer a sedative a half-hour before the procedure. The operator should scrub as for any surgical procedure. Sterile gloves are desirable but not necessary. The skin is shaved if necessary, washed, and cleaned with iodine and alcohol or other suitable antiseptics. The area may be draped with sterile towels, although if care is taken, this is unnecessary. The skin, subcutaneous tissues, and finally the periostum of the bone are infiltrated with procaine. After a suitable time interval the adjustable guard on the special marrow needle is set at a suitable depth and the needle is inserted into the bone with a rotating or boring motion. A "give" is felt when the marrow cavity is entered. The needle is then passed 1 or 2 mm. into the cavity. The stylet is removed from the needle and a dry, sterile, tight fitting 5 ml. syringe is attached. Firm but gentle pressure is applied to the plunger of the syringe until the first drop of marrow appears. If the needle is in the marrow cavity, momentary pain is usually experienced by the patient when suction is applied. If no marrow appears, it is necessary to replace the stylet and move the needle. As soon as one drop of marrow appears in the syringe, the syringe is removed and passed to an assistant who then prepares several smears. If desired, a second dry sterile syringe is then attached and 1 ml. of marrow is withdrawn. After removal of the marrow needle, a small, tight, sterile dressing is applied.

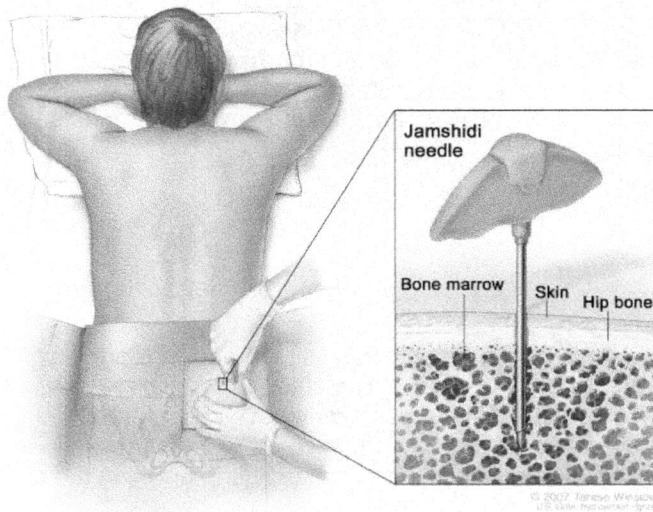

Courtesy of the National Cancer Institute

Preparation of Thin smears

From the several drops of marrow in the first syringe, thin smears are prepared and stained with Wright's stain or Giemsa stain, except that the fixing time and the staining time are increased to about twice that required for blood. Bone marrow smears may also be stained by the myeloperoxidase method, alkaline Phosphatase method or Prussian blue method.

The marrow obtained in the second syringe is placed in a vial containing a small amount of either EDTA or heparin. After proper mixing, a hematocrit tube is filled and centrifuged for 5 minutes at 1000 R.P.M. Four layers may then be distinguished: fat, plasma, nucleated cells, and erythrocytes. Measurement of the volume of these layers can be pipetted off and smears made from the nucleated cell layer diluted with and equal volume of plasma. In this manner concentrated material can be obtained from the nucleated cell layer. This is of particular value when the direct smears are relatively acellular or when a particular abnormal cell type is present in small numbers.

The marrow need not be concentrated routinely.

Peripheral Smear   Wright's stained   Bone Marrow Aspirate

Bone Marrow smears examination

Low magnification

All preparations should be examined first under low power.
1- Observe the various regions of each smear.
2- Define bone marrow cellularity.
3- Define the average number of megakacarycoytes.
4- Search for rare but normal bone marrow cells, usually large in size or those demonstrate specific content.
5- Search for rare and abnormal cells, including: neoplastic cells, abnormal histiocytes (hemophagocytic syndromes, storage disorders).

6- Overview of bone marrow cells: normal bone marrow shows cells that are heterogeneous in size, shape, and color, a homogeneous aspect (all cells look identical), or predominance of one color (many cells are deeply blue for example) hypothesize an abnormal bone marrow.
7- Look for the parts of the smear that are spread at best: those parts of smears will be examined at high magnification.

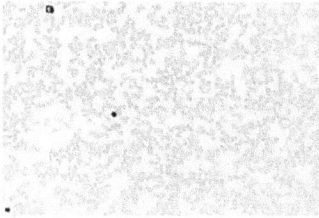
Cellularity=0

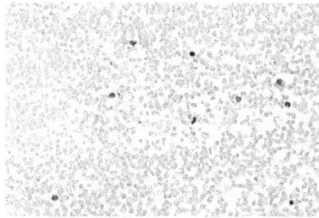
Cellularity= 1+

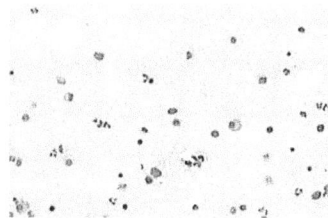
cellularity= 2+

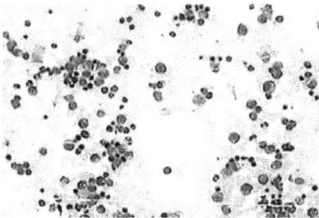
Cellularity= 3+

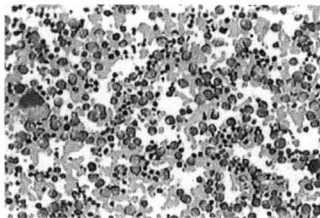
Cellularity= 4+

http://bioimage.free.fr/hem_image/richesse_moelle.htm

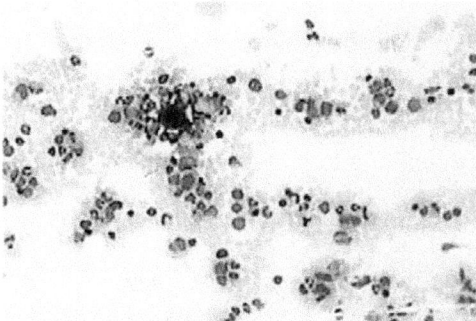
Megakacarycoytes= 1+

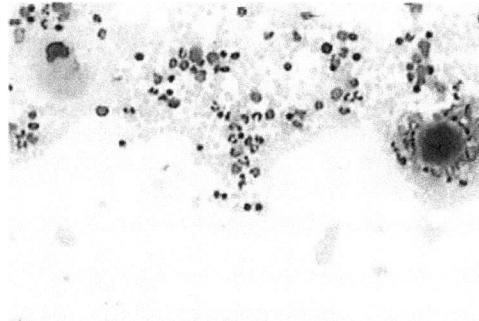
Megakacarycoytes= 2+

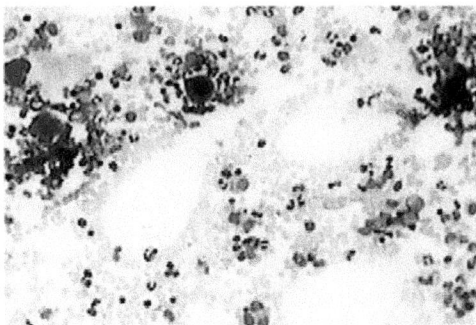

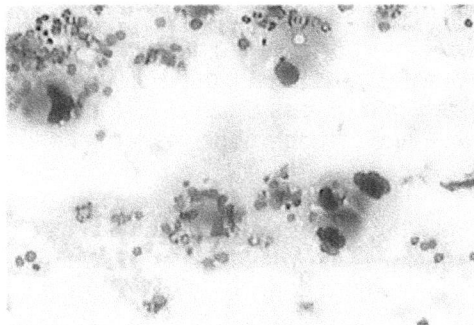

136

Megakaryocytes= 3+   Megakaryocytes= 4+

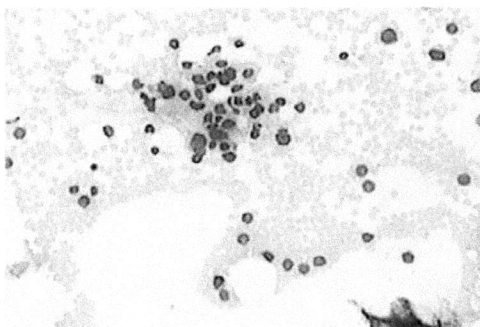

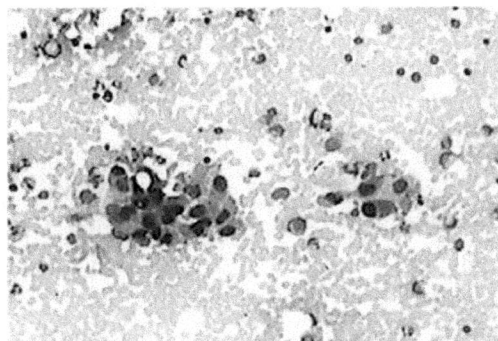

= Metastatic cells =

http://bioimage.free.fr/hem_image/richesse_moelle.htm

High magnification

After the entire area of bone marrow smear has been examined with the low power objective, a good area for detailed examination under the oil-immersion objective is selected. The cells in this area should be almost but not quite touching one another. Cells cannot be identified in an area which is too thick. In the areas which are too thin, the morphology of the cells may be disturbed. Selection of the appropriate area to make the detailed examination is one of the most important steps in the examination of marrow. This should be done with great care.

Morphological examination

1- Look for the cells you can easily recognize: Polymorphonuclears, lymphocytes (size, color, criteria that define such cells). This step gives information on the staining: if staining is not optimal, you will have to modify more or less sharply criteria that define each bone marrow cell, at least color of their various components.
2- Look at cells from the granulocytes series, and define criteria that allow the definition of each morphological stage
3- Look at erythroblastic series, and once again define criteria that allow the definition of each morphological stage.
4- Look at very cell you encounter on the smear. At least the following results must be obtained: morphology of cells from each lineage: normal or abnormal? Describe any morphological abnormality (do these abnormalities help to give rise to a specific diagnostic?)Any abnormal cells? Morphology?

Full bone marrow count

All cells you see must be counted, but some elements are not: Mitotic cells (in most instances cell lineage is rather easy to ascertain, but morphological stage of differentiation it is more difficult to determine). Lysed cells, or destroyed by spreading, or naked nuclei. Rare cells, including normal (mast cells, osteoclasts, and osteoblasts) or abnormal ones (metastatic cells)

In certain circumstances it may desirable to perform a differential cell count. This is done on a total of 300 to 500 cells and the results for each cell type are recorded as a percent of total cells counted.

Calculation of the myeloid: erythroid (M: E) ratio may be helpful. This is done by dividing the total number of myeloid cells (myeloblasts, promyelocytes, myelocytes, metamyelocytes and PMNs) counted by the total number of erythroid (pronormoblasts and normoblasts) cells counted. If information concerning only the M: E ratio is desired, the procedure may be shortened by grouping all of the myeloid cells into one group and the erythroid cells into a second group. The nonmyeloid cells may be ignored and the particular stage of maturation of the myeloid and erythroid cells may be ignored.

Eventually, comments are done (bone marrow within quantitative and qualitative ranges, or any abnormal finding) and whenever possible the diagnosis you can perform, or proposals for convenient interpretation of your findings.

In certain instances it is instructive to plot a "maturation" curve for the myeloid series of cells. This is done by adding up the total number of cells counted in the series and calculating the percentage of each cell type within the series. The percentages are then plotted as illustrated.

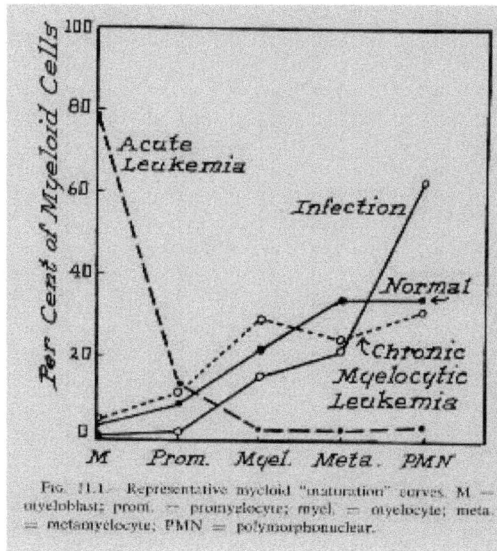

FIG. 11.1.—Representative myeloid "maturation" curves. M = myeloblast; prom. = promyelocyte; myel. = myelocyte; meta. = metamyelocyte; PMN = polymorphonuclear.

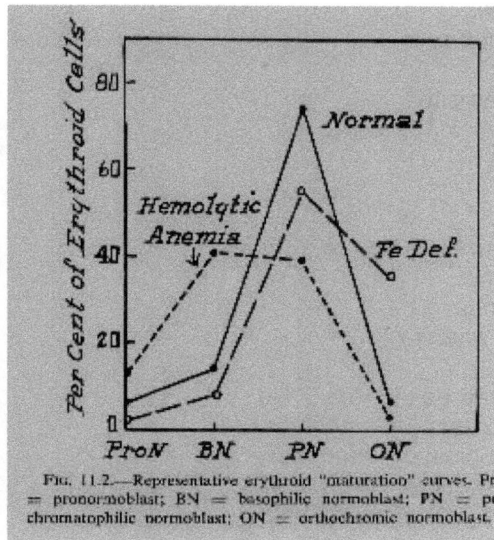

FIG. 11.2.—Representative erythroid "maturation" curves. Pro = pronormoblast; BN = basophilic normoblast; PN = polychromatophilic normoblast; ON = orthochromic normoblast.

A "maturation" curve for the erythroid series of cells may also be obtained.

Normal bone marrow

Neutrophil series		40-60%
Myeloblast	0.5-3.0	
Promyelocytes	1-5	
Myelocytes	5-15	
Metamyelocytes	15-20	
Band cells	10-15	
Polymorphs	25-35	
Eosinophil series	0-5	3%
Basophil series	0-1	1%
Erythroblastic series		15-30%
Proerythroblasts	1-2	
Basophilic erythroblasts	2-5	
Intermediate erythroblasts	6-12	
Late (orthochromatic)	6-10	
Lymphocytes	5-15	5-15%
Plasma cells	1-3	2%
Monocytes	1-5	3%
Megacaryocytes	Present	

Interpretation of thin smears

The normal myeloid-erythroid ratio for adults is 2 to 5:1. The pattern in infants and children is somewhat different from this and varies according to age. The myeloid-erythroid ratio is low at birth (1.8:1), increases rapidly during the first two weeks to values as high as 11:1, and then gradually decreases to 3:1 during the first year. Lymphocytes are low at birth as compared with normal adult values. During the first weeks of life, the lymphocytes increase in number to values as high as 40 percent. They then gradually decrease during the first and second years, thereafter reaching the adults values.

I. Presence of cells which are not normally found in marrow
    1- Myeloma cells
    2- Carcinoma cells
    3- Gaucher cells
    4- Niemann-Pick cells

II. Presence of Parasites
    1-Lishmania
    2-Histoplasma
    3- Malaria

III. M: E Ratio Normal (2-5:1) or Variable
    1- Normal marrow
    2- Aplastic anemia
    3- Myelophtisic anemia

IV. M: E Ration Decreased (0.5-2:1)
    A- Due to Increased in erythroid cells
        1- Normoblastic Hyperplasia
            - Post hemorrhagic anemia
            - Iron Deficiency anemia
            - Hemolytic anemia
            - Cirrhosis of liver
            - Polycythemia Vera
            - Lead Poisoning and thalassemia
        2- Megaloblastic hyperplasia
    B- Due to Decreased in Myeloid cells
        1- Agranulocytosis

V. M: E Ratio Increased (5+:1)
    A. Due to Increased in Myeloid cells
        1- Acute Myeloblastic leukemia
        2-Chronic Myelocytic Leukemia
        3- Infections
        4- Leukemoid reactions
    B. Due to Decreased in erythroid cells (RARE)
        1- Hypoplastic anemia of infancy
        2- Erythroid hypoplastic anemia in adults

VI. Increase in Non Myeloid cells
        1- Acute Lymphocytic leukemia
        2- Chronic Lymphocytic leukemia
        3- Aplastic Anemia
        4- Infectious Mononucleosis

Bone Marrow Biopsy

Using a trephine (Jamshidi) a small cylinder of bone marrow (1,2-1,5 mm in diameter and 15 to 30 mm in length) is obtained. This fragment is immersed into a fixative solution (neutral formalin), treated next with an acidic solution to remove calcium from bone, and eventually dehydrated and embedded in paraffin.

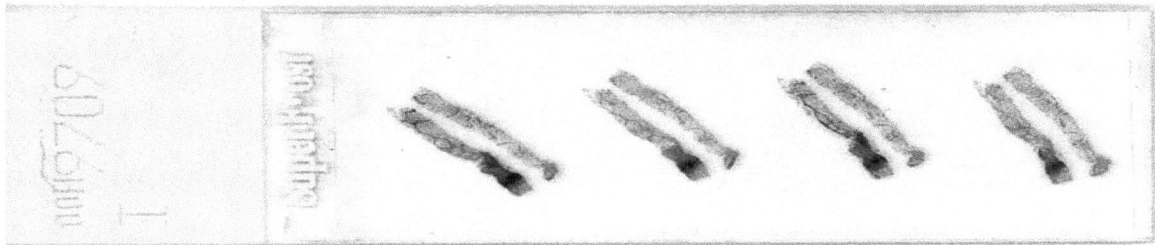

Bone marrow trephine biopsy: four sections, each broken in two parts (H & E staining)

= HEMATOCELL (Prof Marc Zandecki). Used with permission=

Marrow hematopoietic cellularity ranges from 30-70%. Fat cells make up the remainder of the readily visible cells, though fibroblasts and endothelial or sinus lining cells are also present.

Immature myeloid cells are located along the bone trabeculae, with maturing neutrophils, eosinophils, etc., located more centrally, or away from bone.

Erythroid and megakaryocytic elements are found in the central areas, often near marrow sinuses. Erythroid precursors tend to cluster in red cell islands.

Megakaryocytes are relatively few in number.

Lymphocytes, plasma cells, mast cells, and macrophages are scattered about in small numbers.

Bone trabeculae are moderately thick and have only thin rims of osteoid. Occasional osteoblasts and rare osteoclasts are seen (osteoclasts & osteoblasts are common in children).

Examination of the bone marrow includes assessment of hematopoietic tissue cellularity, with an estimate of the relative proportion for each lineage.

The cellularity varies with location of biopsy.
1- The vertebral body is about 10% more cellular than iliac crest.
2- The sternum can show variable cellularity relative to iliac crest.
3- The rib tends to have a lower cellularity than the iliac crest.

Cellularity of hematopoietic tissue as percent of marrow space:
1. Normally most nucleated cells are hematopoietic.
2. Infiltration by lymphocytes, plasma cells, tumor cells, etc. can reduce relative percent of hematopoietic cellularity.

Cellularity:

1- Decreases with age.
2- Combined effect of decreased hematopoietic tissue and reduction in bone.
3- Adipose tissue fills the nonhematpoietic marrow cavity.

4- May be considerable affected by technical factors.
5- Cellularity less than 20% tends to indicate hypoplasia, except in elderly.
6- Cellularity more than 80% tends to indicate hyperplasia, except in patients under 20 years of age.
7- A cellularity of 25- 75% is usually normal cellularity for patients 20-70 years of age.

Myeloid-to-Erythroid Ratio

3. An increase ratio is seen in granulocytic hyperplasia (leukocytosis, myeloproliferative disorders) or depressed erythropoiesis.
4. A decreases ratio is seen in depressed leucopoiesis or erythroid hyperplasia.

In bone marrow smears of good cellularity, normally 1-3 megacaryocytes are seen per 100x (10xobjective, 10x ocular) field.

Normal bone marrow Biopsy

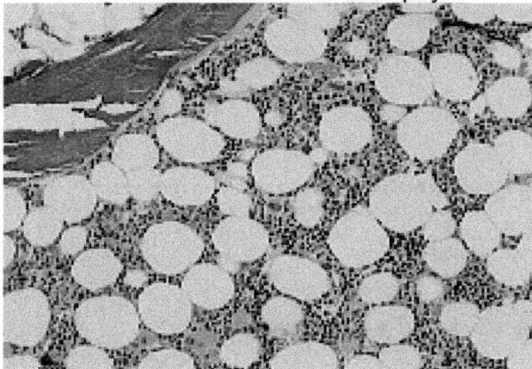

©2007. Rector and visitors of the University of Virginia
Charles E. Hess, M.D. and Lindsey Krstic, B.A. Used with permission

Miscellaneous conditions

Metastatic Carcinoma

In the present day, inspection of the bone marrow is considered one of the most valuable diagnostic tools to evaluate hematologic disorders. Indications have included the diagnosis, staging, and therapeutic monitoring for lymphoproliferative disorders such as chronic lymphocytic leukemia (CLL), Hodgkin and Non-Hodgkin lymphoma, hairy cell leukemia, myeloproliferative disorders, and multiple myeloma. Furthermore, evaluation of cytopenia, thrombocytosis, leukocytosis, anemia, and iron status can be performed.

The application of bone marrow analysis has grown to incorporate other, nonhematologic, conditions. For example, in the investigation for fever of unknown origin (FUO), specifically in those patients with autoimmune deficiency syndrome (AIDS), the marrow may reveal the presence of microorganisms, such as tuberculosis, Mycobacterium avium intracellular (MAI) infections, Histoplasmosis, leishmaniasis, and other disseminated fungal infections. Furthermore, the diagnosis of storage diseases (e.g. Niemann-Pick disease and Gaucher disease), as well as the assessment for metastatic carcinoma and granulomatous diseases (e.g., sarcoidosis) can be performed

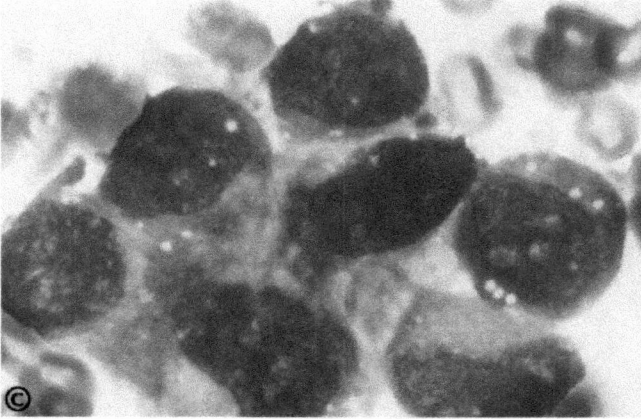

MEDULLOBLASTOMA (BONE MARROW)
=Atlas of Hematology (Nivaldo Medeiros, MD). Used with permission=

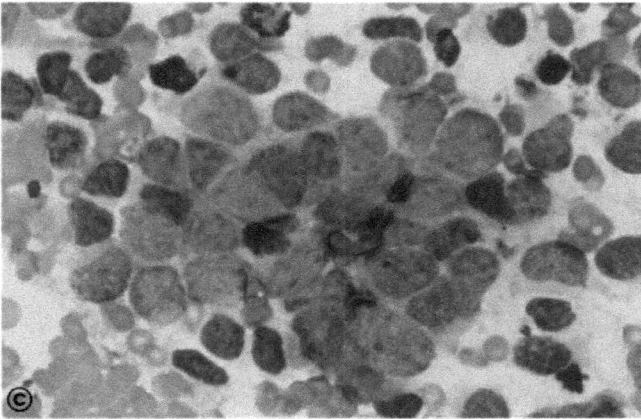

NEUROBLASTOMA (BONE MARROW)
=Atlas of Hematology (Nivaldo Medeiros, MD). Used with permission=

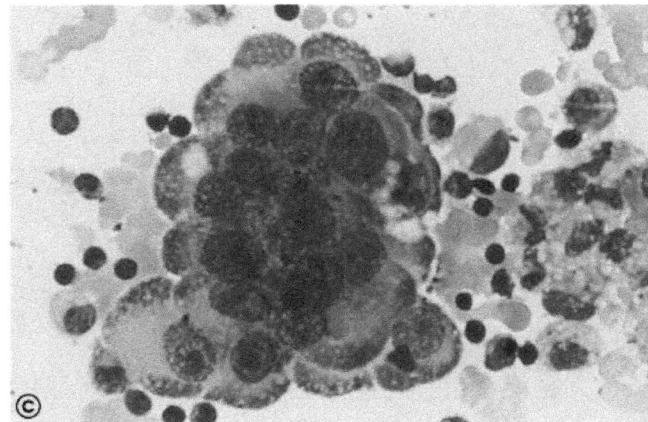

BREAST CARCINOMA (BONE MARROW)

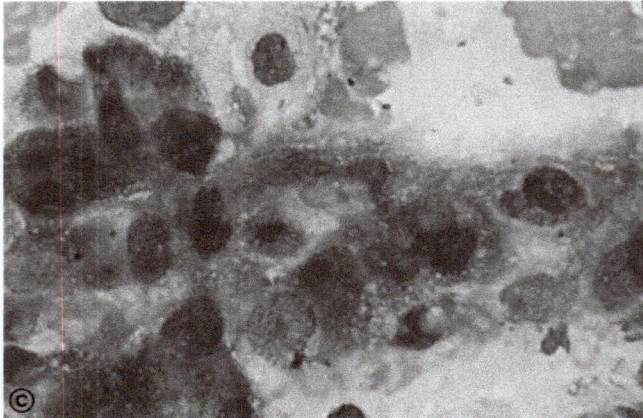

PROSTATE CARCINOMA (BONE MARROW)
=Atlas of Hematology (Nivaldo Medeiros, MD). Used with permission=

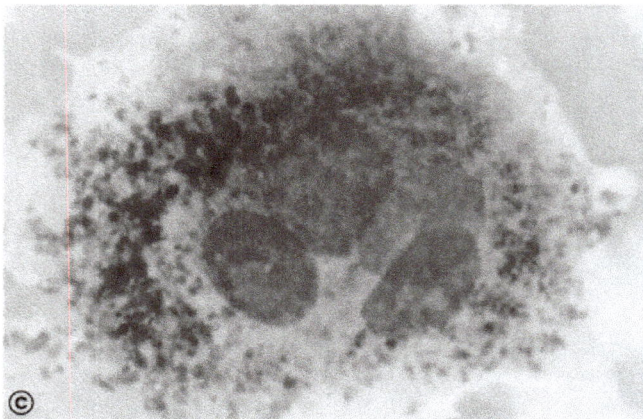

MELANOMA (BONE MARROW)
=Atlas of Hematology (Nivaldo Medeiros, MD). Used with permission=

Parvovirus B19

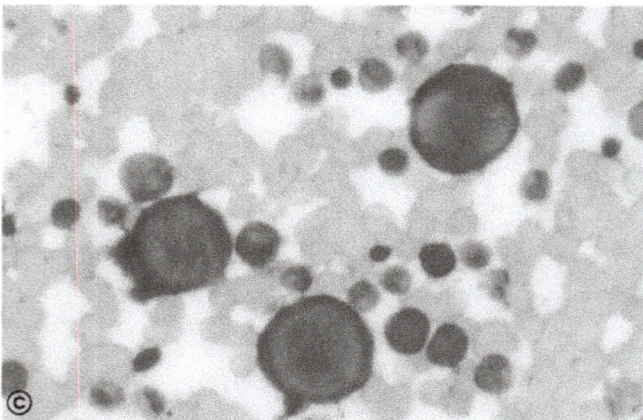

PARVOVIRUSES (BONE MARROW)
=Atlas of Hematology (Nivaldo Medeiros, MD). Used with permission=

Normal cells

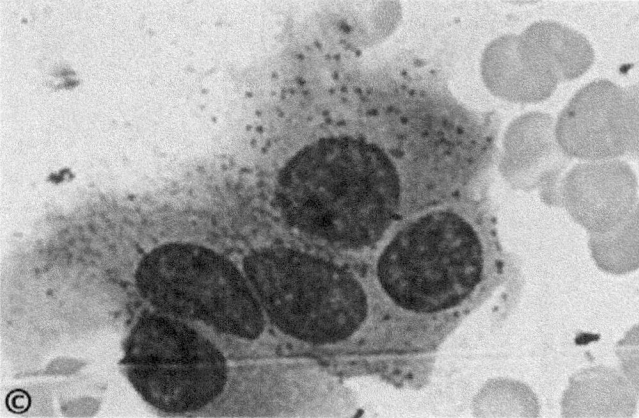

OSTEOCLAST (BONE MARROW)
=Atlas of Hematology (Nivaldo Medeiros, MD). Used with permission=

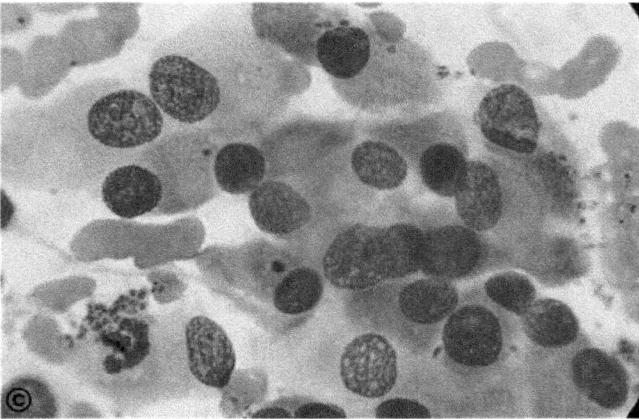

OSTEOBLAST (BONE MARROW)
=Atlas of Hematology (Nivaldo Medeiros, MD). Used with permission=

Parasites

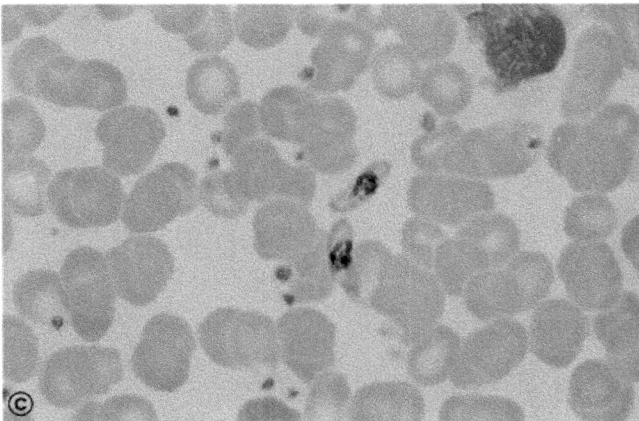

P. Falciparum
=Atlas of Hematology (Nivaldo Medeiros, MD). User with permission=

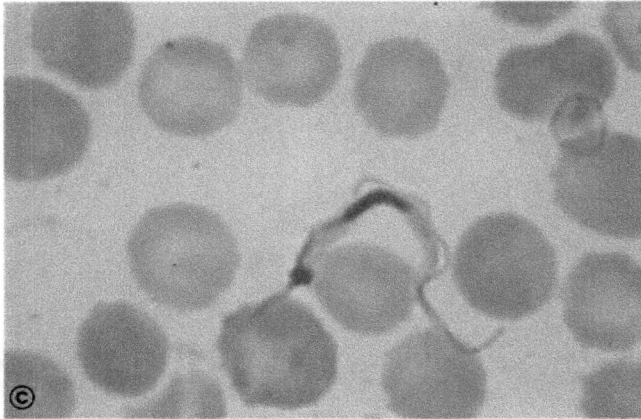

Trypanosome
=Atlas of Hematology (Nivaldo Medeiros, MD). Used with permission=

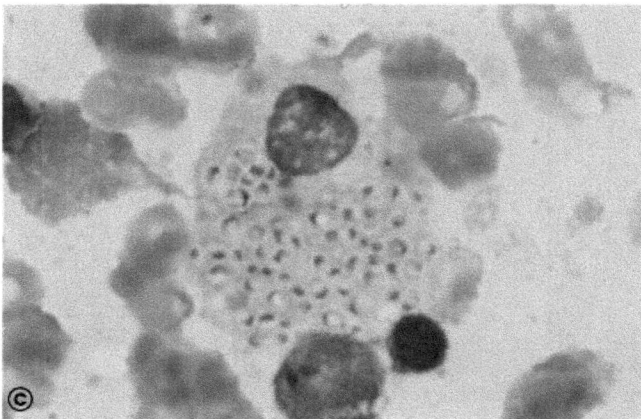

Leishmania
=Atlas of Hematology (Nivaldo Medeiros, MD). Used with permission=

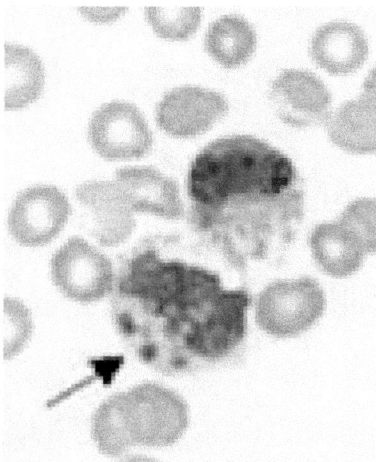

Human monocytic ehrlichiosis

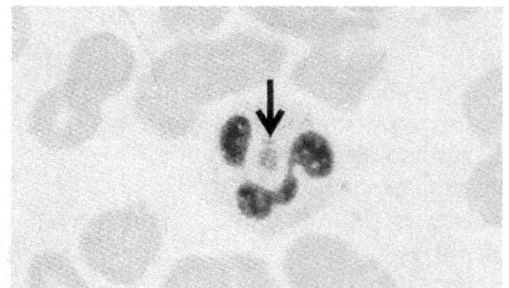

Human granulocytic

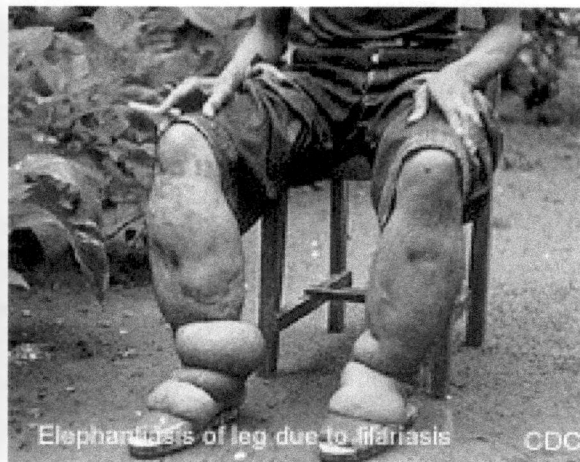

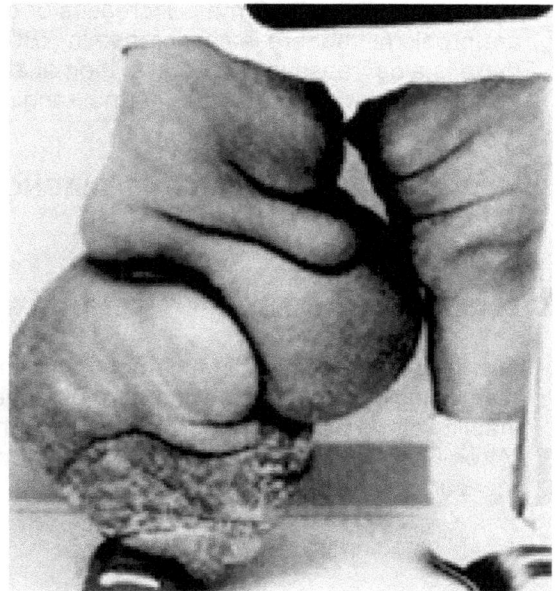

Elephantiasis/Filariasis

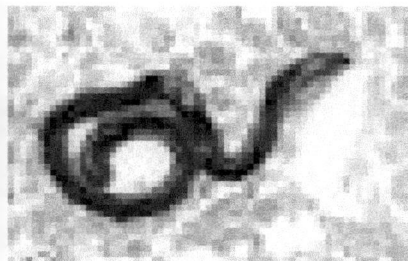

Brugia Malayi

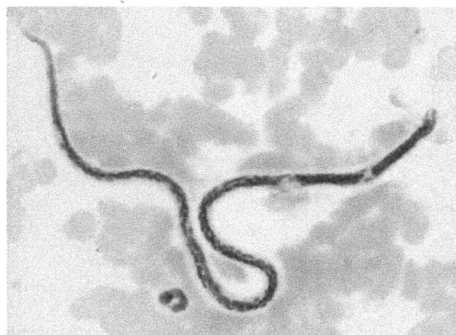

Wuchereria Bancrofti

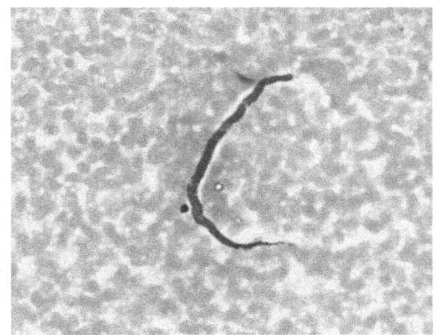

Loa-Loa

= Hematopathology (Pr Nguyen-Nghia). Used with permission

PART SEVEN: APPROACH TO THE DIAGNOSIS OF ANEMIA

Normally the number of erythrocytes and their hemoglobin content remains at a physiologically constant mass. This is designated as RBCs mass. RBCs primary role is to provide oxygen for the cells of the body. If the RBC mass increases or decreases to values outside the normal range, then there are problems. If there is an increase in RBC mass, then polycythemia (erythrocytosis) is suspect. If there is a decrease in RBC mass, then anemia is suspect. The goal of the laboratory is to detect and identify the deviation from the normal range of values as anemia or not.

CHAPTER ONE: DIAGNOSIS AND CLINICAL CONSIDERATIONS

Clinical Considerations

Definition of Anemia

Anemia is due to bleeding, hemolysis or impaired RBC production. Anemia is simply a reduction in the hemoglobin level below the normal range for a population of the same age and sex. Anemia is the inability of the blood to supply the tissue with adequate oxygen for proper metabolic function.
Anemia is a decrease in the whole body red cell mass. Unfortunately there is no good way to rapidly measure this value.

Misleading in:

1- Pregnancy
2- Hemoconcentration
3- Hemodilution

In working up a patient for anemia there are some very basic principles that must always be kept in mind. First and foremost is the principle that anemia is not a disease. It is a manifestation of an underling disease. The goal is to identify the specific cause and treat it appropriately. In the ideal situation, the best definition of anemia is: significantly decrease hemoglobin compared to the baseline that was previously establish for the patient when they were in a stable, well, baseline state.

Based on venous hemoglobin:

1- Adult males   Hgb = <13.5g/dl.
2- Adult females Hgb= <11.5g/dl.
3- Pregnant women Hgb= <10.5g/dl.
4- Ages 10-13 Hgb=<12g/dl.
5- <Age 10 Hgb=< 11g/dl.

Grading systems for anemia

The severity of anemia can range from mild to life threatening. The National Cancer Institute and Cooperative Oncology Groups use a grading system for anemia. Within normal limits (WNL) hemoglobin (Hgb) values are 12.0-16.0 g/dl for women and 14.0-18.0 g/dl for men. There are four grades of anemia, indicating increasing severity:

Grade 1= mild (10.0 to < WNL).
Grade 2= moderate (8.0-10.0).
Grade 3= serious/severe (6.5-7.9).
Grade 4= life-threatening (< 6.5).

Cardiovascular Adaptation in Anemia

The main consequence of anemia is tissue hypoxia. If anemia has developed rapidly, there may not be adequate time for compensatory adjustments to take place, so there is a sudden marked contraction of intravascular volume, resulting in postural hypotension, fall in cardiac output, shunting of blood from skin to central organs. If anemia has slowly installation, many adaptations occur for the oxygen maintenance, such s increasing of plasmatic volume and right shift of the oxygen-hemoglobin dissociation curve.

* Oxygen is carried in blood:

1 - Bound to hemoglobin (98.5% of all oxygen in the blood)
2 - Dissolved in the plasma (1.5%)

Because almost all oxygen in the blood is transported by hemoglobin, the relationship between the concentration (partial pressure) of oxygen and hemoglobin saturation (the % of hemoglobin molecules carrying oxygen) is an important one.

* Hemoglobin saturation:

1- Extent to which the hemoglobin in blood is combined with O2
2- Depends on PO2 of the blood:

The relationship between oxygen levels and hemoglobin saturation is indicated by the oxygen-hemoglobin dissociation (saturation) curve (in the graph below). You can see that at high partial pressures of O2 (above about 40 mm Hg), hemoglobin saturation remains rather high (typically about 75 - 80%). This rather flat section of the oxygen-hemoglobin dissociation curve is called the 'plateau.'

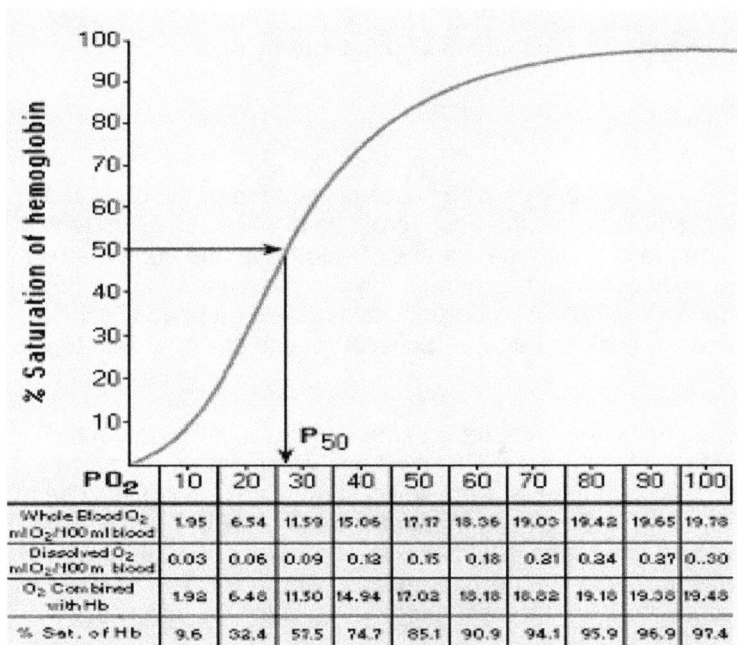

PO_2	10	20	30	40	50	60	70	80	90	100
Whole Blood O_2 ml O_2/100 ml blood	1.95	6.54	11.59	15.06	17.17	18.36	19.03	19.42	19.65	19.78
Dissolved O_2 ml O_2/100 m blood	0.03	0.06	0.09	0.12	0.15	0.18	0.21	0.24	0.27	0..30
O_2 Combined with Hb	1.92	6.48	11.50	14.94	17.02	18.18	18.82	19.18	19.38	19.48
% Sat. of Hb	9.6	32.4	57.5	74.7	85.1	90.9	94.1	95.9	96.9	97.4

http://www.lib.mcg.edu/edu/eshuphysio/program/section4/4ch5/s4ch5_23.htm

Recall that 40 mm Hg is the typical partial pressure of oxygen in the cells of the body. Examination of the oxygen-hemoglobin dissociation curve reveals that, under resting conditions, only about 20 - 25% of hemoglobin molecules give up oxygen in the systemic capillaries. This is significant (in other words, the 'plateau' is significant) because it means that you have a substantial reserve of oxygen. In other words, if you become more active, and your cells need more oxygen, the blood (hemoglobin molecules) has lots of oxygen to provide

When you do become more active, partial pressures of oxygen in your (active) cells may drop well below 40 mm Hg. A look at the oxygen-hemoglobin dissociation curve reveals that as oxygen levels decline, hemoglobin saturation also declines - and declines precipitously. This means that the blood (hemoglobin) 'unloads' lots of oxygen to active cells - cells that, of course, need more oxygen.

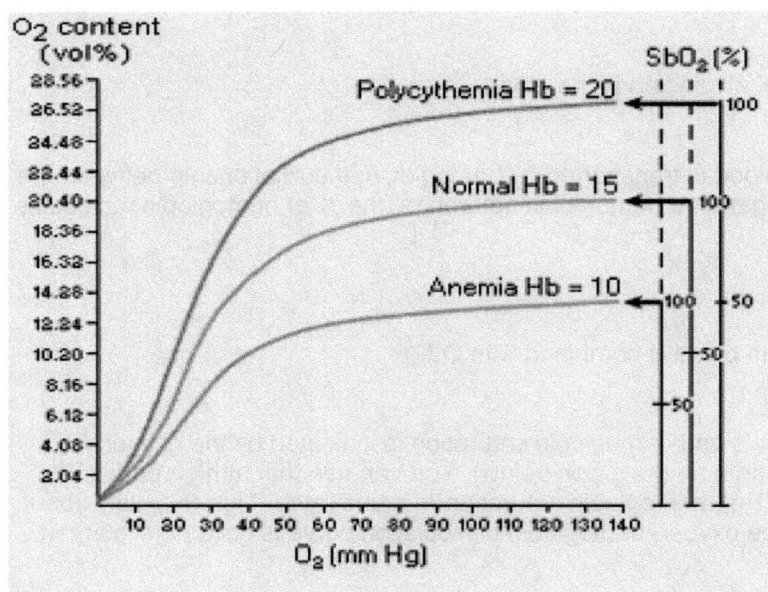

http://www.lib.mcg.edu/edu/eshuphysio/program/section4/4ch5/s4ch5_24.htm

Physiological Process

When the body experiences hypoxia, there is a vasoconstriction in selective areas of the body in an attempt to selectively redistribute blood to critical areas of the body (brain, heart, liver, etc). There will be a corresponding shift to the right in attempt to increase the release of blood from the bone marrow. If the anemia is mild to moderate, then the body can maintain normal oxygen pressure and distribution over the body. If the anemia is moderate to severe, then the heart has to increase outout, which increase stress. Increased stress on the heart is likely to result in tachycardia and this may lead to heart failure, then death.

Other physiological process is initiated when the kidney detects a decreased level of oxygen in the erythrocytes. Erythropoietin is released into the bloodstream. This hormone enters the bone marrow and stimulates the erythrocyte precursors. The pluripotential stem cell is stimulated and it gives rise to the CFU-GEMM cell. It in turn matures into the BFU-E cell and maturates into the CFU-F cell which gives rise to the first identifiable RBC precursor, the proerythroblast. The maturation sequence continues through the basophilic erythroblast follow by the polychromatic erythroblast. The next maturation step is the appearance of the acidophilic erythroblast, then the reticulocyte, and finally the mature red blood cell, the erythrocyte.

Clinical Manifestations in Severe Anemia

[1] Weakness, shortness, and/or loss of breath. This is more obvious after physical exertion because of the redistribution of blood to the more critical parts of the body.
[2] Dizziness and syncope.
[3] Gastrointestinal disturbances which include appetite loss and indigestion.
[4] Confusion. The patient may experience hallucinations and insomnia.
[5] Increase in pallor, noticeable in the mucus membranes and the nail beds.
[6] Leg cramps are usually associated with the blood being redistributed to the critical body parts.
[7] Headaches

149

[8] Tachycardia due to the efforts of the heart to distribute oxygenated blood throughout the body.
[9] NOTE: if the anemia is not corrected and it increases in severity, then the patient will go into a coma, and death is the final outcome.

Causes of Anemia

[1] Acute blood loss (hemorrhage)
[2] Accelerated destruction of RBCs
[3] Nutritional deficiency
[4] Bone marrow replacement
[5] Infection and toxicity
[6] Hematopoietic stem cell arrest or damage
[7] Hereditary or acquired defect

Evaluation of Anemia

An abnormal complete blood count points the diagnosis. First check the WBC and Platelets and differential WBC. Abnormality high or low WBC or platelets may be a clue of an underlying primary blood disease such as leukemia. Pancytopenia suggests marrow aplasia replacement or Hypersplenism. An erythroleukoblastic blood smear (circulating immature cells such as myelocytes or metamyelocytes and nucleated RBCs) could indicate marrow replacement with tumor, fibrosis, leukemia etc.

The characteristics of the RBC are the clue and point the diagnostic.

LOOK AT THE MCV

1. Hematologic

    1. Hematocrit
    2. Hemoglobin concentration. Hgb electrophoresis.
    3. RBC indices: MCV, MCH, MCHC, RBW
    4. Leukocytes count.
    5. Reticulocyte count.
    6. Platelet count.
    7. Stained blood smear: RBC morphology.

2. Urine analysis

    1. Appearance: Color, pH, Clarity.
    2. Test for protein, Bence Jones protein.
    3. Bilirubin, Urobilinogen.
    4. Occult blood, hemosiderin.
    5. Microscopic examination.

3. Stool

    1. Appearance: Color, Consistency.
    2. Occult blood.
    3. Examination of ova, parasites.

4. Serum or Plasma

    1. BUN, Creatinine.
    2. Bilirubin: Direct, Indirect.
    3. Protein. Serum protein electrophoresis

4. Serum iron, TIBC (Total Iron Binding Capacity). Ferritin
5. Haptoglobin. Vitamin B12 and Folate
6. LDH.

5. Special tests in hematology.

1. Coombs'test,
2. G-6PD.
3. Hgb typing.
4. Ham acid test.
5. Sucrose test, Autohemolysis test.
6. Prussian blue stain in bone marrow.

Classification of Anemias

I-Etiologic Classification

A-Impaired RBC Production

1-Abnormal bone marrow

1-1 Aplastic anemia
1-2 Myelophthisis: Myelofibrosis, Leukemia, Cancer metastasis.

2-Essential factors deficiency

2-1 Deficiency anemia: Fe, Vit.B12, Folate, etc.
2-2 Anemia in renal disease: EPO decreased

3- Stimulation factor deficiency

3-1. chronic disease
3-2. hypopituitarism
3-3 .hypothyroidism

B-Excessive Destruction of RBC

1-Hemolytic Anemia

1- Intravascular Defect
1-1 Membrane: Hereditary Spherocytosis
Hereditary Ovalocytes, etc
1-2 Enzymes: G-6PD def, PK def, etc.
1-3 Hemoglobin: Thalassemia, Hemoglobinopathies.
2- Extra corpuscular Defect
2-1 Mechanical: March Hemolytic anemia
MAHA (Microangiopathic HA)
2-2 Chemical/Physical
2-3 Infection: Clostridium tetani
2-4 Antibodies: autoimmune system
2-5 Hypersplenism

C-Blood Loss
1- Acute blood loss: Accident, GI bleeding.
2- Chronic blood loss: Hypermenorrhae
Parasitic infestation

II- Morphologic Classification

1- Macrocytic Anemia: MCV> 100

  1-1- Megaloblastic

    1-1 Vit- B12 deficiency: Pernicious anemia
    1-2 Folic acid deficiency: Nutritional megaloblastic anemia, Sprue, Other Malabsorption.
    1-3 inborn errors of metabolism
    1-4 Abnormal DNA synthesis: Chemotherapy, Anticonvulsant, Oral contraceptives

  1-2-Non-Megaloblastic
    2-1 increased erythropoiesis: Hemolytic anemia response to hemorrhage
    2-3 increased membrane surface area: Hepatic disease, Obstructive jaundice, Post-splenectomy
    2-3 Idiopathic: Hypothyroidism, Hypoplastic and aplastic anemia

2- Microcytic hypochromic Anemia: 80< MCV

 1-Iron Deficiency Anemia
    1-1 chronic blood loss
    1-2 inadequate diet
    1-3 Malabsorptions
    1-4 increased demand
 2-Abnormal Globin Synthesis
    2-1 Thalassemia
    2-2 Hemoglobinopathies
 3- Abnormal Porphyrin and Heme Synthesis
 4- Other Abnormal Iron Metabolism

3- Normocytic Normochromic Anemia: 80<MCV<100

1- Blood loss
2- Increased plasma volume: Pregnancy, over hydration
3- Hemolytic anemia
4- Hypoplastic marrow
5- Infiltrate bone marrow
6- Abnormal endocrine
7- Kidney disease/ Liver disease/ Cirrhosis

III- PHYSIOLOGIC CLASSIFICATION

-RPI (Reticulocyte Production Index) < 2 = Ineffective Erythropoiesis-

 1-Hypoproliferative anemia
            - Hypoplastic anemia-idiopathic/ Chemical/ infectious/Drugs→ Maturation arrest.
            - Myelophtisic anemia (marrow infiltration).
            - Refractory anemia (Dysmyelopoietic syndrome).
    1-1 Normocytic/ Normochromic and Normal RDW
            - Bone Marrow Failure
            - Decrease marrow stimulation
            - Endocrine disease
            - Anemia of chronic disease
            - Renal disease
    1-2 Abnormal RBC morphology and Increased RDW
            - Oval macrocytes: refractory Dysmyelopoietic
            - Dacryocytes/ Tear drops: Myelophtisic
 2-Maturation disorder

2-1 Microcytic, high RDW
- Sideroblastic (Microcytic dimorphic RBC)
- Iron deficiency (Microcytic hypochromic RBC)

2-2 Microcytic, Normal RDW
- Heterozygous, thalassemia syndrome
- Anemia of chronic disease

2-3 Macrocytic
- Liver disease
- Folate deficiency
- Vit. B12 deficiency
- Hemolytic anemia (Normocytic polychromasia)

-RPI (Reticulocyte Production Index) >3= Effective Erythropoiesis-

1-Hemolytic anemia
4- Intrinsic hereditary disorder
5- Extrinsic acquired disorder

2-Blood loss
6- Acute blood loss
7- Chronic blood loss (without treatment→ microcytic, hypochromic anemia)

The RBC indices are a mathematical calculation to yield three parameters useful in diagnosing anemia. The first indice is the Mean Corpuscular Volume (MCV); an average RBC volume is calculated by dividing the hematocrit value by the RBC count value. Normal values are 80 to 100 femtoliters (fl).If the value is below 80 fl, then this indicates microcytic anemia. A value greater than 100 would suggest macrocytic anemia. The second indice is the Mean Corpuscular Hemoglobin (MCH). This describes the hemoglobin content of each RBC and is obtained by dividing the hemoglobin value by the RBC count value. The normal values ranges from 27 to 32 picograms (pg). Values below 27 are suggestive of hypochromic anemia. The third indice is the Mean Corpuscular Hemoglobin Concentration (MCHC), describing the hemoglobin concentration in RBCs. Normal values range from 31 to 36 g/dl. Low value suggests Hypochromia. Anemias may be classified in more that one way.

A-One method is morphologically in which there are three general types of anemia:
1- Macrocytic
2- Microcytic
3- Normocytic

B-A second method is pathophysiological or etiological in which two general groups of anemias appear:

1- One group is those anemias that are caused by a reduction in the number of RBCs due to a maturation defect.
2- The other groups of anemias are those due to increased RBC destruction.

Morphologically classified anemia can be evaluated by blood smear evaluation and biochemical testing. In the blood smear evaluation, the size, shape, and hemoglobin content of the erythrocytes is assessed. In the event of this type of anemia, one might expect to see a large clear area of pallor in the center of the RBC; this indicates a decrease in hemoglobin content or hypochomia. The presence of bluish-tinted erythrocytes are indicators of immaturity (young red blood cells), a condition known a Polychromatophilia or diffuse basophilia. If the patient has hemorrhaged, then the loss of RBCs, the bone marrow will be stimulated and the blood smear will be characterized by Polychromatophilia and Macrocytes.

The four most important types of anemia in the morphological classification are:
1- Normocytic, normochromic anemia

153

2- Microcytic, hypochromic anemia
3- Macrocytic, normochromic anemia

The uniqueness of the morphological classification is that the slide evaluation and biochemical data will to the cause of the anemia and treatment can begin immediately.
Another means of categorizing anemias is by grouping the anemias as fallows.

A- If anemia is due to a decrease or absence in bone marrow production: ineffective erythropoiesis.
B- If the anemia is due to RBC destruction and/or hemorrhage: effective erythropoiesis.

MCV suggests the mechanism of anemia. The Mean Corpuscular Volume is the mean size of RBC as determined by an automated cell counter.

MVC gives an important clue as to the pathophysiology of an anemia as indicated below:

A- LOW MCV- indicates that hemoglobin synthesis is impaired from a number of possible causes.
B- HIGH MCV-indicates that DNA synthesis is impaired or that there is an increase in the RBC membrane.
C- NORMAL MCV- suggests that there is no impairment in hemoglobin or DNA synthesis.

Knowing the MCV thus allows you to take a focused history and order appropriate investigations to determine the cause.

CHAPTER TWO: IRON DIFICENCY ANEMIA: IDA

In developed countries, adequate iron intake is not a problem. The high risk groups who are most likely to develop IDA are [1] infants, [2] rapidly growing adolescents, [3] pregnant women, and [4] women during their child bearing years (losing from 10 to 45 mg/month). The pregnant female needs about 3.4 mg of iron daily (a total of 1000 mg to carry the fetus to term). About 400 mg are needed for the fetal RBS mass. At parturition, approximately 300 mg will be lost and up to 170 mg will be contained in the placenta and umbilical cord.

It has been estimated that a healthy adult male would require about eight years developing IDA if no more iron were absorbed in the diet. Malabsorption is uncommon unless there is a primary problem as [1] sprue, [2] gastrectomy, or [3] atrophic gastritis. Other causes are [1] regular blood donation and [2] paroxysmal nocturnal Hemoglobinuria.

Iron Metabolism

1-Types of iron

People consume two types of iron: non-heme and heme
Iron comes primarily from plants and heme iron comes primarily from meat. Plants do contain tiny traces of heme iron but not enough to make a difference. Meat contains both types of iron. About 55-60% of the iron in meat is non-heme the rest is heme iron.

Nonheme iron represents the majority of iron humans consume in their diets and is the type of iron in most supplements. Non-heme type of iron is inorganic and is found in grains such as rice, wheat, and oats. Non-heme iron is also found in nuts, fruits, vegetables, most iron pills, fortificants, or contaminant iron such as from water, soil or cooking utensils. Unlike heme iron, the iron from all of these sources must be changed before it can be absorbed.

Meat, especially red meat is the best source of heme iron. When we eat meat we consume the blood proteins, the hemoglobin and myoglobin contained in the flesh of the animal. Heme iron is easily absorbed by the body and the best source of iron for people who are iron deficient. Too much heme iron in the diet can increase the risk of disease for some people with abnormal iron metabolism such as hemochromatosis.

For persons with normal iron metabolism only 20 to 25 percent of the heme iron consumed is actually absorbed. For example, a four-ounce hamburger contains about 3 milligrams of iron; about 1.2 milligrams are heme and about 1.8 milligrams are non-heme. The amount of heme iron absorbed from that 4 oz hamburger would be approximately a third of a milligram. Persons with abnormal iron metabolism, such as hereditary hemochromatosis can absorb up to four times the iron as that of a person with normal metabolism. Therefore 80-100% of heme iron can be absorbed or approximately 1.2 milligrams from the same 4oz hamburger!

Many substances can reduce the amount of non-heme iron we absorb; these substances include tannins in coffee or tea, dairy, phytates (fiber), eggs and some types of chocolate. Calcium can impair the absorption of both non-heme and heme iron. Therefore if a person needs more iron, he or she should avoid these items to improve the amount of iron absorbed. But if a person has a problem of too much iron, he or she should use these items to help lower the amount of iron absorbed.

2- Absorption, transport and storage of iron

Iron is primarily absorbed in a portion of the small intestine called the duodenum. Before iron can be absorbed however, it is exposed to stomach acid and changed into a form that is soluble.

Once iron is absorbed it is carried (transported) by a protein called Transferrin. Transferrin is the major transporter of iron and ideally should be about 25-35% saturated with iron. Transferrin molecules that are heavily loaded (saturated) lose the ability to hold onto (bind) iron. Unbound or free iron is highly destructive and dangerous. Unbound iron can trigger free radical activity, which can cause cell death, and destroy DNA.

Free iron can also provide nourishment for bacteria such as Yersinia, Listeria and Vibrio. These bacteria are harmless for people with normal iron levels, but when transferrin is highly saturated with iron Yersinia, , Listeria, and Vibrio, contained in raw shellfish such as oysters, can lead to septicemia (definition will include symptoms). Death by septicemia can occur within hours if a person has very high body iron levels. People with high iron should always take care not to eat raw shellfish or walk barefoot on a beach where they might step on an infected shell.

Some microorganisms are skilled in other ways in obtaining iron from human hosts. Staph, for example can break open red blood cells and extract the iron it needs. Another pathogen, the protozoan that causes malaria, can get into the red blood cell to obtain iron necessary to thrive. And finally, there are bacteria such as the one that causes tuberculosis that grow best inside macrophages that are iron loaded.

Macrophages are white blood cells that protect us against disease; they scavenge for harmful invaders that enter our bloodstream. When the macrophage is called into action, it engulfs the bacteria or harmful debris and traps it so that it cannot thrive and spread disease in the human host. Iron-loaded macrophages are helpless to defend us against opportunistic infection and disease. Overwhelmed with an iron these macrophages can migrate to other parts of the body and release free iron to that organ. An example is iron-loaded alveolar (lung macrophages) that migrate to the bladder and increase the risk of bladder disease. For this reason, people who smoke are at risk for many diseases, especially cancer. Cancer cells thrive on iron.

When working normally, transferrin binds to iron, and transports it to all tissues, vital organs, and bone marrow, so that normal metabolism, DNA synthesis, and red blood cell production can take place. Recently scientists have discovered that transferrin does not work completely alone in the transport of iron. Ceruloplasmin, a protein that binds with copper is involved in iron transport. Iron needs adequate amounts of copper to reach some of its intended destinations, such as the brain.

Besides transferrin, two newly discovered proteins: divalent metal transporter 1 (DMT1) and ferroportin (FPN) are important to the transport of non-heme iron. DMT1 carries iron into the cell, while ferroportin carries iron out of the cell and into the bloodstream.

Ferritin is a protein that acts like a large holding vessel. Ferritin contains iron that we don't presently need. It is sometimes called an iron storage protein. Ferritin is produced by nearly every cell of the body. The brain contains huge amounts of ferritin, so does the liver. Ferritin is a very large molecule; one ferritin molecule alone can hold up to 4, 500 atoms of iron.

Elevated serum ferritin can be a sign that the person has inflammation due to disease, or that potential disease causing factors such as iron overload may be present.

Like transferrin, ferritin can also become unstable, and ineffective. Think of ferritin like a big sink; when this sink gets full, ferritin and its iron can be changed into something called hemosiderin.

Hemosiderin is a yellowish-brown substance that contains ferric oxide (rust). A small amount of hemosiderin in tissues is probably normal and may not be harmful, but when large amounts of the substance are allowed to collect in organs, it then becomes a threat to good health. Hemosiderin can accumulate in cells of the heart, liver, lungs, pancreas, central nervous system, thyroid, reproductive organs, skin, adrenals, pituitary and thyroid gland. When the build up of hemosiderin is great, the organ cannot function properly. For example, when beta cells (insulin producing cells of the pancreas) are loaded with hemosiderin, these cells become unable to produce or store adequate amounts of the hormone insulin, which results in diabetes.

Clearly, inadequate amounts or excessive accumulation of iron can endanger health, but iron can also be harmful to a person's health in yet another way.

3-How much iron is in the body?

Males of average height have about 4 grams of iron in their body, females about 3.5 grams; children will usually have 3 grams or less. These 3-4 grams are distributed throughout the body in hemoglobin, tissues, muscles, bone marrow, blood proteins, enzymes, ferritin, hemosiderin, and transport in plasma.

The greatest portion of iron in humans is in hemoglobin. Except in cases of great blood loss, pregnancy, or growth spurts, where larger amounts of iron are required, our bodies only need about 1 to 1.5 milligrams of iron per day to replace what is lost. Normal daily excretion of iron through urine, vaginal fluid, sweat, feces, and tears total about 1-1.5 milligrams, or the equivalent of what most of us require per day, to function normally.

Nature provides for these periods of increased iron needs by stepping up the amount of iron that is absorbed. This very elaborate regularly system can be observed in females who are menstruating, who will naturally increase the 1.5 milligrams that she usually absorbs up to 3-3.5 milligrams to replenish her iron stores. An unborn child in the third trimester and right before birth gets a tremendous amount of iron from the mother. This vast store of iron is in preparation for a spectacular period of rapid growth and will assure adequate iron is available for the first six months of life. For this reason newborns and infants have exceedingly high serum ferritin and Tsat% (transferrin/iron saturation percentage). The continued assurance of iron during this period is from breast milk or infant formulas. Thereafter, iron needs can be met with solid foods introduced to an infant at the appropriate time.

Iron deficiency anemia is the most common form of anemia. Approximately 20% of women, 50% of pregnant women, and 3% of men are iron deficient. Iron is an essential component of hemoglobin. Iron is normally obtained through the food in the diet and by the recycling of iron from old red blood cells.

The causes of iron deficiency are too little iron in the diet, poor absorption of iron by the body, and loss of blood (including from heavy menstrual bleeding). It is also caused by lead poisoning in children. Anemia develops slowly after the normal stores of iron have been depleted in the body and in the bone marrow.

Women, in general, have smaller stores of iron than men and have increased loss through menstruation, placing them at higher risk for anemia than men. In men and postmenopausal women, anemia is usually due to gastrointestinal blood loss associated with ulcers or the use of aspirin or nonsteroidal anti-inflammatory medications (NSAIDS).

High-risk group include: women of child-bearing age who have blood loss through menstruation; pregnant or lactating women who have an increased requirement for iron; infants, children, and adolescents in rapid growth phases; and people with a poor dietary intake of iron through a diet of little or no meat or eggs for several years.

Risk factors related to blood loss are peptic ulcer disease, long term aspirin use, colon cancer, uterine cancer, and repeated blood loss donation. The incidence is 2 out of 1000 people.

Clinical Syndromes of Iron Metabolism

Iron deficiency anemia develops in stages, from depletion of iron stores through iron-deficient erythropoiesis to fully manifested iron deficiency anemia. This important to consider when morphologically evaluating red blood cells smear because the degrees of microcytosis and hypochomia seen on peripheral blood smear may vary with the stage of iron impairment.

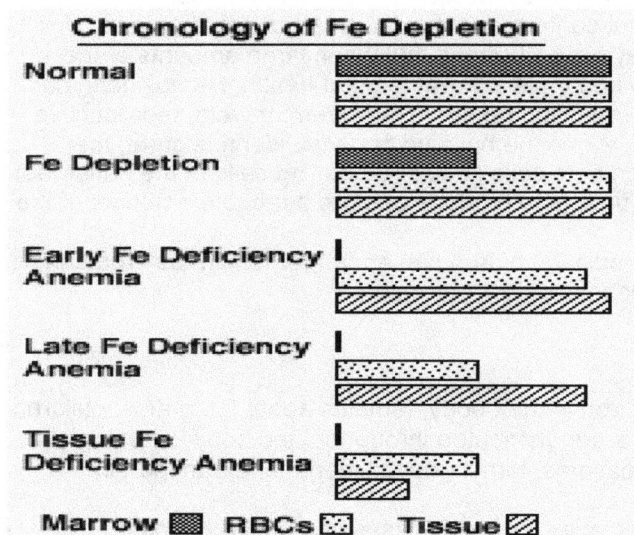

©2007. Rector and visitors of the University of Virginia
Charles E. Hess, M.D. and Lindsey Krstic, B.A. Used with permission

In a normal balanced state, 1-2 mg of iron enters and leaves the body every day.

Dietary iron is absorbed in the duodenum by enterocytes and circulates in the plasma. There it is bound by transferrin, and becomes available for uptake throughout the body by any tissue with transferrin receptors. Liver parenchymal tissue is especially rich in transferrin receptors, and stores large quantities of iron. Most of the circulating iron is used by the bone marrow to generate hemoglobin for red blood cells; while around 10- 15% is utilized by muscle fibers to generate myoglobin. Circulating red blood cells normally comprise the largest iron storage pool. When they become senescent, red blood cells are engulfed by reticuloendothelial macrophages, which make their

157

iron available for redistribution to other tissues using transferrin. Traces of iron are lost each day by sloughing of mucosal cells, loss of epithelial cells, and blood loss. Since the human body has not evolved a mechanism to clear excess iron, disorders of iron balance, such as iron overload and iron deficiency, are among the most common diseases in humans.

Iron Deficiency Anemia (IDA)

Iron deficiency anemia can range from mild to severe. A mild case usually causes no symptoms or problems. However, a severe case can cause extreme fatigue (tiredness) and weakness. Severe iron deficiency anemia can lead to serious problems for young children and pregnant women, and it can affect the heart.
In young children, iron deficiency anemia can cause a heart murmur and delays in growth and development. It puts a child at greater risk for lead poisoning and infections, and it can cause behavior problems.
In pregnant women, iron deficiency anemia can increase the risk of a premature delivery and a low-birth-weight baby.
The heart is affected when there is a lack of oxygen in the body. The heart has to work harder to get enough oxygen throughout the body. Over time, this stress on the heart can lead to a fast or irregular heartbeat, chest pain, an enlarged heart, and even heart failure.

Signs and symptoms of IDA

Symptoms of iron deficiency anemia include unusual cravings for nonfood items such as ice, dirt, paint, or starch. This craving for nonfood items is called pica.
Another symptom of IDA is developing restless legs syndrome (RLS). RLS is a disorder that causes an uncomfortable feeling in the legs that can only be relieved by movement. Sleep is difficult for people with RLS.
In infants and young children, signs and symptoms include a poor appetite, being irritable, and a slower rate of growth and development.
Some of the signs and symptoms of IDA are related to its causes, such as blood loss. Blood loss is most often seen with very heavy or long lasting menstrual bleeding or vaginal bleeding in women after menopause. Other signs of internal bleeding are bright red blood in the stool or black, tarry-looking stools.

Diagnostic test and procedures

Usually, the first test used to diagnose anemia is a complete blood count (CBC). The CBC tells a number of things about a person's blood, including:
1- The Hgb level.
2- The Hct level.
3- The RBC indices.
4- The reticulocyte count.
5- The WBC.
6- The platelet count.

The CBC count documents the severity of the anemia. In chronic IDA, the RBC indices show a microcytic and hypochromic erythropoiesis. If the CBC count is obtained after blood loss, the RBC indices do not enter the abnormal range until most of the erythrocytes produced before the bleeds are destroyed at the end of their normal lifespan (120 days).
Peripheral blood smear in IDA confirm the CBC, the microcytosis is apparent in the smear long before the MVC is decreased after an event producing iron deficiency, Platelets usually are increased in this disorder (> 450,000/ul). This normalizes following iron therapy.
Other laboratory tests are useful to establish the etiology of iron deficiency anemia and to exclude or to establish a diagnosis of one of the other microcytic anemias.

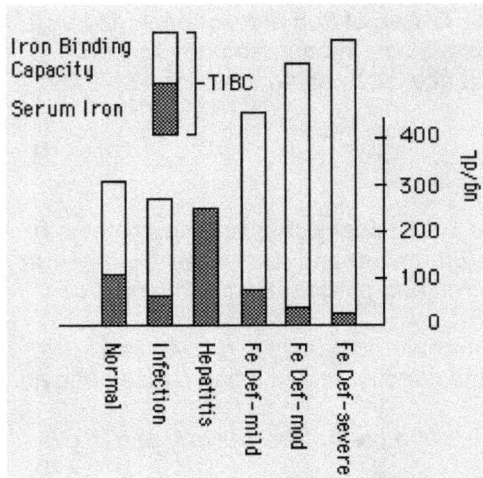

Serum iron test

The adult body contains about 3 to 5 grams of iron, with 2 to 2.5 grams being located in the hemoglobin. A small amount (less than 150 mg) is found in myoglobin (an oxygen binding protein of muscle). Iron is also a ligand or cofactor in enzymes, enabling the enzyme (such as peroxidases, catalases, and cytochromes) to functionally active. Iron can be stored as Ferritin and hemosiderin, which serves as an important storage pool of iron. If an iron deficiency condition arises, these two pools will become diminished. Iron deficiency is one of the most prevalent disorders, affecting 15% of the world population. Iron is decreased in iron deficiency anemia, malnutrition, malignancy, chronic infection, and anemia of chronic disease.

Normal values are shows as follows:

Male (adults):	50 to 160 ug/dL.
Female (16 to 40 y/o):	45 to 150 ug/dL
Child:	50 to 120 ug/dL.
Newborn:	100 to 250 ug/dL

Iron is increased in iron poisoning, hematochromatosis, viral hepatitis, and sideroblastic anemia.

The value of the total iron binding capacity

The total iron binding capacity test (TIBC) is a test procedure that totally saturates the protein transferring (TRF) with iron. The TIBC test measures the resulting iron concentration to arrive at the available amount of transferring. Actually this test tends to over-measure the actual amount of Transferrine because iron can also be bound by albumin and certain other plasma proteins. In normal conditions, when iron values are about 70 to 180ug/dl, an estimated 30 to 35% of the Transferrine molecules are bound with iron. In the TIBC test, from 15 to 50% Transferrine saturation can be demonstrated in the normal individual with values for female being somewhat lower than for the male.

This test can be useful to help diagnose disorders involving iron metabolism or anemias. The TIBC can be calculated indirectly by multiplying the serum transferring value times 1.25.

> Normal value for adult male and female is 250 to 460 ug/dL.

Transferrine and Transferrine saturation test

Transferrine is beta1globin, a glycoprotein that is synthesis in the liver. It transports iron through the circulatory system to cells that require iron. There are transferring receptors on the cell allowing the binding the molecule to attach. The transferring enters the cell via endocytosis and the iron detaches from the transferring molecule and is passed into the cytoplasm where it is bound to Ferritin to be held until ready for use. The transferring molecule does not detach from the cytoplasm membrane receptor and it will be returned back to outside the cell where it dissociates from the receptor and reenters the plasma to pick up more iron.

Normal values for plasma transferring are:

Male (adult):	200 to 380 mg/dL.
Female (16 to 40y/o)	200 to 380 mg/dL.
Child	200 to 360 mg/dL
Newborn	130 to 275 mg/dL

The Transferrin saturation test is also known as the percent saturation test and is simply a mathematical comparison of the serum iron to the TIBC. Calculation it as follows:

Divide the total iron (ug/dL) by TIBC (ug/dL) and multiply by 100% to obtain the % saturation.

Example problem: If the total iron is 100 ug/dL, the TIBC is 350 ug/dL. The % of saturation is 28.57%

Normal values are as follows:

Male (adult):	20 to 55%.
Female (16 to 40 y/o)	15 to 50%
Child, Newborn, Infant:	12 to 50%.

Ferritin test

Ferritin is a multi-unit (24 subunits) protein that takes on the form of a shell and contains approximately 4,500 iron atoms. The iron is deposited in the core of this large molecule as a ferric hydroxyphosphate complex. In this way, the toxic action of extra iron is prevented. If the Ferritin shell is void of iron, it is then known as apoferritin. It is found in most cells and can be quickly mobilized to store iron. Little Ferritin is found in human plasma, but will be elevated if there is an excess of iron. The amount of Ferritin in plasma is used as an index of body iron stores. The synthesis of Ferritin is connected to the level of iron in the cells. When iron levels are high, mRNA (Ferritin type) is activated (or stabilized) to produce more Ferritin. When iron stores are decrease, the Ferritin type mRNA is destabilized (deactivated) and production of Ferritin ceases.

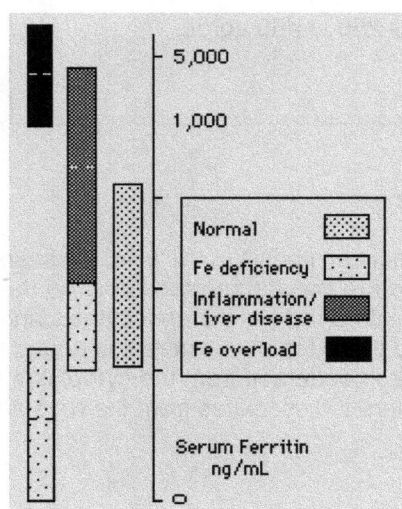

Normal values of Ferritin are as follows:

Male (adult):	20 to 250 ug/L.
Female (16 to 40 y/o)	10 to 120 ug/L
Child:	7 to 140 ug/L.
Newborn:	25 to 200 ug/L.

Ferritin is elevated in sideroblastic anemia and hemochromatosis, but it is decreased in iron deficiency anemia.

Other tests

A bone marrow aspirate can be diagnostic of iron deficiency. The absence of stainable iron in a bone marrow aspirate that contains spicules and a simultaneous control specimen containing stainable iron permit establishment of a diagnosis of iron deficiency without other laboratory tests.

Testing for the presence of hemoglobin is useful in establishing gastrointestinal bleeding as the etiology of IDA. Hemoglobinuria and hemosiderinuria can be detected by laboratory testing. This documents IDA to be due to renal loss of iron and incriminates hemolytic anemia. Hemoglobin electrophoresis and measurement of hemoglobin A2 and fetal hemoglobin are useful in establishing thalassemia or hemoglobinopathy.

Iron excess and Sideroblastic state

The body maintains normal iron homeostasis by regulating the absorption of iron from the diet as well as its distribution within the body. The distribution of iron through the blood is normally accomplished by means of transferrin. When iron is present in excess, it overwhelms the transferrin binding capacity and therefore becomes bound to smaller, low molecular weight molecules in the form of non-transferrin-bound iron (NTBI).Labile plasma iron (LPI), a directly chelatable component of NTBI, is highly toxic as it can catalyze the formation of harmful free hydroxyl radicals. LPI is thought to be the iron that loads cells via an unregulated mechanism other than the transferrin receptor. This is in contrast to the uptake of transferrin-bound iron, which takes place through transferrin receptors in a regulated manner.

Under steady-state conditions serum Ferritin levels correlate with total body iron. However, Ferritin is an acute-phase reactant so can be naturally elevated during the course of disease. Inflammation and infections, ascorbate level, abnormal liver function, and increased erythropoiesis can influence

161

circulating Ferritin levels. As such, a single measure of Ferritin is not clinically useful, although long – term serial assessment is convenient and valuable for estimating body iron stores and for monitoring chelation therapy.

Normal serum Ferritin levels differ for males (<300ng/ml) and females (<150ng/ml). Mild –to-moderate iron overload is indicated by serum Ferritin levels of 300-2500ng/ml, while levels > 2500ng/ml are associated with an increased risk of cardiac disease. The predictive value of serum Ferritin for the major complications of iron overload varies according to the type and severity of underlying anemia and the mechanism of iron loading.

Hemochromatosis

Iron overload can result from either primary or secondary causes:
* Primary iron overload is caused by genetic disorders that create an imbalance in iron metabolism.
* Secondary iron overload is caused by factors that bypass normal iron homeostasis, such as repeated blood transfusions, or iron poisoning.

The increased iron absorption observed in hereditary hemochromatosis leads to the gradual accumulation of storage iron in hepatocytes and other parenchymal cells. Iron accumulation in reticuloendothelial macrophages is, initially at least modest.

For patients with hereditary hemochromatosis the excess iron absorption can be counterbalanced with regular phlebotomy, which reduces the red blood cells iron pool. Excess storage iron in vital organs is redistributed to erythrocytes and then back into the red blood cell, thereby providing effective treatment in the patients whose ability to make new red blood cells is unimpaired.

In transfusional iron overload, phlebotomy is not a viable option. The anemia that originally led to the need for transfusion will have already reduced the red blood cell iron pool. The sudden large increase in the red blood cell iron pool following each transfusion results, after red blood cell degradation, in a gradual redistribution of this iron to reticuloendothelial macrophages. From these cells, it is later shuttled to hepatocytes and other parenchymal cells by transferrin. After repeated transfusions, excess iron storage in reticuloendothelial, parenchymal, and hepatic cells rapidly reaches and exceeds the levels that can be controlled by normal iron homeostatic mechanisms, leading to the formation of non transferrin bound iron and subsequent cellular damage.

The gene for classic hemochromatosis (HFE) was discovered by a team of scientists in California in August 1996. Two major mutations of HFE attributable to iron loading are C282Y and H63D.

In classic hemochromatosis, the iron built up is slow, usually taking 25-30 years before observed damage can be detected. In clinical practice, HHC/iron overload is more often seen in males in their mid to late fifties. For this reason HHC has acquired the mistaken identity of an older male's disease. HHC can be present in females, especially those who no longer menstruate.

Types of hemochromatosis

Type I: Is also called classic hemochromatosis, is due to mutation of HFE, a gene located on chromosome 6. There are more than 20 known mutations of HFE, but the most important for iron loading to date are C282Y and H63D. When a person inherits any two mutations of HFE, the risk for iron overload is increased but inheriting 2 mutated copies of C282Y currently appears to present the greatest risk for iron loading. Type I hemochromatosis is seen mostly in whites (Caucasians), though cases of blacks who are homozygous for C282Y have been documented.

Type II: type II or juvenile form of hemochromatosis is not presently associated with HFE but due to other gene mutations. Type IIa is caused by a mutation G320V on a gene named hemojuvelin found of chromosome 1. Type IIb is associated with chromosome 19, due to a mutation of hepcidin, a protein produced by the liver that is believed to be significant in limiting intestinal iron absorption.
Type II hemochromatosis has an onset prior to age 30 but can be seen in patients as young as 6 years of age.

Type III: type III hemochromatosis is due to a mutation in the transferrin receptor 2 (tRf2) located on chromosome 7. This form can be seen in any ethnicity.

Type IV: type IV hemochromatosis is due to a mutation in ferroportin, a protein that shuttles iron out of the cell and into the bloodstream. This form is different in that it is dominant, requiring only one mutated copy to inherit the disease. Type IV is seen mostly in Africans.

Since the discovery of HFE, genetic testing has become a way to confirm the diagnosis of hemochromatosis. This test is also used to identify family members of a person with genetic hemochromatosis, which provides an opportunity to seek early treatment and prevent disease.

According to the Centers for Disease control and Prevention, people with HHC are misdiagnosed 67% of the time and usually see an average of three doctors before obtaining a successful diagnosis. This remains a critical health concern, because hemochromatosis is common and early detection with treatment can save lives and improve quality of life. Also, if a person with hemochromatosis is diagnosed prior to serum Ferritin greater than 1,000 ng/ml. The chance of cirrhosis is less than 1%.

Sideroblastic anemia

Sideroblastic anemia is an enzyme disorder in which the body has adequate iron but is unable to incorporate it into hemoglobin. Iron enters the developing red blood cell (erythroblasts); here iron accumulates in the mitochondria giving a ringed appearance to the nucleus (ring sideroblast). The mitochondria are overloaded with iron and hemoglobin production (heme synthesis) is defective. Sideroblasts are visible with Prussian blue staining and observable under microscopic examination of bone marrow.

Iron Deficiency vs. Sideroblastic Anemia

	Iron Deficiency	Sideroblastic Anemia
MCV	Reduced proportional to degree of anemia	Very low in congenital type
Serum Iron	Reduced	Raised
TIBC	Raised	Normal or low
Serum Ferritin	Reduced	Raised
Bone Marrow Iron Stores	Absent	Present; often increased
Erythroblast Iron	Absent	Ringed Sideroblasts

Hemosiderin

Hemosiderin is a poorly defined molecule that is formed by the degradation of Ferritin, yet still contains iron, it cab detected by Prussian blue stain and is seen histologically with there is excessive storage of iron. The iron stored in the cell is an insoluble cellular inclusion of fe+++ complexed with ferritin. These complexes form granules (from 1 to 2 um in diameters) that serve as storage form of iron when there are insufficient levels of apoferritin. The iron to ferritin ratio is much greater as hemosiderin than in ferritin. Hemosiderin can release it iron, but does so at a very slow rate. Hemosiderin, when seen on unstained smears, appears as yellow granules. When present in Wright's or Wright's-Giemsa stain, the granules are brownish-blue coloration. The presence or absence of hemosiderin is determined by cytochemical staining of bone marrow using Prussian blue stain which is the preferred and precise technique, which yields bluish granules. It is used to assess body iron stores. If hemosiderin granules are absent, then the body iron stores are depleted. The presence of granules may be reported as a numerical value from 0 to 4+, where 2+ represents a normal or adequate iron store. Normal marrow will have 30 to 50% of the erythroblasts containing specks of hemosiderin.

In the normal metabolism of hemoglobin, iron can be captured by the renal tubules and complexed with storage proteins and ferritin to from tubular hemosiderin. When these cells are sloughed off, hemosiderin can demonstrated in the urine (hemosiderinuria). Normally hemosiderin is not found in the urine, if present, it indicates an unexplained anemia or chronic intravascular hemolysis.

Three categories of sideroblastic anemia are: hereditary, acquired or idiopathic.

1- Hereditary sideroblastic anemia is due to a genetic defect; the gene is an X-linked recessive (not dominant) gene. It may manifest in men and women but seen more commonly in young males, maternal uncles and cousins. Hereditary sideroblastic anemia generally manifests during the first three decades of life especially during adolescence but it has been diagnosed in patients over seventy.
2- Acquired sideroblastic anemia is due to prolonged exposure to toxins like alcohol, lead, drugs or nutritional imbalances such as deficiency in folic acid, deficiency in copper or excess zinc. Other causes are due to disease such as inflammatory conditions like rheumatoid arthritis, cancerous conditions such as leukemia, lymphoma; kidney disorders causing uremia; endocrine disorders such hyperthyroidism; metabolic disorders such porphyria cutanea tarda. Acquired sideroblastic anemia is usually seen in patients over 65 year of age but it can be present as early as mid to late fifties.
3- Idiopathic sideroblastic anemia means the cause is unknown; this category of sideroblastic anemia is referred to as myelodysplastic syndrome (MDS), MDS are generally observed in the early pre-leukemic stages of disease. Myelodysplasia is a bone marrow dysfunction disorder which can develop into aplastic anemia requiring bone marrow or stem cell transplantation.

Porphyrias

Porphyria cutanea tarda (PCT) is an aberration of normal heme synthesis, which is due to a decreased activity of an enzyme (uroporphyrinogen decarboxylase) in the liver. PCT is the most common form of porphyria. The main clinical manifestation is blistering of the skin of sun-exposed areas, such as the back of the hands, forearms, face, eras, and neck.

This photosensitivity is due to the overproduction of porphyrins (building blocks of heme) in the liver, due to the enzyme deficiency, which spills out into the blood, and builds up in the skin. Exposure to light, oxygen, minor bumps and scrapes leads to the chronic skin rash.

Free erythrocyte protoporphyrin (FEP) is a product of the hem synthesis pathway. This molecule escapes from the synthesis pathway and exists as a nonheme protoporphyrin in the erythrocyte. It can be measured and the information it provides is clinically useful. Normal reference levels range from 170 to 770 ug/L. if a condition arises in which there is a iron deficiency or an impairment of the utilization of iron, FER will increase. Also lead poisoning will significantly increase this product. This testing procedure is a helpful screening test for iron deficiency. It was used to screen for lead poisoning, but more sensitive tests have replace it as a screening test. It is also increased in anemia of chronic disease and may be in sideroblastic anemia (but not always). It is usually normal in hemochromatosis and thalassemia trait.

The second most common form of porphyria is due to a deficiency in the enzyme ferrochelatase. It is an autosomal dominant disorder. It is also known as "erythrohepatic protoporphyria". It appears to have a predilection for Caucasians. The enzyme ferrochelatase is though to be deficient in all tissues. Since the bone marrow reticulocyte is important in the final formation of heme, erythrocyte concentrations of protoporphyrin increases. RBC survival time is shortened to as little as 18 days. This creates an excess of protoporphyrin appearing in the blood. Because protoporphyrin is not water soluble it does not appear in the urine. The excess protoporphyrin is excreted into the bile and there is some risk that the large amounts may damage the hepatocytes. The excess protoporphyrins will accumulate in the skin and cause cutaneous photosensitivity.

CHAPTER THREE: MEGALOBLASTIC ANEMIA

Megaloblastic anemias are a group of disorders characterized by defective nuclear maturation caused by impaired DNA synthesis. RBCs are fragile, are larger and have higher nuclear-to cytoplasm ratios compared to normoblastic cells. Lifespan is shortened and many die in the bone marrow which causes elevated LDH. Granulocytes can be hypersegmented, and megacaryocytes are affected as well, resulting in thrombocytopenia.

A hallmark of megaloblastic anemia is ineffective erythropoiesis, as evidence by erythroid hyperplasia in the bone marrow, a decrease peripheral reticulocyte count, and an elevation in lactate dehydrogenase and indirect bilirubin levels. The pathogenesis of these findings is the intramedullary destruction of fragile and abnormal megaloblastic erythroid precursors.

Macrocytosis or an MCV of >100 is a common finding, most often associated with alcohol intake. The second most common cause of macrocytosis is abnormal DNA synthesis due to B12 or folate deficiency.
Hypothyroidism, liver disease, and blood loss or hemolysis is also associated with macrocytosis. Macrocytic anemia resulting from abnormal DNA synthesis is referred to as megaloblastic anemia. Megaloblastic anemia is not to be confused with macrocytic anemia. Macrocytic anemia is a secondary problem due to a primary disorder such as

1- Liver disease.
2- Acute hemorrhage.
3- Severe anemic episode.

Macrocytic anemia is characterized by a MCV range of 105 to 115 fl (indicating thin cells or target cells), although the MVC may go from 100 fl to 130 fl and if severe, may be up to 160 fl. The retic count tends to run from 10 to 25% where it is normal for megaloblastic condition. In megaloblastic anemia the MCV may range from 100 fl to 160 fl with the MCH elevated but the MCHC is usually normal.

Megaloblastic anemia is most often due to a B12 or folate deficiency, but the cause of the deficiency must be determined for proper treatment.

Megaloblastic anemia due to vitamin B12 deficiency caused by a lack of intrinsic factor is specifically referred to as pernicious anemia.

Laboratory testing of B12 and folate are critical to establishing the cause of a megaloblastic anemia.

The megaloblastic changes are most apparent in the polychromatophilic and orthochromatophilic stages. Multinucleate RBCs, abnormal karyorrhexis, increased pyknosis, and Howell-Jolly bodies may be seen.

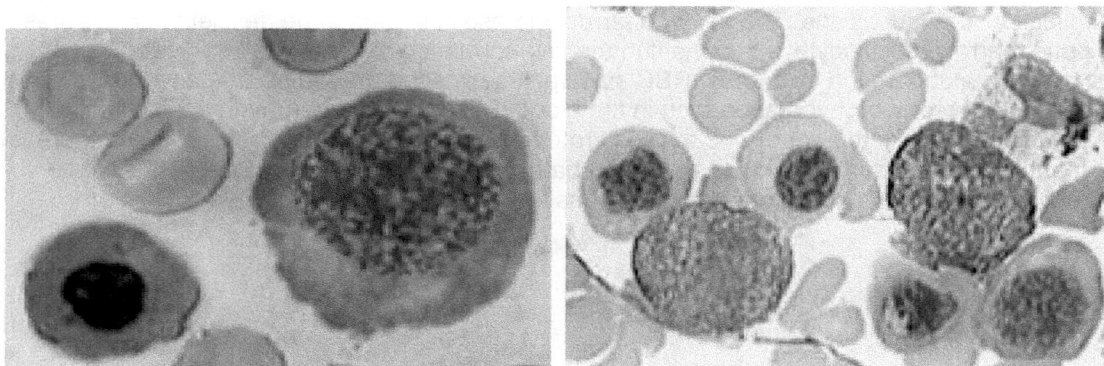

©2007. Rector and visitors of the University of Virginia
Charles E. Hess, M.D. and Lindsey Krstic, B.A. Used with permission

Vitamin B12 (Cyanocobalamin) Deficiency

Dietary intake is the source of cobalamin and folate because humans cannot synthesis these substances. Cobalamin must be bound to intrinsic factor, and this complex is taken up in the terminal ileum. Once absorbed, cobalamin is bound to another protein, transcobalamin II, and is transported to storage sites. Abnormalities in any of these steps in cobalamin transport can lead to deficiencies in this substance.

The major morbidity of cobalamin deficiency is related to the severity of anemia. In cobalamin deficiency, neurological impairment and anemia are major complications.

Folate deficiency during pregnancy can lead to neural tube defects and other development disorders in the fetus. However, folate supplements during pregnancy have reduced this morbidity.

Pernicious anemia usually occurs in individuals older than 40 years, and the prevalence increases in older populations. Dietary folate deficiency also increases in older populations because of poor diets.

Boiling foods in water dilutes folates, and excessive heating destroys folates.

The condition was named "pernicious" anemia because it was often fatal in the years before the cause was discovered to be a lack of vitamin B12, and no specific treatments were available. Now it is easy to treat with vitamin B12 pills or injections.

Some intestinal problems can cause poor absorption of vitamin B12. There problems include:
- An infection caused by parasites or an overgrowth of bacteria in the intestine
- Celiac disease (also known as sprue), a genetic disorder that makes a person unable to tolerate gluten
- Crohn's disease, an inflammatory bowel disease.
- Not enough stomach acid to digest food- a problem that can occur in older adults.

Long-term use of certain drugs may lead to deficiency of vitamin B12.

Megaloblastic anemia is more likely to develop in people who do not eat foods high in vitamin B12 for long periods of time. This includes some vegetarians, elderly, and people with alcoholism.

Folic Acid (Folate) Deficiency

A deficiency of folate, vitamin B12 or vitamin B6 may increase blood levels of homocysteine, and folate supplementation has been shown to decrease homocysteine levels and improve endothelial function. At least one study has linked low dietary folate intake with an increased risk of coronary events. The folic acid fortification program in the U.S. has decreased the prevalence of low levels of folate and high levels of homocysteine in the blood in middle-aged and older adults. Daily consumption of folic-acid fortified breakfast cereal and the use of folic acid supplements have been shown to be an effective strategy for reducing homocysteine concentrations in the blood.

The National Heart, Lung, and Blood Institute of the National Institutes of Health has identified many risk factors for cardiovascular disease, including an elevated LDL-cholesterol level, High blood pressure, a low HDL-cholesterol level, obesity, and diabetes. In recent years, researchers have identified another risk factor for cardiovascular disease, an elevated homocysteine level.

Homocysteine is an amino acid normally found in blood, but elevated levels have been linked with coronary heart disease and stroke. Elevated homocysteine levels may impair endothelial vasomotor function, which determines how easily blood flows through blood vessels. High levels of homocysteine also may damage coronary arteries and make it easier for blood clotting platelets to clump together and form a clot, which may lead to heart attack.

Some evidence associates low blood levels of folate with a greater risk of cancer. Folate is involved in the synthesis, repair, and function of DNA, our genetic map, and there is some evidence that a deficiency of folate can cause damage to DNA that may lead to cancer. Several studies have associated diets low in folate with increased risk of breast, pancreatic, and colon cancer.

Folate deficiency has been observed in alcoholics. A 1997 review of the nutritional status of chronic alcoholics found low folate status in more then 50% of those surveyed. Alcohol interferes with the absorption of folate and increases excretion of folate by the kidney. In addition, many people who abuse alcohol have poor quality diets that do not provide the recommendation intake of folate.

Folate is important for cells and tissues that rapidly divide. Cancer cells divide rapidly, and drugs that interfere with folate metabolism are used to treat cancer. Methotrexate is a drug often used to treat cancer because it limits the activity of enzymes that need folate.

Unfortunately, Methotrexate can be toxic, producing side effects such as inflammation in the digestive tract that may make it difficult to eat normally. There are many studies underway to determine if folic acid supplements can help control the side effects of Methotrexate without decreasing its effectiveness in chemotherapy. It is important for anyone receiving Methotrexate to follow a medical doctor's advice on the use of folic acid supplements.

Lab Studies

 * A CBC count, RBC indices, platelet count, differential count, reticulocyte count, and microscopic examination of the peripheral blood smear should be performed.
 * A typical patient with megaloblastic anemia presents with macrocytic anemia with thrombocytopenia and a decreased reticulocyte count. The mean cell volume can range from 100-150 fL or greater.
 * Hypersegmented neutrophils can be observed on the peripheral smear and represent an early phase of megaloblastosis in persons with nutritional megaloblastic anemias. Hypersegmented neutrophils contain 5 or more lobes, while normal neutrophils contain 3-4 lobes.
 * Macrocytes are oval and have been called macroovalocytes. In persons with severe anemia, macrocytes with nuclear remnants and erythrocytes with megaloblastic nuclei can be present in the peripheral blood. Macrocytes can be found in the peripheral blood in patients with liver disease or hemolytic anemia (because of an increase in reticulocytes) and usually do not have oval features. However, macroovalocytes are characteristic of megaloblastic anemias.
 * In general, the profoundness of megaloblastic changes is proportional to the severity of the anemia.
 * In some cases of megaloblastosis, no anemia is present despite overt neuropsychiatric disease. One cause of this disparity is the administration of folic acid to patients with cobalamin deficiency. This therapy partially corrects the anemia, but the neuropathy is not affected and progresses.
* Macrocytosis due to cobalamin or folate deficiencies may be masked in patients with microcytic anemias because of thalassemia or iron deficiency. However, hypersegmentation of neutrophils may persist. Transfusion therapy or infections may modify the expression of megaloblastosis.
* LDH and indirect bilirubin assays should be ordered, and results are expected to be high because of intramedullary destruction of megaloblastic red cell precursors. LDH fraction 1 (LDH_1) and LDH fraction 2 (LDH_2) are elevated, with LDH_1 being greater than LDH_2. The LDH level is often extremely high, and, following therapy, the fall in the LDH level is an excellent indication of response to or failure of therapy. Increased LDH and indirect bilirubin levels along with a decreased reticulocyte count suggest ineffective hemopoiesis in which intramedullary hemolysis is occurring.
* Serum iron and ferritin assays should be ordered initially and during the treatment of megaloblastic anemias. These parameters may be high. Increased iron turnover occurs in persons with untreated megaloblastosis. However, serum iron and ferritin levels may also decrease because patients respond to therapy and consume iron stores for the production of new RBCs. If iron stores are depleted, patients have an incomplete response to cobalamin or folate therapy.
* Tests for the diagnosis of cobalamin deficiency are described as follows:
* The most important test is measuring the serum cobalamin level. In a typical clinical presentation of megaloblastic anemia, a low serum cobalamin level and a full response to cobalamin may be sufficient to establish a diagnosis. A Schilling test can be performed in patients who have been treated with cobalamin and folate. This test can be used to diagnose cobalamin deficiency and to distinguish between pernicious anemia and ileal malabsorption.
 * Serum for cobalamin levels should be drawn before transfusions or vitamin B-12 therapy. If the test cannot be performed within a reasonable time frame, serum should be frozen to preserve it for testing so that therapy can be started. Serum cobalamin levels are usually low in patients with anemia due to cobalamin deficiency. However, exceptions to this rule exist.
 * Cobalamin levels may be falsely high in patients with megaloblastosis due to nitrous oxide, TCII deficiency, inborn errors in cobalamin metabolism, and myeloproliferative disorders. On the other hand, serum cobalamin levels can be falsely low with normal tissue levels in some patients with folate or iron deficiency, vegetarians, individuals on high doses of ascorbic acid, pregnant women, and persons with transcobalamin I (TCI) deficiency.
 * Serum samples for folate levels should also be obtained and, if necessary, frozen prior to therapy in patients with possible cobalamin deficiency because patients with folate deficiency can have reduced cobalamin levels.
 * A Schilling test is a radiometric test of cobalamin absorption.
The results of the Schilling test may indicate cobalamin malabsorption in patients who have severe and long-standing folate deficiencies. This is because of the effect of severe folate deficiency on the ileal mucosa that leads to a decrease in cobalamin uptake in the terminal ileum. Treating patients with severe folate deficiency with both cobalamin and folate for a month may be advisable to restore the ileal mucosa before performing a Schilling test.
 * Methylmalonic aciduria is another test. Urinary excretion is a reliable index of cobalamin deficiency, provided the patient does not have renal failure.
Serum methylmalonic acid and homocysteine test results are elevated in more than 90% of patients with cobalamin deficiencies.

* Tests for folate deficiency

- Serum folate is the earliest indicator of folate deficiency. Serum samples should be collected prior to therapy or transfusions. If necessary, serum can be frozen until the laboratory can perform the test. Folate levels respond rapidly to changes in dietary folate. A low folate level reflects dietary intake during the previous 2-3 days. Conversely, a single meal with normal folate content can restore serum folate levels to normal.

- The RBC folate level is usually low in patients with folate deficiency. Folate is incorporated into erythrocytes when they are formed, and folate levels do not fluctuate with changes in diet during the lifespan of the RBC. The RBC folate level may not be low in persons with rapidly developing acute folate deficiency. Another limitation of this test is that RBC folate levels are low in more than 50% of patients with cobalamin deficiency, and this test cannot be used to distinguish between these disorders.

* Bone marrow aspiration and biopsy results are useful to confirm the diagnosis, to rule out myelodysplasia, and to assess the iron stores. Marrow is cellular with erythroid hyperplasia. Megaloblastic RBC precursors are abundant, and giant metamyelocytes are present. Iron stores may vary from high to low. The bone marrow begins to convert from megaloblastic to normoblastic within 12 hours, and normalization is complete within 2-3 days. Therefore, bone marrow aspiration should be performed as soon as possible and preferably before therapy if the procedure is considered useful for the patient's treatment.

* On histologic findings bone marrow is hypercellular. An increase in erythropoietic activity is reflected by a decreased or reversed myeloid-to-erythroid ratio. Erythroid precursors have megaloblastic features in that they are larger than normoblastic cells and they have immature nuclear development. Cytoplasmic maturation is normal, but nuclear remnants, Howell-Jolly bodies, may be present in the cytoplasm. Giant bands (neutrophils) may be present. Megakaryocytes may be large and hyperlobulated. Iron stores vary from being increased before therapy to decrease if iron is consumed during therapy for megaloblastosis. Bone marrow studies should be performed before therapy because therapy may restore normoblastic erythropoiesis rapidly.

CHAPTER FOUR: BONE MARROW DISEASE

Aplastic Anemia

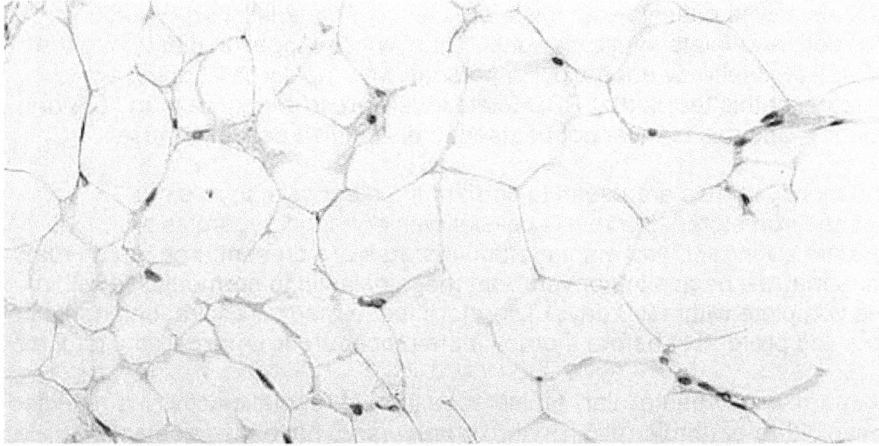

Note the absence of red and white blood cells in this bone marrow biopsy.
90% of area is fat-filled.

Aplastic anemia is a disorder (or group of disorders) characterized by aplasia of bone marrow or its destruction by chemical agents or physical factors. All lines are affected. The disease can be traced back to 1888 when a famous German pathologist Dr. Paul Ehrlich studied the case of a pregnant woman who died of bone marrow failure. However, the disorder was not officially termed as"aplastic" anemia until 1904.

Patients with aplastic anemia typically have low cells counts in all three blood lines. Upon examination, the bone marrow is found to be hypoplastic or aplastic, meaning low growth or no growth of blood-forming stem cells. Chromosomal abnormalities are not typically found in these instances.

Based on the neutrophil count, the aplastic anemia is classified as:

      a.   Moderate (MAA)
      b.   Severe (SAA)
      c.   Very severe (VSAA).

The symptoms of aplastic anemia can include increased bleeding, dyspnea, petechiae, purpura, ecchymoses and mucosal bleeding, and susceptibility to infections.

Aplastic anemia can appear at any age, it is diagnosed more often in children and young adults. Diagnosis begins with a review of history and symptoms, then the laboratory findings in the CBC and the bone marrow biopsy.

This is a Hypoproliferative or defective RBC anemia. It is characterized by a stoppage of RBC production and loss of all hematopoietic elements. There is a peripheral pancytopenia and the presence of hypocellular bone marrow. In all of the aplastic anemias investigated, approximately 60% are idiopathic. Clinically, aplastic anemia presents with three typical symptoms:[1] bleeding due to the thrombocytopenia with the platelet count < 20,000/ul, [2] a normocytic, normochromic anemia, [3] infection characterized by granulocytopenia with a neutrophil count < 500/ul, [4] clinical symptoms include [a] fatigue, [b] weakness, [c] bleeding gums, [d] petechiae, [e]tendency for infections, [f] easily bruised, [g] sleepiness, [h] hepato- and/or [i] splenomegaly as rare occurrences. Diagnosis of aplastic anemia requires the following parameters be demonstrated.

      D- Bone marrow with a 30% or more loss of cellularity.
      E- Granulocytes count less than 500/ul.
      F- Platelets count less than 20,000/ul.
      G- Corrected reticulocyte count < 1.0%.

About 25% of aplastic anemia's occur in individuals > 20y/o. approximately 33% of the cases of this type of anemia occurs in individuals > 60 y/o.

Aplastic anemia is classified as being either primary (constitutional) or secondary.

Primary types of aplastic anemias are due to congenital causes which will show up early in life. Two types of congenital aplastic anemia are Fanconi's anemia (a rare disorder) and familial aplastic anemia (for which is though to be a variant of Fanconi's anemia and can manifest at any age).

Secondary aplastic anemias make up the majority of these types of disorders. This type of anemia occurs because of exposure to a causative agent. The following are known to cause secondary aplastic anemia:

1- Secondary to toxic agent exposure.
2- Infections

Pure red cell aplasia (PRCA) is a disorder that affects only erythrocytes, but not the leukocytes or thrombocytes. It is not a true aplastic anemia since the other cell lines are not affected. It is describes as a unicellular aplasia. This tends to be a rare RBC disorder that affects the middle age adult with less than a thousand cases reported world wide. There are two general categories of this anemia: acquired and congenital. Expected laboratory findings are:

1- Decrease hemoglobin, hematocrit, and RBC count.
2- Reticulocytes are usually absent.
3- NRBCs are absent from the peripheral blood.
4- RBCs in peripheral blood may be normal to slightly macrocytic.
5- Serum erythropoietin is increased.
6- Bone marrow is characterized by absence of RBC precursor cells.

The acquired form of PRCA is the most commonly encountered type and may be either the acute or chronic form. The acute type may be referred to as acute acquired erythroblastopenia. This form is seen most often in children with an infection or is being treated with a particular drug. This form is often reversible. The chronic type (designated as chronic acquired erythroblastopenia) is seen most often in middle age or older adults and appears in females more often than males. Patients diagnosed with the chronic form of PRCA may have an accompanying benign thymoma or myasthenia gravis (MG).

Myasthenia gravis is an autoimmune disorder of neuromuscular transmission. Weakness is seen in the facial muscles and limbs. MG involves an abnormality at the synapse where the autoantibodies combine with autoimmune antigen on the acetylcholine esterase receptors on the muscle fiber end plates resulting in their destruction. This decreases the amount of acetylcholine esterase that can be received and produces rapid fatigue and loss of strength.

Causes of both acute and chronic forms have been attributed to:

1- Another hemolytic disorder as in a sickle cell crisis.
2- Sulfonamides.
3- Chloramphenicol
4- Neoplasm's such as benign thymoma
5- Idiopathic
6- Parvovirus B19 infection.
7- Malnutrition.

Myelophtisic anemia is a pancytopenia that is characterized by the replacement of infiltration of fibrotic, granulomatous, and/or neoplastic cells. Note: granulomatous infers the presence of granulomas. Granulomas are tumors/growths occurring when macrophages cannot destroy foreign bodies and some mycobacteria. The macrophages will surround the foreign material, enclosing it. Immune cells and fibroblast will surround and enclose the macrophages creating an area of inflammation and abnormal growth. Granulomas are common tuberculosis.

The presence of these abnormal growths will cause disruption of the bone marrow and displace its architecture. The increasing granulomatous "stuff" displaces the marrow elements, reducing the amount of marrow hematopoietic tissue. There is a consequential release of immature cells into the peripheral blood. This condition is known to be associated with [1] prostate cancer, [2] breast cancer, and [3] stomach cancer. These patients are prone to DIC.

Congenital Dyserythropoietic Anemia

This has been classified as both a normocytic and macrocytic anemia. It is a pancytopenia that is described as a refractory familial anemia with abnormal and ineffective erythropoiesis. The peripheral blood is pancytopenic picture. RBCs are characterized by abnormal nuclear development and erythroid hyperplasia is seen in the bone marrow. These patients are likely to develop hemosiderosis. There are three types of CDA.

CDA -TYPE I

This is an autosomal, recessive disorder that manifests itself at birth. This is mild to moderate macrocytic anemia characterized by anisocytosis and poikilocytosis. It is a refractory familial anemia with abnormal and ineffective erythropoiesis. The peripheral blood picture is pancytopenic. The following may be observed in a patient diagnosed with this disorder:

3- Cabot rings
4- NRBCs
5- Large platelets
6- Hgb = 8 to 12 gm/dl
7- MCV = 93 to 115 fl.
8- Basophilic stippling
9- Serum iron = Normal to moderately elevated.
10- Haptoglobin=< 70 mg/dl.
11- Acid serum test = Negative
12- Sugar water test = Negative
13- Reticulocyte count = increased.

One distinguishing feature of this anemia is that from 1% to 3% of the immature RBCs will present with binucleation, incomplete nuclear segments; and thin. Fiber-like internuclear chromatin bridges between nuclei. The immature erythroblastic cells also present with multilobated nuclei and megaloblastic changes. This patient tends to lead a normal life.

CDA- TYPE II

This is the most commonly observed form. It is also called hereditary erythroblast multinuclearity with positive acidified serum test (HEMPAS). This RBC membrane in this disorder has more membrane "i antigens" and susceptible to hemolysis by "i antibodies". The anemia that develops can be mild to severe. This disease tends to benign, but can develop into a serious problem requiring medical intervention such as transfusions. It splenomegaly develops. Surgical removal may be required. Laboratory findings are very similar to CDA- type I. Clinical symptoms include jaundice and hepatomegaly. Note: This anemia mimics "Paroxysmal Nocturnal Hemoglobinuria". PNH RBCs will hemolysate in sugar water as cells from the other three types of CDA do not. The bone marrow features distinguish CDA-type I by demonstrating approximately 10% to 50 % of its bone marrow population of immature cells is characterized with nuclear abnormalities.

CDA-TYPE III

This is an autosomal disorder, dominant anemia that tends to run a mild to moderate benign macrocytic anemia. It is also called hereditary benign erythroreticulosis". It has been described as a combination of type I and type II. It is characterized by extreme multinucleation of the erythroid precursor and may be designated as gigantoblasts. The bone marrow may contain up to 30% of these giant, multinucleated "blast" forms. RBCs from this disorder can agglutinates by anti "i" antibodies.

Paroxysmal Nocturnal Hemoglobinuria (PNH)

PNH occurs when abnormal blood-forming stem cells produce RBC with a defective protective layer. An abnormal platelet function is also detectable among patients with Paroxysmal Nocturnal Hemoglobinuria.

Patients with PNH have lower RBC count caused by the destruction, or hemolysis, of red blood cells in the bloodstream. This destruction occurs when the blood cells lack a necessary surface molecule, GP1, they are destroyed by the complement which is the part of the immune system.

Red blood cells destruction often causes the urine to become dark or red in color. The patient may experience other symptoms, such a back pain, easy bruising of the skin, blood clots (thrombosis), abdominal discomfort, and liver failure.

Several tests are used to diagnosis PNH, including: the CBC, Sucrose hemolysis test, Ham Dacie test (acidified serum lysis test), flow cytometry, urinalysis, and serum hemoglobin.

PNH is not inherited. It often occurs as an isolated disorder. However, it also arises in an estimated 30% of aplastic anemia cases and in some patients with MDS. In addition, 5- 10% of PNH may evolve into acute myelogenous leukemia.

Generally the course of treatment is conservative, depending upon the severity of the symptoms experienced by PNH patients.

    d. Transfusion may be needed when hemoglobin decreases.
    e. Stem cell transplantation is the only known therapy for a cure. Best results are achieved in younger patients with a matched sibling donor.

Diagnostic laboratory tests:

    f. Screening test: Sugar water test: Blood is incubated in a solution 10% of sugar water. The low ionic strength of the solution activated complement. And PNH cells are lysed.

g. Confirmation test: Ham's test (acidified Serum Lysis Test). PNH cells incubated in acidified serum will lyse whereas normal cells will not lyse. In order to be called positive, two conditions must be met:1) hemolysis occurs with the patients cells and not with normal cells, 2) hemolysis is enhanced by acidified serum and does not occur with heat activated serum in with complement has been destroyed.

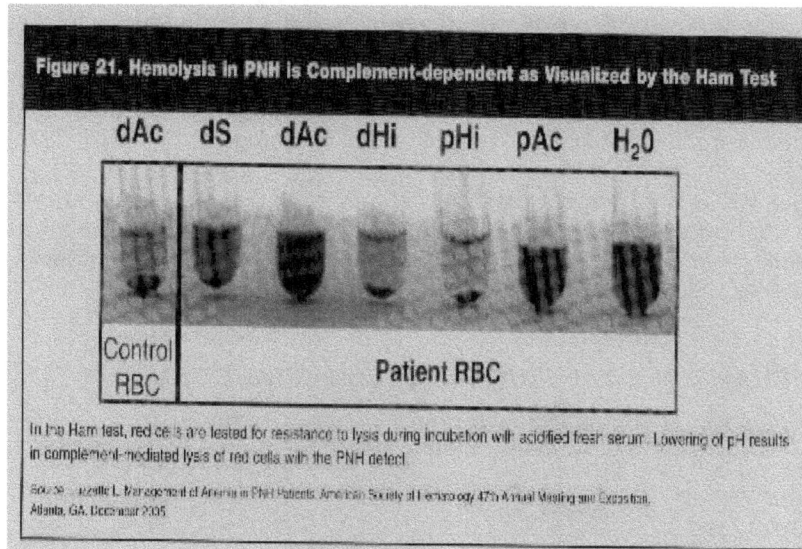

Figure 21. Hemolysis in PNH is Complement-dependent as Visualized by the Ham Test

Credit: THOMSON AMERICAN HEALTH CONSULTANTS

PNH begins between 30 and 50 years of age but may occur at any age. Conditions which may predispose a person to this from of anemia are:
1- Aplastic anemia
2- Viral infections
3- Surgery
4- Menstrual cycle
5- Iron therapy
6- Drugs

It appears that somehow the injury to a stem cell and defective clones are produced that produce the defective RBC membrane. PNH is associated with deficiencies in one to nine proteins. These nine proteins are:
1- Decay accelerating factor (DAF).
2- Membrane inhibition of reactive lysis (MIRL).
3- Homologous restriction factor (HRF).
4- Erythrocyte acetyl cholinesterase.
5- Leukocyte alkaline phosphates
6- Lymphocyte-5'-ectonucleotidase.
7- Lymphocyte function antigen-3 (LFA-3)
8- Neutrophil Fcy III receptor (CD-16).
9- Monocyte antigen (CD- 14).

The PNH patient will demonstrate three types of erythrocytes.
1- Normal appearing RBCs designated as PNH type I cells.
2- PNH type II with moderate sensitivity to complement (about more5x more sensitive than type I).
3- PNH type III with highest sensitivity (about 20x more sensitive than type I).

The degree of severity of PNH is determined by the proportion of the three types of cells. Also the degree of deficiency of cell membrane proteins (in quantity and type) will affect the degree of hemolysis.

PART EIGHT: HEMOLYTIC ANEMIAS

Hemolysis is the premature destruction of erythrocytes, normal RBC survive 100-120 days in the circulation before they are destroyed (mostly in the RES), the normal marrow can compensate for 6 to 8 times the normal rate of hemolysis. Anemia occurs when the rate of hemolysis exceeds the bone marrow's ability to compensate.

Hemolytic anemia is an anemia caused by hemolysis of red blood cells resulting in reduction of normal red cell lifespan. This occurs when bone marrow activity cannot compensate for the erythrocytes loss. In more serious cases, the anemia can be life threatening.

Hemolysis may be either intravascular or extravascular.

In intravascular hemolysis RBCs lyse in the circulation releasing hemoglobin into the plasma. Causes include mechanical trauma, complement fixation, and other toxic damage to the RBC. The RBCs are called schistocytes.

In extravascular hemolysis RBCs are phagocytized be macrophages in the spleen and liver. Causes include RBC membrane abnormalities such as bound immunoglobulin, or physical abnormalities restricting RBC deformability that prevent egress from the spleen. Extravascular hemolysis is characterized by spherocytes.

CHAPTER ONE: INTRACORPUSCULAR DEFECTS

Hereditary Defects of RBC Membrane
A- Defects of the red cell membrane.
B- Enzyme defects.
C- Hemoglobinopathies.
D- Thalassemia syndromes.

Hereditary Spherocytosis

Definition
Spherocytes are seen in a variety of hemolytic anemias, especially those in which the RES is involved in removing the cells. Examples would be immunohemolytic anemias and Hypersplenism. In such cases the spherocytosis is a secondary change due to escape and repair of partially damaged RBCs from the Reticulo Endothelial System.

Hereditary spherocytosis (HS) is an inherited disease that results in the formation of abnormal red blood cells with fragile cells wall. A loss of surface area of the red cell membrane protein (such as spectrin) and membrane protein dysfunction result in the formation of fragile spherocytic red cells.

Because spherocytes cannot change their shape easily, they stay in the spleen longer than normal red blood cell, and the membrane surrounding the cell becomes damaged. After circulating through the spleen many times, the cell eventually becomes so damage that it is destroyed by the spleen.

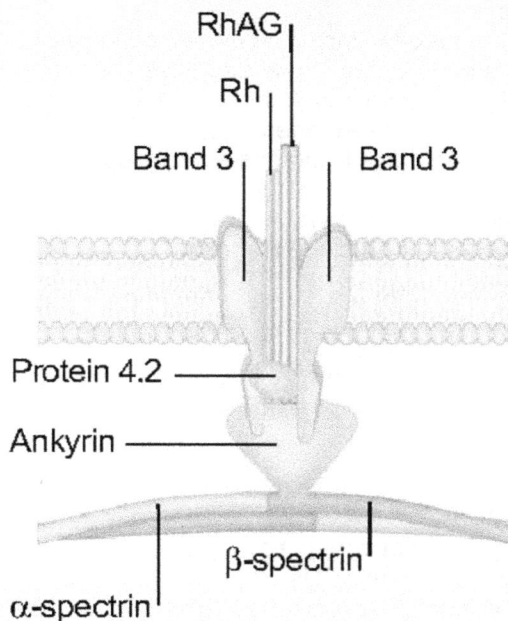

(Illustration by Paulette Dennis)

Membrane defects in HS affect the "vertical" interactions anchoring the membrane skeleton to the lipid bilayer. Deficiency in any one of the protein components (band 3, RhAG, ankyrin, protein 4.2, or spectrin) involved in the anchoring process leads to HS.

Four abnormalities in red cell membrane proteins have been identifiable and include:

1- Spectrin deficiency alone.
2- Combined spectrin and ankyrin deficiency.
3- Band 3 deficiency.
4- Protein 4.2 (pallidin) defects.

Spectrin deficiency is the most common defect. Each is associated with a variety of mutation that results in different protein abnormalities and varied clinical expression. Most cases of HS are heterozygous because homozygous states are lethal.

Signs and symptoms

Symptoms of HS vary depending on the severity of the disease. Many people with HS have a normal hemoglobin level. Most patients have only mild anemia. These patients compensate by producing more reticulocytes. However, infection, fever and stress can stimulate the spleen to destroy more red blood cells than usual. If this occurs anemia may be severe enough to require a red blood cell transfusion.

Anemia, jaundice, and splenomegaly are the clinical features of HS. Splenomegaly is palpable in more than 75% of affected subjects.

Children diagnosed early in life usually have seen a severe form of HS, thus resulting in their early presentation, a family history of HS is present, or the patient may report a history of a family member having had a splenectomy or cholecystectomy before the fourth decade of life.

Adults who remain undiagnosed usually have a very mild form, and they live with the HS remaining undetected until challenged by an environmental stressor.

Laboratory test

1- An increased MCHC values greater than upper limit of normal (35%-36%) are common (this is the only condition in which an MCHC can be truly increased). This increased MCHC is a result of mild cellular dehydration. The MCV in patients with HS actually is low. This relatively low MVC may reflect membrane loss and cell dehydration.

2- RBC morphology is distinctive yet not diagnostic, spherocytes- a smaller than normal RBC with concentrated hemoglobin content and no central pallor, and varying degrees of polychromasia, anisocytosis and poikilocytosis.
3- Biochemical changes of hemolysis also are present, including increased lactate dehydrogenase (LDH), increased unconjugated bilirubin, and decreased serum Haptoglobin.
4- Diagnostic tests: 1)-Osmotic fragility (cells are incubated in decreasing concentration of saline. Spherocytes lyse sooner then normal red cells), 2) - Autohemolysis test (red cells are incubated at 37*C for 48 hours. Degree of hemolysis is increased when spherocytes are present.
5- Red cell membrane is analyzed using gel electrophoresis.
6- The initial workup if hemolysis is suggested should include the following:
    1- Reticulocyte count
    2- LDH
    3- Fractionated bilirubin
    4- Haptoglobin
    5- CBC
    6- Vitamin B12 and folate
    7- Total iron body stores
    8- Herpes simplex virus. HPV type 19 and infections mononucleosis.

Treatment is splenectomy, removing the spleen does not cure the disease, but it does allow the red cell to live longer so that a subject no longer becomes anemic. It is very important that the subject receive all of the normal immunizations and a few special immunizations (pneumococcal and meningococcal immunizations) to prevent infection.

After splenectomy the subject is at an increased risk for certain types of infection. For this reason penicillin is taken twice a day for the rest of life.

The Osmotic Fragility Test

The osmotic fragility test is a measure of the resistance of erythrocytes to hemolysis by osmotic stress. The test consists of exposing red cells to decreasing strengths of hypotonic saline solutions and measuring the degree of hemolysis calorimetrically at room temperature. The percentage of hemolysis is plotted on the vertical axis against decreasing saline concentration on the horizontal axis. A symmetrical curve, sigmoidal in shape, is obtained in most subjects.

1-Reagents:

Stock Solution of buffered sodium chloride (AR) 100 g/L NaCl 90 g
Na2HPO4 13.65 g or Na2HPO4.H2O 17.115 g
NaH2P04.2H2O2.34g
Water to 1 L
From (the stock solution, prepare first a 10 g/L solution by dilution with water. Dilutions equivalent to 9.0, 7.5, 6.5, 6.0, 5.5, 5.0, 4.0, 3.5, 3.0, 2.0, 1.0 g/L are then prepared.

2-Method:

Heparinized venous blood is used. The test should be carried out within 2 hours of collection or within 6 hours if kept at 4° C.
1. Deliver 5.0 mL of the 11 saline solutions in test tubes. Add 5.0 mL of water to tube 12.
2. Add to each tube 50 uL (microliter) of well mixed blood and mix immediately by inverting the tubes for several times avoiding foam.
3. Incubate at room temperature for 30 min. Mix again and centrifuge.
4. Remove supernatant and estimate the amount of lysis in a colorimeter at 540 nm. Use as blank the supernatant in tube 1.
5. Assign a value of 100 % lysis to tube 12 (water).
Factors affecting osmotic fragility tests: Three variables capable of markedly affecting the results, apart from the accuracy of saline concentrations:
1. The relative volumes of blood and saline.
2. The final pH of the blood in saline suspension.
3. The temperature at which the tests are carried out.

A proportion of 1 volume of blood to 100 volumes of saline is chosen to render the effect of the plasma on the final tonicity of the suspension negligible. The fragility of the red cells is increased by a fall in pH. A rise in temperature decreases the fragility, a rise of 5° C being equivalent to an increase in saline concentration of about 0.1 g/L

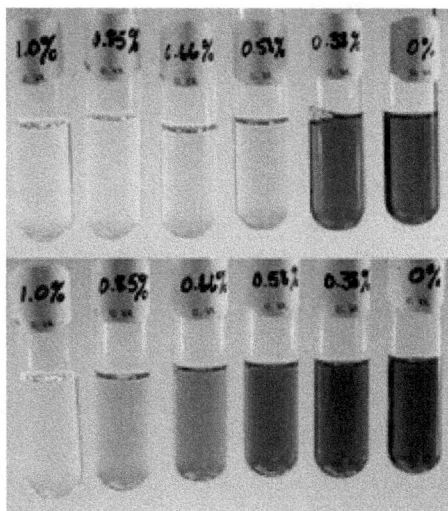

©2007. Rector and visitors of the University of Virginia
  Charles E. Hess, M.D. and Lindsey Krstic, B.A. Used with permission

3-Results recording:

 Osmotic fragility can be described in terms of the saline concentration at which lysis begins (initial lysis or minimum resistance normally 4.5 - 5.0 g/L) and at which lysis appears to be complete (complete lysis or maximum resistance, normally 3.0 - 3.3 g/L). It is essentially useful to record the concentration of saline causing 50 % lysis, i.e. the Median Corpuscular Fragility (MCF), normally 4, 0 - 4.45 g/L. and to inspect the entire curve.

Test-tube No.	Concentration of buffered Sodium chloride solution (g/L)	Distilled water (ml)	Absorbance (wavelength = 540 nm)	Percentage lysis
1	9.0	1.0	0.000	0.00
2	7.5	2.5	0.003	0.33
3	6.5	3.5	0.018	1.99
4	6.0	4.0	0.026	2.88
5	5.5	4.5	0.035	3.73
6	5.0	5.0	0.033	3.66
7	4.0	6.0	0.121	13.43
8	3.5	6.5	0.638	70.81
9	3.0	7.0	0.842	93.45
10	2.0	8.0	0.865	97.00
11	1.0	9.0	0.885	98.22
12	0.0	10.0	0.901	100.00

Table 1

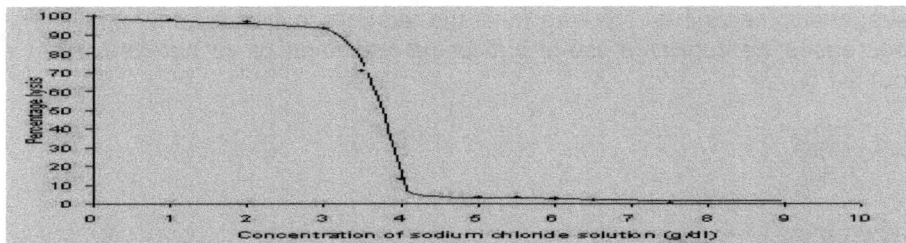

Fig. 1. Graph of percentage lysis against concentration of sodium chloride solution.

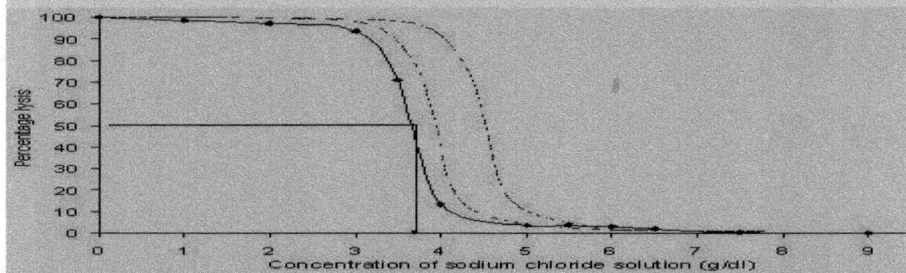

Fig. 2. Graph of percentage lysis against concentration of sodium chloride solution (including normal range).

Discussion: The shape of the curve is only one aspect of the test. The position of the curve on the axes relative to reference values must also be considered. It is essentially useful to record the concentration of sodium chloride solution causing 50% lysis, i.e. the Median Corpuscular Fragility (MCF). This value is normally 4.0-4.5 g/L. Other useful values include the concentration at which lysis begins (minimum resistance) and that at which lysis appears to be complete (maximum resistance). These are normally 4.5-5.0 g/L and 3.0-3.3 g/L respectively. On adding a sketch of the normal range of relevant values to the same axes, it is observed that the experimental curve lies slightly to the left, outside the normal range.

The mean corpuscular fragility (MCF) is obtained as 3.65 g/L of sodium chloride, when the normal range, as indicated earlier, is 4.0-4.45 g/L. The significance of the 'shifting' of the graph to the left may involve an imbalance in intracellular sodium level.

The osmotic fragility test is most useful in the diagnosis of congenital spherocytosis, but here this is most probably not the case. In hereditary spherocytosis, there is abnormal morphology due to a lack of spectrin, a key red blood cell cytoskeletal membrane protein. This produces membrane instability that forces the cell to the smallest volume-a sphere. This is shown by increased osmotic fragility, which causes the entire curve to 'shift to the right' or most of it may be within the normal range, but with a 'tail' of fragile cells. In these patients, intravascular hemolysis results in hemoglobinemia, and the circulating hemoglobin is excreted in the urine, imparting it a red colour. Therefore, a urine sample would have been helpful in this case.

Another possibility could have been hereditary elliptocytosis. As above, the defect is a structural abnormality of spectrin or a deficiency of the red cell membrane protein (4.1), without anemia and usually with no splenomegaly and only mild hemolysis. Most patients are asymptomatic, but the number of elliptocytes does not correlate with the severity of hemolysis. Osmotic fragility is usually normal, but may be similar to that of hereditary spherocytosis, but with less marked changes. 'Idiopathic' acquired hemolytic anemia is also associated with increased osmotic fragility. However, considering the position of the curve, it is more likely that the disease is associated with decreased osmotic fragility. The osmotic fragility curve of patients suffering from b-thalassemia major is outside the normal range and its shape is also altered. Usually not sigmoidal, but shows a steady slope. The mean corpuscular fragility is decreased in all forms of thalassemia, except in some a-thalassemia heterozygotes. The subject being investigated may suffer from some sort of thalassemia (apart from b-thalassemia major and some a-thalassemia) since the whole curve is 'left shifted'. Since ß-thalassemia major patients have severe transfusion dependent anemia and nearly all patients have hepatomegaly and splenomegaly, the diagnosis of this disease could be relatively easily confirmed. The life span of patients with ß-thalassemia major is short, most dying before adulthood. Sickle cell anemia also shows the 'shifting' of the curve to the left. The decreased osmotic fragility is another consequence of the presence of HbS. The latter is poorly soluble in low oxygen tension situations, forming a gel and polymerizing into fibrilary structures or tactoids. This distorts the red cells causing them to become rigid and sickled. But the sickle cell solubility test is the widely used method for screening for sickle cell anemia. The sickle cell solubility test relies on the relative insolubility of HbS in concentrated

177

phosphate buffers compared to HbA and other hemoglobin variants. HbS precipitates causing a cloudy solution. This test can be used to confirm any conclusion of sickle cell anemia.

4-Conclusion:

Although the curve is outside the normal range, suggesting that the patient may be suffering from a hemoglobinopathy, this alone does not provide enough data for tangible definitive conclusions, especially since the deviation from normality is only slight. Experimental conditions might have caused the decrease in fragility: a rise in pH decreases osmotic fragility. This explanation is plausible since the discrepancy is only in the position and not the overall shape of the graph (Fig. 2.). It can be concluded that there may be nothing abnormal with the subject. But it would be safer to carry out the test once more to ensure that experimental errors have not affected the results significantly, before diagnosing sickle cell anemia, some thalassemia, or any condition associated with decreased osmotic fragility.

Increased osmotic fragility (OF):

Hereditary spherocytosis (HS) Entire curve may be shifted to the right or most of it may be within the normal range, but with a 'tail' of fragile cells

Hereditary elliptocytosis (HE) As in HS, but in general, changes are less marked. Abnormal OF usually correlates with severity of hemolysis, i.e. OF is normal in non-hemolytic HE.

Decreased osmotic fragility (OF):

Thalassemia MCF decreased in all forms of thalassemia, except some a-thalassemia heterozygotes; usually the entire curve is left shifted.

Enzyme abnormalities OF usually normal (anemia usually referred to as hereditary non-spherocytic), but tail of highly resistant cells may be seen on account of high reticulocytosis.

Hereditary Elliptocytosis

A defect in the red cell membrane skeleton results in the formation of elliptocytic red cells that are sensitive to mechanical stress.
1- CBC usually normal but mild anemia may exist in some patients.
2- Peripheral smear – marked increase in elliptocytosis or Ovalocytes.
3- Treatment is usually not necessary, but if patients have hemolysis, splenectomy is beneficial.

Hereditary Enzyme Deficiency

Glucose-6-Phosphate Dehydrogenase Deficiency, G-6PD

G6PD deficiency is a hereditary sex-linked anemia in which denatured hemoglobin precipitates in the RBC after exposure to oxidative stress causing hemolysis.

The World health organization has divided G6PD deficiency into five classes:
- h. Class I is the most severe of hemolytic expressions.
- i. Class II hemolytic episodes are mild.
- j. Class III presents with hemolytic episodes.
- k. Class IV and Class V does not manifest hemolytic episodes.

Each of these classes is characterized by different genetic expressions, levels of G6PD enzyme activity and deficiency, and electrophoretic test patterns.

This deficiency is most common in West Africa, the Mediterranean, Middle East, and South Asian Nations. In order to expression of the severity of this disorder the following expresses as follows: Mediterranean Populations> Oriental Populations> Middle East Populations> Black Populations. There are more than 150 variant forms of this disease and are named According to their location, Using G as G6PD the following are example of variants.
[1] G (B+): NORMAL, Found in all populations.
[2] G (A+): ABNORMAL, found in African populations.
[3] G (A-): ABNORMAL, Found in American Black population.
[4] G (Med): ABNORMAL, Found in Mediterranean populations.
[5] G (CANTON): ABNORMAL, Found in Southeast Asian populations.
[6] G (MAHIDOL): ABNORMAL, Found in Thailand and Vietnam populations.

Physiology of G6PD

The G6PD enzyme catalyzes an oxidation/reduction reaction. Oxidation/reduction reactions function in transferring electrons from one molecule to another, oxidation is the loss of electrons and reduction is the gain of electrons. As illustrated, the G6PD enzyme functions in catalyzing the oxidation of glucose-6-phosphate to 6- phosphogluconate, while concomitantly reducing nicotinamide adenine dinucleotide phosphate (NADP+to NADPH); or, in terms of electron transfer, glucose-6-phosphate loses two electrons to become 6-phosphogluconate and NADP+ gains two electrons to become NADPH. This is the first step in the pentose phosphate pathway.

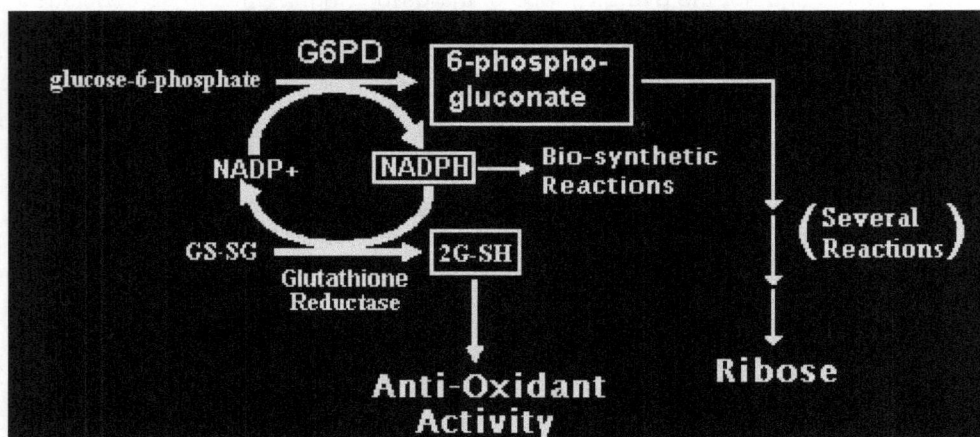

The Pentose Phosphate Pathway. Note the importance of G6PD in the production of reduced G-SH, ribose, and NADPH (adapted from: Yoshida and Beutler, 1986, pg.8).
   * NADP+ = nicotinamide adenine dinucleotide phosphate
   * NADPH = reduced nicotinamide adenine dinucleotide phosphate
   * GS-SG = oxidized glutathione
   * G-SH = reduced glutathione
There are other metabolic that can generate NADPH in all cells, except in red blood cells where other NADPH-producing enzymes are lacking. This has a profound effect on the stability of red blood cells since they are especially sensitive to oxidative stresses in addition to having only one NADPH-producing enzyme to remove these harmful oxidants. This is why G6PD deficient individuals are not prescribed oxidative drugs, because the red blood cells in these individuals are not able to handle this stress and consequently hemolysis ensues.

Clinical Aspects of G6PD Deficiency

When the red blood cell can no longer transport oxygen effectively throughout the body, hemolytic anemia arises. In addition to hemolytic anemia, G6PD deficiency individuals can expect several other clinical manifestations of their condition. These include neonatal jaundice, abdominal and/or/ back pain, dizziness, headache, dyspnea, and palpitation. Neonatal jaundice is a common condition in all newborns, but when it persists, G6PD deficiency is suspected. Hemolytic anemia is another condition which may cause problems for G6PD deficient individuals. An anemic response can be induced in affected individuals by certain oxidative drugs, fava beans, or infections. In order to prevent a severe reaction or even death, G6PD deficiency individuals are prohibited from taking certain drugs such as, antipyrine, aspirin, quinine and sulfacetamide for example, the common theme shared among these drugs is that they are oxidizing agents.
The severe case of G6PD deficiency is called FAVISM.

Laboratory Tests

Tests most frequently upon are
   1- CBC
   2- Peripheral Blood Smear Evaluation
   3- Retic Count
   4- Heinz Body Stain

5- RBC Enzyme Screen
6- Urine Hemoglobin
7- Serum Haptoglobin
8- Serum Indirect Bilirubin
9- LDH With LDH-1 and LDH-2

Pyruvate Kinase (PK) Deficiency

 The PK enzyme is found in the Embden-Meyerhof Pathway, commonly known as the glycolysis pathway. It catalyzes the conversion of phosphoenolpyruvate to pyruvate and generates an ATP molecule. This disorder causes a mild to severe hemolytic anemia in homozygotes. People of northern European descent are more prone toward this anomaly, inheriting it as an autosomal recessive trait. If the anomaly is severe, it will manifest itself in infancy. If a mild form of the disorder, then it will manifest in adulthood. If the individual is heterozygous for the trait, pyruvate kinase levels are a bout 50% that of the normal individual. They will remain asymptomatic throughout life with no anemia or morphological changes.
 Clinical manifestations are variable. The patient readily tolerates the anemia as a rule. Such patients may demonstrate gallstones, splenomegaly, or jaundice. If the hemozygotic infant has a serious episode, an exchange transfusion may be required. Expected clinical laboratory finding include the following:

1- Anemia with a hemoglobin level ranging from 6 to 12 gm/dl.
2- RBCs are usually normocytic and normochromic.
3- MVC=> 100 fl (indicating the presence of macrocytes).
4- Reticulocytes = up to 15%, (if a splenectomy, then count may be up to 55%, the reticulocyte is vulnerable to hemolysis in PK deficiency, easily destroyed in the spleen).
5- Stained blood smear morphology (usually there is no remarkable morphologic features, but the following may be observed). Anisocytosis, poikilocytosis, polychromasia, echinocytes, no Heinz bodies or spherocytes, NRBCs are seen.
6- Pyruvate = Decrease.
7- Lactate= Decrease.
8- Osmotic fragility = Normal.

The Hemoglobinopathies

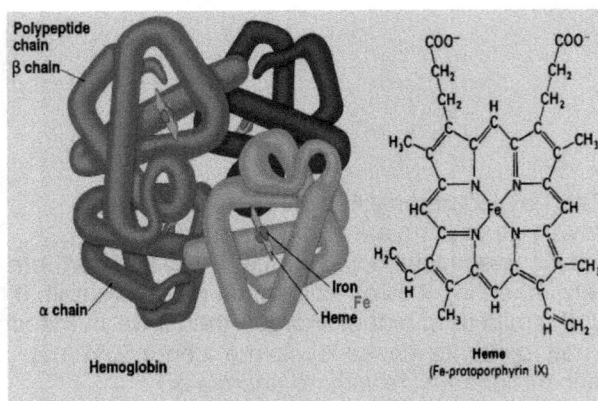

Hemoglobin synthesis requires the coordinated production of heme and globin. Heme is the prosthetic group that mediates reversible binding of oxygen by hemoglobin. Globin is the protein that surrounds and protects the heme molecule.

Heme Synthesis

Heme is synthesized in a complex series of steps involving enzymes in the mitochondrion and in the cytosol of the cell. The first step in heme synthesis takes place in the mitochondrion, with the condensation of succinyl CoA and glycine by ALA synthase to form 5-aminolevulic acid (ALA). This molecule is transported to the cytosol where a series of reactions produce a ring structure called coproporphyrinogen III. This molecule returns to the mitochondrion where an addition reaction produces protoporphyrin IX.

The enzyme ferrochelatase inserts iron into the ring structure of protoporphyrin IX to produce heme. Deranged production of heme produces a variety of anemias. Iron deficiency, the world's most common cause of anemia, impairs heme synthesis thereby producing anemia. A number of drugs and toxins directly inhibit heme production by interfering with enzymes involved in heme biosynthesis. Lead commonly produces substantial anemia by inhibiting heme synthesis, particularly in children.

Globin Synthesis

Two distinct globin chains (each with its individual heme molecule) combine to form hemoglobin. One of the chains is designated alpha. The second chain is called "non-alpha". With the exception of the very first weeks of embryogenesis, one of the globin chains is always alpha. A number of variables influence the nature of the non-alpha chain in the hemoglobin molecule. The fetus has a distinct non-alpha chain called gamma. After birth, a different non-alpha globin chain, called beta, pairs with the alpha chain. The combination of two alpha chains and two non-alpha chains produces a complete hemoglobin molecule (a total of four chains per molecule).

The combination of two alpha chains and two gamma chains form "fetal" hemoglobin, termed "hemoglobin F". With the exception of the first 10 to 12 weeks after conception, fetal hemoglobin is the primary hemoglobin in the developing fetus. The combination of two alpha chains and two beta chains form "adult" hemoglobin, also called "hemoglobin A". Although hemoglobin A is called "adult", it becomes the predominate hemoglobin within about 18 to 24 weeks of birth.

The pairing of one alpha chain and one non-alpha chain produces a hemoglobin dimer (two chains). The hemoglobin dimer does not efficiently deliver oxygen, however. Two dimers combine to form a hemoglobin tetramer, which is the functional form of hemoglobin. Complex biophysical characteristics of the hemoglobin tetramer permit the exquisite control of oxygen uptake in the lungs and release in the tissues that is necessary to sustain life. The genes that encode the alpha globin chains are on chromosome 16. Those that encode the non-alpha globin chains are on chromosome 11. Multiple individual genes are expressed at each site. Pseudo genes are also present at each location. The alpha complex is called the "alpha globin locus", while the non-alpha complex is called the "beta globin locus". The expression of the alpha and non-alpha genes is closely balanced by an unknown

181

mechanism. Balanced gene expression is required for normal red cell function. Disruption of the balance produces a disorder called thalassemia.

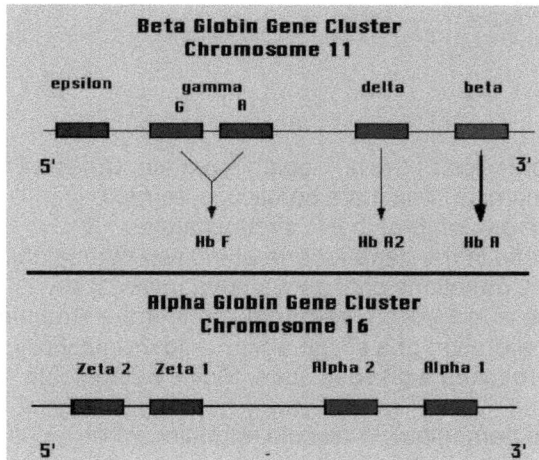

Beta Globin Gene Cluster
Chromosome 11

epsilon   gamma   delta   beta
                G   A

5'   3'

Hb F   Hb A2   Hb A

Alpha Globin Gene Cluster
Chromosome 16

Zeta 2   Zeta 1   Alpha 2   Alpha 1

5'   -   3'

The lower panel shows the alpha globin locus that resides on chromosome 16. Each of the four alpha globin genes contributes to the synthesis of the alpha globin protein. The upper panel shows the beta globin locus. The two gamma globin genes are active during fetal growth and produce hemoglobin F. The "adult" gene, beta, takes over after birth.

Alpha Globin Locus

Each chromosome 16 has two alpha globin genes that are aligned one after the other on the chromosome. For practical purposes, the two alpha globin genes (termed α1 and α2) are identical. Since each cell has two chromosomes 16, a total of four α globin genes exist in each cell. Each of the four genes produces about one-quarter of α globin chains needed for hemoglobin synthesis. The mechanism of this coordination is unknown. Promoter elements exist 5' to each α globin gene. In addition, a powerful enhancer region called the locus control region (LCR) is required for optimal gene expression. The LCR is many kilo bases upstream of α globin locus. The mechanism by which DNA elements so distant from the genes control their expression is the source of intense investigation. The transiently expressed embryonic genes that substitute for α very early in development, designated zeta are also in α globin locus.

Beta Globin Locus

The genes in the β globin locus are arranged sequentially from 5' to 3' beginning with the gene expressed in embryonic development (the first 12 weeks after conception; called epsilon). The β globin locus ends with the adult β globin gene. The sequence of the genes is: epsilon, gamma, delta, and beta. There are two copies of the gamma gene on each chromosome 11. The others are present in single copies. Therefore, each cell has two beta globin genes, one on each of the two chromosomes 11 in the cell. These two β globin genes express their globin protein in a quantity that precisely matches that of the four alpha globin genes. The mechanism of this balanced expression is unknown.

Ontogeny of Hemoglobin Synthesis

The globin genes are activated in sequence during development, moving from 5' to 3' on the chromosome. The zeta gene of the alpha globin gene cluster is expressed only during the first few weeks of embryogenesis. Thereafter, the alpha globin genes take over. For the beta globin gene cluster, the epsilon gene is expressed initially during embryogenesis. The gamma gene is expressed during fetal development. The combination of two alpha genes and two gamma genes forms fetal hemoglobin or hemoglobin F. Around the time of birth, the production of gamma globin declines in concert with a rise in beta globin synthesis. A significant amount of fetal hemoglobin persists for seven or eight months after birth. Most people have only trace amounts, if any, of fetal hemoglobin after infancy. The combination of two alpha genes and two beta genes comprises the normal adult hemoglobin, hemoglobin A. The delta gene, which is located between the gamma and beta genes on chromosome 11, produces a small amount of delta globin in children and adults. The product of the delta globin gene is called hemoglobin A2, and normally comprises less than 3.5% of hemoglobin in adults, is composed of two alpha chains and two delta chains.

Hemoglobin Disorder

Hemoglobin is produced by genes that control the expression of the hemoglobin protein. Defects in these genes can produce abnormal hemoglobins and anemias, which are conditions, termed "Hemoglobinopathies". Abnormal hemoglobins appear in one of three basic circumstances:
- Structural defects in the hemoglobin molecule. Alterations in the gene for one of the two hemoglobin subunit chains, alpha or beta are called mutations. Often, mutations change a single amino acid building block in the subunit. Most commonly the change is innocuous, perturbing neither the structure nor function of the hemoglobin molecule. Occasionally, alteration of a single amino acid dramatically disturbs the behavior of the hemoglobin molecule and produces a disease state. Sickle hemoglobin exemplifies this phenomenon.
- Diminished production of one of the two subunits of the hemoglobin molecule. Mutations that produce this condition are termed "thalassemia" Equal numbers of hemoglobin alpha and beta chains are necessary for normal function. Hemoglobin chain imbalance damages and destroys red cells thereby producing anemia. Although there is a dearth of the affected hemoglobin subunit, with most thalassemia the few subunits synthesized are structurally normal.
- Abnormal associations of otherwise normal subunits. A single subunit of the alpha chain (from the alpha-globin locus) and a single subunit from the beta-globin locus combine to produce a normal hemoglobin dimer. With severe alpha-thalassemia, the beta-globin subunits begin to associate into groups of four (tetramers) due to the paucity of potential alpha-chain partners. These tetramers of beta-globin subunits are functionally inactive and do not transport oxygen. No comparable tetramers of alpha globin subunits form with severe beta-thalassemia. Alpha subunits are rapidly degraded in the absence of a partner from the beta-globin gene cluster (gamma, delta, beta globin subunits).

Types of hemoglobins

There are hundreds of hemoglobin variants that involve genes both from the alpha and beta gene clusters. The list below touches on some of the more common and important hemoglobin variants.

Normal Hemoglobins

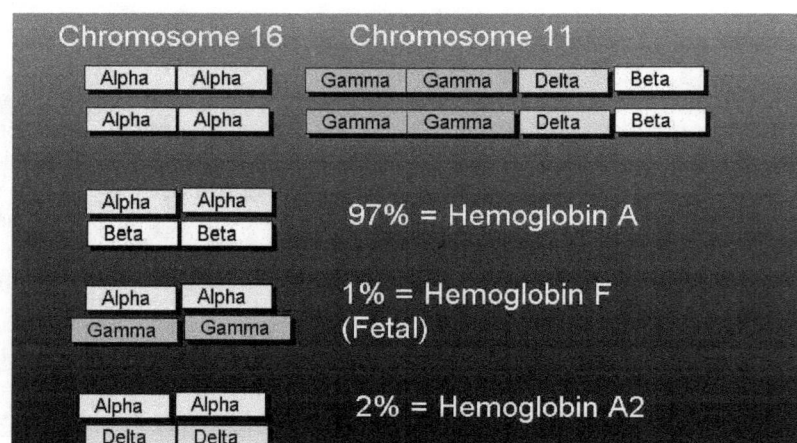

Credit: James R. Eckman, M.D., SERGG Workshop 1992

1- Hemoglobin A. This is the designation for the normal hemoglobin that exists after birth. Hemoglobin A is a tetramer with two alpha chains and two beta chains

2- Hemoglobin A2. This is a minor component of the hemoglobin found in red cells after birth and consists of two alpha chains and two delta chains Hemoglobin A2 generally comprises less than 3.5% of the total red cell hemoglobin.

3- Hemoglobin F. Hemoglobin F is the predominant hemoglobin during fetal development. The molecule is a tetramer of two alpha chains and two gamma chains

The genes for Hb F and Hb A are closely related, existing in the same gene cluster on chromosome 11. Hemoglobin F production falls dramatically after birth, although some people continue to produce small amounts of hemoglobin F for their entire lives.

Clinically Significant Variant Hemoglobins

1-Hb S

Hemoglobin S is the predominant hemoglobin in people with sickle cell disease. The alpha chain is normal. The disease-producing mutation exists in the beta chain. People who have one sickle mutant gene and one normal beta gene have sickle cell trait which is benign.

2-Hb C

Hemoglobin C results from a mutation in the beta globin gene and is the predominant hemoglobin found in people with hemoglobin C disease. Hemoglobin C disease is relatively benign, producing a mild hemolytic anemia and splenomegaly. Hemoglobin C trait is benign.

3-Hb E

This variant results from a mutation in the hemoglobin beta chain. People with hemoglobin E disease have a mild hemolytic anemia and mild splenomegaly. Hemoglobin E trait is benign. Hemoglobin E is extremely common in S.E. Asia.

4-Hb Constant Spring

Hemoglobin Constant Spring is a variant in which a mutation in the alpha globin gene produces an alpha globin chain that is abnormally long. The quantity of hemoglobin in the cells is low for two reasons. First, the messenger RNA for hemoglobin Constant Spring is unstable. Some is degraded prior to protein synthesis. Second, the Constant Spring alpha chain protein is itself unstable. The result is a thalassemic phenotype. (The designation Constant Spring derives from the isolation of the hemoglobin variant in a family of ethnic Chinese background from the Constant Spring district of Jamaica.)

5-Hb H

Hemoglobin H is a tetramer composed of four beta globin chains. Hemoglobin H occurs only with extreme limitation of alpha chain availability. Hemoglobin H forms in people with three-gene alpha thalassemia as well as in people with the combination of two-gene deletion alpha thalassemia and hemoglobin Constant Spring.

6-Hb Barts

Hemoglobin Barts develops in fetuses with four-gene deletion alpha thalassemia. During normal embryonic development, the epsilon gene of the alpha globin gene locus combines with genes from the beta globin locus to form functional hemoglobin molecules. The epsilon gene turns off at about 12 weeks, and normally the alpha gene takes over. With four-gene deletion alpha thalassemia no alpha chain is produced. The gamma chains produced during fetal development combine to form gamma chain tetramers. These molecules transport oxygen poorly. Most individuals with four-gene deletion thalassemia and consequent hemoglobin Barts die in utero (hydrops fetalis).

The abnormal hemoglobin seen during fetal development in individuals with four-gene deletion alpha thalassemia was characterized at St. Bartholomew's Hospital in London. The hospital has the fond sobriquet, St. Barts, and the hemoglobin was named "hemoglobin Barts."

Compound Heterozygous Conditions

Hemoglobin is made of two subunits derived from genes in the alpha gene cluster on chromosome 16 and two subunits derived from genes in the beta gene cluster on chromosome 11. Occasionally someone inherits two different variant genes from the alpha globin gene cluster or two different variant genes from the beta globin gene cluster (a gene for hemoglobin S and one for hemoglobin C, for instance). This condition is called "compound heterozygous". The nature of two genes inherited determines whether a clinically significant disease state develops. The compound heterozygous states tends to consist of common groupings (e.g., hemoglobin SC), due to the geographic clustering of hemoglobin variants around the world.

5-3 -1 Hemoglobin SC disease

Patients with hemoglobin SC disease inherit a gene for hemoglobin S from one parent, and a gene for hemoglobin C from the other. Hemoglobin C interacts with hemoglobin S to produce some of the abnormalities seen in patients with sickle cell disease. On average, patients with hemoglobin SC disease have milder symptoms than do those with sickle cell disease. This is only an average, however. Some people with hemoglobin SC disease have a condition equal in severity to that of any patient with sickle cell disease. A number other syndromes exist that involve a hemoglobin S compound heterozygous state. They are less common than hemoglobin SC disease, however. Ironically, hemoglobin SC disease is often a much more severe condition than is homozygous hemoglobin C disease. The expression of a single hemoglobin S gene normally produces no problem (i.e., sickle cell trait). The hemoglobin C molecule disturbs the red cell metabolism only slightly. However, the disturbance is enough to allow the deleterious effects of the hemoglobin S to be manifested.

5-3-2-Sickle/beta-thalassemia

In this condition, the patient has inherited a gene for hemoglobin S from one parent and a gene for beta-thalassemia from the other. The severity of the condition is determined to a large extent by the quantity of normal hemoglobin produced by the beta-thalassemia gene. (Thalassemia genes produce normal hemoglobin, but in variably reduced amounts). If the gene produces no normal hemoglobin, beta (0)-thalassemia, the condition is virtually identical to sickle cell disease. Some patients have a gene that produces a small amount of normal hemoglobin, called beta (+)-thalassemia. The severity of the condition is dampened when significant quantities of normal hemoglobin are produced by the beta (+)-thalassemia gene. Sickle/beta-thalassemia is the most common sickle syndrome seen in people of Mediterranean descent (Italian, Greek, and Turkish). Beta-thalassemia is quite common in this region, and the sickle cell gene occurs in some sections of these countries. Hemoglobin electrophoresis of blood from a patient with sickle/beta (0)-thalassemia shows no hemoglobin A. Patients with sickle/beta (+)-thalassemia have an amount of hemoglobin A that depends of the level of function of the beta (+)-thalassemia gene.

5-3-3 Hemoglobin E/beta-thalassemia

The combination of hemoglobin E and beta-thalassemia produces a condition more severe than is seen with either hemoglobin E trait or beta-thalassemia trait. The disorder manifests as a moderately severe thalassemia that falls into the category of thalassemia intermediate. Hemoglobin E/beta-thalassemia is most common in people of S.E. Asian background.

5-3-4 Alpha thalassemia/Hemoglobin Constant Spring

This syndrome is a compound heterozygous state of the alpha globin gene cluster. The alpha globin gene cluster on one of the two chromosomes 16 has both alpha globin genes deleted. On the other chromosome 16, the alpha1 gene has the Constant Spring mutation. The compound heterozygous condition produces a severe shortage of alpha globin chains. The excess beta chains associate into tetramers to form hemoglobin H.

6- Sickle cell Disease

Sickle cell disease has been referred to as "sickle cell anemia". Physicians, researchers, and those affected by this hemoglobin disorder prefer to use the term disease since it is a syndrome with many manifestations. There are no true cures for this disease. Hydroxyurea (a drug used to treat certain malignancies) has been found to increase the production of fetal hemoglobin. Hemoglobin F in higher concentrations tends to prevent the sickling phenomenon. Nitric oxide is an alternative treatment that causes the hemoglobin-S molecule to retain its oxyhemoglobin form in preference to the deoxyhemoglobin form, which hinders the tendency of the cell to sickle.

The signs and symptoms of sickle cell (Drepanocytes) anemia appear about 6 months of age. By this time enough of the HbS has replaced HbF that the trait can express itself. What the parent sees and the physician records in the medical chart is a child that is not growing as it should, there is increased susceptibility to infections (especially pneumonia), and a general failure to thrive. The patient should be tested for sickle cell anemia.

Sickle cell disease or sickle cell anemia is due to a defective gene in the beta hemoglobin chain. The sixth amino acid (glutamic acid) from the "N" terminal end of the globulin molecule is replaced by valine. The alpha and beta chains can combine to form the hemoglobin molecule, but it is abnormal. The seriousness of this disease is due the tendency of the sickle cell hemoglobin molecule to form aggregates in the low oxygen atmospheres and under go polymerization. The cell forms a type of a rigid filamentous gel as the membrane shrinks and the cell undergoes changes in shape and the RBC loses it flexibility and cannot deform to move through the capillaries. This deformity phenomenon is known as "sickling". There is a corresponding hemolysis of the deformed cells resulting in the patient experiencing anemia and jaundice.

Sickle cell patients can be heterozygous or homozygous; therefore there can be levels of the defective hemoglobin molecule. If the patient does not have more than 40% of their hemoglobin in the sickle cell form (HbS), they are asymptomatic and never have any difficulty with this disease. If the amount of HbS is between 40% and 80%, the patient may have mild to moderate manifestations of this disease. Those who have 80% or more of their hemoglobin as the HbS type, they will display the typical symptoms of the disease are true homozygotes. Sickle cell anemia is prevalent among the American black population. It is estimated that 1 in 650 blacks will have sickle cell anemia. This gene is found in the Mediterranean basin, Middle East, and India.

Sickling crises are induced by fever, respiratory diseases, and physical activity: anything that can cause anoxia. This includes pregnancy. When a crisis occurs, the sickled RBCs occlude the capillaries and small blood vessels over the body. This sets up areas of infarction and causes pain, especially in the bones, abdomen, and chest. Other areas include the kidney, retina, brain (about 25% of these patients will have a neurological disturbance), spleen, lungs, cancellous areas of the long bones, and lower limbs. If the patient lives into adulthood, the spleen will have been damaged because of the many infarctions and it will be reduced to a functionless, atrophic structure. These patients often demonstrate ulcerations around the ankles of the legs. Infections tend to be common and recurrent.

Patients with sickle cell disease undergo episodes referred to as crises. An episode is an event in which something happens. Examples of crises are:

[1] Hemolytic crisis in which RBCs have a shortened life span producing a decrease in hemoglobin and hematocrit. Reticulocytes are increased and jaundice is possible.

[2] The vaso-occlusive crisis is the trademark symptom of this disease and occurs most often in the bones, brain, lungs, penis, and spleen. When the small blood vessels are occluded by the sickled RBCs, there are strong manifestations of pain.

[3] Sequestration is a crisis characterized by the sudden and intense pooling of RBC's in the spleen, depriving the vascular system of cells. If a peripheral blood sample were taken during this time, the hemoglobin value can be as low as 6 mg/dL. This occurs most often in children and infants. It can be fatal in infants.

Sickle cell anemia is characterized a high mortality rate, even with the best of medical intervention. Most patients die in early adulthood.

Clinical laboratory findings include:

WBC count	10,000 to 30,000/μL
RBC count	1.0 to 4.0 X 106/μL
Hgb	3 to 11 gm/dL
Hct	9 to 33%
Retic count	5-20%

* WBC Differential: Look for shift-to-left with possible metamyelocytes and myelocytes. Also look for the following which are usual findings in the differential: [a] sickle cells, [b] NRBCs, [c] anisocytosis, [d] basophilic stippling, [e] target cells, [f] Howell-Jolly bodies, [g] Polychromatophilia, [h] spherocytes, and [i] poikilocytosis.
* Platelet count . . . . up to 500,000/μL
* a positive hemoglobin electrophoresis test for HbS-S or Hb-SC
* Serum Bilirubin   1.0 to 3.0 mg/dL
* a bone marrow examination will feature a 40 to 70% increase in NRBCs.
* RBC osmotic fragility test will be decreased.

7- Hemoglobin C Disease

Hemoglobin C disease is a disorder where the normal hemoglobin production is suppressed. It is a disease that is found principally in up to 28% of the black population of West African descent. This is a disorder that does not require specific medical intervention. Hemoglobin C disease is usually asymptomatic. When symptoms do occur, the homozygous patient complains of pain in the abdomen and joints. This patient may also experience fatigue, splenomegaly, and hemolytic episodes. It can become a problem if there is the presence of an infection. Hemoglobin C differs from normal hemoglobin when lysine is substituted for the sixth positioned glutamic acid in the beta chain. This substitution results in decreased hemoglobin solubility and if RBC dehydration occurs. The hemoglobin will precipitate out in the form of crystals. The formation of crystals within the cell causes increased cellular rigidity, decreasing the life span of the erythrocyte up to 55 days.

In the true homozygous C patient, hemoglobin A_1 is absent. In the heterozygous individual, up to 60% of the hemoglobin is of the A_1 type, up to 40% is hemoglobin C, and there remainder is hemoglobin A_2.

Clinically, this disorder manifests with a mild, chronic, normocytic, normochromic hemolytic anemia. The peripheral blood smear is characterized by up to 90% targets cells, along with folded cells, Microspherocytes, poikilocytes, and a variety of fragmented cells. Intra-erythrocytes Hemoglobin C crystals are present. (NOTE: If the RBCs are washed in saline and then resuspended in sodium citrate, crystals can be observed.) Hemoglobin C crystals are pyramid shaped and tetragonal shaped.

Other lab findings are [1] increased reticulocytes, [2] decreased osmotic fragility due to the target cells, and [3] NRBCs may be observed. (NOTE: If the blood smear is allowed to dry slowly, hemoglobin C crystals will likely be demonstrated on the blood film.)

8- Hemoglobin S/C Disease

This is due to a patient having both an Hb S and Hb C gene. This is a double heterozygous disorder due to a defect in the beta-globulin chains. This means that the individual does not have a normal hemoglobin chain which can result in moderately severe manifestations. One beta-globulin chain will have the glutamic acid replaced by valine (Hb S) and the other, lysine replaces glutamic acid.
One parent donates the Hb S gene and the other donates the Hb C gene. The RBC contains approximately equal amounts of Hb C and Hb S with up to 8% hemoglobin F. No hemoglobin A is present.
This genetic disorder may not express itself until the teen years. Clinical symptoms include:
[1] increased blood viscosity   [5] femoral head necrosis
[2] splenomegaly   [6] increased incidence of spontaneous abortions
[3] retinal hemorrhage   [7] vaso-occlusion crises
[4] renal papillary necrosis
This disorder can express itself in a mild form or can be as complicated as a sickle cell crisis.

Clinical laboratory observations include any combination of the following:

[1] Hemoglobin ranging from 10 to 14 g/dL
[2] Hematocrit is usually above 25%
[3] The MCHC is usually increased
[4] The MCH and MCV is variable
[5] Up to 90% target cells
[6] Hemoglobin C crystals may be demonstrated in the peripheral smear
[7] Mild to severe anisocytosis and/or poikilocytosis.

9- Hemoglobin D Disease

This is a β-chain disorder in which glutamine substitutes for glutamic acid at the 126 position. This is a disorder that remains somewhat benign in either the homozygous or heterozygous state. Patients have been reported as presenting with an enlarged spleen.
The indices are normal. Any poikilocytosis is usually limited to a few target cells. The osmotic fragility test is usually decreased. There are about 16 Hb D beta-chain variants reported, all of which are benign conditions. Electrophoretically, this hemoglobin migrates identical to Hb S. The sickle cell test (to differentiate) is negative. There are six known alpha-chain variants of Hb D.

10- Hemoglobin E Disease

Hemoglobin E disease is a beta- variant where lysine substitutes for glutamic acid at the 26th position. This is the third most prevalent world wide hemoglobinopathy being found predominately in oriental populations. This trait is generally asymptomatic and the only clinical manifestation is the presence of splenomegaly in the homozygous state. In the homozygous state it may present as a mild anemia characterized by microcytes and target cells. The presence of the microcytes is due the unstable nature of Hb E under oxygen stress. Clinical lab findings may include any of the following: [1] microcytes, [2] target cells, [3] MCV = 65 to 70 fL (indicating microcytosis), and [4] decreased osmotic fragility if microcytes are present. The homozygous individual will have up to 97% Hb E with Hb A_2 and Hb F. The heterozygous individual will have up to 70% Hb A, up to 30% Hb E, and a small amount of A_2. If Hb E is present and the patient has IDA, then the diagnosis of Hb E may be masked.

11- Hemoglobin G Disease

Hemoglobin G is a variant of hemoglobin D. It is an alpha-chain variant. The Hb G Philadelphia in which the amino acid lysine substitutes for asparagines in the 68th position. This disorder is asymptomatic in the heterozygous state and is found in the American black population (those of West African descent). The homozygous condition is not compatible with life. In the heterozygote, hemoglobin G makes up to 40% of the total hemoglobin. Hemoglobins A1, A_2, and F are part of the hemoglobin composition.

12- Hemoglobin M Disease

Also known as methemoglobinemia, this disorder is the result of tyrosine substituting for histidine in the alpha- or beta -globulin chains. These substitutions allow the iron ion to be auto-oxidized from the Fe^{++} (ferrous) to the Fe^{+++} (ferric) state. In this oxidized ferric state, it cannot combine with oxygen. This in turn will cause cyanosis when methemoglobin levels reach levels of 20% to 40%. This is an autosomal dominant disorder and is found worldwide. If the individual is born in the homozygous state, the condition is incompatible with life. The only known variants are heterozygotes and are asymptomatic.

Clinically, a child has born with the beta-chain variant do not express symptoms of cyanosis until after the second or third month of life. This is when the gamma-chains (fetal hemoglobin) have completed switching to the beta-chains. If the substitution is located in the alpha-globulin chain, then cyanosis will occur at birth. The cyanotic color of the skin is due to the circulating methemoglobin which gives the blood a chocolate-brown color. The affected heterozygote will have up to 50% of their hemoglobin of the M type. Other clinical symptoms include: [a] clubbing of the fingers, [b] a bluish slate-gray or brown cyanosis of the skin, lips, and nail beds.

Clinical laboratory findings are:
[1] Presence of Heinz bodies
[2] urine with a brown color and blood serum with a brownish-green or brownish-gray color.
There is no effective treatment for this condition. This condition should be accurately diagnosed to prevent unwarranted and unnecessary treatment for other conditions (example: cyanotic heart disease.) Methemoglobinemia is a problem to the patient because it is cosmetically embarrassing.

Acquired methemoglobinemia (caused by toxic drug effects) is the most prevalent form of the three types of methemoglobinemia. The drug will cause oxidation of hemoglobin and the level of exposure to the drug determines the degree of methemoglobin formation. Treatment can be effective with the use of methylene blue or ascorbic acid. The formation of methemoglobin by a toxic drug may be less serious, if the methemoglobin reducing system can keep up with it, since the drug may have the potential to initiate a severe hemolytic crisis. In such an event, the serum bilirubin will elevate with the appearance of possible marked anemia. Heinz body formation may strikingly obvious.
Causes for this form of methemoglobin have included [a] eating meats or drinking well water containing high levels of nitrates and nitrites, [b] burn patients treated with silver nitrate, [c] exposure to ionizing radiation, [d] eating crayons or chalk containing aniline dyes, and [e] products containing nitrobenzene .
Examples of chemicals known to be associated with methemoglobin formation include: [a] phenacetin, [b] sulfonamides, [c] pyridium, [d] benzocaine, [e] lidocaine, [e] nitroglycerin, [f] acetophenetidin, [g] dinitrotoluene [h] resorcinol, and [i] hydroquinone.

13- Hemoglobin O Arab

Hemoglobin O Arab is a hemoglobin variant found in people from the Balkans (Bosnia, Bulgaria, Croatia, and Serbia) and the Middle East, and occasionally in African-Americans. The beta chain of hemoglobin O Arab contains a lysine substituted for the glutamic acid at position 121. Hemoglobin O Arab migrates with hemoglobin C (slower than sickle hemoglobin) on cellulose acetate electrophoresis at pH 8.4. The mobility of these hemoglobins differs on agar gel electrophoresis at pH 6.2 and they can be distinguished by this method

Patients who have hemoglobin O Arab trait (A/O Arab) will have no associated health problems. Testing the partner of pregnant patients with hemoglobin O Arab trait is recommended to determine the risk of the couple having a child with a symptomatic hemoglobinopathy. The more common hemoglobin traits that can cause a symptomatic hemoglobinopathy in combination with hemoglobin O Arab are: sickle cell trait, beta-thalassemia trait, and hemoglobin O Arab (resulting in homozygous hemoglobin O Arab).

Hemoglobin S/O Arab is similar to homozygous sickle cell anemia (S/S) with vaso-occlusive manifestations and severe hemolytic anemia. Children with this condition may develop hand-foot syndrome and acute splenic sequestration crises. As with all newborns with sickle cell disease, newborns with hemoglobin S/O Arab need to be placed on prophylactic penicillin beginning at two months of age.

Hemoglobin O Arab/beta°-thalassemia causes a moderately severe anemia with a hemoglobin level of 6 to 8 g/dl and splenomegaly. Several such cases have been reported from Bulgaria.
The homozygous state for hemoglobin O Arab may also be a relatively severe disorder.

Thalassemia Syndromes

The thalassemias are a group of disorders in which the normal hemoglobin protein is produced in lower amounts than usual. The genes are defective in the amount of hemoglobin they produce, but that which they produce (generally) is normal. The thalassemias are a complex group of disorders because of the genetics of hemoglobin production and the structure of the hemoglobin molecule. The fundamental abnormality in thalassemia is impaired production of either the alpha or beta hemoglobin chain. Thalassemia is a difficult subject to explain, since the condition is not a single disorder, but a group of defects with similar clinical effects. More confusion comes from the fact that the clinical descriptions of thalassemia were coined before the molecular basis of the thalassemias was uncovered. As a result, the organizational structure is somewhat disorderly. Review of thalassemia is best approached by separately examining its genetic basis and clinical expression. Thalassemia includes disorders affecting the alpha hemoglobin chain genes and the beta hemoglobin chain gene.

Clinical Classifications of the Thalassemias

Alpha Thalassemia

Alpha thalassemia occurs when one or more of the four alpha chain genes fails to function. Alpha chain protein production, for practical purposes, is evenly divided among the four genes. With alpha thalassemia, the "failed" genes are almost invariably lost from the cell due to a genetic accident.
[1] – Silent carrier.
The loss of one gene diminishes the production of the alpha protein only slightly. This condition is so close to normal that it can be detected only by specialized laboratory techniques that, until recently, were confined to research laboratories. A person with this condition is called a "silent carrier" because of the difficulty in detection.
[2]- Alpha-Thalassemia trait.
The loss of two genes (two-gene deletion alpha thalassemia) produces a condition with small red blood cells, and at most a mild anemia. People with this condition look and feel normal. The condition can be detected by routine blood testing, however.
[3]- Hemoglobin H disease.
The loss of three alpha genes produces a serious hematological problem (three-gene deletion alpha thalassemia). Patients with this condition have a severe anemia, and often require blood transfusions to survive. The severe imbalance between the alpha chain production (now powered by one gene, instead of four) and beta chain production (which is normal) causes an accumulation of beta chains inside the red blood cells. Normally, beta chains pair only with alpha chains. With three-gene deletion alpha thalassemia, however, beta chains begin to associate in groups of four, producing abnormal hemoglobin, called "hemoglobin H". The condition is called "hemoglobin H disease". Hemoglobin H has two problems. First it does not carry oxygen properly, making it functionally useless to the cell. Second, hemoglobin H protein damages the membrane that surrounds the red cell, accelerating cell destruction. The combination of the very low production of alpha chains and destruction of red cells in

hemoglobin H disease produces a severe, life-threatening anemia. Untreated, most patients die in childhood or early adolescence.

[4]- Hemoglobin Bart's hydrops fetalis syndrome.

The loss of all four alpha genes produces a condition that is incompatible with life. The gamma chains produced during fetal life associate in groups of four to form abnormal hemoglobin called "hemoglobin Barts". Most people with four-gene deletion alpha thalassemia die in utero or shortly after birth. Rarely, four gene deletion alpha thalassemia has been detected in utero, usually in a family where the disorder occurred in an earlier child. In utero blood transfusions have saved some of these children. These patients require life-long transfusions and other medical support.

Beta Thalassemia

The fact that there are only two genes for the beta chain of hemoglobin makes beta thalassemia a bit simpler to understand than alpha thalassemia.Unlike alpha thalassemia, beta thalassemia rarely arises from the complete loss of a beta globin gene. The beta globin gene is present, but produces little beta globin protein. The degree of suppression varies. Many causes of suppressed beta globin gene expression have been found. In some cases, the affected gene makes essentially no beta globin protein (beta-0-thalassemia). In other cases, the production of beta chain protein is lower than normal, but not zero (beta-(+)-thalassemia). The severity of beta thalassemia depends in part on the type of beta thalassemic genes that a person has inherited.

[1]- One-gene beta thalassemia has one beta globin gene that is normal, and a second, affected gene with a variably reduced production of beta globin. The degree of imbalance with the alpha globin depends on the residual production capacity of the defective beta globin gene. Even when the affected gene produces no beta chain, the condition is mild since one beta gene functions normally. The red cells are small and a mild anemia may exist. People with the condition generally have no symptoms. The condition can be detected by a routine laboratory blood evaluation. (Note that in many ways, the one-gene beta thalassemia and the two-gene alpha thalassemia are very similar, from a clinical point of view. Each results in small red cells and a mild anemia).

[2]- Two-gene beta thalassemia produces a severe anemia and a potentially life-threatening condition. The severity of the disorder depends in part on the combination of genes that have been inherited: beta-0-thal/ beta-0-thal; beta-0-thal/ beta-(+)-thal; beta-(+)-thal/ beta-(+)-thal. The beta-(+)-thalassemia genes vary greatly in their ability to produce normal hemoglobin. Consequently, the clinical picture is more complex than might otherwise be the case for three genetic possibilities outlined.

Thalassemia minor or thalassemia trait

These terms are used interchangeably for people who have small red cells and mild (or no) anemia due to thalassemia. These patients are clinically well, and are usually only detected through routine blood testing. Physicians often mistakenly diagnose iron deficiency in people with thalassemia trait. Iron replacement does not correct the condition.

The primary caution for people with beta-thalassemia trait involves the possible problems that their children could inherit if their partner also has beta-thalassemia trait. These more severe forms of beta-thalassemia trait are outlined below.

Thalassemia intermedia.The most important fact to remember is that thalassemia intermedia are a description, and not a pathological or genetic diagnosis. Patients with thalassemia intermedia have significant anemia, but are able to survive without blood transfusions.

The factors that go into the diagnosis are:

- The degree to which the patient tolerates the anemia
- The threshold of the physician to transfuse patients with thalassemia

With regard to the tolerance of the anemia, most patients with thalassemia have substantial symptoms with an Hgb of much below 7 or 8 gm/dl. With hemoglobins of this level, excess energy consumption due to the profound hemolysis can produce small stature, poor weight gain, poor energy levels, and susceptibility to infection. Further, the extreme activity of the bone marrow produces bone deformities of the face and other areas, along with enlargement of the spleen. The long bones of the arms and legs are weak and fracture easily. Patients with this clinical condition usually do better with regular transfusions. The need for regular transfusions would then place them under the heading of thalassemia major. On the other hand, some patients with marked thalassemia can maintain hemoglobin of about 9 to 10 gm/dl. The exercise tolerance of these patients is significantly better. The question then becomes whether the accelerated bone marrow activity needed to maintain this level of hemoglobin causes unacceptable side-effects such as bone abnormalities or enlarged spleen. This is a judgment decision. A given patient at the critical borderline would be transfused by some physicians to prevent these problems, even if they are slight. The patient then would be clinically classified as having thalassemia major. Another physician might choose to avoid the complications of chronic transfusion. The same patient then would be clinically classified as thalassemia intermedia. The patient has thalassemia that is more severe than thalassemia trait, but not so severe as to require chronic transfusion as do the patients with thalassemia major.

A patient can change status. The spleen is enlarged in these patients. The spleen plays a role in clearing damaged red cells from the blood stream. Since all of the red cells in patients with severe thalassemia have some degree of damage, clearance by the spleen accelerates the rate of cell loss. Therefore the bone marrow has to work harder to replace these cells. In some patients, removal of the spleen slows the rate of red cell destruction just enough, that they can manage without transfusion, and still not have the unacceptable side-effects. In this case, the patient converts clinically from thalassemia major to thalassemia intermedia.

Thalassemia major

This is the condition of severe thalassemia in which chronic blood transfusions are needed. In some patients the anemia is so severe, that death occurs without transfusions. Other patients could survive without transfusions, for a while, but would have terrible deformities. While transfusions are life-saving in patients with thalassemia major, transfusions ultimately produce iron overload. Chelation therapy, usually with the iron-binding agent, is needed to prevent death from iron-mediated organ injury.

The advent of modern molecular biology permits the genetic classification of thalassemias. A rough correlation exists between the clinical and genetic classifications. The relationship between genetics and clinical state is not absolute, however:
- Thalassemia trait (minor)- normal beta gene/ thalassemia gene (beta zero or +)
- Thalassemia intermedia- often two beta-(+)-genes
- Thalassemia major- two beta-(+)-genes (where the plus is not substantial); beta-(+)-gene/ beta-0-gene; beta-0-gene/ beta-0-gene

This anemia is known as Cooley's anemia. This hemoglobin anomaly is more common in the regions of southern Italy and Greece, Middle East, India, Pakistan, and Southeast Asia. It is described as a common genetic disorder and is found world-wide. Its pathophysiology is due to an imbalance in one or more of the beta-globulins.

Types of Beta-Thalassemia Anemia's

(Note: Each parent will carry a variable type of beta-chain gene and each offspring inherits one beta gene each from their parents.)

[1] Beta gene allows for normal Beta-chain production.
[2] Beta (0) gene will result in little (if any) Beta-chain production. Consider that production totally blocked.
[3] Beta (+) gene will permit some Beta-chain production. This means this gene is partially blocking Beta-chain production. It is estimated that there is between 10% and 50% normal chain productions.
[4] If the genotype is B0/B0, then hemoglobin A is absent . . . .
   A. Hemoglobin A2 will make up to 6% of the adult hemoglobin.
   B. Hemoglobin F will make up to 98% of the adult hemoglobin.
   C. The body is tying to compensate for the deficiency in hemoglobin A.
   D. This form is designated as Thalassemia major.
[5] If the genotype is B^+/B^+ (Mediterranean form). . . .
   A. A small amount of hemoglobin A is present.
   B. Up to 9% of the total hemoglobin is type A_2.
   C. Up to 95% of hemoglobin will be F type.
   D. This form is designated as Thalassemia major.
[6] If the genotype is B^0/B^+ . . . .
   A. A small amount of adult hemoglobin A is present.

B. Up to 6% of the total hemoglobin is type A_2.
C. More that 75% of the hemoglobin is F type.
D. This form is designated as Thalassemia major.

N O T E

Clinical symptoms have a widely varied range that includes: [1] frequent infections, [2] abdominal enlargement due to hepatosplenomegaly, [3] mental retardation, [4] mongoloid-like facial features, and [5] a distinctive RBC morphology.

Beta - thalassemia is a serious hemoglobin disorder with an imbalance in the B-globulin chains. This may be the most severe of all the congenital hemolytic anemias. There are four genotypes associated with this specific anemia. Each causes severe RBC dysfunction and results is significantly increased RBC destruction in the bone marrow by macrocytes. The erythropoiesis is ineffective and the bone marrow produces red blood cell that are of extremely poikilocytic forms. This anemic disorder will express itself within the first year of life. This patient will require blood transfusion support to have a quality of life. Treatment for this patient is supportive with neocytes being the preferred cell for transfusion. Patients are administered a medication (as desferrioxamine) to prevent accumulation of iron in the tissues and iron toxicity. If there is no medical intervention, the hemoglobin will range from 2.0 to 6.5 gm/dL.
 Clinical symptoms include: [1] slow growth rate, [2] delayed onset of sexual characteristics, [3] odd skin color due to icterus, melanin deposition, and pallor, [4] enlarge malar (cheek) bones to give a "chipmunk" facial appearance, [5] cardiomegaly, [6] hepatomegaly, [7] splenomegaly, and [8] prone to congestive heart failure. Since life expectancy is short, most do not survive to adulthood.

Clinical laboratory features for the β-thalassemia major syndrome are:

[1] Hemoglobin may be as low as 2.0 g/dL   [9] slight leukocytosis
[2] Hypochromic-microcytic anemia.   [10] thrombocytosis
[3] MCV = 65 fL (mean value)   [11] NRBC
[4] MCH = < 27 pg   [12] Serum iron = increased
[5] MCHC = < 32%   [13] Serum ferritin = increased
[6] Anisocytosis   [14] Polychromasia
[7] Basophilic stippling   [15] Retic count = < 10%
[8] *Osmotic fragility = strikingly decreased   [16] RPI = <3
[17] Poikilocytosis (with schistocytes, Dacryocytes, Ovalocytes, and target cells)
[18] Free erythrocyte protoporphyrin = normal
[19] Urine = brown color due to presence of hemoglobin precursors
[20] Bone marrow is hypercellular with ringed sideroblasts present. There is marked erythroid hyperplasia. Note: Gaucher's cells have been reported in the bone marrow.

The B-thalassemia minor syndrome is typically an asymptomatic disorder with little or no evidence of anemia. If the laboratory examines a stained blood smear, the RBC morphology will be definitely abnormal. The following genotypes are expressed as one of the variants of β-thalassemia minor syndrome:
 The mean hemoglobin level in this patient will be about 15% lower than the average adult, with a higher RBC count, and the presence of microcytes. Any anemia, if present, will be mild. As a rule, no medical intervention is required for these individuals.
Clinical laboratory findings will include any combination of the following:
[1] decrease in the MCV and MCH
[2]   normal or slightly decreased MCHC
[3] hemoglobin levels range between 10.5 to 13.9 grams/dL (The hematocrit will be <31%)
[4] The stained blood film will present with [a] microcytes, [b] target cells, [c] hypochromic RBC's, [d] anisocytosis, [e] poikilocytosis, [f] basophilic stippling, [g] polychromasia, [h] an absence of NRBCs, and [i] normal serum iron.
[5] The bone marrow is essentially normal with mild erythroid hyperplasia.

Iron and Thalassemia

Thalassemia and iron metabolism are closely linked. Iron deficiency and mild forms of thalassemia (e.g., thalassemia trait) are often confused. Both are associated with mild to moderate anemia and microcytosis (small red cells). At the other end of the spectrum, severe forms of thalassemia frequently produce iron overload. Excess iron accumulates due to enhanced iron absorption produced by thalassemia, repeated blood transfusions or both. A number of questions are frequently asked regarding thalassemia and iron.

Iron replacement tablets or iron-supplemented vitamins should be taken only as directed by a physician to treat actual iron deficiency or to prevent iron deficiency in high risk circumstances (e.g., pregnancy). People with thalassemia trait (thalassemia minor) are not per se at greater risk of complications from iron in the diet than anyone else in the general population. There are instances, however, in which coincident conditions can increase the risk of iron overload. For example, people with thalassemia trait who also inherit the gene for hereditary hemochromatosis can accumulate dangerous levels of iron by using dietary iron supplements.

In the absence of concomitant iron deficiency, iron supplementation will neither correct nor improve anemia due to thalassemia. For people with both iron deficiency and thalassemia, iron replacement will lessen the severity of the anemia, until the iron deficiency is corrected. The blood count will level off and no further improvement will occur. Excess iron, accumulation is a leading cause of clinical deterioration, and often death in patients with severe forms of thalassemia. The excess iron can be removed from the patient's body only by iron-binding drugs called chelators. The most widely used chelator is desferrioxamine, whose trade name is Desferal®. This medication can prevent many of the complications associated with iron overload. The drug is most effective when given daily over periods of time ranging from 12 to 16 hours. A special pump that the patient wears slowly gives the medication under the skin. Desferal® has been given as an intravenous infusion at the time of blood transfusion. This method of delivery does not effectively remove iron. Desferal® is not effective when given by mouth. A new oral agent called deferipone or L1 continues to be tested in people. The drug effectively removes iron from many patients with substantial iron overload. The key unknown with this agent is its safety.

Iron Deficiency vs. Thalassemia Minor

	Iron Deficiency	Thalassemia Minor	Combined
MCV	Low	Very Low	Very Low
RDW	High	Normal or High	High
Red Cell Count	Low	Normal or High	Normal or Low
Marrow Iron	Absent	Normal	Absent
Serum Iron	Low	Normal	Low
TIBC	High	Normal	High
Serum Ferritin	Low	Normal	Low
Hemoglobin A2	Low	High	Normal

Inheritance Pattern

Alpha Thalassemia

Four genes (two from each parent) are needed to make enough alpha globin protein chains. If one or more of the genes is missing, you will have alpha thalassemia trait or disease. This means that you don't make enough alpha globin protein.

If you have only one missing gene, you're a silent carrier and won't have any signs of illness.

If you have two missing genes, you have alpha thalassemia trait (also called alpha thalassemia minor). You may have mild anemia.

If you have three missing genes, you likely will have hemoglobin H disease (which a blood test (can detect). This form of thalassemia causes moderate to severe anemia.

Very rarely, a baby will have all four genes missing. This condition is called alpha thalassemia major or hydrops fetalis. Babies with hydrops fetalis usually die before or shortly after birth. The diagram shows one example of how alpha thalassemia is inherited. The alpha globin genes are located on chromosome 16. A child inherits four alpha globin genes—two from each parent. In this example, the father is missing two alpha globin genes and the mother is missing one alpha globin gene.

Therefore, each child has a 25 percent chance of inheriting two missing genes and two normal genes (thalassemia trait), three missing genes and one normal gene (hemoglobin H disease), four normal genes (no anemia), or one missing gene and three normal genes (silent carrier).

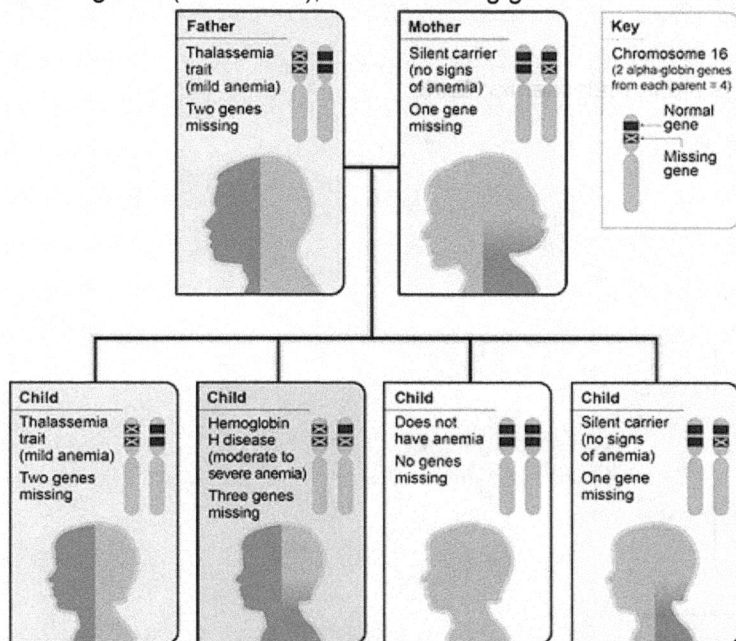

Credit: Department of Health and Human Services National Institutes of Health National Heart, Lung, and Blood Institute

Four genes (two from each parent) are needed to make enough alpha globin protein chains. If one or more of the genes is missing, you will have alpha thalassemia trait or disease. This means that you don't make enough alpha globin protein.
If you have only one missing gene, you're a silent carrier and won't have any signs of illness.
If you have two missing genes, you have alpha thalassemia trait (also called alpha thalassemia minor). You may have mild anemia.
If you have three missing genes, you likely will have hemoglobin H disease (which a blood test (can detect). This form of thalassemia causes moderate to severe anemia.

Very rarely, a baby will have all four genes missing. This condition is called alpha thalassemia major or hydrops fetalis. Babies with hydrops fetalis usually die before or shortly after birth. The diagram shows one example of how alpha thalassemia is inherited. The alpha globin genes are located on chromosome 16. A child inherits four alpha globin genes—two from each parent. In this example, the father is missing two alpha globin genes and the mother is missing one alpha globin gene.

Therefore, each child has a 25 percent chance of inheriting two missing genes and two normal genes (thalassemia trait), three missing genes and one normal gene (hemoglobin H disease), four normal genes (no anemia), or one missing gene and three normal genes (silent carrier).

Alpha-Globin Genotypes and Clinical Syndromes

Genotype	Clinical Syndrome
a-/aa	Silent carrier or mild alpha thalassemia minor; alpha+ thalassemia trait
a-/a-	Homozygous alpha+ thalassemia or --/aa alpha0 thalassemia trait
a-/--	Hemoglobin H disease
--/--	Hydrops fetalis or homozygous alpha thalassemia; Barts hemoglobin

Beta Thalassemia

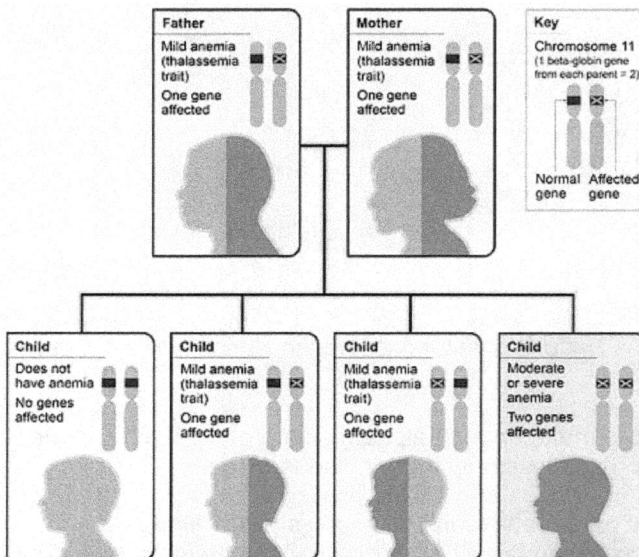

Credit: Department of Health and Human Services National Institutes of Health National Heart, Lung, and Blood Institute

Two genes (one from each parent) are needed to make enough beta globin protein chains. If one or both of these genes are altered, you will have beta thalassemia. This means that you don't make enough beta globin protein.

If you have one altered gene, you're a carrier. This condition is called beta thalassemia trait or beta thalassemia minor. It causes mild anemia.

If both genes are altered, you will have beta thalassemia intermedia or beta thalassemia major (also called Cooley's anemia). The intermedia form of the disorder causes moderate anemia. The major form causes severe anemia.

The diagram shows one example of how beta thalassemia is inherited. The beta globin gene is located on chromosome 11. A child inherits two beta globin genes—one from each parent. In this example, each parent has one altered beta globin gene.

Therefore, each child has a 25 percent chance of inheriting two normal genes (no anemia), a 50 percent chance of inheriting one altered gene and one normal gene (beta thalassemia trait), or a 25 percent chance of inheriting two altered genes (beta thalassemia major).

Laboratory detection of Hemoglobinopathies

The suggested protocol for the detection and identification of hemoglobinipathies consist of initial screening by electrophoresis, following by further confirmatory testing.

Alkaline electrophoresis on cellulose acetate (pH 8.6) is a testing principle that takes advantage of charged particles migrating in an electric field. The hemoglobin molecule carries an electrical charge because it contains both carboxyl (COO^-) and protonated nitrogen ($NH3^+$) groups. The number of these two groups determines the strength of the charge on the molecule. If the hemoglobin molecule contains more carboxyl groups, the molecule will carry a stronger negative charge that cancels out the weaker positive charge from the protonated groups. In an electric field this molecule will migrate toward the positive electrode (the anode). If the protonated groups predominate, then the molecule will migrate toward the cathode (negative charged electrode). There are several factors that affect the rate at which the molecule will migrate toward an electrode. These are the net charge on the molecule, the size (mass) of the molecule, the shape of the molecule, the strength of the electrical field, the chemical and physical properties of the supporting medium, and the temperature of the electrophoresis system.

The hemoglobin molecule is made up of repeating units of amino acids and the number and type of amino acids determine its charge. There are more than 450 known variants of hemoglobin that result form amino acid substitutions made in the hemoglobin molecule. For example, sickle cell hemoglobin differs from normal (A_1) hemoglobin by a single amino acid. Sickle cell hemoglobin contains valine instead of glutamic acid at the sixth position on the β-globulin chain. Substitutions can alter the solubility, stability, and function of the hemoglobin molecule. As a result of this one amino acid molecule difference, sickle cell hemoglobin will migrate slower than normal adult hemoglobin.

If hemoglobin migrates in an electric field faster than normal adult hemoglobin, it is designated as fast hemoglobin. If it migrates slower, then it is slow hemoglobin. The rate at which a hemoglobin molecule migrates in an electric field is known as its RF value.

Routine hemoglobin electrophoresis tests are routinely performed first on cellulose acetate strips at a pH of 8.6. When two or more hemoglobin species (such as Hgb D, Hgb S, and Hgb G) are found to migrate at the same speed, then the electrophoresis may be repeated on a different or secondary system such as citrate agar at a pH of 6.0. Note that hemoglobins A_2, C, E, and O Arab will migrate at the same RF value on cellulose acetate strips at a pH of 8.6 and have to be differentiated using citrate agar at a pH of 6.0.

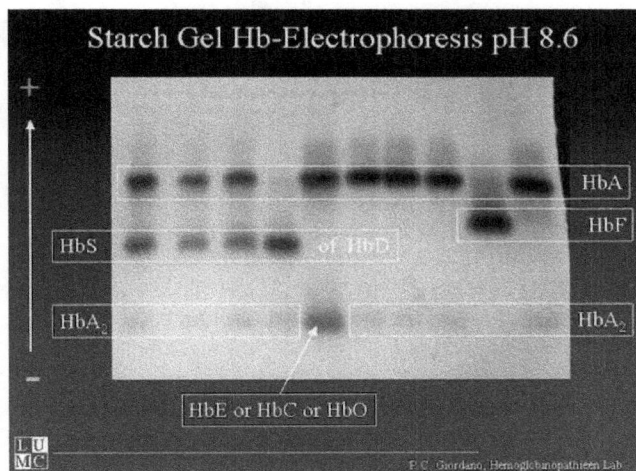

=Hemoglobinopathies Laboratory. (PC Giordano). Used with permission=

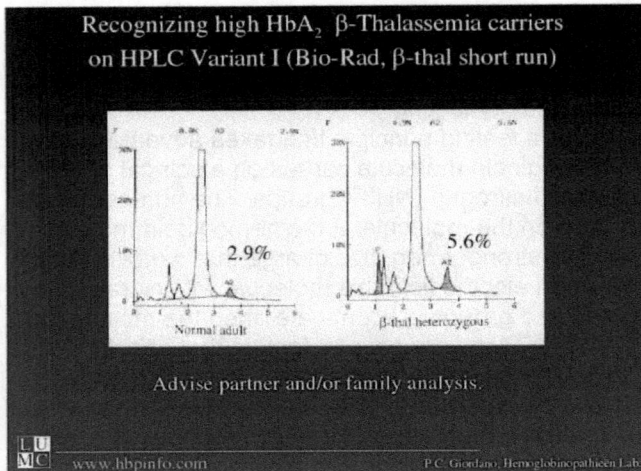

Recognizing high HbA₂ β-Thalassemia carriers
on HPLC Variant I (Bio-Rad, β-thal short run)

2.9%
5.6%

Normal adult
β-thal heterozygous

Advise partner and/or family analysis.

www.hbpinfo.com
P.C. Giordano; Hemoglobinopathieën Lab.

HgbA₂ values between 3.5 and 8 % indicate β-thalassemia heterozygosity (The normal HbA₂ value has no diagnostic significance in babies younger than 6 months and in rare cases of ß-thalassemia heterozygosity associated normal HbA₂ values (2,5-3.5%).
HgbA₂ values lower than 2.5% in absence of iron depletion may indicate the presence of α-thalassemia (specialized analysis is needed).
HgbF values higher than 1% are unusual after the age of 2. In β-thalassemia heterozygosity the HgbF level can be slightly to strongly elevated (1-8% in point mutation carriers 5-30% in deletion carriers).

Hb-electrophoresis or Hb-chromatography (HPLC) and estimate the level of the HgbA₂ and HgbF fractions. By this method the presence and estimation of the normal and abnormal Hgb fraction are semi- or fully automatically obtained. Hemoglobin electrophoresis separates hemoglobin into different types. Hemoglobin Bart is elevated at birth in patients with alpha thalassemia. In hemoglobin H disease, 20-40% of total hemoglobin is of hemoglobin Bart; however, in the silent carrier alpha thalassemia condition, the percentage is only 1-2% with low or normal amounts of hemoglobin A₂. Hemoglobin electrophoresis is generally not sufficiently sensitive to diagnose silent carrier alpha thalassemia.

Currently, genetic testing is used to establish the diagnosis in patients with a suggestive family history and/or hematologic findings suggestive of alpha thalassemia.
1-Recombinant DNA technology can be diagnostic but is still a research tool.
2-Gene mapping
3-Polymerase chain reaction (PCR)
4-Restriction endonucleases
5-Anti-L globin monoclonal antibodies
The diagnosis of beta thalassemia minor usually is suggested by the presence of an isolated, mild microcytic anemia, target cells on the peripheral blood smear, and a normal red blood cell count. An elevation of Hgb A2 (2 alpha-globin chains complexed with 2 delta-globin chains) demonstrated by electrophoresis or column chromatography confirms the diagnosis of beta thalassemia trait. The Hgb A2 level in these patients usually is approximately 4-6%. In rare cases of concurrent severe iron deficiency, the increased Hgb A2 level may not be observed, although it becomes evident with iron repletion. The increased Hgb A2 level also is not observed in patients with the rare delta-beta thalassemia trait.

An elevated Hgb F level is not specific to patients with the beta thalassemia trait.

Free erythrocyte porphyrin (FEP) tests may be useful in situations in which the diagnosis of beta thalassemia minor is unclear. FEP level is normal in patients with the beta thalassemia trait, but it is elevated in patients with iron deficiency or lead poisoning.

Alpha thalassemia is characterized by genetic defects in the alpha-globin gene, and this variant has features similar to beta thalassemia. Patients with this disorder have normal Hgb A2 levels. Establishing the diagnosis of the alpha thalassemia trait requires performing genetic tests of the alpha-globin cluster (by Southern blot or polymerase chain reaction tests).

Iron studies (iron, transferrin, and ferritin) are useful in excluding iron deficiency and the anemia of chronic disorders as the cause of the patient's anemia.

Patients may require a bone marrow examination to exclude certain other causes of microcytic anemia. Physicians must perform an iron stain (Prussian blue stain) to diagnose sideroblastic anemia (ringed sideroblasts).

The Mentzer index is defined as mean corpuscular volume per red cell count. An index of less than 13 suggests that the patient has the thalassemia trait, and an index of more than 13 suggests that the patient has iron deficiency.

Molecular diagnostic tests can precisely determine whether a mutation is present any time after approximately 8 weeks of gestation. The physician can establish the diagnosis in utero using DNA obtained from amniocentesis or by chorionic villus sampling. In most laboratories, the DNA is amplified using the polymerase chain reaction technique and then is analyzed for the presence of the thalassemia mutation using a panel of oligonucleotide probes corresponding to known thalassemia mutations.

Severe forms of thalassemia intermedia must be differentiated from beta thalassemia major; this is mainly a clinical differentiation based on close monitoring to determine whether the patient's Hgb level can be maintained at 6-7 g/dL without blood transfusions.

The severe anemia, if associated with thrombocytopenia, hypersplenism, and the immature leukocytes often observed on peripheral blood films, raises the question of acute leukemia or metastatic lymphoma. Milder cases, on the other hand, must be differentiated from thalassemia trait or even anemias related to iron deficiency or chronic inflammation. Unlike the intermedia forms, beta thalassemia trait rarely produces an Hgb level less than 9 g/dL. Iron deficiency anemia is characterized by a normal Hgb electrophoresis pattern and abnormal iron study results.

The following tests are usually adequate to suggest a diagnosis of thalassemia major or intermedia:

CBC count and differential reveal anemia with marked hypochromasia and microcytosis. An Hgb level below 7-8 g/dL indicates a severe case; whether the thalassemia is major or intermedia can be determined only after adequate monitoring.

Hgb electrophoresis shows an abnormal pattern. An elevated Hgb A_2 fraction up to 7% indicates a beta thalassemia, typically beta thalassemia trait or certain forms of thalassemia intermedia. However, absence of Hgb A_2 does not exclude the diagnosis of beta thalassemia. In the intermedia type overall, Hgb F ranges from 20-100%, Hgb A from 0-80%, and A_2 up to 7% of total.

Peripheral blood film examination usually reveals marked hypochromasia and microcytosis, polychromasia, target cells, and significant variation in the size of the RBCs.

Iron studies should be performed, either as baseline in anticipation of iron overload in the future or for diagnosis and management of this condition when suspected.

1-Ferritin level is an adequate tool for screening but is not the perfect test for a precise evaluation of the progress of iron overload and the development of tissue damage as a complication. It is a noninvasive test that is easy to obtain and is of value in the early stages of iron overload process; however, it becomes inaccurate when iron accumulates heavily, it lacks sensitivity and specificity, and it correlates poorly with hepatic iron concentration. It is also known to be a positive plasma reactant, which rises in association with inflammation.

2-Serum transferrin saturation may provide some information about the patient's iron status; however, it lacks sensitivity. Twenty-four–hour desferrioxamine-induced urinary iron excretion is a beneficial test in deciding when chelation therapy should be started (presence of adequate iron available for chelation); it is not a practical test to evaluate iron overload, however. Urine aliquots are not usually collected correctly, the ratio of stool-to-urine iron is variable, and furthermore, it correlates poorly with hepatic iron deposits.

3-Either bone marrow grading of iron stores or monitoring the numbers of nucleated red blood cells in the peripheral blood may reflect the stage of iron overload. Patients with thalassemia intermedia tend to develop iron overload somewhat later than those with thalassemia major regardless of whether they are on a transfusion schedule.

4-Once the patient is started on blood transfusions, the onset of iron overload should be expected earlier than in patients who are not receiving transfusion, and closer follow-up is required.

1-Tests to identify endocrine disturbances such as diabetes mellitus or thyroid, adrenal, or other gland dysfunction are also required.

2-Liver function tests are needed at diagnosis and during follow-up, especially in patients who are receiving blood transfusions.

Flow chart 2

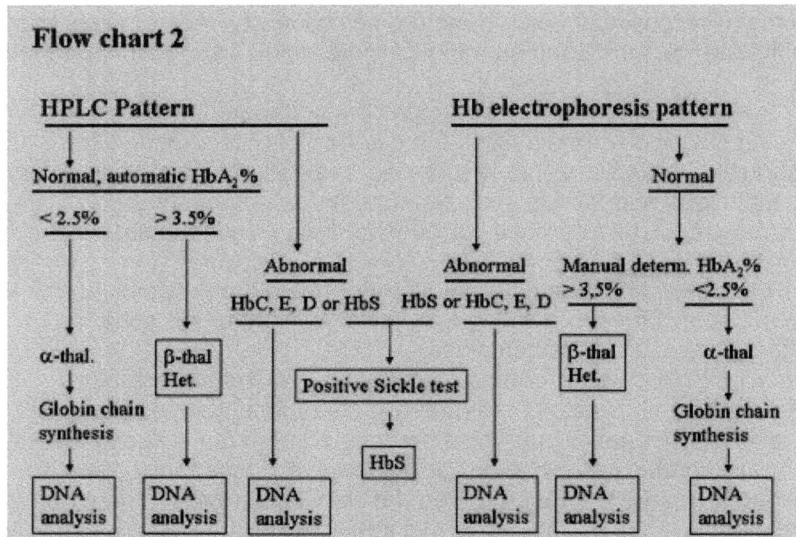

The Kleihauer-Betke test is a semi quantitative test that detects fetal hemoglobin F. A thin maternal blood smear is made and allowed to air dry for up to 60 minutes. The slide may be fixed in 80% ethanol. The slide is placed in prewarmed (37 ^{0}C) citric acid-phosphate buffer for 5 minutes. During the incubation the slide(s) should be dipped up and down several times at one minute and at 4 minutes. After 5 minutes, remove the slide(s) and rinse with distilled water. Allow slides to air dry. Stain in Mayer's hematoxylin for 3 minutes. Remove and rise with distilled water. Place slides in erythrosine B for 4 minutes. Remove and rise with distilled water and allow to air dry. Examine under oil immersion objective and look for fetal cells that stain a dark red-orange color. The normal maternal cells will appear as ghost cells. Normal adult cells will have <1% Hb F and at this level will appear as ghost cells. Infant values will run from 70 to 90% and readily take up the stain.

The maternal RBCs are citrate-buffer sensitive and hemoglobin A washes out. The fetal RBCs (with hemoglobin F) resist the elution, remaining in the RBCs. When stained, the maternal RBCs appear as ghosts and the fetal cells take up the stain. If a maternal/fetal bleed has occurred, then count 2000 ghost cells and note the number of fetal cells. Divide the number of fetal cells counted by the number of "ghost" cells counted and multiply by 100. This give a percent estimate of fetal RBCs in maternal circulation. Multiply the % fetal cells times 50 and the resulting answer is an estimate of the amount of fetal blood (in mL) that escaped into maternal circulation. This value determines the amount of prophylactic RhoGamm required for administering to the mother. The prescription for administering is 300 µgm of RhoGamm per 15 mL of fetal RBCs. RhoGamm is Rh immune globulin or Rh$_o$IgG.

CHAPTER TWO: EXTRAVASCULAR DEFECTS

Immune Hemolytic Anemia

1- Intravascular

Intravascular immune hemolysis occurs within the vascular system and results from activation of the classic complement pathway via immunoglobulin G (IgG) or (IgM) antibodies. Antibodies bind to antigens on red cells and activate complement resulting in lysis of the cell.

2-Extravascular

Antibody coated red cells are fully or partially phagocytized by cells in the reticuloendothelial system (RES), particularly in the spleen and liver. Partially phagocytized cells are seen as spherocytes on the peripheral smear.

3-Classification

Auto-immune Hemolytic Anemia (AIHA)

In autoimmune anemia's, the mechanism to control auto reactive antibodies is lost, allowing for antibodies to be formed that react against the patient's own RBC's. The antibodies bind to the RBC membrane and cause hemolysis. Warm autoimmune hemolytic anemia (WAIHA) is the most common form of the autoimmune hemolytic anemias (AIHA) most often appearing in individuals over the age of 40. The optimum serological activity is at 37 °C. When this anemia is initiated, it can develop into a severe form in 2 to 3 days. In 60% of the cases, the cause is not known. The remaining 40% can be secondary to such things as:

[1] Infection [4] stress
[2] trauma [5] neoplastic disease
[3] surgery [6] rheumatoid arthritis.

Clinical symptoms include:

[1] Dizziness [5] splenomegaly (if anemia is severe)
[2] jaundice [6] jaundice
[3] weakness [7] pallor
[4] mild to moderate hepatomegaly [8] pyrexia.

Hemolysis is affected by IgG antibodies. Note that compliment is not required. Hemolysis is an extra-vascular phenomenon. The antibody will attach to the RBC membrane antigen receptor, leaving its Fc component free (unattached). As the cell with its attached antibody flows through the vascular system of the spleen (which is the major side of RBC destruction), macrophages with their Fc receptors, will bind the Fc component. If the antibody-antigen complex holds, the RBC is phagocytized. If the "complex" breaks, then the RBC is pitted and the RBC re-anneals to form a smaller RBC's, spherocytes and fragmented RBC's. Human anti-globulin sera can react with this IgG antibody to give a positive Coomb's test.
Clinical laboratory findings include:

[1] Increased retic count, with RPI = >2 (values to 6 and 7).
[2] Peripheral blood smears with spherocytes, schistocytes, poikilocytosis, polychromasia, and anisocytosis.
[3] Erythrophagocytosis by monocytes (Intact RBC's will appear red in the monocyte. If the RBC has been hemolyzed, there will be a clear appearing vacuole.)
[4] WBC count is increased.
[5] Platelet count will be normal or decreased.
[6] Bilirubin will be elevated. Values up to 5.0 mg/dL reported.
[7] Osmotic fragility: increased.
[8] Urobilinogen: >1.0
[9] DAT: positive

If the WAIHA is severe, with a significant hemolytic episode, then one or more of the following will appear: [1] hemoglobinemia, [2] Hemoglobinuria, [3] methemoglobinemia, [4] hemosideruria.

Treatment strategy does not usually include transfusion therapy, but splenectomy, steroids, and immunosuppressant.

Direct Coombs test / Direct antiglobulin test

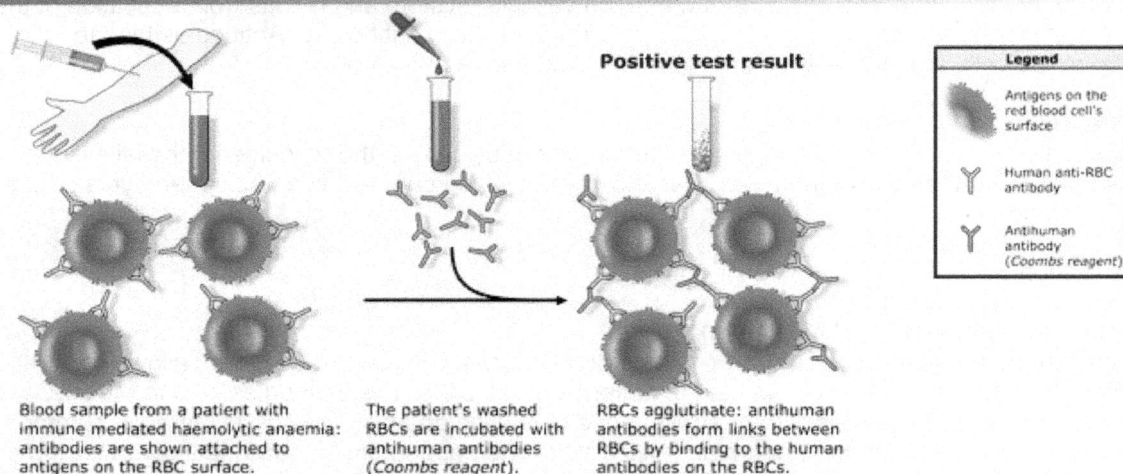

Positive test result

Legend

Antigens on the red blood cell's surface

Human anti-RBC antibody

Antihuman antibody (*Coombs reagent*)

Blood sample from a patient with immune mediated haemolytic anaemia: antibodies are shown attached to antigens on the RBC surface.

The patient's washed RBCs are incubated with antihuman antibodies (*Coombs reagent*).

RBCs agglutinate: antihuman antibodies form links between RBCs by binding to the human antibodies on the RBCs.

Indirect Coombs test / Indirect antiglobulin test

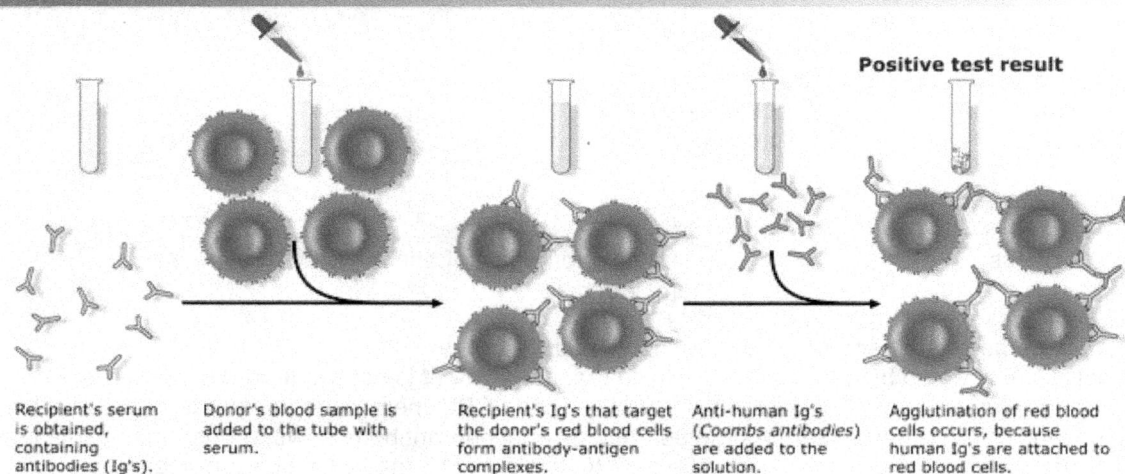

Positive test result

Recipient's serum is obtained, containing antibodies (Ig's).

Donor's blood sample is added to the tube with serum.

Recipient's Ig's that target the donor's red blood cells form antibody-antigen complexes.

Anti-human Ig's (*Coombs antibodies*) are added to the solution.

Agglutination of red blood cells occurs, because human Ig's are attached to red blood cells.

□ Description: schematic of the Coombs (or antiglobulin) test, showing what is performed and the micro- and macroscopic changes that occur. With a - direct or indirect - negative test result (not shown), agglutination will not occur and the tube will look exactly like it was in the previous step.
□ Author: A. Rad
□ Date: March 16, 2006
□ License: GFDL-self
http://en.wikipedia.org/wiki/Image:Coombs_test_schematic.png

Drug-Induced AIHA

   This anomaly resembles warm autoimmune hemolytic anemia (WAIHA). Examples of drugs known to be associated with this form of anemia are:
 [1] Phenacetin (analgesic),
[2] Acetaminophen (analgesic),
[3] Sulfonamides,
 [4] Insectides,
 [5] Cephalosporins, and
 [6] Penicillin.

   It is estimated that up to 20% of the autoimmune hemolytic anemias are drug induced. One concept is the drug appears to bind to the RBC membrane and form a new, but strange antigen complex. The body then produces antibodies against this complex and causes hemolysis. Penicillin is thought to interact this way. The other concept assumes that the drug binds to a serum protein to form a new, but strange immune complex. The body forms antibodies against this complex. The new antibody is specific enough to bind to the RBC membrane and form an immune complex and also activating complement. Hemolysis results. This is called the "innocent bystander mechanism".

AIHA (Cold-Reacting Antibodies)

All normal human sera contain cold-reacting antibodies. These are usually IgM antibodies and require the presence of compliment to function. These cold, autoimmune antibodies are made up of anti-I, anti-H, and anti-IH types. The majority of the human population contains the H and I antigens on the membranes of the RBC's. As a rule, the anti-I, anti-H, and anti-HI antibodies are not clinically significant. They are reactive in a limited thermal range of 4 oC (39.2 0F) to 22 oC. (71.6 0F) There are three groups of autoimmune cold antibody anemia pathologies:
[1] Cold Autoimmune Hemolytic Anemia (CAIHA),
[2] Secondary Cold Autoimmune Hemolytic Anemia, and
[3] Paroxysmal Cold Hemoglobinuria (PCH).

Research conducted by M. L. Beck and P. D. Issett finds that cold-reacting antibodies are present in all normal human sera. These types of antibodies are too weak to react. This is not the case in autoimmune hemolytic anemia.

Cold autoimmune hemolytic anemia (CAIHA) is an IgM antibody that activates compliment. Synonyms for CAIHA are Idiopathic Cold Agglutinin Syndrome, Cold Hemagglutinin Disease (CHD), and Cold Idiopathic Autoimmune Hemolytic Anemia. Hemolysis occurs in this fashion:

This type of anemia is not usually a severe disease, but tends to be seasonal, manifesting itself during the winter months. There are medical cases in which air conditioning has "triggered" this disorder. Clinical symptoms tend to be pallor, weakness, weight loss, and slight jaundice.
Clinical laboratory findings are:
[1]   Positive DAT, due to C3b coating the RBCs,
[2]   Reticulocytosis,
[3]   Hemoglobinuria,
[4]   Peripheral smear with: Rouleaux, polychromasia, mild to moderate anisocytosis, poikilocytosis,
[5]   Bilirubin: increased (usually around 3.0 mg/dL),
[6]   Haptoglobin: decreased.

When collecting blood for cold autoimmune antibody testing . . . . Remember:

[1]   These antibodies are dissociated at 37 °C.
[2]   If blood specimen is allowed to cool to room temperature (22 to 26 °C), the
        antibodies will begin to bind to the RBC membranes causing auto agglutination.
[3]   If blood tests performed on this blood in the cooled state, will yield false results:
        a.   RBC count will be decreased.
        b.   RBC count will not correlate to the hemoglobin and hematocrit.
        c.   The MCV and MCHC will be falsely elevated.
        d.   The MCH will be normal or increased.
[4]   To correct the problem, warm the sample back to 37 °C and repeat the test.
        The antibodies will dissociate and the results should be in the correct parameters.
[5] WBCs and platelets are not affected.

The body's peripheral temperatures drop, allowing the cold antibody to agglutinate the RBC's in the capillaries of the skin. This stasis or sludging action causes a sense of vasospasms and numbness in the extremities. This phenomenon is known as Raynaud's syndrome. Compliment is also fixed to the RBC membrane. As the RBC's return to the warmer parts of the body, the cold antibody (agglutinin) elutes from the RBC, leaving the compliment attached to the RBC membrane. The activated complement completes it activation/cascade cycle and lysis the RBC. If the RBC enters the liver, macrophages sensitive to C3B/iC3B will remove the RBC from circulation. If the patient's RBC (with the C3d compliment) tested with polyspecific antisera (containing anti-C3d antiglobulin), then a positive DAT test

Secondary Cold AIHA

This is a transient disorder secondary to infections. The disorder often occurs in respiratory infections and the principle microorganism known to be involved is Mycoplasma pneumoniae. It is suggested that the antibody produced in this disorder is a cold autoantibody specific to the mycoplasmal antigens. Unfortunately, this antibody is also cross-specific to the red cell "I" antigen. In this case the problem is self limiting. When the infections are cured, the antibody disappears. Clinical symptoms include jaundice and pallor. Clinical lab findings are similar to other AIHA disorders. Note: Episodes are also observed in infectious mononucleosis and lymphoproliferative disorders.

Paroxysmal Cold Hemoglobinuria (PCH)

This is the least common of the cold autoimmune hemolytic anemias. It was once observed in patients diagnosed with syphilis. This is no longer a problem as syphilis is controlled by antibiotics. It does occur in patients with viral disorders (mumps, measles, chicken pox, flu, and infectious mononucleosis. This is a self-limiting disorder, disappearing when the primary problem is resolved. The antibody is a cold-reacting IgG and is called "autohemolysin or "biphasic hemolysis". This antibody is also known as a Donath-Landsteiner (L-D) antibody. It is capable of binding to the patient's RBC's and fixing complement. The site of attachment is at the "P" blood group antigen site on the RBC membrane. The following occurs: the cold reacting IgG binds to RBC's at lower temperatures and in doing so "fixes" complement.

When the RBC's returns to the core temperature of the body, the IgG releases from the RBC's and complement causes hemolysis. This phenomenon is called "biphasic hemolysis".

Clinical symptoms include: [1] chills, [2] pyrexia, [3] cephalgia, [4] Raynaud's phenomenon (diffuse pain in the legs, back, and abdomen with pallor and cyanosis). [5] Hemoglobinuria usually appears with symptoms, and [6] jaundice.

Clinical lab findings include:

[1] hemoglobin as low as 5 g/dL
[2] leucopenia with a shift-to-the-left
[3] bilirubin greater than 1.5 mg/dL
[4] spherocytes
[5] decrease in serum complement
[6] peripheral blood smear with erythrophagocytosis by monocytes

---

DONATH-LANDSTEINER TEST

This is included for its historical interest. It is the classic diagnostic procedure for diagnosing PCH. A patient's blood sample is divided into two aliquots and maintained at two different temperatures. Set up as follows:

STEP ONE.

	incubate 30 min	incubate 30 min
aliquot #1	37 °C	37 °C
aliquot #2	4 °C	37 °C

STEP TWO. Centrifuge and observe for hemolysis.

INTERPRETATION. If no hemolysis in either tube the test is negative. The patient does not have PCH. If hemolysis occurs in both tubes, the test is inconclusive. If no hemolysis in aliquot #1 but hemolysis in aliquot #2, the patient has PCH.

Erythroblastosis Fetalis

This is an anemia (also known as hemolytic disease of the newborn, HDN) that is the consequences of warm-reacting antibodies. It occurs with a Rh-D negative mother is pregnant with a fetus that has a Rh-D positive blood type. What happens occurs during gestation period, there is a placental leakage of the fetus's red blood cells into the maternal circulation. It takes about 1.0 mL of blood to initiate this hemolytic response. Most sensitizations to the Rh-D positive antigen occur at delivery, which is why the first child is rarely affected by this type of anemia. There are "small" amounts (less than 0.5 mL) of fetus to maternal "bleeds" during the last four months of pregnancy and these are usually insufficient to stimulate production of antibodies. When the sensitized female becomes pregnant and carries a fetus with Rh-D positive RBC's, if a small amount of RBC's escape into maternal circulation, her antibody titer will significantly increase and the antibodies that are produced will escape across the placenta and attack the fetus's RBC's, causing hemolysis. The degree of antibody titer will determine the severity of erythroblastosis fetalis. This phenomenon gives rise to the term "alloimmune disease of the newborn". The most extreme form of this anemia will cause death in utero which is known as hydrops fetalis. If the problem is mild, the only external evidence that a problem exists is the presence of jaundice, which will vary with the severity of the problem. Jaundice indicates that bilirubin (from RBC hemolysis) is present and the danger that arises from this hemoglobin breakdown product is that increased levels are toxic to the brain cells. If the bilirubin rises to increased levels (greater than 20 mg/dL), it will cross the blood brain barrier and deposit in the basal ganglia cells, causing permanent neuron damage.

The Rh-type HDN accounts for about 33% of HDN and is the severest form of HDN. It is estimated that about 5% of Rh-negative women (even with multiple pregnancies) ever deliver infants with erythroblastosis fetalis. There is an immunoprophylaxis that will prevent this disorder. When a Rh-negative female delivers a Rh-positive infant, if she is administered anti-D immunoglobulin (trade name = RhoGamm) within 12 hours of delivery, this will prevent maternal immunization and the anemia is prevented. If the woman has been already been sensitized, the administration will be medically useless. It has been reported that if the baby is typed with either the A or B blood group and Rh antigen, with the mother typed as an O group and Rh negative, then the Rh sensitization is blocked. It seems that naturally occurring isoagglutinins of group O will destroy the group A or B cell which results in the destruction of the Rh antigen.

The ABO-type HDN is more common. It is usually characterized by a mild hemolytic anemia. This type of disorder is observed in group A or group B infants with group O mothers. NOTE: There are ABO-like substances in food that can stimulate anti-A or anti-B antibody production in group O mothers. At birth, if anemia is present in an ABO type of HDN, the anemia will be mild and require little or no medical intervention. A CBC will be normal with this exception; spherocytes will be seen in the peripheral blood smear. The spherocytes is usually not observed in Rh-type HDN.

NOTE

If you see spherocytes, NRBCs, macrocytes, microcytes, target cells, etc., look for another cause of anemia than the ABO-type HDN. Severe ABO-HDN anemias are very rare.

If you suspect an Rh-type HDN, then look for the following clues.

[1] Cord blood hemoglobin: The Hb should be <14 gm/dL. Capillary blood will be higher by about 3 to 6 gm/dL the cord blood value tends to reflect the severity of the anemia.
[2] After birth, the Hb can fall at a rate of up to 3.0 gm/dL per day. This can create a crisis requiring transfusion therapy to rid the infant of maternal antibodies.
[3] The WBC count can be as high as 30,000/μL.
[4] The blood film should be characterized by a shift-to-the-left.
[5] The platelet count is usually normal, however if the HDN is severe, look for a decrease.
[6] The RBC "picture" will be macrocytic, normocytic.
[7] NRBCs may range from 10 to 100/100 WBC.
[8] Reticulocytes will be elevated. Values as high as 60% have been reported
[9] Polychromatophilia is common.
[10] Anisocytosis
[11] Poikilocytosis, if present, will be absent to mild.
[12] Spherocytes are rarely seen.
[13] Bilirubin testing of cord blood will be <5.5 mg/dL and does not reflect the severity of HDN. Note: Some hospitals will perform an exchange transfusion if the cord blood level of bilirubin is 4.5 mg/dL. Venous level has been reported up to 50.0 mg/dL which is quite serious. Bilirubin is soluble and crosses the placenta readily. When the bilirubin levels reach 15 to 20 mg/dL, medical intervention may be required in the form of transfusion therapy. If bilirubin is rising at the rate of 0.5 mg/dL each hour or at a rate of 10 mg/dL in 24 hours, transfusion therapy is the usual rule.
[14] The Coomb's test will be positive.

At birth the infant's liver cannot conjugate bilirubin effectively. This is a function that is handled by the mother for the fetus during gestation. During the first week after birth, the rate of conjugation of bilirubin is slow in the normal infant. The bilirubin concentration will elevate initially and then begin to fall as the liver function takes over. This slight increase in serum bilirubin is normal and is termed physiological jaundice. If the unconjugated bilirubin continues elevates with the liver failing to conjugate the bilirubin, then it is deposited into the nuclei of neurons, this is termed "kernicterus". Should this continue, neuronal death will occur, resulting in brain damage and mental retardation? Continued neuron death and increasing jaundice is eventually fatal to the newborn. If you are assessing anemia in the newborn, use cord blood. The arterial and venous hemoglobin will be 3 to 6 g/dL higher. the cord blood hemoglobin value is <14 g/dL, then the infant is anemic. If the hemoglobin is <12 g/dL, then an exchange transfusion may be required.

Hemolytic Anemia due to a transfusion reaction

This form of anemia is the consequence of transfusing incompatible blood that is characterized by intravascular hemolysis. If the transfusion reaction is immediate, the ABO system is the most likely cause. The anti-A and anti-B antibodies are IgM and can cause immediate cell destruction. The IgM antibody will fix complement and the activated complement constitutes an activated hemolysin unit that causes membrane lysis and release of hemoglobin into the plasma.

There is a "delayed" hemolytic reaction that sets in from 2 to 14 days following the transfusion. The IgG antibody is most often the cause. This is a less potent reaction and IgG antibody coated cell represents a sensitized cell that are sequestered and destroyed, primarily in the spleen. The delayed reaction may not be as severe as the immediate transfusion reaction.

Clinical symptoms include [a] facial flushing, [b] anxiety, [c] nausea, [d] clammy skin, [e] chest pain, [f] back pain, [g] leg pain, [h] pyrexia, [i] chills, [j] pain and/or burning at infusion site, [k] hypo-tension, [l] chest pain, [m] dyspnea, [n] Hemoglobinuria, [o] oliguria or anuria, [p] generalized bleeding, and [q] shock.

If the patient has a delayed transfusion reaction, symptoms are usually mild. A laboratory follow-up is designed to identify the antibody to prevent future problems. Medical intervention is usually not required.

Intervention strategy in the event of an immediate transfusion reaction:
[1]   Immediately stop the transfusion.
[2]   Begin to hydrating the patient (lysed RBC stoma can clog and damage renal tubules) to stimulate renal function.
[3]   Evaluate urine for hemoglobin.
[4]   Evaluate patient's blood plasma for hemoglobinemia per lab protocol.
[5]   The blood bank repeats cross-matching steps and check-out process for the problem unit of blood.
[6]   The D-dimer (D-d dimer) test may be required to evaluate degree if intravascular clotting if any.
[7]   Tests for urobilinogen and serum bilirubin may be required.

Non-immune Hemolytic Anemia

These anemias represent a group of conditions that lead to the shortened survival of red cells by various mechanisms.

I-Intracellular infections

1-Malaria.: This is the most common infectious disease in the world that causes a hemolytic anemia. Species of malaria include:
   1- Plasmodium Vivax.
   2- P.Malariae- uncommon
   3- P.Oval – uncommon
   4- P. Falciparum. Most fatal

2- Babesiosis. Tick-borne parasites.
  A variety of organisms, both intracellular and extracellular, may be found in the blood and bone marrow:

3-Microfilaria, trypanosomes, and borrelia are extracellular.

4-Histoplasma, toxoplasma, Leishmania, mycobacterium avium intracellular, and fungi and bacteria (rods, cocci) are generally phagocyted by macrophages (histiocytes), monocytes, and sometimes even by granulocytes, but may also be seen extracellularly.

II--Extracellular infections

III--Mechanical etiologies

1-Cardiac prothesis (RBC fragments)
2- March Hemoglobinuria (caused by traumatic destruction of the red cells in strenuous and sustained physical activity such as marching).
3-Microangiopathic hemolytic anemia (Caused by fragmentation of the red cells by fibrin strands as they pass through abnormal arterioles, The fibrin strands are the results of intravascular thrombocytopenia purpura (TTP).
4- Venoms (some spiders contain enzymes that lyse the red cells membrane; Snake venoms rarely cause lysis in vivo).
5- Osmotic effects (Burns over more than 15% of the body can cause hemolysis

PART NINE: ANEMIA ASSOCIATED WITH SYSTEMIC NONHEMATOLOGIC DISORDERS

Anemia of Chronic Disease

This is a morphological anemia that is similar to iron deficiency anemia. Two distinguishing features are: [a] decreased transferrin level and [b] a normal RDW value. Diseases which are characterized by a secondary anemia are [a] infections, [b] liver disease, [c] malignancy (lymphoma and carcinoma), [d] renal failure, [e] systemic lupus erythematosus, [f] tissue injury, and [g] rheumatoid arthritis. The anemia is rarely severe and the degree of anemia is dependent upon the primary disease. It is thought that the disease may interfere with heme synthesis and blocks the release of iron from the macrophages for recycling. It is not known why, but erythropoietin stimulation and subsequent production does not occur. This anemia is alleviated by successful treatment of the underlying cause. Clinical laboratory findings include:

[1]   low hemoglobin (seldom <9.0 gm/dL) [N: F = 12 -16 g/dL; M = 14 - 18 g/dL]
[2]   low hematocrit (seldom <27%) [N: F = 37 - 47%; M = 40 - 54%]
[3]   Normocytic, normochromic RBC's
[4]   reticulocyte production index is usually <2.0
[5]   plasma iron = 10 to 65 mg/dL [60 - 160 mG/dL]
[6]   TIBC = 100 to 300 µG/dL [N: 250 - 350 µG/dL]
[7]   serum ferritin may be increased (but is often normal) [N: 20 - 200 mG/dL]
NOTE: If the bone marrow is examined, the M: E ration is increased, sideroblasts are decreased, and macrophages have increased hemosiderin.

Anemia of Chronic Renal Failure

The principle cause of this type of anemia is due to failure of the kidney to produce and/or release erythropoietin. Medical research indicates that there is a unidentified inhibitory substance in the plasma of some patients with chronic renal failure. Decreased erythropoietin = decreased RBC production.

The anemia may be associated with dialysis therapy that accompanies chronic renal failure. There are acquired defects in the sodium-potassium ATPase pump and the pentose-phosphate shunt. The consequence of these defects leaves the RBC more susceptible to hemolysis. The "stress" initiated through the oxidants introduced through the dialysis fluid can induce Heinz body formation and promote early hemolysis of the cell. These patients may develop hypersplenism, shortening RBC survival. Uremic toxins may contribute to the early hemolysis of the RBC. These toxins can also suppress the erythroid precursors. The dialysis process can create electrolyte disturbances that produce crenated/burr cells.

Anemia related to renal failure is often Hypoproliferative, normochromic, and normocytic. This type of anemia can progress into disseminated intravascular coagulation (DIC). When examining peripheral blood smears, look for schistocytes and microcytes, which are indicators of DIC.

Anemia associated with infections

This type of anemia usually expresses itself in a patient when the infection (bacterial or fungal) persists for two weeks or longer. Examples of microorganisms that are known to induce anemic conditions are:

Features of this type of anemia may be characterized by weight loss, fever, and the presence acute-phase reactants (inflammatory products). Clinical laboratory findings include the following:
01   Increased WBC count
02   normochromic and normocytic RBC's
      A.   If the disease increases in severity, then it becomes hypochromic.
03   MCHC and MCV will be normal or low
04   Serum iron tends to be decreased.
05   Serum ferritin usually increases.
06   Total iron binding capacity (TIBC) usually decreases.
07   C-Reactive Protein and Amyloid A Protein tests are positive.
08   ESR is increased.
09   If sepsis, then bacteria and fungi may be demonstrated in the blood.
10   Presence of neutrophils with toxic granulation and vacuolation.

Anemia associated with liver Disease

The liver is the largest organ of the human body lying under the diaphragm and is attached to it. It weights between 2.9 and 3.3 pounds. It has a rich blood supply from two sources. One is the portal vein that carries blood from the alimentary tract. The other is the hepatic artery that delivers oxygenated blood. The classical manifestation of liver disease is jaundice (yellow discoloration of the plasma, skin, sclera, and mucus membranes) which results from bilirubin accumulation. If there are changes occurring in the hepatic blood flow, then portal hypertension is another manifestation. A third clinical event in disease is enlargement (hepatomegaly). Anemia usually appears when there is some chronic disease involving the liver. The degree of anemia does not correlate with the degree or severity of hepatic failure. In liver disease, there is often altered lipid metabolism which produces the characteristic acanthocytes and target cells. Macrocytes may also be present as well as reticulocytosis. If there is a chronic or acute blood loss with liver disorders, then a microcytic, hypochromic anemia may develop.

In most cases of liver disease the clinical lab may find the following:

01   MCV that falls between 100 and 110 fL.
02   Normocytic and normochromic RBC's.
03   Increase in the number of retic cells.
04   A decrease in the hematocrit. NOTE: This may be due to the pooling of the RBCs in the spleen or venous system. There may also be an increase in plasma volume which dilutes the RBCs.

Anemia associated with alcoholism

Ethanol is toxic to bone marrow cells, especially the erythrocytes. The rubriblasts tend to be vacuolated and the rate of mitotic activity in the erythroid precursors falls. Anemia associated with ethanol consumption is usually macrocytic with evidence of hypochomia. Alcoholism causes cirrhosis, esophageal varices, intestinal bleeding, and folate deficiencies which may lead to an anemia that resembles that of iron deficiency. It is not unusual to observe a dimorphic RBC population in a stained blood smear. In chronic alcoholism, there is likely cirrhosis with nutritional deficiencies and altered metabolism. Increased cholesterol alters cell membrane formation and acanthocytes and target cells form the basis of acanthocytosis or spur-cell anemia.

Anemia associated with connective tissue

Rheumatoid arthritis (RA), Systemic Lupus Erythematosus (SLE), mixed connective tissue disease (MCTD), scleroderma, dermatomyosis and Sjogren's syndrome. Many factors contribute to this anemia.

PART TEN: DIAGNOSTIC BLOOD SMEARS

The blood smear remains a crucial diagnostic aid. It is important for laboratory hematologists to know what they are looking for and should be looking for in a smear. Blood smear often make the diagnosis very straightforward.

A laboratory-initiated request for a blood smear is usually the result of an abnormality in the complete blood count or a response to "FLAGS" produced by an automated instrument.

Below is the listing of criteria used to determine a positive smear finding for the study of suggested criteria for action following automated CBC and WBCs differential analysis?

1. Morphology
a.   RBC morphology at either 2+ / Moderate or greater. The only exception is Malaria, where any finding will be considered a positive finding.
b.   PLT morphology (giant platelets) at either 2+ / Moderate or greater.
c.   Platelet Clumps at > rare / occasional
d.   Dohle bodies at either 2+ / Moderate or greater
e.   Toxic granulation at either 2+ / Moderate or greater
f.   Vacuoles at either 2+ / Moderate or greater

2. Abnormal Cell Types
a.   Blast > 1
b.   Meta > 2
c.   Myelo / Promyelocyte > 1
d.   Atypical Lymphs > 5
e.   NRBC > 1
f.   Plasma Cells > 1

The International Society for Laboratory Hematology (ISLH) has published consensus criteria for the laboratory-initiated review of blood smears on the basis of the results of the automated blood count. The indications for smear review differ according to the age and sex of the patient, whether the request is an initial or a subsequent one, and whether there has been a clinically significant change from a previous validated result (referred to as a failed delta check). All laboratories should have a protocol for the examination of a laboratory-initiated blood smear, which can reasonably be based on the criteria of the International Society for Laboratory Hematology. Regulatory groups should permit the examination of a blood smear when such protocols indicate that it is necessary. There are numerous valid reasons for a clinician to request a blood smear, and these differ somewhat from the reasons why laboratory workers initiate a blood-smear examination. Sometimes it is possible for a definitive diagnosis to be made from a blood smear.

Laboratory-initiated examinations of blood smears for patients with anemia are usually the result of a laboratory policy according to which a blood smear is ordered whenever the hemoglobin concentration is unexpectedly low. This policy should be encouraged, since the consideration of the blood smear and the red-cell indices is a logical first step in the investigation of any unexplained anemia. Initiating a smear as a reflex test also means that a further blood sample does not have to be taken for this purpose. Modern automated instruments impart valuable information about the nature of anemia. They provide not only a red-cell count, MCV, MCH, and the MCHC but also newer variables that give information that previously could be derived only from a blood smear. These variables usually include the RDW, which correlates on a blood smear with anisocytosis, and they may also include the hemoglobin-distribution width and the percentages of hypochromic and hyperchromic cells, which correlate with anisochromasia, hypochomia, and hyperchromia. A variety of histograms and scatter plots give a visual representation of red-cell characteristics.

Clinical indications of blood smears

Morphologic abnormalities of erythrocytes may be due either to production of abnormal erythrocytes in the bone marrow or to pathologic processes to which the erythrocytes are exposed in the circulation.
Macrocytes usually reflect abnormal erythropoiesis in which there are a reduced number of cell divisions during maturation of erythroid precursors.
Hypochromia generally arises because of impaired hemoglobinization of erythroid cells in the marrow.

209

Spherocytes can be due to an inherited membrane abnormality of erythrocytes (hereditary spherocytosis) or can result from the action of phagocytes on erythrocytes sensitized with antibodies wherein the phagocytes remove portions of the red cell membrane, creating spherocytes. In addition, both spherocytes and schistocytes result from the action of abnormal physical forces in the circulation (particularly shear stress) that causes fragmentation of normal erythrocytes. Stomatocytes are over hydrated cells, which in three-dimensional views are bowl shaped; they may appear as an intermediate form in the transformation of diskocytes to spherocytes.

The target cell is a bell-shaped cell with a relative excess of membrane; in patients with obstructive liver disease a significant increase in the total membrane content of cholesterol leads to the increase in cell surface area.

The spur cells (acanthocytes) of chronic alcoholic liver disease have increased cholesterol but, in contrast to target cells, normal content of phospholipids. The echinocytes of pyruvate kinase deficiency form because of decreased ATP generation resulting in loss of water and potassium from the red cells.

Sickle cells result from aggregation in the deoxygenated state of molecules of hemoglobin S, which have the substitution of valine for glutamic acid of the sixth amino acid position of the beta chain of hemoglobin. In hereditary elliptocytosis, the elliptical shape of the cell is due to membrane protein abnormalities. Infiltrative disorders of the bone marrow, with disruption of the vasculature of the marrow, are associated with the formation of elliptocytes and teardrop erythrocytes. Bite cells apparently arise when a phagocyte removes a portion of the red cell along with a Heinz body.

Howell–Jolly bodies are remnants of DNA; they are ordinarily removed from red cells by the spleen. Basophilic stippling occurs in conditions in which the biosynthesis of hemoglobin is impaired; the stippled particles are aggregates of ribosomes or, in the case of Pappenheimer bodies, aggregates of ferritin, lysosomes, ribosomes, and degenerating mitochondria.

Pelger–Hüet cells occur in a hereditary disorder in which the granulocytes function normally and no hematologic illness exists. As an acquired disorder, Pelger–Hüet cells generally reflect neutrophilic granulocytic dysplasia.

Two abnormalities of erythrocytes can be recognized by low-power microscopic examination of the blood. Rouleaux of erythrocytes are related to very high serum protein concentrations, generally due to multiple myeloma or to macroglobulinemia. Agglutination of red cells on the slide is usually due to cold agglutinins.

Macrocytes (frequently oval) in substantial numbers are observed in patients with megaloblastic anemias (vitamin B12 or folic acid deficiency) often with considerable anisocytosis (with some microcytes present as well). In addition, macrocytes may be prominent in individuals with erythroleukemia, myelodysplastic disorders, acquired sideroblastic anemia, and with antimetabolite or androgen drug therapy. A lesser degree of macrocytosis is seen commonly in alcoholic patients. Polychromatophilic macrocytes usually indicate a high reticulocyte count.

A predominance of hypochromic microcytic cells is found in iron deficiency anemia, thalassemia, and hereditary sideroblastic anemia, and in some patients with the anemia of chronic disorders and with lead intoxication. For individuals with mild anemia, the degree of microcytosis is usually substantially greater in patients with thalassemia minor than those with iron deficiency. Anisochromasia with the presence of a dimorphic red cell population (hypochromic and normochromic) is observed in acquired sideroblastic anemia, patients with thalassemia minor after transfusions, and persons with iron deficiency following transfusions or treatment with iron.

Examination of peripheral blood films of normal persons reveals small numbers of poikilocytes, usually less than 2%. In the assessment of the significance of poikilocytosis, one must identify the predominant abnormal morphologic form and exclude artifactual alterations of the red cells.

Spherocytes are the predominant morphologic abnormality in patients with hereditary spherocytosis, autoimmune hemolytic anemia, and hemolytic transfusion reactions, and are common, along with schistocytes, in patients with red cell fragmentation disorders. Spherocytes may also be observed in less common hemolytic states such as the Heinz body hemolytic anemias and clostridial sepsis. Stomatocytes are seen in large numbers in alcoholics and in the rare disorder of hereditary stomatocytosis, and in small numbers in normal persons. There are four major circumstances in which target cells appear as the major morphologic abnormality: thalassemia, hepatic disease with jaundice, hemoglobin C disorders, and the postsplenectomy state. Lesser numbers of target cells are found in sickle cell anemia, iron deficiency, and lead intoxication. Leptocytes are seen in thalassemic disorders and with obstructive liver disease. Sickle cells and dense, deformed poikilocytes ("irreversibly sickled cells") are characteristic of sickle cell anemia, hemoglobin SC disease, hemoglobin S-thalassemia, and hemoglobin C-Harlem, but are not observed in sickle cell trait.

A large number of elliptocytes (25 to 75% of the red cells) usually indicates hereditary elliptocytosis. Moderate numbers of elliptocytes are seen in thalassemia and myelofibrosis, and lesser numbers in iron deficiency and hypersplenic states. Teardrop erythrocytes (usually with elliptocytes) are particularly prominent in patients with myelofibrosis with myeloid metaplasia and occur frequently in patients with other infiltrative disorders of the bone marrow such as leukemia and metastatic carcinoma. Acanthocytes are the principal morphologic abnormality in abetalipoproteinemia and in the "spur cell anemia" associated with severe alcoholic liver disease. Acanthocytes are found along with other poikilocytes after splenectomy. Conditions associated with the appearance of echinocytes are pyruvate kinase deficiency of erythrocytes, uremia, carcinomas, and immediately after the transfusion of aged or metabolically depleted blood (echinocytes form during storage of the blood). Correction of the metabolic abnormalities of uremia results in disappearance of echinocytes. Schistocytes are the morphologic hallmark of the hemolytic anemias associated with red cell fragmentation (i.e., the microangiopathic hemolytic anemias and those hemolytic anemias associated with malfunctioning cardiac prostheses). Schistocytes also may form during disseminated intravascular coagulation. Bite cells are principally related to the various Heinz body hemolytic anemias, such as glucose-6-phosphate dehydrogenase deficiency.

Howell–Jolly bodies are found in patients who have had splenectomy or are hyposplenic (e.g., sickle cell anemia) and rarely in megaloblastic anemias. The three disorders particularly associated with coarse basophilic stippling are lead poisoning, sideroblastic anemia, and thalassemia.

Nucleated erythrocytes, usually in small numbers (in adults), may appear in the blood when the marrow is under intense stimulation due to severe hemolysis, hemorrhage, or hypoxia. In addition, nucleated red cells and immature myeloid cells may be recognized with infiltrative disorders of the marrow such as myelofibrosis, leukemia, and metastatic carcinoma. In patients with megaloblastic anemias the nucleated erythrocytes in the blood have megaloblastic nuclear features.

Cytoplasmic vacuolization of granulocytes is observed in patients with bacteremia or other severe infections. Toxic granulation, a rather nonspecific finding, is found in a variety of disorders including infections and metabolic derangements. Dohle bodies are seen in patients with infections and burns, during pregnancy, after cytotoxic chemotherapy (particularly with cyclophosphamide), and with the May–Heggelin anomaly. Pelger-Hüet cells, on an acquired rather than hereditary basis, are particularly associated with myelodysplastic and myeloproliferative disorders. Hypersegmented neutrophils usually are an important clue to the presence of vitamin B12 or folic acid deficiency but are occasionally found in patients with myelodysplasia or myeloproliferative disorders.

The diagnosis of leukemia is commonly obvious by recognition of abnormal numbers and stages of development of myeloid or lymphoid cells in the blood. Immature monocytes suggest either leukemia or myelodysplasia. A significant increase in the number of basophils usually indicates a myeloproliferative disorder.

A high percentage of reactive lymphocytes may be seen in viral illnesses such as infectious mononucleosis, viral hepatitis, cytomegalovirus infection, HIV infection and rubella, or with reactions to drugs such as phenytoin and para-aminosalicylic acid. Lymphocytes with convoluted nuclei may be found in T cell lymphomas and in the Sezary syndrome.

An increased number of large platelets are observed in thrombocytopenia with immune-mediated hyperdestruction, disseminated intravascular coagulation, myeloproliferative disorders (particularly myelofibrosis), megaloblastic anemias, the Bernard–Soulier syndrome, and the May–Hegglin anomaly. Platelet size is normal in hypersplenic states. Microthrombocytes are found in the Wiskott–Aldrich syndrome. Hypogranular platelets are seen in the myeloproliferative disorders.

Sometimes the blood smear provides the primary or the only evidence of a specific diagnosis, such as myelodysplastic syndrome, leukemia, lymphoma, or hemolytic anemia. It is important that, if possible, such blood smears be stored over the long term, just as a tissue that provides a histologic diagnosis is stored over the long term. In practice, such storage is easily achieved if a patient has also had a bone marrow aspirate (since a blood smear should always be stored with an aspirate), but it is harder to achieve if the peripheral blood smear alone has provided the diagnosis. Individual laboratories should have a mechanism to make possible the retention of such smears or an image derived from them. Some laboratories retain all smears that have been reviewed by a laboratory hematologist or pathologist; this can create a storage problem, and it is likely that, increasingly, digital images of important abnormal smears will be stored. The continuing importance of the blood smear is highlighted by the recent introduction of photographs of blood smears as a regular feature in both the journal Blood, by ongoing efforts to develop image-recognition technology for the automated examination of blood smears, and by the development of telehematology to permit the remote interpretation or second opinions of blood smears. Even in the age of molecular analysis, the blood smear remains an important diagnostic tool. Physicians should request a blood smear when there are clinical indications for it. Members of the laboratory staff should make and examine a blood smear whenever the results of the complete blood count indicate that a blood smear is essential for the validation or the further elucidation of a detected abnormality. If error is to be avoided, sophisticated modern investigations of hematologic disorders should be interpreted in the light of peripheral-blood features as well as the clinical context.

Approach to Abnormal WBCs

KEEP IT SIMPLE.

Given a patient with an abnormal WBC, your approach should be very straightforward. Basically you want to determine:
Which cell type or types are abnormal? Is abnormality reactive (due to an infection), if not, is it neoplastic?
The differential leukocyte count is essential.
=Is maturation normal? Are immature cells present? Are there any blasts?
=Are cells marker studies needed for lineage identification?
=Are clonality studies needed to identify neoplastic causes?
=If this is an emergency problem.

Granulocytosis.

Causes of reactive granulocytosis include:

* Infection: Inflammatory cytokines (IL-2, TNF) released by lymphocytes and neutrophils as well as endotoxin result in increased bone marrow production and release of granulocytes from storage pools as well as demargination.
    * Chronic Inflammation
    * Stress: hypoxemia, exercise, epinephrine
    * Drug-induced:
        Steroids: increased release of neutrophils from marrow, demargination and decreased egress to tissue pool
        Granulocyte colony stimulating factor
        Lithium: increased production of colony stimulating factors
* Non-hematologic malignancy: paraneoplastic syndrome; increased neutrophils secondary to release of G-CSF from tumor; or with metastatic disease, may result from inflammation and necrosis;
    * Asplenia/hyposplenism: loss of site of pooling/sequestration of WBCs
    * Chronic marrow stimulation: chronic hemolytic anemias, immune thrombocytopenia
    * "Rebound leukocytosis" following recovery from marrow suppression.

Elevation of the granulocyte count may result from a primary bone marrow disorder resulting in autonomous proliferation of cells or it may be a secondary response to an underlying condition. There are a few, rare syndromes associated with granulocytosis without an underlying cause.
Primary bone marrow disorders associated with granulocytosis include hematopoietic stem cell disorders. The mechanism(s) leading to excessive proliferation of cells in these disorders are not clear, but may be related to molecular events (gene mutations and translocations) that induce cell proliferation or suppress apoptosis (programmed cell death).
The mechanisms of secondary or reactive granulocytosis include: increased bone marrow production, increased bone marrow release, demargination of granulocytes and decreased egress of granulocytes from the circulating pool to the tissues. Cytokines and chemotactic factors elicited during infection, inflammation and tissue damage are the mediators of these events. When the reactive granulocytosis is dramatic (leukocytosis >50,000/mm3) and associated with an increase in early neutrophil precursors (bands, metamyelocytes, myelocytes) it is referred to as a Leukemoid reaction.
Chronic Idiopathic Neutrophilia: a syndrome of chronic leukocytosis (WBC counts between 10 and 40 x 109/L) of unknown etiology in patients who are otherwise well.
Leukocyte Adhesion Factor Deficiency: impaired neutrophil Chemotaxis and inability to phagocytose opsonized particles; defect in adherence; Neutrophils lack surface receptor for C3bi; clinically: leukocytosis, recurrent infections
Familiar Cold Urticaria and leukocytosis: leukocytosis, fever, Urticaria, rash, muscle and skin tenderness on exposure to cold.

Hematopoietic stem cell disorders associated with granulocytosis:
- Acute myelogenous leukemia (AML)

AML is a clonal, hematopoietic stem cell disorder characterized by uncontrolled proliferation of myeloid cells. In addition, there is impaired differentiation of the stem cells so that they do not mature into functioning blood cells. The myeloid cells that accumulate in the blood and bone marrow are immature cells called "blasts".

- The myeloproliferative disorders
    * Chronic Myelogenous Leukemia (CML)
    * Polycythemia Vera (PV)
    * Agnogenic Myeloid Metaplasia (AMM)
    * Essential Thrombocythemia (ET)
The myeloproliferative disorders are a group of acquired, clonal, hematopoietic stem cell disorders characterized by excessive proliferation of blood cells without the arrest in maturation seen with acute leukemia. Granulocytosis is the hallmark of CML, but is commonly seen in PV. It is a less constant feature of AMM and ET.

Neutropenia.

Neutropenia is a decrease in circulating neutrophils in the peripheral blood. The absolute neutrophil count (ANC) number defines neutropenia. An abnormal ANC value contains fewer than 1500 cells per mm3. African Americans may have a lower but normal ANC value of 1000 cells per mm3 with a normal total WBC count. The ANC is calculated by multiplying the percentage of bands and neutrophils (segmented neutrophils or granulocytes) on a CBC differential times the total white WBC count.

Note that many modern automated instruments actually calculate and provide the ACN number in their reports. These instruments usually do not separate bands from segmented neutrophils, and so the combined number is termed the granulocyte number. Thus, in such an instrument report, the ANC is equivalent to the absolute segmented neutrophil or granulocyte number. If a band number is reported separately, then add it to the granulocyte number.

The severity of neutropenia is categorized as mild when the ANC is 1000-1500 cells per mm3, moderate when the ANC is 500-1000 cells per mm3, and severe when the ANC is less than 500 cells per mm3. The risk of bacterial infection is related to both the severity and duration of neutropenia.

Eosinopenia

This condition is not easy to identify. Normal values in the peripheral blood are normally low. It is possible to perform a differential and not count any eosinophils (EO). An absolute count of 50/µL is considered to be eosinopenia. Causes of eosinopenia include [1] stress, [2] acute infections, [3] neoplasms, and [4] severe injuries (for example: burns). To determine if the patient has eosinopenia, use the 10X objective and scan the blood smear. If NO eosinophils are observed, then the patient may have eosinopenia.

NOTE. If the blood levels of glucocorticoids are elevated for any reason, there will be most likely, a decreased peripheral concentration of EO's.

Eosinophilia

Leukocytosis is observed in allergies, asthma, drug hyper-sensitivities, parasitic infections, terminal Hodgkin's disease, and chronic hepatitis. Bacterial infections (leprosy, tuberculosis, scarlet fever), fungal infections, ulcerative colitis, and certain skin diseases. Counts >500/µL are required in the peripheral blood. When you are performing a differential count and you note the increased presence of eosinophils (EO), look for increased rupture of EO cytoplasmic membranes. Eosinophils tend to be more fragile when increased.

- Drugs (eosinophils may reach 10 G/l), chemical and physical agents
        Many drugs, including: liver extracts, antibiotics, fungicides, analgesics, ant tubercular, anti-inflammatory, psychotropic drugs...
        Irradiation, chronic cigarette smoking, haemodialysis, phosphorus, mercury, benzene
- Various hematologic disorders

Non malignant diseases: recovery phase of agranulocytosis, graft versus host disease, after splenectomy

Myeloproliferative disorders: chronic myelocytic leukemia (frequent, may be quite important)
Hodgkin disease (not consistent, often < 1G/l)
Non-Hodgkin Lymphomas (some situations, such as angioimmunoblastic lymphadenopathy)
Acute leukemias (a few cases)
Hypereosinophilic syndrome: very rare situation related to huge eosinophilia, the latter seriously affecting lungs, kidneys and nervous system
- Gastrointestinal disorders
Crohn's and Whipple diseases
- Solid tumours
Namely if necrosis occurs, or after metastasis (breast, lung)
- Some bacterial infections.
- Allergic disorders (most cases show number of eosinophils < 1.5 G/l)
Bronchial asthma
Angioneurotic oedema
Eczema
Hives
Allergic rhinitis (hay fever)

- Parasitic infections (eosinophils may reach 10-20 G/l, and at times up to 50 G/l)
Mainly helminth, especially those that invade the tissues:
Ascaris, Fasciola hepatica, Trichinelle spiralis
Larva migrans viscerale (Toxocara canis and catis)
Echinococcus granulosus
Eosinophilia is moderate of absent in pure bowel parasitism (oxyuris, Trichocephalus trichuris)
In tropical areas: Schistosoma, Filaria

- Skin disorders: mainly those related to allergy
Pemphigus, dermatitis herpetiformis

There is a hyper-eosinophilia in which the count will be >1,500/µL this highly elevated count is due to a systemic disorder such as polyarteritis (a disorder involving the medium sized arteries) or Löffler's syndrome (an allergic response to helminth parasites). In hyper-eosinophilia, hepatosplenomegaly may be observed and also Charcot-Leyden crystals in exudates and tissues.

TROPICAL EOSINOPHILIA
This is a syndrome of acute and chronic lung disease with clinical symptoms that include [1] low-grade fever, [2] weight loss, [3] paroxysmal cough, and [4] adenopathy, with swelling. This disorder occurs only where microfilaria are endemic (such as Wuchereria bancrofti and Brugia malayi. Eosinophil counts >3,000/µL are the rule.

Basopenia

Basopenia is even more difficult to identify than eosinopenia. It is not unusual to perform a differential count and not record a basophil, even when counting 200 WBCs. Use the same strategy as when screening for eosinopenia. If no basophils can be observed on a stained blood film, then that patient may have basopenia. Until the development of flow cytometry, with it capability of identifying the basophils in a population of 10,000 or more WBCs, the identification of basopenia was a problem. Decreased basophils are observed in anaphylaxis and other allergic reactions, hemorrhage, stress, myxedema, myelofibrosis, chronic hemolytic anemia, glucocorticoid therapy, acute infections, neoplasms, Polycythemia Vera, colitis, and severe injuries (as in burns).

Basophilia

Basophilia is diagnosed when the absolute basophil count is >100/µL. Another criterion for basophilia is that more than 2% of the total WBC count will be basophils. This increase will most often be observed in chronic myelogenous leukemia, colitis, Polycythemia Vera, myelofibrosis, nephrotic, radiation exposure, chronic hemolytic anemia, myxedema, and hypothyroid conditions.

Basophils are involved in inflammatory processes and hypersensitivity reactions. These cells synthesize and store histamine and other inflammatory mediator chemicals. These biologically active materials when released will cause
[1] vasodilatation (increasing vascular permeability),
[2] initiate smooth muscle contractions,
[3] Increase secretions,
[4] Exert an inhibitory effect upon certain parts of the coagulation mechanism.
Basophils (and tissue basophils/mast cells) have receptors for IgE. If the appropriate antigens for IgE are present, then degranulation occurs with release of histamine with a clinical manifestation of a form of hypersensitivity is seen in [1] bronchial asthma, [2] Urticaria, [3] allergic rhinitis, and [4] hyper-sensitivity to drugs, insect venom, and other antigens.

Lymphocytosis

Lymphocytosis or increased blood lymphocyte count is common and occurs at some time in most people, usually in association with viral infections. Lymphocytosis is commonly short lived, and investigation of such cases by Immunophenotyping is usually unrewarding. Uncommonly, Lymphocytosis may indicate a lymphoproliferative disorder.
The first step in the investigation of Lymphocytosis is to assess the major lymphocyte subsets: T cells, B cells and NK cells. The T cells are further divided into CD4 T cells (helper cells) and CD8 T cells (cytotoxic cells).
In a healthy person, roughly 70-80% of lymphocytes are T cells, and approximately equal proportions of the remainder are B cells and natural killer (NK) cells. Of the T cells, the ratio of CD4 to CD8 cells is normally about 2:1. A full blood count tube must be collected at the same time, to determine the absolute lymphocyte count. The absolute counts of the various subsets are then calculated, and these values are usually more informative than the percentages. In children up to 6 years of age, the absolute lymphocyte count is significantly higher than in adults, and the absolute counts of the various subsets are also higher. .

In viral infection, the elevation in total lymphocyte count is caused by an increase in the absolute count of CD8 T cells. This occurs most dramatically in Epstein-Barr virus infection, but is also associated with other viruses such as acute CMV infection. The cytotoxic CD8 cells are able to kill infected cells, thereby limiting the dissemination of the virus. The CD8 count may remain markedly elevated for many months after the patient recovers. Other infectious diseases that may cause Lymphocytosis include toxoplasmosis, in which CD8 T cells are selectively increased, and pertussis, in which all subsets are increased. However, in many infections the blood lymphocyte count remains within normal limits. Patients who have undergone splenectomy, or whose splenic function is otherwise reduced, may have a Lymphocytosis. All lymphocyte subsets may be increased, especially NK cells, and the Lymphocytosis itself is not clinically significant.
The most serious cause of Lymphocytosis is a lymphoproliferative disorder. If the clinical notes indicate that such a disease is suspected, and immunophenotypic analysis is requested, the laboratory tests the blood sample with a large panel of antibodies, to determine whether the lymphocytes have abnormal markers, and whether there is evidence of monoclonality.
All mature B cells express either kappa or lambda antibody light chains. In a normal individual, there is a mixture of kappa and lambda B cells. In a neoplastic disorder, with a monoclonal population derived from a single B cell, there is a predominance of either kappa or lambda cells. The test for kappa and lambda is simple and reliable.
CD4 T cell, CD8 T cell and NK lymphoproliferative disorders are much less common than their B cell counterparts, and classification is less satisfactory. It may be difficult to distinguish a reactive Lymphocytosis from a lymphoproliferative disorder. If an elevated T cell count is detected as an isolated finding in an otherwise healthy individual, the lymphocyte subset determination should be repeated every 3-6 months. If the condition is post-infectious, the T cell counts are likely to fall gradually; increasing counts favor the possibility of a lymphoproliferative disorder.
Immunophenotyping can detect monoclonality in about half the cases of CD4 or CD8 T cell lymphoproliferative disorders by specialized methods.
Lymphocytosis is characteristic of viral infections, certain chronic infections, and certain disorders. (Examples include: lymphocytic leukemia, tuberculosis, pertussis, toxoplasma infection, and

hyperthyroidism). A normal absolute lymphocyte count (adult) ranges from 1,500 to 4,000/µL. In lymphocytosis, look for absolute lymphocytes concentrations >4,000/µL in adults. In children, the normal absolute count varies.

Consider the following examples:

1. Birth = 2,000 to 11,000/µL
2. 1 y/o = 4,000 to 10,500/µL
3. 4 y/o = 2,000 to 8,000/µL
4. 6 y/o = 1,500 to 6,500/µL

An absolute lymphocyte count for lymphocytosis will be greater than the maximum values listed. Remember when determining absolute lymphocytosis, there will be an increase in the lymphocyte count along with an increase in the overall WBC count. Also there should be almost no smudge cells present as in CLL.

- If the increase in lymphocytes is due to small lymphocytes (with diameters of 6 to 8 µ and a small amount of cytoplasm) then it is most likely this is a benign response. Note. LESS THAN 10% of the total lymphocytes will be larger forms with increased cytoplasm and an "immature appearing" nucleus that may resemble a monocyte. Conditions in which this type of mature lymphocyte predominates are [1] hyperthyroidism, [2] pertussis, [3] disseminated tuberculosis, [4] acute infectious lymphocytosis (a children's disorder), [5] early chronic lymphocytic leukemia, and [6] advance chronic lymphocytic leukemia.

- If the increase in lymphocytes is characterized by >10% of the total lymphocyte of the larger form with increased cytoplasm and an "immature appearing" nucleus that may resemble a monocyte, then you may be observing reactive lymphocytosis. This type of increase may due to any of the following viral infections: [1] infectious mononucleosis (Epstein-Barr virus), [2] cytomegalovirus infection, [3] viral hepatitis, [4] mumps, [5] measles, [6] upper respiratory infections, and [7] human immuno-deficiency virus.

Absolute lymphocytosis (due to an increase in lymphocytes) must be distinguished from relative lymphocytosis (which is due to a decrease in neutrophils).

Lymphopenia

Lymphocytopenia for the adult occurs when the absolute lymphocyte count drops below 1,500/µL in the child, dependent on the age, the absolute count will be <1,500 to 2,000/µL.
Causes for Lymphocytopenia include

[1]	Chemotherapy	[4]	radiation therapy
[2]	Malnutrition	[5]	systemic lupus erythematosus
[3]	Stress	[6]	drugs (such as corticosteroids),

Put the lymphocyte count into clinical context. The history is taken with knowledge of the main causes of lymphocytosis and lymphopenia.
A physical examination is done to determine:
1- Presence of lymphadenopathy, location, size and texture of the glands.
2- Presence of local inflammation or neoplastic disease.
3- Is splenomegaly present?
A laboratory investigations is performed to determine cell type (reactive or blast) and clonality (in B-cell kappa or lambda).

Monocytosis

Monocytosis occurs when the monocyte concentration is >1000/µL. (Normal is an absolute count of 100 to 1000/µL) In children up to 1 y/o, the normal absolute count may be up to 1,100/µL. Such increases are associated with [1] Monocytic leukemia, [2] tuberculosis, [3] syphilis, [4] 62% of all malignancies, [5] Chronic neutropenia, [6] Hemolytic anemias, [7] Polycythemia Vera, [8] 25% of patients with Hodgkin's disease, and [9] connective tissue diseases.

Caution: When you are interpreting a Wright's stained blood smear, do not confuse these cells with reactive lymphocytes that may be encountered in a variety of diseases.

Monocytopenia

Monocytopenia occurs when the absolute monocyte count drops below 50/µL. Decreased monocytes occur in [1] hairy cell leukemia, [2] massive infections, and [3] glucocorticoid (steroid) therapy. If monocytopenia occurs in a massive infection, it is probable that there is also neutropenia.

- The Normal Large Lymphocyte.
 Look for nuclear chromatin that tends to be clumped rather than linear. The clumping is more obvious at the periphery of the nucleus. The cytoplasm stains a pale sky blue with a structureless appearance. There may be the appearance of fine bluish interlacing fibrils. There may be a few well-defined bluish-red granules with uneven distribution. The cytoplasm tends to be relatively clear, with a non-granular background. The cytoplasmic membrane is easily indented by neighboring cells.

 - The Normal Monocyte.
 The nuclear chromatin tends to be linear, not clumped. The nucleus may have the appearance of brain-like convulsions. The cytoplasm will appear a dull grey-blue and is finely granular. It also has a ground-glass appearance. Distinct bluish red granules are present and are interspersed among numerous fine granules. The monocyte will project blunt pseudopods and tend to compress cells rather than be indented by them.
To identify the reactive lymphocyte, look for the following features in the:
[1] NUCLEUS. Begin by looking for a chromatin pattern that "lies" between that of a small lymphocyte and monocyte. The nucleus can be blast-like in appearance with nucleoli present. This nucleus may look almost exactly like that of a monocyte. Nuclear descriptions have included [1] cleaved, [2] convoluted, [3] bean-shape, and [4] oblong.
[2] CYTOPLASM. Look for the presence of distinctive red granules, vacuoles, and a bubbly or foamy appearance. These are not regular features. The cytoplasm will have an increased degree of basophilia with or without a patchy appearance. Examine the cytoplasm near the nucleus, looking for linear or rod-like clear and unstained areas. Note if the edge of the cytoplasm is scalloped and a deeply basophilic periphery is present. The cytoplasm has a tendency to be indented by adjacent cells.
 When enumerating the "reactive" lymphocyte, follow the established laboratory criteria for your laboratory. It is normal for "normal" lymphocytes to have slight degrees of variation. It may be deemed to be wise policy to ignore the slight variations and have established criteria for more distinctive variations. Lymphocytes react readily to a variety of antigens in the blood and will "transform" according to the degree of stimulus. Because reactive and malignant lymphocytes may exhibit immature-appearing cells, remember that malignant lymphocytes are usually clonal and all abnormal cells should appear very similar to each other with consistency in appearance to its nucleus, cytoplasm, and size and shape. The "reactive" lymphocyte should present somewhat inconsistent, with variation in the appearance of its nucleus, cytoplasm, and size and shape.

217

Infectious Mononucleosis (IM)

This acute and contagious viral disorder was first described by Emil Pfeiffer as "glandular fever". It received it current name in 1920 by T.P. Sprunt and F.A. Evans when they associated the disease with the cellular morphology of the blood. The relationship to the Epstein-Barr virus was discovered in 1968. This disorder affects primarily young adults, preferably in the age range of 14 to 20 years. Eighty to ninety percent of the adults have antibodies to the virus and are immune. I. M. can be transmitted by saliva, hence its name "kissing disease".

Clinical symptoms include [a] pyrexia, [b] pharyngitis, [c] lethargy, [d] cervical lymph node enlargement, [e] splenomegaly (in 75% of the patients), [f] hepatomegaly (in 25% of the patients), [g] vomiting (in 20% of the patients), [h] headaches (in 20% of the patients), [i] jaundice (in 5% of the patients). If I. M. infects a child under ten years of age, that child will be heterophil negative. Infectious mononucleosis can be either heterophil negative or positive. Expected clinical laboratory findings include:

[1]   WBC count = 12,000 to 25,000/μL
[2]   The stained blood film will contain >10% reactive lymphocytes and >50% of the WBCs are lymphocytes.
[3]   Platelet count will be decreased but seldom <1.0 X 10^5/μL
[4]   About heterophil testing: If the test is negative repeat in 7 to 10 days. Heterophil antibodies are not elevated until the second or third week of the disease. The titer will increase and hold till about the eighth week, after which time it decreases. If the heterophil testing continues to be negative, look for another cause for the presence of reactive lymphocytes.
[5] The liver function tests will be abnormal:
    A. Bilirubin = upper limits of normal is the rule,
    B. AST (SGOT) = >30 IU/L (look for values eight times normal)
    C. ALT (SGPT) = >30 IU/L (look for values up to three times normal) RBC, Hct, Hgb, MCV, MCH, MCHC = usually within normal parameters. Coomb's test = negative.

Infectious lymphocytosis is a disease of young children with an unknown etiology. Clinical symptoms include [1] diarrhea, [2] gastrointestinal distress, [3] headache, [4] respiratory infection, [5] vertigo, [6] fever; [7] lymphadenopathy is not present. Expected laboratory findings include: [1] WBC count = 40,000 to 50,000/μL. [2] Sixty to ninety percent of the WBCs seen on the stained blood film are small, normal-like lymphocytes. Reactive lymphocytes are not the rule. As the leukocytosis recedes, the eosinophil count tends to increase, with absolute values up to 3,000/μL being reported. [3] Other hematology parameters are normal.

Chediak-Steinbrink-Higashi Syndrome

This is an autosomal recessive disorder, more apt to be referred to as Chediak-Higashi Syndrome. It is a hereditary anomaly of neutrophils with a very poor prognosis. It appears in infancy and most children die before their tenth year of life. Clinical symptoms include hepatosplenomegaly and partial albinism (seen in the hair, eyes, and skin). These patients tend to bleed easily and have low resistance to infections (infections tend to be overwhelming and are the usual cause of death). If the affected individual lives into their teen years, the condition will develop into a fatal lymphoma. Expected laboratory findings include:

[1]   WBC = 2,000 to 3,000/μL (leukocytopenia). There is a persistent and mild granulocytopenia.
[2]   The stained peripheral blood smear is characterized by:
    A. giant cytoplasmic lysosomes which are defective and peroxidase positive. They are the result of the fusion of primary and secondary granules which are fused to the cytoplasmic membrane and cannot enter into a phagosome to kill ingested bacteria. The lysosomes stain a distinctive blue color with Wright's stain.
    B. granulocytes are irregular in size and shape.
    C. eosinophils have over-large granules.
    D. monocytes have large cytoplasmic granules
    E. lymphocytes may have large cytoplasmic granules (not peroxidase positive).
[3] Decreased platelet count.
[4] Bleeding time is prolonged due to thrombocytopenia. Other coagulation tests are usually normal.

May-Hegglin Anomaly

This is more of a platelet disorder than it is of neutrophils. It is an autosomal dominates disorder that is of rare occurrence. The peripheral blood smear presents with thrombocytopenia and the presence of giant agranular platelets. Some of the platelets may have bizarre appearances. If the thrombocytopenia is significant, the patient will have bleeding problems. The clot retraction test will be prolonged and the capillary fragility test will be positive.

This patient tends to present with mild neutropenia and the granulocytes are characterized by the presence of blue staining Dohle-like bodies in the cytoplasm. These bodies are composed of glycogen and RNA material. These bodies stain best with methyl green pyronin stain but appear as blue-grey structures with Wright's stain. These spindle-shaped bodies may be observed in lymphocytes and monocytes. These presence of these inclusions do not appear to seriously impair WBC functions as most persons are found to be in good health and asymptomatic.

Wiskott-Aldrich Syndrome

Wiskott-Aldrich syndrome (designated as a congenital immunodeficiency disorder) is a sex-linked, recessive disorder characterized by a decrease in T-lymphocytes and normal B-lymphocytes. This patient has a poor prognosis because of their inability to generate an appropriate T-lymphocyte response. Affected boys present with bleeding problems in infancy and most do not survive beyond ten years of age, dying of bleeding complications, infections, or lymphoreticular malignancy. Transplantation of histocompatible bone marrow from a normal donor has corrected this syndrome anomaly. The problem appears to lie in the inability of the antibody system to synthesize antibodies to the polysaccharide antigens. Clinical symptoms include: eczema, susceptibility to infections, and bleeding tendencies. Clinical laboratory findings include: [1] thrombocytopenia, [2] normal lymphocyte counts, and [3] decreased serum IgM. The platelets are structurally abnormal, with deficiencies in alpha and dense granules. The platelets tend to be small.

Severe Combined Immune Deficiency (SCID) Syndrome

Severe Combined Immune Deficiency (SCID) syndrome (lymphopenic agammaglobulinemia, Nezelof's syndrome, thymic alymphoplasia) is a gross functional impairment of both humoral (implies circulating antibodies) and cellular immunity. It affects both the B- and T-lymphocytes and plasma cells.   It can be inherited as either a sex- or autosomal-linked recessive disorder. Affected infants are susceptible to all types of infections and rarely survive beyond their first year. Infections with common organisms as measles virus, Candida albicans, Pneumocystis carinii, cytomegalovirus, varicella (varicella-herpes virus), and vaccinia (pox virus) are likely to result in death. Transplantation of histocompatible bone marrow has proven to be a successful form of therapy. Clinical symptoms include: retarded growth, frequent infections, wasting, and diarrhea. Clinical laboratory findings include: [a] decreased T-lymphocytes, [b] decreased or absence of gamma globulins, [c] decreased B-lymphocytes, and [d] absence of plasma cells.
CAUTION: It is important that this disorder be identified early. If an infant should be given a blood transfusion, it may result in fatal graft-versus-host disease.

Ataxia Telangiectasia

Ataxia Telangiectasia is a rare, autosomal recessive genetic disorder. This is a complex disorder involving abnormalities in the nervous, immunological, hepatic, endocrine, and cutaneous systems. This disorder begins to express itself about the third year of life. It is a progressive disease with the patient becoming confined to the wheel chair at about the age of ten. There is no known treatment that will reverse this disorder. Only symptomatic treatment is available. The most frequent causes of death are chronic pulmonary disease (due to decreased IgA) and malignancy. Expected laboratory findings include: [a] absence of serum IgA (in up to 80% of the patients), [b] decreased serum IgG, [c] decreased serum IgE, and [d] lymphopenia. IgM and IgD are usually normal.

Nadir

When discussing chemotherapy side effects often you will hear the word nadir, mainly in reference to the blood counts, particularly white blood cell count and platelet count. Nadir basically means low point, however further explanation may clarify this term in connection with chemotherapy treatment.

When chemotherapy is given it not only affects the rapidly dividing cancer cells but it also affects some of the normal cells of the body. These effects particularly occur on normal cells that divide rapidly such as, the hair, the lining of the mouth, the cells lining the intestinal tract and the blood cells (white and red blood cells as well as platelets).

In the bone marrow, the spongy inner core of the larger bones in the body is where blood cells are made. There are very immature cells called stem cells, from which the various types of blood cells develop. These stem cells do not reproduce quickly and are less likely to be affected by chemotherapy. As cells are maturing there are certain phases in which they divide faster. It is during these times that the cells are most sensitive to chemotherapy. The more mature cells can continue to become fully mature cells for several days after chemotherapy is given. When these cells live out their life span, the circulating supply is depleted and the blood counts fall to a low point, the nadir.

The blood counts will return to normal within three to four weeks, after the body's feedback system has told the stem cells in the bone marrow to increase production and begin making new cells. If chemotherapy is given at the time that the stem cells in the bone marrow are increasing their production this could cause permanent bone marrow damage. The timing of chemotherapy cycles takes this process into account. For example some chemotherapy drugs are given on day 1 and day 8 of a 28-day cycle. The second dose of chemotherapy, one week after the first, is tolerated because the stem cells have not yet increased their production (they are still at the nadir). They have not increased their production because the second treatment is given before the count of the circulating blood has reached its nadir.

The nadir time is usually about 10 days after treatment, although this may vary depending on the drugs given. The concern during the nadir time is that the body's first line of defense against infection, white blood cells and the platelets, which help to clot the blood, are low leaving a person more susceptible to infection and bleeding. The next dose of chemotherapy is given only after a person's blood counts have left the nadir and recovered to a safe level.

Pancytopenia

1- Definition:
      1- Hemoglobin < 13 g/dl (male) or 12 g/dl (female)
      2-Neutropenia < 1.5 G/l
      3-Thrombocytopenia < 150 G/l
[If only two parameters from the full blood count are low (= bicytopenia) the diagnostic approach is the same as for pancytopenia]

2 -Pancytopenia related to peripheral origin
     - All disorders leading to enlargement of the spleen
     - Immune disorders (the spleen may be affected or not)
        -Lupus (SLE)
        -Rheumatoid arthritis with splenomegaly and neutropenia < 0.5 G/L (Felty syndrome)
      -Immune anemia + immune thrombocytopenia
     - Increased plasma volume (related to elevated monoclonal Ig, mainly IgM; some cardiac disorders)
     - End of pregnancy

3- Pancytopenia related to bone marrow production

   3-1 the bone marrow is acellular:
      * Aplastic or hypoplastic anemia
Bone marrow biopsy is necessary to ascertain the diagnosis
Poorer prognosis is related to   neutropenia < 0.5 G/L
                         Thrombocytopenia < 20 G/L
                         Reticulocytes < 20 G/L

Main situations:
Origin is unknown in at least 50% of cases

Chemical and physical agents
Infections (mainly viruses (hepatitis, human immunodeficiency disease, EBV, B19 parvovirus)
Familial: Fanconi's anemia
One peculiar and rare subgroup of myelodysplastic syndromes: hypoplastic myelodysplastic syndrome.
    * Gelatinous transformation of the bone marrow (starving conditions)
    * Bacterial or virus associated hemophagocytic syndromes

3-2- the bone marrow is cellular:
Abnormal cells are observed on bone marrow smears
        * Acute leukemias
        * Chronic lymphocytic leukaemia
        * Non-Hodgkin lymphomas
        * Myeloma, Waldenstrom's disease
        * Some metastatic carcinomas
Bone marrow cells demonstrate dysplastic features:
        * Secondary bone marrow dysplasia: B12 or folate deficiency, chemicals, drugs
        * Primitive: myelodysplastic syndromes
Bone marrows smears fail to demonstrate any abnormality:
        Is it any spleen enlargement?
        Overwhelming infections (excess of mature histiocytes is not infrequent)

3-3 -Bone marrow is poor in cells but bone marrow biopsy is cellular: myelofibrosis must be considered
    Bone marrow aspiration is often difficult to perform, smears are devoid of cells; bone marrow biopsy is cellular and special stains for reticulin and/or collagen may demonstrate fibrosis
        * Agnogenic myeloid metaplasia
        * Megakaryocytic leukaemia
        * Hairy cell leukaemia
        * Some acute lymphoid leukemia
        * generalized mastocytosis
        * Some metastatic carcinomas
        * Malignant myelosclerosis
        * Rarely: Hodgkin's disease, Polycythemia rubra Vera.

3-4- miscellaneous conditions:
 1- Paroxysmal Nocturnal Hemoglobinuria.
 2- Decreased bone marrow production, and splenomegaly (liver cirrhosis, B12 or folate deficiency and drugs or alcohol).

Immature Granulocytes

    Immature granulocytes (metamyelocytes, myelocytes, and even promyelocytes) may be observed on the blood smear: total number < 2% is devoided of any significance; values over 2% and observed in at least two separated instances need explorations:

1- Immature granulocytes without neutrophilia
  - Solid tumours invading the bone marrow
      Some erythroblasts and schistocytes are present.
      Early step of an acute hematological disorder
   - Recovery after bone marrow hypoplasia or agranulocytosis
   -Myelofibrosis (some cases)
   -Severe bacterial infections
      Bone marrow tuberculosis

2- Immature granulocytes with neutrophilia
-Myeloproliferative disorders:
    Up to 50% immature granulocytes: Chronic Myeloid Leukemia (CML)

Up to 10-20% (and some erythroblasts are present): Agnogenic myeloid metaplasia (idiopathic myelofibrosis)

Less than 5% or absent: Polycythemia Rubra Vera, essential thrombocythemia.

-Myeloproliferative/myelodysplastic syndromes:

.Atypical CML

If Monocytosis > 1 G/L: Chronic Myelomonocytic Leukemia (CMML) in adult or in infant

.Acute bone marrow regeneration

.Acute hemorrhage

.After chemotherapy or after stem cell transplantation

.After growth factor therapy

.After acute drug-induced agranulocytosis

.Overproduction related to severe infections

.The so-called "Leukemoid blood picture"

Such situations correspond to non malignant situations related to high leukocyte counts (> 50 G/L) with a large number of immature granulocytes (some blast cells or myeloblasts may be present), mimicking leukemic disorders. So far, infections (meningitis, pneumonia), intoxications, malignant tumours disseminating to bone marrow are to be considered first.

Transient leukemic disorder in the newborn is a peculiar situation, quite frequent in Down syndrome at birth, mimicking leukemia, but spontaneous improvement is observed within a few weeks or months (a true leukaemia may appear one or several years later).

Approach to Abnormal Platelet Counts

1- Platelet Evaluation:

Peripheral blood smears prepared from blood collected in EDTA is preferred.

1. Examine the Wright stained blood smear under oil immersion lens (100X) and check 10 or more fields in order to determine the number of platelets per field. A normal blood smear will show about 7-25 platelets per oil field. The platelet estimate is generally recorded as normal, decreased, or increased.

2. Platelet clumps, giant platelets and/or bizarre platelets should also be recorded.

3. Platelet Diameter and Morphology

2.5 μm diameter	Average normal diameter
4 μm diameter	Large physiologic platelets may indicate increased turnover with shortened marrow release time
>7 μm diameter	Giant platelets imply myeloproliferative disorder, myelodysplastic syndrome, May-Hegglin anomaly
Gray platelets	Slightly enlarged gray platelets seen in Bernard-Soulier syndrome or alpha-granule deficiency (Gray platelet syndrome)
Platelet clumps	Clotting due to improper specimen management or agglutination due to EDTA-dependent antibody
Platelet satellitism	Artifact of EDTA-dependent antibody

2- Platelet Disorders:

- The normal platelet count is 150,000/mm3 to 450,000/mm3. The platelet count may be decreased (thrombocytopenia) or increased (thrombocytosis or thrombocythemia) with or without impairment of their function.

-Thrombocytopenia: Bleeding time is prolonged and the clot retraction is abnormal (delayed, decreased or absent). Although the bleeding time is prolonged, the PT (prothrombin time) and APTT (activated partial thromboplastin time) are not prolonged even when there is marked thrombocytopenia.

- Relative Thrombocytosis: The platelet count is usually in the range of 450,000/mm3 to 1 million/mm3. The thrombocytosis is benign and transient.

-Thrombocythemia: A persistent increase (months or years) in platelets to usually over a million/mm3. The peripheral blood smear usually shows clumps of platelets, giant forms and bizarre platelets. The platelet function tests are often abnormal.

- Platelets are distributed between the circulation (2/3) and the spleen (1/3).

- The platelet count falls due to pooling when the spleen is enlarged and rises after splenectomy.

- The total mass of platelets remains fairly constant whether spleen is enlarged or absent.
-Platelets normally survive 10 to 14 days in the circulation.

1- Causes of thrombocytopenia
    1-1 increased destruction may be due to:
      - Antibodies.
      - DIC and Microangiopathy.
      - TTP
      - Hypersplenism
    1-2 Decreased production
      - Stem cell diseases.
      - Immune mechanisms.
      - Chemotherapy.
      - Marrow infiltration.
   1-3 splenic sequestration occurs with
  - Portal hypertension and inflammatory and infiltrative causes of splenomegaly.
Disorders that involve the breakdown of platelets include:
Immune thrombocytopenic purpura(ITP)
Drug-induced immune thrombocytopenia
Drug-induced Nonimmune thrombocytopenia
Thrombotic thrombocytopenic purpura
Disseminated intravascular coagulation(DIC)
Hypersplenism
Disorders that involve low production in the bone marrow include:
Aplastic anemia
Cancer in the bone marrow
Infections in the bone marrow (rare)
Drugs (very rare)

In an adult, a normal count is about 150,000 to 450,000 platelets per microliter of blood. If platelet levels fall below 20,000 per microliter, spontaneous bleeding may occur and is considered a life-threatening risk. Patients who have a bone marrow disease, such as leukemia or another cancer in the bone marrow, often experience excessive bleeding due to a significantly decreased number of platelets (thrombocytopenia). As the number of cancer cells increases in the bone marrow, normal bone marrow cells are crowded out, resulting in fewer platelet-producing cells. Low number of platelets may be seen in some patients with long-term bleeding problems (e.g., chronic bleeding stomach ulcers), thus reducing the supply of platelets. Decreased platelet counts may also be seen in patients with Gram-negative sepsis.

Individuals with an autoimmune disorder (such as lupus or idiopathic thrombocytopenia purpura (ITP), where the body's immune system creates antibodies that attack its own organs) can cause the destruction of platelets.

Certain drugs, such as acetaminophen, quinidine, sulfa drugs, digoxin, vancomycin, valium, and nitroglycerine, are just a few that have been associated with drug-induced decreased platelet counts. Patients undergoing chemotherapy or radiation therapy may also have a decreased platelet count. Up to 5% of pregnant women may experience thrombocytopenia at term.

Platelet consumption may be observed in renal diseases. Thrombocytopenic purpura (TTP) and Hemolytic Uremic syndrome (HUS) are seen in renal failure and can result in fewer circulating platelets in the blood. Similarly, a condition known as splenic sequestration, where platelets pool within the spleen, can also cause a platelet decrease.

More commonly (up to 1% of the population), easy bruising or bleeding may be due to an inherited disease called von Willebrand's disease. While the platelets may be normal in number, their ability to stick together is impaired due to a decrease in von Willebrand's factor, a protein needed to initiate the clotting process. Many cases may go undiagnosed due to the mild nature of the disease. Many cases are discovered when a patient has to have surgery or a tooth extraction or when delivering a baby. However, some cases are more severe and can be aggravated by use of certain drugs, resulting in a life-threatening situation.

Increased platelet counts (thrombocytosis) may be seen in individuals who show no significant medical problems, while others may have a more significant blood problem called myeloproliferative disorder. Some, although they have an increased number of platelets, may have a tendency to bleed due to the lack of stickiness of the platelets; in others, the platelets retain their stickiness but, because they are increased in number, tend to stick to each other, forming clumps that can block a blood vessel and cause damage, including death (thromboembolism).

2- Causes of thrombocytosis
The causes of reactive (secondary) thrombocytosis are described below.

1-Infection
Infections can cause a high or low platelet count. In children, an infection is often accompanied by a raised platelet count. This is thought to be due to the hormones, called cytokines that are produced as part of the body's normal defense against infection.
A high platelet count is less common in adults who have infections.
The thrombocytosis usually resolves as the infection recovers, although it may take longer to settle.

2-Inflammatory responses
These conditions may cause a high platelet count in a similar way to infections.
Kawasaki's disease is a rare condition, mainly affecting children, in which there is widespread inflammation of the arteries. It is associated with a high platelet count that gradually resolves in the recovery phase. In adults either a high or low platelet count may accompany other symptoms of autoimmune diseases such as rheumatoid arthritis.

3-Blood loss
in event of an injury, the response of the bone marrow to blood loss is to produce more red blood cells and more platelets.

4- Malignancy
Some cancers can cause a high platelet count either by causing damage to tissues, causing blood loss (for example from the bowel) or by erroneously producing a response from the immune system that stimulates the bone marrow to produce platelets.

5- Chemotherapy
Some chemotherapy drugs work directly on dividing cells in the body - including the bone marrow where platelets are made. When the body is recovering from the effects of chemotherapy, a temporary overproduction of some cells can occur.

3- Causes of thrombocythemia
Until recently, the cause of ET was a mystery. Now there have been several breakthroughs.

In 2005 scientists around the world discovered that many patients with bone marrow diseases (MPDs) had a mutation in a molecule called JAK2.

JAK2 is a protein that functions as a signal to regulate cell functions. It sends messages in the cell, telling it to grow and make more cells, or else to stop when the body does not need more cells.

Researchers believe that in MPD patients, the mutation in JAK2 enhances messages asking for more cell production. The result is too many blood cells which clog the blood and make it sticky.

The JAK2 mutation (also called the V617F JAK2) is found in about:
half of patients with too many platelets in their blood (ET)
half of patients with too many fibroblasts in their blood (MF)
95 per cent of patients with too many red cells in their blood (PV).
It's thought the JAK2 mutation is likely to occur as a result of some damage to the bone marrow, for example as a result of viral infections or background radiation. While unusual, ET can be hereditary; this is known as familial thrombocytosis.

Research has found that affected members of some families have the JAK2 mutation whereas others do not.

In some of these families there is a disruption in the production of a hormone (cytokine) called thrombopoietin, which regulates platelet production.

The Nonmalignant Lymphocyte Disorder: AIDS

This is a lethal immunodeficiency disease that is characterized by a decrease in CD4 T lymphocytes (helper-inducer cells). It is known as acquired immune deficiency syndrome (AIDS). It was first described in 1981 and initially given the name of gay-related immunodeficiency disease (GRID), but later changed. The destruction of the CD4 T lymphocytes immulogically compromises the host and they become very susceptible to a wide variety of opportunistic pathogens.
The following is a partial listing of such pathogens:

Mycobacterium avium	Herpes simplex virus
Mycobacterium intracellular	Cytomegalovirus (CMV)
Pneumocystis carinii	Histoplasma capsulatum

It is a three stage disease where the first stage is asymptomatic carrier stage, which gives way to the AIDS-related complex (ARC) stage where mild symptoms are evident. The third stage is the symptomatic AIDS stage.

Laboratory evidence of a patient having AIDS is the presence of serological antibody tests positive for the AIDS virus (human immunodeficiency virus type (HIV-1). This includes:
[1]   Positive HIV nucleic acid (either DNA or RNA).
[2]   Positive HIV cultures.

If a child is born to an infected HIV mother, it will show a positive anti-HIV IgG antibody test as the maternal antibodies will readily transfer across the placental barrier. This is not a reliable test for the infant. Testing should be performed when the infant is one-month of age in which case, if the test is positive, then the virus is present.

The clinical laboratory should watch for the following findings when testing patient with AIDS.
[1]   Anemia will onset early in most patients and will become progressively worse as the disease progresses. Opportunistic infections facilitate the worsening of the anemia.
       A.   Macrocytic anemia is the rule for most of these patients.
[2]   Pancytopenia develops as the disease progresses.
[3]   Up to 20% of the patients, with hypergammaglobulinemia, will develop
       anti-erythrocyte antibodies that will act like polyagglutinins and cause a positive DAT (direct antiglobulin test) or Coomb's test.
[4]   Many patients will develop immune thrombocytopenia which is
       indistinguishable from idiopathic thrombocytopenic purpura (ITP)
       resulting in the destruction of platelets.

Epstein - Barr virus (National Center for Infectious Diseases)

1- Disease information
Epstein-Barr virus, frequently referred to as EBV, is a member of the herpesvirus family and one of the most common human viruses. The virus occurs worldwide, and most people become infected with EBV sometime during their lives. In the United States, as many as 95% of adults between 35 and 40 years of age have been infected. Infants become susceptible to EBV as soon as maternal antibody protection (present at birth) disappears. Many children become infected with EBV, and these infections usually cause no symptoms or are indistinguishable from the other mild, brief illnesses of childhood. In the United States and in other developed countries, many persons are not infected with EBV in their childhood years. When infection with EBV occurs during adolescence or young adulthood, it causes infectious mononucleosis 35% to 50% of the time.
Symptoms of infectious mononucleosis are fever, sore throat, and swollen lymph glands. Sometimes, a swollen spleen or liver involvement may develop. Heart problems or involvement of the central nervous system occurs only rarely, and infectious mononucleosis is almost never fatal. There are no known associations between active EBV infection and problems during pregnancy, such as miscarriages or birth defects. Although the symptoms of infectious mononucleosis usually resolve in 1 or 2 months, EBV remains dormant or latent in a few cells in the throat and blood for the rest of the person's life. Periodically, the virus can reactivate and is commonly found in the saliva of infected persons. This reactivation usually occurs without symptoms of illness.
EBV also establishes a lifelong dormant infection in some cells of the body's immune system. A late event in a very few carriers of this virus is the emergence of Burkitt's lymphoma and nasopharyngeal

carcinoma, two rare cancers that are not normally found in the United States. EBV appears to play an important role in these malignancies, but is probably not the sole cause of disease.

Most individuals exposed to people with infectious mononucleosis have previously been infected with EBV and are not at risk for infectious mononucleosis. In addition, transmission of EBV requires intimate contact with the saliva (found in the mouth) of an infected person. Transmission of this virus through the air or blood does not normally occur. The incubation period, or the time from infection to appearance of symptoms, ranges from 4 to 6 weeks. Persons with infectious mononucleosis may be able to spread the infection to others for a period of weeks. However, no special precautions or isolation procedures are recommended, since the virus is also found frequently in the saliva of healthy people. In fact, many healthy people can carry and spread the virus intermittently for life. These people are usually the primary reservoir for person-to-person transmission. For this reason, transmission of the virus is almost impossible to prevent.

The clinical diagnosis of infectious mononucleosis is suggested on the basis of the symptoms of fever, sore throat, swollen lymph glands, and the age of the patient. Usually, laboratory tests are needed for confirmation. Serologic results for persons with infectious mononucleosis include an elevated white blood cell count, an increased percentage of certain atypical white blood cells, and a positive reaction to a "mono spot" test.

There is no specific treatment for infectious mononucleosis, other than treating the symptoms. No antiviral drugs or vaccines are available. Some physicians have prescribed a 5-day course of steroids to control the swelling of the throat and tonsils. The use of steroids has also been reported to decrease the overall length and severity of illness, but these reports have not been published.

It is important to note that symptoms related to infectious mononucleosis caused by EBV infection seldom last for more than 4 months. When such an illness lasts more than 6 months, it is frequently called chronic EBV infection. However, valid laboratory evidence for continued active EBV infection is seldom found in these patients. The illness should be investigated further to determine if it meets the criteria for chronic fatigue syndrome, or CFS. This process includes ruling out other causes of chronic illness or fatigue.

2- Diagnosis of EBV Infections

In most cases of infectious mononucleosis, the clinical diagnosis can be made from the characteristic triad of fever, pharyngitis, and lymphadenopathy lasting for 1 to 4 weeks. Serologic test results include a normal to moderately elevated white blood cell count, an increased total number of lymphocytes, greater than 10% atypical lymphocytes, and a positive reaction to a "mono spot" test. In patients with symptoms compatible with infectious mononucleosis, a positive Paul-Bunnell heterophile antibody test result is diagnostic, and no further testing is necessary. Moderate-to-high levels of heterophile antibodies are seen during the first month of illness and decrease rapidly after week 4. False-positive results may be found in a small number of patients, and false-negative results may be obtained in 10% to 15% of patients, primarily in children younger than 10 years of age. True outbreaks of infectious mononucleosis are extremely rare. A substantial number of pseudo-outbreaks have been linked to laboratory error, as reported in CDC's Morbidity and Mortality Weekly Report, vol. 40, no. 32, on August 16, 1991.

When "mono spot" or heterophile test results are negative, additional laboratory testing may be needed to differentiate EBV infections from a mononucleosis-like illness induced by cytomegalovirus, adenovirus, or Toxoplasma gondii. Direct detection of EBV in blood or lymphoid tissues is a research tool and is not available for routine diagnosis. Instead, serologic testing is the method of choice for diagnosing primary infection.

4-EBV-Specific Laboratory Tests

Laboratory tests are not always foolproof. For various reasons, false-positive and false-negative results can occur for any test. However, the laboratory tests for EBV are for the most part accurate and specific. Because the antibody response in primary EBV infection appears to be quite rapid, in most cases testing paired acute- and convalescent-phase serum samples will not demonstrate a significant change in antibody level. Effective laboratory diagnosis can be made on a single acute-phase serum sample by testing for antibodies to several EBV-associated antigens simultaneously. In most cases, a distinction can be made as to whether a person is susceptible to EBV, has had a recent infection, has had infection in the past, or has a reactivated EBV infection.

Antibodies to several antigen complexes may be measured. These antigens are the viral capsid antigen, the early antigen, and the EBV nuclear antigen (EBNA). In addition, differentiation of immunoglobulin G and M subclasses to the viral capsid antigen can often be helpful for confirmation.

When the "mono spot" test is negative, the optimal combination of EBV serologic testing consists of the antibody titration of four markers: IgM and IgG to the viral capsid antigen, IgM to the early antigen, and antibody to EBNA.

IgM to the viral capsid antigen appears early in infection and disappears within 4 to 6 weeks. IgG to the viral capsid antigen appears in the acute phase, peaks at 2 to 4 weeks after onset, declines slightly, and then persists for life. IgG to the early antigen appears in the acute phase and generally falls to undetectable levels after 3 to 6 months. In many people, detection of antibody to the early antigen is a sign of active infection, but 20% of healthy people may have this antibody for years. Antibody to EBNA determined by the standard immunofluorescent test is not seen in the acute phase, but slowly appears 2 to 4 months after onset, and persists for life. This is not true for some EBNA enzyme immunoassays, which detect antibody within a few weeks of onset.

Finally, even when EBV antibody tests, such as the early antigen test, suggest that reactivated infection is present, this result does not necessarily indicate that a patient's current medical condition is caused by EBV infection. A number of healthy people with no symptoms have antibodies to the EBV early antigen for years after their initial EBV infection.

Therefore, interpretation of laboratory results is somewhat complex and should be left to physicians who are familiar with EBV testing and who have access to the entire clinical picture of a person. To determine if EBV infection is associated with a current illness, consult with an experienced physician.

4- Additional Information about EBV Antibody Tests and Interpretation

Antibody tests for EBV can measure the presence and/or the concentration of at least six specific EBV antibodies. By evaluating the results of these different tests, the stage of EBV infection can be determined. However, these tests are expensive and not usually needed for the diagnosis of infectious mononucleosis.

It is not appropriate for CDC to interpret test results or to handle counseling for the public. We suggest that questions be directed to a local physician who is familiar with the patient's history and laboratory test results. In addition, CDC cannot recommend specific physicians for referral. Our general recommendation is for patients to consult with an infectious disease specialist or their local or state public health department.

5- Summary of Interpretation

The diagnosis of EBV infection is summarized as follows:

- Susceptibility

if antibodies to the viral capsid antigen are not detected, the patient is susceptible to EBV infection.

- Primary Infection

Primary EBV infection is indicated if IgM antibody to the viral capsid antigen is present and antibody to EBV nuclear antigen, or EBNA, is absent. A rising or high IgG antibody to the viral capsid antigen and negative antibody to EBNA after at least 4 weeks of illness is also strongly suggestive of primary infection. In addition, 80% of patients with active EBV infection produce antibody to early antigen.

- Past Infection

if antibodies to both the viral capsid antigen and EBNA are present, then past infection (from 4 to 6 months to years earlier) is indicated. Since 95% of adults have been infected with EBV, most adults will show antibodies to EBV from infection years earlier. High or elevated antibody levels may be present for years and are not diagnostic of recent infection.

- Reactivation

In the presence of antibodies to EBNA, an elevation of antibodies to early antigen suggests reactivation. However, when EBV antibody to the early antigen test is present, this result does not automatically indicate that a patient's current medical condition is caused by EBV. A number of healthy people with no symptoms have antibodies to the EBV early antigen for years after their initial EBV infection. Many times reactivation occurs subclinically.

-Chronic EBV Infection

Reliable laboratory evidence for continued active EBV infection is very seldom found in patients who have been ill for more than 4 months. When the illness lasts more than 6 months, it should be investigated to see if other causes of chronic illness or CFS are present.

URL:http://www.cdc.gov/ncidod/diseases/ebv.htm
Updated: 11/09/2008 19:59:34

PART ELEVEN: THE CONCEPT OF LEUKEMIA

Leukemia (a generic term) is a malignant disease of white blood cells. Leukemias can involve any of the white blood cells in all of their varying stages of maturity. All leukemias have three complications in common.

[1] Leukemias always infiltrate the bone marrow. For this reason physicians will request a bone marrow biopsy to confirm the diagnosis of leukemia.

[2] Peripheral blood will contain increased leukocytes and may contain an increased number of immature cells.

[3] The three following complications are common: anemia, recurring infections, and bleeding.

As leukemia progresses, it infiltrates (with uncontrolled proliferation) the body organs and replaces the precursors of normal leukocytes, erythrocytes, and thrombocytes. As the liver cells are overwhelmed, coagulation factor productions is suppressed which causes the patient to have a bleeding tendency. Massive infections are often the major cause of death in leukemic patients. Leukemia can occur at any age and in any population of people. Certain forms of leukemia may have predilection for age groups, genders, or race. Leukemias that present in children are often of the acute form (up to 85%). The adult populations contend with the chronic forms of leukemia.

Consider the following four leukemias:

[1] Acute lymphoblastic leukemia (ALL) is the most common form of leukemia in children and is increased in older adults. It occurs twice as often in whites as it does in blacks. About 20% of the total leukemias are of this type.

[2] Acute myelogenous leukemia (AML) occurs in all age groups, but is most common in the older individual. About 40% of all leukemias are of this type.

[3] Chronic myelogenous leukemia (CML) rarely occurs before adolescence, affect the older person. About 15% of all leukemias are of this type.

[4] Chronic lymphocytic leukemia (CLL) is rarely diagnosed in individuals under 40 years of age, It incidence in adults increases as the adult ages. About 25% of all leukemias are of this type.

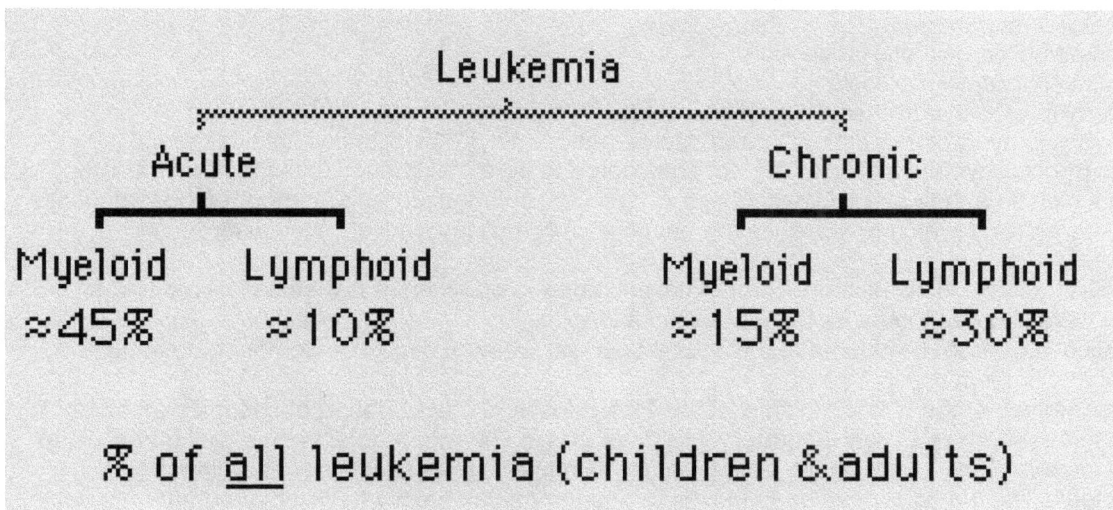

Leukemia

Acute		Chronic	
Myeloid	Lymphoid	Myeloid	Lymphoid
≈45%	≈10%	≈15%	≈30%

% of all leukemia (children &adults)

A- Etiology of Leukemia

The causes of leukemia are not clearly understood. There are several factors that have been identified that are associated with the risk of leukemia. The term host factor implies those conditions that predispose a person for increased risk of leukemia.

[1] Hereditary. There is no hard evidence that leukemia can be inherited. What appears to be the problem is that mutations and alterations in genetic expression are the origins of leukemia. What is known is that certain unique and recurring chromosomal abnormalities do predispose a person for a malignancy. If a family line has a recurring history of a certain disease, the risk or incidence is increased for that family.

[2] Chromosome Abnormalities. The statistical data supports chromosome abnormalities to be linked to an increased risk for leukemia.

A. the Philadelphia chromosome biases that person for a high risk of chronic myelogenous leukemia (CML). Ninety percent of patients with CML will demonstrate the Philadelphia chromosome. This chromosome is the result of a translocation of chromosome material between the long arms of chromosomes 9 and 22. The fusion of these two genes is thought to result in the formation of a protein that overcomes the regulatory mechanism of a normal cell. This chromosome is also observed in twenty percent of patients with acute lymphocytic leukemia.

B. Other chromosomes known to undergo translocation are:

    a. Chromosome 8 and 21. This is observed in acute myeloid leukemia

    b. Chromosome 15 and 17. This is observed in acute promyelocytic leukemia.

    c. Down's syndrome, a 21 trisomy, has a high risk for acute leukemia, especially in the first decade of their life.

[3] Congenital Immunodeficiency. Hereditary linked immunodeficiencies have been statistically linked to malignant disorders.

A. Fanconi's anemia appears to leukemogenic. This is an idiopathic refractory anemia (with pancytopenia) and there is a significant risk for this patient to develop an acute leukemic disorder (usually acute monomyelocytic leukemia).

B. Wiskott-Aldrich syndrome patients (which have a survival rate of about 5 years) have a 10% increased risk for hairy cell leukemia or lymphoma.

C. Bloom's syndrome (photosensitivity syndrome) has a high risk of leukemia (either AML or lymphoma or cancer).

D. Chediak-Higashi syndrome has a high risk of leukemia.

[4] Chronic Marrow Dysfunction. Statistical data for patients with the following disorders indicated a significant risk for the development of acute leukemia.

A. Aplastic anemia.

B. Proximal nocturnal Hemoglobinuria.

C. Myeloblastic syndromes:

    - Chronic Myelomonocytic leukemia

    - Chronic erythremic myelosis

    - Myelodysplastic syndromes. Examples include: [1] refractory anemia, [2] dyspoietic megakaryocytic hyperplasia with 5q⁻ chromosome abnormality, [3] single cell aplasia, and [4] idiopathic thrombocythemia. These are not considered to be a malignancy until they reach a later stage, at which time they can undergo transformation to acute leukemia. A number of these patients will die before they develop acute leukemia because of complications from their disorder.

[5] Ionizing Radiation. This is an environmental influence in which there is a statistical relation-ship of leukemia developing to exposure to ionizing radiation.

A. Statistical data from Hiroshima and Nagasaki nuclear weapon exposure demonstrate a high occurrence of leukemia

B. In the decades of the 60's a biologist at the TVA (Muscle Shoals, Alabama) occupied an office adjacent to the energized x-ray laboratory. His desk was in line with a defect in the wall that allowed radiation into his office. He hung his jacket with the film badge on a coat rack out-of-line of the radiation leak. The biologist developed leukemia and the office defect was discovered after his death.

[6] Chemicals and Drugs. This is an environmental influence. Two chemicals known to have high carcinogenic potential are [a] benzene and [b] benzidine (extremely carcinogenic). Other chemicals include:

A. Chloramphenicol: antibiotic

B. Phenylbutazone: synthetic steroid

C. Cytotoxic therapeutic agents: Alkylating drugs are potentially hazardous, especially if they are used in conjunction with therapeutic ionizing radiation. The Alkylating chemicals can introduce an alkyl radical (hydrocarbon) into a compound to replace the hydrogen ion. Peptides may be cleaved in the process.

    a. Patients at increased risk are those with Hodgkin's disease and Multiple Myeloma.

    b.   Examples of Alkylating drugs are: cyclophosphamide, fluorouracil, mercapto-purine, Hydroxyurea, Methotrexate, and doxorubicin hydrochloride.

[7] Viruses.   Evidence for viral causes of leukemia is not conclusive, although the link has been established. Feline leukemia has been proven to be caused by a virus designated as FeLV.

   A. Adult T-cell Leukemia-lymphoma (ATL) has been linked to the HTLV-I (human T-cell leukemia-lymphoma) virus.

   B. Atypical hairy cell leukemia is linked to the HTLV-II (human T-cell leukemia-lymphoma) virus.

   C. Type C RNA viruses are tumor viruses linked with animal leukemia and lymphoma.

   D. Epstein-Barr virus is linked to the African form of Burkitt lymphoma.

   E. Human adenovirus type 3 is known to cause malignant tumors in hamsters.

   F. Human wart virus causes benign growths (warts) in humans.

Classification strategies for Leukemia

[1]   W. Ebstein (1888-1889) classified leukemia into two categories: [1] acute and [2] chronic. This system is popular and in continued use. Acute implies a disorder with a predominance of immature cells and chronic infers a predominance of mature cells.

[2]   The medical profession tends to categorize leukemias into two predominant cell types. The lymphoid or myeloid (non-lymphoid). In this form of classification, the acute stages tend to be very difficult to differentiate.

[3]   Another classification scheme is on the basis of duration. Those with the acute type have a short life expectancy.

[4]   A fourth method is on the basis of the leukocyte count and morphology in the peripheral blood. This method classifies leukemia as [1] leukemic, [2] subleukemic, and [3] aleukemic.

   A. If leukemic leukemia, then the WBC count is higher than normal. This value is usually taken to be >15,000/µL (1.5×10^9/L). Abnormal cells are present.

   B. If subleukemic leukemia, then the WBC count is not elevated. There are abnormal cells present in the peripheral blood to indicate the presence of leukemia.

   C. If aleukemic leukemia, the WBC count is less than normal. Abnormal cells will be present in the bone marrow, but should not be present in the blood.

Reasons for classifying leukemias

[1]   A mechanism is provided to allow the comparison of different therapeutic regimens.

[2]   A system to identify and compare clinical features and laboratory findings.

[3]   Permits association of Cytogenetic abnormalities with the disease.

[4]   Morphological evaluation of the Leukemias.

A laboratory work-up is required to identify the type of leukemia. Anemia will be a consistent finding. Thrombocytopenia will (as a rule) be present. The WBC count will range from decreased to significantly increased values. The peripheral blood smear will demonstrate "blasts" and other immature forms. When evaluating the peripheral blood morphology, it is best to use non-anticoagulant blood. A finger-stick prepared smear is an appropriate specimen.

Caution is to be exercised if using EDTA anticoagulant treated blood. A smear made immediately will be suitable for a cellular evaluation. EDTA is capable of causing morphological artifacts of nucleated cells and platelets. If the blood is allowed to "stand" in the anticoagulant for >30 minutes, the following will likely be observed: [a] artifactual vacuolation of monocytes and neutrophils, [b] induced aberrant nuclear shape changes, [c] cellular swelling, and [d] platelet degranulation.

Principle studies

The principle studies include:
1- Morphology (peripheral blood smear and bone marrow aspirate and biopsy)
2- Cytochemistry

3- Genetic analysis-chromosomal and molecular
4- Immunology
The first and most important determination when deciding on chemotherapy and prognosis is to determine whether the blasts are myeloid or lymphoid.

The morphology of the blasts yields strong evidence of the blast lineage. Most of the time (probably >80%) one can accurately predict the blast type from morphology alone. The key features are the chromatin pattern and the character of the cytoplasm.

	Lymphoblasts	Myeloblasts
Similarities	Round-Oval Nuclei	Round-Oval Nuclei
Differences Nuclear	Coarse chromatin which tends to aggregate into masses	Fine delicate chromatin
Cytoplasmic	More basophilic no azurophilic granules no Auer rods may have non-specific cytoplasm granules	Less basophilic has primary azurophilic granules may have Auer rods

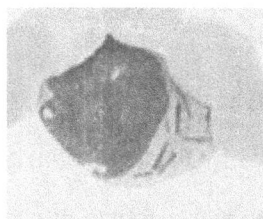

Myeloblast with Auer rods

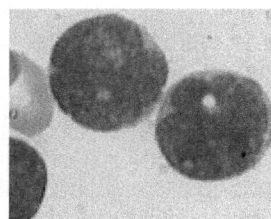

Lymphoblats

Effect of Acute Leukemia upon the body

Clinical features include an invasion of the bone marrow that is unchecked will result in displacement of the normal cells, which leads to organ failure and eventually death. The bone marrow will undergo a series of changes due to the sequels (conditions and effects that result from a disease) of invasion that is characterized by [a] anemia, [b] thrombocytopenia, and [c] granulocytopenia.

Because of the aggressiveness of acute leukemia, the symptoms appear suddenly. The patient notices that they are weak, easily fatigued. They complain of flu-like symptoms and if they wound themselves, they notice that it takes longer for the bleeding to stop. The find that infections that at one time did not deter them, now causes problems. These patients are likely to die of infections or bleed to death before the leukemia kills them. Other disorders that cause death are hepatic, renal, pulmonary, and cardiac failures. Such failures are due the invasive nature of the leukemia and the overwhelming leukemic infiltration of the organ causes it to cease functioning and death occurs. The uncontrollable proliferation of WBCs causes an increase in blood viscosity that result in "sludging" with causes infarction or organ rupture leading to hemorrhage.

231

Comparison of Acute and Chronic

Presentation	Acute	Chronic
Age	Affects all ages	Predilection for adults
Clinical Onset	Sudden	Slow and insidious
Prognosis (untreated)	< 6 months	< 6 years
Leukemic cell type	immature forms predominate	mature forms predominate
Anemia	prominent	mild, less prominent
Thrombocytopenia	prominent mild	less prominent
WBC count	variable	elevated
Lymphadenopathy	mild, less prominent	present
Splenomegaly	mild, less prominent	present
Hepatomegaly	mild, less prominent	present

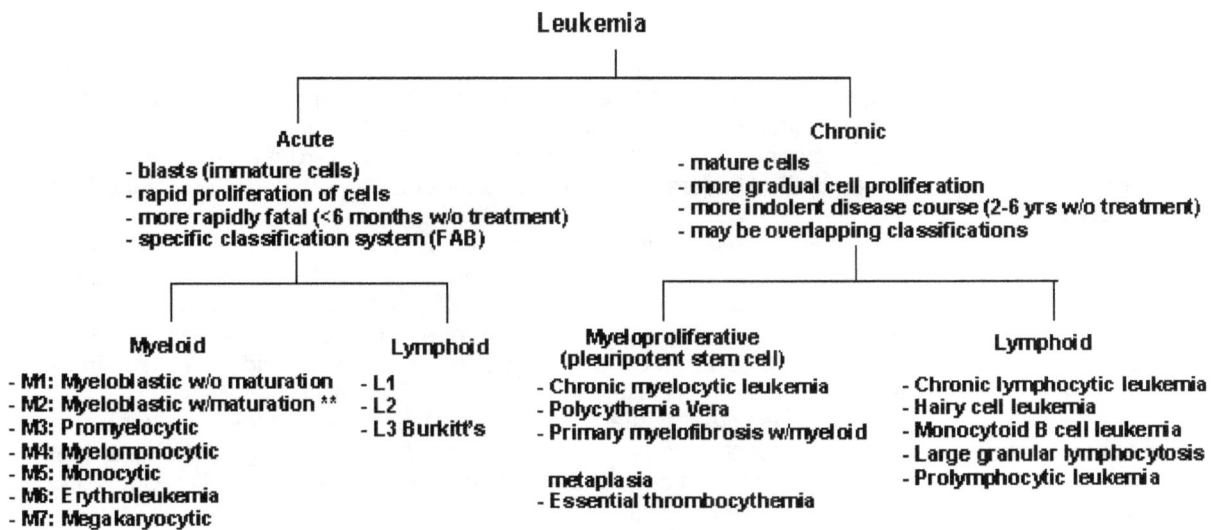

Leukemia

Acute
- blasts (immature cells)
- rapid proliferation of cells
- more rapidly fatal (<6 months w/o treatment)
- specific classification system (FAB)

Chronic
- mature cells
- more gradual cell proliferation
- more indolent disease course (2-6 yrs w/o treatment)
- may be overlapping classifications

Myeloid
- M1: Myeloblastic w/o maturation
- M2: Myeloblastic w/maturation **
- M3: Promyelocytic
- M4: Myelomonocytic
- M5: Monocytic
- M6: Erythroleukemia
- M7: Megakaryocytic

Lymphoid
- L1
- L2
- L3 Burkitt's

Myeloproliferative (pleuripotent stem cell)
- Chronic myelocytic leukemia
- Polycythemia Vera
- Primary myelofibrosis w/myeloid metaplasia
- Essential thrombocythemia

Lymphoid
- Chronic lymphocytic leukemia
- Hairy cell leukemia
- Monocytoid B cell leukemia
- Large granular lymphocytosis
- Prolymphocytic leukemia

CHAPTER ONE: CHRONIC LEUKEMIAS

Chronic Myelogenous Leukemia (CML)

Chronic myelogenous leukemia (CML) is a malignant disease of myeloid cell precursors, generally limited to the granulocyte cell line. Synonyms are [1] chronic myeloid leukemia and [2] chronic granulocytic leukemia. Patients diagnosed with CML generally present with immature granulocytes (myeloblasts, promyelocytes myelocytes, and metamyelocytes), basophilia, anemia, thrombocytosis, splenomegaly, and hepatomegaly. Immature granulocytes are found in the peripheral blood and WBC counts will exceed 100,000/mm^3. This disease onsets insidiously, the patient may see the physician for other reasons and in the medical evaluation discover the presence of CML. If platelet defects are present, the patient bruises easy and hemorrhagic episodes may occur. CML patients exhibit tiredness, lack endurance, and are prone to infections. This disorder is designated as a chronic myeloproliferative disorder and account for about 15% of all leukemias (There are statistical sources that state CML accounts for up to 20% of all leukemias). It affects adults between the ages of 25 to 60 y/o. The peak occurrence of CML is between 35 and 45 y/o. It is seen occasionally in adolescents and rarely in infancy.

Pathophysiology

CML was the first malignancy to be linked to a clear genetic abnormality, the chromosomal translocation known as the Philadelphia chromosome. This chromosomal abnormality is so named because it was first discovered and described in 1960 by two scientists from Philadelphia, Pennsylvania: Peter Nowell of the University of Pennsylvania and David Hungerford of the Fox Chase Cancer Center.

In this translocation, parts of two chromosomes (the 9th and 22nd by conventional karyotypic numbering) switch places. As a result, part of the BCR ("breakpoint cluster region") gene from chromosome 22 is fused with the ABL gene on chromosome 9. This abnormal "fusion" gene generates a protein of p210 or sometimes p185 weight (p is a weight measure of cellular proteins in kDa). Because abl carries a domain that can add phosphate groups to tyrosine residues (a tyrosine kinase), the bcr-abl fusion gene product is also a tyrosine kinase.

The fused bcr-abl protein interacts with the interleukin 3beta(c) receptor subunit. The bcr-abl transcript is continuously active and does not require activation by other cellular messaging proteins. In turn, bcr-abl activates a cascade of proteins which control the cell cycle, speeding up cell division. Moreover, the bcr-abl protein inhibits DNA repair, causing genomic instability and making the cell more susceptible to developing further genetic abnormalities. The action of the bcr-abl protein is the pathophysiologic cause of chronic myelogenous leukemia. With improved understanding of the nature of the bcr-abl protein and its action as a tyrosine kinase, targeted therapies have been developed (the first of which was imatinib mesylate) which specifically inhibit the activity of the bcr-abl protein. These tyrosine kinase inhibitors can induce complete remissions in CML, confirming the central importance of bcr-abl as the cause of CML.

Approximately 90% of the patients diagnosed with CML will demonstrate a Philadelphia (Ph[1]) chromosome. This chromosome can be demonstrated in neutrophils, monocytes, RBC, thrombocyte, and basophil precursors. It has been isolated in the B-lymphocyte. The presence of the Ph[1] chromosome is considered to be diagnostic of CML. On an average, about three males are affected by this disorder for every two females.

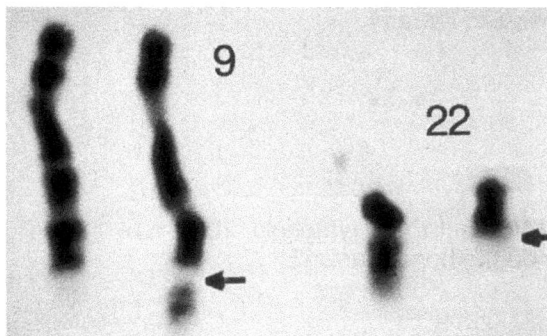

The Philadelphia chromosome, which is a diagnostic karyotypic abnormality for chronic myelogenous leukemia, is shown in this picture of the banded chromosomes 9 and 22. Shown is the result of the reciprocal translocation of 22q to the lower arm of 9 and 9q (c-abl to a specific breakpoint cluster region [bcr] of chromosome 22 indicated by the arrows). Courtesy of Peter C. Nowell, MD, Department of Pathology and Clinical Laboratory of the University of Pennsylvania School of Medicine.

Classification

CML is often divided into three phases based on clinical characteristics and laboratory findings. In the absence of intervention, CML typically begins in the chronic phase, and over the course of several years progresses to an accelerated phase and ultimately to a blast crisis. Blast crisis is the terminal phase of CML and clinically behaves like an acute leukemia. One of the drivers of the progression from chronic phase through acceleration and blast crisis is the acquisition of new chromosomal abnormalities (in addition to the Philadelphia chromosome). Some patients may already be in the accelerated phase or blast crisis by the time they are diagnosed.
Once diagnosed with CML the patient will live for about 3 to 4 years in the chronic phase. In approximately 66% of the CML patients, the initial or stable phase will revert to an accelerated phase known as the blast stage. The blast stage tends to be refractive and is a signal that death is soon pending. It is estimated that 50-60% of CML patients will convert to the blast stage. It is interesting to note that up to 30% of the CML patients will demonstrate lymphoblastic morphology not myeloblastic morphology. This would infer that the pluripotential stem cell is involved and holds some degree of "uncommitment". The mechanism for this is not known.

Morphology-Chronic Phase

Peripheral blood:
* Leukocytosis (median 170k), due mainly to neutrophils (peak in myelocytes and PMNs); no significant dysplasia; blasts <2%
* Absolute basophilia: invariably present; eosinophilia
* Monocytes: can be increased in absolute numbers, but usually <3%
* Thrombocytosis common, thrombocytopenia rare

BM:
* Hypercellular
* increased immature neutrophils
* Megakaryocytes are small and hypolobated nuclei
* Pseudo-Gaucher cells in aspirate (seen as foamy cells in biopsy), 30%

Spleen: infiltration of red pulp by granulocytic precursors

Morphology-Accelerated Phase

- Blasts 10-19% in PB or BM
- Basophils
- 20% in PB
- Plt <100k, unrelated to therapy
- Plt >1,000k, despite therapy

☐　　Increasing WBC count and spleen size, unresponsive to therapy
☐　　Evidence of clonal evolution

Morphology- Blast Phase

☐　　≥20% blasts in PB or BM
☐　　Extramedullary proliferation of blasts
☐　　Large aggregates and clusters of blasts in BM bx(Myeloid: 70%; lymphoid: 20-30%) -
Development of a chloroma (solid focus of leukemia outside the bone marrow)

Signs and symptoms

Clinical symptoms known to manifest are: [a] malaise, [b] fatigue, [c] pyrexia, [d] sweating, [e] loss of weight, [f] bone pain, [g] hepatosplenomegaly (causes fullness in abdomen), [h] recurring headaches, [i] unusual infections, [j] ankle edema, [k] priapism (males only), [l] gouty arthritis, with elevated uric acid, [m] peripheral vascular insufficiency, and [n] hemorrhage manifestations (petechiae, hematuria, ecchymosis, and retinal hemorrhages).

Laboratory findings

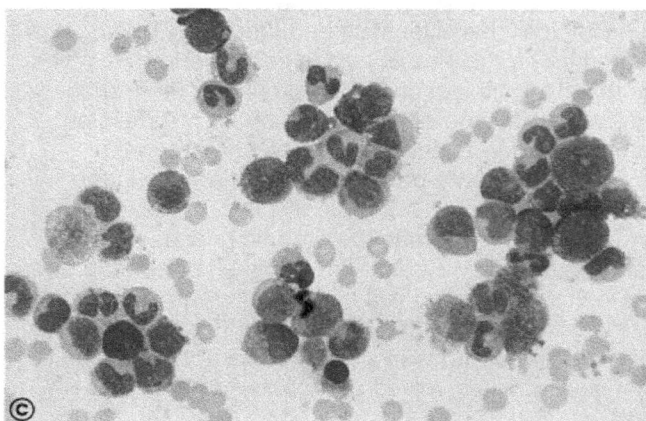

=Atlas of Hematology (Nivaldo Medeiros, MD). Used with permission=

[1]　Leukocytosis with an average range of $2.0 \times 10^5/\mu L$ to $5.0 \times 10^5/\mu L$. Counts up to and over one million/uL have been reported.
[2]　Thrombocytopenia is uncommon in CML. Counts range from $1.0 \times 10^5/\mu L$ to $6.0 \times 10^5/\mu L$. If CML converts to the blast stage, the thrombocytopenia with counts ranging between $5.0 \times 10^4/\mu L$ to $1.5 \times 10^5/\mu L$. Platelet function is usually abnormal.
[3]　RBC count = 2.0 to $3.0 \times 10^6/\mu L$. Anemia will be normocytic/normochromic and will worsen as the disease progresses.
[4]　Hemoglobin in the asymptomatic stage will range from 9 to 13 g/dL. As CML progresses the range will drop to 4 to 8 g/dL
[5]　The peripheral blood smear presents a distinct shift-to-the-left. The following is a sample CML differential:
Myeloblasts =　1% (both myeloblasts and promyelocytes will not exceed 20% of the total count)
promyelocytes =　3%
Myelocytes =　6% (can be up to 50% of the total count)
Metamyelocytes =　4% (can be up to 25% of the total count)
Bands =　6%
Neutrophils =　55%
Lymphocytes =　6% (are usually increased)
Eosinophils =　5%　(can be 7% to 8% of the total count)
Basophils =　9%　(can be >20% of the total count if in the blast stage.

Note: that the presence of basophilia may herald a blast crisis.)
    NRBC =   may range from 4 to 12 per 100 WBCs
    Pseudo-Pelger Hüet anomaly may be demonstrated.
[6] Other laboratory findings are:
    LAP score = decreased (<13)
    Anisocytosis may present toward the end of stage 2.
    Reticulocyte count = up to 3%
    LDH = >200 IU/L
Uric acid = >8.0 mG/dL
Total serum B_{12} = >950 pG/mL
[7]   Bone marrow demonstrates intense cellularity. The myeloid: erythroid ratio
    is 10 to 50:1. Normal M:E ratio = 2 to 4:1. Immature granulocytes dominate
    the bone marrow. <30% of the bone marrow population will be made up of
    blasts.

The clinical course of these disease transverses through three stages:

STAGE1: the asymptomatic and proliferate stage
[1]   It may take up to eight years for CML to develop any symptoms.
[2]   This is the pre-leukemic stage, chronic stage.
[3] Ph^1 chromosome can be identified in the bone marrow cells.
[4]   WBC count is normal.

STAGE2. The symptomatic stage with hyper proliferation
[1]   Occurs about 6.3 years after the appearance of the Ph^1 chromosome.
[2]   Immature granulocytes may be found in the peripheral blood, the
    shift-to-the-left manifestation.
[3]   WBC count begins to elevate indicating that the disease is accelerating.
[4]   After the onset of leukocytosis, then about 19 months will lapse before
    the clinical symptoms begin to appear?
[5]   Diagnosis is often made in this stage.
[6]   Patients, once diagnosed in this stage, will live only 3 to 4 years.

STAGE3. Accelerated stage with uncontrolled hyper proliferation
[1]   Once the blast stage manifests, then the chronic form becomes the acute
    form of leukemia.
[2]   There is a rapid and inexorable progression to death.
[3]   This stage is refractory to any treatment.

Chronic Eosinophilic Leukemia / Hypereosinophilic Syndrome (CEL / HES)

• Definition
– Persistently increased numbers of eosinophils in the blood ($\geq$1.5 x 10^9/L), bone marrow, and peripheral tissues.
– Organ damage occurs as result of leukemic infiltration or the release of cytokines, enzymes, or other proteins by the eosinophils.

• To make the Dx of HES
– Exclude all causes of reactive eosinophilia
– Exclude all neoplastic disorders in which eosinophils are part of the neoplastic clone
– Exclude T cell population with aberrant phenotype and abnormal cytokine production

• To make the Dx of CEL
Same as HES, and
• Evidence of eosinophilic clonality
• Or > 2% but < 20% myeloblasts in PB
• Or > 5% but < 20% myeloblasts in BM

- Epidemiology
- Rare
- True incidence is unknown
- HES
- M:F = 9:1
- Peak in 4th decade
- CEL
- Marked male predominance

- Site of involvement
- PB and BM always involved
- Spleen and liver involved in 30-50% of cases
- Heart, lungs, CNS, skin, GI tract

- Clinical features
- Asymptomatic (10%)
- Constitutional symptoms (Fever, fatigue, cough, angioedema, muscle pains, pruritis, diarrhea)
- Most serious findings are cardiac
- Endomyocardial fibrosis with restrictive cardiomyopathy
- Mitral/tricuspid valve scarring with regurgitation and embolization
- Other frequent findings
- Peripheral neuropathy, CNS dysfunction, pulmonary sxs, rheumatologic sxs

- Etiology
Unknown

- PB Morphology
- Striking eosinophilia (mainly mature eos.)
- Possible eosinophil abnormalities
- Sparse granulation with clear areas of cytoplasm
- Cytoplasmic vacuolization
- Nuclear hypersegmentation or hyposegmentation
- Enlarged size
- Neutrophilia
- Monocytosis
- If blasts >2%, consider CEL

- BM Morphology
- Hypercellular (due to proliferation of eosinophils).
- Orderly eosinophilic proliferation
- Charcot-Leyden crystals in macrophages
- Normal erythropoiesis and megakaryopoiesis
- If blasts 5%-19%, consider CEL
- Possible fibrosis

- Cytochemistry / immunophenotype
MPO positive (cyanide-resistant)

Chronic Neutrophilic Leukemia

- Definition
- Sustained PB neutrophilia
- BM hypercellularity
- Hepatosplenomegaly
- Should exclude
- All causes of reactive neutrophilia
- All other myeloproliferative diseases

- Epidemiology

- True incidence is unknown
- <100 cases reported
- Generally affects older adults
- No gender predilection

- Sites of involvement
- PB and BM: always involved
- Spleen, liver: usually show leukemic infiltrates

- Clinical features
- Most constant feature: splenomegaly
- Hepatomegaly usually present
- Up to 30% of cases: h/o bleeding from mucocutaneous surfaces or GI tract
- Gout
- Pruritis

- Etiology
- Unknown
- a/w multiple myeloma (up to 20% of cases)

- PB Morphology
- Neutrophilia ($\geq$25 x 10^9/L)
- Mostly segs (+/- toxic granules) and bands (>80% of WBC)
- Immature granulocytes (<10% of WBC)
- Blasts almost never seen (<1% of WBC)
- No dysplasia

- BM morphology
- Hypercellular (neutrophilic proliferation)
- M:E may reach 20:1
- No increase in myeloblasts (<5% of nucleated marrow cells) and promyelocytes
- Myelocytes and mature granulocytes increased
- No dysplasia (if present, consider atypical CML)
- Look for plasma cell dyscrasia

- Cytochemistry/immunophenotype
- Increased Leukocyte Alkaline Phosphatase (LAP)

Chronic Lymphocytic Leukemia (CLL)

Estimated new cases and deaths from chronic lymphocytic leukemia (CLL) in the United States in 2008:
New cases: 15,110.
Deaths: 4,390.

Chronic lymphocytic leukemia (CLL) is a malignant disease of lymphoid cells in which there is a clonal proliferation of immunologically immature and functionally inadequate small B-type lymphocytes. The CLL lymphocyte is strikingly similar to the normal lymphocyte. As this disease progresses the lymphocytes will invade the lymphatic system, causing enlargement of the spleen and lymph nodes. There may some hepatomegaly. There follows and invasion of the bone marrow. The increase in abnormal cells gradually replaces normal tissues compromising normal functions. CLL is an indolent or sluggishly progressing disorder that takes years to effect death in the patient. Because of the slow nature of this disorder, chemotherapy treatment is not satisfactory and is not offered to the patient.

Clinically, diagnosis is confirmed by a WBC count that indicates lymphocytosis with an absolute lymphocyte count of 5,000/mm^3 (> 2 months) or more with a characteristic immunophenotype (CD5 and CD23 positive B cells). As assays have become more sensitive for detecting monoclonal B-CLL–like cells in peripheral blood, researchers have detected a monoclonal lymphocytosis of undetermined significance (MLUS) (i.e., MLUS in analogy to the monoclonal gammopathy of undetermined significance, MGUS) in 3% of adults older than 40 years and 6% in adults older than 60 years. Such early detection and diagnosis may falsely suggest improved survival for the group and may unnecessarily worry or result in therapy for some patients who would have remained undiagnosed in their lifetime, a circumstance known in the literature as overdiagnosis or pseudodisease. At the present time, the natural history or clinical significance of these findings is unknown.

As the disease progresses, severe anemia, thrombocytopenia, and neutropenia are characteristic. The patient complains of tiredness and absence of endurance (these are the earliest symptoms). Other symptoms include splenomegaly (in 50% of the patients), hepatomegaly, anorexia, weight loss; low grade fever, night sweats, lymphadenopathy, and is prone to infections. Discrete lymph nodes are easily palpable in about 75% of the patients. The prognosis is variable. Some patients live as few as two years and others may survive for 20 years and longer. Most patients die in about eight years from recurring infections, uncontrolled progressive leukemic infiltration of vital organs, bleeding, or extreme inanition (inability of the body to use food for whatever reason and the body starves to death).

The disease rarely occurs in individuals under 40 y/o. 90% of the patients are >50 y/o and 66% of these are over 60 y/o. Men are affected more than women by a 2 to 1 ratio. It has been estimated that about 25% of the patients diagnosed with CLL are discovered at the physician's office when they are there for some other reason. There are no known characteristic chromosome abnormalities described. The chromosome aberrations have been observed in CLL: [a] an extra chromosome 12 to form a trisomy, [b] deletion of the long arms on chromosome 6, and [c] translocation to the long arm of chromosome 14 from some other chromosome.

Classification

WHO Classification of Chronic Leukemias (with modification):
B cell chronic lymphocytic leukemias (CLL), represents more than 90% of all chronic lymphocytic leukemias. Clonal cells cannot be distinguished from normal, small peripheral blood lymphocytes. This subtype is often referred to as chronic lymphocytic leukemia (CLL), the inference being that they are of B cell lineage. Other B cell chronic leukemias are uncommon and include:
Mantle cell leukemia
Hairy cell leukemia
Chronic Prolymphocytic B cell leukemia
Leukemic phase of splenic lymphoma with villous lymphocytes
Leukemic phase of marginal zone lymphoma
Leukemic phase of lymphoplasmacyte lymphomas
T and NK cell chronic lymphocytic leukemias
Large granular lymphocyte (LGL) syndrome
Leukemic phase of mycosis fungoides
Chronic Prolymphocytic leukemia (CPLL)
Chronic small lymphocytic T cell leukemia

There are two different systems for staging chronic lymphocytic leukemia.
The Rai classification is used more often in the United States, whereas the Binet system is used more widely in Europe.
The Rai stages can be separated into low, intermediate, and high-risk categories. Stage 0 is considered low-risk, 1 and 2 are considered intermediate-risk, and 3 and 4 are considered high-risk.

Comparison of Rai and Binet Staging Systems

Criteria	Rai Stage 0	I	II	III	IV
Lymphocytosis (> 15,000/µL)	+	+	+	+	+
Lymphadenopathy		+	+/–	+/–	+/–
Hepatosplenomegaly			+	+/–	+/–
Anemia (hemoglobin < 11 g/dL)				+	+/–
Thrombocytopenia (< 100,000/µL)					+

Criteria	Binet Stage A	B	C
Lymphocytosis (> 15,000/µL)	+	+	+
Lymphadenopathy (> 3 sites), including hepatosplenomegaly		+	+/–
Anemia (hemoglobin < 10 g/dL) or thrombocytopenia (< 100,000/µL)			+

Rai K, Sawitsky A, Cronkite E, et al: Clinical staging of chronic lymphocytic leukemia. *Blood* 46:219-234, 1975. Binet JL, Auquier A, Dighiero G, et al: A new prognostic classification of chronic lymphocytic leukemia derived from a multivariate survival analysis. *Cancer* 48:198-206, 1981.[10,11]

Laboratory findings

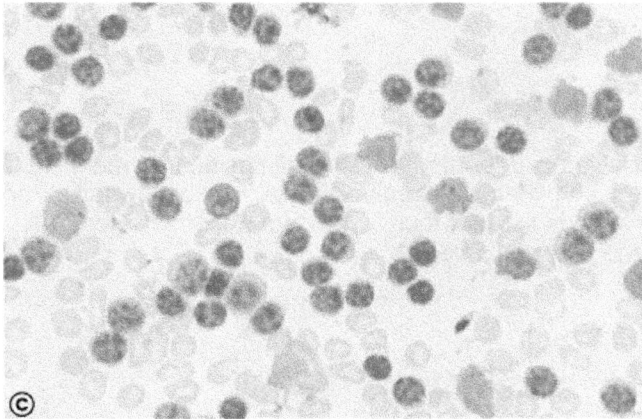

=Atlas of Hematology (Nivaldo Medeiros, MD). Used with permission=

[1] WBC counts may go as high as 1.0×10^6/µL (higher values have been reported).
[2] Absolute lymphocytosis. This may range for 10,000 to 150,000/µL. Lymphocytes are always increased and may represent >97% of the total WBC count.
[3] Anemia
[4] Smudge cells (fragile Lymphs) are typical for CLL. The number of smudge cells per 100 WBCs on a stained blood film may equal or exceed the number of WBCs counted. (Note: if it is necessary to demonstrate that the smudge cells are lymphocytes, then add a few drops of 22% bovine albumin to a few drops of patient's blood and make a blood smear and stain when dry. The albumin will help prevent the lymphocyte from forming into smudge cells.
[5] As CLL advances the following parameters appear
A. Thrombocytopenia
B. Neutropenia
C. Autoimmune hemolytic anemia
D. Total bilirubin (may reach levels >10 mG/dL)

E. Hypogammaglobinemia (Consider obtaining serum quantitative immunoglobulin levels in patients developing repeated infections because monthly intravenous immunoglobulin administration in patients with low levels of immunoglobulin G (<500 mg) may be beneficial in reducing the frequency of infectious episodes).

F. Elevated uric acid (normal = males (3.5 to 8.0 mG/dL) and females (2.5 to 7.0 mG/dL)

[6] A bone marrow biopsy is generally not required to diagnose this type of leukemia. Immunological markers for CLL include: weak sIg (surface Immunoglobulin), HLA-DR, CD5, CD19, CD20, CD23, CD24, CD2, CD3, CD8, T-cell CLL.

[7] The differential diagnosis of CLL includes several other entities, such as hairy cell leukemia, which is moderately positive for surface membrane immunoglobulins of multiple heavy-chain classes and typically negative for CD5 and CD21. Prolymphocytic leukemia has a typical phenotype that is positive for CD19, CD20, and surface membrane immunoglobulin and negative for CD5. Large granular lymphocytic leukemia has a natural killer cell phenotype (CD2, CD16, and CD56) or a T-cell immunotype (CD2, CD3, and CD8). The pattern of positivity for CD19, CD20, and the T-cell antigen CD5 is shared only by mantle cell lymphoma.

MLUS is distinguish from CLL by the ALC < 5-8000/mm3 and CD5-.

Complications:

Hypogammaglobinemia and impaired T-cell function associated with CLL predispose patients to potentially serious infections. Patients who demonstrate a pattern of repeated infections, such as pneumonia and septicemia, should be treated monthly with prophylactic parenteral gamma globulin. Anemia secondary to bone marrow involvement with CLL, splenic sequestration of red blood cells, and autoimmune hemolytic anemia associated with a positive Coombs test are included in the differential diagnosis of a patient with anemia who has CLL. Thrombocytopenia: The causes of low platelets in patients with CLL are very similar to the causes of anemia in patients with CLL and include bone marrow involvement, splenic sequestration, and immune thrombocytopenia. A variety of clinical factors, including beta-2-microglobulin, lymphocyte doubling time, and cytogenetic abnormalities, may be helpful in predicting progression of disease.

Prolymphocytic Leukemia

Prolymphocytic leukemia is a lymphoproliferative disorder that has a predisposition for men over the age of 60. It onset is sudden and is characterized by fatigue, weakness, weight loss, sweating, and pyrexia. The prognosis for this disorder is more serious than for CLL. Lymphadenopathy is not a problem, but there is a marked enlargement of the liver and spleen.

Clinical laboratory findings include:

[1]   WBC count = 2.5×10^4/μL to 1.0×10^6/μL.

[2]   Normocytic/normochromic anemia.

[3]   Thrombocytopenia.

[4]   Peripheral blood smears:

    A.   immature agranulocytes

    B.   Nucleated RBC's with rubriblasts.

Monocytosis (Note: An absolute count may be >800/μL.)

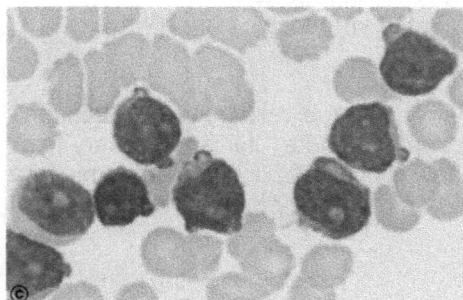

= Atlas of Hematology (Nivaldo Medeiros, MD). Used with permission=

241

The prolymphocyte is the predominate cell and can totally replace the bone marrow by aggressive infiltration. This cell is a large mononuclear lymphocyte with a round to oval nucleus. Chromatin is coarse in appearance. The nucleus may present with one or more large nucleoli. The cytoplasm is agranular and basophilic.

Immunological markers are: strong sIg (surface Immunoglobulin), HLA-DR, CD22, CD19, CD20, CD 24, CD2, CD3, CD4, CD5, CD7. CD10 and CD8 may or may not be present.

Hairy Cell Leukemia (HCL)

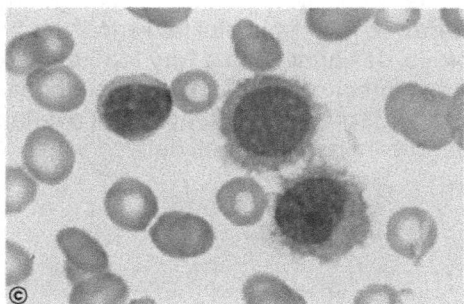

=Atlas of Hematology (Nivaldo Medeiros, MD). Used with permission=

It was first described in 1923 by O. Ewald (Germany). It represents about 2% of all leukemias and occurs about 4 times more often in men than women. It onsets in the middle-aged individual (average age is about 50).

 Clinical findings includes [1] Splenomegaly, in up to 90% of the patients, [2] hepatomegaly, in up to 40% of the patients, [3] pancytopenia in up to 66% of the patients, and the presence of petechiae, indicating the presence of thrombocytopenia. Hairy cell leukemia (HCL) tends follow an indolent course in most patients. Patients have been reported as living 27 years.

 The usual prognosis is about 7 years for most patients. HCL is a chronic lymphoproliferative leukemic disorder. What is the hairy cell in this form of leukemia? It is a medium size to large lymphocyte that has the appearance of a reticuloendothelial cell that has multiple cytoplasmic projections from the cell membrane that resembles hairs.   They are B-lymphocytes. They are larger than the normal, small lymphocyte with a cytoplasm that stains from clear to sky blue. Azurophilic granules may be present and if vacuoles are present, they are most likely to be small. The nucleus may be rounding, reniform, or oval in shape. Nuclear shapes that are folded or dumb-bell in appearance have been reported. Its chromatin resembles that of the medium size lymphocyte. Nucleoli are usually absent. If a nucleolus is present, it will be single and small.

The hairy cell is rich in type 5 tartrate-resistant acid phosphatase. Note the presence of a hairy cell is not sufficient for a diagnosis. Acid phosphatase exists in five isoenzyme forms. Most WBCs are deficient in type-5 acid phosphatase isoenzyme. If the hairy cell lymphocyte is pre-incubated in a tartrate buffer, then stained with acid phosphatase, the stain is not destroyed. The tartrate-resistant acid phosphatase stain (TRAP) is a distinctive test to differentiate hairy cell leukemia from other leukemias.

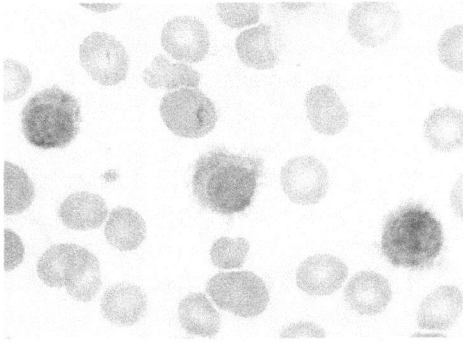

Blood film at X1000 magnification demonstrating tartrate-resistant acid phosphatase (TRAP) activity of lymphocytes. Photographed by U. Woermann, MD, Division of Instructional Media, Institute for Medical Education, University of Bern, Switzerland

Cytochemical staining is not helpful in differentiating HCL The hairy cell cytoplasm tend to fragment and such fragments may be confused as platelets. The bone marrow biopsy is useful in diagnosing HCL. It is always involved. Bone marrow aspirates are often fibrotic, designated as a "dry tap", and are characterized by the presence of lots of reticulum (produced by the tumor cells). If a reasonable bone marrow tap is procured, then the stained smear should contain widely spaced cells that do not overlap or touch each other. Mitotic figures are not likely to be observed. The cells will be well defined with a clear cytoplasm and "bland" nucleus.

Expected clinical laboratory findings include:
[a] granulocytopenia,
[b] Possible monocytopenia,
[c] Abnormal platelets,
[d] Absence of hairy cells in other body fluids (unusual in that most leukemic cells tend to infiltrate all body fluids), and
[e] Anemia.
Immunological markers include: HLA-DR, CD19, CD20, CD22, CD24, CD25, CD103, sIg (surface immunoglobulin).
HCL may behave as a chronic leukemia without causing any symptoms. Approximately 10% of cases, usually in elderly men with moderate splenomegaly and mild decrease in blood counts, never require therapy.
The standard criteria for initiating therapy include the following:
Symptoms or blood transfusion requirement
Significant anemia with hemoglobin of 8-10 g/dL or less
Thrombocytopenia with platelet counts of 50,000-100,000/mL or less
Neutropenia with an absolute neutrophil count of 500-1000/mL or less
Less common indications for therapy include the following:
Leukocytosis with a high proportion of hairy cells
Repeated life-threatening infections
Symptomatic splenomegaly
Bulky or painful lymphadenopathy
Vasculitis
Bony involvement

Large Granular Lymphocytic Leukemia

- Uncommon: 2-3% of cases of small lymphocytic leukemia
- Involves peripheral blood, bone marrow, liver and spleen; usually not lymph nodes.
- Most cases are indolent
- Severe neutropenia, with or without anemia. May have red cell hypoplasia due to cytokine production.
- Lymphocytosis usually not marked 2,000-20,000.
- Moderate splenomegaly is the main physical finding.

243

- Rheumatoid arthritis, autoantibodies, circulating immune complexes and hypergammaglobulinemia are also common.

Large granular lymphocytes with abundant cytoplasm and fine or coarse azurophilic granules
- Granules contain proteins involved in cytolysis such as perforin and granzyme B
- Bone marrow involvement is variable
- Can be divided into groups based on the predominant cell markers:

Common variant (80% of cases)
* CD3+, TCRαβ+, CD4-, CD8+

Rare variants
* CD3+, TCRαβ+, CD4+, CD8-
* CD3+, TCRαβ+, CD4+, and CD8+
* CD3+, TCRγδ+

* CD11b, CD56 and CD57 are variably expressed; CD57 is often expressed in the common type
* TIA-1 is usually positive

- Prognosis: May be indolent and nonprogressive, raising the possibility of a reactive lymphocytosis which may be clonal in some circumstances.
- Morbidity is associated with neutropenia, but usually not mortality.
- May progress to a more aggressive disease with transformation to a PTCL of large cells.

CHAPTER TWO: ACUTE LEUKEMIAS

Acute Lymphoblastic Leukemia

This type of leukemia (designated as ALL) is characterized by a massive invasion of the bone marrow with small to large immature blast cells. There is a corresponding spillage into the peripheral blood containing a significant increase in immature lymphoid cells. The etiology of this malignancy is not known. This disease has a rapid course and the patient is afflicted with recurring infections, weakness, and bleeding. Lymph nodes are enlarged and splenomegaly and hepatomegaly are present.. Without medical intervention, ALL is fatal within six months. Current chemotherapy is producing a cure rate in about 60% of those treated with children having a better prognosis than adults. Females have a better survival rate than males. About 90% of all patients treated can expect a full remission.
Note: Estimated new cases and deaths from acute lymphoblastic leukemia (ALL; also called acute lymphocytic leukemia) in the United States in 2008:
New cases: 5,430.
Deaths: 1,460

Morphologic Classification

Acute lymphoblastic leukemia can be separate into three FAB morphological groups as follows:
L1. This leukemia is characterized by small, uniform lymphoblasts. The nucleus is round with an indistinct/inconspicuous nucleolus. The cytoplasm is scanty and stains blue. Some basophilia may be seen. Cytoplasmic vacuoles may or may not be present. This "blast" cell will be about up to 2.5 times larger than the normal small lymphocyte. The cell is fairly homogenous, consistent in its appearance. 71% of the ALL cases will be of this type. This disorder tends to occur in individuals >15 y/o. This has the best prognosis of the three types. The age groups of 2 to 10 have the best prognosis and if the patient is less than 1 y/o, then they have the poorest prognosis.

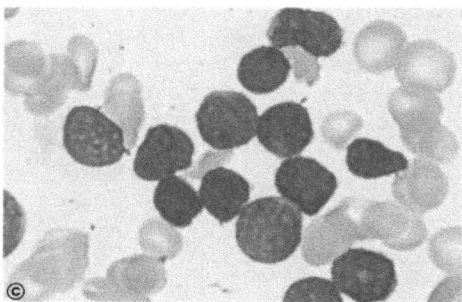

=Atlas of Hematology (Nivaldo Medeiros, MD). Used with permission=

L2. This form tends to appear most often in adults. Predominate lymphoblast is from 2 to 3 times larger than the small lymphocyte. Cell size is not consistent; it has a degree of variability. It has a mod of cytoplasm surrounding a nucleus with a irregular nuclear membrane. One or more nucleoli are visible and large. The nucleus tends to be irregular with clefting or indenting. Cytoplasmic vacuolation and some basophilia may be present.

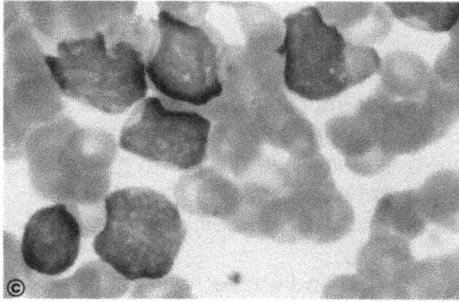

L3. This leukemia affects all age groups equally and has the worst prognosis. The lymphoblast is large, with a nucleus containing from 3 to 5 nucleoli. The nucleus is round to oval, not given to clefting or indenting. The cytoplasm is abundant and very basophilic. The cytoplasm has prominent vacuolation. This type is a B-cell malignancy arts prognosis. Vacuoles will stain with Oil Red O which helps to identify this type ALL. The lymphocyte is designated as a Burkitt type-lymphocyte.

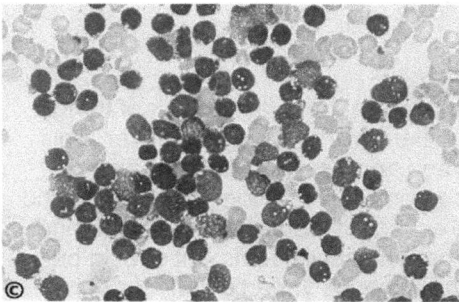

Burkitt's lymphoma is a disorder small malignant lymphoid cell. It is usually seen in children but may appear in adults. Burkitt's lymphoma is endemic to Africa, but is found worldwide. The disease has a predilection for males. There are clinical variations of this malignancy, but all variations are characterized by diffuse proliferation of small neoplastic lymphoid cells that are interspersed with histiocytes (that stains lightly compare to the darker staining lymphoid cells). This result in a microscopic view described as a "starry sky" pattern that consists of benign macrophages interspersed among the B-lymphocyte tumor cells. The Burkitt lymphoid cell presents with a round and noncleaved nucleus containing clumped chromatin, multiple nucleoli, and mitotic patterns. Nucleoli are present. There is scanty basophilic cytoplasm containing lipid filled vacuoles. The Burkitt cell is described as being monotonously uniform. Diagnosis is made using histological and cytoimmunological techniques of lymph nodes and affected tissues. Chromosomal studies demonstrate t(8;14), t(2;8), and t(8:22) translocations.

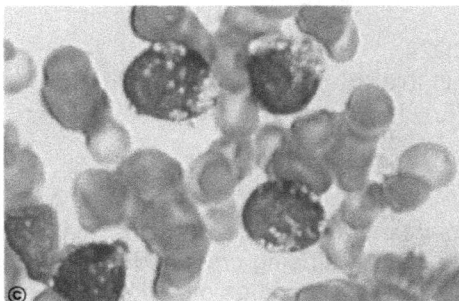

The Epstein-Barr virus (EBV) has been implicated strongly in the African form, while the relationship is less clear in the sporadic form. EBV is associated with about 20% of sporadic cases. Rare adult cases are associated with immunodeficiency, particularly AIDS. The lymphocytes have receptors for EBV and are its specific target. In the African form, the hosts are believed to be unable to mount an appropriate immune response to primary EBV infection, possibly because of coexistent malaria or another infection that is immunosuppressive. Months to years later, excessive B cell proliferation occurs.

Lymph node involvement occurs. Burkitt cells are homogeneous in size and shape, with round to oval nuclei and slightly coarse chromatin, with multiple nucleoli, and with intensely basophilic vacuolated cytoplasm that contains neutral fat. Frequent mitotic figures usually are observed. A starry sky appearance is imparted by scattered macrophages with phagocyte cell debris.

Various staging systems have been proposed.

The National Cancer Institute (NCI) system
A - Single solitary extra-abdominal site
AR - Intra-abdominal, more than 90% of tumor resected
B - Multiple extra-abdominal tumors
C - Intra-abdominal tumor
D -Intra-abdominal plus one or more extra-abdominal sites

Patients with Burkitt lymphoma, especially those with extensive disease, have a high risk of tumor lysis syndrome even before chemotherapy is initiated because of the rapid tumor cell turnover. This emergent life-threatening clinical situation should be anticipated and addressed prior to starting treatment. Patients should receive prophylactic allopurinol and aggressive hydration with alkalinization starting as soon as Burkitt lymphoma is diagnosed. Electrolytes, especially potassium, calcium, and phosphorus, as well as uric acid and creatinine, should be monitored closely. Treatment should be performed at a facility where renal dialysis is available should it be necessary, particularly for patients with extensive disease.

The WHO classifies the L1 and L2 subtypes of ALL as precursor B lymphoblastic leukemia/lymphoblastic lymphoma or precursor T lymphoblastic leukemia/lymphoblastic lymphoma depending on the cell of origin. The L3 subtype of ALL is included in the group of mature B-cell neoplasms, as the subtype Burkitt lymphoma/leukemia.
Cytogenetic abnormalities occur in approximately 70% of cases of ALL in adults. These abnormalities included balanced translocations as occur in cases of AML. However, abnormalities of chromosome number (hypodiploidy, hyperdiploidy) are much more common in ALL than in AML.

Immunologic Classification

The acute leukemic lymphoblast can be identified immunologically by the presence of certain lymphocyte leukemic antigens present on the membrane. There are six immunological subtypes of acute lymphoblastic leukemia based upon these antigens.
[1] B ALL . Corresponds to L3.
  A. Contains antigens for HLA-DR, CD19, and sIg. CD10 may be present.
  B. Up to 5% of all cases fall in this category. This type has the worse prognosis.
[2] C ALL. Corresponds to L1/L2.
  A. Contains antigens for TdT, HLA-DR, CD10, CD19, and CD24.
  B. Up to 75% of children and 40% of adult cases of ALL fall in this category.
 [3] pre-B ALL . Corresponds to L1/L2.
  A. Contains antigens for HLA-DR, CD10, CD19, TdT (CD7), and sIg.
  B. Percentage of cases unknown.
[4] pre-T ALL . Corresponds to L1/L2.
  A. Contains antigens for TdT and T antigen. CD10 marker may be present. Also contains the enzyme focal acid phosphatase. (The term focal means that the enzyme is being produced by the affected cell and does not come from another source.) The enzyme can be used as a marker for this leukemia.

B. Exact percentage of cases unknown.
[5] T ALL. Corresponds to L1/L2.
   A. Contains antigens for sheep erythrocyte receptors, T antigen, and TdT. cALLa may be present. Also contains the enzyme focal acid phosphatase.
   B. Up to 15% of children and 15% of adult cases of all fall in this category.
[6] μALL. . Corresponds to L1/L2.
   A. Designated as null or unclassified ALL, this type contains the antigens TDT and HLA-DR,
   B. About 10% of children and 40% of adult cases of ALL fall in this category.

Prognosis indicators

[A] If the child is <1 y/o or >13 y/o, the prognosis tend to be less favorable.
[B] If the child is between 3 and 7 y/o, the prognosis tends to be the most favorable.
[C] If the WBC count at the time of presentation is:
   - < 10 x 10^6/μL, the prognosis tends to be favorable.
   - > 20 x 10^6/μL, the prognosis tends to be less favorable.
   - > 100 x 10^6/μL, the prognosis tends to be very unfavorable

Patients with ALL are divided into 3 prognostic groups.
[1]- Good risk includes (1) no adverse cytogenetics, (2) age younger than 30 years, (3) WBC count of less than 30,000/μL, (4) complete remission within 4 weeks.
[2] - Intermediate risk does not meet the criteria for either good risk or poor risk.
[3]- Poor risk includes (1) adverse cytogenetics [(t9;22), (4;11)], (2) age older than 60 years, (3) precursor B-cell WBCs with WBC count greater than 100,000/μL, or (4) failure to achieve complete remission within 4 weeks.
   General clinical symptoms include [a] fatigue, [b] pallor, [c] pyrexia (an infection may be present), [d] weight loss, [e] anorexia, [f] bone pain in 80% of the cases, [g] petechiae and/or ecchymoses in 50% to 60% of the cases, [h] cephalalgia, [i] splenomegaly, [j] lymphadenopathy, [k] hepatomegaly, and/or [l] vomiting.

Laboratory findings

[1] WBC count may be aleukemic (decreased), subleukemic (normal range) and a few blasts may be present, or leukemic (increased) and blasts will be present.
[2] Thrombocytopenia (<150,000/μL).
[3] RBC: normocytic, normochromic anemia is the rule. Anisocytosis, poikilocytosis, and NRBC/s are not usually present.
[4] If the CBC results support pancytopenia, this is the aleukemic stage.
[5] If there is a hyperleukocytosis, then hyperkalemia, hypocalcemia and hyperphosphatemia is most likely to be present.
[6] Chromosome anomaly may be present:
   A. Look for the Ph^1 chromosome in 10 to 15% of the children diagnosed with ALL.
   B. Translocations of the following chromosomes are known to have occurred.
      a. Fragmentation from 8 to 14 (seen most often in ALL type-L3)
      b. Fragmentation from 4 to 11.
[7] Bone marrow is hypercellular and infiltrated with lymphocytic cells.

   - 85% of cases of ALL are derived from B cells. The primary distinction is between (1) early (pro-B) ALL, which is TDT positive, CD10 (CALLA) negative, surface Ig negative; (2) precursor B ALL, which is TDT positive, CD10 (CALLA) positive, surface Ig negative; and (3) mature B cell (Burkitt) ALL, which is TdT negative, surface Ig positive.
   - 15% of cases are derived from T cells. These cases are subclassified into different stages corresponding to the phases of normal thymocyte development. The early subtype is surface CD3 negative, cytoplasmic CD3 positive and either double negative ($CD4^-$, $CD8^-$) or double positive ($CD4^+$, $CD8^+$). The latter subtype is surface CD3 positive, CD1a negative and positive for either CD4 or CD8, but not both.

Immunophenotyping of ALL Cells - ALL of B-Cell Lineage (85% of cases of adult ALL)

ALL Cells	TdT	CD19	CD10	CyIg*	SIg†
Early B-precursor ALL	+	+	-	-	-
Pre–B-cell ALL‡	+	+	+	+	-
B-cell ALL	-	+	+/-	+/-	+

*Cytoplasmic immunoglobulin

Immunophenotyping of ALL Cells - ALL of T-Cell Lineage (15% of cases of adult ALL)

ALL Cells	TdT	surface CD3	CD4/CD8
Early T-precursor ALL	+	-	+/+ or -/-
T-cell ALL	+	+	+/- or -/+

1- Negative myeloperoxidase stain and a positive TdT is the hallmark of the diagnosis of most cases of ALL. However, positive confirmation of lymphoid (and not myeloid) lineage should be sought by flow cytometric demonstration of lymphoid antigens, such as CD3 (T-lineage ALL) or CD19 (B-lineage ALL), in order to avoid confusion with some types of myeloid leukemia (e.g., M0, acute monocytic leukemia), which also stain negative with myeloperoxidase. Although more than 95% of cases of the L1 or L2 subtype of ALL are positive for TdT, TdT is not specific for ALL. TdT is present in some subtypes of AML such as M0. Additionally, TdT is absent in cases of L3 type ALL. However, TdT helps distinguish ALL from malignancies of more mature lymphocytes (i.e., NHL).

2- In cases of acute leukemia that are MPO negative, TdT positive, the distinction between AML and ALL is made based on the analysis of flow cytometry results. Patients with AML demonstrate myeloid markers such as CD33, whereas patients with ALL demonstrate lymphoid markers. Further confusion arises because some patients with ALL have aberrant expression of myeloid markers, such as CD13. However, if the cells are TdT-positive, myeloperoxidase-negative, and CD33-negative and demonstrate lymphoid markers, the leukemia is considered ALL.

3-Studies for bcr-abl analysis by polymerase chain reaction or cytogenetics may help distinguish patients with Philadelphia chromosome positive ALL from those with the lymphoid blastic phase of chronic myelogenous leukemia. Most patients with Ph+ ALL have the p190 type of bcr-abl, whereas patients with lymphoid blastic CML have the p210 type of bcr-abl.

4- Newer studies are analyzing ALL subtypes by gene expression profiling. In children with ALL, Bogni et al distinguished 3 groups of patients. Interestingly, one of these groups had a significantly increased risk of developing treatment-related AML following chemotherapy for their ALL.

Ph1-positive ALL has a worse prognosis than most other types of ALL, though many children and some adults with Ph1-positive ALL may have complete remissions following intensive ALL treatment clinical trials. Imatinib mesylate, an orally available inhibitor of the BCR-ABL tyrosine kinase, has been shown to have clinical activity as a single agent in this disease.

Laboratory evaluation DNA index

The number of chromosomes or ploidy of leukemic cells is especially important in childhood ALL, where the hyperdiploid ALLs have a better prognosis than diploid or hypodiploid ALL.

Approximately 25-30% of childhood ALLs are hyperdiploid (>50 chromosomes); 15% are hyperdiploid (47-50 chromosomes); 5-10% are hypodiploid (<46 chromosomes); <1% are tetraploid or near tetraploid; and the remainder diploid.

Ploidy is determined by karyotype or by measurement of cellular DNA content.

Cells are stained with a fluorescent dye (propidium iodide) that binds to DNA. The fluorescence is measured by flow cytometry. The degree of fluorescence reflects the amount of cellular DNA. A DNA index of >1.15 corresponds to >52 chromosomes or hyperdiploidy. A DNA index of 1.0-1.15 is diploid or hyperdiploid 47-50. A DNA index of <1.0 corresponds with hypodiploidy.

Formula for Calculating DNA Index $\dfrac{\text{leukemic } G_0/G_1}{\text{normal } G_0/G_1}$ = DNA index

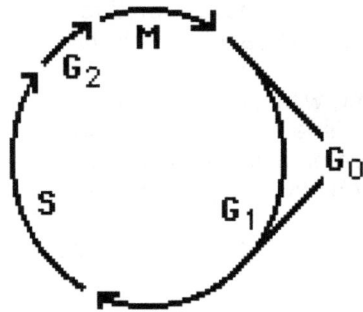

The Cell Cycle

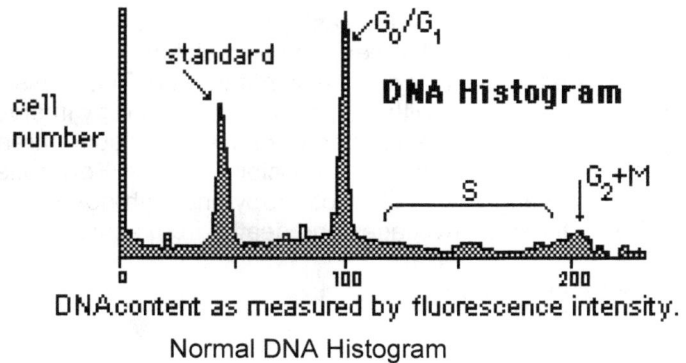

DNA Histogram

cell number

G_0/G_1

standard

S

G_2+M

0   100   200

DNA content as measured by fluorescence intensity.

Normal DNA Histogram

Examples:

In A, the DNA index of a leukemic bone marrow (60% blasts; 40% normal myeloid & erythroid) is abnormally high (>1.15) indicating hyperdiploidy. Note the normal G0/G1 peak from the normal marrow cells present.

In B, marrow cells (>90% blasts) with features of ALL-L3 Burkitt's are hypodiploid (DNA index <1.0). There is a high proliferative fraction, as measured by the cells in S phase. This is characteristic of high grade leukemia/lymphoma

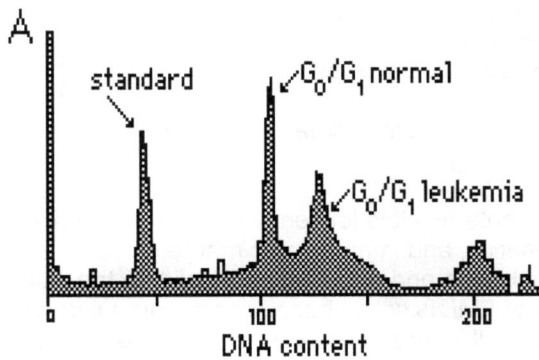

A

standard

G_0/G_1 normal

G_0/G_1 leukemia

0   100   200

DNA content

DNA index = $\dfrac{\text{leukemic } G_0/G_1}{\text{normal } G_0/G_1}$ = 1.28

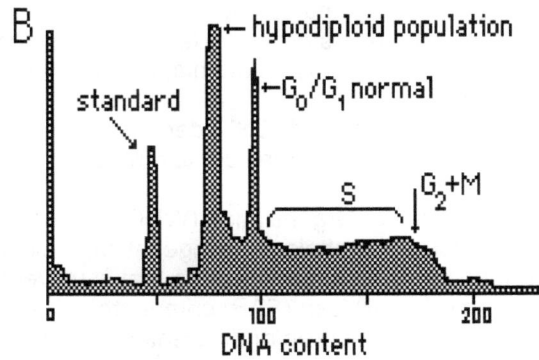

B

← hypodiploid population

←G_0/G_1 normal

standard

S

G_2+M

0   100   200

DNA content

DNA index = $\dfrac{\text{leukemic } G_0/G_1}{\text{normal } G_0/G_1}$ = 0.84

Acute Myeloid Leukemia (AML)

Introduction

Acute myeloid leukemia (AML), also known as acute myelogenous leukemia represents a heterogenous group of diseases arising from a neoplastic transformation of the multipotential Hemopoietic stem cell that can express it consequences in granulocytes, monocytes, erythrocytes, or megacaryocytes. This neoplastic cell does not mature beyond the blast stage and will spill its immature forms into the peripheral circulation.

AML is a rapidly fatal disease is not treated. The remission rate is low, with some patients surviving more than 15 years with supportive chemotherapy intervention. It is estimated that if the patient is younger (under 60 years of age) remission for up to three years can be obtained in 70% of the patients treated. Long term remissions are low. Few patients live beyond five to six years. Treatment consists of aggressive chemotherapy and high-dose radiation.

Note: Estimated new cases and deaths from acute myeloid leukemia (AML) in the United States in 2008:

New cases: 13,290.

Deaths: 8,820.

Acute myelogenous leukemia shares several clinical features with acute lymphocytic leukemia. In both types, the initial symptoms are present within three months. A sample listing of similarities include the following:

[1]   Pancytopenia without circulating blasts.

[2]   Normal leukocyte count or a marked increased leukocyte count.

[3]   Leukocytosis when the blast count exceeds 100.0 X 10^9/L (1.0 X 10^5/µL). This marked number of blasts causes hypo fusion of vital organs and occlusion of their micro-circulation. Infarcts may occur.

[4]   Anemia

[5]   Dyspnea and fatigability on mild exertion or exercise.

[6]   Laboratory analysis of glucose, potassium, and blood gases will be altered.

[7]   Thrombocytopenia with bleeding and coagulation defects.

[8]   Infection is a frequent and a serious complication as the disease progresses. Gram-negative bacteria, gram-positive cocci, and Candida species are common pathogens for the compromised acute leukemia patient.

[9]   Hepatomegaly and splenomegaly varies with the type of acute leukemia.

[10]   Bone pain and sternal tenderness are symptoms in about ½ of the patients.

[11]   Hyponatremia, hyperkalemia, increased LDH, and hyperuricemia result from metabolic abnormalities.

[12]   Cerebrospinal fluid (CSF) demonstrates presence of blast cells, increased total protein, decreased glucose, and may contain blood.

The World Health Organization (WHO) classification of acute myeloid leukemia (AML) incorporates and interrelates morphology, cytogenetics, molecular genetics, and immunologic markers in an attempt to construct a classification that is universally applicable and prognostically valid. In the older French-American-British (FAB) criteria, the classification of AML is solely based upon morphology as determined by the degree of differentiation along different cell lines and the extent of cell maturation.

FAB Classification

There are seven variant forms of AML as designated by the French-American-British (FAB) system. This is a classification system (proposed in 1976) that assumes to categories of acute leukemia: lymphoblastic and myeloblastic. This classification is based upon the basis of the morphology of the cells from bone marrow and peripheral blood smears using Romanowsky stain along with cytochemical stains (myeloperoxidase, Sudan Black B, periodic acid Schiff, Naphthol AS-D chloroacetate (specific), α-Naphthol acetate esterase (non-specific), α-Naphthol butyrate esterase (non-specific), and leukocyte alkaline phosphatase. Cell markers for B- and T-lymphocytes, Terminal DNA nucleotidyltransferase testing, and membrane immunoglobulin testing are examples of testing strategies to classify acute leukemias.

WHO classification

AML with recurrent genetic abnormalities
AML with t(8;21)(q22;q22), (AML1/ETO)
AML with abnormal bone marrow eosinophils and inv(16)(p13q22) or t(16;16)(p13)(q22), (CBFB/MYH11)
APL with t(15;17)(q22;q12), (PML/RARa) and variants
AML with 11q23 (MLL) abnormalities
AML with multilineage dysplasia
Following myelodysplastic syndrome (MDS) or MDS/myeloproliferative disease (MPD)
Without antecedent MDS or MDS/MPD but with dysplasia in at least 50% of cells in 2 or more lineages
AML and MDS, therapy related
Alkylating agent or radiation-related type
Topoisomerase II inhibitor type
Others
AML, not otherwise classified
AML, minimally differentiated
AML, without maturation
AML, with maturation
Acute myelomonocytic leukemia
Acute monoblastic or monocytic leukemia
Acute erythroid leukemia
Acute megakaryoblastic leukemia
Acute basophilic leukemia
Acute panmyelosis and myelofibrosis
Myeloid sarcoma

[1] Acute myeloblastic leukemia, minimally differentiated (FAB Classification M0)

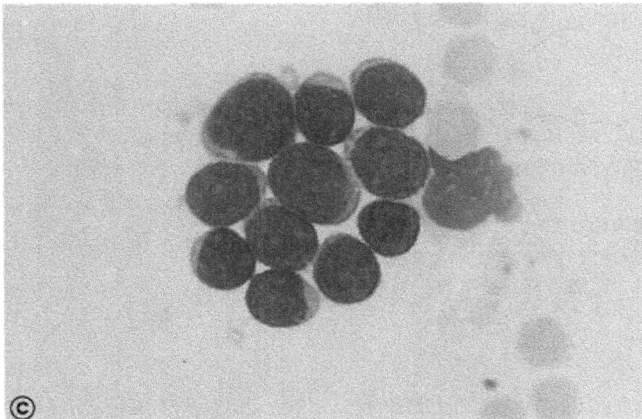

=Atlas of Hematology (Nivaldo Medeiros, MD). Used with permission=

 This AML shows no evidence of myeloid differentiation by morphology and light microscopy cytochemistry. The myeloid nature of the blasts is demonstrated by immunophenotyping and/or ultrastructural studies. Immunophenotyping studies must be performed to distinguish this acute leukemia from acute lymphoblastic leukemia (ALL). Cases of AML, minimally differentiated, comprise approximately 5% of cases of AML. Patients with this AML typically present with evidence of marrow failure, thrombocytopenia, and neutropenia.
Morphologic and cytochemical features include the following:
- Medium-sized blasts with dispersed nuclear chromatin.
- Agranular cytoplasm
- Occasionally small blasts that resemble lymphoblasts

- Cytochemistry negative for myeloperoxidase (MPO), Sudan Black B (SBB), and naphthol - ASD chloroacetate esterase (<3% positive blasts)
- Cytochemistry negative for alpha naphthyl acetate and butyrate esterases
- Markedly hypercellular marrow

Immunophenotyping reveals blast cells that express one or more panmyeloid antigens (CD13, CD33, and CD117) and are negative for B and T lymphoid-restricted antigens. Most cases express primitive hematopoietic-associated antigens (CD34, CD38, and HLA-DR). The differential diagnosis includes ALL, acute megakaryoblastic leukemia, biphenotypic/mixed lineage acute leukemia, and, rarely, the leukemic phase of large cell lymphoma. Immunophenotyping studies are required to distinguish these disorders. Although no specific chromosomal abnormalities have been found in AML, minimally differentiated point mutations of the AML1 gene have been observed in approximately 25% of cases. This mutation appears to correlate clinically with a higher white blood cell count and greater marrow blast involvement. Mutation of FLT3, a receptor tyrosine kinase gene, occurs in approximately 25% of cases and has been associated with short survival. The median overall survival is approximately 10 months.

[2] M1 or acute myeloblastic leukemia (without maturation).

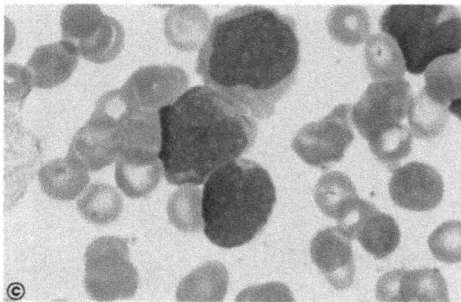

=Atlas of Hematology (Nivaldo Medeiros, MD). Used with permission=

AML without maturation is characterized by a high percentage of bone marrow blasts with little evidence of maturation to mature neutrophils and comprises approximately 10% of cases of AML. Most patients are adults. Patients usually present with anemia, thrombocytopenia, and neutropenia.

Common morphologic and cytochemical features include the following:
- Myeloblasts of 90% or more of the nonerythroid cells in the bone marrow.
- Myeloblasts that may have azurophilic granules and/or Auer rods.
- Myeloblasts that resemble lymphoblasts.
- MPO and SBB positivity in blasts of 3% or more.
- Typically markedly hypercellular marrow.

Immunophenotyping reveals blasts that express at least two myelomonocytic antigens (CD13, CD33, and CD117) and/or MPO. CD34 is often positive. The differential diagnosis includes ALL in cases of AML without maturation with no granules and a low percentage of MPO positive blasts, and AML with maturation in cases of AML with maturation with a high percentage of blasts.
Although no specific chromosomal abnormality has been identified for AML without maturation, mutation of the FLT3 gene has been associated with leukocytosis, a high percentage of bone marrow blast cells, and a worse prognosis.

[3] M2 or acute myeloblastic leukemia (with maturation), one of the two most common subtypes.

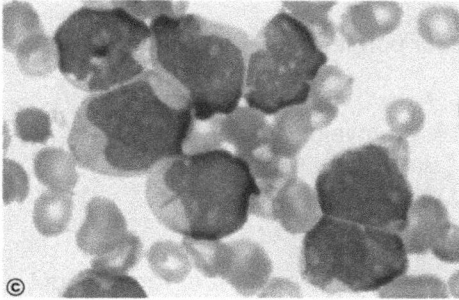

=Atlas of Hematology (Nivaldo Medeiros, MD). Used with permission=

AML with maturation is characterized by 20% or more myeloblasts in the blood or bone marrow and 10% or more neutrophils at different stages of maturation. Monocytes constitute less than 20% of bone marrow cells. This AML comprises approximately 30% to 45% of cases of AML. While it occurs in all age groups, 20% of patients are less than 25 years and 40% of patients are 60 years or older .
Patients frequently present with anemia, thrombocytopenia, and neutropenia.
Morphologic features include the following:
- Myeloblasts with and without azurophilic granules.
- Auer rods.
- Promyelocytes, myelocytes, and neutrophils 10% or more of the bone marrow cells.
- Abnormal nuclear segmentation in neutrophils.
- Increased eosinophil precursors (frequently).
- Hypercellular marrow (usually).
- Blasts and maturing neutrophils reactive with antibodies to MPO and lysozyme.
    With immunophenotyping, the blasts typically express one or more myeloid-associated antigens (CD13, CD33, and CD15). The differential diagnosis includes: RAEB in cases with a low blast percentage, AML without maturation when the blast percentage is high, and AMML in cases with increased monocytes.
    Approximately 33% of karyotypically abnormal cases of AML with maturation are associated with t(8; 21)(q22;q22). Such cases have a favorable prognosis. Rare cases with t(6; 9)(q23; q34) are reported to have a poor prognosis.

[4] M3 or acute promyelocytic leukemia

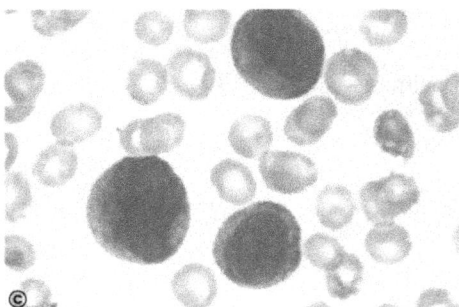

=Atlas of Hematology (Nivaldo Medeiros, MD). Used with permission=

Acute promyelocytic leukemia (APL) AML with t(15; 17)(q22; q12) is an AML in which promyelocytes predominate. APL exists as two types, hypergranular or typical APL and microgranular (hypogranular) APL. APL comprises 5% to 8% of cases of AML and occurs predominately in adults in midlife. Both typical and microgranular APL are commonly associated with disseminated intravascular coagulation

(DIC). In microgranular APL, unlike typical APL, the leukocyte count is very high with a rapid doubling time.

Common morphologic features of typical APL include the following:
- Kidney-shaped or bilobed nuclei.
- Cytoplasm densely packed with large granules (bright pink, red, or purple in Romanowsky stains).
- Bundles of Auer rods within the cytoplasm (faggot cells).
- Larger Auer rods than in other types of AML.
- Strongly positive myeloperoxidase (MPO) reaction in all leukemic promyelocytes.
- Only occasional leukemic promyelocytes in the blood.

Common morphologic features of microgranular APL include the following:
- Bilobed nuclear shape.
- Apparent scarce or absent granules (submicroscopic azurophilic granules).
- Small number of abnormal promyelocytes with visible granules and/or bundles of Auer rods (faggot cells).
- High leukocyte count in the peripheral blood.
- Strongly positive MPO reaction in all leukemic promyelocytes.

APL has a specific sensitivity to treatment with all-trans retinoic acid (ATRA, tretinoin), which acts as a differentiating agent. High complete remission rates in APL may be obtained by combining ATRA treatment with chemotherapy.

[5] M3m or microgranular promyelocytic leukemia (M3V)

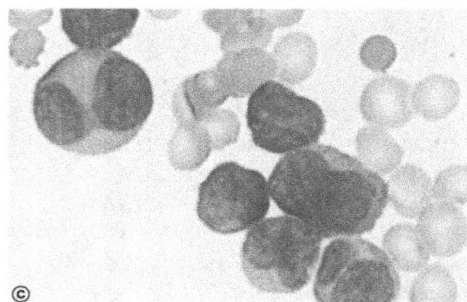

=Atlas of Hematology (Nivaldo Medeiros, MD). Used with permission=

A.   The granules in the promyelocyte are so small that they cannot be resolved in the microscope (requires the electron microscope to discern), therefore the cytoplasm of the cell will appear clear. For this reason the condition is referred to as microgranular not hypogranular.
B.   The nucleus is often reniform or bilobed. Its cytochemistry is similar to M1, M2, and M3.
C.   This type has been confused the M5 (acute monocytic leukemia).
D.   There is also an increased incidence of DIC.
E.   Auer rods may be observed, sometimes in multiple forms (fagot cell).

[6] M4 or acute myelomonocytic leukemia, one of the two most common subtypes.

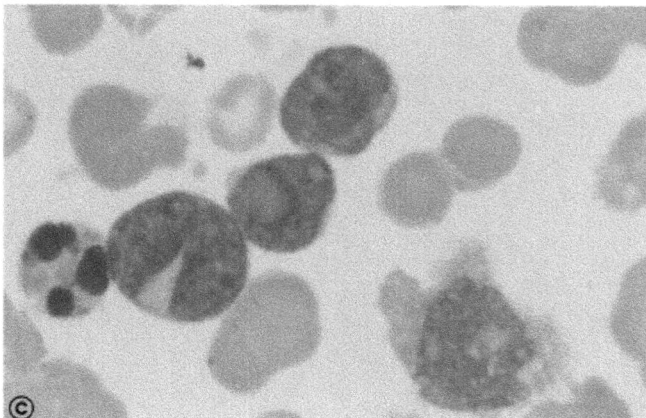

=Atlas of Hematology (Nivaldo Medeiros, MD). Used with permission=

Acute myelomonocytic leukemia (AMML) is characterized by the proliferation of neutrophil and monocyte precursors. Patients usually present with anemia and thrombocytopenia. This classification of AML comprises approximately 15% to 25% of cases of AML, and some patients have a previous history of chronic myelomonocytic leukemia (CMML). This type of AML occurs more commonly in older individuals.

Morphologic and cytochemical features include the following:
- 20% or more blasts in the bone marrow.
- 20% or more neutrophils, monocytes, and their precursors in the bone marrow (to distinguish AMML from AML with or without maturation and to increase monocytes).
- 5 x 10^9/L or more monocytes in the blood.
- Large monoblasts with round nuclei, abundant cytoplasm, and prominent nucleoli.
- MPO positivity in at least 3% of blasts.
- Monoblasts, promonocytes, and monocytes typically nonspecific esterase- (NSE) positive.

Immunophenotyping generally reveals monocytic differentiation markers (CD14, CD4, CD11b, CD11c, CD64, and CD36) and lysozyme. The differential diagnosis includes AML with maturation and acute monocytic leukemia.

Most cases of AMML exhibit nonspecific cytogenetic abnormalities. Some cases may have an 11q23 genetic abnormality. Cases with increased abnormal eosinophils in the bone marrow associated with a chromosome 16 abnormality have a favorable prognosis.

[7] M4E or Acute myelomonocytic leukemia with bone marrow eosinophilia.

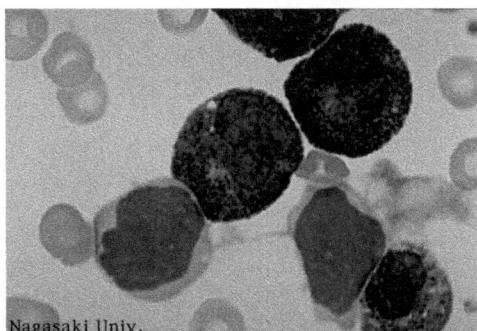

Credit of Nagoya University School of Medicine Department of Medicine the Branch Hospital

A. Similar to M4 except abnormal and immature eosinophils are present in the marrow.

256

B.   Chromosome 16 has an abnormal inversion
C.   This subtype has a better remission rate that M4.

[8] M5a or acute monocytic leukemia poorly differentiated.

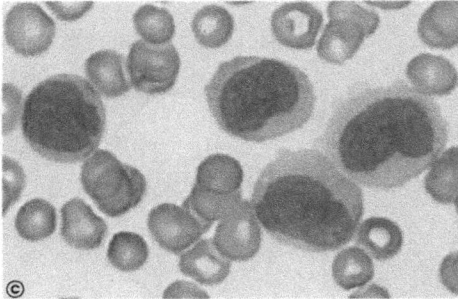

=Atlas of Hematology (Nivaldo Medeiros, MD). Used with permission=

A.   >80% of the bone marrow cells are monoblasts with delicate
      chromatin, at least one prominent nucleoli, abundant blue-gray
      cytoplasm that has the appearance of budding.
B.   The remaining cells tend to be monocytes. Note that a distinguishing
      feature is that promonocytes are seldom observed.
C.   This cell tends to be confused with M1 type acute leukemia.
D. M5a is observed most often in the young adult (median age of 16)

[9] M5b or acute monocytic leukemia well differentiated.

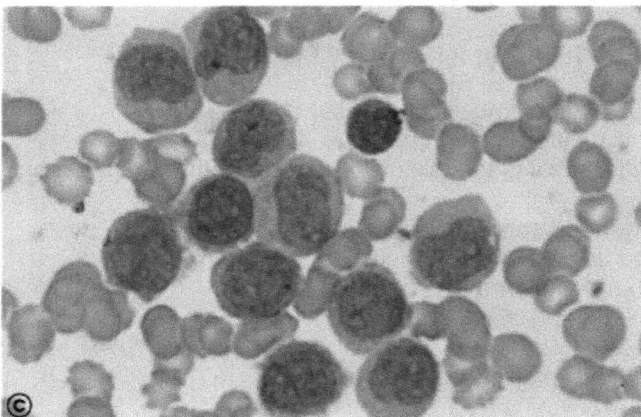

=Atlas of Hematology (Nivaldo Medeiros, MD). Used with permission=

   Acute monoblastic and acute monocytic leukemia are AMLs in which 80% or more of the leukemic
cells are of a monocytic lineage. These cells include monoblasts, promonocytes, and monocytes.
These two leukemias are distinguished by the relative proportions of monoblasts and promonocytes.
In acute monoblastic leukemia, most monocytic cells are monoblasts (usually ≥80%). In acute
monocytic leukemia, most of the monocytic cells are promonocytes. Acute monoblastic leukemia
comprises 5% to 8% of cases of AML and occurs most commonly in young individuals. Acute
monocytic leukemia comprises 3% to 6% of cases and is more common in adults. Common clinical
features for both acute leukemias include bleeding disorders, extramedullary masses, cutaneous and
gingival infiltration, and central nervous system involvement.
Morphologic and cytochemical features of acute monoblastic leukemia include the following:
-Large basophilic monoblasts with abundant cytoplasm, pseudopod formation, round nuclei, and one
or more prominent nucleoli.

- Rare Auer rods.
- Typically intensely NSE positive and MPO negative.
- Hypercellular marrow with large numbers of monoblasts.
- Lysozyme positive.
Morphologic and cytochemical features of acute monocytic leukemia include the following:
- Promonocytes with an irregular nuclear configuration with a moderately basophilic cytoplasm and cytoplasmic azurophilic granules.
- Typically intensely NSE positive.
- Occasional MPO positivity.
- Lysozyme positive.
- Hemophagocytosis (erythrophagocytosis).

 The extramedullary lesions of these leukemias may be predominantly monoblastic or monocytic or an admixture of the two cell types. Immunophenotyping of these leukemias may reveal expression of the myeloid antigens CD13, CD33, CD117, CD14 (+), CD4, CD36, CD 11b, CD11c, CD64, and CD68. The differential diagnosis of acute monoblastic leukemia includes AML without maturation, minimally differentiated AML, and acute megakaryoblastic leukemia. The differential diagnosis of acute monocytic leukemia includes AMML and microgranular APL.
 An abnormal karyotype has been observed in approximately 75% of cases of acute monoblastic leukemia while approximately 30% of cases of acute monocytic leukemia are associated with an abnormal karyotype. Almost 30% of cases of acute monoblastic leukemia and 12% of cases of acute monocytic leukemia are associated with 11q23 genetic abnormalities involving the MLL gene. Mutation of FLT3, a receptor tyrosine kinase gene, has been observed in about 30% of cases of acute monocytic leukemia (approximately 7% in acute monoblastic leukemia). The translocation t(8;16)(p11; p13) (strongly associated with acute monocytic leukemia, Hemophagocytosis by leukemic cells, and a poor response to chemotherapy).

[10] M6 or acute erythroleukemia.

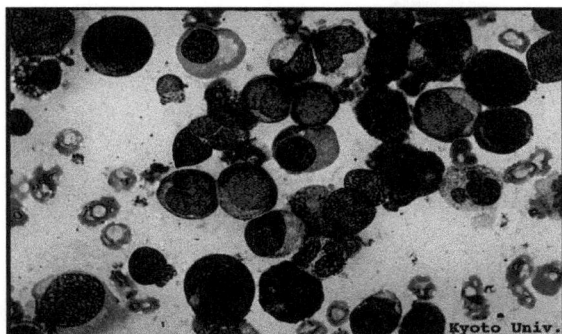

Credit of Nagoya University School of Medicine Department of Medicine the Branch Hospital

	The two subtypes of the acute erythroid leukemias, erythroleukemia and pure erythroid leukemia are characterized by a predominant erythroid population and, in the case of erythroleukemia, the presence of a significant myeloid component. Erythroleukemia (erythroid/myeloid; M6a) is predominantly a disease of adults, comprising approximately 5% to 6% of cases of AML. Pure erythroid leukemia (M6b) is rare and occurs in all age groups. Occasional cases of chronic myeloid leukemia (CML) may evolve to one of the acute erythroid leukemias. Erythroleukemia may present de novo or evolve from an MDS, either RAEB or RCMD-RS or RCMD.

Morphologic and cytochemical features of erythroleukemia include the following:
- 50% or more erythroid precursors in the entire nucleated cell population of the bone marrow.
- 20% or more myeloblasts in the nonerythroid population in the bone marrow.
- Dysplastic erythroid precursors with megaloblastoid nuclei.
- Multinucleated erythroid cells.
- Myeloblasts of medium size, occasionally with Auer rods.
- Ringed sideroblasts.
- Positive PAS stain in the erythroid precursors.
- Hypercellular bone marrow.

- Megakaryocytic dysplasia.

Morphologic and cytochemical features of pure erythroid leukemia include the following:
- Medium- to large-sized erythroblasts with round nuclei, fine chromatin, one or more nucleoli, deeply basophilic cytoplasm, and occasional coalescent vacuoles.
- Erythroblasts reactive with alpha-naphthyl acetate esterase
- Acid phosphatase
- PAS.

   Immunophenotyping in erythroleukemia reveals erythroblasts that react with antibodies to Glycophorin A and hemoglobin A and myeloblasts that express a variety of myeloid-associated antigens (CD13, CD33, CD117, c-kit, and MPO). Immunophenotyping in acute erythroid leukemia reveals expression of Glycophorin A and hemoglobin A in differentiated forms. Markers such as carbonic anhydrase 1, Gero antibody against the Gerbich blood group, or CD36 are usually positive. The differential diagnosis for erythroleukemia includes RAEB and AML with maturation with increased erythroid precursors and AML with multilineage dysplasia (involving ≥50% of myeloid or megakaryocyte-lineage cells). If erythroid precursors are 50% or more and the nonerythroid component is 20% or more, the diagnosis is erythroleukemia, whereas, if the nonerythroid component is less than 20%, the diagnosis is RAEB. The differential diagnosis for pure erythroid leukemia includes megaloblastic anemia secondary to vitamin B_{12} or folate deficiency, acute megakaryocytic leukemia, and ALL or lymphoma.

[11] M7 or acute megakaryocytic leukemia.

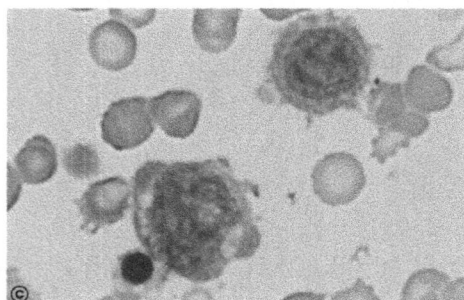

=Atlas of Hematology (Nivaldo Medeiros, MD). Used with permission=

   Acute megakaryoblastic leukemia, in which 50% or more of blasts are of the megakaryocyte lineage, occurs in all age groups and comprises approximately 3% to 5% of cases of AML. Clinical features include cytopenias; dysplastic changes in neutrophils and platelets; rare organomegaly, except in children with t(1; 22); lytic bone lesions in children; and association with mediastinal germ cell tumors in young adult males.
Morphologic and cytochemical features include the following:
- Medium- to large-sized megakaryoblasts with round or indented nucleus and one or more nucleoli.
- Agranular, basophilic cytoplasm with pseudopod formation.
- Lymphoblast-like morphology (high nuclear-cytoplasmic ratio) in some cases.
- Circulating micromegakaryocytes, megakaryoblastic fragments, dysplastic large platelets, and hypogranular neutrophils.
- Stromal pattern of marrow infiltration mimicking a metastatic tumor in infants.
Negative stains for SBB and MPO.
- Blasts reactive with PAS, acid phosphatase, and nonspecific esterase.
   Immunophenotyping reveals megakaryoblasts expression of one or more platelet glycoproteins: CD41 (glycoprotein IIb/IIIa) and/or CD61 (glycoprotein IIIa). Myeloid markers CD13 and CD33 may be positive; CD36 is typically positive. Blasts are negative with the anti-MPO antibody and other markers of myeloid differentiation. In bone marrow biopsies, megakaryocytes and megakaryoblasts may react positively to antibodies for Factor VIII. The differential diagnosis includes minimally differentiated AML, acute panmyelosis with myelofibrosis, ALL, pure erythroid leukemia, and blastic transformation of

chronic myeloid leukemia or idiopathic myelofibrosis and metastatic tumors in the bone marrow (particularly in children).

.

[12]-Myeloid sarcoma

Myeloid sarcoma (also known as extramedullary myeloid tumor, granulocytic sarcoma, and chloroma) is a tumor mass that consists of myeloblasts or immature myeloid cells, occurring in an extramedullary site; development in 2% to 8% of patients with AML has been reported. Clinical features include occurrence common in subperiosteal bone structures of the skull, paranasal sinuses, sternum, ribs, vertebrae, and pelvis; lymph nodes, skin, mediastinum, small intestine, and the epidural space; and occurrence de novo or concomitant with AML or a myeloproliferative disorder.
Morphologic and cytochemical features include the following:
- Granulocytic sarcoma composed of myeloblasts, neutrophils, and neutrophil precursors with three subtypes based on degree of maturation (i.e., blastic, immature, and differentiated).
- Monoblastic sarcoma preceding or occurring simultaneously with acute monoblastic leukemia.
- Tumors with trilineage hematopoiesis occurring with transformation of chronic myeloproliferative disorders.
- Myeloblasts and neutrophils positive for MPO.
- Neutrophils positive for naphthol ASD chloroacetate esterase.
Immunophenotyping with antibodies to MPO, lysozyme, and chloroacetate are critical to the diagnosis of these lesions. The myeloblasts in granulocytic sarcomas express myeloid-associated antigens (CD13, CD33, CD117, and MPO). The monoblasts in monoblastic sarcomas express acute monoblastic leukemia antigens (CD14, CD116, and CD11c) and usually react with antibodies to lysozyme and CD68. The main differential diagnosis includes non-Hodgkin lymphoma of the lymphoblastic type, Burkitt lymphoma, large-cell lymphoma, and small round cell tumors, especially in children (e.g., Neuroblastoma, Rhabdomyosarcoma, Ewing/primitive neuroectodermal tumors, and Medulloblastoma).

[13]- Acute Leukemias of Ambiguous Lineage

Acute leukemias of ambiguous lineage (also known as acute leukemias of undetermined lineage, mixed phenotype acute leukemias, mixed lineage acute leukemias, and hybrid acute leukemias) are types of acute leukemia in which the morphologic, cytochemical, and immunophenotypic features of the blast population do not allow classification in myeloid or lymphoid categories; or the types have morphologic and/or immunophenotypic features of both myeloid and lymphoid cells or both B and T lineages (i.e., acute bilineal leukemia and acute biphenotypic leukemia). These rare leukemias account for less than 4% of all cases of acute leukemia and occur in all age groups but are more frequent in adults. Clinical features include symptoms and complications caused by cytopenias, i.e., fatigue, infections, and bleeding disorders.
Morphologic and immunophenotypic features of these acute leukemias include the following:
- Undifferentiated acute leukemia in which the leukemic cells lack any differentiating characteristics and lack markers for a given lineage.
- Bilineal acute leukemia in which a dual population of blasts exhibits morphologic features and markers of two distinct lineages, i.e., myeloid and lymphoid or B and T.
Biphenotypic acute leukemia in which the blasts exhibit the morphological features of only one lineage but express markers of more than one lineage.
The differential diagnosis includes myeloid antigen-positive ALL or lymphoid-positive AML (from which biphenotypic acute leukemia should be distinguished) and minimally differentiated AML (from which undifferentiated acute leukemia must be distinguished).
Cytogenetic abnormalities are observed in a high percentage of bilineal and biphenotypic leukemias. Approximately 33% of cases have the Philadelphia chromosome, and some cases are associated with t(4; 11)(q21; q23) or other 11q23 abnormalities. In general, the prognosis appears to be unfavorable, particularly in adults; the occurrence of the translocation t(4; 11) or the Philadelphia chromosome are especially unfavorable prognostic indicators.

[14]- Acute Myeloid Leukemia with Multilineage Dysplasia

In the WHO classification, refractory anemia with excess blasts in transformation (RAEB-t) is no longer considered a distinct clinical entity and is instead included within the broader category "AML with multilineage dysplasia" as one of the following:
- AML evolving from an MDS.
- AML following an MDS.
AML with multilineage dysplasia is characterized by 20% or more blasts in the blood or bone marrow and dysplasia in two or more myeloid cell lines, generally including megakaryocytes. To make the diagnosis, dysplasia must be present in 50% or more of the cells of at least two lineages and must be present in a pretreatment bone marrow specimen. AML with multilineage dysplasia may occur de novo or following MDS or a myelodysplastic and myeloproliferative disorder (MDS and MPD). The diagnostic terminology "AML with multilineage dysplasia evolving from a myelodysplastic syndrome" should be used when an MDS precedes AML.

This category of AML occurs primarily in older patients. Patients with this type of AML frequently present with severe pancytopenia.
Common morphologic features include the following:
- Multilineage dysplasia in the blood or bone marrow.
- Dysplasia in 50% or more of the cells of two or more cell lines.
- Dysgranulopoiesis (neutrophils with hypogranular cytoplasm, hyposegmented nuclei or bizarrely segmented nuclei).
- Dyserythropoiesis (megaloblastic nuclei, karyorrhexis, or multinucleation of erythroid precursors and ringed sideroblasts).
- Dysmegakaryopoiesis (micromegakaryocytes and normal size or large megakaryocytes with monolobed or multiple separated nuclei).

The differential diagnosis of AML with multilineage dysplasia includes acute erythroid-myeloid leukemia and acute myeloblastic leukemia with maturation (FAB classifications M6a and M2). Some cases may overlap two morphologic types.
As evidenced in several Southwest Oncology Group studies, such as SWOG-8600 and SWOG-9031. The numerous chromosome abnormalities observed in AML with multilineage dysplasia are similar to those found in MDS and frequently involve gain or loss of major segments of certain chromosomes, predominately chromosomes 5 and/or 7. The probability of achieving a complete remission has been reported to be affected adversely by a diagnosis of AML with multilineage dysplasia.

[15] -Acute Myeloid Leukemias and Myelodysplastic Syndromes, Therapy-Related

This category includes AML and MDS that arise secondary to cytotoxic chemotherapy and/or radiation therapy. The therapy-related (or secondary) MDS are included because of their close clinicopathologic relationships to therapy-related AML. Although these therapy-related disorders are distinguished by the specific mutagenic agents involved, a recent study suggests this distinction may be difficult to make because of the frequent overlapping use of multiple potentially mutagenic agents in treating cancer.

The alkylating agent/radiation-related acute leukemias and myelodysplastic syndromes typically occur 5 to 6 years following exposure to the mutagenic agent, with a reported range of approximately 10 to 192 months. The risk for occurrence is related to both the total cumulative dose of the alkylating agent and the age of the patient. Clinically, the disorder commonly presents initially as an MDS with evidence of bone marrow failure. This stage is followed by dysplastic features in multiple cell lineages with a blast percentage that is usually less than 5%. In the MDS phase, approximately 66% of cases satisfy the criteria for refractory cytopenia with multilineage dysplasia (RCMD), with approximately 33% of these cases exhibiting ringed sideroblasts in excess of 15% (RCMD-RS). Another 25% of cases satisfy the criteria for refractory anemia with excess blasts 1 or 2 (RAEB-1; RAEB-2). The MDS phase may evolve to a higher grade MDS or AML. Although a minority of patients may present with acute leukemia, a substantial number of patients succumb to the disorder in the MDS phase.
Common morphologic features include the following:
- Panmyelosis.
- Dysgranulopoiesis.
- Dyserythropoiesis.
- Ringed sideroblasts (60% of cases; >15% in 33% of cases).
- Hypercellular bone marrow (50% of cases).

Cases may correspond morphologically to acute myeloid leukemia with maturation, acute monocytic leukemia, AMML, erythroleukemia, or acute megakaryoblastic leukemia (FAB classifications M2, M5b, M4, M6a, and M7, respectively).

Immunophenotyping of AML Cells

Marker	Lineage
CD13	Myeloid
CD33	Myeloid
CD34	Early precursor
HLA-DR	Positive in most AML, negative in APL
CD11b	Mature monocytes
CD14	Monocytes
CD41	Platelet glycoprotein IIb/IIIa complex
CD42a	Platelet glycoprotein IX
CD42b	Platelet glycoprotein Ib
CD61	Platelet glycoprotein IIa
Glycophorin A	Erythroid
TdT	Usually indicates acute lymphocytic leukemia, however, may be positive in M0 or M1
CD11c	Myeloid
CD117 (c-kit)	Myeloid/stem cell
CD56	NK-cell/stem cell

Laboratory findings

 * CBC count with differential demonstrates anemia and thrombocytopenia to varying degrees. Patients with acute myelogenous leukemia (AML) can have high, normal, or low WBC counts.
 * Prothrombin time/activated partial thromboplastin time/fibrinogen/fibrin degradation products. The most common abnormality is disseminated intravascular coagulation (DIC), which results in an elevated prothrombin time, a decreasing fibrinogen level, and the presence of fibrin split products. Acute promyelocytic leukemia (APL), also known as M3, is the most common subtype of AML associated with DIC.
 * Peripheral blood smear
Review of peripheral blood smear confirms the findings of the CBC count. Circulating blasts are usually seen. Schistocytes are occasionally seen if DIC is present.
*Chemistry profile
 Most patients with AML have an elevated lactic dehydrogenase level and, frequently, an elevated uric acid level.
Liver function tests and BUN/creatinine level tests are necessary prior to the initiation of therapy. Appropriate cultures should be obtained in patients with fever or signs of infection, even in the absence of fever.
Perform HLA or DNA typing in patients who are potential candidates for allogeneic transplantation.
*Bone marrow aspiration
 A blast count can be performed with bone marrow aspiration. Historically, by French-American-British (FAB) classification, AML was defined by the presence of more than 30% blasts in bone marrow. In the newer World Health Organization (WHO) classification, AML is defined as the presence of greater than 20% blasts in the marrow.
 The bone marrow aspirate also allows evaluation of the degree of dysplasia in all cell lines.
*Flow cytometry (Immunophenotyping) can be used to help distinguish AML from acute lymphocytic leukemia (ALL) and further classify the subtype of AML. The immunophenotype correlates with prognosis in some instances.
*Cytogenetic studies performed on bone marrow provide important prognostic information and are useful to confirm a diagnosis of APL, which bears the t(15;17) and is treated differently.

Adult Acute Myeloid Leukemia in Remission

Adult acute myeloid leukemia (AML) in remission is defined as a normal peripheral blood cell count (absolute neutrophil count >1,000/mm^3 and platelet count >100,000/mm^3) and normocellular marrow with less than 5% blasts in the marrow and no signs or symptoms of the disease. In addition, no signs or symptoms are evident of central nervous system leukemia or other extramedullary infiltration. Because the vast majority of AML patients meeting these criteria for remission have residual leukemia, modifications to the definition of complete remission have been suggested, including cytogenetic remission, in which a previously abnormal karyotype reverts to normal, and molecular remission, in which interphase fluorescence in situ hybridization (FISH) or multiparameter flow cytometry are used to detect minimal residual disease. Immunophenotyping and interphase FISH have greater prognostic significance than the conventional criteria for remission.

Cytochemical stains

7-1 Myeloperoxidase stain
This is dependent upon the peroxidase enzyme found in the primary granules of granulocytes, eosinophils, and (to a lesser degree) in monocytes. In the granulocyte cell line, this enzyme is found in the promyelocyte and subsequent stages. This enzyme should be designated as myeloperoxidase (MPO) to differentiate it from other cellular peroxidases. The neutrophil line of cells will give the strongest peroxidase reaction. The value of this stain lies in differentiating acute myeloid leukemia (FAB type M1, M2, and M3) from acute lymphocytic leukemia. As a rule, more than 80% of the myeloid blast cells will be peroxidase positive. Auer rods are also emphasized with this stain. Lymphocytic blasts are negative, that is <3% of the blast cells demonstrate some degree of peroxidase activity. Monocytes will be weakly or diffusely positive. The fact that the more mature granulocytes are peroxidase positive does not contribute to the diagnosis. It is the immature forms that are diagnostic. Look for a blue-black precipitate that is identified as coarse granulation in the cytoplasm of cells. Note: Early myeloblasts, rubriblasts, lymphoblasts, mature basophils, and plasma cells are myeloperoxidase negative.

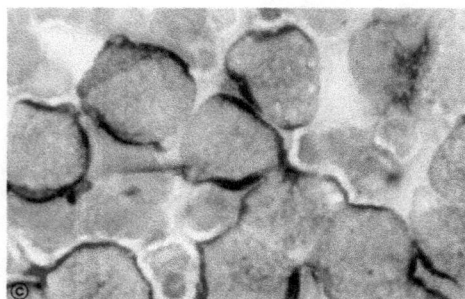

ACUTE MYELOID LEUKEMIA (AML-M2 + PEROXIDASE)
=Atlas of Hematology (Nivaldo Medeiros, MD). Used with permission=

Interpretation is as follows:

[01]   Look for positive activity in the more mature cells. Generally, the reactivity in the mature cells (bands and 'segs') is not significant in differentiating acute leukemias.
[02]   Monocyte peroxidase activity will be slight (weakly positive). In acute monocytic leukemia, the monoblasts are usually negative. The positive reactions are noted in the more mature monocytes.
[03]   Auer rods are strongly peroxidase positive. This stain readily demonstrates their presence.
[04]   Eosinophilic granules are strongly peroxidase positive.
[05]   The following cells are usually peroxidase negative:
   A. early myeloblasts
   B. Erythroblasts
   C. Lymphocytes
   D. Mature basophils
   E. Plasma cells

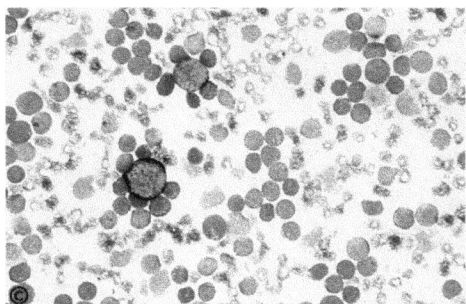

(ALL-L2) NEGATIVE PEROXIDASE

=Atlas of Hematology (Nivaldo Medeiros, MD). Used with permission=

7-2 Sudan Black B stain

   Sudan Black B (SBB) stain is a lipid soluble dye. Cells that stain with SBB are designated as sudanophilic, the lipids are found in the primary, secondary, and tertiary granules of the granulocytes. Lipids are found in the lysosomal granules of monocytes and macrophages, but to a lesser extent. Myelocytic cells stain most strongly and monocytes are weakly or diffusely staining. Early myeloblasts, lymphocyte series, erythrocyte series, mature basophils, and platelets are negative for the SBB stain. Note: Burkitt's lymphoma cells have been found to be sudanophilic. The presence of brown-black granules in the cytoplasm is positive for SBB stain. This procedure is useful to differentiate acute myelocytic leukemia form acute lymphocytic leukemia.

   Observations regarding SBB are: [1] peripheral smears, bone marrow slides, fresh capillary slides, and slides made for EDTA, Heparinized, or oxalated bloods are suitable to this staining technique. [2] If the SBB stain is old, increase the staining time. [3] Hematoxylin or Giemsa stains are satisfactory as a counterstained.
7-3 Periodic Acid-Schiff stain
   Periodic acid-Schiff (PAS) stain detects the presence of intracellular glycogen. This stain detects muco-proteins, glycoproteins, and high molecular weight polysaccharides. A positive stain is a cell with a fuschia-pink color. Staining reactions are as follows:
[01] Eosinophil granules do not take up the stain, but the cytoplasmic background
        stains positively. This is a normal finding.
[02] Early granulocytes show weak staining reactions, but the more mature forms react
        strongly.
[03] Lymphocytes stain positive with varying degrees of intensity and patterns. The
        staining reaction is usually weak.
[04] Megakaryocytes and platelets stain positively with varying degrees of intensity
        and patterns.
[05] Monocytes stain positively with varying degrees of intensity and patterns. The
        stain is usually a weak positive.
[06] Nucleated red blood cells are negative, EXCEPT in patients with thalassemia
        and erythroleukemia (DiGuglielmo's disease).
[07] Basophils stain positive.
 The PAS reaction in abnormal hematological cells are as follows:
[A] The erythroblast (in M6 erythroleukemia) stains positive.
[B] The lymphoblast (in 80% of ALL cases) is positive.
[C] The myeloblast (in 10% of the AML cases) is positive.
   In the PAS reaction, complex carbohydrates are oxidized to aldehydes to yield a red--colored insoluble precipitate (aldehyde-fuscin-sulphurous acid molecule). Basic fuscin is responsible for the red color.

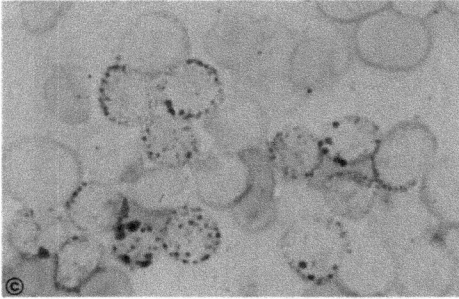

(ALL-L2) POSITIVE-PAS
=Atlas of Hematology (Nivaldo Medeiros, MD). Used with permission=

The procedure requires fixing the slides, followed by a rinsing sequence, after which the slides are treated with periodic acid. Stain in Schiff's reagent, rinse, and then counter stain with hematoxylin. Coverslip with permount (or its equivalent) and examine.

Comments regarding this stain: [1] the mature neutrophils on the slide may be used as positive controls. [2] If the patient is diagnosed with Burkitt's leukemia, the lymphoblasts will be PAS negative. [3] A Wright's stained smear (even if years old) may be PAS stained. [4] Schiff's reagent is colorless or light yellow. Add a drop to 37% formalin, if a purple color, then the reagent is okay, otherwise discard. If the Schiff's reagent turns pink, discard. [5] PAS stain should not be used to try to differentiate types of leukemia. There is too much variability in the staining reactions to be reliable.

7-4 Leukocyte alkaline phosphate (LAP) stain

Synonyms: alkaline phosphatase score, alkaline phosphatase cytochemical test, and alkaline phosphatase activity of neutrophils. Leukocyte alkaline phosphatase (LAP) enzyme is found in the cytoplasmic of mature neutrophils (neutrophil, band, and metamyelocyte) and this feature is used to differentiate a Leukemoid reaction from chronic myelogenous leukemia. LAP activity increases as the granulocyte matures. The enzyme is found in the tertiary (microvesiuclar) granules of the neutrophil. The quantity of LAP enzyme varies within the neutrophil in various diseases. LAP score values range from a low of zero to a maximum of 400. The normal value rage is 13 to 100. Disorders with values less than 13 are chronic granulocytic leukemia, acute granulocytic leukemia, marked eosinophilia, paroxysmal hemoglobinuria, sideroblastic anemia, hereditary hypophosphatasia, infectious mononucleosis, and sickle cell anemia. Values less than 13 have been reported in normal individuals. Elevated LAP scores may be observed in neutrophilic Leukemoid reactions, last trimester of pregnancy, corticosteroid therapy, multiple myeloma, polycythemia vera, obstructive jaundice, myelofibrosis, and meningitis.

A blood specimen, fingersticks or heparinized specimens, is collected, smears prepared and air dried. The smear is fixed in an acetone and citrate buffer, and then stained in freshly prepared staining solution at a temperature between 18°C and 26°C. Smears may be counterstained in hematoxylin. The patient's smear should be stained along with a negative/normal and positive control to validate the staining characteristics. The blood from a woman in the 3rd trimester or a female on oral contraceptives will provide a positive control and the blood from a healthy individual will serve for a normal control.

To perform the LAP score, count 100 neutrophils and bands. Grade the degree of staining as follows:
[01]   Zero = no evidence of stain,
[02]   1+ = slight staining, very diffuse and faint without distinctive granular
                appearance,
[03]   2+ = pale stain with small amount of granular appearance,
[04]   3+ = strong coloration, with moderate granular appearance,
[05]   4+ = intense coloration with large amount of granular, practically obscuring the
        cytoplasm.

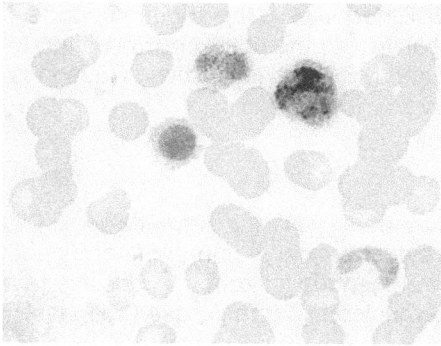

The top two neutrophils in this image are scored as 1 and 2+ respectively while the bottom neutrophil is scored as 0 (no cytoplasmic staining). Note the nucleated RBC next to the top two neutrophils does not stain.

The test principle employs a substrate, such as naphthol AS-BI phosphate, which is hydrolyzed in the presence of leukocyte alkaline phosphatase enzyme. The hydrolyzed substrate complexes with a dye that precipitates at the site of enzyme activity. When performing a LAP test, use slides with a monolayer, so that the neutrophils do not touch the RBC's. If a thick slide is used, it is very likely to falsely elevate the LAP score. Do not attempt to include cells other than neutrophils and bands in the count. The slides once made, tend to deteriorate quickly. Perform the LAP score evaluation quickly. Do not allow the stained slides to remain in direct light. Control slides can be prepared and held ahead of time if fixed and wrapped in a plastic film such as parafilm. Store such slides in a -70°C freezer. If the lab uses commercial LAP staining kits, follow the manufacturer's directions closely. Note normal value may vary from lab to lab. Other normal values reported are [1] 11 to 95 and [2] 30 to 185.

LEUKOCYTE ALKALINE PHOSPHATE SCORE

100 neutrophils and bands are counted and each cell is graded 0 to 4+. Step one: multiply the number of cells in each LAP grade times its rating. Add the scores in the five categories to determine the LAP score. See the following example.

grade	# cells counted	value calculated
0	30	0
1+	35	35
2+	20	40
3+	10	30
4+	5	20
	Total score	125

This test should be reported out as abnormal when using the normal range as 13 to 100. Negative/normal and positive controls should also be reported.

7-5 α-Naphthol AS-D Esterase stain

Also designated as specific esterase (SE) stain, this reagent stain is specific for early myeloid cells. It advantage lies in identify precursor cells in myelogenous leukemia. It is used it identify M1, M2, M3, and M5 acute leukemias. The myeloblasts usually stain positive. The dye stains the neutrophil line strongly, but the monocyte line is weakly or diffusely stained. Auer rods are well stained by this technique.

7-6 α-Naphthol butyrate stain

Also designated as nonspecific esterase (NSE) stain, this reagent stain is less sensitive than α-naphthol AS-D stain, but it is more specific. Its value lies in identifying early monocytes and macrophages if used with a sodium fluoride inhibition step. Macrophages, plasma cells, monocyte, and megakaryocytes are NSE positive. Granulocytes tend to be NSE negative. If the sodium fluoride step is added, the macrophages and monocytes become NSE negative, but the other NSE positive cells remain positive. This stain is advantageous in identifying M4 and M5 acute leukemias. Caution is to be used in interpreting this stain. T-lymphocytes can stain positive.

7-7 Terminal Deoxynucleotidyl Transferase

Terminal deoxynucleotidyl transferase (TdT) is a nuclear enzyme that is present in immature (precursor) B- and T-lymphocytes and stem cells. It is an immuno cytochemical or immunofluorescent technique to distinguish acute lymphocytic leukemia from acute myelogenous leukemia. A positive test is indicated by a staining pattern of the nucleus. The terminal deoxynucleotidyl transferase (TdT) test is a means of identifying
lymphoblasts (primitive lymphoid cells). This is an enzyme, deoxyribonucleic acid polymerase, found in the nucleus of pre-B lymphocytes and T lymphoblasts. This enzyme identifies L1 and L2 acute leukemias. This test can differentiate acute lymphocytic leukemia from acute myelogenous leukemia. There are three methods used to assay TdT: immunofluorescence, immuno peroxidase technology, and radioimmunoassay.
Conduct the test as-soon-as-possible. Do not stain if the slide is over seven days old. Fix the test slides, then rinse and hydrate in a phosphate buffer solution. Apply antibody to the slide and incubate for 30 minutes. Rinse. Apply the second antibody and incubate for 30 minutes. Rinse, dry, and prepare for examination. The nuclei of positive cells will fluorescence at 496 nm.
Record degree of fluorescence from zero to 4+

CHAPTER THREE: CHRONIC MYELOPROLIFERATIF DISORDERS

Chronic Idiopathic Myelofibrosis (CIMF)

Synonyms: Agnogenic Myeloid metaplasia, primary myelofibrosis, aleukemic myelosis, splenomegalic myelophthisis, and leukoerythroblastic anemia. Myelofibrosis is a chronic myeloproliferative disorder characterized by an unchecked proliferation of hemopoietic elements. Involvement may include one, two, or three cell lines (erythrocytes, granulocytes, and/or platelets). Usually only one or two cell lines are involved. This is a progressive bone marrow fibrosis that occurs secondary to the abnormal cell line. It can be very severe. Fibroblasts appear and give rise to reticulin (type III collagen) and other collagen fibers. Splenic enlargement occurs due to the spleen assuming an extramedullary role in hemopoiesis. Islands of proliferating erythroid, myeloid, and megakaryocyte elements appear. This is seen in 85% of the cases. Hepatomegaly occurs for the same reason and is observed in 50% of the cases.

> Myelophthisis describes the replacement of normal bone marrow tissue with abnormal tissue.

This disorder occurs in middle aged or older adults. 60% of the cases appear in individual between 50 to 70 years of age. There is no gender preference. When the disease onset, the following symptoms appear over time and cause the patient to seek the assistance of the physician: [1] gouty arthritis, [2] increased abdominal girth due to hepatosplenomegaly, [3] bone pain, [4] petechiae (seen in 25% of patients), [5] jaundice (about a 15% occurrence), [6] ascites (about 15% occurrence), [7] weight loss, and [8] pallor.   Expected laboratory findings include:
[1] Mild to moderate normocytic/normochromic anemia (hemoglobin ranges from 9 to 13 g/dL).
[2] Reticulocytosis = 2 - 15% (counts of 60,000/μL reported).
[3] Increased Polychromatophilia (correlates with retic count) as disease progresses.
[4] RBC morphology changes:
A. In beginning states, Dacryocytes are characteristic and distinctive feature.
B. As diseases progresses, severe anisocytosis and poikilocytosis appear.
C. Increased basophilic stippling with progression.
D. Normoblastosis with progression
[5] WBC counts = variable. Counts are decreased in 15% of cases, normal in 33% of cases, and elevated in 52% of cases. Elevated counts range from 15,000 to 30,000/μL and counts of 70,000/μL have been reported.
[6] WBC morphology.
A. Immature granulocytes are the rule with up to 10% blasts.
B. False Pelger-Huet.
C. Basophilia
D. Eosinophilia
[7] Platelet counts are variable, being higher in the early stages and thrombocytopenia developing in the later stages. Morphologically, micro-megacaryocytes, naked megacaryocytes, and megakaryocyte fragments have been reported. The platelet and megakaryocyte observations are important in differentiating this disorder.
[8] Other lab findings include:
 [A] Increased uric acid
 [B] Increased LDH.
[9] Bone marrow biopsies are required for diagnosis. Aspirates are difficult and "dry taps" are not uncommon. A bone marrow specimen that presents with a sectional area with fibrosis is required for positive diagnosis.
[10] Cytogenetics: The Ph[1] chromosome is not present, but deletions of the long arm of chromosome 13 are reported.

Polycythemia Vera

Polycythemia is the increase of the red blood cell count, hemoglobin, and total red blood cell volume, accompanied by an increase in total blood volume. This must be distinguished from relative erythrocytosis secondary to fluid loss or decreased intake; this distinction can be made easily on a clinical basis. Polycythemia accompanies increased total blood volume, whereas relative erythrocytosis does not. Two basic categories of polycythemia exist:
Primary polycythemias are due to factors intrinsic to red cell precursors and include the diagnoses of primary familial and congenital polycythemia (PFCP) and polycythemia Vera (PV).
Secondary polycythemias are caused by factors extrinsic to red cell precursors.

Earlier diagnostic criteria for polycythemia Vera included the following (based on the Polycythemia Vera Study Group Diagnostic Criteria):
Red cell mass greater than 36 mL/kg for men and greater than 32 mL/kg for women
Arterial oxygen saturation greater than 92%
Splenomegaly or 2 of the following:
Thrombocytosis greater than 400×10^9/L
Leukocytosis greater than 12×10^9/L
Leukocyte alkaline phosphatase activity greater than 120 U/L in adults (reference range, 30-100 U/L) without fever or infection
Serum vitamin B-12 greater than 900 pg/mL (reference range, 130-785 pg/mL)
Unsaturated vitamin B-12 binding capacity greater than 2200 pg/mL
Polycythemia Vera (PV) is a stem cell disorder characterized as a panhyperplastic, malignant and neoplastic marrow disorder. The most prominent feature of this disease is an elevated absolute red blood cell mass because of uncontrolled red blood cell production. This is accompanied by increased white blood cell (myeloid) and platelet (megakaryocytic) production, which is due to an abnormal clone of the hematopoietic stem cells with increased sensitivity to the different growth factors for maturation.
Several reasons suggest that a mutation on the Janus kinase-2 gene (JAK2) is the most likely candidate gene involved in PV pathogenesis since JAK2 is directly involved in the intracellular signaling following exposure to cytokines to which PV progenitor cells display hypersensitivity. A recurrent unique acquired clonal mutation in JAK2 was recently found in most patients with PV and other myeloproliferative diseases (MPDs) including essential thrombocythemia and idiopathic myelofibrosis. A unique valine to phenylalanine substitution at position 617 (V617F) in the pseudokinase JAK2 domain has been identified called JAK2 V617F leading to a permanently turned on signaling at the affected cytokine receptors. How these mutations interact with the wild type kinase genes and how they manifest into different forms of MPDs need to be elucidated.
* Sites of Involvement
- Bone marrow
- Peripheral blood
- Liver (extramedullary hematopoiesis)
- Spleen (extramedullary hematopoiesis)
* WHO Criteria
- A_1: RBCs >25% above normal, or Hb >18.5g/dL in men and 16.5g/dL in women
- A_2: No cause of secondary erythrocytosis (Hypoxia, abnormal Hb, familial conditions)
- A_3: Splenomegaly
- A_4: Clonal genetic abnormalities (but not Ph+)
- A_5: Endogenous erythroid colony formation in vitro

- B_1: Thrombocytosis >400×10^9/L
- B_2: WBCs >12×10^9/L
- B_3: BM Bx with panmyelosis, erythroid and megakaryocytic hyperplasia
- B_4: Low serum erythropoietin levels

* Diagnosis of Polycythemia Vera
- $A_1 + A_2$ and any other category A, or
- $A_1 + A_2$ and any two of category B

* Clinical Features
- Thrombosis (25%)
- Hemorrhage

- Stroke
- Plethora (70%)
- Splenomegaly (70%)
- Hepatomegaly (40%)
- Leukocyte Alkaline Phosphatase (LAP): normal

* Polycythemic Stage
- Erythroid proliferation in BM
- Normochromic, normocytic RBCs in PB
- If bleeding, RBCs hypochromic and microcytic
- Neutrophilia
- Basophilia
- Thrombocytosis (>50%)
- BM cellularity 35-100% (median 80%)
- Panmyelosis (Erythroid, granulocytic, and megakaryocytic proliferation)
- Blasts not increased
- Megakaryocytes: increased, clustered (parasinusoidal and paratrabecular); sinusoids dilated, pleomorphic, nuclear hyperlobulation, but not dysplastic
- No stainable iron in 95% of cases
- Only 30% with fibrosis (reticulin increased)
- Spleen and liver congested
- Extramedullary hematopoiesis: minimal
- 10-50% progress to fibrotic stage

* "Spent" Phase - Post-Polycythemic Myelofibrosis and Myeloid Metaplasia
- Red cell mass decreases
- BM cellularity decreases
- BM fibrosis (reticulin and collagen increased)
- Splenomegaly - Extramedullary hematopoiesis
- Leukoerythroblastic blood smear: RBC poikilocytosis with tear-drop cells, NRBCs, immature granulocytes
- Megakaryocytes still prominent and clustered
* Prognosis
PV is a chronic disease, and its natural history of 1.5-3 years of median survival in the absence of therapy has been extended to at least 10-20 years because of new therapeutic tools. The major causes of morbidity and mortality are as follows:
Thrombosis has been reported in 15-60% of patients, depending on the control of their disease. It is the major cause of death in 10-40% of patients. Venous and arterial thromboses have resulted in pulmonary emboli, renal failure from renal vein or artery thrombosis, intestinal ischemia from mesenteric vein thromboses, or peripheral arterial emboli.
Hemorrhagic complications occur in 15-35% of patients and lead to death in 6-30% of these patients. Bleeding is usually the consequence of vascular compromise resulting from ischemic changes from thrombosis or hyperviscosity.
Peptic ulcer disease is reported to be associated with PV at a 3- to 5-fold higher rate than that of the general population. This has been attributed to increased histamine serum levels.
Myelofibrosis and pancytopenia occur in 3-10% of patients, usually late in the disease, which is considered the spent phase of PV. In these patients, infections and bleeding complications may be the most serious health threats, and red blood cell transfusions may be required to maintain adequate red blood cell counts and to improve fatigue and other anemia-related symptoms. Persistently elevated platelet counts are associated with increased risk of developing myelofibrosis. Development of myelofibrosis does not have adverse prognostic implications if increased reticulin is an isolated finding, but spent phase with extramedullary hematopoiesis is associated with a poor prognosis.
Acute leukemia or a myelodysplastic syndrome develops in 1.5% of patients treated with phlebotomy alone. The transformation risks increase to 13.5% within 5 years with treatment using chlorambucil and 10.2% within 6-10 years in patients treated with ^{32}P.

Essential Thrombocythemia

Essential thrombocytosis (ET), first described by Epstein and Goedel in 1934, is a nonreactive, chronic myeloproliferative disorder. ET is associated with sustained megakaryocyte proliferation that increases the number of circulating platelets. Traditionally, ET was considered a clonal disorder that involved pluripotent stem cells; however, recent studies indicate that some patients may have polyclonal hematopoiesis.

ET is characterized by a platelet count greater than 600,000/$\Box$L, megakaryocytic hyperplasia, splenomegaly, and a clinical course complicated by hemorrhagic and/or thrombotic episodes.

The mechanism by which thrombocythemia produces hemorrhage or thrombosis is not well defined
Several defects have been described, including a decrease in aggregation, hyperaggregation, and intracellular concentration of various chemicals. In addition, reports show a decrease in von Willebrand ristocetin cofactor activity and high molecular weight von Willebrand factor multimers. Some reports show patients with an acquired deficiency of antithrombin III, protein C, and protein S.

In most patients, physical examination findings are unremarkable. Approximately 40-50% of patients present with splenomegaly; 20% present with hepatomegaly.

The etiology and predisposing factors for ET development remain unclear. Genetic transmission of this disorder is rare, although reports show several families with multiple members affected by ET. Research suggests that a thrombopoietin production or receptor abnormality can cause familial ET.

Lab Studies:

CBC count

This panel is essential for ET diagnosis.

The hallmark of ET is a sustained, unexplained thrombocytosis.

Leukocytosis, erythrocytosis, and mild anemia may be found.

The peripheral blood may show occasional immature precursor cells (eg, myelocytes, metamyelocytes). Large platelets (thrombocytes) are typically identifiable on routine peripheral blood smear.

Mild basophilia and eosinophilia may be found.

Bone marrow

Approximately 90% of patients show an increase in bone marrow cellularity.

Megakaryocytic hyperplasia is common.

Giant megakaryocytes are often observed. Clusters of megakaryocytes may be present; significant dysplasia of the megakaryocytes is unusual.

Hyperplasia of granulocyte and reticulocyte precursors is common.

Bone marrow reticulin is usually increased, but collagen fibrosis is uncommon.

Iron stores may be absent in the bone marrow. This may be due to gastrointestinal tract bleeding or menorrhagia. However, in ET, as in other myeloproliferative disorders, bone marrow iron stain results may be negative even when other studies do not support the presence of iron deficiency.

Platelet aggregation studies

The results of the prothrombin time and activated partial thromboplastin time studies are usually within reference ranges. The bleeding time may or may not be prolonged.

Platelet aggregation study findings are abnormal and show impaired platelet aggregation to epinephrine, adenosine diphosphate, and collagen but not to ristocetin and arachidonic acid.

Some patients may present with spontaneous platelet aggregation.

Chemistries

Chemistries reveal elevated uric acid levels in 25% of patients at diagnosis.

Pseudohyperkalemia may occur, and falsely elevated phosphorous and acid phosphatase levels may be noted.

Pseudohypoxemia may develop from extreme thrombocytosis.

Vitamin B-12 levels are increased in 25% of patients.

Cytogenetic study results are usually normal. Molecular studies (e.g., polymerase chain reaction, Southern [genomic] blotting) may be used as sensitive means of excluding chronic myelogenous leukemia.

Elevation of C-reactive protein, fibrinogen, and interleukin-6 levels suggests the presence of secondary thrombocytosis, because these are acute-phase reactants.

Conduct an RBC mass study to exclude polycythemia vera. In ET, the RBC mass is without abnormality.

Conduct a sensitivity test to interleukin-3, which shows an increase in the formation of endogenous erythroid and/or megakaryocytic colonies and indicates the presence of abnormal hematopoietic progenitor cells (primarily a research tool).

Bone marrow aspirate and biopsy

A bone marrow aspirate and biopsy are useful. Use specialized needles to obtain the aspirate and biopsy material over the posterior iliac crest.

Obtaining an aspirate over the sternum may also be helpful, although most physicians prefer the posterior iliac crest.

Do not attempt to obtain a biopsy from the sternum.

Approximately 90% of patients show an increase in bone marrow cellularity. Megakaryocytic hyperplasia is present. Giant megakaryocytes are frequently observed, and clusters of megakaryocytes may be present. Significant dysplasia of the megakaryocytes is unusual. Hyperplasia of granulocyte and reticulocyte precursors is common. Bone marrow reticulin is usually increased, but collagen fibrosis is uncommon.

In ET, as in other myeloproliferative disorders, bone marrow iron stain results may be negative when other studies do not support the presence of iron deficiency. For practical purposes, a ferritin level that is within the reference range or increased, along with an RBC mean corpuscular volume that is within the reference range, is sufficient to exclude reactive thrombocytosis secondary to iron deficiency and the possibility of polycythemia vera masked by iron deficiency.

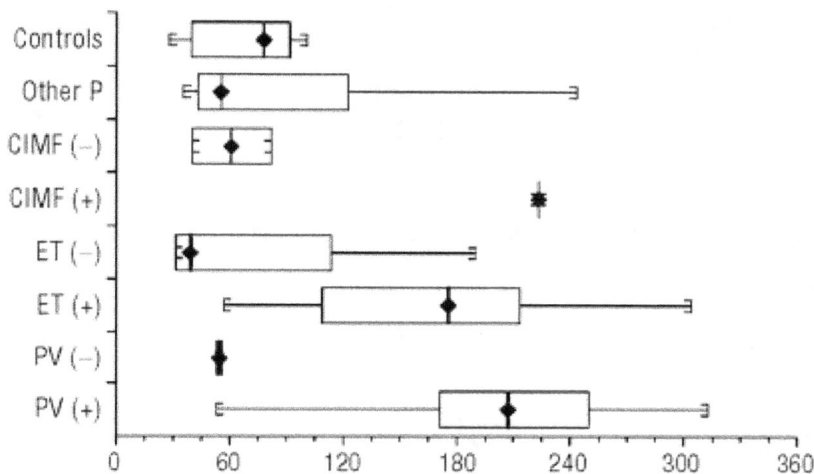

Source: http://www.haematologica.org/cgi/content/full/92/5/704/F10920704

Leukocyte Alkaline Phosphatase (LAP) scores in granulocytes of peripheral blood. LAP values obtained in different categories of patients and controls are shown in a box plot where the diamond indicates median. Differences between the groups studied are statistically significant (Kruskal-Wallis test; $p < 0.0001$). PV: Polycythemia Vera; ET: essential thrombocythemia; CIMF: chronic idiopathic myelofibrosis; (+) or (−) are JAK2 V617F positive or negative respectively.

CHAPTER FOUR: MYELODYSPLASTIC / MYELOPROLIFERATIVE DISEASES

Chronic Myelomonocytic Leukemia (CMML)

Monoclonal hematopoietic disorder of bone marrow stem cells in which monocytosis is a major defining feature

1-Diagnostic criteria
· Persistent monocytosis (>1 x 10^9/L) in PB
· No Ph or BCR/ABL
· <20% blasts in PB or BM (CMML Blasts: Myeloblasts, monoblasts and promonocytes)
· Dysplasia in one or more myeloid lineages (not necessary)
· If dysplasia is minimal or absent, CMML can be diagnosed if:
o Clonal cytogenetic abnormality in marrow cells, or
o Monocytosis persistent for at least 3 mo, and all other causes of monocytosis have been excluded (such as tumor, infection, or inflammation)

2-Epidemiology
· 3/100,000 over the age of 60, annually
· Median age at diagnosis 65-75 years
· Male predominance 1.5-3:1

3-Clinical features
· Sites of involvement
   - PB and BM always involved
   - Most common sites of extramedullary leukemic infiltration: spleen, liver, skin, and LNs
· ~50% of patients
   - WBC count normal or slightly decreased
   - MDS-like picture
· ~50% of patients
   - WBC count increased
   - MPD-like picture
· Fatigue, weight loss, fever, night sweats, infection, and bleeding

4-Etiology
· Unknown
· Occupational or environmental carcinogens, ionizing irradiation and cytotoxic agents in some cases

5-PB Morphology
· Monocytosis (>1 x 10^9/L), hallmark of CMML
· Monocytes >10% of WBC
· Monocytes are usually mature with unremarkable morphology, but can exhibit:
   - Abnormal granulation
   - Unusual nuclear lobation
   - Finely dispersed chromatin
· Blasts <20% of WBC
· WBC count decreased, normal, or increased
· Promyelocytes and myelocytes <10% of WBC
· Mild basophilia
· Eosinophils normal or slightly increased.
· If >1.5 x 10^9/L, then DX: CMML with eosinophilia
· Dysgranulopoiesis present in most cases, and may be more prominent in cases with normal or low WBC count
· Neutrophil nuclear hypolobation
· Neutrophil abnormal cytoplasmic granulation
· Mild anemia, common
· Moderate thrombocytopenia with atypical platelets often present

6-BM Morphology
· Hypercellular in >75% of cases
· Granulocytic proliferation
· Monocytic proliferation
  - Alpha naphthyl acetate esterase
  - Alpha naphthyl butyrate esterase +/- naphthol ASD chloroacetate esterase
· Dysgranulopoiesis in most cases
· Dyserythropoiesis (>50% of cases)
  - Megaloblastic changes, abnormal nuclear contours, ringed-sideroblasts
· Megakaryocytic dysplasia (up to 80% of cases)
  - Abnormal nuclear lobation and micromegs
· Variable degree of fibrosis (30% of cases)

Other organ systems
· Splenic enlargement
  - Red pulp infiltration by leukemic cells
· Lymph nodes
  - Uncommon involvement
  - If seen→ sign of transformation to a more acute phase
  - LN may be diffusely infiltrated by myeloid blasts
· Plasmacytoid monocytes
  - Sometimes diffusely infiltrate LNs or spleen
  - Generalized lymphadenopathy due to plasmacytoid monocyte infiltration may be presenting manifestation of CMML
  - Proposed to be of monocytic lineage, but not proven to be clonally related to the neoplastic cells of CMML

7-Classification
· CMML-1
  - Blasts <5% in PB or <10% in BM
· CMML-2
  - Blasts 5-19% in PB or 10-19% in BM (or Auer rods with <20% blasts in BM or PB)
  - May be at risk of rapid transformation to acute leukemia and poor prognosis
· CMML with eosinophilia:
  - CMML criteria + PB eosinophilia > 1.5 x 10^9/L
  -May have extensive tissue damage related to eosinophil degranulation

8-Immunophenotype
· CD33 and CD13 +, variable CD14, CD64, and CD68
· Increased % of CD34+ cells may be associated with early transformation to acute leukemia
· Plasmacytoid monocytes
  - Characteristic phenotype: CD14, CD43, CD56, CD68, and CD4
  -CD2, CD5 often present, but T-cell derivation disproved

9-Genetics
Nonspecific cytogenetic abnormalities in 20-40%
· +8
· -7/del (7q)
· Structural abnormalities of 12p
· Abnormalities of 11q23 uncommon (suggest acute leukemia)
 10-Prognosis/predictive factors
· Prognosis
  - Median survival 20-40 months
  - 15-30% progress to acute leukemia
· Predictive factors
  - PB and BM blast % (most imp. survival determinant)
  - Splenomegaly
 - Severity of anemia
  - Degree of leukocytosis

Atypical Chronic Myeloid Leukemia (aCML)

- Leukemic disorder with MDS and MPD features at initial diagnosis
- Leukocytosis with principle involvement of dysplastic immature and mature neutrophils
- Multilineage dysplasia common
- No Ph or BCR/ABL

1-Epidemiology
- Unknown incidence
- Estimated 1-2 cases for every 100 cases of Ph+, BCR/ABL+ CML
- Median age 7th-8th decades
- M:F = 1-2.5:1

2-Sites of involvement
- PB and BM always involved
- Spleen and liver involvement common

3-Clinical features
- Few reports
- Most patients have symptoms related to
  - Anemia
  - Thrombocytopenia
  - Splenomegaly

4-Etiology
- Unknown

5-Diagnostic criteria
- PB leukocytosis (mature and immature neutrophils)
- Prominent dysgranulopoiesis (major feature): pseudo Pelger-Huet cells abnormally condensed nuclear chromatin, abnormal nuclear segmentation, or abnormal granules.
- No Ph or BCR/ABL
- Neutrophil precursors (promyelos, myelos, metamyelos) 10% of WBC
- Basophils <2% of WBC
- Monocytes < 10% of WBC
- Hypercellular BM with granulocytic proliferation and dysplasia +/- erythroid and megakaryocytic dysplasia
- <20% blasts in PB and BM

6-BM morphology
- BM megakaryopoiesis and erythropoiesis are variable in quantity
- M:E >10:1
- Increased reticulin fibers at diagnosis or later in course of disease

7-Cytochemistry/Immunophenotype
- No specific abnormalities

8-Genetics
- +8, +13, del(20q), i(17q), del(12p)
  - 80% of cases
  - Not specific
  - No Ph or BCR/ABL

9-Course and prognosis
- Median survival < 20 months
- Poor prognostic factors
  - Thrombocytopenia
  - Marked anemia
- 25-40% evolves to acute leukemia

·   Remainder dies of marrow failure

10-aCML Variant: Syndrome of abnormal chromatin clumping
·   PB morphology
     - High % of immature and mature neutrophils with exaggerated clumping of chromatin
     - Nuclear hypolobation and cytoplasmic hypogranularity are common
     - WBC count usually increased
     - Severe anemia and thrombocytopenia
·   BM morphology
     - Hypercellular
     - Granulocytic proliferation with nuclear abnormalities similar to PB
     - Moderate dysplasia in erythroid and megakaryocytic lineages
·   Survival is similar to aCML

Juvenile Myelomonocytic Leukemia (JMML)

·   Monoclonal hematopoietic disorder of childhood characterized by proliferation of the granulocytic and monocytic lineages
·   Erythroid and megakaryocytic abnormalities common
·   Bone marrow stem cell with multilineage potential in the myeloid series

1-Diagnostic Criteria
·   PB monocytosis > 1×10^9/L
·   Blasts < 20% of WBCs in the blood and of the nucleated bone marrow cells
·   No Ph chromosome or BCR/ABL
·   Plus two or more of the following:
     - Hemoglobin F increased for age
     - Immature granulocytes in PB
     - WBC>10 x 109/L
     - Monoclonal chromosomal abnormality
    - GM-CSF hypersensitivity of myeloid progenitors in vitro

2-Epidemiology
·   1.3 per million children ages 0-14, annually
·   <2-3% of all childhood leukemias
·   20-30% of all cases of myeloproliferative and myelodysplastic diseases in patients less than 14 years old.
·   75% occur in children <3 years old
·   Male predominance of ~ 2:1
·   10% of patients have NF-1

3-Sites of Involvement
·   PB and BM always involved
·   Leukemic infiltration
    - Liver and spleen, virtually in all cases
    - LN
    - Skin
    - Respiratory tract

4-Clinical Features
·   Constitutional symptoms (including malaise, pallor, and fever or infection)
·   Bleeding
·   Bronchitis or tonsillitis in (50%)
·   Maculopapular skin rash (40-50%)
·   Café-au-lait spots in pts with NF-1
·   Hepatosplenomegaly (~100%)

5-Etiology
·   Unknown

- Some genetic predisposition
- Association with neurofibromatosis type 1

6-PB Morphology
- Leukocytosis
  -WBC 25-35 x 10^9/L
  - >100 x 10^9/L in 5-10%
  - Neutrophils (including promyelocytes and myelocytes) and monocytes
  - Blasts usually < 5%, always < 20%
  - Eosinophilia and basophilia in minority
- Anemia
  - NRBCs frequent
  - RBCs typically normocytic, but may be microcytic, or macrocytic (a/w monosomy 7)
- Thrombocytopenia (may be severe)

7-BM Morphology
- Hypercellular bone marrow
  -Granulocytic proliferation
  - Monocot's usually 5-10%
  - Blasts < 20%
  No Auer rods
  Dyspoiesis/dysplasia usually minimal
  - Pseudo-Pelger-Huet neutrophils
  - Hypogranularity of neutrophil cytoplasm
  - Megaloblastic changes in erythroid precursors

8-Morphology in Other Organs
- Leukemic infiltration
  - Skin
  Superficial and deep dermis
  - Lung
  Peribronchial lymphatics into adjacent alveolar septae
  - Spleen
  Red pulp
  Predilection for trabecular and central arteries
  - Liver
  Sinusoids and portal tracts

9-Cytochemistry/Immunophenotype
- No specific abnormalities
- Lysozyme should be used for detection
  - Myelo-peroxidase may be weakly expressed
- Alpha naphthyl acetate esterase
- Butyrate esterase +/- napthol ASD chloroacetate esterase
- LAP scores decreased in 50% of cases, not helpful for Dx

10-Genetics
- No Ph or BCR/ABL
- Monosomy 7 (30-40%)
- Point mutations in RAS (20%)
- Loss of NF1 allele
  -Associated with NF-1
- Loss of heterozygosity for NF1
  - Patients lacking NF-1 phenotype

11-Prognosis
- Overall poor prognosis
- Better Prognosis:
  <1 year of age

- Worse prognosis:
  - 2 years old
  - PLT <33 x 10^9/L
  - Hbg F >15%
- If untreated, 30% die in one year
- Median survival from 5 months to 4 years
- Most die from organ failure (leukemic infiltration)
- 10-20% evolves to acute leukemia
- Response to chemotherapy often poor
- BMT demonstrated to improve survival time

Myelodysplastic/myeloproliferative disease, unclassifiable (MDS/MPD, U)

· Cases with clinical, laboratory and morphologic features that support a diagnosis of both MDS and MPD, but do not meet criteria for other entities in the MDS/MPD category
· Proliferation of one or more myeloid lineages that is ineffective and/or dysplastic, and, simultaneously effective proliferation +/- dysplasia in one or more of the other
  lineages

1-Diagnostic Criteria
- Features of MDS (RA, RARS, RCMD, RAEB), and
- Features of MPD (e.g., plt>600k, WBC≥13k), and
- No h/o CMPD or MDS, no drug causes, no Ph or BCR/ABL, del (5q), t(3;3)(q21;q26) or inv(3)(q21q26)
  OR
- Features of MDS and MPD, but cannot be assigned to any other MDS, CMPD or MDS/MPD

Exclusion Criteria
- Patients with a previous, well-defined myloproliferative disease who develop dysplastic features associated with transformation to a more aggressive phase
- Ph, BCR/ABL

2-Incidence
- Unknown

3-Sites of Involvement
- BM and PB always involved
- Spleen
- Liver
- Other extramedullary tissues

4-Clinical Findings
- Similar to those of both MDS and MPD patients
- Splenomegaly and hepatomegaly

5-Etiology
- Unknown

6-PB Morphology
- Anemia +/- macrocytosis
  - Dimorphic RBCs
- Evidence of effective proliferation in one or more lineages
  - Thrombocytosis (> 600 x 10^9/L)
  - Leukocytosis (> 13 x 10^9/L)
- Dysplasia
- Giant or hypogranular platelets
- Blasts < 20%
  - >10% indicates transformation to aggressive phase

7-BM Morphology
· Hypercellular bone marrow
· Proliferation of one or all of the myeloid lineages
· Dysplastic features present simultaneously in at least one cell line

MDS/MPD, U-Refractory anemia with ringed-sideroblasts (RARS) associated with marked thrombocytosis

· Clinical and morphologic features of RARS
· Markedly elevated platelet count (>600 x 10^9/L)
· BM Morphology
 >15% of erythroid precursors are ringed-sideroblasts
 - Megakaryocytic proliferation
 Normal or enlarged Megas, similar to those in ET
· ? Distinct entity
· ? Spectrum of RARS
· ? Simultaneous occurrence of two diseases
· Disease entities with similar findings
 - 5q- syndrome
 - MDS or AML and abnormalities of 3q21q26
 Thrombocytosis with micromegs
· Genetics
 - Not specific
· No Ph, BCR/ABL
· Cell of origin
 - Unknown
· Prognosis/predictive factors
 - Unknown

CHAPTER FIVE: MYELODYSPLASTIC SYNDROME (MDS)

1-Subtypes:
- Refractory anemia (RA)
- Refractory anemia with ringed sideroblasts (RARS)
- Refractory cytopenia with multilineage dysplasia (RCMD)
- Refractory anemia with excess blasts (RAEB)
- Myelodysplastic syndrome, unclassifiable
- Myelodysplastic syndrome a/w isolated del (5q) chromosome abnormality (5q- syndrome)

2-General:
- Dysplasia
- Ineffective haematopoiesis
- Blasts <5% in PB and < 20% in BM

3-Clinical Features:
- Related to:
  - Anemia, most frequently
  - Neutropenia, thrombocytopenia
  - Organomegaly is infrequently observed

4-Etiology:
- Primary MDS: virus, benzene, cigarette smoking, Fanconi's anemia
- Therapy related: alkylating agents

5-Morphology:
- Dyserythropoiesis
- Dysgranulopoiesis
- Megakaryocytic dysplasia
- BM: hypercellular (sometimes normo- or hypocellular)

6-Differential:
- Non-clonal disorders with dysplastic changes:
  - Congenital dyserythropoietic anemia
  - Parvovirus B19
  - G-CSF: hypergranularity, Dohle bodies, blasts can be 10% or more
  - PNH

7-Prognosis:
- Poor with more blasts
- Karyotype:
  - Normal, -Y,-5q, -20q → good
  - 3 or more chromosome abnormalities, chromosome 7 → poor
- Poor with cytopenia: Hgb<10; Neutrophils <1500; Plt < 100 K

Refractory Anemia (RA)

General:
- 5-10% of MDS
- Unequivocal dyserythropoiesis
- Exclude: drug, toxin, viral, immunologic, congenital disease, vitamin deficiency
(B12/folate)
- Blasts:
  - Blood: <1%
  - BM: <5%
- Etiology: unknown
- Sites: blood and BM
- Genetics: abnormal in 25% of cases, usually -20q, +8, abnormal 5, 7

·   Prognosis:
- Median survival 66 months
- Rate of progression to AML ~6%

Refractory Anemia with Ringed Sideroblasts (RARS)

General:
·   Epidemiology: 10-12% of MDS
·   Findings in RA plus 15% or more of erythroid precursors being ringed sideroblasts (RS)
·   RS: erythroid precursor in which 1/3 or more of the nucleus is encircled by 10 or more siderotic granules
·   Blasts in BM <5%
·   BM morphology:
  -Erythroid hyperplasia
  -Dysplasia, restricted to erythroid lineage
   Nuclear lobation
   Megaloblastoid features
 - Abundant hemosiderin-laden macrophages
·   Rule out: antituberculosis medication, alcoholism, sideroblastic anemia
·   Sites: blood, BM, liver and spleen
·   Clinical features: moderate anemia, progressive iron overload
·   Etiology: unknown
·   Genetics: <10% of cases clonal (if developed during the course of the disease→reevaluate and appropriately reclassify patient)
·   Prognosis:
- Median survival 6y
- 1-2% of cases → leukemia

Refractory cytopenia with multilineage dysplasia (RCMD)

·   Morphology
  -Dysplastic changes in 10% of the cells in 2 or more myeloid cell lines
 - Neutrophils may show hypogranulation and/or hyposegmentation
 - Erythroids may show
   Cytoplasmic vacuoles
   Marked nuclear irregularity including
·   Multilobation
·   Multinucleation
   Megaloblastoid nuclei
 - Megakaryocytes may show
   Hypolobation
   Small size
 - Blasts <5%
·   Prognosis
- 11% progress to acute leukemia
- Overall median survival 33 months

Refractory anemia with excess blasts (RAEB)

·   PB Morphology:
·   Uni- or multilineage abnormalities
   RBC: anisopoikilocytosis with macrocytes
   Neutrophils: hypogranulation and nuclear hyposegmentation
   Atypical platelets
   0-19% blasts
·   BM Morphology:
  -Usually hypercellular (hypocellular in 10-15%)
 - Abnormal localization of immature precursors (ALIP): cluster of 5-8 cells (blasts and promyelocytes), 3 or more/section → recheck smear and BM, note in report.
   -Dysgranulopoiesis, dyserythropoiesis, dysmegakaryopoiesis

- 5-19% blasts (myeloid phenotype CD13/ CD33/ CD117)
- RAEB-1, Blasts, <5 % (blood) or 5-9% (BM)
- RAEB-2, Blasts, 5-19 % (blood) or 10-19% BM
  · Epidemiology:
  >50 years old
  - ~40% of pts with MDS
  · Prognosis:
  - RAEB-1→25% progress to AML
  - RAEB-2→33% progress to AML
  - Remainder→BM failure
  - Median survival
    RAEB-1 ~18 months
    RAEB-2 ~10 months

Myelodysplastic syndrome, unclassifiable (MDS, U)

-Myelodysplastic syndrome which lacks findings appropriate for classification as RA, RARS, RCMD, RAEB
· Morphology
- No specific findings
- Dysplasia restricted to neutrophils or megakaryocytes (may be marked)

5q- Syndrome

·

A myelodysplastic syndrome a/w an isolated del (5q)
· <5% blasts in PB and BM
· Epidemiology
-Middle age to older women (predominantly but not exclusively)
· PB Morphology
-Marked macrocytic anemia
- Slight leukopenia
- Platelet count normal or elevated
<5% blasts
· BM Morphology
- Normocellular or hypercellular
- Megakaryocytes normal or increased in number, many hypolobated
- Variable degree of erythroid dysplasia
<5% blasts
- Scattered aggregates of small lymphocytes
· Genetics
- Del (5q), between bands q31 and q33
- Break points and size of deletion are variable
- No other cytogenetic abnormalities, by definition
· Prognosis and predictive factors
- Long survival
- Karyotypic evolution is uncommon
- Additional cytogenetic abnormalities a/w evolution to AML or MDS of higher grade
- Significance of isolated del (5q) and >5% blasts is not clear

Dyserythropoiesis

Dyserythropoiesis is commonly characterized by the presence of oval macrocytes in the peripheral blood. Also found are target cells. Abnormal erythrocyte development will feature anisocytosis, basophilic stippling, cytoplasmic vacuoles, Howell-Jolly bodies, nucleated RBC's, poikilocytosis, reticulocytopenia, sideroblasts, and/or siderocytes. Hemoglobin F is usually increased up to 6%. Other anomalies reported are the presence of Hemoglobin H, altered A, B, and/or I membrane antigens, and membrane changes that resemble that of proximal nocturnal hemoglobinuria.

In the bone marrow, erythrocyte precursors will contain abnormal nuclear shapes and/or multiple nucleoli. Giant forms can be found. Karyorrhexis, nuclear budding and/or lobes will be observed. Ringed sideroblasts are a common finding. The vitamin B_{12} and folic acid serum values will be normal, yet there will be megaloblastoid features in the developing erythrocytes. The bone marrow may demonstrate either hypoplasia or hyperplasia in the erythrocyte line.

Whether in the peripheral blood or bone marrow, irregular staining properties will manifest. Cytoplasmic borders of erythrocytes may be indistinct or ragged. A dimorphic RBC population of hypochromic and normochromic cells is the rule.

Dysgranulopoiesis

This abnormality is considered to be more subtle that the other two forms. One distinctive feature of this disorder is a persistent basophilia. Other distinctive peripheral blood findings are abnormal granulation (either hypogranular or agranularity) of the neutrophils. Granules present may be larger than normal. The neutrophil line may be characterized by peripheral basophilia and/or hypersegmentation. Abnormal granulation is common in the leukocytes and includes agranulation.

In the bone marrow the promyelocyte may be void of primary granules or have overly large granules. This is a primary finding for this anomaly. Both myelocytes and promyelocytes tend to have a central nucleus and may be agranular or hypogranular. (Agranular promyelocytes may be mistaken for blasts.) Auer rods may sometimes be seen. The myelocyte line is characterized by nuclear/cytoplasmic asynchrony. Nuclear anomalies include false Pelger-Hüet cells and twinning deformity. Twinning is represented by an abnormal large tetraploid cell. Low CD4 helper T-type lymphocyte counts may be observed in the bone marrow.

Dysmegakaryopoiesis

The megakaryocyte population in the bone marrow may display abnormal morphology as large mononuclear megacaryocytes, micromegakaryoblasts, and/or micromegakaryocytes. Look for nuclei in these cells to be either bilobed or have numerous small separated nuclei.   In the peripheral blood, look for large and/or bizarre platelets. Other atypical platelets may have balloon-like budging of the membranes. Numbers may be decreased, increased, or normal.

The role of blasts in MDS

The blast count and identification is an important prognostic indicator for this disorder. The diagnosis of MDS is limited to less than 20 % blasts. If the percentage is higher, then the diagnosis will be that of an acute leukemia. The dysgranulopoiesis of the blast cells affects principally the primary azurophilic granules. A normal blast is classified as having a central nucleus composed of fine chromatin material, high nuclear to cytoplasm ratio, very basophilic cytoplasm, and an agranular cytoplasm.

There are three types of blasts to be recognized in MDS.

First is Type I which includes the classic myeloblast and the unclassified immature cells. Prominent nucleoli (1 to 5 in number) are scattered among the nuclear chromatin in a round to oval nucleus. The nuclear to cytoplasm ratio tends to be variable, usually averaging a ration of 4:1. Granules are absent in the cytoplasm.

The Type II blast also has a centrally located nucleus and somewhat resembles the Type I blast. Its cytoplasm will contain less than 20 azurophilic primary granules. The usual number of granules is from 1 to 6. The nuclear to cytoplasmic ratio is shifted so there is slightly more cytoplasm than nucleus.

The Type III blast resembles the Type II blast but will have more than 20 azurophilic primary granules in the cytoplasm.

The promyelocyte is characterized by an eccentric nucleus containing more condensed chromatin material. A clear area (hoof) is located adjacent to the nucleus and represents the Golgi body. Increased cytoplasm gives a smaller nuclear to cytoplasm ratio. The cytoplasm is characterized by many azurophilic primary granules. The promyelocyte is not included in the blast count when diagnosing MDS.

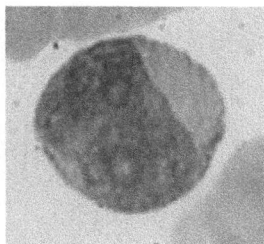

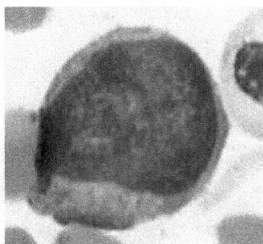

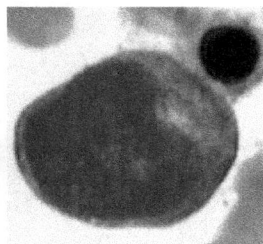

Myeloblast Type I

No azurophilic primary granules.
No Auer rods.

Myeloblast Type II

Few (<20) azurophilic primary granules.
Auer rods may be seen.

Myeloblast Type III

>20 azurophilic primary granules without a Golgi zone.
Auer rods may be seen.

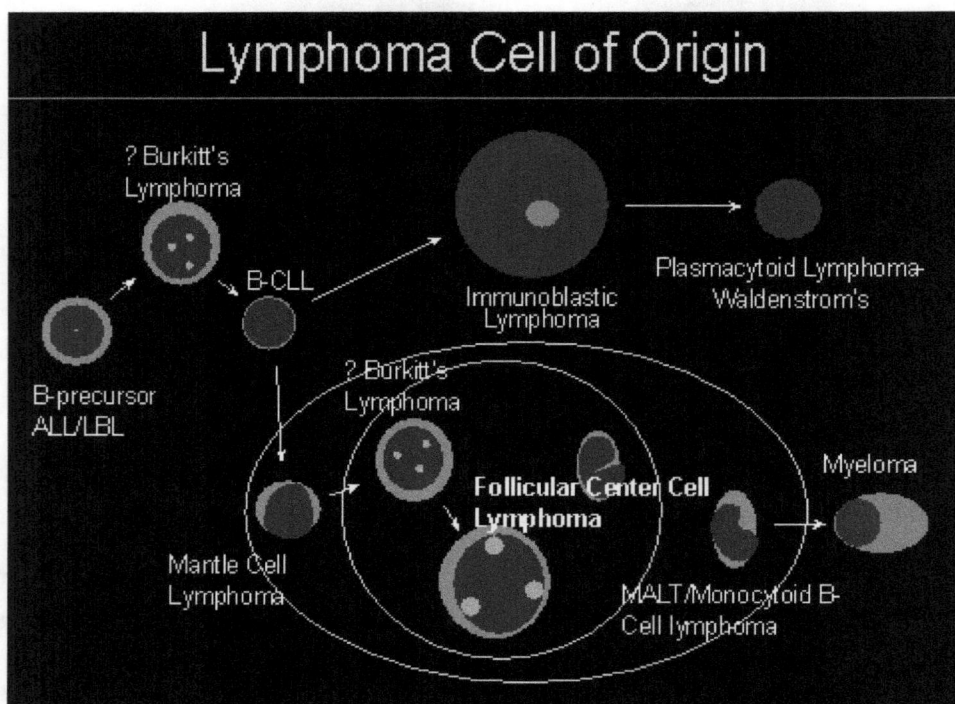

=Hemepath Tutorial (Prof David Weissmann) Used with permission=

Updated REAL/WHO Classification

B-cell neoplasms
 -Precursor B-cell neoplasm: precursor B-acute lymphoblastic leukemia/lymphoblastic lymphoma (LBL). - Peripheral B-cell neoplasms.
- B-cell chronic lymphocytic leukemia/small lymphocytic lymphoma.
- B-cell prolymphocytic leukemia.
- Lymphoplasmacytic lymphoma/immunocytoma.
- Mantle cell lymphoma.
- Follicular lymphoma.
- Extranodal marginal zone B-cell lymphoma of mucosa-associated lymphatic tissue (MALT) type.
- Nodal marginal zone B-cell lymphoma (± monocytoid B-cells).
- Splenic marginal zone lymphoma (± villous lymphocytes).
- Hairy cell leukemia.
- Plasmacytoma/plasma cell myeloma.
- Diffuse large B-cell lymphoma.
- Burkitt lymphoma.
T-cell and putative NK-cell neoplasms
 - Precursor T-cell neoplasm: precursor T-acute lymphoblastic leukemia/LBL.
 - Peripheral T-cell and NK-cell neoplasms.
 - T-cell chronic lymphocytic leukemia/prolymphocytic leukemia.
 - T-cell granular lymphocytic leukemia.
 - Mycosis fungoides/Sezary syndrome.
 - Peripheral T-cell lymphoma, not otherwise characterized.
 - Hepatosplenic gamma/delta T-cell lymphoma.
 - Subcutaneous panniculitis-like T-cell lymphoma.
 - Angioimmunoblastic T-cell lymphoma.

- Extranodal T-/NK-cell lymphoma, nasal type.
- Enteropathy-type intestinal T-cells lymphoma.
- Adult T-cell lymphoma/leukemia (human T-lymphotrophic virus [HTLV] 1+).
- Anaplastic large cell lymphoma, primary systemic type.
- Anaplastic large cell lymphoma, primary cutaneous type.
- Aggressive NK-cell leukemia.
Hodgkin lymphoma
- Nodular lymphocyte–predominant Hodgkin lymphoma.
- Classical Hodgkin lymphoma.
- Nodular sclerosis Hodgkin lymphoma.
- Lymphocyte-rich classical Hodgkin lymphoma.
- Mixed-cellularity Hodgkin lymphoma
-Lymphocyte-depleted Hodgkin lymphoma.

Lymph node anatomy

A. The lymph node has 7 major subdivisions.

1. The lymph node capsule, which surrounds the lymph node
2. The subcapsular sinus- the initial entryway of lymphatic fluid and antigenic material into the node via afferent lymphatics
3. The lymph node cortex- beneath the subcortical sinus-the location of primary and secondary lymphoid follicles
a. In the absence of immune stimulation, the cortical lymphoid follicles are primary follicles primary follicles, composed of small B lymphocytes which may be virgin B lymphocytes or recirculating memory B cells. There is also a fine meshwork of dendritic reticulin cell cytoplasm, which is invisible without special immunolabelling techniques
b. With antigenic stimulation, antigen recognizing B cells are stimulated to replication and differentiation. This converts the primary follicle into a secondary follicle or germinal center, surrounded by a mantle zone of transient small lymphocytes, and a central area containing replicating "follicular center cells" and their differentiating progeny- see below.
4. The paracortex- the region surrounding and beneath the germinal centers
5. The medulla- deep to the cortex/paracortex, and composed of medullary cords and medullary sinuses
6. Medullary vessels- artery and vein
7. Afferent and efferent lymphatic vessels
B. After initial maturation in the primary immune organs, "virgin" B and T lymphocytes are released into the peripheral blood and home to specific sites within the lymph node (and the other secondary organs), controlled by incompletely understood homing receptors. Hence these regions are enriched for one type of lymphocyte T or B. The separation of B and T lymphocytes is not absolute however, and both cell types are present throughout the lymph node, necessary for coordinated lymphoid immune response.
C. The sites of B cell homing include:
1. The primary and secondary follicles of the lymph node cortex-the sites of antigen presentation to B cells, and subsequent proliferation and differentiation in response to same.
2. The medullary cords, where plasma cells aggregate, and release their immunoglobulins into the efferent lymph.
D. The site of T cell homing is the paracortex.
E. Normal lymphocytes recirculate, passing from blood into and through the lymph nodes, and then into efferent lymphatics, surveilling for the presence of the antigen for which they have a unique and specific receptor on their surface. If this antigen is not present, the lymphocytes leave the node.
F. Virgin lymphocytes have a finite lifespan, numbered in weeks, unless they come in contact with antigen.

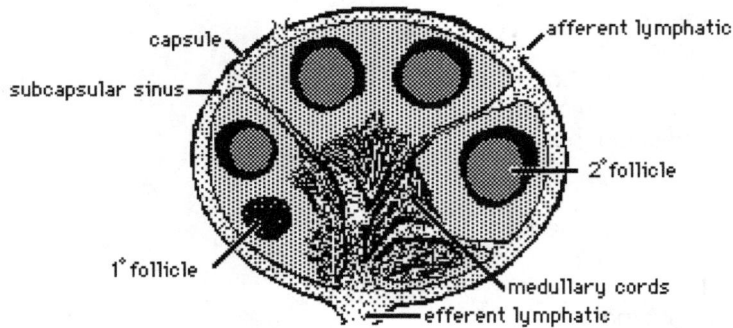

Labels on diagram: capsule, subcapsular sinus, afferent lymphatic, 2° follicle, 1° follicle, medullary cords, efferent lymphatic

©2007. Rector and visitors of the University of Virginia
    Charles E. Hess, M.D. and Lindsey Krstic, B.A. Used with permission

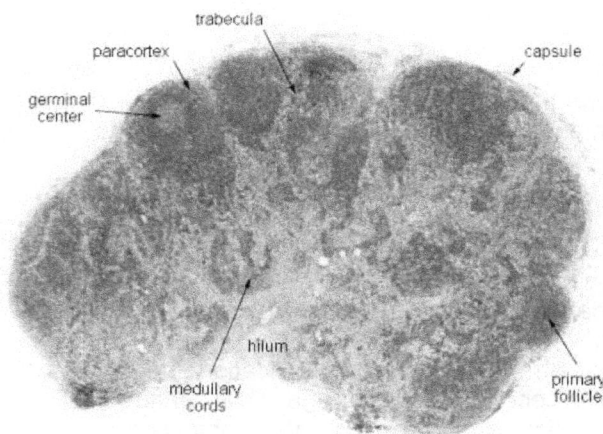

Labels on image: trabecula, paracortex, germinal center, capsule, hilum, medullary cords, primary follicle

=Hemepath Tutorial (Prof David Weissmann) Used with permission=

Cytology of the lymph node

A. The lymph node is thus a dynamic organ, composed of transient B and T lymphocytes, antigen processing and presenting cells, replicating B and T lymphocytes (in response to antigen), persistent and transient final effector cells. Some of these functional subgroups are cytologically unique, and others are cytologically indistinguishable. The ultimate microscopic impression, with practice, is one of cytologic heterogeneity, and histologic organization.
B. Cell types:
    1. Small lymphocytes-
a. Small round dark blue dots. Round nucleus, clumped chromatin, small or absent nucleolus
b. The dullest looking cells hiding the greatest level of functional heterogeneity. Can be T or B cell, virgin (unexposed to antigen) or differentiated effector/memory cell. Most likely lineage guessed by location within the node, but lineage and state of differentiation must be confirmed by immunologic/molecular techniques
c. Locations:
1). B cells- primary follicles, mantle zone of secondary follicles, medullary cords
2). T cells- paracortex, minor population within germinal center.
d. Kinetically, clumped chromatin tells us that the cell is no proliferating- not activated to enter the cell cycle and replicate
2. Follicular (germinal) center cells- replicating and post-replicating B cells.
a. Noncleaved cells, large and small
1). Replicating populations within the germinal center-expanding the number of cells reactive with entrapped antigen.

287

a). Have round nuclei like small lymphocytes, but larger, with open or vesicular chromatin pattern, and recognizable nucleoli. Nucleus clear because genetic material unwound for replication. Size, large or small, based on comparison with nucleus of macrophage.

b. Cleaved cells, small (and large)- post mitotic memory or plasma cell precursors

1). Small cleaved cells have clumped chromatin like small lymphocytes, but irregular folded and cleaved nuclear profiles. Large cell variant may have nucleolus

2). No proliferating population

3. Immunoblasts- Proliferating large cells found outside the germinal centers. May be of B or T cell type. Again have characteristics or replicating lymphocytes- vesicular chromatin, nucleoli

4. Accessory cells

a. Antigen processing cells-process and present antigen to B and T lymphocytes- invisible in normal lymph node

1). T cell paracortex- interdigitating reticulum cells

2). B cell germinal centers- dendritic reticulum cells

b. Macrophages (histiocytes)-

1). Tingible body macrophages of germinal centers

2). Main cells of medullary sinuses- Abundant pale cytoplasm, oval nucleus, single small nucleolus

Pathology of lymph node

In lymphoma, normal lymph node architecture is distorted or effaced by the proliferating malignant lymphoid cells.

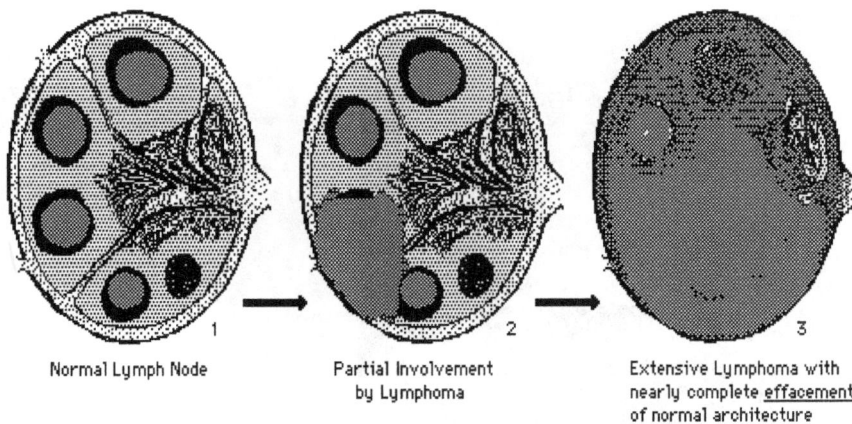

Normal Lymph Node   Partial Involvement by Lymphoma   Extensive Lymphoma with nearly complete <u>effacement</u> of normal architecture

©2007. Rector and visitors of the University of Virginia
Charles E. Hess, M.D. and Lindsey Krstic, B.A. Used with permission

The effacement of nodal architecture may be either diffuse (left) or follicular (center). The follicular pattern may evolve into a diffuse pattern (right). The growth pattern is observed at low magnification while high magnification is used for assessment of cell type. Note the growth or extension of lymphoma outside of the capsule. This is typical of lymphoma.

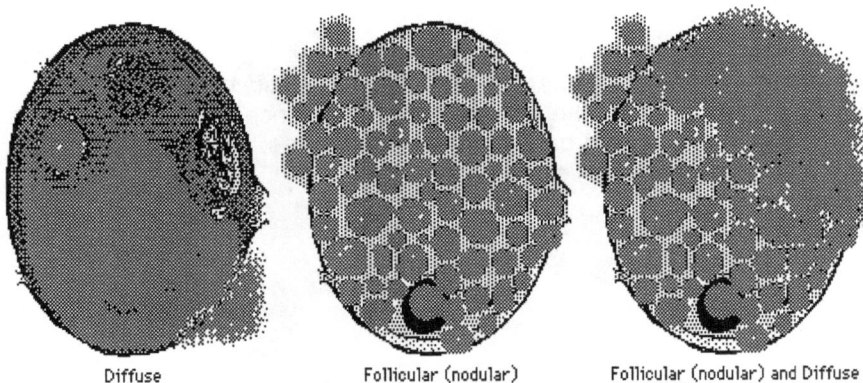

Diffuse   Follicular (nodular)   Follicular (nodular) and Diffuse

©2007. Rector and visitors of the University of Virginia

288

Charles E. Hess, M.D. and Lindsey Krstic, B.A. Used with permission

A. Reactive hyperplasias

1. Exaggerations of normal histology. Expansion of all regions or selective expansion of one. Some types characteristic of certain diseases, but most not
2. Follicular hyperplasia- increase in number and size of germinal centers, spread into paracortex, medullary areas
a. Collagen vascular diseases
b. Systemic toxoplasmosis
c. Syphilis
3. Interfollicular hyperplasia- paracortex-
a. Skin diseases
b. Viral infections
c. Drug reactions
4. Sinus histiocytosis- expansion of the medullary sinus histiocytes-
a. Adjacent cancer
b. Infections

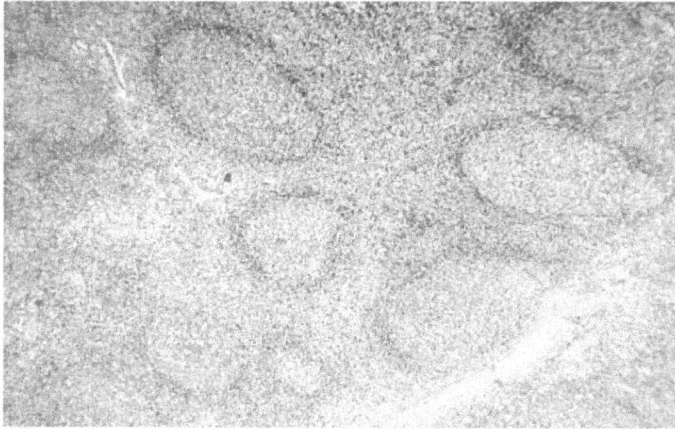

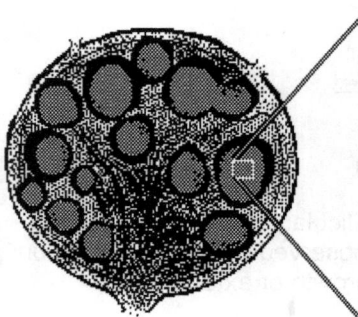

Reactive Node : Follicular Hyperplasia   Mixture of Cell Types

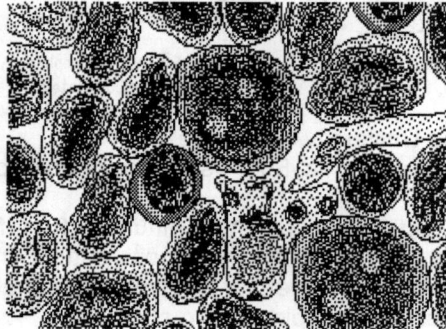

This example of Reactive lymphoid hyperplasia is characterized by hyperplasia of follicular (germinal) centers. Note the variability in the size of the follicles and the presence of a mantle zone in the reactive node. Most important is the mixture of large and small lymphocytes; plasma cells (green) and "tangible body" macrophages (blue) in the reactive germinal center.

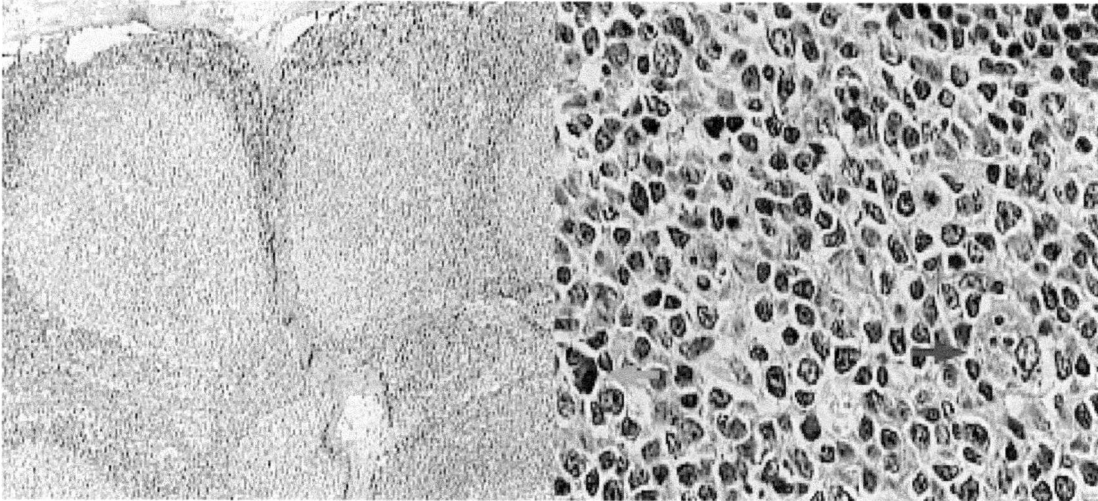

Reactive node: Follicular Hyperplasia   Mixture of Cell Types

©2007. Rector and visitors of the University of Virginia
   Charles E. Hess, M.D. and Lindsey Krstic, B.A. Used with permission

B-Malignant lymphomas (Non-Hodgkins' lymphomas-NHLs)

1. Malignancies of the lymphoid system in which the primary manifestations of disease occur outside the bone marrow, at the sites of normal lymphoid homing
a. Lymph nodes
b. Spleen
c. MALT
d. Anywhere
e. (Lymphomas outside lymph nodes and spleen are referred to as extranodal lymphomas)
   2. Since there are several cytologically recognizable stages of normal lymphoid maturation, there are several cytologic types of lymphomas
   3. Clonal malignancies, all derived from a single cell that has undergone a malignant transformation, mutation
   4. Best conceptualized as two major clinical types
           a. Indolent lymphomas (slow-growing)
           b. Aggressive lymphomas (fast-growing)
   In malignant lymphoma the proliferative cell is usually monomorphous (one type of cell); in reactive conditions, the proliferations are polymorphous (multiple types of cells). In this illustration we see a proliferation of small lymphocytes in a diffuse pattern or malignant lymphoma, small lymphocytic (ML, SL).

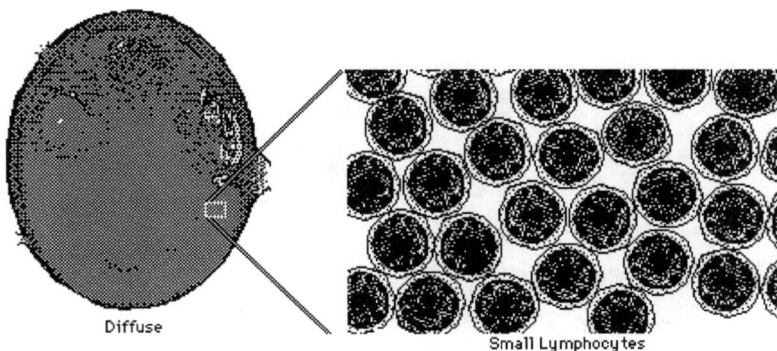

Diffuse

Small Lymphocytes

   Here we see a case of malignant lymphoma, small lymphocytic (ML, SL). Note the proliferation of small lymphocytes in a diffuse pattern.

290

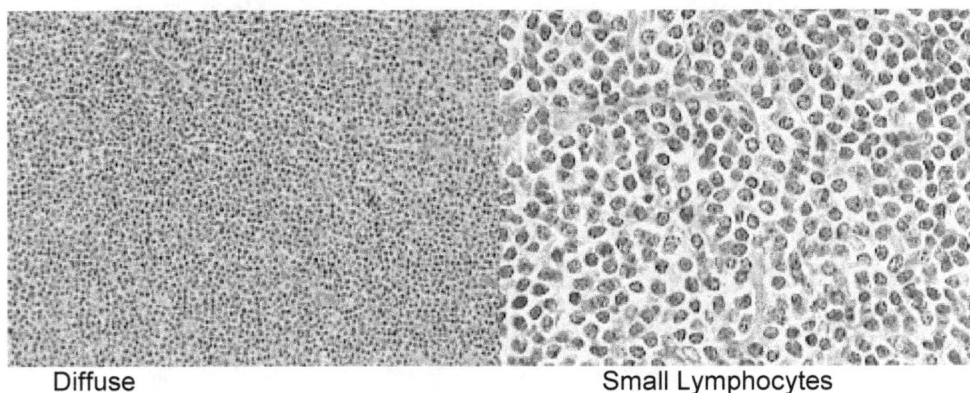

Diffuse   Small Lymphocytes

Here we see a follicular pattern of growth with follicular structures growing beyond the capsule. Looking inside one of the follicles you see a predominance of one cell type-in these case small cleaved lymphocytes. Thus, you can make a diagnosis of malignant lymphoma, follicular, small cleaved cell (ML, SCC, follicular).

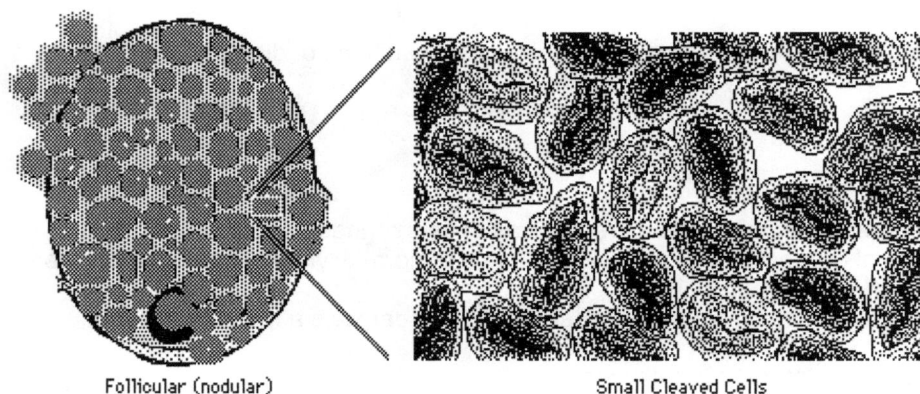

Follicular (nodular)   Small Cleaved Cells

Here is an actual case of malignant lymphoma, follicular, small cleaved cell (ML, SCC, follicular). Note the follicular pattern of growth. At right is a high magnification view of a follicle with a predominance of one cell type-in this case small cleaved lymphocytes.

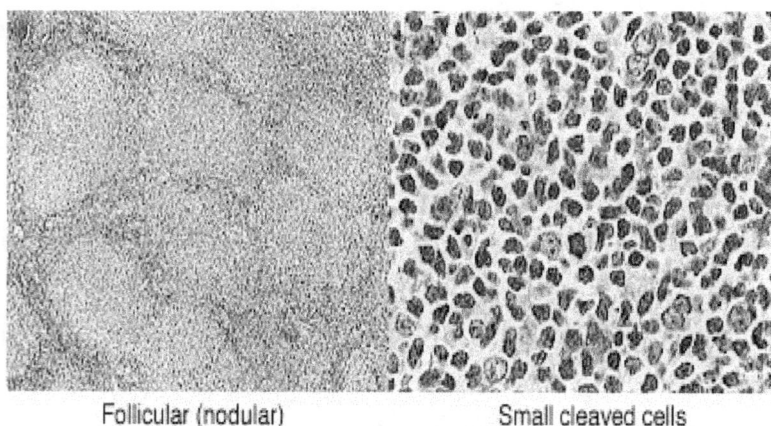

Follicular (nodular)   Small cleaved cells

291

Definition

Lymphoma should be distinguished from leukemia, although this is not always easily done.

- Lymphoma - Primarily of lymph node origin, generally forming a tumor mass

- Leukemia - Of bone marrow origin, generally manifest in the peripheral blood
- can also refer to the systemic proliferation of an abnormal hematopoietic cell throughout the marrow and vascular compartments as is seen in some lymphomas, i.e. Common in lymphoblastic ML and Burkitt's ML

The malignant lymphomas (ML) constitute a heterogeneous group of neoplasms arising from the immune system and primarily involving lymphoid cells.

ML is classified based on 1) the cell type and 2) the architectural (growth) pattern. In this way, two large categories: the Hodgkin's and the Non-Hodgkin's lymphomas are defined.

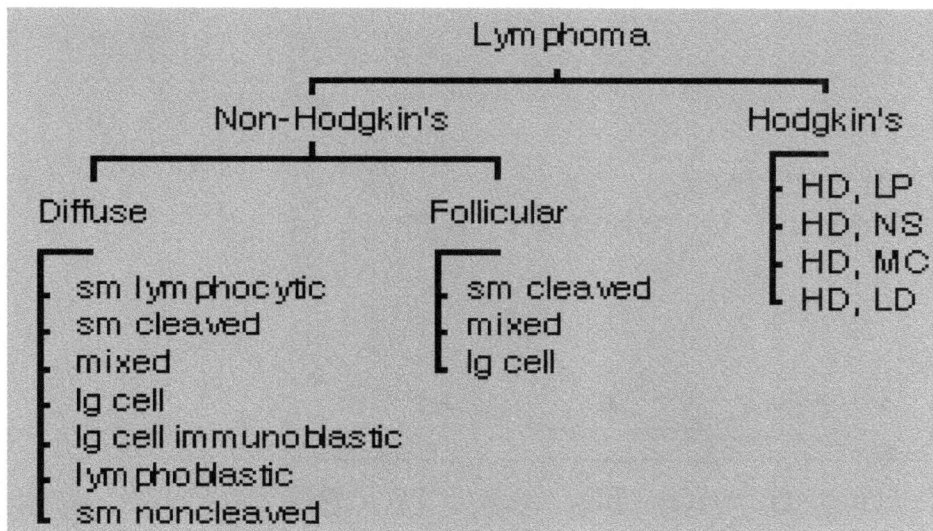

Lymphoma
- Non-Hodgkin's
  - Diffuse
    - sm lymphocytic
    - sm cleaved
    - mixed
    - lg cell
    - lg cell immunoblastic
    - lymphoblastic
    - sm noncleaved
  - Follicular
    - sm cleaved
    - mixed
    - lg cell
- Hodgkin's
  - HD, LP
  - HD, NS
  - HD, MC
  - HD, LD

CHAPTER ONE: HODGKIN'S LYMPHOMA

Epidemiology

In the United States the incidence of HL in recent years has been 2.9 per 100,000, with whites more affected than blacks. Each year about 7,400 new cases and 1,400 deaths are expected. Mostly because of increasingly effective therapy, the prognosis for HL is good. Compared to 30 years ago, the death rate has declined about 60% and the five-year survival rate is 82% versus 40%.

The age distribution in developed countries shows 2 modal peaks: young adults (15-34 y) and older adults (50+ y). In developing countries, the young adult peak is replaced by a childhood (0-14 y) form. This difference in pattern between developed and developing countries has suggested to some investigators that exposure to an infectious disease plays a role in HL's etiology. In fact epidemiology, serologic studies, and tissue probes all tend to associate many cases with Epstein-Barr virus. Nonetheless the etiologic role of the virus is controversial, and sensitive techniques are unable to find tissue evidence of the virus in half the cases.

Hodgkin's lymphomas are characterized by the presence of giant bilobed or multinucleate Reed-Sternberg cells in a reactive appearing cellular background. In contrast, the non-Hodgkin's lymphomas generally consist of a uniform proliferation of cells.

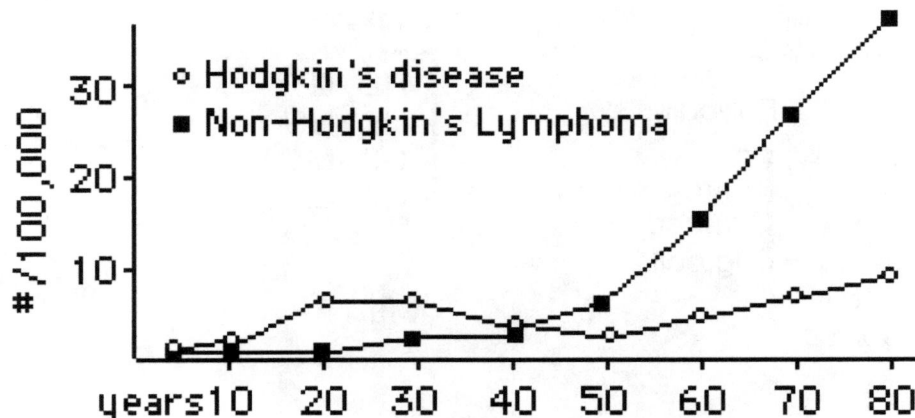

©2007. Rector and visitors of the University of Virginia
Charles E. Hess, M.D. and Lindsey Krstic, B.A. Used with permission

Signs and Symptoms

The major clinical manifestation of malignant lymphoma is painless lymph node enlargement. Such nodes are usually firm or rubbery, often multiple and fixed in place,   Systemic symptoms include fever, malaise, night-sweats, weight loss, and pruritis. As lymphoma progresses, spread may occur to spleen, liver, bone marrow, and other organs.

Common primary sites of lymphoma include cervical, supraclavicular, mediastinal, axillary, periaortic, and inguinal lymph nodes.

Common extranodal sites of lymphoma include the gastrointestinal tract, CNS, skin, spleen, bone marrow, pharyngeal tissues, salivary glands, thymus, and lung among others.

The physical presence of disease and the presence or absence of symptoms is the measures for the respective pathologic and clinical staging of lymphoma.

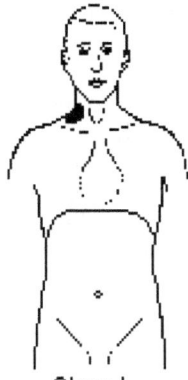 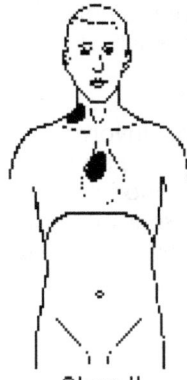 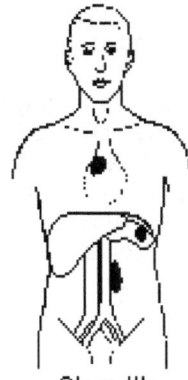 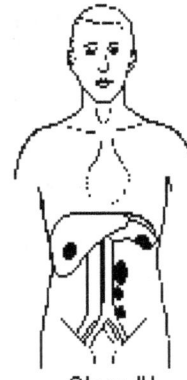

Stage I	Stage II	Stage IIIs	Stage IV
single lymph node region or single extranodal site	two or more sites, same side of diaphragm or c̄ contiguous extranodal site (IIe)	both sides of diaphram or c̄ spleen (IIIs) or contiguous extranodal site (IIIe)	extranodal sites ± nodal disease

Stage subdivision: A-asymptomatic B-unexplained weight loss>10% in 6m and/or fever and/or night sweats

Definition

Hodgkin lymphoma is a neoplastic proliferation of lymphoid cells predominantly involving lymphoid tissues. The malignant cell is the Reed-Sternberg cell. Reed-Sternberg (R-S) cells are essential to the diagnosis of Hodgkin lymphoma. The presence of R-S cells is necessary, but as R-S cells are not unique to HD, R-S cells alone are not sufficient for the diagnosis. The Reed-Sternberg cell is a lymphoid cell and in most cases, is a B cell, and clonal. R-S cells are very large with abundant pale cytoplasm and two or more oval lobulated nuclei containing large nucleoli (red on H & E).

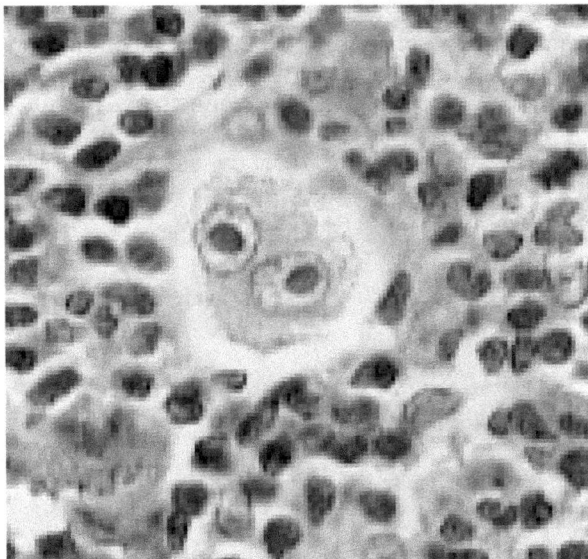

Hodgkin lymphoma was first described by Thomas Hodgkin in an 1832 series of tumors of the absorbent (lymph) glands. The characteristic Reed-Sternberg cell was decribed by Carl Sternberg (1898) and Dorothy Reed (1902).

294

Hodgkin lymphoma is separated from non-Hodgkin lymphoma not only by a unique histologic appearance, but also because the systemic manifestations (such as fever) and the clinical presentation are distinctive.

Hodgkin lymphoma generally presents as regional enlargement of a single group of peripheral lymph nodes, as opposed to non-Hodgkin lymphoma in which nodal involvement is more widely disseminated. Hodgkin lymphoma generally involves contiguous nodes. Non-Hodgkin lymphoma is noncontiguous. In addition, Hodgkin lymphoma is rarely extranodal whereas extranodal involvement is frequent in non-Hodgkin lymphomas. At presentation, bone marrow involvement by HD is highly unusual (< 5%).When Hodgkin lymphoma involves the spleen or liver it generally presents as a mass lesion rather than as diffuse involvement.

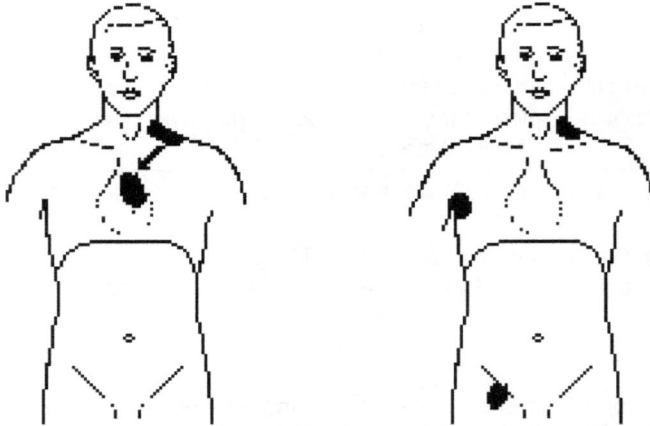

Hodgkin's Lymphoma   Non-Hodgkin's Lymphoma
©2007. Rector and visitors of the University of Virginia
Charles E. Hess, M.D. and Lindsey Krstic, B.A. Used with permission

Etyology

The etiology of HD is unknown. Possible etiologic factors associated with the development of Hodgkin lymphoma (no conclusive evidence supporting any factor) include: prior EBV infection and frequent bcl-2 translocations. Epstein-Barr virus has been detected in approximately 40% of the cases of classical HL, and it is clonal; suggesting that EBV might play a role in the pathogenesis of at least some types of HL.

Rearrangements of immunoglobulin genes are found in Hodgkin lymphoma. Most cases are B-cell derived and the Hodgkin cells are clonal.

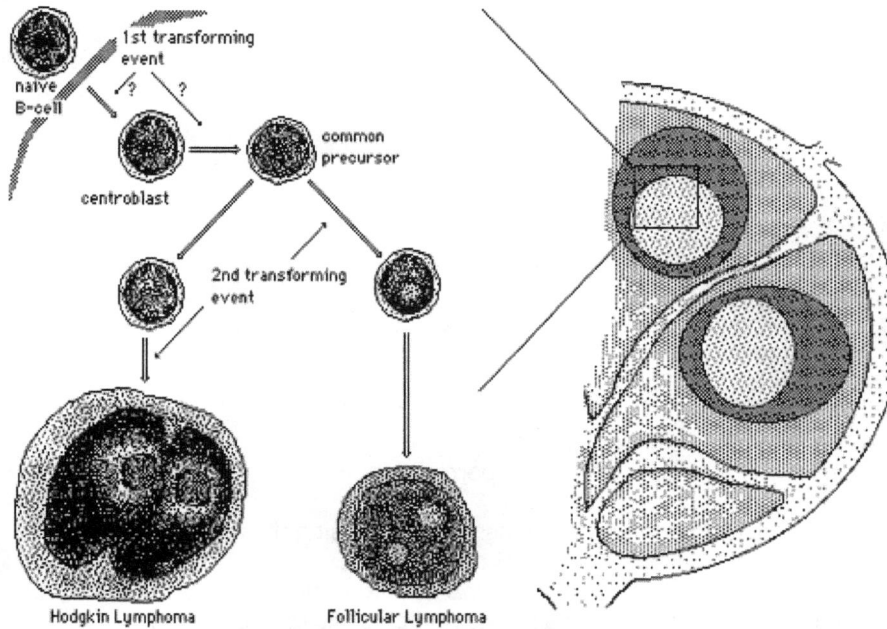

Abnormal cellular immunity is a feature of HD. Combined with chemotherapy it may lead to infectious complications. Further evidence of an immune defect is the lymphopenia seen in 40-50% of people with HD and which is more common in late stages.

Classic Reed-Sternberg cells are large (15-45μ m) with abundant pale cytoplasm and two or more oval lobulated nuclei containing prominent "owl-eye" eosinophilic (H&E) nucleoli.

In some R-S cell variants the cytoplasm shrinks during formalin fixation and processing of tissue, leaving an empty space around the nucleus. Such R-S variants are known as "lacunar cells".

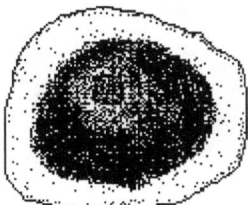

"lacunar" cell

Another R-S variant is the "L&H" or "popcorn" cell with a fluffy, lobulated nucleus having fine chromatin and small nucleoli.

"popcorn" cell

Other common R-S variants are mononuclear Hodgkin cells and "mummified" cells.

296

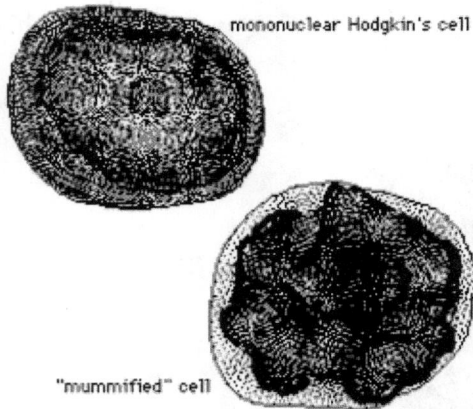

mononuclear Hodgkin's cell

"mummified" cell

The accompanying cellular background of lymphocytes, plasma cells, eosinophils, histiocytes, and stromal cells is variable and is reactive to the neoplastic R-S cells.

The relative frequency of lymphocytes, eosinophils, and plasma cells and the character and amount of fibrosis in lymph nodes, are further clues as to the diagnosis and classification of Hodgkin lymphoma. The primary diagnosis of Hodgkin lymphoma from the histopathologic examination of a lymph node requires the identification of Reed-Sternberg cells in an appropriate, reactive cellular background. If a diagnosis of HD has been established on lymph node biopsy, the criteria for diagnosis of extranodal sites can be relaxed - requiring only mononuclear R-S cells and their variants in appropriate background- not classic bilobed R-S cells. Of course, benign reactive disorders must be ruled out by an experienced hematopathologist.

Classification

Classification of Hodgkin's disease-Rye Classification
Are characteristic patterns of involvement and characteristic variants of Reed Sternberg cell associated with different subtypes?

a. Lymphocyte predominant (5%)
1) Usually presents with limited disease in the neck of young adults
2) May be nodular or diffuse histology
3) Lymphocyte is predominant cell- classic R-S cells infrequent
4) Associated with L and H (lymphocytic and histiocytic) cell (popcorn cell) variant RS cell

Though hard to discern its outline, a single nodule almost fills this picture. The large, paler cells in the midst of the small lymphocytes are either the neoplastic "L & H" cell variants of Reed-Sternberg cells or epithelioid histiocytes.

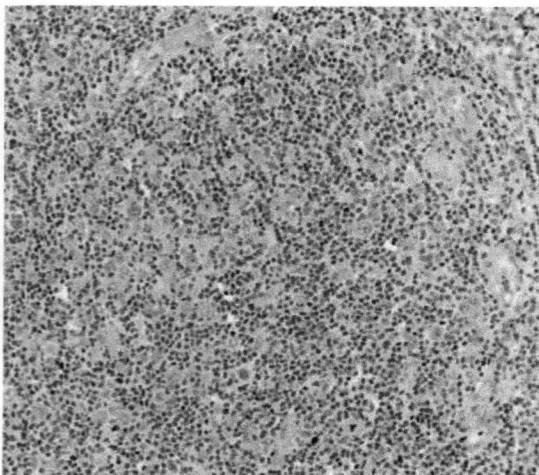

b. Nodular sclerosis (70%)

1) Most common type of HD in industrialized countries
2) Usually presents in the anterior mediastinum and neck of young adult females
3) Lymph node or thymus divided into variably sized nodules by collagenous bands ("sclerosis") extending from a thickened capsule
4) Nodules composed of mix of lymphocytes, eosinophils, histiocytes, classic R-S cells and
5) Lacunar variant Reed Sternberg cell
    Lacunar cells are a feature of nodular sclerosis Hodgkin lymphoma and are not found in other subtypes. In formalin-fixed tissue, the cytoplasm around Reed-Sternberg cell nuclei retracts, leaving a cleared space possibly spanned by a few shreds of cytoplasm. The nuclei are also contracted and have diminished nucleoli.

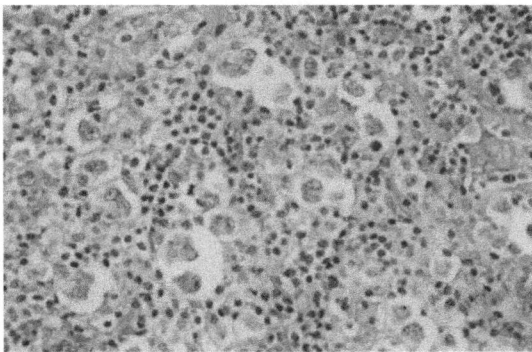

=Hemepath Tutorial (Prof David Weissmann) Used with permission=

c. Mixed cellularity (20%)

1.) Contains a mixture of lymphocytes, eosinophils, histiocytes, and larger numbers of R-S cells
2.) Increased numbers of mononuclear variant R-S cells
As its name implies, the background inflammatory component of mixed cellularity Hodgkin lymphoma sports a variety of different cell types. It lacks the fibrous bands of the nodular sclerosis subtype, generally has more numerous Reed-Sternberg cells, and has a slightly worse prognosis. A high power image like this, however, could easily have come from the center of a nodule of a case of nodular sclerosis Hodgkin lymphoma.

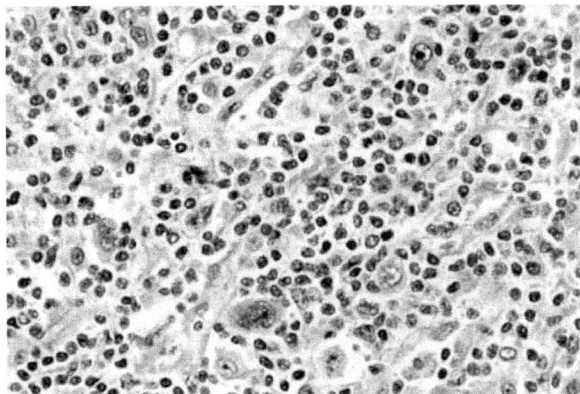

= Hemepath Tutorial (Prof David Weissmann) Used with permission=

d. Lymphocyte depleted (5%)

1) Uncommon type HD; now know many cases previously diagnosed as LD HD were in fact Non-Hodgkins lymphomas

2) Can present in retroperitoneum, without peripheral nodal disease
3) Tissues contain precollagenous sclerosis, and pleomorphic RS cell variants
   A Reed-Sternberg cell occupies the center, surrounded by not-too-many lymphocytes and fibrosis that might be described as disorganized. When viewed through polarized light, it is not birefringent, unlike the fibrous bands of nodular sclerosis

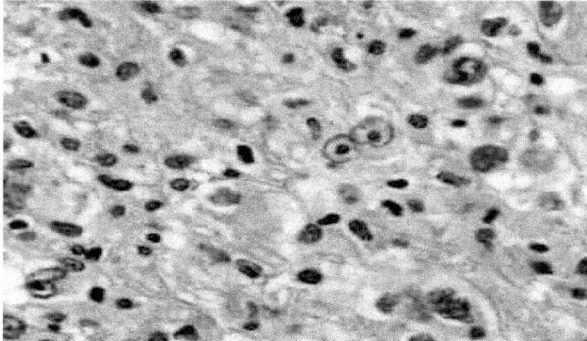

=Hemepath Tutorial (Prof David Weissmann) Used with permission=

Monoclonality

  Reed-Sternberg cells and most Hodgkin variants express the monoclonal antigens CD15 (Leu M-1) and CD30 (Ki-I), but are CD45 (LCA-leukocyte common antigen) negative.
  The exception is the Hodgkin cell of LP, HD - the "L&H" or "popcorn" cell, which is CD45 positive; CD15 negative, CD20 (L26) positive, and light-chain restricted (monoclonal). Therefore HD, LP is immunologically distinct from the other types of HD.
Despite recent advances and although there is good evidence that most if not all Hodgkin lymphomas are B-cell in origin, the etiology and pathogenesis of Hodgkin lymphoma remains largely unknown.

Immunophenotype
The immunophenotypes of the Reed-Sternberg cells and variants in the two subgroups of HL are mirror images:

	CD15	CD30	LCA (all leukocytes)	CD20 (B-cells)	EMA
Classic Hodgkin	+	+	-	-	-
Lymphocyte Predominance	-	-	+	+	+

CHAPTER TWO: NON-HODGKIN'S LYMPHOMA

Epidemiology

In the United States the incidence of NHL in the last few years has been 17.9/100,000 in males and 11.5/100,000 in females. The table below shows estimated new case and death data in 2000 for NHL and HD in comparison to 2 other common cancers. At these rates, NHL is the fifth or sixth most common cause of both new cases of cancer and cancer deaths. The rate of NHL is twice as high in whites as in blacks.

	Non Hodgkin's Lymphomas	Hodgkin's Disease	Prostate Cancer	Breast Cancer
New Cases	54,900	7,400	180,400	184,200
Deaths	26,100	1,400	31,900	41,200

The non-Hodgkin lymphomas are neoplasms of the immune system arising almost anywhere in the body, but most frequently (80%) developing in lymph nodes.
The pathology of a lymphoma depends on:
1- The cell lineage
2- On the degree of cell differentiation
3- On the location of the cell of origin (humoral factors, i.e. growth factors)
The histologic appearance of the lymphoma and its clinical behavior are determined by the above three factors. The histologic appearance of the lymphoma can be used to predict behavior.
Survival can vary from 0.7 - 7.2 years and can be predicted by the histologic appearance. Thus classification (by histology and phenotype) of the non-Hodgkin lymphoma is important for determining proper treatment and predicting prognosis.
The diagnosis of non-Hodgkin lymphoma is based on 1) partial or complete obliteration of the lymph node by a usually monomorphous lymphoid cell type and 2) the pattern of growth.
The two most often encountered patterns of growth are 1) follicular (sometimes referred to as nodular) in which the lymphoma mimics follicular center structures and 2) diffuse in which the lymphoid cells proliferate in an apparently unorganized fashion.
The histiologic classification schemes in use today reflect past and ongoing controversy over the nature of malignant lymphoma. The application of modern immunologic concepts to the classification of malignant lymphoma has led to modifications of old classifications and to the invention of new schemes.
Each system requires the identification of tumor cell types and patterns of growth.
The classification of a lymphoma should provide prognostic and therapeutic information for the clinician.

Non-Hodgkin Lymphoma: Cytology

The size; nuclear and cytoplasmic features of lymphoma cells allow for the morphologic identification of the lymphoma. Generally speaking, non-Hodgkin ML is a proliferation of a uniform (monomorphous) type of cell. One does not see reactive background cells as in Hodgkin lymphoma, nor does one usually see Reed-Sternberg cells (R-S like cells are occassionly found in non-HD, especially T-immunoblastic ML). Cytology can predict biologic behavior, patterns of growth and prognosis. For instance, the involvement of the bone marrow is uncommon (<10%) with large cell lymphoma, but common (60-70%) with ML, follicular, small cleaved cell. In another example, lymphomas composed of lymphoblasts or small noncleaved lymphocytes have a rapid growth rate and a poor prognosis.

Non-Hodgkin Lymphoma: Pattern

The pattern by which a lymphoma infiltrates and replaces a previously normal lymph node is predictive of its biological behavior. The architectural pattern of the proliferating process, that of either a diffuse or a follicular appearance, is of prognostic value - follicular MLs have a better prognosis than diffuse MLs and are rare below the age of 20.

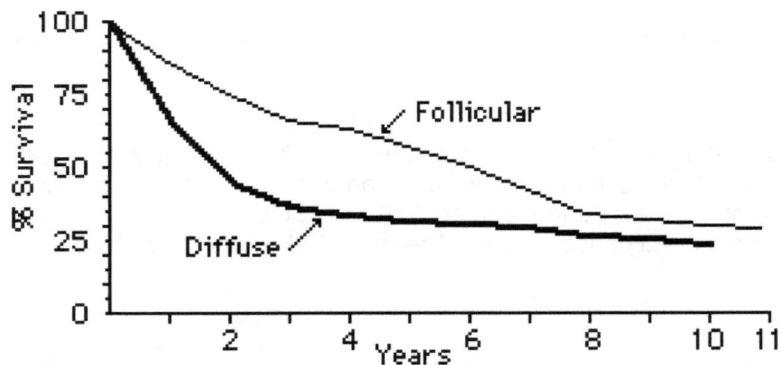

The natural history of follicular lymphoma is to retain the follicular pattern for extended periods; progress to a diffuse aggressive form in 25 -30% of patients. Follicular lymphomas frequently (50-60%) have bone marrow involvement at presentation. The follicular structure implies B cell immunologic lineage. Follicular lymphomas must be carefully distinguished from reactive follicular hyperplasia.

Non-Hodgkin Lymphoma: Phenotype

Certain lymphomas, such as marginal zone B cell MLs, tend to grow filling lymph node sinuses. Still others home toward vessels causing a rare primary intravascular ML (intercellular adhesion molecules on the lymphoma and endothelial cells key to this pattern of growth and unique biologic behavior). Most lymphomas are of B cell phenotype (75-85%), while about 20% are T cell lymphomas. There are prognostic and some treatment differences between T and B cell processes.

Immunochemistry allows for phenotypic determination of cell lineage. Surface or cytoplasmic Ig and/or surface B cell restricted molecules (CD19; CD20) identify cells as of B cell phenotype. Antigens (CD2; CD3; CD7) identify T cells, while (CD13; CD14; CD33) indicate myeloid or monocytic lineage. Malignant lymphomas of B cell origin are monoclonal, that is they exclusively express one light chain (lambda or kappa). Reactive lymphoid populations are polyclonal.

Phenotyping assists in: 1) the distinction between non-hematopoietic and hematopoietic neoplasms, 2) the identification and subclassification of MLs, and 3) the distinction between reactive and malignant lymphoid populations.

It is especially useful in the case of B-cell lymphomas that express surface immunoglobulin (and most of them do). Immunoglobulin molecules contain a light chain and a heavy chain. In a random, benign collection of lymphoid cells, the kappa light chains are present on roughly 2/3rds of the cells and lambda light chains on 1/3rd. If you applied an antibody to kappa light chains, it would mark 2/3rds of the cells; an antibody to lambda would mark 1/3rd. On the other hand, a malignant collection of lymphoid cells is monoclonal, at least at first approximation. By definition, then, all the cells will bear identical surface immunoglobulin molecules with either kappa or lambda light chains, but not a mixture. Thus an antibody to a specific kind of light chain (kappa or lambda) will mark either all or none of the cells.

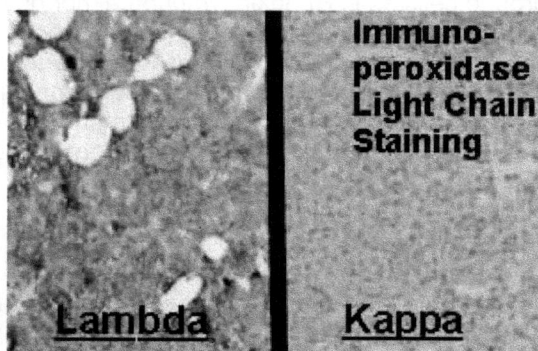

Immuno-peroxidase Light Chain Staining

Lambda   Kappa

=Hemepath Tutorial (Prof David Weissmann) Used with permission=

The image above shows immunoperoxidase light chain staining, where each of 2 frames represents the same tissue stained with antibodies to different light chains. All the cells stained by lambda antibody are positive (deep orange).
* All lymphoid cells (well, almost all): Lymphoid cells are reactive for CD45 (leukocyte common antigen, or LCA). Immature cells and plasma cells in particular, however, may be negative.
* B-cells: Almost all of these are reactive for CD19, CD20 and CD22. Certain low-grade B-cell lymphomas are reactive for two markers otherwise usually found on T-cells: CD5 and CD43. Follicular center cell lymphomas (as well as very different fish, lymphoblastic lymphomas) are frequently CD10 (+).
* T-cells: Pan T-cell markers (present on almost all T-cells) include CD2, CD3, CD5, and CD7. Most T-cells mark with either CD4 (helper cells) or CD8 (suppressor cells or cytotoxic cells). Immature thymus T-cells may not conform to these generalities.
Natural-killer cells: These tough guys are frequently associated with CD16, CD56, or CD57.

Non-Hodgkin Lymphoma: Genotype

In T cell lymphomas and in some B cell lymphomas clonality cannot be determined by phenotyping. Molecular genetic studies, in particular analysis, can detect clonality by probes to immunoglobulin and T cell receptor genes. Thus, both lineage and clonality can be identified. In addition, oncogene probes can detect rearrangements of oncogenes associated with particular types of lymphomas, i.e. c-myc with small non-cleaved cell ML or bcl-2 with nodular B cell ML. Another molecular genetic technique, PCR (Polymerase Chain Reaction), can detect minute quantities of abnormal DNA allowing for detection of residual disease following therapy.
Chromosomal translocations have been associated with specific types of lymphoma.
Follicular lymphomas are associated (>80%) with a t(14;18). Translocation of the bcl-2 gene from 18q21 to 14 at a site adjacent to the J-region of the Ig-heavy chain results in unregulated expression of the bcl-2 protein. Normally Bcl-2 prevents apoptosis of germinal center lymphocytes and in reactive germinal centers is "turned off" thus increasing cell turnover. In neoplastic cells bcl-2 is over expressed thus promoting cell survival and allowing neoplastic lymphocytes to accumulate in the germinal center. The translocation t(11;14) (q13;q32)causes a similar unregulated expression of the bcl-1 protein cyclin D1 controlling the cell cycle. Normal lymphoid cells do not express cyclin D1. The bcl-1 protein overexpression appears to be specific for mantle cell lymphoma (rare cases of large cell ML; myeloma reported).
    Burkitt's lymphoma (small noncleaved lymphoma) is associated with the t(8;14) leading to unregulated production of the oncogene protein c-myc, a DNA transcription factor. The translocations t(8;2) and (8;22) produce similar deregulation of the c-myc oncogene.
    Knowledge of these molecular markers is useful for understanding the pathogenesis of lymphoma; as an aid in the diagnosis and subclassification of lymphoma.

Non-Hodgkin Lymphoma Grade

    Morphology (cytology and pattern) remains the "gold standard" by which malignant lymphomas are classified, although the morphologic diagnosis is supplemented by phenotypic and genotypic information. We will study the "New Working Formulation for Clinical Use", the most widely used system in the US.
"New Working Formulation for Clinical Use"
Low-Grade
A. Small lymphocytic (lymphocytic; plasmacytoid)
B. Follicular, predominantly small cleaved cell
C. Follicular, mixed, small cleaved and large cleaved cell
Intermediate-Grade
D. Follicular, predominantly large cell, cleaved and/or non-cleaved
E. Diffuse, small cleaved cell
F. Diffuse, mixed, large and small cell
G. Diffuse, large cell, cleaved or noncleaved
High-Grade
H. Large cell, immunoblastic - (B- or T-cell type)
I. Lymphoblastic
J. Small noncleaved cell (Burkitt's and non-Burkitt's)

Miscellaneous
The Low-Grade MLs have 5 year survival rates of 50-70%.
"New Working Formulation for Clinical Use"
Low-Grade
A. Small lymphocytic (lymphocytic; plasmacytoid) - 4% *
B. Follicular, predominantly small cleaved cell - 25%
C. Follicular, mixed, small cleaved and large cleaved cell - 8%

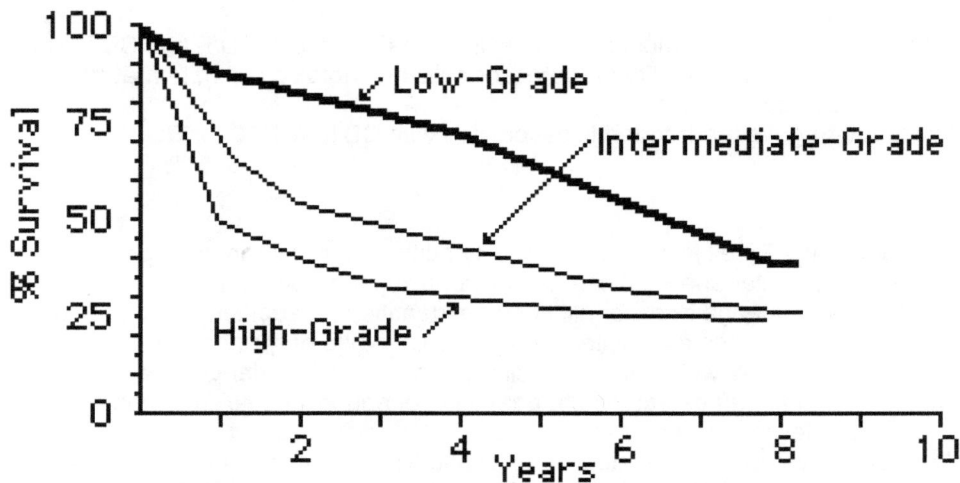

* Percent of all malignant lymphoma

Lymphoplasmacytic Lymphoma (LPL) / Waldenström Macroglobulinemia (WM)

1- Definition
• Neoplasm of small B-lymphocytes, plasmacytoid lymphocytes, and plasma cells
• Usually involves: BM, LNs, and spleen
• Usually lacks CD5
• Has a serum monoclonal protein with hyperviscosity or cryoglobulinemia in most cases
• Plasmacytoid variants of other lymphomas must be excluded (B-CLL, MZL, FL)
2-Epidemiology
• Rare disease (1.5% of nodal lymphomas)
• Older adults (median age 63y/o)
• Slight male predominance (53%)
3- Sites of involvement
• Commonly involves BM, LNs, and spleen
• May involve: PB, extranodal sites with lung, GI, skin (most previously diagnosed cases are MZL of MALT-type)
4- Clinical features
• In most cases, monoclonal IgM paraprotein (>3g/dl in Waldenström macroglobulinemia)
• M-component may result in
    – Hyperviscosity (10-30% of patients) which causes: RBC sludging or Rouleaux formation, reduced visual acuity, increased risk of CVA
        – autoimmune reactions
        – cryoglobulinemia
        – neuropathies (10%)
• Paraprotein deposition in: skin, GI tract (causes diarrhea)
• Coagulopathy, due to binding of IgM to: clotting factors, platelets, fibrin
• Waldenstrom macroglobulinemia is NOT synonymous with LPL,
  IgM paraprotein present in other diseases
        – Splenic MZL
        – B-CLL
        – Extranodal MZL of MALT type (rarely)

5-Etiology
- Hepatitis C virus
  - In patients with HCV, cryoglobulinemia, and LPL, decreasing viral load with interferon is associated with regression of the lymphoma
    - Mechanism is unclear: HCV has transforming potential, or LPL is antigen-driven
- Genetic susceptibility
- Occupational exposures

Morphology in LNs
- Growth pattern
  - diffuse
  - may be interfollicular with sparing of sinuses
- No pseudofollicles
- Neoplastic cells
  - Small lymphocytes
  - Plasmacytoid lymphocytes
  - Plasma cells, with or without Dutcher bodies
- Progression to diffuse large cell (immunoblastic) lymphoma may occur

Morphology in BM and PB
- BM: nodular and/or diffuse lymphoid infiltrate

- PB: if involved, WBC count typically is less than that in CLL
- Aspirate smears show a mixture of: small lymphocytes, plasmacytoid lymphocytes, and plasma cells

6- Immunophenotype
- sIg and cIg positive (usually IgM; sometimes IgG, rarely IgA)
- IgD negative
- CD19/ CD20/ CD22/ CD79a positive
- CD38 positive
- CD5/ CD10/ CD23 negative
- CD43 is variable

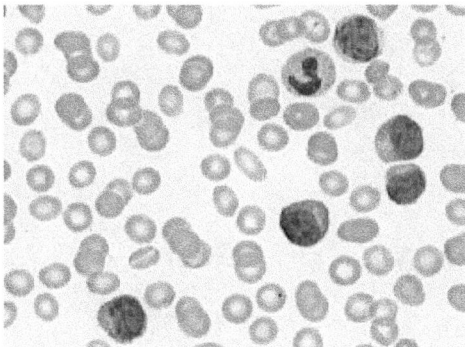

Splenic Marginal Zone Lymphoma (SMZL)

* Definition
  · B-cell neoplasm
  · Small lymphocytes that surround and replace the splenic white pulp germinal centers, efface the follicle mantle and merge with a peripheral (marginal) zone of larger cells including scattered transformed blasts
  · Both small and larger cells infiltrate the red pulp
  · Hilar lymph nodes and BM are often involved
  · PB: villous lymphocytes may be seen

* Epidemiology
·   Rare, <1% of lymphoid neoplasms
·   May account for most cases of otherwise unclassifiable chronic lymphoid leukemias that are CD5-
·   Most patients above 50 y/o, F=M
* Site of Involvement and Clinical Features
·   Splenomegaly
·   Splenic hilar lymph nodes
·   BM, usually positive
·   PB villous lymphocytes, variable
·   Liver in some cases
·   Peripheral lymph nodes typically not involved
·   Autoimmune thrombocytopenia or anemia, sometimes
·   Extranodal infiltration, extremely uncommon
·   Small monoclonal serum protein, 1/3 of cases. Marked hyperviscosity and hypergammaglobulinemia are uncommon.

* Morphology-Spleen
·   White pulp/central zone: small round lymphocytes surround, or, more commonly replaces reactive germinal centers with effacement of the normal follicle mantle
·   Peripheral zone of small to medium-sized lymphocytes with more dispersed chromatin and abundant pale cytoplasm resembling marginal zone cells and are interspersed with transformed blasts
·   Red pulp: always infiltrated, small nodules of larger cells and sheets of the small lymphocytes, which often invade sinuses
·   Epithelial histiocytes: may be present in the lymphoid aggregates
·   Plasmacytic differentiation: may occur. Rarely, clusters of plasma cells may be present in the centers of the white pulp follicles.

* Morphology-Hilar LN
·   Sinuses are dilated
·   Lymphoma surrounds and replaces germinal centers
·   The two cell types (small lymphocytes and marginal zone cells) are often more intimately mixed without the formation of a distinct "marginal" zone

* Morphology-BM
·   Nodular interstitial infiltrate, cytologically similar to that in the lymph nodes
·   Occasionally neoplastic cells surround reactive follicles
·   Intrasinusoidal lymphoma cells are characteristic

* Morphology-PB
·   When present, usually show lymphocytes with short polar villi (villous lymphocytes)
·   Some lymphocytes may appear plasmacytoid

* Morphology-Differential Diagnosis
·   Other small B-cell lymphoma/leukemias: CLL, HCL, MCL, FL, LPL
·   Nodular pattern on BM excludes HCL, but BM morphology may not be sufficient to distinguish SMZL from others
·   PB villous lymphocytes are helpful
·   PB or BM flow cytometry results are helpful
·   A diagnosis of exclusion in the absence of splenectomy

* Immunophenotype
·   Positive: sIgM, sIgD, CD20, CD79a
·   Negative: CD5, CD10, CD23, CD43, cyclin D1, CD103

Marginal zone B-cell lymphoma of mucosa-associated lymphoid tissue (MALT lymphoma)

- Definition:

An extranodal lymphoma comprising morphologically heterogeneous small B-cells including marginal zone (centrocyte-like) cells, cells resembling monocytoid cells, small lymphocytes, and scattered immunoblast and centroblast-like cells. There is plasma cell differentiation in a proportion of the cases.
- The infiltrate is in the marginal zone of reactive B-cell follicles and extends into the interfollicular region. In epithelial tissues, the neoplastic cells typically infiltrate the epithelium, forming lymphoepithelial lesions.

- Epidemiology:

MALT lymphoma comprises 7-8% of all B-cell lymphomas and up to 50% of primary gastric lymphoma.
- Most cases occur in adults with a median age of 61 and a slight female preponderance (M:F ratio 1:1.2). There appears to be a higher incidence of gastric MALT lymphomas in north-east Italy and a special subtype called immunoproliferative small intestinal disease (IPSID) occurs in the Middle East and the Cape region of South Africa.
- Precursor lesions and conditions: in many cases of MALT lymphoma, there is a history of chronic inflammatory, often autoimmune disorders that result in accumulation of extranodal lymphoid tissue. Examples: H. pylori associated chronic gastritis, Sjögren syndrome or Hashimoto thyroiditis.

- Sites of involvement:

The gastrointestinal (GI) tract is the most common site of MALT lymphoma, comprising 50% of all cases, the stomach is the most common location (85%). The small intestine and colon are typically involved in IPSID. Other common sites include lung (14%), head & neck (14%), ocular adnexae (12%), skin (11%), thyroid (4%), and breast (4%).

- Clinical features:

The majority of pts present with stage I or II disease. Aprox. 20% of patients have bone marrow involvement, but the frequency seems to vary among primary sites, being lower for gastric cases and higher for primary ocular adnexal or pulmonary cases. Multiple extranodal sites may be involved in up to 10% of the cases at the time of presentation.
- Despite plasmacytic differentiation in many of the cases, a serum paraprotein (M-component) is rare in MALT lymphomas. The major exception is IPSID, in which an aberrant alpha heavy chain can usually be found in the peripheral blood.
- The term "high-grade MALT lymphoma" should not be used, and the term "MALT lymphoma" should not be applied to a large B-cell lymphoma even if it has arisen in a MALT site.

- Differential diagnosis:

Distinction from reactive processes is based mainly on the presence of destructive infiltrates of extrafollicular B cells, typically with the morphology of marginal zone cells. In borderline cases, immunophenotyping or molecular genetic analysis to assess B-cell clonality are necessary to establish or exclude a diagnosis of MALT lymphoma. Distinction from other small B-cell lymphomas is based on a combination of the characteristic morphologic and immunophenotypic features.

- Immunophenotype:

Tumour cells typically express IgM, and less often IgA or IgG, and show light chain restriction. The tumour cells are CD20+, CD79a+, CD5-, CD10-, CD23-, CD43+/-, CD11c+/-(weak).
- In IPSID, both the plasma cells and marginal zone cells express alpha heavy chain without any light chain
- There is no specific marker for MALT lymphoma at present.
- Genetic abnormalities and oncogenes:

o   - Trisomy 3 is found in 60% and t(11;18)(q21;q21) has been observed in 25-50% of the cases.
o   - In contrast, t(11;18) is not found in primary large B cell gastric lymphoma. Recently, analysis of the t(11;18) breakpoint has shown fusion of the apoptosis-inhibitor gene API2 to a novel gene at 18q21, named MLT.

- Postulated cell of origin:
  Post germinal centre, marginal zone B-cell.

- Prognosis:

 MALT lymphomas run an indolent natural course and are slow to disseminate. Recurrences may involve other extranodal sites. The tumours are sensitive to radiation therapy, and local treatment may be followed by prolonged disease-free intervals. Involvement of multiple extranodal sites and even bone marrow involvement do not appear to confer a worse prognosis.
- Protracted remissions may be induced in H. pylori-associated gastric MALT lymphoma by antibiotic therapy for H. pylori. Cases with the t(11;18)(q21;q21) appear to be resistant to H. pylori eradication therapy.
- In IPSID, remissions have followed therapy with broad spectrum antibiotics.
- Transformation to diffuse large B-cell lymphoma may occur.

Nodal Marginal Zone B-cells lymphoma

- Definition:

 NMZL is a primary nodal B-cell neoplasm that morphologically resembles lymph nodes involved by marginal zone lymphomas of extranodal or splenic types, but without evidence of extranodal or splenic disease. Monocytoid B-cells may be prominent.

- Epidemiology:

 Nodal marginal zone lymphoma is a rare disease, comprising only 1.8% of lymphoid neoplasms

- Sites of involvement:

 Peripheral lymph nodes, occasionally bone marrow and peripheral blood

- Clinical features:

 Most patients present with localized or generalized peripheral lymphadenopathy, with good performance status

- Morphology:

 The marginal zone and interfollicular areas of the lymph node are infiltrated by marginal zone (centrocyte-like) B-cells, monocytoid B-cells, or small B lymphocytes, with scattered centroblast- and immunoblast-like cells.
- Two types described:
o   - One that closely resembles nodal involvement by MALT lymphoma
o   - One that resembles splenic marginal zone lymphoma
- Plasma cell differentiation is a feature of some cases
- Follicular colonization may be present
- Transformation to large B-cell lymphoma may occur
- In patients with extranodal (MALT) lymphoma, Hashimoto thyroiditis or Sjögren Syndrome, nodal involvement by marginal zone lymphoma should be considered secondary involvement by MALT lymphoma.

Follicular Lymphoma

Definition:
- Neoplasm of follicular centre B cells, with at least a partially follicular pattern. The lymphoma cells consist of two types: centrocyte (cleaved follicle centre B cells), and centroblasts (non-cleaved follicle centre B cells)
- Predominantly adults, median age 59 yrs; male to female ratio of 1:1.7
- 70% of low grade lymphomas
- Most patients have widespread disease at diagnosis (bone marrow involvement in 40-50%)
- Patients are usually asymptomatic at diagnosis, except for lymph node enlargement

Morphology:
- Follicular architecture
- Neoplastic follicles are: poorly defined and closely packed, no mantle zone, no polarization, no tingible body macrophages

Pattern:
- Follicular   > 75% follicular
- Follicular and diffuse   25-75% follicular
- Minimally follicular   < 25% follicular

Grading:
- Grade 1: 0-5   centroblasts / hpf
- Grade 2: 6-15 centroblasts / hpf
- Grade 3: > 15 centroblasts / hpf
- o   -3a: Some centrocytes present
- o   -3b: Solid sheets of centroblasts

Immunophenotype:
- Surface Ig +
- Express B-cell antigens: CD 19, CD 20, CD 22, CD 79a
- CD 10 +
- BCL 2 + (can help distinguishing from reactive follicles; however, grade 3 and cutaneous type may be negative)
- BCL 6 +

Genetics:
- t(14;18) (q32;q21)

BCL 2 rearrangement, present is 70-95% cases
Confers a survival advantage on B cells; failure to switch off BCL 2 during blast transformation may contribute to development of lymphoma by preventing apoptosis

Prognosis:
- Grades 1 and 2: indolent
- Grade 3: aggressive; treatment as for DLBCL
- 25-33% cases progress to DLBCL

Variants:

(1) Diffuse Follicle Centre Lymphoma:
Centrocytes and centroblasts (minority) but no follicles
Both cell types must have follicle centre cell phenotype (SIg+, CD 10+, BCL2+, BCL6+)
If centroblasts predominate, or if the small cells are T cells, DLBCL is the diagnosis

(2) Cutaneous Follicle Centre Lymphoma:
Partially follicular pattern
Composed of cells those resemble centrocytes (often large) and centroblasts
Often BCL2 –
Occur on head and trunk; tend to remain localized to the skin; amenable to local therapy

Mantle Cell Lymphoma

Definition
☐ B-cell neoplasm of monomorphous small to medium-sized cells that resemble
  centrocytes
☐ Median age: 60 yrs
☐ Male predominance (at least about 2:1)
☐ Extranodal sites: bone marrow (50-60%), GI (30%, multiple lymphomatous polyposis in large intestine), and Waldeyer's ring
☐ Most patients present with lymphadenopathy, hepatosplenomegaly

Morphology
☐ Monomorphic proliferation of small to medium-sized lymphoid cells that resemble centrocytes
☐ Vague nodular/ diffuse / mantle zone growth pattern
☐ Hyalinized small blood vessels

Immunuphenotype
☐ Intense sIg (IgM +/- IgD)
☐ CD5 +, CD43 +, BCL-2 +, Cyclin D1 +
☐ Cyclin D1 seen in 70-80% of cases
☐ CD10 -, BCL-6 –

Genetics
☐ t(11;14) (q13;q32): chr 11 Cyclin D1, chr14 Ig heavy chain
Blastoid Variant
☐ Cells resemble lymphoblasts with dispersed chromatin
☐ High mitotic rate (>10/10 hpf)

Prognosis
☐ Median survival 3-5 yrs
☐ Vast majority cannot be cured

Diffuse Large B -Cell Lymphoma

Definition
☐ Diffuse proliferation of large neoplastic B lymphoid cells
☐ Nuclear size equal to or exceeding normal macrophage nuclei or more than twice the size of a normal lymphocyte

Epidemiology
☐ 30-40% of adult non-Hodgkin lymphomas in western countries; higher proportion in developing countries
☐ Broad age range (median: 7th decade) including children
☐ Slightly more common in males
☐ Increasing incidence, independent of HIV

Site of Involvement
☐ Nodal or extra-nodal
☐ Up to 40% are at least initially confined to extranodal sites
☐ Most common extranodal site: GI (stomach or ileo-coecal region)
☐ Virtually any extranodal location
☐ Primary tumor in BM and/or PB is rare

Clinical Features
☐ A rapidly enlarging, often symptomatic mass at a single nodal or extranodal site
☐ With staging evaluation, many patients have disseminated disease

☐ Usually de novo but can represent progression / transformation of a less aggressive lymphoma

□ Immunodeficiency is a significant risk factor
□ DLBCL in the setting of immunodeficiency are more often EBV-positive than sporadic DLBCL

Morphologic Variants
 Centroblastic
- Medium to large cells with oval to round, vesicular nuclei with fine chromatin and 2-4 nucleoli. The cytoplasm is generally scanty and amphophilic to basophilic
- May have a monomorphic or polymorphic appearance. Cells may be multilobated. Centroblast-like cells may be admixed with multilobated cells and up to 90% immunoblasts
- Immunoblastic
- Immunoblasts > 90%, with a single centrally located nucleolus and an appreciable amount of basophilic cytoplasm
-Centroblasts <10%
- Plasmacytoid differentiation may be present
- Clinical and/or immunophenotypic findings may be essential in differentiating from extra-medullary involvement by a plasmablastic variant of plasma cell myeloma
- T-Cell / Histiocyte Rich
- Majority of cells are T-cells with or without histiocytes; <10% large neoplastic B-cells
- Histiocytes may or may not be epithelioid. The large cells may resemble L&H cells, centroblasts, immunoblasts, or Reed-Sternberg cells
- B-cells are rare to infrequent. Increased B-cells: possibility of NLPHL (especially vaguely nodular growth pattern)
- Immunophenotypic studies may be essential in the differential diagnosis with classical HL. Many diffuse mixed lymphoma cases in the working formulation represent the this variant of DLBCL
- Anaplastic
- Very large round, oval, or polygonal cells with bizarre pleomorphic nuclei which may resemble RS cells
- The cells may grow in a cohesive pattern mimicking carcinoma and may show a sinusoidal pattern of growth
- These cases are biologically and clinically unrelated to ALCL of cytotoxic T-cell derivation

Mycosis Fungoides/Sezary Syndrome

 Mycosis fungoides (MF) and Sezary syndrome are T-cell lymphomas involving the skin with widespread dissemination. The characteristic proliferating T cells are large with highly convoluted or cerebriform nuclei. In MF the cerebriform lymphocytes infiltrate the upper dermis and epidermis, sometimes creating. 'Pautrier's microabscesses in the epidermis. The lesions are erythematosus with eczematous, plaque, and tumor stages.
 It is the presence of the cerebriform cells in the peripheral blood that characterizes the Sezary syndrome. Both MF and Sezary's are clonal and usually expresses a T helper phenotype with aberrant expression of T cell antigens.

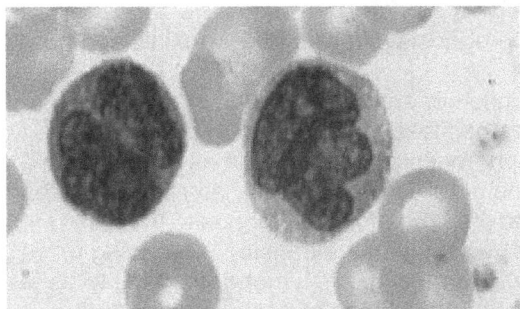

©2007. Rector and visitors of the University of Virginia
Charles E. Hess, M.D. and Lindsey Krstic, B.A. Used with permission

Adult T-cell leukemia/lymphoma

Adult T cell leukemia/lymphoma (ATL/L) is a T cell lymphoma with leukemic manifestations involving lymph nodes, skin, spleen and liver. The neoplastic circulating cells vary in size, but characteristically are large multilobulated lymphoid cells. They are T cells, nearly always T helper cells (CD 4 positive) and show aberrant expression of T cell antigens. The ATL/L cells express CD 25 (the interleukin 2 receptor). This is important in that CD 25 is the receptor used by HTLV1 to gain access to lymphocytes.

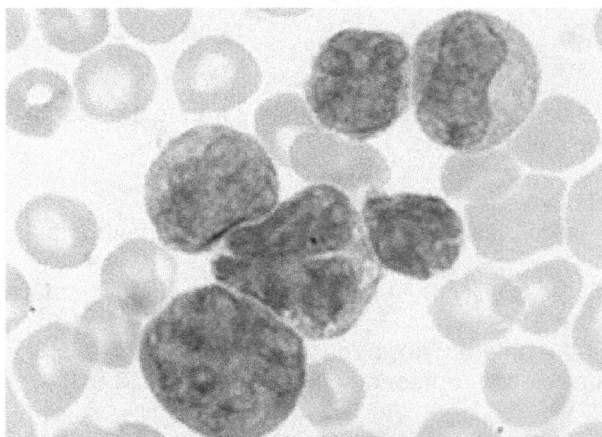

©2007. Rector and visitors of the University of Virginia
Charles E. Hess, M.D. and Lindsey Krstic, B.A. Used with permission

The goal of the physician is to establish a diagnosis, determine the extent of disease (stage), and institute appropiate therapy for the patient.

Clinical Presentation
Signs & symptoms
Laboratory tests- including biopsy & when appropriate FNA
Staging
Treatment
Chemotherapy
Radiation
Observe and do no harm
Because the clinical presentation, staging, treatment and prognosis different for Hodgkin's and non-Hodgkin's lymphomas they will be considered separately.

The clinical manifestations of Hodgkin lymphoma are, while not entirely unique, distinctive for the most part. Hodgkin lymphoma most commonly presents as painless enlargement of peripheral (superficial) lymph nodes. Cervical or supraclavicular lymph nodes are enlarged in as many as 80% of patients at presentation. Mediastinal involvement is common (10% initially; >50% later). In more than 90% of patients disease is located above the diaphragm at the time of initial diagnosis. In most instances, Hodgkin lymphoma appears to spread or grow by contiguous extension (spreading from one lymph node to adjacent nodes or to extranodal tissue). Non-Hodgkin's lymphomas tend to be less defined in their growth pattern, commonly being diffuse, without evidence of contiguous spread.

The lymphadenopathy is often (approximately 25% of cases) accompanied by fever, night sweats (drenching the bedclothes or sheets), and weight loss (>10% in 6 months). Pruritis, usually generalized, is noted in about 10% of cases. An interesting, but rare symptom is pain in the involved lymph nodes secondary to alcohol ingestion.

Often there are no symptoms, but about 40% of people will have some vague signs of the disease. If symptoms do occur, they may include:
Persistent, painless swelling of lymph nodes, especially in the neck, underarm, or groin

Unexplained fevers, tiredness, night sweats, weight loss, and itching
Cough shortness of breath, chest discomfort
Enlarged spleen
Alcohol-induced pain

Laboratory findings:

[1] Normocytic/normochromic anemia that is from mild to moderate in nature.
 In most patients, the anemia is due to the suppressive action of the
 malignancy upon the RBC precursors.
[2] Increased ESR
[3] Normal reticulocyte count is the rule, but may be decreased in some patients.
[4] Reactive lymphocytes may be encountered on the smear in the early stages.
[5] Neutrophilic leukocytosis is moderated to marked (Normal = 2000 to
 7000/µL)
   A.   The neutrophilic count may be so elevated that it suggests chronic
        myelogenous leukemia.
   B.   Toxic granulation may be present.
[6]   Large monocytes, with vacuolation, may be present.
[7]   Lymphocytopenia seen in <15% of patients (<1000/µL).
[8]   Eosinophilia (mild form) is usually present.
[9]   Thrombocytosis with bizarre forms present.
[10]   AHG Test: usually negative. If the patient develop autoimmune hemolytic anemia this test will be
positive. If hypersplenism is present, then the test is positive
[11]   If the liver is involved, then liver function tests will be positive.
[12]   The Epstein-Barr virus titer is usually elevated.
[13]   The bone marrow biopsy tends to reveal little useful data.
[14]   Plasma cells may be observed in the peripheral blood smear.

   The Reed-Sternberg cells are observed mostly in lymph node biopsies. It is a giant bi-lobed cell
with eosinophilic nucleoli. There is perinuclear clearing that forms a halo around the nuclei. The
nuclear membrane is thick and well defined. The abundant cytoplasm stains pale with a slight degree
of eosinophilia.

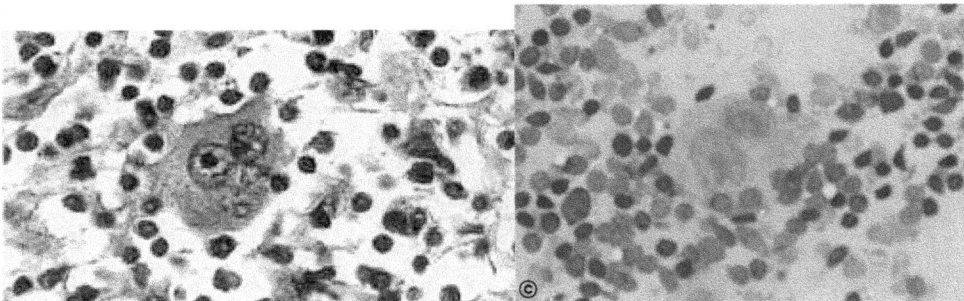

=Atlas of Hematology (Nivaldo Medeiros, MD). Used with permission=

PART THIRTEEN: PLASMA CELL DISORDERS

Multiple Myeloma (MM)

• Plasma cell myeloma
• Plasmacytoma
• Monoclonal immunoglobulin deposition disease
>   1- Primary amyloidosis
>   2- Monoclonal light and heavy chain deposition disease
>   3- Osteosclerotic myeloma (POEMS syndrome)
>   4- Heavy chain diseases
>>   - Gamma heavy chain disease
>>   - Mu heavy chain disease
>>   - Alpha heavy chain disease

•   Immunosecretory disorders result from the expansion of a single clone of immunoglobulin secreting, terminally differentiated, end-stage B-cells
•   These monoclonal proliferations of either plasma cells or plasmacytoid lymphocytes are characterized by secretion of a single homogeneous immunoglobulin product known as the M-component or monoclonal component
•   The prominence of the M-component in serum and urine protein electrophoresis (SPE, UPE) has led to various designations for these disorders including monoclonal gammopathies, dysproteinemias and paraproteinemias
•   The M-components, although monoclonal, may be seen in malignant conditions (plasma cell myeloma and Waldenström macroglobulinemia) and benign or premalignant disorders (MGUS)
•   Variants of plasma cell myeloma include syndromes defined by the consequence of tissue immunoglobulin deposition, including primary amyloidosis (AL) and light and heavy chain deposition diseases

There are several risk factors for this disorder. Four are listed as follows:
[1] Genetic predisposition.   Families which have MM diagnosed relatives have a higher risk of presenting with this disease.
[2] Ionizing radiation.   Medical follow up of the victims of the Hiroshima and Nagasaki atomic bombings statistically has a fivefold increase in this disease.
[3] Chronic infections.   Chronic infections (examples: osteomyelitis and rheumatoid arthritis) have been statistically linked to an increased risk to presenting with MM.
[4] Chromosome abnormalities.   Chromosome studies in some MM patients have demonstrated translocations, trisomy, and monsomy (absence of one chromosome of a chromosome pair).

History

In the clinical diagnosis of this disease, the following features have been presented:
[1]   Diffuse sheets or nodular aggregates of plasma cells in the bone marrow.
[2]   Presence of monoclonal serum M-component paraproteins.
[3]   Radiological demonstration of bone lesions in the skull, spine, ribs, and other flat bones.
[4]   Bone pain in the vertebrae and ribs.
[5]   Anemia, hypercalcemia, and renal insufficiency.
[6]   Amyloidosis (metabolic disorder with amyloid, a protein-polysaccharide complex, being deposited in the tissues.
[7]   Bence-Jones protein demonstrated in the urine.
[8]   Decreased levels of normal serum immunoglobulins due the suppression of normal B-lymphocytes and an increase in the catabolic rate of IgG, in other words, an immunodeficiency.
[9]   Clotting disorders, indicating a serious risk for bleeding/hemorrhage.

Multiple myeloma (MM) is refractory to treatment; hence it is an incurable disease. With the best of medical care, the patient may survive up to 3 years. Without medical intervention, the patient will die in six months or less. Death usually comes because of infection or kidney failure.

There is several type of multiple myeloma:

[1] Smoldering myeloma. An inactive, sluggish form of the disease, that in its early stages, it appears to be of uncertain significance. It will take several years for this stage to develop into a "full-blown" case of MM.

[2] Non-secretory myeloma. Multiple myeloma cells are present and are highly undifferentiated (they are primitive, embryonic, without distinct morphology). they have invasive capability and can cause bone lesions.

[3] Plasma cell leukemia. This disorder, though included as a subtype of multiple myeloma is considered by some to be a separate disease. It is suggested that plasma cell leukemia is the fulminant conclusion of multiple myeloma.

Multiple myeloma has a predilection for the middle aged and elderly. The median age is about 60 y/o. It occurs in the black population more often than the white. It is rarely observed in patients under 40 y/o. It makes up about 1% of all cancers and about 10% of hematologic malignant tumors.

3- Clinical symptoms:

[1]   Bone pain (major symptom in about 60% of the patients),
[2]   Renal insufficiency (in about 25% of the patients),
[3]   Infections (in about 10% of patients,
[4]   Bleeding disorders,
[5]   Constipation,
[6]   Back pain,
[7]   Amyloidosis (about 15% of patients).

Clinical laboratory findings

[1] There are two hallmark features:
    A.   Erythrocyte sedimentation rate = very high (100 mm/hr has been reported).
    B.   Rouleaux formation on stained blood films.

[2]   The stained blood film of the peripheral smear usually has a bluish background due to the excess abnormal plasma proteins.

[3]   Hemoglobin is usually <10 g/dL. Ranges reported to be 7.0 to 12 g/dL.

[4]   WBC count: at the initial presentation of the disease, the count is usually normal. As the disease progresses, neutropenia may be observed.

[5]   Platelet count: usually normal at onset but can progress to thrombocytopenia as the disease progresses.

[6]   The peripheral blood smear tends to yield a leukoerythroblastic (presence of immature granulocytes and erythrocytes) picture.

Serum Protein Electrophoresis and Immunofixation

MM results in the production of massive amounts of immunoglobulins of a single class. IgG is the most common globulins followed by IgA, IgM, IgD then IgE. Both light and heavy chains are produced, with light chains in the greatest abundance. These light chains (known as Bence-Jones protein) are rapidly excreted in the urine. These light chain proteins can precipitate in the tubules. If urine flow is poor, precipitation can result with blockage, impaired tubular function, and possible damage. The increase in these abnormal globulins causes a decrease in normal immunoglobulins. The typical MM electrophoresis peak is illustrated below with a normal peak, and different patterns.

Normal Pattern

Note the relative sizes and shapes of the globulin fractions. There is no evidence of Monoclonal Gammopathy.

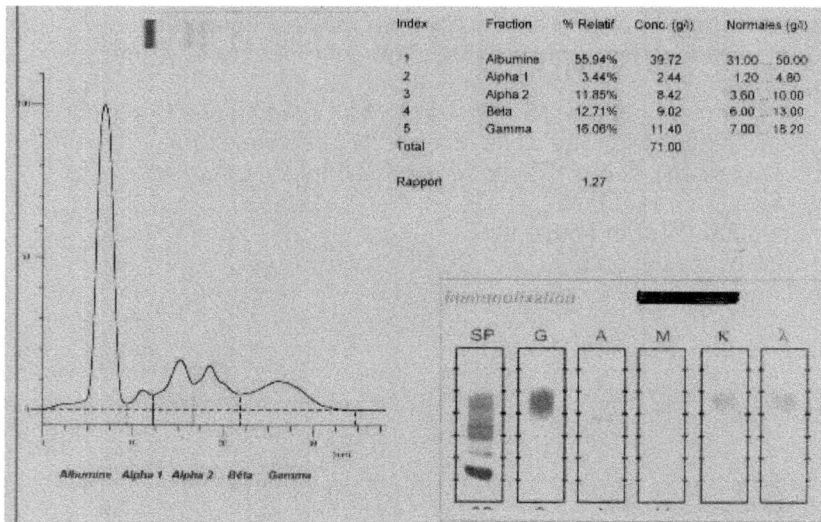

Index	Fraction	% Relatif	Conc. (g/l)	Normales (g/l)
1	Albumine	55.94%	39.72	31.00 ... 50.00
2	Alpha 1	3.44%	2.44	1.20 ... 4.80
3	Alpha 2	11.85%	8.42	3.60 ... 10.00
4	Beta	12.71%	9.02	6.00 ... 13.00
5	Gamma	16.06%	11.40	7.00 ... 15.20
Total			71.00	
Rapport			1.27	

Courtesy of Dr N. Lazrak, Laboratoire du Maghreb

Polyclonal Gammopathy

- Usually secondary to many chronic diseases. IFE excluded the possibility of a monoclonal protein. Much increased gamma without any "spike"
"Polyclonal gammopathy" occurs in chronic liver disease, sarcoidosis, collagen-vascular disease, etc,
An increase in proteins lying between the beta and gamma regions ("beta-gamma bridging") may be seen in polyclonal gammopathy of any etiology, though it is best known for its association with liver disease.

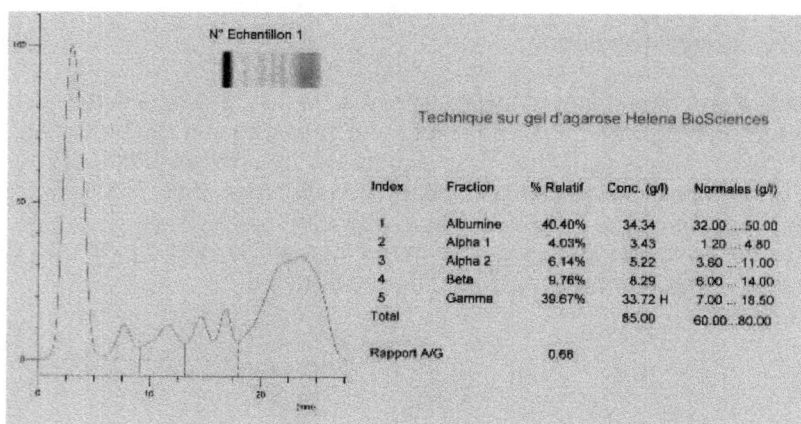

Technique sur gel d'agarose Helena BioSciences

Index	Fraction	% Relatif	Conc. (g/l)	Normales (g/l)
1	Albumine	40.40%	34.34	32.00 ... 50.00
2	Alpha 1	4.03%	3.43	1.20 ... 4.80
3	Alpha 2	6.14%	5.22	3.60 ... 11.00
4	Beta	9.76%	8.29	6.00 ... 14.00
5	Gamma	39.67%	33.72 H	7.00 ... 18.50
Total			85.00	60.00 ... 80.00
Rapport A/G			0.68	

Courtesy of Dr N. Lazrak, Laboratoire du Maghreb

315

Nephrotic Patterns

The nephrotic pattern illustrates the long term loss of lower molecular weight proteins (Examples: albumin, IgG) and retention of higher molecular weight proteins (example alpha-2-macroglobulin.) This patient was a 43 year old man with dialysis. Her daily total urinary protein loss exceeded 4200 mg. (Normal loss is less that 150 mg/day.)

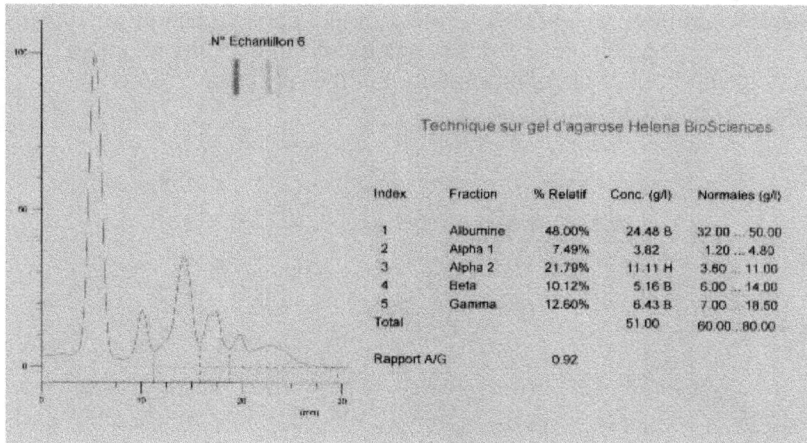

Index	Fraction	% Relatif	Conc. (g/l)	Normales (g/l)
1	Albumine	48.00%	24.48 B	32.00 ... 50.00
2	Alpha 1	7.49%	3.82	1.20 ... 4.80
3	Alpha 2	21.79%	11.11 H	3.80 ... 11.00
4	Beta	10.12%	5.16 B	6.00 ... 14.00
5	Gamma	12.60%	6.43 B	7.00 ... 18.50
Total			51.00	60.00 ... 80.00
Rapport A/G		0.92		

Courtesy of Dr N. Lazrak, Laboratoire du Maghreb

The combination of low total protein, low albumin, high alpha-2 globulins (Haptoglobin and alpha-2 macroglobulin) and beta lipoproteins is suggestive of severe nephrotic syndrome. There is no evidence of a Monoclonal Gammopathy. However, light chains that may be associated with nephrotic syndrome are seldom seen on serum electrophoresis.

Cirrhotic Patterns

Patient was a 46 year old male with end stage liver disease. In the cirrhotic pattern, the distinction between beta and gamma globulin is blurred and is sometimes referred to as the "beta-gamma bridge" pattern.

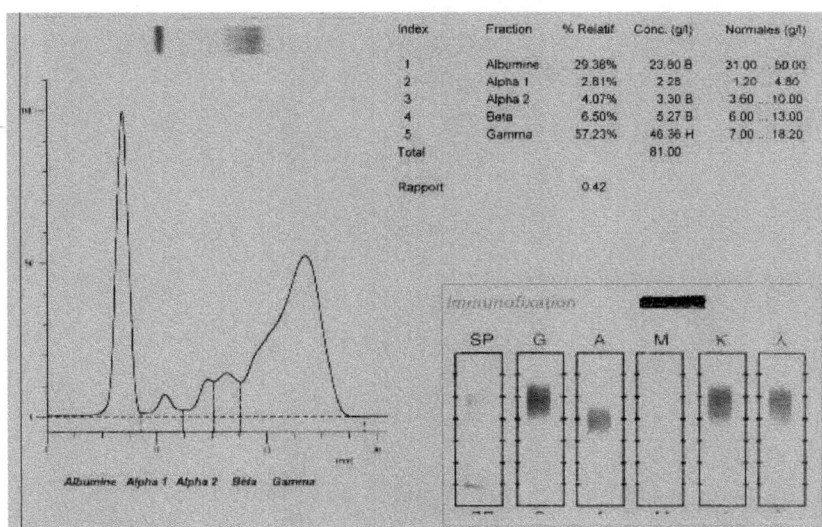

Index	Fraction	% Relatif	Conc. (g/l)	Normales (g/l)
1	Albumine	29.38%	23.80 B	31.00 ... 50.00
2	Alpha 1	2.81%	2.28	1.20 ... 4.80
3	Alpha 2	4.07%	3.30 B	3.60 ... 10.00
4	Beta	6.50%	5.27 B	6.00 ... 13.00
5	Gamma	57.23%	46.36 H	7.00 ... 18.20
Total			81.00	
Rapport		0.42		

Courtesy of Dr N. Lazrak, Laboratoire du Maghreb

Acute inflammatory patterns

This patient was a 34 year old female who presented with a temperature of 40 degrees C and was diagnosed with pneumonia. In the acute inflammatory pattern albumin is decreased and alpha-2-globulin becomes very prominent. "acute-reaction protein pattern" involves increases in fibrinogen, anti-trypsin, Haptoglobin, Ceruloplasmin, CRP, the C3 portion of complement, and acid glycoprotein. Often, there are associated decreases in the albumin and transferrin levels. The combination of hypogammaglobulinemia and severe inflammation suggests an immunologic abnormality or an autoimmune disease. Measurements of immunoglobulin subclasses and auto antibodies might be helpful. Hypergammaglobulinemia is a sign of chronic inflammation, but the absence of other abnormalities is unusual. No gammopathy is identified.

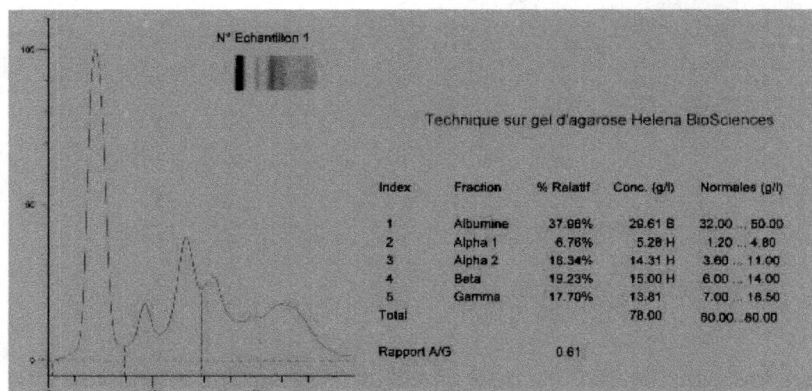

N° Echantillon 1

Technique sur gel d'agarose Helena BioSciences

Index	Fraction	% Relatif	Conc. (g/l)	Normales (g/l)
1	Albumine	37.96%	29.61 B	32.00 ... 50.00
2	Alpha 1	6.76%	5.28 H	1.20 ... 4.80
3	Alpha 2	18.34%	14.31 H	3.60 ... 11.00
4	Beta	19.23%	15.00 H	6.00 ... 14.00
5	Gamma	17.70%	13.81	7.00 ... 18.50
Total			78.00	60.00 ... 80.00
Rapport A/G		0.61		

Courtesy of Dr N. Lazrak, Laboratoire du Maghreb

Monoclonal (M) Protein Present

The patient was a 72 year old male who presented with lower back pain. Quantitative immunoglobulin measurements showed a large increase in serum IgG, but decreased IgA and IgM. Bone marrow exam revealed a large increase in plasma cells. IFE on this patient's serum showed the M protein was IgG kappa. A diagnosis of multiple myeloma was made.

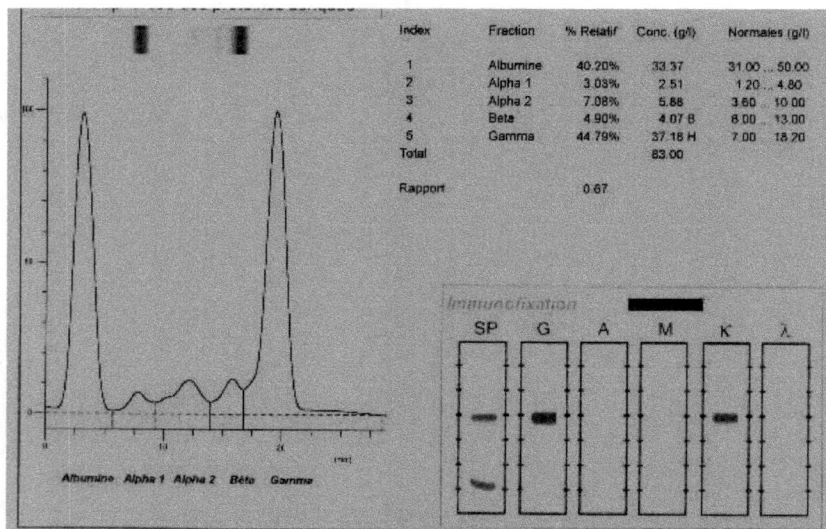

Index	Fraction	% Relatif	Conc. (g/l)	Normales (g/l)
1	Albumine	40.20%	33.37	31.00 ... 50.00
2	Alpha 1	3.03%	2.51	1.20 ... 4.80
3	Alpha 2	7.08%	5.88	3.60 ... 10.00
4	Beta	4.90%	4.07 B	6.00 ... 13.00
5	Gamma	44.79%	37.18 H	7.00 ... 18.20
Total			83.00	
Rapport		0.67		

Albumine Alpha 1 Alpha 2 Bêta Gamma

Immunofixation

SP G A M K λ

Courtesy of Dr N. Lazrak, Laboratoire du Maghreb

Biclonal Gammopathy

This sample is from a 70 year old male who presented with weight loss and fatigue. He was found to have multiple myeloma. In this disease, Biclonal gammopathies are rare, occurring in about 2.0 % of patients. IFE showed the 2 M proteins to be IgG- Lambda.

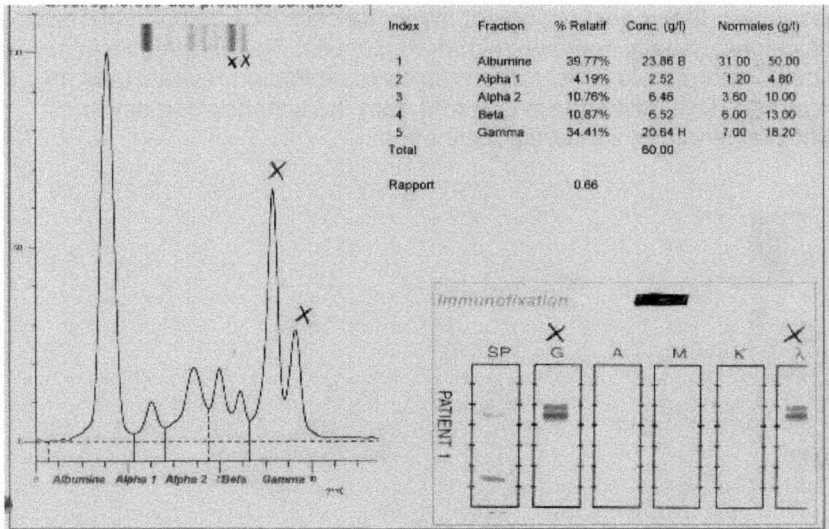

Index	Fraction	% Relatif	Conc. (g/l)	Normales (g/l)
1	Albumine	39.77%	23.86 B	31.00 .. 50.00
2	Alpha 1	4.19%	2.52	1.20 .. 4.80
3	Alpha 2	10.76%	6.46	3.60 .. 10.00
4	Beta	10.87%	6.52	6.00 .. 13.00
5	Gamma	34.41%	20.64 H	7.00 .. 18.20
Total			60.00	
Rapport		0.66		

Courtesy of Dr N. Lazrak, Laboratoire du Maghreb

IBone marrow aspirate and biopsy

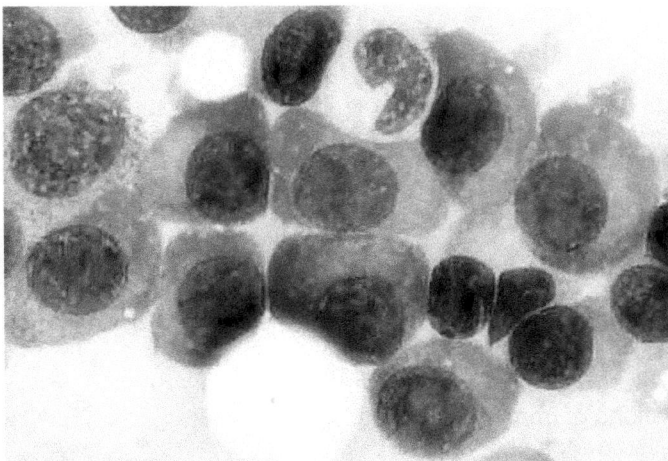

These plasma cells are more clearly malignant. In addition to large nuclei, they have fine chromatin, occasional nucleoli, and atypical cytoplasmic features.

=Hemepath tutorial (Prof. David Weissmann). Used with permission=

Obtain samples to calculate the percent of plasma cells in the aspirate (reference range, <3%) and to look for sheets or clusters of plasma cells in the biopsy specimen.

- Cytogenetic analysis of the bone marrow may contribute significant prognostic information. Abnormalities of chromosome 13 (predominantly monosomy 13) predict a poor outcome. In addition, in persons with MGUS, the presence of monosomy 13 may correlate with the subsequent development of myeloma.
- Histologic Findings: In patients with myeloma, plasma cells proliferate within the bone marrow, typically in sheets. Plasma cells are 2-3 times larger than typical lymphocytes; they have eccentric nuclei that are smooth (round or oval) in contour with clumped chromatin and have a perinuclear halo or pale zone. The cytoplasm is basophilic. Many descriptions of myeloma cells include characteristic, but not diagnostic, cytoplasmic inclusions, usually containing immunoglobulin. The variants include Mott cells, Russell bodies, grape cells, and morula cells. Bone marrow examination reveals plasma cell infiltration, often in sheets or clumps. This infiltration is different from the lymphoplasmacytic infiltration observed in patients with Waldenström's macroglobulinemia.

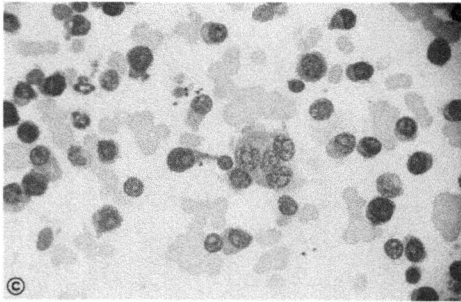

=Atlas of Hematology (Nivaldo Medeiros, MD). Used with permission=

- Bone marrow is marked by hypercellularity due to plasma cell proliferation. The plasma cell is a large mono- or bi-nucleated cell with prominent nucleoli. The nuclear chromatin can be fine or coarse. The nucleus can stain with differing intensity. There is abundant cytoplasm with the degree of basophilia determined by the amount of RNA present. Bizarre plasma cells may be present which confuses the evaluation. Two intracellular inclusions are noted in the MM cell:
A. Dutcher bodies may be present in the nucleus. These are PAS positive inclusions, also seen in abnormal lymphocytes.

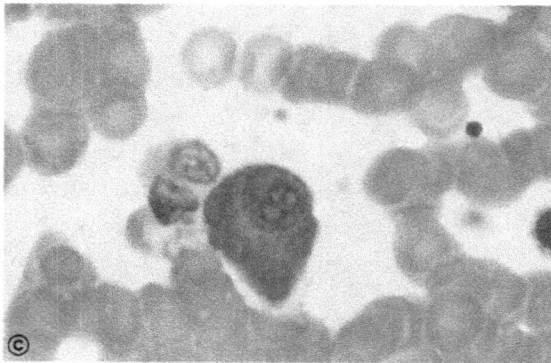

B. If the cytoplasm contains rounded accumulations of immunoglobulins, these are Russell bodies. Such a cell is called a Mott cell, morula cell, or plasma cell with Russell bodies.

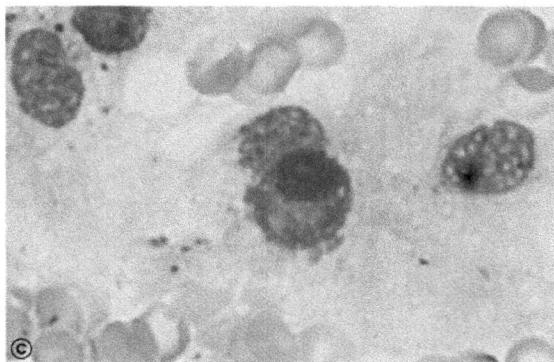

C. If the cytoplasm contains ribosomal proteins then the cytoplasm, when stained will take on a reddish hue (called a flame cell).

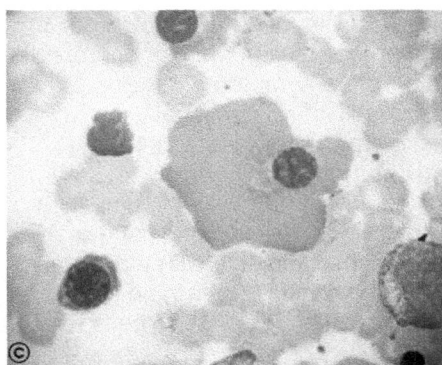

=Atlas of Hematology (Nivaldo Medeiros, MD). Used with permission=

Multiple myeloma is not a curable disease. In the United States, approximately 10,000 persons per year die of multiple myeloma. Without treatment, most patients die in less than 1 year; with treatment, life expectancy may be extended 2-3 years. Death usually occurs in less than two years.

The following are the most important diagnostic criteria for MM:

[1]   More than 30% of the cells in the bone marrow are plasma cells.
[2]   Presence of a monoclonal (M) spike on the electrophoresis test that
        consist of >3.5 g/dL of serum IgG or >2.0 g/dL of serum IgA or
        >1.0 g/dL of lambda or kappa urinary light chains.
[3]   Multiple bone lesions.
[4]   Beta-2 microglobulin is a very strong predictor of outcome; some studies suggest it is more powerful than stage; it is a surrogate marker for the overall body tumor burden. The level of beta-2 microglobulin is increased in patients with renal insufficiency without myeloma, which is one reason that it is a useful prognosticator in myeloma. The prognosis with myeloma and impaired renal function is reduced.

Staging

Staging is a cumulative evaluation of all of the diagnostic information garnered and is a useful tool for stratifying the severity of patients' disease. The staging system for myeloma is somewhat complex, but it is well correlated with outcome.
The Durie-Salmon staging system uses a more complex system taking into account several test results, and is broken into Stage I (low), Stage II (intermediate), and Stage III (high).

Stage I involves all of the following:
Hemoglobin level greater than 10 g/dL

Calcium level less than 12 mg/dL
Radiograph showing normal bones or solitary plasmacytoma
Low M protein values (i.e., IgG <5 g/dL, IgA <3 g/dL, urine <4 g/24 h)
Stage II involves criteria that fit neither stage I nor stage III.
Stage III involves any one of the following:
Hemoglobin level less than 8.5 g/dL
Calcium level greater than 12 mg/dL
Radiograph showing advanced lytic bone disease
High M protein value (i.e., IgG >7 g/dL, IgA >5 g/dL, urine >12 g/24 h)
Subclassification A involves a creatinine level of less than 2 g/dL.
Subclassification B involves a creatinine level greater than 2 g/dL.
Stage I is associated with median survival of longer than 60 months, stage II is 41 months, and stage III is 23 months. Stage B disease has a significantly worse outcome (e.g., 2-12 mo in 4 separate series).

Treatment

People who develop multiple myeloma can present with smoldering multiple myeloma, which is characterized by increased plasma cells in the bone marrow and the presence of monoclonal proteins, without the symptoms of multiple myeloma. Often it can be 2-3 years before symptoms develop, and there have been no studies that have shown a benefit to early treatment. Therapy is usually not started in patients with smoldering multiple myeloma or asymptomatic stage I disease. Generally, therapy for Stage II or III multiple myeloma starts with "conventional chemotherapy", which is traditional chemotherapy. Stem cell transplantation is a mainstay of treatment now as well, usually after conventional chemotherapy, but some studies have shown it may be beneficial as initial therapy. The preferred initial treatment for people who are thought to be potential transplant is with thalidomide and dexamethasone or lenalidomide and dexamethasone. Prior regimens used Melphan; an alkylating chemotherapy which can damage the stem cells, causing problems with collection of stem cells for future transplant.
Treatment is given in three phases for transplants: induction therapy -> consolidation therapy-> maintenance therapy:
Induction therapy: Several combinations of various agents can be used as induction therapy. Dexamethasone, vincristine and doxorubicin can be used in combination, or else Dexamethasone with thalidomide or Dexamethasone alone can be used. Occasionally total body radiation can be used. These treatments are used to try to decrease the number of myeloma cells prior to harvesting stem cells from the blood or bone marrow.
Consolidation therapy: People are then treated with high dose chemotherapy, such as Melphan to destroy as many myeloma cells as possible. The harvested stem cells are then infused and take root in the bone marrow and begin to grow and replace the old marrow.
Maintenance therapy: Used to try to maintain remission, people can be treated with steroids, thalidomide, or no treatment may be necessary.
Almost all patients with multiple myeloma are at risk for an eventual relapse. Generally, for relapses that occur within the first six months, another cycle of the same initial chemotherapy is given. Alternatively, in people who have had stem cells harvested and saved, an autologous stem cell transplant can be used as salvage therapy.

Follow-up Testing

Follow up appointments to check for recurrences are very important in people with multiple myeloma. Generally, after completion of treatment the patients must be following up every one to three months. The follow up visit usually entails a physical exam, X-Rays, blood tests and urine tests. X-Rays are used to check for bone disease and blood and urine tests are used to check for the level of monoclonal proteins. Blood tests to check kidney function, calcium levels, and cell counts are also done routinely. Repeated bone marrow biopsies may also be needed to check for myeloma cells in the bone marrow.

Refractory Plasma Cell Neoplasm

There are two main types of refractory myeloma patients:
- Primary refractory patients who never achieve a response and progress while still on induction chemotherapy.
- Secondary refractory patients who do respond to induction chemotherapy but do not respond to treatment after relapse.

Subgroups of patients who do not achieve a response to induction chemotherapy have stable disease and enjoy a survival prognosis that is as good as that for responding patients. When the stable nature of the disease becomes established, these types of patients can discontinue therapy until the myeloma begins to progress again. Others with primary refractory myeloma and progressive disease require a change in therapy.

The myeloma growth rate, as measured by the monoclonal (or myeloma) protein-doubling time, for patients who respond to their initial therapy, increases progressively with each subsequent relapse and remission durations become shorter and shorter. Marrow function becomes increasingly compromised as patients develop pancytopenia and enter a refractory phase; occasionally the myeloma cells dedifferentiate and extramedullary plasmacytomas develop. The myeloma cells may still be sensitive to chemotherapy, but the regrowth rate during relapse is so rapid that progressive improvement is not observed.

Plasma Cell Leukemia

Plasma cell leukemia is diagnosed when a significant number (>10% of the total cells or 2,000/μL) of plasma cells appear in peripheral blood. It is an unusual disease with leukocytosis. These neoplastic cells are found in advanced stages of multiple myeloma. Plasma cells will diffuse throughout the body, infiltrating and aggregating in the liver, spleen, bone marrow, and lymph nodes. The "blood picture" is leuko-erythroblastic (presence of both immature granulocytes and erythrocytes).

This patient will present with one or more of the following: [1] lymphadenopathy, [2] proteins with M-component, [3] bone lesions, and [4] hepatosplenomegaly. As this stage progresses, the following is typical:
[1] WBC count = 10,000 to 15,000/μL. (Higher values, up to
        90,000/μL, have been reported)
[2] Plasmablasts and proplasmacytes appear in the blood and will
        make up from 10% to 90% of the total leukocyte count.
[3] Thrombocytopenia occurs in 50% of the patients.
[4] Anemia develops.
[5] Bleeding manifestations (petechiae, ecchymoses, hemorrhage)
[6] The presence of hypergammaglobulinemia with marked amounts
        of IgD and IgE.
Plasma cell leukemia is refractive to therapy and the patient dies in a few months from a blast crisis.
Plasma cell leukemia is considered to have clinicopathological differences with multiple myeloma, but may only represent a phase of multiple myeloma.

Macroglobulinemia

Macroglobulinemia is a proliferation of plasmacytoid lymphocytes secreting an IgM M protein. Patients often have lymphadenopathy and hepatosplenomegaly, but bony lesions are uncommon. No generally accepted staging system exists.

The term macroglobulinemia describes an increase in the serum concentration of a monoclonal IgM. Most patients are asymptomatic and do not require treatment. The most common symptoms and signs are fatigue, manifestations of hyperviscosity (e.g., headache, epistaxis, and visual disturbances), and neurologic abnormalities. Serum or plasma viscosity (relative to water) measures the risk of symptoms. The normal viscosity level is 1.7 to 2.1; symptoms may rarely appear between 3.0 and 4.0 but more commonly appear above 4.0. Emergent therapy (i.e., plasmapheresis and chemotherapy) is usually required above a viscosity level of 4.0. Lymphadenopathy and splenomegaly are found in about 33% of patients. The increased intravascular concentration of high molecular weight IgM leads to an expansion of the plasma volume, a Dilutional anemia, and in extreme cases, congestive heart failure. Sludging of the blood can be seen in conjunctival and retinal veins with dilatation and segmentation of vessels (i.e., a link of sausage appearance), retinal hemorrhages, and papilledema.

Similar problems with the circulation of blood in the central nervous system can cause ataxia, nystagmus, vertigo, confusion, and disturbances of consciousness.

The various disorders associated with the appearance of a monoclonal IgM include:

- Monoclonal Gammopathy of Undetermined Significance (MGUS). Patients are asymptomatic, the M protein is stable, and no lymphadenopathy, splenomegaly, or bony lesions are present.

- Waldenström's Macroglobulinemia (WM). This entity is called lymphoplasmacytic lymphoma in the World Health Organization/Revised European-American Lymphoma classification system. Patients are symptomatic, have lymphoplasmacytic marrow infiltration, and a rising serum IgM concentration, and may have lymphadenopathy or splenomegaly. Rarely, patients with WM have lytic bone lesions.

- Absolute lymphocyte count exceeding 5,000 cells/mm^3. The patient may be classified as having chronic lymphocytic leukemia (CLL) if the lymphocytes are of the small, well-differentiated variety. CLL must be differentiated from the lymphoplasmacytosis that may occur as a peripheral blood manifestation of WM.

- Chronic cold agglutinin disease. Patients have a high cold agglutinin titer and no morphologic evidence of neoplasia. These patients often have a hemolytic anemia that is aggravated by cold exposure. The IgM has kappa light chains in more than 90% of these types of patients.

Waldenstrom's Macroglobulinemia

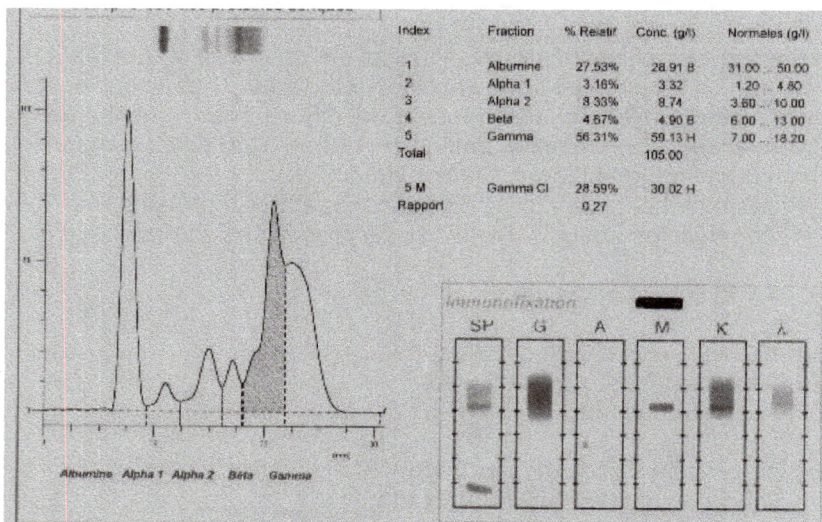

Courtesy of Dr N. Lazrak, Laboratoire du Maghreb

Waldenström's macroglobinemia is an immuno-lymphoproliferative disorder that has features of both malignant lymphoma and multiple myeloma. This is a disease of older adults, usually men with a median age of around 60. Clinical symptoms are [1] weight loss, [2] fatigue, [3] blurred vision, [4] epistaxis and other bleeding episodes.

Clinical laboratory findings include:

[1]   Normocytic/normochromic anemia.
[2]   Prolonged prothrombin time with low fibrinogen values.
[3]   Lymphocytes with variation, resembling plasmacytoid cells.
[4]   Serum IgM monoclonal antibody = >3 g/dL (or >15% of the total
        serum globulins).
[5]   No Bence-Jones protein is present.
[6]   Serum precipitate is present which may be erroneously counted as
        platelets to produce a spurious count, if performing an electronic
        count.
[7]   Hyperviscosity of the blood.
[8]   Bone marrow is hypercellular. Predominate/significant cell is
        lymphoplasmacyte-like cell.

[9]   Characteristic bruising is called cryoglobulinemic purpura.
[10] Cryoglobulins precipitate on exposure to cold.

Cryoglobulinemia

Cryoglobulinemia results from abnormal proteins that precipitate at reduced temperatures. It is associated with PCDs and chronic inflammation. Cryoglobulins can be 1) monoclonal immunoglobulins (Type I) as in myeloma or Waldenstrom's, 2) monoclonal proteins (usually IgM k) complexed to IgG (Type II), or 3) polyclonal immune complexes with no monoclonal component (Type III). Types II and III are associated with connective tissue and autoimmune disorders. Through the formation of protein gels at reduced body temperatures, precipitated cryoglobulins can occlude small vessels giving rise to Raynaud's phenomenon, vascular purpura (cold urticaria) and arthralgia.

   Therapy is based on the treatment of the underlying disease and/or plasmapheresis and, of course, avoidance of cold.

Note that cold agglutinins which are RBC antibodies are different from cyroglobulins.

Monoclonal Gammopathy of Undetermined Significance

Patients with MGUS have an M protein (< 3g/L) in the serum without findings of multiple myeloma, macroglobulinemia, Amyloidosis, or lymphoma, and with less than 10% of plasma cells in the bone marrow. These types of patients are asymptomatic and should not be treated. They must, however, be followed carefully since about 1% to 2% per year will progress to develop one of the symptomatic B-cell neoplasms and may then require therapy. Risk factors predicting progression include an abnormal serum-free light chain ratio, non-IgG class MGUS, and a high serum M protein level (≥15 g/L).

"Nonsecretory" myeloma

In which immunoglobulin is not synthesized (true Nonsecretory) or secreted but not excreted, is rare (<5%). Cases have been reported in which there is production of J chain but no heavy or light chain. Clinical, hematologic, and radiologic findings are similar to those of standard myeloma. Some have reported fewer problems with infection and less renal damage (no increase in circulating monoclonal immunoglobulin) but survival appears no better than the average myeloma patient.

Plasmacytoma

•   Clonal proliferation of plasma cells (cytologically, morphologically, and immunophenotypically identical to myeloma cells) with localized growth pattern
•   Localized growth pattern
     . Osseous: solitary plasmacytoma of bone
     . Extraosseous (extramedullary) plasmacytoma

Solitary Plasmacytoma of Bone
•   Osseous plasmacytoma
•   Localized bone tumor
•   Solitary lytic lesion on X-rays
•   No plasmacytosis in bone marrow away from lesion
•   Epidemiology: rare (5% of plasma cell neoplasms)
•   Sites of involvement: most commonly in marrow areas of most active hematopoiesis (vertebrae, ribs, skull, pelvis, femur, clavicle, and scapula)
•   Clinical features
     . Presentation: bone pain, or pathological fracture
     . No serum or urine M-protein (if present, it usually disappears after treatment)
•   Morphology, immunophenotype, and genetics: identical to plasma cell myeloma
•   Treatment: radiation therapy
•   Prognosis at 10 years
     . 55% develop plasma cell myeloma
     . 35% cured

. 10% local recurrence or develop another solitary lesion at different sites

Extraosseous Plasmacytoma
- Extraosseous and extramedullary tumor
- Epidemiology
  . 3-5% of plasma cell neoplasms
  . Adults (median age 55)
  . Males: Female=2:1
- Sites of involvement
  . Upper respiratory tract (80%): oropharynx, nasopharynx, sinuses, larynx
  .Other sites of involvement: GI tract, urinary bladder, central nervous system, breast, thyroid, testis, parotid gland, lymph nodes, skin
- Clinical features
  . No evidence of plasma cell myeloma on bone marrow examination and by radiography
  . May have monoclonal gammopathy (15-20%)
  . No evidence of anemia, hypercalcemia, or renal insufficiency
- Morphology
  . Similar to osseous plasmacytoma
  . Some cases (particularly in GI) may represent MALT lymphoma with plasmacytic differentiation
- Differential diagnosis: reactive plasma cell infiltrates with polyclonal kappa and lambda light chain expression
- Immunophenotype and genetic features
  . Not extensively studied
  . Appear to be identical to those of plasma cell myeloma
- Treatment: radiation therapy
- Prognosis
  . 25% of cases with regional recurrences
  . 15% of cases develop plasma cell myeloma

Monoclonal Immunoglobulin Deposition Disease (MIDD)

Visceral and soft tissue Ig deposition, resulting in compromised organ function
Two major categories

1- Primary amyloidosis: fibrillary protein with a beta-pleated sheet structure, which binds Congo red with apple-green birefringence, and contains amyloid-P component. Predominant lambda light chain

2- Monoclonal light chain and heavy chain deposition diseases: abnormal light chain or heavy chain (or both) that does not have a beta-pleated sheet configuration and does not bind to Congo red nor contain amyloid-P component. Predominantly kappa light chain

Primary amyloidosis

Amyloid stained with Congo red   Polarized birefringent amyloid

*   Rare disease in adults, 80% with monoclonal immunoglobulin, 20% having overt plasma cell myeloma
*   15% myeloma patients have or will develop primary amyloidosis
*   Most frequently lambda light chain

1-Sites of involvement
*   Plasma cell-related amyloid (AL) accumulates in: heart (congestive heart failure), liver (hepatomegaly), kidneys (nephrotic syndrome and/or renal failure), gut (malabsorption), tongue (macroglossia), nerves (sensorimotor peripheral neuropathy and loss of sphincter control), bone, and blood vessel (bleeding due to vessel fragility)
*   Diagnostic sites: abdominal subcutaneous fat-pad, BM, or rectum

2- Pathophysiology
*   AL: primary or immunoglobulin-light chain (myeloma-associated) amyloidosis
*   AA: secondary amyloidosis (inflammation-associated)
*   AF: familial amyloidosis
*   b2M: b-2 microglobulin amyloidosis (hemodialysis-associated)
*   AL: intact immunoglobulin light chains secreted by monoclonal plasma cells, ingested, processed and discharged by macrophages into the extracellular matrix.
*   Macroscopy: dense "porcelain-like" or waxy appearance.

3- Microscopy:
    H&E: amorphous, eosinophilic, waxy-appearing substance, with a characteristic cracking artifact, focally in thickened blood vessel walls, on basement membranes, and in the interstitial of tissues such as adipose tissue or bone marrow.
    Congo red: pinkish red by standard light microscopy and "apple-green" birefringence by polarization microscopy.

4- Immunophenotype: light chains: useful in distinguishing primary from secondary amyloidosis but background may be high in paraffin-embedded sections.

5- Prognosis: patients with plasma cell myeloma and amyloidosis have a shorter survival period than those with myeloma alone.

Monoclonal light chain and heavy chain deposition diseases (LCDD and HCDD)

Epidemiology

Rare (<70 cases described)
Age range: 33-79 years (56 year median)
Usually associated with MGUS or myeloma
No ethnicity effect and equal incidence in male and female

Site of involvement: many organs, most commonly kidneys, liver, heart, nerves, blood vessels and occasionally joints. Prominent deposition of aberrant Ig on basement membranes, elastic and collagen fibers. Vascular occlusion and microaneurysm formation may occur

Clinical Features
*   Organ dysfunction: nephrotic syndrome, renal failure, arthritis, congestive heart failure, and coagulopathy due to liver involvement
*   IgG3 or IgG1: hypocomplementemia
*   Monoclonal gammopathy: 85% of cases
*   No M-component: 15% of cases; representing strong tissue binding of the aberrant Ig

Pathophysiology
Monoclonal Ig: structural changes due to deletion and mutation. Alteration in physiochemical properties or aberrant glycosylation, which favor tissue binding and deposition
HCDD
CH1 deletion: secreted prematurely
Substitutions in variable regions: increase in tissue deposition and binding blood elements
LCDD
Multiple mutations in light chain variable regions, with V_{kIV} over-represented, favoring tissue binding
Most frequently kappa light chain (80% of cases)

Morphology
*   Monoclonal Ig deposit: non-amyloid, nonfibrillary, amorphous eosinophilic material, negative for Congo red
*   Refractile eosinophilic material in glomerular and tubular basement membranes, but may also be seen in bone marrow and other tissues
*   EM: discrete, dense punctate granular, nonfibrillary deposits
*   X-ray diffraction: absence of the beta-pleated sheet structure
*   Typically few plasma cells in the organs with Ig deposition; Ig produced in the BM and reach the site via circulation
*   BM plasmacytosis: 50-60% cases

Immunophenotype
*   BM: aberrant kappa/lambda ratio, even without overt plasmacytosis

Prognosis: very poor, fatal within 1-2 years even in the absence of aggressive plasma cell proliferation

Heavy Chain Disease

1-Gamma Heavy Chain Disease

A lymphoplamacytic neoplasm that produces a truncated gamma chain, which lacks light-chain binding sites and does not bind to light chains to form a complete immunoglobin molecule

Sites of involvement: lymph nodes, Waldeyer's ring, bone marrow, liver, spleen, peripheral blood
·   Epidemiology: rare, median age: 60
·   Clinical features
*   Associated with lymphoplasmacytic lymphoma
*   No lytic bone lesions
*   SPE: normal-looking or sometimes broad band (infection-like)
*   Immunofixation: IgG (truncated) without light chains
*   Urine protein: <1g/24h
*   Median survival 12 months

2-Mu Heavy Chain Disease

* Extremely rare, associated with B-cell neoplasm resembling CLL, with truncated mu heavy chain, slowly progressive
* Involves: spleen, liver, bone marrow, peripheral blood. Lymph nodes are usually spared
* Routine SPE: frequently negative
* Immunofixation: Mu fragments in diverse sizes
* Urine Bence-Jones light chains: in 50% of cases, mostly kappa (cannot bind to Mu chains)
* Monoclonal cytoplasmic Mu heavy chains without light chains
* Pan B-cell Antigens (+), CD5 (-), CD10 (-)
* Bone marrow: vacuolated plasma cells with small lymphocytes
* Prognosis: slowly progressive

3-Alpha Heavy Chain Disease

* A variant of MALT (immunoproliferative small intestinal disease or IPSID), in which a defective alpha heavy chain is secreted
* Involves GI tract in young adults resulting in diarrhea, malabsorption
* May respond to antibiotics but may also lead to high grade lymphoma
* Peak incidence in second and third decades
* Common in areas bordering Mediterranean
* Plasma cells and marginal zone cells: monoclonal cytoplasmic alpha heavy chains without light chains
* Pan B-cell Antigens (+), CD5 (-), CD10 (-)
* Early phase may completely remit with antibiotic therapy
*   However, many transform to DLBCL, and frequently fatal

Osteosclerotic Myeloma (POEMS Syndrome)

Osteosclerotic myeloma often associated with
  Polyneuropathy: sensorimotor demyelination
    Organomegaly: liver, spleen
      Endocrinopathy: diabetes mellitus, gynecomastia, testicular atrophy, impotence
        Monoclonal gammopathy
          Skin changes: hyperpigmentation
·   Other associations: Castleman disease (angiofollicular hyperplasia)
·   1-2% of plasma cell dyscrasias
·   Adults (median age 50 years)
·   Male-to-female ratio 1.4:1
·   Some association with Kaposi sarcoma and Herpes Virus 8 (HHV 8)
·   Monoclonal cIg (IgG or IgA heavy chain type), light chain lambda in >90%
·   Prognosis: survival 60% at 5 years (better than that for multiple myeloma)

Immunoglobulin free light chain

MM results in the production of massive amounts of immunoglobulins of a single class. IgG is the most common globulins followed by IgA, IgM, IgD then IgE. Both light and heavy chains are produced, with light chains in the greatest abundance. These light chains (known as Bence-Jones protein) are rapidly excreted in the urine. These light chain proteins can precipitate in the tubules. If urine flow is poor, precipitation can result with blockage, impaired tubular function, and possible damage. The increase in these abnormal globulins causes a decrease in normal immunoglobulins.
Mutations in the immunoglobulin genes may result in myeloma cells producing:
    - Light chains only, a condition called Bence Jones myeloma
    - Heavy chains only
    - Molecular fragments of immunoglobulins
The overproduction of this monoclonal protein, present in a variety of shapes and sizes, is common to multiple myeloma and AL amyloidosis.

  Urine is formed by ultrafiltration of plasma across the glomerular capillary wall that has a sieving effect on larger plasma proteins into the ultrafiltrate.
  The passage of plasma proteins across the glomerular barrier is a function of molecular size, electrical charge and molecular configuration.
  All the molecules greater than 50,000 Daltons are retained by the glomerular barrier.
  Albumin and transferrin with a molecular weight of respectively 65,000 and 80,000 Daltons are almost completely retained, only about 0.1 % of each ultrafiltrates.
  All the plasma proteins with a molecular mass under 50,000 Daltons pass through the glomerular wall, but all are reabsorbed by the proximal tubule cells, and are degraded by enzymes in to amino acids which are returned to the blood.
  The final filtrate usually contains some traces of albumin and transferrin (under 0.1% of the total proteinuria).
  Proteins normally present in urine are albumin and transferrin in low quantity.
The physiological proteinuria is about 150 mg / 24 hours. Abnormal proteins in urine can be present even with a normal level of proteinuria.

It is recommended to analyze fresh urine as soon as possible because some proteins are denaturated in alkaline urine and some others in acid urine (for example, b2 microglobulin is denaturated at a pH under 5.5, while Retinol Binding Protein (RBP) is denaturated at alkaline pH).

Immunoglobulin free light chains, or Bence Jones proteins, pass from the serum into the urine and are therefore considered the tumor marker for multiple myeloma. Thus, their detection in urine provides valuable information for the initial diagnosis and follow-up.

Tests for the screening and the investigation of multiple myeloma also include electrophoretic methods with high sensitivity and specificity for the detection of free light chains.

Immunofixation electrophoresis (IFE) is a laboratory method used to define the biochemical identity and homogeneity of immunoglobulins or light chains, when suspected monoclonal components are detected in protein electrophoretic patterns of biological fluids. IFE Bence Jones method combines the resolution of protein fractions by electrophoresis with the specific recognition of free light chains using antibodies raised against heavy chains of human immunoglobulins (IgG, IgM, and IgA) and their light chains, kappa and lambda, either bound or free. The binding between the specific antibody and the monoclonal protein, namely the complete immunoglobulin and/or bound and free light chains, results in the formation of a band of precipitate in the corresponding lane that identify the type of immunoglobulin, either heavy chain and/or light chain.

1-Free Light Chains in Serum

FLCS are seen in two conditions:
In conjunction with a typical monoclonal protein, example IgG kappa with free kappa light chain.
In free light chain disease in which the monoclonal free light chain is the only monoclonal protein, example free light chain kappa or lambda (IgD and IgE heavy chains must be ruled out).

2- Free light chains in Urine

Light chain disease is a monoclonal gammopathy in which only kappa or lambda monoclonal light chains are produced. These light chains are not attached to the heavy chain portion of the immunoglobulin molecule and are known as PBJ.

Due to their small molecule size, free light chain filter through the glomerulus with little observation and accumulate in the tubule. Renal impairment can result from the accumulation of light chains. Pathological changes range from relatively benign tubular proteinuria to acute renal failure or Amyloidosis.

Light chain disease comprises 10% to 15% of all monoclonal gammopathies, occurring about as often Waldenstrom's macroglobulinemia. Its diagnosis presents difficulties not associated with other common monoclonal gammopathies.

A- Progression of light chain disease

1-Early stage
The kidney is only mildly affected, excretion and reabsorption continue normally but only partial catabolism occurs. Free light chain may be detected in the serum.

2-Primary Intermediate stage
Progression renal involvement impairs reabsorption. Diminished reabsorption with decreased catabolism results in free light chain in both serum and urine.

3- Secondary Intermediate stage
Reabsorption is totally blocked. Free light chains are present in urine only.

4- Terminal stage
Uremia occurs and renal clearance is affected. FLC again appear in serum. Very small amounts of PBJ in serum an often associated with significant clinical problems, especially pathologic renal changes. Detection and identification of monoclonal free light chains are essential; appropriate therapy may guard against renal failures.

B- How to evaluate Free Light chains

Current laboratory protocols for multiple myeloma diagnosis are generally based on the detection of whole immunoglobulin monoclonal protein (M-protein) in serum by serum protein electrophoresis (SPE). This is followed by immunofixation electrophoresis (IFE) to confirm monoclonality and class of the M-protein. As 15% of all cases of Multiple Myeloma are Light Chain (Bence Jones) Multiple Myeloma with little or no detectable protein in the serum, further analysis is required. A 24-hour urine sample is concentrated x100 then analyzed for the presence of Bence Jones protein by electrophoresis. Quantification may be performed by densitometric scanning of the gel.

1- Limitations of Current Practice
Detection of paraproteins in urine may occur late in disease
Patient compliance with 24 hour urine collections
Sample variability
Transport and storage of large volumes of urine and the associated costs
Labour intensive process
Sensitivity of current methods
Semi-quantitative measurement only
Imprecision of densitometric scanning can make monitoring difficult

2- Initial Investigation Protocol
Conventional laboratory analysis has involved serum protein electrophoresis (SPE) or capillary zone electrophoresis (CZE) plus urine protein electrophoresis (UPE) (for Light Chain Multiple Myeloma, Bence Jones Protein), followed by immunofixation electrophoresis (IFE).
Now, with Freelite, a more sensitive and specific protocol can be implemented to significantly increase detection of B cell dyscrasia.
In the initial laboratory investigation a strategy of performing serum protein electrophoresis and serum Freelite analysis will allow identification of all significant monoclonal proteins and negate the requirement for urine Bence Jones protein samples for screening.

3- Evidence for the Initial Investigation Protocol
In all recent studies the addition of serum Freelite assays to SPE as a first line test increased the detection of B cell dyscrasia.
A prospective analysis in a veterans population, published in Spring 2006 showed adoption of the Freelite plus SPEP protocol resulted in the additional detection of 15 Multiple Myeloma, 1 lymphoma and 1 patient with bladder transitional cell carcinoma.
Further evidence from a prospective study of 1003 serum samples published in August 2005, indicated detection increased by 56% when Freelite assays were added to CZE.
Shortly after that, (December 2005), Freelite assays were shown to be "...significantly more sensitive for detecting monoclonal FLC than urine IFE analysis".
This screening strategy replaces the need for urine testing for Bence Jones proteins
Two recently published studies indicate clearly that if you replace urine Bence Jones Protein tests with serum assays including Freelite free light chains, during the initial investigation for Multiple Myeloma, all patients requiring medical intervention are identified.
"Urine tests are no longer necessary as part of the screening algorithm for identifying monoclonal gammopathies..."
"..No significant pathology would have been missed by replacing BJP with serum FLCs."

C- Interpretation of serum free light chain results
Freelite results should be considered under the following categories and investigated appropriately.

1. Normal samples. Serum κ, λ and κ/λ ratio are all within the normal ranges. If accompanying serum electrophoretic tests are normal it is most unlikely that the patient has a monoclonal gammopathy.

2. Abnormal κ/λ ratios. Support the diagnosis of a monoclonal gammopathy and require an appropriate tissue biopsy. Borderline elevated κ/λ ratios occur with renal impairment and may require appropriate renal function tests.

3. Low concentrations of κ, λ or both. Indicate bone marrow function impairment.

4. Elevated concentrations of both κ and λ with a normal κ/λ ratio. May be due to the following:
Renal impairment (common)
Over-production of polyclonal FLCs from inflammatory conditions (common)
Biclonal gammopathies of different FLC types (rare)

5. Elevated concentrations of both κ and λ with an abnormal κ/λ ratio.
Suggest a combination of monoclonal gammopathy and renal impairment.

D- Serum reference ranges
   The most extensive serum free light chain normal range study has been conducted at The Mayo Clinic, USA, using The Binding Site Freelite assays for the BN™II. In this study serum samples from 287 normal subjects aged from 20 to 90 years were assayed for free kappa and free lambda. The results from this trial are shown in the table below.

Normal Adult Serum	Mean Concentration	Median Concentration	95 Percentile Range
Free Kappa	8.36 (mg/L)	7.30 (mg/L)	3.30-19.40 (mg/L)
Free Lambda	13.43 (mg/L)	12.40 (mg/L)	5.71-26.30 (mg/L)
	Mean	Median	Total Range
Kappa/Lambda ratio	0.63	0.60	0.26-1.65

   The combination of individual concentrations of the free light chains and their ratio distinguishes a monoclonal increase from excess polyclonal production and renal dysfunction.
The ratio of kappa to lambda in serum is the opposite of that seen in urine, with kappa being lower than lambda. This is despite the fact that there are approximately twice as many kappa producing plasma cells as lambda producing cells.
The explanation for this is kappa molecules (25kDa) that are normally present in serum as monomers, are filtered through the kidney at approximately three times the rate of the lambda molecules (50kDa) which are present as dimers. So although the production rate of lambda in normal patients is lower than kappa, the serum concentration of lambda is actually higher, due to slower renal clearance. This also explains why, in the urine, the reverse is seen with kappa being present at approximately twice the level of lambda.

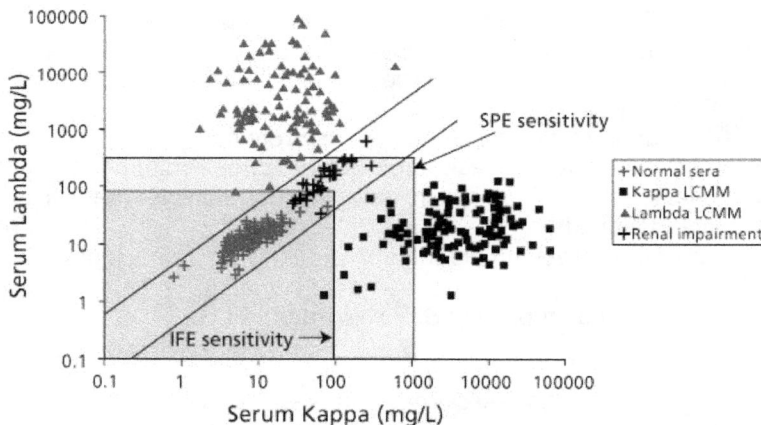

Credit: Warde Medical Laboratory © 2007

Serum FLC concentrations in normal individuals and patients with monoclonal gammopathies

   This figure illustrates the utility of the κ/λ ratio for diagnosis of monoclonal gammopathies. Quantitation of FLCs in normal sera shows a κ/λ ratio between 0.26 and 1.65 (values between the diagonal lines). The κ/λ ratio in patients with monoclonal gammopathies is either higher or lower than this range, such as shown here for Kappa Light Chain Multiple Myeloma (Kappa LCMM) or for Lambda LCMM. Note that an increase in FLC levels due to renal impairment or polyclonal gammopathy can be distinguished from a monoclonal gammopathy because patients with renal impairment or polyclonal gammopathy present with a normal κ/λ ratio (between the diagonal lines). The light gray box indicates the limit of sensitivity for SPE, while the dark gray box indicates the limit of sensitivity for IFE. The limits of sensitivity for SPE and IFE are as presented in and published elsewhere

Intact Immunoglobulin Multiple Myeloma (IIMM)

The serum FLC assay would present two areas of advantage over other laboratory methods for diagnosis and monitoring of IIMM patients. IIMM patients are monitored by following changes in total immunoglobulin levels, as measured by nephelometry, and in monoclonal immunoglobulins, as measured by densitometry of SPE gels. Both of these methods are insensitive at low levels. Hence, sensitive serum FLC measurements would be useful when monoclonal immunoglobulin production is low, especially if a significant proportion of IIMM patients produced excess levels of FLCs.

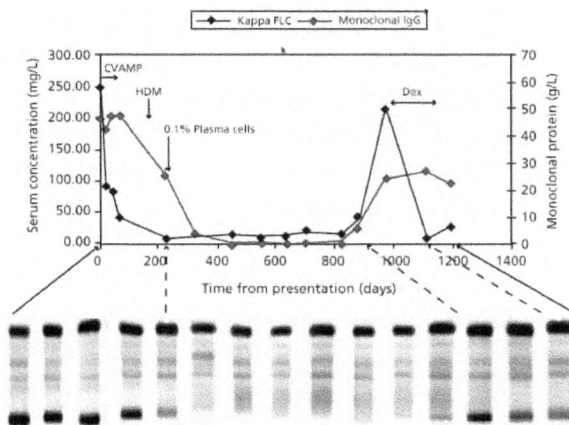

Credit: Warde Medical Laboratory © 2007

Following treatment in an IIMM patient with whole immunoglobulin, SPE, and serum FLC

Whole immunoglobulin was quantitated using nephelometry. Note that both sFLC level and IgG level fell following initiation of treatment, but that the sFLC level decreased sooner and reached plateau in advance of the IgG level. A bone marrow plasma cell count of 0.1% was made at the time when the sFLC level had fallen within in the normal range. At this time, there continued to be a considerable level of IgG present in serum. Relapse was detected by both serum FLC and whole immunoglobulin assays, but only the serum FLC assay detected the response to subsequent treatment with dexamethasone.

Summary of Plasma Cell Dyscrasia

A-Plasmacytosis

1-1- Plasmacytosis due to monoclonal plasma cell proliferation (Malignant plasmacytosis)
- Multiple myeloma
- Plasma cell leukemia
- Macroglobulinemia
- Benign monoclonal gammopathy
- Others: malignancies,
especially IL-1- or IL-6-producing tumors

332

Acute Plasmocytic Leukemia

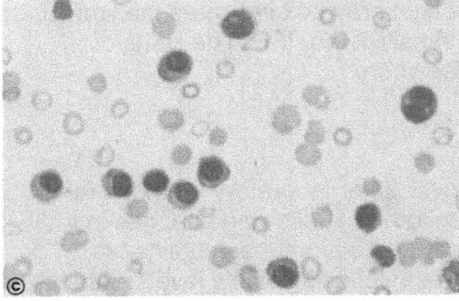

=Atlas of hematology (Prof Nivaldo Medeiros, MD). Used with permission=

1-2- Plasmacytosis due to increased mobilization of plasma cells (Reactive plasmacytosis)
    1- Monoclonal plasmacytosis
      a) benign monoclonal gammopathy
      b) others: malignancies
    2- Polyclonal plasmacytosis
      a) inflammation
      b) collagen disease
      c) liver disease
      d) others: malignancies

B-Diagnostic Criteria for Multiple Myeloma (American Group)

major criteria	minor criteria
I. the presence of plasmacytoma in the tissue biopsy	a.10~30% plasma cells in the BM
II. more than 30% of plasma cells in the BM	b.serum M-protein level lowere than that of major criteria III
III. marked amounts of M-protein in the serum	c. bone lytic lesion(+)
IgG > 3.5 g/dl	d.suppression of residual normal serum Ig
IgA > 2.0 g/dl	IgM < 50 mg/dl
or marked amounts of L chain in the urine	IgA < 100 mg/dl
K or L > 1.0 g/day	or IgG < 600 mg/dl

If diagnosed as myeloma, the following should be satisfied:

      I + b, I + c, I + d (I + a not sufficient)
      II + b, II + c, II + d
      III + a, III + c, III + d
      a + b + c, a + b + d

C- Diagnostic Criteria for MGUS, Indolent Myeloma or Smoldering Myeloma (American Group)

1. MGUS (Monoclonal Gammopathy with Undetermined Significance)
i) M-protein (+) in the serum
ii) M-protein; IgG < 3.5 g/dl, IgA < 2.0 g/dl, BJ protein < 1.0 g/day

iii) Plasma cells in the BM < 10%
iV) No bone lesion
V) No symptoms

2. Indolent Myeloma
i) Bone lesion; no or localized lesion without compression fracture
ii) M-protein; IgG < 7 g/dl, IgA < 5 g/dl
iii) No symptoms or no symptoms associated with myeloma
a) Performance status > 70%
b) Hb > 10 g/dl
c) Serum Ca level; normal
d) Serum creatinine level < 2.0 mg/dl
e) No infection

3. Smoldering Myeloma
diagnosed as myeloma or indolent myeloma, and also has the following:
i) No bone lesion
ii) Plasma cells in the BM < 30%
D-Phenotype of Plasma cells

Phenotypic differences between normal and malignant plasma cells

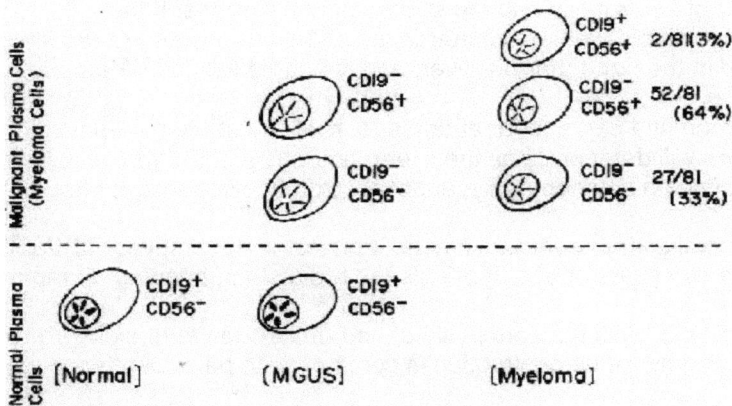

From left, CD19/CD38, CD56/CD38, CD49e/CD38 and MPC-1/CD38

http://web.cc.yamaguchi-u.ac.jp/~plasma/msg/nextpage/plasma02.html

Phenotypic analysis of plasma cells (myeloma cells) was recently improved by 3-color staining with anti-CD38 antibody. Plasma cells alone express CD38 Ag strongly (CD38++), while other hematopoietic cells do not express CD38 (CD38-) or express it weakly (CD38+).
This 3-color analysis revealed as follows:
1) With regard to the expression of CD19 and CD56, normal plasma cells are clearly distinguished from malignant plasma cells (myeloma cells). Normal plasma cells are CD19+CD56-, while malignant plasma cells are mostly CD19-CD56+, partly CD19-CD56- and rarely CD19+CD56+. [Blood 81:2658-2663, 1993]
2) Furthermore, plasma cells consist of MPC-1$^-$CD45$^+$CD49e(VLA-5)$^-$, MPC-1$^-$CD45$^-$CD49e$^-$ immature, MPC-1$^+$CD45$^-$CD49e$^-$, MPC-1$^+$CD45$^+$CD49e$^-$ intermediate and MPC-1$^+$CD45$^+$CD49e$^+$mature cells. [Blood 82:564-570, 1993, Br. J. Haematol. in press, 1999]

PART FOURTEEN: LIPID (LYSOSOMAL) STORAGE DISORDERS

Lipid storage disorders are also called lysosomes storage diseases. These rare occurring, autosomal recessive traits that express early in childhood. They are due to defects in lipid enzymes and are characterized by the accumulation of unmetabolized material in the lysosomes of a variety of cells. Lysosomes are a type of intracellular digestive tract and breakdown selected macromolecules. The cells responsible for much of this digestive activity are the monocytes and macrophages. When such an enzyme deficiency occurs, there is a subcellular accumulation of undigested lipids. Designated as lipid storage diseases, these phagocytic cells will infiltrate the bone marrow and replace the normal cells causing depressed organ function. Other organs affected are the spleen and liver. Diagnosis is dependent upon identifying an enzyme deficiency or a clinically distinct cell. The three best known of these disorders are [a] Gaucher's disease, [b] Niemann-Pick disease, and [c] Tay-Sachs disease. These three disorders have a predilection for Jewish people. Therapy strategies include bone marrow transplantation, which has been considered to be successful in some cases. These disorders may be referred to as a non-malignant WBC disorder.

Gaucher's Disease

Gaucher's disease is a glucosylceramide lipidosis due to a deficiency in the enzyme glucosylceramidase. It is characterized by hepatomegaly and is a progressive neural disorder that terminates in death. It is the most common of the lysosomal storage diseases. The source of glucocerebrosides is the neutral glycolipid of neutrophils and the stroma of erythrocytes. If the macrophage enzymes are normal, these glycolipid wastes of neutrophils and erythrocytes are readily degraded. These macrophages are found in the bone marrow, liver, and lymphoid tissues. There are three types of Gaucher's disease.

Type I: Adult form. This is the most common and can appear at any age. It will most often manifest in childhood or early adulthood. Liver function will deteriorate as the liver macrophages interfere with liver circulation. Diagnosis usually occurs with finding splenomegaly, anemia, thrombocytopenia, and/or leukopenia.

Type II: Infantile form. This is an acute or malignant neuropathic type. It onsets in the first year of life. It is progressive with death occurring before two years of age. It affects the brain stem, bringing on rapid neurological death.

Type III: Juvenile or subacute neuropathic type. This appears in childhood (from one y/o to eight y/o). It is characterized by rapid hepatosplenomegaly. Bone destruction is common with pain. Death occurs in late childhood or adolescence.

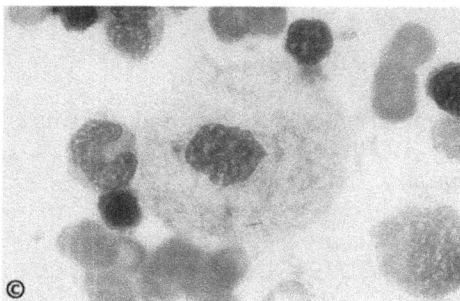

=Atlas of Hematology (Nivaldo Medeiros, MD). Used with permission=

Clinical lab findings include:

[1] Normocytic and hypochromic anemia.
[2] Hemoglobin = >8.0 g/dL
[3] WBC = 2,000 to 3,000/µL (usually there is a relative lymphocytosis)
[4] Platelet count = 50,000 to 100,000/µL
[5] Serum Acid Phosphatase = >1.9 IU/L (N = 0.11 -0.60 IU/L)
[6] As the disorder progresses, the following will occur:
   A. pancytopenia in the late stages of the disease

B. as liver involvement increases, clotting factor abnormalities increase.

[7] The diagnostic cell is the Gaucher's cell, a macrophage that if filled with lipids. It is a large, with a diameter from 20 μ to 80 μ, with a small eccentric nucleus. The cytoplasm is filled with pale staining lipids that have a crumpled appearance. Gaucher's cells may occasionally found in peripheral blood, but are readily found in the bone marrow and spleen.

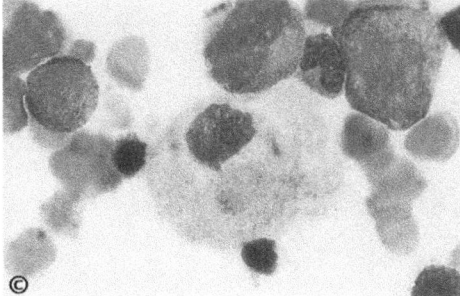

Niemann-Pick Disease

Niemann-Pick disease is the second most commonly occurring lipid disorder with a defect in the enzyme sphingomyelinase. Common clinical manifestations are hepatosplenomegaly and impaired mental development. It affects girls more than boys, with death occurring before the third year of life. The defective enzyme allows the macrophage to accumulate unmetabolized sphingomyelin and cholesterol, constituents of the cell membrane. These lipid-laden, foamy-like macrophages are readily found in the bone marrow, liver, lungs, lymph nodes, spleen, and other tissues.

The lipid filled macrophage is known as a Niemann-Pick cell. It is diagnostic for this disease. Enzyme analysis of leucocytes and fibroblasts for the absence of sphingomyelinase is diagnostic. The Niemann-Pick cell measures from 20 μ to 90 μ in diameter. Wright's stain will cause the lipids (appearing as droplets due to the lipid filled vacuoles) in the cell to take on a very pale to light blue color. The nucleus takes on a purplish-red to darker blue coloration. This cell reacts positively with Sudan black B, luxol fast blue, acid phosphatase, nonspecific esterase, and oil red O stains. The myeloperoxidase stain is negative. NOTE: No treatment is available.

There are five variations of this disorder. This information is compiled from medical textbooks.

[1] Type A: Infantile or classic Niemann-Pick disease. The most common and severest form, making up to 85% of the known cases. It onsets as early as three months and is progressive with marked liver and nerve dysfunction, resulting in death within one to four years.

[2] Type B: Similar to Type A, but without nervous system involvement. The disease is less severe. Life threatening risks are primarily from pulmonary infections and hypersplenism. A reasonable life span is possible with medical intervention.

[3] Type C: This disorder onset in childhood and then presents with neurological disorders (seizures, behavioral disorders, and/or mental retardation). Hepatosplenomegaly and/or hypertelorism (abnormal distance between paired organs) may occur. This is a progressive disorder and is fatal.

[4] Type D: Rare. Known to occur only in a Nova Scotian population. It resembles Type C.

[5] Type E. Known to not involve the nervous system and does not have a sphingomyelinase deficiency. Its biochemistry is not understood.

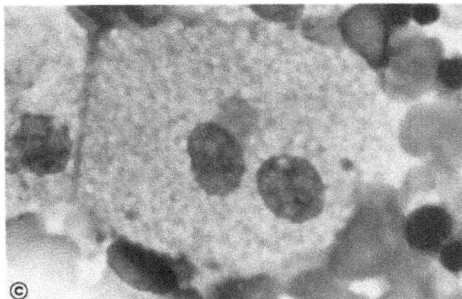

Other clinical laboratory findings include:

[A] Leukocytopenia
[b] Thrombocytopenia
[c] Vacuolation in lymphocytes and monocytes (ranging from 2 to 20 vacuoles per cell)
[d] Anemia (may be present).

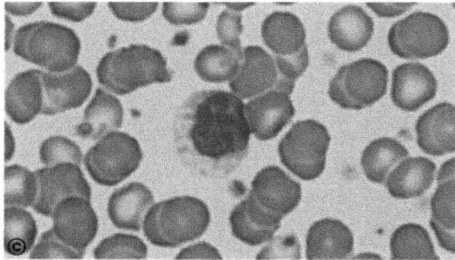

=Atlas of Hematology (Nivaldo Medeiros, MD). Used with permission=

Histiocytosis

Also known as Sea-Blue Histiocytes Syndrome. This is an autosomal-recessive benign genetic disorder that generally occurs in adults less than 40 y/o. The patient presents with hepatomegaly and splenomegaly. There is a tendency for bleeding (epistaxis, purpura, and gastrointestinal bleeding). The younger the affected individual, the more severe the disease. There is a medical opinion that Histiocytosis is an adult form of Niemann-Pick disease.

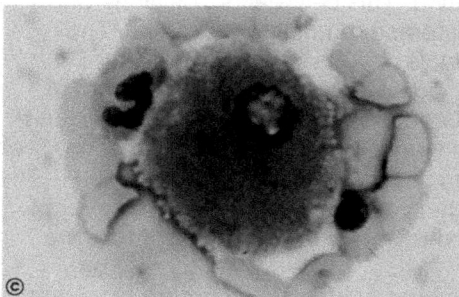

=Atlas of Hematology (Nivaldo Medeiros, MD). Used with permission=

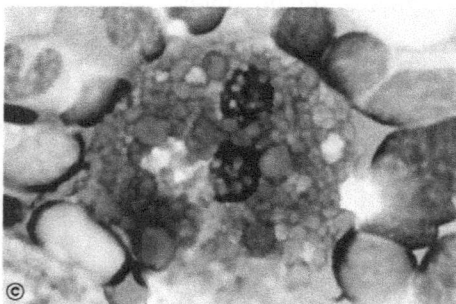

=Atlas of Hematology (Nivaldo Medeiros, MD). Used with permission=

Clinical laboratory findings include:

[a] thrombocytopenia (common finding),
[b] Normal liver function tests in most cases,
[c] WBC counts = normal or decreased,
[d] Other lab tests (includes the lipids) are within normal limits.

Bone marrow biopsy is required for diagnosis. The diagnostic cell is a bright sky-blue Wright's stained macrophage with an eccentric nucleus and the blue cytoplasm containing blue or blue-green lipid rich granules. The diagnostic cells will stain positive with PAS, Sudan Black B, Oil Red O, and acid-fast stains. The diameter of these cells range from 50 μ to 60 μ and can also be found in the liver and spleen.

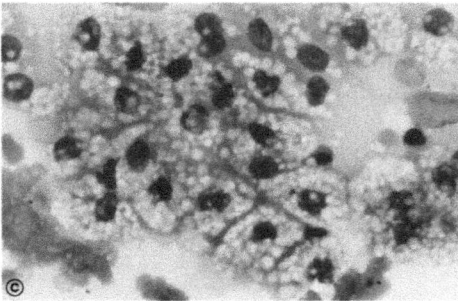

=Atlas of Hematology (Nivaldo Medeiros, MD). Used with permission=

PART FIFTEEN: ORGANOMEGALY

Lymphadenopathy

1-1 Clinical approach: Put lymphadenopathy in clinical context.

Take the history with the main causes of lymphadenopathy in mind.
Examine for extent, size, texture, and local disease.
Biopsy when you suspect malignancy.

1-2 Main causes of lymphadenopathy.

- Normal immune response to antigen- a polymorphic response.
- Infection – inflammatory cells.
- Lymphoma – malignant lymphocytes.
- Metastatic carcinoma – carcinoma cells.

1-3 Normal immune response = Polyclonal Lymphadenopathy.

Antigen stimulates macrophages and lymphocytes.
Blood flow increase 10 to 25 times.
Node size increases due to increased ingress, decreased egress and proliferation of T and B-lymphocytes,
Node may increase 15 times normal size after 5 to 10 days of antigenic stimulation.
Normal reactive glands are seldom larger than 1 cm.
Inguinal glands may be normally 0.5 to 2 cm.

The discovery of enlarged nodes represents an important physical finding that demands a systemic evaluation. In most patients with lymphadenopathy, a diagnosis can be made after a careful history, physical examination, and appropriate testing including hematologic investigations, serologic tests, skin tests, and routine x-rays. As in all diagnostic work-up, these tests should be performed in a goal-directed manner in order to evaluate specific hypotheses.

Glands in several areas are particularly worrisome.

- Large non tender glands.
- No evidence of regional or systemic infection.
- Hard, rubbery, or stoney glands or glands matter together.
- Suspicious location. (e.g. hilar, retroperitoneal, supraclavicular, femoral).

1-4 When to Biopsy an enlarged node

Slap et al develop on algorithm in 1984 which could used to determine if an enlarged lymph node in a child, adolescent or young adult should be biopsied.

Patient population:

- The patients were 9-25 years of age.
- The patients were seen at the hospital of the University of Pennsylvania form 1953 to 1983 or the Children's Hospital of Philadelphia from 1969 to 1983.
Endpoints:

- Those patients who did not require lymph node biopsy to determine treatment: normal, hyperplasic or benign inflammatory conditions. The last group included bacterial lymphadenitis and toxoplasmosis, since these could be diagnosed by lymph node aspiration or serology respectively.

- Those patients with significant disease who needed lymph node biopsy to determine treatment: granulomatous disease, malignant lymphoma, metastatic tumor.

Parameters used in discriminate stepwise analysis.

1-Chest roentgenogram

    Normal finding (Original Coefficient = 0), (Simplified Coefficient= 0)
        Abnormal finding (OC= 2.36), (SC = +5)
2-Lymph node diameter

> 2 cm (OC = 1.59), (SC = +3)
      <=2 cm (OC= 0), (SC = 0).
3-Ear, nose, and throat symptoms

Present (OC = -1.56), (SC= -3)
Absent (OC= 0), (SC= 0).

4-Discriminate score= SUM (simplified coefficient values for the findings present)

        Minimum score= -5, Maximum score= +6

If the score is <= 0, the biopsy is not required.
If the score is > 0, then it is likely that the patient has a diagnosis that will require lymph node biopsy to determine treatment.

5-Performance:
Sensitivity= 95%
Specificity= 96%
Positive predictive value=95%
Negative predictive value=96%.

1-5 Recommendations for biopsy

    Indications for biopsy of the enlarged lymph node- any of the following:

Patient age > 40 years
Supraclavicular lymph node
Diameter > 2cm
Nontender
Rock hard consistency
Fixed and matted together
Persistence >2 weeks.

    If none of the indications are present then the patient can be observed for 2to 4 weeks.

Splenomegaly

    Splenomegaly commonly occurs as a manifestation of diseases involving the spleen or hematopoietic organs. Then it seldom presents a diagnostic problem.
    Splenomegaly may also be an incidental finding on clinical examination, or turn up on imaging studies, where it does present a diagnostic problem.
    In the latter scenario, a fishing expedition is mounted to elucidate the cause. Often the investigations draw a blank, and the splenomegaly resolves without ever being explained. Sometimes it persists.
    Sometimes the spleen becomes so large that it causes a life threatening situation. The big spleen syndrome is potentially disastrous.

2-1 Causes of splenomegaly

The spleen is a major component of reticulo-endothelium- system, is involved in many disease processes. The main causes of splenomegaly are:

- Chronic passive congestion (due to portal hypertension).
- Increased workload (by removing abnormal or antibody coated blood cells).
- Normal response to antigen.
- Infection – inflammation cells.
- Lymphoma/Leukemia.
- Metastatic carcinoma.

2-2 Hypersplenism

Hypersplenism is a removal of normal blood cells by an enlarged spleen-(filtering, pooling and phagocytosis). Microanatomy is important:
- Increased portal pressure.
- Congestion of sinuses.
- Sluggish flow, decreased pH, glucose deprivation and abnormalities of other factors.
- Hemophagocytosis.

2-2-1 Causes of diagnostic:

1- Splenomegaly
2- One or more cytopenias.
3- Appropriate marrow response.
4- Cure by splenectomy.

Mechanisms of the different cytopenias:

- RBCS (increased pooling and stasis Hemophagocytosis).
- WBCS (increased margination).
- Platelets (increased pooling).

2-3- Massive spleens cause big problems

Mechanical problems:

- Early satiety
- Diarrhea and continence.

Circulatory problems:

- Splenic infarction
- Dilutional anemia
- High cardiac outpout
- Hypermetabolism
- Contributes to portal hypertension

2-4- Indications for splenectomy

- Increased RBC destruction.
- Severe hereditary spherocytosis.
- Autoimmune hemolytic anemia.
- Agnogenic (unknown origin) myeloid metaplasia.
- Severe refractory hemolytic anemia.
- Certain platelet defect syndromes.
- Sickle cell disease causing splenic infarcts.

- Hypersplenism due to cirrhosis of the liver, thrombosis, vascular stenosis, aneurysm of the splenic artery, or cysts.

2-5- Hematological response to splenectomy

Splenectomy may be considered in diseases where sequestration is believed to a significant contributor to one or more cytopenias. Criteria to evaluate the change in hematological parameters can help determine how effective the procedure was.

1-RBCs: Hemoglobin increase> 3g/dl, response = excellent.
2-Platelets: increase platelet count >= 50.000/ul, response= excellent.
3- Neutrophils: increase in neutrophil count >= 1.000/ul, response= excellent.

Evaluation for effectiveness should be done after the body has stabilized from the blood loss and other changes induced by surgery.

Hepathomegaly

The liver, a life essential organ, becomes non-hematopoietic after birth. In is involved in the followings ways:

It is affected by storage disease of monocytes and macrophages. The liver will engorge and enlarge, a condition known as hepatomegaly. These are enzymatic diseases, such as, Gaucher's disease, Niemann-Pick disease.
The liver sequesters damaged erythrocytes. The liver will segregate defective RBCs and remove then from circulation. This prevents initiating intravascular hemolysis by these cells.
In hemolytic anemia episodes, the rate of conjugation of bilirubin is increased.
In anemic conditions, the liver will increase it storage rate of iron.

BIBLIOGRAPHY

- http://training.seer.cancer.gov; funded by the U.S. National Cancer Institute's Surveillance, Epidemiology and End Results (SEER) Program, via contract number N01-CN-67006, with Emory University, Atlanta SEER Cancer Registry, Atlanta, Georgia,
- Bunn and Forget: Hemoglobin: Molecular, Genetic and Clinical Aspects. Philadelphia, W.B. Saunders Company, 1986.
- Huntsman RG: Sickle Cell Anemia and Thalassemia. Canadian Sickle Cell Society, 1987, p. 27.
- Scriver, Charles R. et al. The Metabolic Basis of Inherited Disease. New York, McGraw Hill, 1995.
- Weatherall and Clegg: The Thalassaemia Syndromes. Oxford, Blackwell Scientific Publications 1981, p 381
- Giardina P, Hilgartner M. Update on thalassemia. Pediatr Rev 1992; 13:55-62.
- Rund, D Rachmilewitz, E. Thalassemia major 1995: older patients, new therapies. Blood Rev 1995; 9:25-32
- Piomelli S, Loew T. Management of thalassemia major (Cooley's anemia). Hematol Oncol Clin North Am 1991; 5:557-69.- Bessis M. Red cell shapes. An illustrated classification and its rationale. Nouv Rev Fr Hematol 1972; 12: 721-46. (Pub Med)
-Bessis M, Lessin LS, Beutler E. Morphology of the Erythron. In: Williams WJ, Beutler E, Ersler AJ, Lichtman MA, eds. Hematology. 3rd Ed. New York: McGraw-Hill, 1983; 257-79.
- Garg SK, Lackner H, Karpatkin S. The increased percentage of megathrombocytes in various clinical disorders. Ann Intern Med 1972; 77: 361-69. (Pub Med)
- Lessin LS, Klug PP, Jensen WN. Clinical implications of red cell shape. In: Stollerman GH, ed. Advances in internal medicine. Chicago: Year Book Medical Publishers, 1976; 21:451–99.
- Schwartz SO, Stansbury F. Significance of nucleated red blood cells in peripheral blood. Analysis of 1,496 cases. JAMA 1954; 154: 1339-40. (Pub Med)
-Zeigler Z, Murphy S, Gardner FH. Microscopic platelet size and morphology in various hematologic disorders. Blood 1978; 51: 479-86. (Pub Med)
- http://fr.wikipedia.org/wiki/Oxyh%C3%A9moglobine
- http://www.gs-im3.fr/hemoglobine/HbStructure1.html
- http://www.umass.edu/microbio/chime/hemoglob/2frmcont.htm
- http://sickle.bwh.harvard.edu/hemoglobinopathy.html
- http://www.nlm.nih.gov/MEDLINEPLUS/ency/article/001291.htm
- http://www.netdoctor.co.uk/diseases/facts/thrombocytopenia.htm
- http://www.emedicine.com/Med/topic3480.htm
- http://www.umm.edu/ency/article/000586.htm
- http://www.mayoclinic.com/health/thrombocytopenia/DS00691/DSECTION=causes
- http://www.drugs.com/enc/thrombocytopenia.html
- http://www.cancer.gov/Templates/db_alpha.aspx?CdrID=45365
- http://www.medscape.com/viewarticle/569207
- http://www.medicinenet.com/neutropenia/article.htm
- http://www.emedicine.com/MED/topic1640.htm
- http://www.cancersymptoms.org/neutropenia/index.shtml
- http://www.mayoclinic.com/health/polycythemia-vera/DS00919
- http://www.polycythemia.org/
-Leitner, S. J. Britton, C, J, C, and Neumark, E: Bone Marrow Biopsy. New York, Grune & Stratton, 1949.
- Sunders, R. D: Sternal aspiration. Staff Meet. Bull. Hosp. Univ. Minnesota 17 (26): 389, 1949.
-Hayhoe, F. G. J. Quaglino, D, and Doll, R: The cytology and cytochemistry of acute leukemia. Her Majesty's Stationary office, London, 1964.
- Hayhoe, F. G. J. Quaglino, D, and Flemans, R, J: Consecutive use of Romanowsky and Periodic-Acid-Schiff techniques in the study of blood and bone marrow cells. Britt. J. Heamat. 6: 23, 1960.
- http://www.hbpinfo.com/en/.
- http://www.cdc.gov/ncidod/diseases/ebv.htm
- Thomson American Health Consultants
- Narla Mohandas[1] and Patrick G. Gallagher[2]
[1] Red Cell Physiology Laboratory, New York Blood Center, New York, NY; and [2] Department of Pediatrics, Yale University School of Medicine, New Haven, CT
.- Lukes RJ, Craver LF, Hall TC, Rappaport H, Ruben P: Report of the nomenclature committee. Cancer Res. 1966; 26:1311.

343

- Willemze R, Kerl H, Sterry W, et al: EORTC classification for primary cutaneous lymphomas: A proposal from the Cutaneous Lymphoma Study Group of the European Organization for Research and Treatment of Cancer. Blood. 1997; 90:354-371.

. - Harris NL, Jaffe ES, Diebold J, et al: World Health Organization classification of neoplastic diseases of the hematopoietic and lymphoid tissues: Report of the Clinical Advisory Committee Meeting - Airlie House, Virginia, November 1997. J Clin Oncol. 1999; 17:3835-3849.

- Jerry A. Katzmann, Raynell J. Clark, Roshini S. Abraham, Sandra Bryant, James F. Lymp, Arthur R. Bradwell, and Robert A. Kyle.
"Serum Reference Intervals and Diagnostic Ranges for Free κ and free λ Immunoglobulin Light Chains: Relative Sensitivity for Detection of Monoclonal Light Chains"
Clin Chem 2002; 48:9:1437-1444

- Freelite Pocket Guide (English International, Non-USA)

- Freelite Pocket Guide (English, USA Only)

- http://www.freelite.co.uk/interpretationofresults-27.asp

-Warde Medical Laboratory © 2007

- Bradwell AR, Carr-Smith HD, Mead GP, Harvey TC, Drayson MT. Serum test for assessment of patients with Bence Jones myeloma. Lancet 2003; 361(9356): 489-91.

- Drayson M, Tang LX, Drew R, Mead GP, Carr-Smith H, Bradwell AR. Serum free light-chain measurements for identifying and monitoring patients with nonsecretory multiple myeloma. Blood 2001; 97(9): 2900-2.

- Mead GP, Carr-Smith HD, Drayson MT, Morgan GJ, Child JA, Bradwell AR. Serum free light chains for monitoring multiple myeloma. Br J Haematol 2004; 126(3): 348-54.

- Katzmann JA, Clark RJ, Abraham RS, Bryant S, Lymp JF, Bradwell AR, Kyle RA. Serum reference intervals and diagnostic ranges for free kappa and free lambda immunoglobulin light chains: Relative sensitivity for detection of monoclonal light chains. Clin Chem 2002; 48(9): 1437-44.

- Rajkumar SV, Kyle RA, Therneau TM, Clark RJ, Bradwell AR, Melton LJ, 3rd, Larson DR, Plevak MF, Katzmann JA. Presence of monoclonal free light chains in the serum predicts risk of progression in monoclonal gammopathy of undetermined significance. Br J Haematol 2004; 127(3): 308-10.

- Kyle RA. Sequence of testing for monoclonal gammopathies. Arch Pathol Lab Med 1999; 123(2): 114-8.

- Levinson SS, Keren DF. Free light chains of immunoglobulins: Clinical laboratory analysis. Clin Chem 1994; 40(10): 1869-78.

- McLaughlin P, Alexanian R. Myeloma protein kinetics following chemotherapy. Blood 1982; 60(4): 851-5.

- Abraham GN, Waterhouse C. Evidence for defective immunoglobulin metabolism in severe renal insufficiency. Am J Med Sci 1974; 268(4): 227-33.

- Solomon A, Waldmann TA, Fahey JL, McFarlane AS. Metabolism of Bence JSones proteins. J Clin Invest 1964; 43: 103-17.

- Wochner RD, Strober W, Waldmann TA. The role of the kidney in the catabolism of Bence Jones proteins and immunoglobulin fragments. J Exp Med 1967; 126(2): 207-21.

- Bradwell AR. Serum free light chain analysis, Second ed. Birmingham, UK: The Binding Site, Ltd., 2004.

- Bradwell AR, Carr-Smith HD, Mead GP, Tang LX, Showell PJ, Drayson MT, Drew R. Highly sensitive, automated immunoassay for immunoglobulin free light chains in serum and urine. Clin Chem 2001; 47(4): 673-80.

- Malpas JS, Bergsagel DE, Kyle RA. Myeloma: Biology and management, 1st. ed. Oxford; New York: Oxford University Press, 1995.

- Kyle RA, Therneau TM, Rajkumar SV, Offord JR, Larson DR, Plevak MF, Melton LJ, 3rd. A long-term study of prognosis in monoclonal gammopathy of undetermined significance. N Engl J Med 2002; 346(8): 564-9.

- Rajkumar SV, Kyle RA, Therneau TM, Melton LJ, Bradwell AR, Clark RJ, Larson DR, Plevak MF, Katzmann JA. Presence of an abnormal serum free light ratio is an independent risk factor for progression in monoclonal gammopathy of undetermined significance (mgus). Blood 2004; 104(11).

- Junghans RP, Anderson CL. The protection receptor for igg catabolism is the beta2-microglobulin-containing neonatal intestinal transport receptor. Proc Natl Acad Sci U S A 1996; 93(11): 5512-6.

- Abraham RS, Clark RJ, Bryant SC, Lymp JF, Larson T, Kyle RA, Katzmann JA. Correlation of serum immunoglobulin free light chain quantification with urinary Bence Jones protein in light chain myeloma. Clin Chem 2002; 48(4): 655-7.

- Tricot G, Jagannath S, Vesole D, Nelson J, Tindle S, Miller L, Cheson B, Crowley J, Barlogie B. Peripheral blood stem cell transplants for multiple myeloma: Identification of favorable variables for rapid engraftment in 225 patients. Blood 1995; 85(2): 588-96.
- Bradwell AR, Carr-Smith HD, Mead GP, Drayson MT. Serum free light chain immunoassays and their clinical application. Clinical and Applied Immunology Reviews 2002; 3(1-2): 17-33.
- Alyanakian MA, Abbas A, Delarue R, Arnulf B, Aucouturier P. Free immunoglobulin light-chain serum levels in the follow-up of patients with monoclonal gammopathies: Correlation with 24-hr urinary light-chain excretion. Am J Hematol 2004; 75(4): 246-8.
- Turesson I, Grubb A. Non-secretory or low-secretory myeloma with intracellular kappa chains. Report of six cases and review of the literature. Acta Med Scand 1978; 204(6): 445-51.
- Coriu D, Weaver K, Schell M, Eulitz M, Murphy CL, Weiss DT, Solomon A. A molecular basis for nonsecretory myeloma. Blood 2004; 104(3): 829-31.
- Buxbaum J. Aberrant immunoglobulin synthesis in light chain amyloidosis. Free light chain and light chain fragment production by human bone marrow cells in short-term tissue culture. J Clin Invest 1986; 78(3): 798-806.
- Kyle RA, Gertz MA. Primary systemic amyloidosis: Clinical and laboratory features in 474 cases. Semin Hematol 1995; 32(1): 45-59.
- Keren DF, Alexanian R, Goeken JA, Gorevic PD, Kyle RA, Tomar RH. Guidelines for clinical and laboratory evaluation patients with monoclonal gammopathies. Arch Pathol Lab Med 1999; 123(2): 106-7.
- Lachmann HJ, Gallimore R, Gillmore JD, Carr-Smith HD, Bradwell AR, Pepys MB, Hawkins PN. Outcome in systemic al amyloidosis in relation to changes in concentration of circulating free immunoglobulin light chains following chemotherapy. Br J Haematol 2003; 122(1): 78-84.
- Abraham RS, Katzmann JA, Clark RJ, Bradwell AR, Kyle RA, Gertz MA. Quantitative analysis of serum free light chains. A new marker for the diagnostic evaluation of primary systemic amyloidosis. Am J Clin Pathol 2003; 119(2): 274-8.
- Gertz MA, Comenzo R, Falk RH, Fermand J-P, Hazenberg BO, Hawkins PN, Merlini G, Moreau P, Ronco P, Sanchorawala V, Sezer O, Solomon A, Grateau G. Definition of organ involvement and treatment response in primary systemic amyloidosis (al): A consensus opinion from the 10th international symposium on amyloid and amyloidosis. Blood 2004; 104(11).
- http://training.seer.cancer.gov; funded by the U.S. National Cancer Institute's Surveillance, Epidemiology and End Results (SEER) Program, via contract number N01-CN-67006, with Emory University, Atlanta SEER Cancer Registry, Atlanta, Georgia,
- http://learn.genetics.utah.edu/units/disorders/karyotype/chrompictures.cfm
- University of Illinois at Chicago, department of Biological Sciences
- National Cancer Institute
- http://www.pathology.washington.edu/clinical/cytogenetics/
- http://www.cancer.gov
- http://uhaweb.hartford.edu/bugl/immune.htm
- Sources: Fairweather D, Rose NR. Women and autoimmune diseases. Emerg Infect Dis. 2004 November. Available from http://www.cdc.gov/ncidod/EID/vol10no11/04-0367.htm
- National Human Genome Research Institute.
- Bitton G, Marshall KC: Adsorption of Microorganisms to Surfaces. John Wiley & Sons, New York, 1980
Draser BS, Hill MJ: Human Intestinal Flora. Academic Press, London, 1974.
- Tannock GW: Normal Microflora. Chapman and Hall, London, UK, 1995
- National Institutes of Health Autoimmune Disease Coordinating Committee Report, 2002. Bethesda (MD): The Institutes; 2002.
- Rose, NR. An immunology primer. In: Morton CC, Fagan T, editors. Proceedings from Sex Differences in Immunology and Autoimmunity, Society for Women's Health Research, Boston, MA, 8 Nov 2001. Washington: Society for Women's Health Research; 2002. p. 7–9.
- IMMUNOBIOLOGY the Immune System in Health and Disease by Charles Janeway et al. (6th Edition, Garland Publishing, 2001
- Janet M. Decker, PhD, Senior Lecturer
- Department of Veterinary Science and Microbiology –
- http://microvet.arizona.edu/Courses/VSC519/vsc519syllabus.html
- http://student.ccbcmd.edu/~gkaiser/goshp.html
- http://www.healthcare.utah.edu/healthinfo/adult/infectious/immune.htm
- http://en.wikipedia.org/wiki/ABO_blood_group_system
- U.S. National Library of Medicine

- http://www.med.univ-angers.fr
- Adapted from Leffell, M. S., A. D. Donnenberg, and N. R. Rose. Handbook of Human Immunology. CRC Press, Boca Raton, 1997.
-Teacher'sDomain.How Cancer cells Grow and Divide, published September 26,2003,retrieved on November 1, 2008,http://www.teachersdomain.org/resource/tdc02.sci.life.stru.oncogene/
- Dr. Art Anderson's Immunology Lecture
- http://www.geocities.com/artnscience/
- http://cellular-immunity.blogspot.com/2007/12/b-cells.html#lymphopoiesis
- http://www.cancerquest.org/index.cfm?page=31&lang=english
- http://www.udel.edu/biology/Wags/histopage/colorpage/ch/ch.htm
- http://www.octc.kctcs.edu/GCaplan/anat2/notes/Notes6%20Blood%20Cells.htm
-http://student.ccbcmd.edu/courses/bio141/lecguide/unit5/index.html#bcell
- http://atlasgeneticsoncology.org//index.html-
- http://www.innerbody.com/image/lympov.html
- http://www.ndsu.edu/instruct/tcolvill/435/erythrocytes.htm
- http://www.path.uiowa.edu/cgi-bin-pub/vs/fpx_browse.cgi?cat=o_hemato&div=iowa
- http://www.vet.uga.edu/vpp/clerk/Smith/index.php
- J. Krause, R.N. McLay, 15 July 1997, Dr. John Krause's Hematopathology Homepage, Tulane University School of Medicine, today's date, -
(http://www.tmc.tulane.edu/classware/pathology/medical_pathology/Krause/Krause.htm
- http://www.embryology.ch/anglais/qblood/blut03.html
- http://www.fda.gov/cder/drug/infopage/RHE/default.htm
- http://www.tau.ac.il/~inter05/
- http://www.virology.net/
- http://www.hematologyatlas.com/
- http://www1.umn.edu/hema/pages/matchart.html
--Faderl S, Talpaz M, Estrov Z, Kantarjian HM (1999). "Chronic myelogenous leukemia: biology and therapy." Annals of Internal Medicine 131 (3): 207-219.
-Tefferi A, Thiele J, Orazi A, Kvasnicka HM, Barbui T, Hanson CA, Barosi G, Verstovsek S, Birgegard G, Mesa R, Reilly JT, Gisslinger H, Vannucchi AM, Cervantes F, Finazzi G,
- Hoffman R, Gilliland DG, Bloomfield CD, Vardiman JW (2007). "Proposals and rationale for revision of the World Health Organization diagnostic criteria for polycythemia Vera, essential thrombocythemia, and primary myelofibrosis: recommendations from an ad hoc international expert pane". Blood 110 (4): 1092-10.
-Nowell PC (2007). "Discovery of the Philadelphia chromosome: a personal perspective". Journal of Clinical Investigation 117 (8): 2033-2035.
-Karbasian Esfahani M, Morris EL, Dutcher JP, Wiernik PH (2006). "Blastic phase of chronic myelogenous leukemia". Current Treatment Options in Oncology 7 (3): 189-199.
-Hasford J, Pfirrmann M, Hehlmann R, Allan NC, Baccarani M, Kluin-Nelemans JC, Alimena G, Steegmann JL, Ansari H (1998). "A new prognostic score for survival of patients with chronic myeloid leukemia treated with interferon alfa. Writing Committee for the Collaborative CML Prognostic Factors Project Group". Journal of the National Cancer Institute 90 (11): 850-858
-Sokal J, Baccarani M, Russo D, Tura S (1988). "Staging and prognosis in chronic myelogenous leukemia." Semin Hematol 25 (1): 49-61.
- Talpaz M, Silver RT, Druker BJ, et al: Imatinib induces durable hematologic and cytogenetic responses in patients with accelerated phase chronic myeloid leukemia: results of a phase 2 study. Blood 2002 Mar 15; 99(6): 1928- 37.
- Cancer news
- Leukemia links
-Lymphoma resource pages
-International Myeloma Foundation
- UC Davis hematology site
- Blood line
-America Society of Hematology
-Society for hematology
-Perdue University
-Pathology Education Instructional Resource
-The Pathology Guy
-University of Utah International Pathology Laboratory
-Immunoquery

-Bristol Biomed Image Archive
-Iowa Virtual Slide box
- Pathmax
- University of Virginia
- Harvard Medical School, IRIM2005, Diagnosis and management of Leukemias and Lymphomas
- http://www.emedicine.com/hematology/index.shtml
-

- Case Study One -

A 40 year old man, resident of the United States, presents to an emergency room with a 5-day history of fever, chills, nausea, vomiting, and myalgias. He returned 2 weeks ago from a 16-day visit to Zambia.

Question 1: What chemoprophylaxis regimen (if any) should be recommended for travel to Zambia? (More than one might apply)
1-Chloroquine
2-Chloroquine-proguanil
3-Sulfadoxine-pyrimethamine
4-Mefloquine
5-Doxycycline
6-Atovaquone-proguanil (Malarone®)

Question 1: Final Correct Answer

Mefloquine, Doxycycline, or atovaquone-proguanil (Malarone®)

These three regimens would be appropriate for chemoprophylaxis during travel to Zambia. Chloroquine and chloroquine-proguanil are not recommended because Chloroquine-resistant Plasmodium Falciparum has been reported in Zambia. Sulfadoxine-pyrimethamine is not recommended because of its association with severe cutaneous adverse events (Stevens Johnson syndrome); in addition, P. Falciparum resistant to Sulfadoxine-pyrimethamine is increasingly reported from eastern Africa.
For this travel to Zambia, the patient had been prescribed Chloroquine. However, he took only a few doses during his visit. On the return flight home, the patient had fever, nausea, and myalgias. Upon arrival to the United States, the symptoms dissipated and the patient did not seek medical care. Nine days later, he had again fever, chills, nausea, vomiting, and myalgias. He went to an outpatient clinic where he was diagnosed with viral syndrome and sent home.

Question 2: Based on the observed time intervals, could the symptoms experienced by the patient be due to malaria?

1- Malaria could not have caused the symptoms experienced during the return flight, nor could it have caused the symptoms that started after return to the U.S.
2-Malaria could have caused the symptoms experienced during the return flight, but not the symptoms that started after return to the U.S.
3-Malaria could not have caused the symptoms experienced during the return flight, but could have caused the symptoms that started after return to the U.S.
4-Malaria could have caused both the symptoms experienced during the return flight and the symptoms that started after return to the U.S.

Question 2: Correct Answer

Malaria could have caused both the symptoms experienced during the return flight and the symptoms that started after return to the U.S.

The shortest incubation period occurs in Plasmodium Falciparum malaria, where symptoms may occur as early as 8 days after the infecting mosquito bite. Thus, the symptoms that developed during the patient's return flight (16 days after first possible exposure to infective Anopheles) and after the patient's return to the United States (25 days after first possible exposure) both occurred after the minimum incubation period, and are compatible with malaria. The time intervals in this case are well within the longest possible incubation periods. These can be much extended due to drug intake or immunity, both of which can delay the appearance of symptoms.

Some days later, the patient was seen at another clinic, where on routine CBC malaria parasites were seen. He was then referred to a hospital, where he presents to the emergency room, at 4 am, with continuing fever, nausea, vomiting, and myalgias. On physical examination, the patient is febrile

(102°F), tachycardic. Jaundiced and pale. He is well oriented but slow in answering questions. A thin blood smear obtained while in the emergency room is read as Plasmodium, species not determined. Other laboratory findings include: hematocrit 33%, creatinine 3.6 mg/dL, and total bilirubin 11.0 mg/dL. The urine is dark, with a measured output of 40 mL/6 hours.

Question 3: Which one of the following would be the best next step in the clinical management of this case?
1-Send the patient home with a prescription for mefloquine
2-Keep the patient under observation in the emergency room until the Plasmodium species is determined; in the meantime, initiate treatment with Chloroquine
3-Admit the patient and treat with oral quinine and oral Doxycycline
4-Admit the patient and treat with IV quinidine plus Doxycycline

Question 3: Correct Answer

Admit the patient and treat with IV quinidine plus Doxycycline

In the presence of a diagnosis of malaria, species undetermined, in a patient returning from Zambia, the safest approach is to treat this as Chloroquine-resistant P. Falciparum. In addition, since the patient is slow in answering questions and signs of renal failure are present, it is best to treat this as a case of severe malaria. The patient should be given quinidine by intravenous infusion and Doxycycline. (An additional argument for parenteral treatment is the patient's vomiting.) Because of the potential cardio toxicity of quinidine, the patient should be admitted to the intensive care unit to allow continuous monitoring of the ECG and frequent checks of the blood pressure. All possible efforts should be made to have as rapidly as possible a definitive identification of the malaria species, and a quantitative estimate of parasite density.

The patient is admitted to the medical intensive care unit and treated with oral quinine and Doxycycline. Later that day, the blood smear is reviewed by more experienced personnel for speciation.

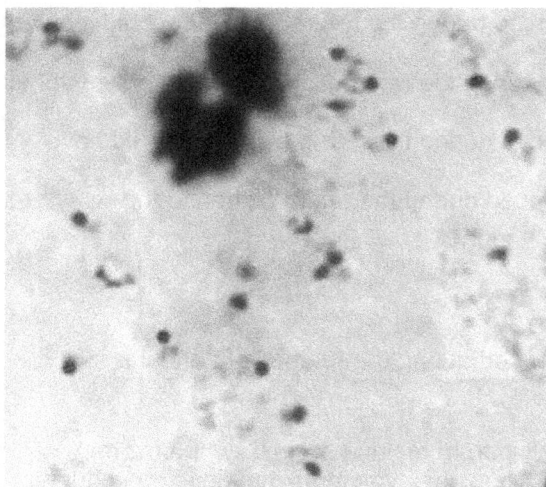

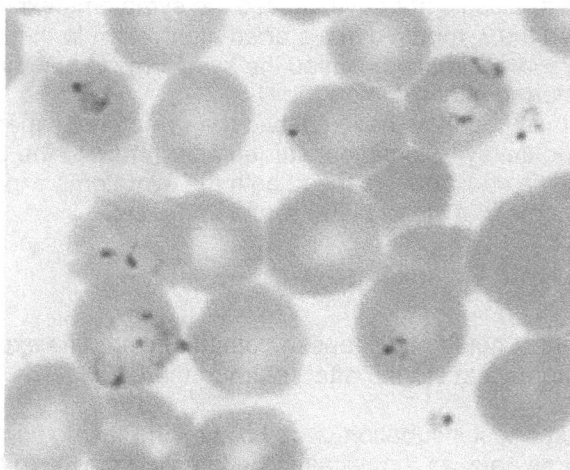

Question 4: What is the diagnosis?
1-Plasmodium Falciparum
2-Plasmodium Vivax
3-Plasmodium ovale
4-Plasmodium malariae
5-Not malaria

Question 4: Correct Answer

Plasmodium Falciparum

The thin smear shows intra-erythrocytic parasites, all at the ring stage. Some erythrocytes are multiply infected, and some parasites are in "appliqué" forms (pushed against the edge of the erythrocyte). All these characteristics are compatible with P. Falciparum. A high proportion of the erythrocytes are infected, an indication that this infection might be severe. (The thick smear shows many parasites and a leukocyte; thick smears are more sensitive than thin smears for detecting parasites, but thin smears are needed for species determination.)
The smears are diagnosed as P. Falciparum, and parasite quantification shows that 17% of the erythrocytes are infected. The patient's mental status deteriorates and his urine output decreases.

Question 5: Which of the following measures would be appropriate?
1-Continue existing treatment (oral quinine and Doxycycline)
2-Switch treatment to intravenous quinidine and Doxycycline
3-Switch treatment to intravenous clindamycin
4-Consider exchange transfusion

Question 5: Final Correct Answer

Switch treatment to intravenous quinidine and Doxycycline and consider an exchange transfusion

This is a case of severe P. Falciparum malaria, and oral treatment is not appropriate. Parenteral (intravenous) treatment with quinidine and Doxycycline should be initiated urgently. An intravenous treatment with clindamycin alone would not be sufficient (clindamycin should be administered in combination with quinidine). In addition, given the high parasitemia and signs of cerebral and renal complications, an exchange transfusion should be considered. Corticosteroids have no role in the management of malaria, and in fact can be harmful.
Treatment with oral antimalarials is continued and an exchange transfusion is ordered. While preparing for the exchange transfusion, the patient becomes hypotensive, requiring a dopamine drip. During the exchange transfusion, the patient becomes increasingly tachypneic and develops atrial flutter, which exacerbates the hypotension. DC cardioversion is attempted without success. The patient develops asystole and expires 17 hours after admission to the medical intensive care unit.

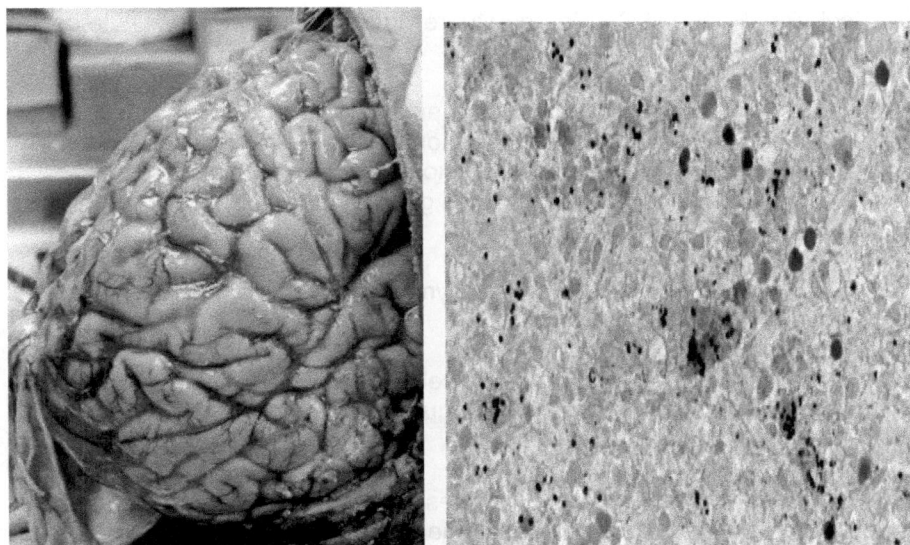

An autopsy was performed, but after a delay of 8 days. The gross findings show a slight swelling of the cerebral gyri, with consequent narrowing of the sulci; some blood vessels are engorged, with scattered petechial hemorrhage. The hematoxylin-eosin section of the brain shows autolysis, some

pycnotic nuclei, and scattered pigment felt to be malarial in origin. The pigment and pinpoint hemorrhages are felt to be pre-mortem.

TAKE HOME MESSAGES, IMPORTANT TO RECOGNIZE AND DON'T FORGET PERIPHERAL BLOOD SMEARS.

Main points:
1) Visitors to malaria endemic areas should take appropriate prophylaxis.
2) Malaria should always be suspected in a febrile patient who has recently traveled in a malaria endemic area.
3) Blood smears for malaria should be examined by experienced staff, without delay.
4) When there is suspicion of severe malaria, the patient should be hospitalized and parenteral treatment should be initiated urgently.
5) Exchange transfusion should be considered when parasite density is high (>10%) or when signs of cerebral or renal complications develop (another indication, not present in this case, is non-overload pulmonary edema).

Content source: Division of Parasitic Diseases
National Center for Zoonotic, Vector-Borne, and Enteric Diseases (ZVED), CDC MALARIA BRANCH.
Used with permission.

-Case study two-

Gérard J / Ly-Sunnaram B / Clech Ph / Pangault C / Mareau-Dupré C / Goasguen JE Université de Rennes I

Clinical features: A 15-month-old male child with previous severe entero-virus infection which caused a pericarditis and a thrombopenia. The child had been followed monthly for a splenomegaly and lymphocytosis (15G/L) .At the age of 15 months, 2 recent skin lesions and cervical and inguinal adenopathy were discovered. The patient's general condition was good. A diagnosis of leukemia was brought up.

Peripheral blood: Hb 111g/L, Pl 263G/L, WBC 27.5G/Lwith 54% lymphocytes, 29% neutrophils, 12% monocytes and a minimal myelemia.

Peripheral blood immunophenotypic features: On total lymphoid cells: T cells 53% (CD4 41% and CD8 12%) and B cells 30%. Conclusion: there was no immunologic argument for clonality. Classified as reactional lymphocytosis.

Bone marrow aspiration: Normal granulosus and erythroid lineages. Excess of various sized lymphoid cells, smaller cells predominating with high nucleocytoplasmic ratio and a condensed chromatin (47%). Small quantity of blastic cells (9%).
Conclusion: Proliferation of polymorphic lymphoid cells, it makes leukemia unlikely.

Bone marrow immunophenotypic features: On lymphocytes area. B cells 77% expressed CD19, CD10 (low), CD24, CD9, CD79a intra, Mµ intra CD45, CD20 (low and partially), CD38 (bright) and lacking CD34 and CD58. One may think for a pre-B ALL (CD19+, CD10+, CD79a intra +, Mµ intra +) but the

CD38 bright and lacking of CD58 and CD34 are not in favour of this proposition; these are actually immature B cells named hematogones
This is confirmed by the negativity of B monoclonality (immunoglobulin gene rearrangement) by PCR on bone marrow cells.

Discussion: Hematogones are mysterious bone marrow cells with condensed nuclear chromatin but homogenous (sometimes reticular with nucleoli) and a scanty cytoplasm. They resemble lymphocytes. They have B cell precursor immunophenotype. There is a significant decrease of hematogones with increasing age (maximum rate before 5 years old); in some instances they constitute 5 to 50% of bone marrow cells. They may be particularly prominent in the regeneration phase following chemotherapy or bone marrow transplantation and in patients with autoimmune and congenital cytopenias, neoplasms, and AIDS.

Conclusion: Every immunophenotype must be linked with cytology analysis. The striking fact of this case report is the high percentage of hematogones (47%) in the bone marrow.

Reference:

- McKenna R, Washington L, Aquino D, Picker L, Kroft S. Immunophenotypic analysis of hematogones (B-lymphocyte precursors) in 662 consecutive bone marrow specimens by 4-color flow cytometry. Blood, 15 Octobre 2001, Vol. 98, Nƒ 8, pp 2498-2507.
- Duval M, Fenneteau O, Cave H, Gobillot C, Rohrlich P, Guidal C, Lescoeaur B, Legac S, Schlegel N, Sterkers G, Vilmer E. Expansion of polyclonal B-cell precursors in bone marrow from children treated for acute lymphoblastic leukemia. Hematol Cell Ther. 1997 Juin, 139-147

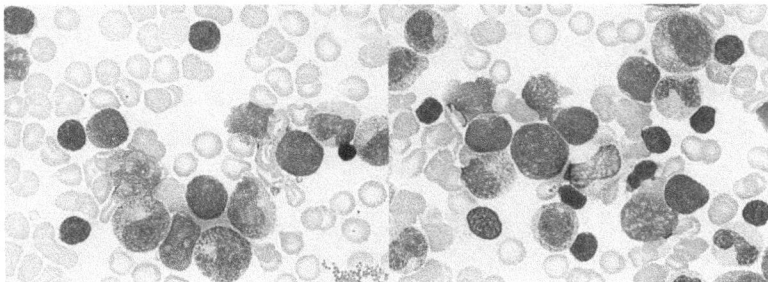

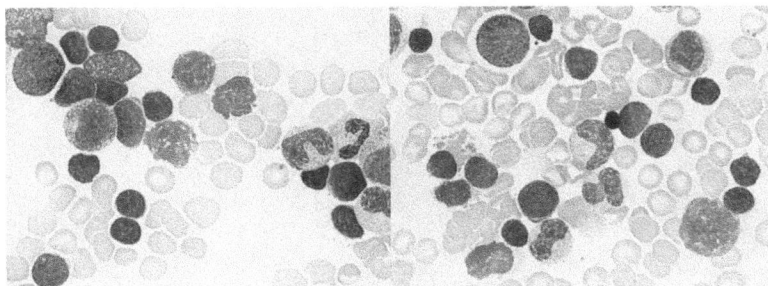

WWW.med.univ-rennes1.fr-r576-Microsoft Internet Explorer

352

References

- American Cancer Society. Cancer Facts and Figures 2008. Atlanta, Ga.
. - Harris NL, Jaffe ES, Stein H, et al: A revised European-American classification of lymphoid neoplasms: A proposal from the International Lymphoma Study Group. Blood. 1994; 84:1361-92.
. - The Non-Hodgkin's Lymphoma Pathologic Classification Project. National Cancer Institute sponsored study of classifications of non-Hodgkin's lymphomas: summary and description of a Working Formulation for clinical usage. Cancer. 1982; 49:2112-2135.
. - Lennert K, Feller AC: Histopathology of non-Hodgkin's lymphomas (Based on the Updated Kiel Classification). 2nd ed. Berlin: Springer-Verlag, 1992.
. - Chan JKC, Banks PM, Cleary ML, et al: A revised European-American classification of lymphoid neoplasms proposed by the International Lymphoma Study Group. Am J Clin Pathol. 1995; 103:543-560.

- Case Study Three-

15 year old asymptomatic female with a mediastinal mass and a lung nodule on chest x-ray.

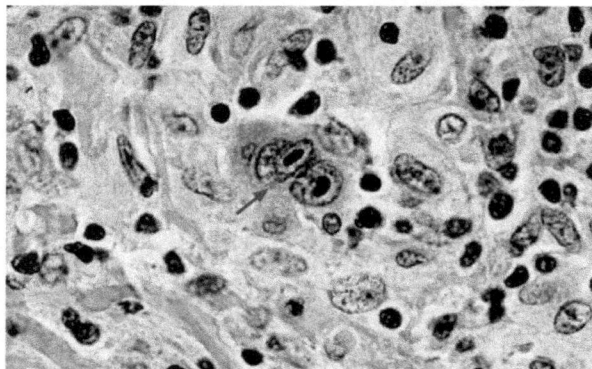

The "Reed-Sternberg" cell in the center is the Diagnostic neoplastic cell in Hodgkin's disease. Note the bilobed nucleus with prominent inclusion-like nucleoli.

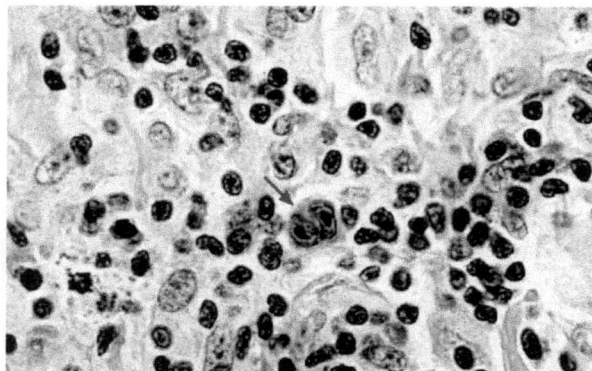

The" Reed-Sternberg" cell in the center is just starting to degenerate, or "mummify" and is taking on a dark staining quality.

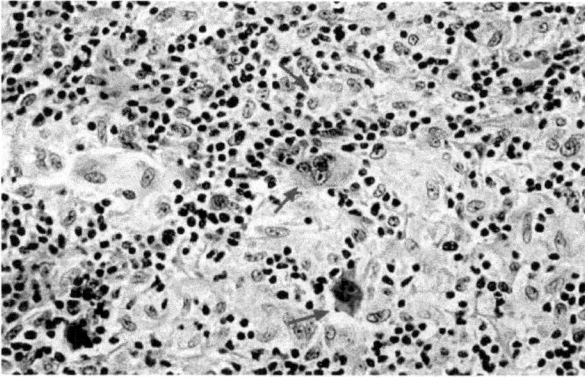

- top (arrow). These are aggregates of histiocytes and lymphocytes

- Center (arrow). This is a multinucleated Reed-Sternberg cell

- Bottom (arrow). This is a mummified cell

What is the outcome of this disease? Does the absence of symptoms or the presence of a lung nodule affect the therapy? Why?

If only the mediastinum is involved, with no symptoms, this is stage IA Hodgkin's disease, and the prognosis is excellent, with appropriate therapy. If the nodule in the lung is also Hodgkin's disease, this makes this stage IVA.

Therapy would probable include irradiation of the lung field as well as chemotherapy, and would result in greater toxicity, and the prognosis would become poorer. In general, if patients respond to therapy and achieve a disease-free survival of 3 years after primary treatment, there is an excellent chance that they will be cured.

Contents:
Robert Hutchison, M.D.
Sharad Mathur, M.D.

Web Design:
Jannie Woo, Ph.D.

Technical Assistance:
John Yowpa, MSIII
Brian Fengler, MSII

SUNY Upstate Medical University
Syracuse, NY

- Case Study Four-

John Kim Choi, MD, PhD
Director of Pediatric Hematopathology
Department of Pathology
Children's Hospital of Philadelphia

Assistant Professor
Department of Pathology and Laboratory Medicine

University of Pennsylvania
Philadelphia, PA, USA

Diagnosis: Severe Congenital Neutropenia (Kostmann Syndrome)

Introduction

Severe neutropenia (absolute neutrophil count < 500 / uL) results in increased risk of bacterial infection [1]. Most neutropenias result from extrinsic causes that include infection, drugs (including chemotherapy), autoimmune disorders, and marrow-occupying malignancies such as chronic or acute lymphoid leukemia [2, 3]. Less common ly, severe neutropenia may result from intrinsic defects in neutrophil proliferation, maturation, and survival [4]. Most intrinsic defects in adults are acquired; this is the case in myelodysplastic syndrome (MDS) and acute myeloid leukemias (AMLs). In contrast, most intrinsic defects in children are congenital or inherited and are usually diagnosed in the newborn and young infants (Table 1). The most common inherited isolated neutropenia is severe congenital neutropenia (SCN), also called Kostmann syndrome. SCN presents with characteristic clinical and pathologic features that are demonstrated in this case presentation.

Clinical History

The patient was delivered by C aesarean section at 41 weeks of gestation and she was discharged following an uneventful 5-day hospital stay. However, a week later, the patient was seen in the emergency department (ED) for fever (101 ° C) and upper respiratory infectious symptoms (cough and rhinorrhea). The latter responded to treatment with a vaporizer. Two days later, the patient returned to the ED for a small cutaneous vesicular lesion on her neck. Two days later, the patient was admitted for fever and cellulitis of the neck. Laboratory studies were significant for an absolute neutrophil count (ANC) of 0 with normal hemoglobin and increased platelets. The patient was started on antibiotics with resolution of the cellulitis. Serial CBCs over 2 weeks showed persistent absence of neutrophils, ANC of 0. (Fig. 1) A bone marrow aspirate was performed and the findings were consistent with SCN. The patient was started on G-CSF at 15 ug/kg/day with prompt elevation in the ANC. She was subsequently followed mostly in the outpatient clinic.

The patient is now 14 years old and has received a daily injection of G-CSF that maintains her ANC between 1000 and 3000 / uL. She has had only a few hospitalizations for fevers, herpes stomatitis, dental abscesses, and pneumonia. She suffers from chronic gingivitis, hepatosplenomegaly, severe osteoporosis with vertebral compression fractures, and short stature. She has being doing well in school, receiving honors. Her marrow is examined on an annual basis by morphology and cytogenetics. Bone marrow aspirates and biopsies have not shown definitive evidence of MDS or AML and the karyotypes have been normal 46, XX.

Pathology

The patient's bone marrow has been evaluated many times at our institution over the past14 years. As typical in most pediatric hospitals, most of the marrow examinations have been via bone marrow aspirate smears, although biopsies were performed at ages 2 months, 11 months, 7 years, 8 years, and 12 years. All of the marrow studies showed similar morphology.

The bone marrow aspirate smears showed normocellular to hypercellular marrow

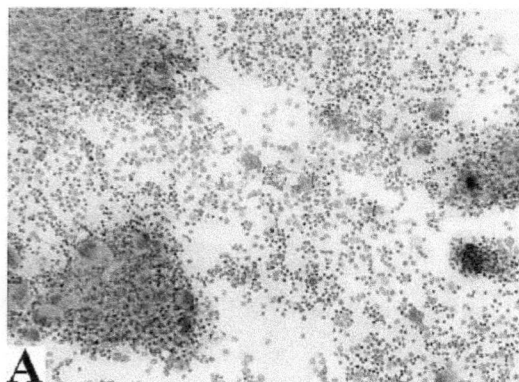

Figure 2a: Bone marrow aspirate smear - 100 X magnifications, Wright stain.

With granulocytic hypoplasia and maturation arrest, with most of the cells arrested at the promyelocyte to myelocyte stage

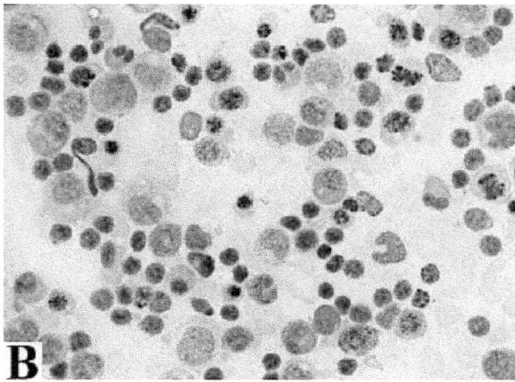

Figure 2b: Bone marrow aspirate smear - 500 X magnifications, Wright stain.

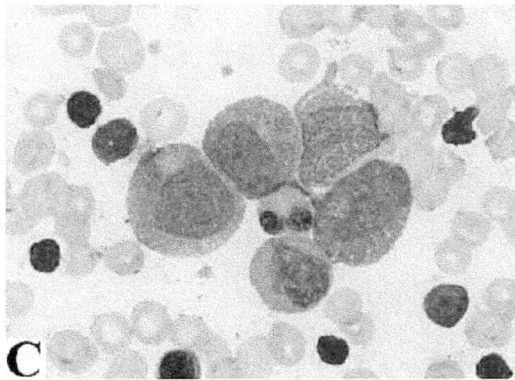

Figure 2c: Bone marrow aspirate smear - 1000X magnification, Wright stain.

The myelocytes showed asynchronous maturation of cytoplasm and nucleus, with the presence of secondary granules without chromatin condensation. The promyelocytes contained decreased numbers of primary granules. The decreased number of mature neutrophils (0 - 8% of marrow cellularity) was strikingly disparate from the increased number of maturing eosinophils (7 – 13%). Monocytes were also increased in number (2 - 9%, normal less than 1%). Erythroid precursor cells were relatively increased in number and showed normal maturation. The megakaryocytes were normal to increased in number and showed normal maturation. Aspirate smears at younger ages showed increased numbers of lymphocytes and immature-appearing lymphocytes consistent with hematogones. Blasts were not increased in number.

The biopsies generally confirmed the aspirate findings. In addition, there was prominent expansion of the myeloid precursors that was confined to the paratrabecular region

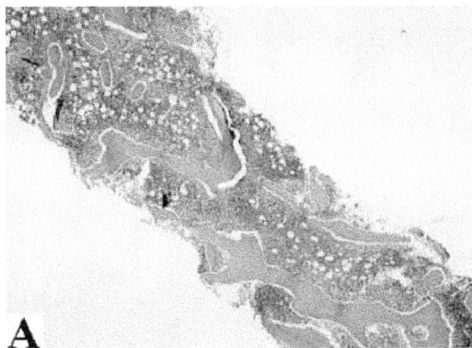

356

Figure 3a: Bone marrow biopsy - 25X - magnification, hematoxylin and eosin stain.

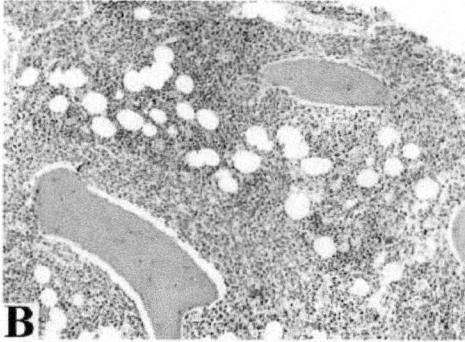

Figure 3b: Bone marrow biopsy - 100X - magnification, hematoxylin and eosin stain.

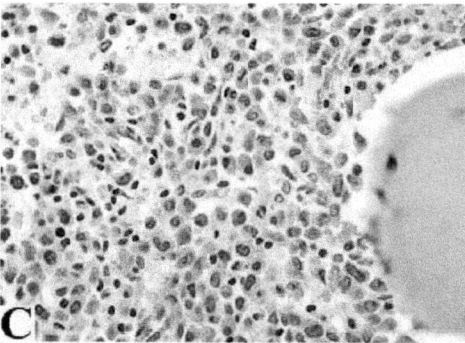

Figure 3c: Bone marrow biopsy - 400X - magnification, hematoxylin and eosin stain.

In the non-paratrabecular regions, there was normal maturation of erythroid precursors in small collections (Erythron), scattered megakaryocytes, and maturing eosinophils

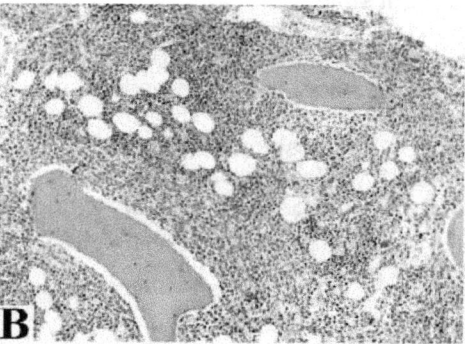

Figure 3b: Bone marrow biopsy - 100X - magnification, hematoxylin and eosin stain.

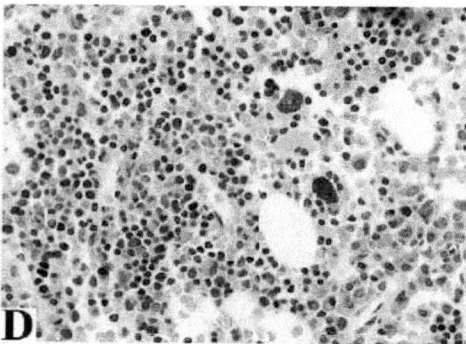

Figure 3d: Bone marrow biopsy - 400X - magnification, hematoxylin and eosin stain.

Mature neutrophils were rare to absent throughout the marrow, suggesting that the mature neutrophils seen on the aspirate smears represented peripheral blood components. The thickened paratrabecular regions that contained the myeloid precursor cells were sharply delineated from the intertrabecular regions that contained erythroid elements, eosinophils, and megakaryocytes.

Discussion

Definition: SCN is an inherited disorder presenting in the newborn with severe chronic neutropenia (ANC less than 500 / ul) and little to moderate anemia/thrombocytopenia. Often the ANC is less than 200 / ul even shortly after birth. SCN should be distinguished from cyclic neutropenia, another intrinsic defect in granulopoiesis that shares many similarities but does not progress to MDS or AML.

Synonyms: Congenital agranulocytosis, infantile congenital agranulocytosis, Kostmann's syndrome, Kostmann syndrome, congenital neutropenia, congenital severe chronic neutropenia. Some authors distinguish SCN from Kostmann syndrome, reserving the latter for the first described family or to those cases with documented autosomal recessive inheritance pattern. Others, including this author, use these terms interchangeably.

Epidemiology: SCN is a rare disease with approximately 1-2 cases / million population [5] . The first cases were reported in 1950 and 1956 by Rolf Kostmann, who designated the disease as infantile genetic agranulocytosis [6]. These cases were transmitted in an autosomal recessive pattern of inheritance. Since then, other cases of SCN have been described, some with autosomal dominant [7] or sporadic pattern of inheritance. Similar to SCN, cyclic neutropenia is a rare disease with less than 1 case / million populations. The inheritance pattern of cyclic neutropenia is autosomal dominant or sporadic [8].

Clinical features: The patients have neutropenia at birth that deteriorates to agranulocytosis with recurrent infections, typically bacterial sepsis or pneumonia (Staphylococcus aureus, Escherichia coli, Pseudomonas aeruginosa). Prior to 1994, most patients were treated with prophylactic antibiotics [9] and rarely, bone marrow transplant [10] . The prognosis in these patients was poor with median age of death as low as 0.8 - 2 years [11, 12] . In addition, there was a 2% incidence of acute leukemia.

In the late 1980s and early 1990s, multiple studies demonstrated the clinical effectiveness of G-CSF in the treatment of SCN [9, 13] . In 1994, G-CSF became widely available and dramatically changed the clinical course of this disease. Also, an international registry (Severe Chronic Neutropenia International Registry, SCNIR, http://depts.washington.edu/registry) was established permitting close clinical follow up of this and other diseases with severe chronic neutropenia. As of 2003, 853 patients have been registered, of which 348 are SCN [5] . Over 90% of the patients respond to G-CSF injections (0.15-60 ug / kg/ day) with the ANC increasing to 1,500 - 10,000 / ml. The median life expectancy is 17.3 years and increasing. Death from infection still occurs (35% of deaths) but is more commonly due to leukemia and its complications (37% of deaths). Even more worrisome is the increasing incidence of MDS / AML, 1% / year for the first four years; this accelerates to approximately 13% cumulative risk after 8 years on G-CSF treatment. The accelerating rate suggests that the incidence and percentage of deaths from MDS/AML will continue to increase. In addition to leukemia, other medical complications are becoming evident with increasing age. Many of the patients exhibit hepatomegaly (20-35% of the patients), osteopenia / osteoporosis (59%), and growth retardation (27-51% were less than the tenth percentile). Less frequent are vasculitis (4%) and glomerulonephritis.

Similar to SCN, cyclic neutropenia may present with severe neutropenia. However, cyclic neutropenia is characterized by a 21 day oscillating neutrophil count with ANC ranging from 0 to 1.5K/ul. Severe infections can occur at the nadir of the neutrophil count. G-CSF treatment has also ameliorated the clinical course of this disease. However, approximately 10% of these patients die, exclusively secondary to infection [5]. Unlike SCN, cyclic neutropenia has not been associated with MDS / AML. As of 2003, 145 patients with cyclic neutropenia have been registered in the SCNIR.

Morphology: The aspirate smear findings in this case are typical of SCN cases . The typical SCN bone marrow aspirate shows a maturation arrest of the myeloid precursors at the promyelocyte/myelocyte stage of differentiation with increased numbers of eosinophils and monocytes. The promyelocytes have normal [14, 15] to abnormally lucent primary granules [16] with paucity of secondary granules in the more mature myeloid cells. The cytoplasm and nucleus show asynchronous maturation [16, 17] . Occasional myeloid precursors showed cytoplasmic vacuolation [14, 16] . In one published case, the promyelocytes and myelocytes were enlarged and multinucleated but this appears to be the exception to the rule [18] . All of these changes, including left shift in myeloid maturation, enlarged myeloid cells, hypogranulation, nuclear to cytoplasmic maturation asynchrony, cytoplasmic vacuolation , eosinophilia, and monocytosis, have been associated with G-CSF treatment [19, 20] and thus, it is unclear how much chronic G-CSF treatment contributes to these morphologic changes. However, such changes are seen in SCN without G-CSF treatment, indicating that they may be intrinsic to SCN. Finally, prominent and increased azurophilic granulation, typical of G-CSF effect, is not seen.

The bone marrow biopsies have been generally described as showing a left shift in myeloid maturation but detailed descriptions are lacking. For example, increased numbers of eosinophils and monocytes have not been noted in the biopsies but given the aspirate findings, one would expect to find that they are also increased in the biopsy. Our case details specific findings that have not been previously described for bone marrow biopsies of patients with SCN. The marrow biopsies showed thickened paratrabecular region comprised exclusively of immature myeloid cells. The non-paratrabecular regions showed normal erythroid precursors, normal to increased megakaryocytes, increased numbers of maturing eosinophils, and the near absence of mature neutrophils. The last point is particularly interesting because normal numbers of mature neutrophils are found in the peripheral blood with G-CSF treatment, suggesting that segmented neutrophils are immediately released from the bone marrow upon maturation or that maturation to neutrophils occurs outside the marrow from circulating immature cells. This would suggest that the mature neutrophils seen in the bone marrow aspirate smears [21] represent peripheral blood contamination. We have seen virtually identical biopsy findings in another case of SCN (data not shown), suggesting that these findings are defining features of a subset of SCN on chronic G-CSF.

The differential diagnosis is limited for the expanded myeloid precursors in the paratrabecular regions with zonation of the myeloid from the erythroid, eosinophils, and megakaryocytes. Possible diagnoses include acute response to G-CSF therapy, early regeneration of the myeloid cells from a toxic event, and MDS. Clinical history excludes the first two possibilities. In theory, autoimmune neutropenia could present with similar morphology if the antibodies react against myelocytes and metamyelocytes. In practice, autoimmune neutropenia typically results in compensatory myeloid hyperplasia in the marrow and occasional neutrophil phagocytosis [2, 22] . The paratrabecular myeloid expansion is unlikely to be a manifestation of MDS because this feature was present for 14 years without any evidence of significant anemia, thrombocytopenia, increased blasts, or cytogenetic abnormalities. Furthermore, MDS often shows disorganization of erythroid precursors from their usual Erythron and immature myeloid cells in the interparatrabecular areas (atypical localization of immature precursors). Finally, the paratrabecular myeloid expansion is unlikely to result solely from chronic G-CSF therapy. While G-CSF therapy can initially cause paratrabecular expansion, prolonged treatment (> 1 month) leads to normalization of the myeloid maturation and localization [19].

Bone marrow findings reported in cyclic neutropenia have been based mostly on bone marrow aspirate smears. The marrow findings range from those similar to SCN at the nadir of the neutrophil count to those similar to normal marrow at normal neutrophil counts. The two disease s can be distinguished by serial CBCs over several weeks [23].

Immunophenotype: Very few studies of the immunophenotype of bone marrow cells from SCN patients have been reported. Flow cytometry analysis of SCN bone marrow without G-CSF demonstrates normal numbers of the very early CD34+, CD38- hematopoietic progenitor cells but decreased numbers of the slightly more committed CD34+, CD38+ hematopoietic progenitor cells [24]. Apoptotic CD34+ progenitor cells and CD33+ or CD15+ more committed myeloid cells are increased in number in cultured SCN bone marrow but not in freshly isolated marrow cells [25] . Peripheral neutrophils in SCN on G-CSF appear to have increased expression of CD64, CD32, CD14, HLA-DR, decreased expression of CD16, and constant expression of CD11b/CD18, CD11a/CD18 [26]. However, later studies indicate that most if not all changes are secondary to G-CSF effect [27, 28] . Currently, there is no consensus immunophenotype that characterizes SCN.

Molecular mechanism: The molecular defect in a subset (57 – 88 %) of SCN cases has been localized to point mutations in the neutrophil elastase 2 gene (ELA-2) [29, 30], a component of primary granules. A mutation in the transcription factor Gfi1, which regulates the expression of ELA-2 gene, has been identified in a minor subset of SCN cases without ELA-2 mutations [31]. The identified mutations are heterozygous and cannot explain the autosomal recessive form of SCN [30, 32] . Additional unidentified mutations remain to be identified. The ELA-2 gene is also mutated in 100% of cyclic neutropenia, although most of the point mutations are different from those in SCN (http://archive.uwcm.ac.uk/uwcm/mg/search/118792.html). However, occasional mutations are shared between the two diseases [33], resulting in the perplexing question of how the same point mutations in ELA-2 cause different diseases.

The identification of ELA-2 using linkage analysis of cyclic neutropenia [34] was a major step in understanding the molecular mechanism s of both cyclic neutropenia and SCN [29]. The obligatory role of ELA-2 was questioned following the identification of a family with two symptomatic children with an ELA-2 mutation and an asymptomatic father with the identical mutation [35]. Later study demonstrated that in such cases the asymptomatic parent was a mosaic for the ELA-2 mutation and the normal ELA-2 genes predominated in the neutrophils, strongly supporting the hypothesis that ELA-2 mutations are sufficient to cause neutropenia [36].

Despite the identification of the offending gene in the majority of SCN cases and the detection of increased apoptosis in the myeloid precursors [37], the exact mechanism of disease remains poorly understood. Early models predicted that normal ELA-2 was necessary for normal granulopoiesis and ELA-2 mutations led to loss of the elastase activity of the mutated ELA-2 protein and the normal ELA-2 protein in a dominant negative manner. Most studies appear to be inconsistent with this model. Mouse models that lack ELA-2 [38] or express ectopic mutated ELA-2 [39] have normal neutrophil development. In vitro assay of the mutated ELA-2 proteins demonstrated varying elastase activities including supranormal levels [40]. Finally, mutated Gli1 leads to the overexpression and not suppression of ELA-2 [31]. These findings have led to an alternative model in which abnormal activity or intracellular localization of ELA-2 leads to apoptosis of the neutrophils [41].

This model is supported by the identification of the molecular defect in a dog model of cyclic neutropenia [42]. This mutated gene encodes an adaptor protein complex b subunit that is important for directing proteins to specific membranes. This model does not explain the mouse studies, but preliminary studies suggest species differences such that mutated ELA-2 alters human but not murine myelopoiesis [43] . Finally, this model also does not define the relationship between abnormal ELA-2 and apoptosis. The relationship may involve the anti-apoptotic protein bcl-2 since bcl-2 is decreased in patients with SCN and is restored to normal levels with G-CSF treatment [44] .

Prognosis and clinical course: The life expectancy in SCN has been greatly increased by the advent of G-CSF. Numerous complications are being identified with increased age of the patients (see clinical course). Of these, the most worrisome is the increasing incidence of MDS / AML that has overtaken infection as the leading cause of mortality. The conversion to AML is associated with the acquisition of G-CSF receptor mutations, loss of chromosome 7, and ras mutations [45].

Table 1: Partial Differential Diagnosis for Severe Neutropenia

Extrinsic
Infection
Drug
Immune-mediated: immunodeficiency, autoimmune, aplastic anemia
Nutritional deficiency: B12, folate
Marrow compromise by tumor
Pseudo-neutropenia secondary to neutrophil clumping
Intrinsic (often seen in newborn / young infant)
Severe congenital neutropenia (Kostmann syndrome)
Cyclic neutropenia
Schwachman-Diamond Syndrome
Chediak-Higashi syndrome
Dyskeratosis congenita
Cartilage hair hypoplasia

Griscelli syndrome
Myelokathexis (WHIM syndrome)
Glycogen storage disease Ib
Myelodysplastic syndrome

References

Dinauer MC. The Phagocyte System and Disorders of Granulopoiesis and Granulocyte Function. in Hematology of Infancy and Childhood, D.G. Nathan, S.H. Orkin, D. Ginsburg, and A.T. Look, Editors. 2003, W.B. Saunders Company: Philadelphia. p. 923-1010.

Foucar K, Duncan MH, and Smith KJ. Practical approach to the investigation of neutropenia. Clin Lab Med. 1993. 13(4): p. 879-94.

Al-Mulla ZS and Christensen RD. Neutropenia in the neonate. Clin Perinatol. 1995. 22(3): p. 711-39.

Boxer L and Dale DC. Neutropenia: causes and consequences. Semin Hematol. 2002. 39(2): p. 75-81.

Dale DC, Cottle TE, Fier CJ, Bolyard AA, Bonilla MA, Boxer LA, Cham B, Freedman MH, Kannourakis G, Kinsey SE, Davis R, Scarlata D, Schwinzer B, Zeidler C, and Welte K. Severe chronic neutropenia: treatment and follow-up of patients in the Severe Chronic Neutropenia International Registry. Am J Hematol. 2003. 72(2): p. 82-93.

Kostmann R. Infantile genetic agranulocytosis; agranulocytosis infantilis hereditaria. Acta Paediatr. 1956. 45(Suppl 105): p. 1-78.

Briars GL, Parry HF, and Ansari BM. Dominantly inherited severe congenital neutropenia. J Infect. 1996. 33(2): p. 123-6.

Palmer SE, Stephens K, and Dale DC. Genetics, phenotype, and natural history of autosomal dominant cyclic hematopoiesis. Am J Med Genet. 1996. 66(4): p. 413-22.

Bonilla MA, Gillio AP, Ruggeiro M, Kernan NA, Brochstein JA, Abboud M, Fumagalli L, Vincent M, Gabrilove JL, Welte K, and et al. Effects of recombinant human granulocyte colony-stimulating factor on neutropenia in patients with congenital agranulocytosis. N Engl J Med. 1989. 320(24): p. 1574-80.

Rappeport JM, Parkman R, Newburger P, Camitta BM, and Chusid MJ. Correction of infantile agranulocytosis (Kostmann's syndrome) by allogeneic bone marrow transplantation. Am J Med. 1980. 68(4): p. 605-9.

Carlsson G and Fasth A. Infantile genetic agranulocytosis, morbus Kostmann: presentation of six cases from the original "Kostmann family" and a review. Acta Paediatr. 2001. 90(7): p. 757-64.

Freedman MH, Bonilla MA, Fier C, Bolyard AA, Scarlata D, Boxer LA, Brown S, Cham B, Kannourakis G, Kinsey SE, Mori PG, Cottle T, Welte K, and Dale DC. Myelodysplasia syndrome and acute myeloid leukemia in patients with congenital neutropenia receiving G-CSF therapy. Blood. 2000. 96(2): p. 429-36.

Dale DC, Bonilla MA, Davis MW, Nakanishi AM, Hammond WP, Kurtzberg J, Wang W, Jakubowski A, Winton E, Lalezari P, and et al. A randomized controlled phase III trial of recombinant human granulocyte colony-stimulating factor (filgrastim) for treatment of severe chronic neutropenia. Blood. 1993. 81(10): p. 2496-502.

Wriedt K, Kauder E, and Mauer AM. Defective myelopoiesis in congenital neutropenia. N Engl J Med. 1970. 283(20): p. 1072-7.

Parmley RT, Ogawa M, Darby CP, Jr., and Spicer SS. Congenital neutropenia: neutrophil proliferation with abnormal maturation. Blood. 1975. 46(5): p. 723-34.

Parmley RT, Crist WM, Ragab AH, Boxer LA, Malluh A, Lui VK, and Darby CP. Congenital dysgranulopoietic neutropenia: clinical, serologic, ultrastructural, and in vitro proliferative characteristics. Blood. 1980. 56(3): p. 465-75.

Zucker-Franklin D, L'Esperance P, and Good RA. Congenital neutropenia: an intrinsic cell defect demonstrated by electron microscopy of soft agar colonies. Blood. 1977. 49(3): p. 425-36.

Lightsey AL, Parmley RT, Marsh WL, Jr., Garg AK, Thomas WJ, Wolach B, and Boxer LA. Severe congenital neutropenia with unique features of dysgranulopoiesis. Am J Hematol. 1985. 18(1): p. 59-71.

Schmitz LL, McClure JS, Litz CE, Dayton V, Weisdorf DJ, Parkin JL, and Brunning RD. Morphologic and quantitative changes in blood and marrow cells following growth factor therapy. Am J Clin Pathol. 1994. 101(1): p. 67-75.

Schmitz LL, Litz CE, and Brunning RD. Morphologic and quantitative alterations in hematopoietic cells associated with growth factor therapy: review of the literature. Hematol Pathol. 1994. 8(3): p. 55-73.

Zeidler C and Welte K. Kostmann syndrome and severe congenital neutropenia. Semin Hematol. 2002. 39(2): p. 82-8.

Shimizu H, Sawada K, Katano N, Sasaki K, Kawai S, and Fujimoto T. Intramedullary neutrophil phagocytosis by histiocytes in autoimmune neutropenia of infancy. Acta Haematol. 1990. 84(4): p. 201-3.

Dale DC and Hammond WP. Cyclic neutropenia: a clinical review. Blood Rev. 1988. 2(3): p. 178-85.

Papadaki HA, Gibson FM, Psyllaki M, Gordon-Smith EC, Marsh JC, and Eliopoulos GD. Assessment of bone marrow stem cell reserve and function and stromal cell function in patients with severe congenital neutropenia. Eur J Haematol. 2001. 67(4): p. 245-51.

Aprikyan AA, Kutyavin T, Stein S, Aprikian P, Rodger E, Liles WC, Boxer LA, and Dale DC. Cellular and molecular abnormalities in severe congenital neutropenia predisposing to leukemia. Exp Hematol. 2003. 31(5): p. 372-81.

Elsner J, Roesler J, Emmendorffer A, Zeidler C, Lohmann-Matthes ML, and Welte K. Altered function and surface marker expression of neutrophils induced by rhG-CSF treatment in severe congenital neutropenia. Eur J Haematol. 1992. 48(1): p. 10-9.

Spiekermann K, Emmendoerffer A, Elsner J, Raeder E, Lohmann-Matthes ML, Prahst A, Link H, Freund M, Welte K, and Roesler J. Altered surface marker expression and function of G-CSF-induced neutrophils from test subjects and patients under chemotherapy. Br J Haematol. 1994. 87(1): p. 31-8.

Spiekermann K, Emmendoerffer A, Elsner J, Raeder E, Lohmann-Matthes ML, Welte K, and Roesler J. Changes in light-scatter profile, membrane depolarization and calcium mobilization of neutrophils induced by G-CSF in vivo. Br J Haematol. 1994. 88(3): p. 506-14.

Dale DC, Person RE, Bolyard AA, Aprikyan AG, Bos C, Bonilla MA, Boxer LA, Kannourakis G, Zeidler C, Welte K, Benson KF, and Horwitz M. Mutations in the gene encoding neutrophil elastase in congenital and cyclic neutropenia. Blood. 2000. 96(7): p. 2317-22.

Bellanne-Chantelot C, Clauin S, Leblanc T, Cassinat B, Rodrigues-Lima F, Beaufils S, Vaury C, Barkaoui M, Fenneteau O, Maier-Redelsperger M, Chomienne C, and Donadieu J. Mutations in the ELA2 gene correlate with more severe expression of neutropenia: a study of 81 patients from the French Neutropenia Register. Blood. 2004. 103(11): p. 4119-25.

Person RE, Li FQ, Duan Z, Benson KF, Wechsler J, Papadaki HA, Eliopoulos G, Kaufman C, Bertolone SJ, Nakamoto B, Papayannopoulou T, Grimes HL, and Horwitz M. Mutations in proto-oncogene GFI1 cause human neutropenia and target ELA2. Nat Genet. 2003. 34(3): p. 308-12.

Ancliff PJ, Gale RE, Liesner R, Hann IM, and Linch DC. Mutations in the ELA2 gene encoding neutrophil elastase are present in most patients with sporadic severe congenital neutropenia but only in some patients with the familial form of the disease. Blood. 2001. 98(9): p. 2645-50.

Aprikyan AA and Dale DC. Mutations in the neutrophil elastase gene in cyclic and congenital neutropenia. Curr Opin Immunol. 2001. 13(5): p. 535-8.

Horwitz M, Benson KF, Person RE, Aprikyan AG, and Dale DC. Mutations in ELA2, encoding neutrophil elastase, define a 21-day biological clock in cyclic haematopoiesis. Nat Genet. 1999. 23(4): p. 433-6.

Germeshausen M, Schulze H, Ballmaier M, Zeidler C, and Welte K. Mutations in the gene encoding neutrophil elastase (ELA2) are not sufficient to cause the phenotype of congenital neutropenia. Br J Haematol. 2001. 115(1): p. 222-4.

Ancliff PJ, Gale RE, Watts MJ, Liesner R, Hann IM, Strobel S, and Linch DC. Paternal mosaicism proves the pathogenic nature of mutations in neutrophil elastase in severe congenital neutropenia. Blood. 2002. 100(2): p. 707-9.

Aprikyan AA, Liles WC, Rodger E, Jonas M, Chi EY, and Dale DC. Impaired survival of bone marrow hematopoietic progenitor cells in cyclic neutropenia. Blood. 2001. 97(1): p. 147-53.

Belaaouaj A, McCarthy R, Baumann M, Gao Z, Ley TJ, Abraham SN, and Shapiro SD. Mice lacking neutrophil elastase reveal impaired host defense against gram negative bacterial sepsis. Nat Med. 1998. 4(5): p. 615-8.

Grenda DS, Johnson SE, Mayer JR, McLemore ML, Benson KF, Horwitz M, and Link DC. Mice expressing a neutrophil elastase mutation derived from patients with severe congenital neutropenia have normal granulopoiesis. Blood. 2002. 100(9): p. 3221-8.

Li FQ and Horwitz M. Characterization of mutant neutrophil elastase in severe congenital neutropenia. J Biol Chem. 2001. 276(17): p. 14230-41.

Horwitz M, Benson KF, Duan Z, Li FQ, and Person RE. Hereditary neutropenia: dogs explain human neutrophil elastase mutations. Trends Mol Med. 2004. 10(4): p. 163-70.

Benson KF, Li FQ, Person RE, Albani D, Duan Z, Wechsler J, Meade-White K, Williams K, Acland GM, Niemeyer G, Lothrop CD, and Horwitz M. Mutations associated with neutropenia in dogs and humans disrupt intracellular transport of neutrophil elastase. Nat Genet. 2003. 35(1): p. 90-6.

Aprikyan AA, Garwicz D, Aprikian P, and Dale DC. Impaired Survival and Proteolytic Activity of Human but Not Murine Myeloid Progenitor Cells Expressing Mutant Neutrophil Elastase. Abstracts of the 44th Annual Meeting of the American Society of Hematology. 2002.

Carlsson G, Aprikyan AA, Tehranchi R, Dale DC, Porwit A, Hellstrom-Lindberg E, Palmblad J, Henter JI, and Fadeel B. Kostmann syndrome: severe congenital neutropenia associated with defective expression of Bcl-2, constitutive mitochondrial release of cytochrome c, and excessive apoptosis of myeloid progenitor cells. Blood. 2004. 103(9): p. 3355-61.

Freedman MH and Alter BP. Risk of myelodysplastic syndrome and acute myeloid leukemia in congenital neutropenias. Semin Hematol. 2002. 39(2): p. 128-33.

- Case Study Five-

Sarah Navina, M.D.
Resident, Dept. of Laboratory Medicine and Pathology
Fairview-University Medical Center
University of Minnesota Medical School
Minneapolis, Minnesota

Kathy Frey, M.D.
Department of Pathology
Fairview-Southdale Medical Center
Edina, Minnesota

Phuong L. Nguyen, M.D. *
Director, Division of Hematopathology & Associate Professor
Dept. of Laboratory Medicine and Pathology
University of Minnesota Medical Center
Minneapolis, Minnesota

* Current Address: Division of Hematopathology
Mayo Clinic
Rochester, Minnesota

Diagnosis: Symptomatic Parvovirus B19-induced Anemia in a Patient with Previously Undiagnosed Band 3 Protein Defect-associated Hereditary Spherocytosis

---

Introduction

Parvovirus B19 infection is common. In immunocompetent and hematologically normal hosts, it is largely self-limited and asymptomatic. However, in patients who may have an underlying hematologic disorder with increased red cell turnover or who are immunocompromised, the infection can result in symptomatic aplastic crises or prolonged red cell aplasia, respectively [1]. Therefore, symptomatic parvovirus B19 infection should prompt an evaluation for an underlying immunologic or hematologic disorder.

Clinical History

A 37-year-old man presented in early summer with severe fatigue of approximately ten days' duration following a brief febrile episode. His past medical history was significant for reported non-Hodgkin's lymphoma at the age of 12 years for which he was treated with combination chemotherapy and radiation therapy. (Details related to this illness and treatments were not available to us). Otherwise, the patient has been reportedly well in the interval. The physical examination was notable for splenomegaly. Laboratory evaluation revealed pancytopenia with severe anemia (Table 1). The patient underwent a bone marrow aspiration and biopsy.

Table 1: Hemogram following post-packed RBC transfusion

		Reference range
Hgb	8.7	(13.3 - 17.7 g/dL)
MCV	88.8	(78 - 100 fL)
MCH	31.5	(26.5 - 35.0 pg)
MCHC	35.5	(32.0 - 36.0 g/dL)
WBC	3.0[56^N 30^L]	(4.0 - 11.0 x 109/L)
Plt	53	(150 - 450 x 109/L

Pathology

Peripheral blood: The blood smear showed a normochromic, normocytic anemia with an abnormal population of spherocytes (Figs. 1-2) and pincered or "mushroom-shaped" erythrocytes (Figs. 1-2).

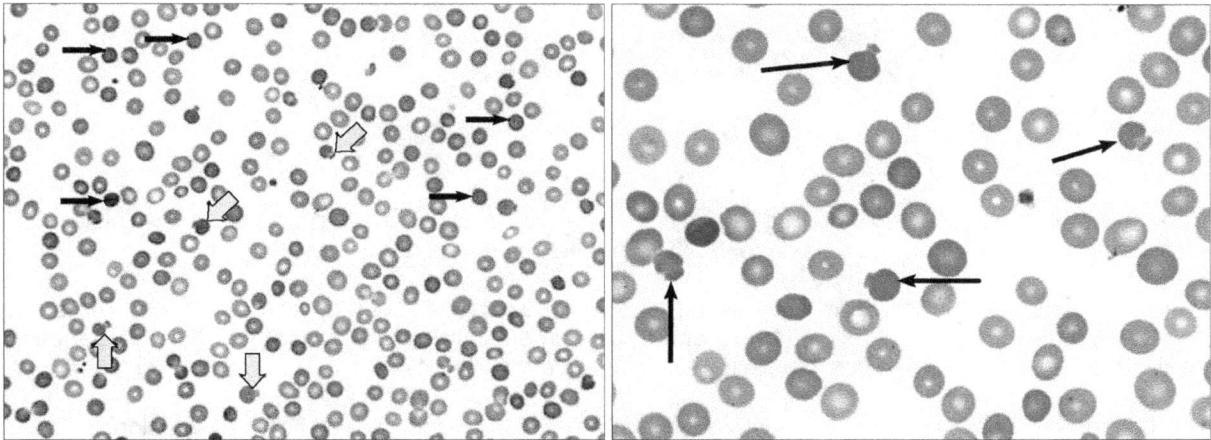

Peripheral blood smear showing spherocytosis (arrows) and pincered or mushroom shaped erythrocytes (block arrows) (Wright-Giemsa stain; x 500).

Polychromasia was not increased. There was a leukopenia with a possible borderline neutropenia and without lymphopenia (Table 1). A thrombocytopenia was also noted.

Bone Marrow he bone marrow aspirate smear showed markedly left-shifted erythroid maturation with a relative predominance of pronormoblasts and basophilic normoblasts (Fig. 3). Dysmyelopoietic features were not identified. Sections of the core biopsy showed a hypercellular marrow (90%) with left-shifted erythroid hyperplasia (Fig. 4). A few giant pronormoblasts with nuclear inclusion were identified (Fig. 5), suspicious for parvovirus B19 infection.

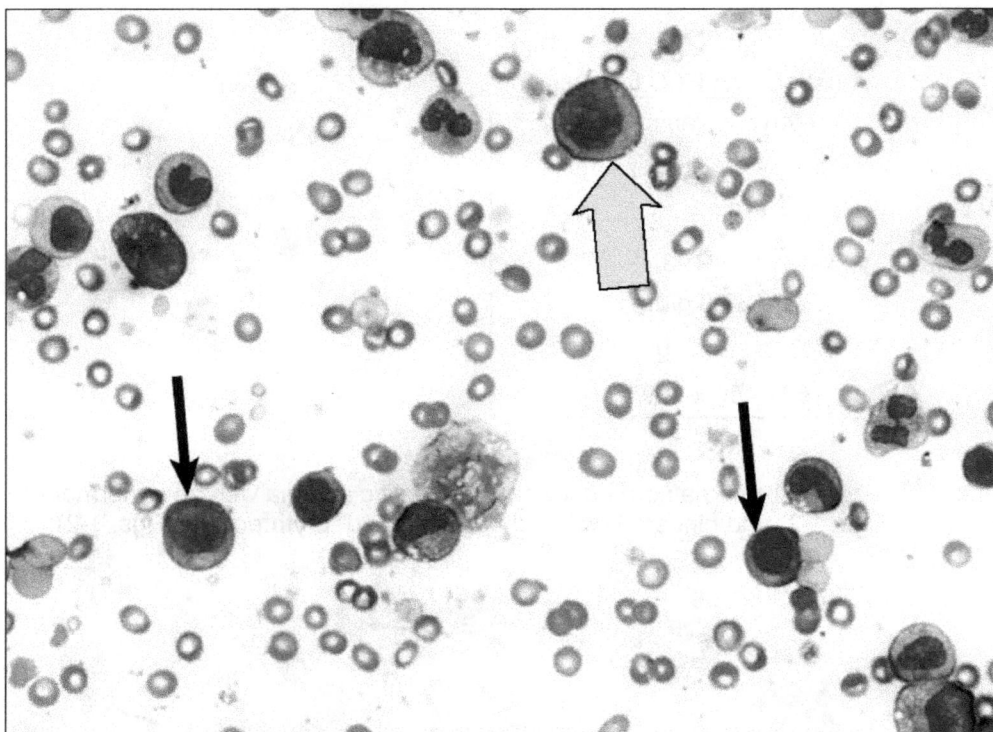

Bone marrow aspirate smear showing left-shifted erythroid maturation with pronormoblasts (block arrow) and basophilic normoblasts (arrows) (Wright-Giemsa stain; x500)

Other laboratory evaluation: Serologic testing for parvovirus B19 was confirmatory, with elevated anti-parvovirus B19 IgM and IgG levels (10.6U and 3.2U, respectively; normal range: <1.1U). Cytogenetic analysis of the bone marrow sample revealed a normal male karyotype.

In addition, the finding of a presumably high MCHC value (35.5 after packed RBC transfusion), spherocytes, and splenomegaly pointed to underlying hereditary spherocytosis. The presence of the so-called "mushroom-shaped" or pincered erythrocytes furthermore suggested that the spherocytosis was due to a defect of band 3 protein. Subsequent testing for osmotic fragility and band 3 fluorescence staining of erythrocytes established the diagnosis of hereditary spherocytosis.

Lastly, the increased number of normal-appearing megakaryocytes in the core biopsy sections indicated that the patient's thrombocytopenia was likely due to peripheral sequestration of platelets secondary to hypersplenism.
Discussion

  Parvovirus B19 infection is common and affects individuals of all ages. Prevalence rates range from approximately 50% among 15-year-old adolescents to over 90% in the elderly [1, 2]. The virus contains a single DNA strand of approximately 5600 nucleotides and forms a small capsid of approximately 25 nm in diameter [3]. It spreads by respiratory droplets, with peak infectivity in the spring in temperate climates [4].

The selective tropism of this virus for erythroid progenitors has been shown to be due to its targeting of the globoside receptor that is present on pronormoblasts and some CFU-E [5, 6]. Death of such infected cells is due to expression of nonstructural viral protein. Recovery of erythropoiesis occurs 10–12 days after infection with development of anti-B19 neutralizing IgM and IgG antibodies. In particular, antibodies to the amino-terminus of VP1 are necessary for viral clearance [7].

Clinically, fever and influenza-like symptoms occur during viremia, with the onset of a cutaneous eruption and rheumatic symptoms occurring approximately 2 weeks later, corresponding to the appearance of antiviral antibodies. Normal hosts with a normal red cell life span or with an intact antibody response show a transient arrest of erythropoiesis with spontaneous recovery following the development of anti-parvovirus B19 antibodies [1]. Aside from the mild rash illness seen in children with parvovirus B19 infection ("fifth disease"), and aside from a subset of adults who may develop a self-limited arthropathy that is thought to be due to immune complex deposition, in most normal hosts, infection with parvovirus B19 is usually asymptomatic.

However, parvovirus B19 infection in individuals with an underlying chronic hemolytic anemia or immunosuppression can result in a clinically significant anemia or possibly pancytopenia. In patients with increased red cell turnover such as hereditary spherocytosis or sickle cell disease, for examples, the destruction of erythroid progenitors is superimposed upon an already shortened red cell life-span and results in transient aplastic crises [8, 9, 10, and 11]. In individuals whose antibody response is compromised by immunosuppression or immunodeficiency, failure to produce appropriate anti-parvovirus B19 antibodies results in prolonged red cell aplasia or pancytopenia [1, 12].

The laboratory diagnosis of parvovirus B19 infection in immunocompetent hosts is made by serologic demonstration of elevated anti-parvovirus B19 IgM antibodies, which are detectable at the time of presentation in patients with fifth disease and within a few days after the onset of transient aplastic crisis [1]. These antibodies persist for 2-3 months after acute infection. The presence of anti-parvovirus B19 IgG can be seen following prior exposure and does not necessarily indicate current infection. In immunocompromised hosts whose antibody production may be minimal to none, demonstration of parvovirus B19 DNA in infected erythroblasts is necessary, typically by hybridization methods [1]. Immunohistochemical assays are also available to demonstrate the presence of parvovirus B19 VP1 and VP2 capsid proteins in infected giant pronormoblasts [2].

In the current patient, results of serologic studies indicate acute or recent parvovirus B19 infection. The increased but left-shifted erythropoiesis in the marrow suggests early recovery from a recent aplastic crisis 1-2 weeks earlier, a finding that is compatible with the timeline of the patient's reported onset of febrile illness and fatigue approximately 10 days earlier.

That this otherwise apparently healthy patient should be symptomatic from such an infection prompts an evaluation for a possible underlying hematologic or immunologic disorder, however. In addition to the presence of splenomegaly, examination of the patient's red blood cell indices and blood smear reveals a presumably high MCHC (>36) prior to packed RBC transfusion and the presence of spherocytes, all of which are consistent with a spherocytic hemolytic anemia which appears to have been undetected. Additional testing was confirmatory, with increased erythrocyte osmotic fragility and decreased band 3 fluorescent staining. Moreover, the presence of pincered or mushroom-shaped erythrocytes in the blood smear (Figs. 1-2) suggests that the spherocytosis is associated with a defect in band 3 protein [13, 14].

Hereditary spherocytosis (HS) shows clinical, biochemical, genetic, and molecular heterogeneity. Approximately 75% of Caucasian cases follow an autosomal dominant pattern of inheritance; others show an autosomal recessive pattern. In some series, up to 25% of cases appear to represent de novo mutations [15]. The prevalence of disease is highest in people of northern European descent, with prevalence rates of up to1: 5000, although this may be an underestimation since patients with a mild form of HS that is detected only by osmotic fragility testing may not have been included in such calculations.

Clinically, HS may present without symptoms, or as mild or severe forms of disease. Typical presentation is with mild anemia from the neonatal period, acholuric jaundice and splenomegaly. Mild or asymptomatic HS may be detected incidentally later in life during evaluation of asymptomatic splenomegaly or study of other family members. Aggravation of symptoms related to anemia occurs when there is suppression of compensatory erythropoiesis by viral infections such as parvovirus B19, Epstein-Barr virus, and hepatitis.

Hemolytic anemia in HS results from deficiencies or dysfunction of various proteins within the supporting cytoskeleton of the red cell membrane and requires the presence of a functionally intact spleen. There are several molecular and biochemical subsets of HS. Among Caucasians, mutations in the ANK1 gene encoding ankyrin account for approximately 50% of HS [13]. Mutations in the SPTB gene encoding the b-chain of spectrin account for 20% of cases [13]. Approximately 15-20% of HS cases among Caucasians are due to mutations in the SLC4A1 gene encoding the anion exchanger 1 or band 3 protein [13]. Some cases of HS are due to a combination of spectrin and ankyrin deficiency. Rare cases of HS have been reported that are due to mutations in the EPB42 gene encoding protein

4.2 or mutations in the SPTA1 gene encoding the a-chain of spectrin. Although the proportions appear to differ among different ethnic groups with HS, the affected red cell membrane proteins are the same [16, 17, and 18].

Hereditary spherocytosis due to band 3 protein deficiency typically follows an autosomal dominant pattern inheritance and shows the characteristic presence of pincered or mushroom-shaped erythrocytes, similar to those seen in the blood smear of our patient (Figs. 1-2) [13, 14] . Whereas the disease is mild in heterozygotes, severe clinical symptomatology has been reported in compound heterozygotes [19, 20]. Reported mutations affecting the SLC4A1 gene encoding the anion exchanger 1 or band 3 protein have included nonsense and frameshift mutations resulting in decreased production and/or stability of mutant mRNA as the cause of decreased band 3 protein synthesis, as well as substitutions of highly conserved amino acids and in-frame deletion that result in the presence of comparable levels of normal and mutant band 3 mRNA [21, 22].

The laboratory evaluation of all types of HS usually involves demonstration of increased erythrocyte destruction and turnover; morphologic evidence of spherocytes in the peripheral blood smear; and physical documentation of spherocytosis demonstrated by osmotic fragility test, which shows increased lysis of erythrocytes in patients with HS compared to normal subjects, especially after 24-hour incubation (glucose deprivation). Since a positive osmotic fragility test does not distinguish between spherocytosis due to immune-mediated hemolysis versus that due to HS, correlation with other clinical and laboratory parameters may be necessary for the diagnosis of HS.

More recently, a flow cytometric test utilizing the dye eosin-5-maleimide has been proposed as an adjunct in the laboratory evaluation of HS [23, 24]. The maleimide moiety of the dye binds covalently with Lys-430 in the first extracellular loop of band 3 proteins, and eosin lies in a pocket deep within the transmembrane core of band 3. Reduced fluorescence and light scatter signals of cells thus reflect a deficiency of band 3 protein, which is thought to reflect loss of membrane surface area.

Lastly, for more complete characterization of the type of red cell membrane skeletal protein deficiency, SDS-PAGE of red cell membrane proteins is employed. Because many of the mutations observed in HS are private, molecular testing for HS may not be practical in the clinical setting, at least in the near future.

The benefits of splenectomy in patients with HS need to be weighed against the risks of post-splenectomy infection. All the same, severe symptomatic hemolysis, mild symptomatic hemolysis and gallstones, and family history of gallstones are considered to be clear indications for splenectomy.

Splenectomy in HS is thought to be beneficial because it prevents of the loss of young erythrocytes. Recent in vitro studies show that in HS patients with defect involving ankyrin and/or spectrin, splenectomy also prolongs survival of more mature erythrocytes. However, such a benefit was not observed with erythrocytes from patients with HS due to band 3 protein deficiency [25]. Thus, although at present therapeutic decisions in HS do not involve precise knowledge of the type of affected protein; it is possible that management of HS patients in the future may require such information.

References
-Young NS, Brown KE. Parvovirus B19. NEJM 2004; 350:586-597
-Imhof A, Kronenberg A, Walter RB, et al. Acute severe anaemia in an elderly patient with hereditary spherocytosis. Postgrad Med J 2003; 79:244-245
-Zhi N, Zadori Z, Brown KE, et al. Construction and sequencing of an infectious clone of the human parvovirus B19. Virology 2004; 318; 142-152
-Human parvovirus B19 infections in United Kingdom 1984-86. Lancet 1987; 1:738-739.
-Mortimer PP, Humphries RK, Moore JG, et al. A human parvovirus-like virus inhibits haematopoietic colony formation in vitro. Nature 1983; 302:426-429
-Brown KE, Anderson SM, Young NS. Erythrocyte P antigen: cellular receptor for B19 parvovirus. Science 1993; 262:114-117
-Saikawa T, Anderson S, Momoeda M, et al. Neutralizing linear epitopes of B19 parvovirus cluster in the VP1 unique and VP1-VP2 junction regions. J Virol 1993; 67:3004-3009
-Beland SS, Daniel GK, Menard JC, et al. Aplastic crisis associated with parvovirus B19 in an adult with hereditary spherocytosis. J Ark Med Soc 1997; 94:163-164

-Lefrere JJ, Courouce AM, Girot R, et al. Six cases of hereditary spherocytosis revealed by human parvovirus infection. Br J Haematol 1986; 62:653-658

-Lee YM, Tsai WH, You JY, et al. Parvovirus B19 infection in Taiwanese patients with hematological disorders. J Med Virol 2003; 71:605-609

-Smith-Whitley K, Zhao H, Hodinka RL, et al. Epidemiology of human parvovirus B19 in children with sickle cell disease. Blood 2004; 103:422-427

-Hayes-Lattin B, Seipel TJ, Gatter K, et al. Pure red cell aplasia associated with parvovirus B19 infection occurring late after allogeneic bone marrow transplantation. Am J Hematol 2004; 75:142-145

-Reinhart WH, Wyss EJ, Arnold D, et al. Hereditary spherocytosis associated with protein band 3 defect in a Swiss kindred. Br J Haematol 1994; 86:147-155

-Delaunay J. Molecular basis of red cell membrane disorders. Acta Haematol 2002; 108:210-218

-Miraglia del Giudice E, Nobili B, Francese M, et al. Clinical and molecular evaluation of non-dominant hereditary spherocytosis. Br J Haematol 2001; 112:42-47

-Lee YK, Cho HI, Park SS, et al. Abnormalities of erythrocyte membrane proteins in Korean patients with hereditary spherocytosis. J Korean Med Sci 2000; 15:284-288

-Yawata Y, Kanzaki A, Yawata A, et al. Characteristic features of the genotype and phenotype of hereditary spherocytosis in the Japanese population. Int J Hematol 2000; 71:118-135

-Sanchez-Lopez JY, Camacho AL, Magana MT, et al. Red cell membrane protein deficiencies in Mexican patients with hereditary spherocytosis. Blood Cells Molecules Dis 2003; 31:357-359

-Alloisio N, Texier P, Vallier A, et al. Modulation of clinical expression and band 3 deficiency in hereditary spherocytosis. Blood 1997; 90:414-420

-Dhermy D, Burnier O, Bourgeois M, et al. The red blood cell band 3 variant (band 3Biceetrel:R490C) associated with dominant hereditary spherocytosis causes defective membrane targeting of the molecule and a dominant negative effect. Mol Membr Biol 1999; 16:305-312

-Jarolim P, Murray JL, Rubin HL, et al. Characterization of 13 novel band 3 gene defects in hereditary spherocytosis with band 3 deficiency. Blood 1996; 88:4366-4377

-Dhermy D, Galand C, Bournier O, et al. Heterogeneous band 3 deficiency in hereditary spherocytosis related to different band 3 gene defects. Br J Haematol 1997; 97:32-40

-Stoya G, Baumann E, Junker U, et al. Flow cytometric analysis of band 3 protein of human erythrocytes. Acta Histochem 1997; 99:29-36

-King M-J, Behrens J, Rogers C, et al. Rapid flow cytometric test for the diagnosis of membrane cytoskeleton-associated haemolytic anaemia. Br J Haematol 2000; 111:924-933

-Reliene R, Mariani M, Zanella A, et al. Splenectomy prolongs in vivo survival of erythrocytes differently in spectrin/ankyrin- and band 3-deficient hereditary spherocytosis. Blood 2002; 100:2298-2215

ABOUT AUTHOR

Dr. Agourram Taieb was born in Amizmiz; a small town in Morocco approximately 55 kilometers South of Marrakech (Capital of the Mid South-Western Economic Region), and educated in its public school system. The author attended National School of Medical Technologists at National Institute of Public Health. After completing an internship at this school, he chose to undergo an additional training at the Laboratoire du Maghreb Analyses Medicales. His career began at this laboratory in 1974. It is here the author developed an integrative basic and clinical research program involving, respectively, the education in clinical laboratory Hematology under supervision of Dr N. Lazrak.

He is married to Hoda and has five children.